VOTAIRE'S BASTARDS

NOVELS BY JOHN RALSTON SAUL

The Birds of Prey
Baraka
The Next Best Thing
The Paradise Eater

John Ralston Saul

VOLTAIRE'S
BASTARDS

John Ralston Saul holds a Ph.D. in history from King's College
(London), ran a Paris-based investment firm, worked as a Canadian oil executive, and has written extensively about North Africa
and Southeast Asia. His most recent novel, *The Paradise Eater*,
won the Premio Letterario Internazionale in 1990.

VOLTAIRE'S BASTARDS

The Dictatorship of Reason in the West

John Ralston Saul

VINTAGE BOOKS

A DIVISION OF RANDOM HOUSE, INC.

NEW YORK

FIRST VINTAGE BOOKS EDITION, NOVEMBER 1993

Copyright © 1992 by John Ralston Saul

Published in the United States by Vintage Books, a division of
Random House, Inc., New York. Originally published in hardcover
by The Free Press, a division of Macmillan, Inc., New York, in 1992.
This edition is reprinted by arrangement with The Free Press, a division of Macmillan, Inc.

Library of Congress Cataloging-in-Publication Data
Saul, John Ralston.
Voltaire's bastards: the dictatorship of reason in the West / John
Ralston Saul.—1st Vintage Books ed.
p. cm.
Originally published: New York: Free Press: Maxwell Macmillan
International, 1992.
ISBN 0-679-74819-9
1. Reason. 2. Rationalism. 3. Civilization, Western. I. Title.
[BC177.S28 1993]
909'.09821—dc20   93-1296
CIP

Manufactured in the United States of America
10 9

For

MAURICE STRONG

who taught me that a sensible relationship

between ideas and action is possible.

Ecartons ces romans qu'on appelle systèmes;
Et pour nous élever descendons dans nous-mêmes.
VOLTAIRE

Contents

PART III

SURVIVING IN FANTASY LAND
The Individual in the World of Reason

PART I

Argument

Reason is a narrow system
swollen into an ideology.

With time and power it has
become a dogma, devoid of
direction and disguised as
disinterested inquiry.

Like most religions, reason
presents itself as the solution
to the problems it has created.

1

In Which the Narrator
Positions Himself

In moments of great passion, the mind tends to be flooded with a warm vision of the person in our arms. We are unlikely, at that point, to be analyzing their flaws, real or hypothetical. Even less likely if lying in darkness. As for the possible product of our intercourse, only the most peculiar lover would be fretting, while in the act, over whether such a child might or might not be an appropriate and worthy creation.

Voltaire and the other thinkers of the eighteenth century could be criticized, with the facility of hindsight, for the passion with which they embraced reason. But they lived in societies still ruled by the demeaning vagaries of court life. All of them had been thrown in jail or risked it simply for expressing their opinions. In most countries justice still used torture as an official method of interrogation and the condemned faced a variety of brutal punishments; being broken on the wheel, for example. This and other tools of arbitrary power constituted a social form of darkness. The philosophers of Europe, England and America threw themselves into the arms of reason, convinced that birth would be given to new rational elites capable of building a new civilization. This love affair was fertile to the point of being miraculous and society was subsequently reformed for the better beyond what any of these thinkers had imagined.

And yet the exercise of power, without the moderating influence of any ethical structure, rapidly became the religion of these new elites. And their reforms included an unparalleled and permanent institutionalization of state violence. This was accompanied by a growing struggle between democratic and rational methods, with the rational increasingly at an advantage.

Were Voltaire to reappear today, he would be outraged by the new structures, which somehow deformed the changes for which he struggled. As for his descendants — our ruling elites — he would deny all

Argument

legal responsibility and set about fighting them, as he once fought the courtiers and priests of eighteenth-century Europe.

It is difficult now to reconstruct the impact that Voltaire had on his times. He was the single most famous individual of the eighteenth century. In spite of neither being a philosopher nor having an integrated philosophy, he set the Western agenda for much of the nineteenth century. His life was filled with contradictions. On the negative side, he was consumed by social and financial ambition. A product of the middle class, he wasted a good part of his life trying to win acceptance from the aristocracy and attempting to succeed as a courtier. The son of a provincial businessman, he made a fortune out of farming, manufacturing and the money market, but in the process was involved in endless ugly scandals and lawsuits. On the other hand, he was driven by an uncontrollable belief in social reform. And he alone of the eighteenth-century Western writers knew how to carry that argument into the public place.

Two unforeseen catastrophes forced him to favour the positive side of his character. In 1726 he was thirty-two years old and imprisoned in the Bastille for the second time. The authorities offered him freedom if he would go into exile. He went to England for two and a half years and was thus exposed to the country "where men think free and noble thoughts." In fact, he returned to France exaggerating the virtues of England as a way of encouraging change at home.

The most important part of his exile may have been the three months spent with Jonathan Swift in the house of Lord Peterborough. The pamphlets and novels he subsequently wrote were built upon the irony and ridicule which Swift had first perfected, but which Voltaire turned into unbeatable populist weapons. "All styles," as he said, "are good, except the boring." His *Philosophical Letters* in 1733 was one of the first great blows against the established powers. His book *The Century of Louis XIV* was the beginning of modern historical method. He carried out exhaustive research and wrote not about a king, but about society.

The second catastrophe came with his failure as a courtier, first at Versailles and then at the court of Frederick the Great. He was already the leading playwright in Europe and most-talked-about man. Then abruptly Voltaire was fleeing the Prussian court and welcome nowhere else. He settled at Ferney, an estate just inside France but for safety just across the Swiss border. There, far from capitals and courts, he was forced to rely on the written word.

Having failed to influence the monarchs and men of power to whom he had access, Voltaire turned towards the citizenry and became the leading defender of human rights and the most ingenious advocate of practical reforms. "Our dominant passion must be for the public weal" sums up the last two decades of his life. He inundated Europe with pamphlets, novels, poems, letters, all of them political.

Professional philosophers, now as then, criticized the absence of grand and integrated ideas in his writing. But grand, integrated ideas don't necessarily change societies. Voltaire concentrated on six basic freedoms — of the person (no slavery), of speech and the press, of conscience, civil liberty, security of private property and the right to work. By addressing himself to the citizenry and not to the rulers and other thinkers, he invented modern public opinion. By successfully establishing the new "acceptable" vocabulary for all civilized men, he forced even those in power to fight on his terms. He was a one-man guerrilla army and, as he put it, "God is not on the side of the heavy battalions, but of the best shots."[1]

In the last year of his life, 1778, Voltaire came back to Paris in triumph. For months on end he was lionized, courted and cheered by all classes of the population. They seemed to be using the reappearance of the old man in the greatest city of Europe as an excuse to demonstrate that they had been converted to the idea of government by a new philosophical coalition of reason balanced with humanism. The arbitrary powers of church and state appeared suddenly quite fragile, in place only until some appropriate crisis brought change. In the meantime, Voltaire himself gave in to the pleasures of being adored. The adulation gradually wore him out and he died.

When the crisis came, it spread immediately throughout Europe. By 1800 all the negatives of the new methods were as obvious as their positives. Looking back on this disorder, our eyes tend to be drawn by the particular political battles of the day. But with the advantage of distance we can also see that the central assumption of Voltaire — of his friends throughout Europe and of the English and the Americans — had been wrong. Humanism was proving itself unable to balance reason. The two seemed, in fact, to be enemies.

A civilization unable to differentiate between illusion and reality is usually believed to be at the tail end of its existence. Our reality is dominated by elites who have spent much of the last two centuries, indeed of the last four, organizing society around answers and around structures designed to produce answers. These structures have fed upon expertise and that expertise upon complexity. The effect has been to render universal understanding as difficult as possible. "What we cannot speak about," Ludwig Wittgenstein said, "we must pass over in silence."[2] The writer's most effective weapons against such silence have always been simplicity and common sense. But never have the custodians of the word been so cut off from the realities of power. Never, for that matter, have people so adept at manipulating the word held the levers of power. Western culture, as a result, has become less and less a critical reflection of its own society.

Ours is a civilization astonishing in the degree to which it seems to see and to know. Never before in history have there been such enormous elites carrying such burdens of knowledge. This success story dominates our lives. Elites quite naturally define as the most important and admired qualities for a citizen those on which they themselves have concentrated.

The possession, use and control of knowledge have become their central theme — the theme song of their expertise. However, their power depends not on the effect with which they use that knowledge but on the effectiveness with which they control its use. Thus, among the illusions which have invested our civilization is an absolute belief that the solution to our problems must be a more determined application of rationally organized expertise. The reality is that our problems are largely the product of that application. The illusion is that we have created the most sophisticated society in the history of man. The reality is that the division of knowledge into feudal fiefdoms of expertise has made general understanding and coordinated action not simply impossible but despised and distrusted.

When we look around at the influence and strength of money, of armies, of legal officials, or indeed at the ease with which writers are silenced through censorship, violence and imprisonment, it seems that the word is a fragile blossom. But one step back from this immediacy is enough to reveal the power of language. Nothing frightens those in authority so much as criticism. Whether democrats or dictators, they are unable to accept that criticism is the most constructive tool available to any society because it is the best way to prevent error. The weakness of rationally based power can be seen in the way it views criticism as an even more negative force than a medieval king might have done. After all, even the fool has been banished from the castles of modern power. What is it which so frightens these elites?

Language — not money or force — provides legitimacy. So long as military, political, religious or financial systems do not control language, the public's imagination can move about freely with its own ideas. Uncontrolled words are consistently more dangerous to established authority than armed forces. Even coercive laws of censorship are rarely effective for more than short periods in limited areas.

There is nothing particularly original about breaking down the intellectual, political, social and emotional walls behind which language has been imprisoned, freeing it, then watching while the poor thing is recaptured and locked up again. That process has been repeated endlessly throughout history. The wordsmiths who serve our imagination are always devoted to communication. Clarity is always their method.

Universality is their aim. The wordsmiths who serve established power, on the other hand, are always devoted to obscurity. They castrate the public imagination by subjecting language to a complexity which renders it private. Elitism is always their aim. The undoubted sign of a society well under control or in decline is that language has ceased to be a means of communication and has become instead a shield for those who master it.

If reason is an idea and rational society an abstraction, then the whole age has turned and continues to turn upon language. Just as the unleashing of ideas and myths in the seventeenth and eighteenth centuries cleared the way for endless changes in state and social structures, so the subsequent pinning down and splitting up of language into feudal states has now made it impossible for the citizen to participate seriously in society. The inviting humanist irony of the early days has given way to the off-putting rational cynicism and sloganeering of our time. And if there was something fatally flawed in those original changes — a sort of grave misunderstanding at the heart of reason — then that flaw must still be there, locked up inside the byzantine and inaccessible structures of our society.

The idea of universal understanding still survives in our memory. Stéphane Mallarmé, who was later echoed by T. S. Eliot, said that we should "purify the dialect of the tribe." What follows here is a mere purification rite; a stripping away of byzantine structures in search of our historical outline and our contemporary reality. This is not an attempt to realign ideas, merely a demonstration of their common sense alignment.

Here, in a few pages, four hundred years are rushed through without due process. Philosophical stop signs and one-way streets are more or less ignored. Here the principal fields of modern expertise are jumbled together as if they were one and not, as they present themselves, autonomous territories of self-contained power. And here the proclaimed justifications of nations are obscured by the sameness of our modern elites, of our structures and of the form which power has taken in this, the dotage of the Age of Reason.

2

The Theology of Power

Some twenty years ago the democratic, industrialized, developed world began a false but ferocious internal struggle which was said to be between the Left and the Right. It was, in fact, the death rattle of the Age of Reason. The slogans assigned to the two camps in this imaginary battle were remarkably familiar. Words such as *reform, socialist, social democrat* and *government intervention* were pitted against *capitalist, conservative, individualism* and *established values*.

The struggle appears to have been set off by two successive crises. First, the loss of the Vietnam War by the United States destroyed a whole set of assumptions based upon American infallibility and accepted until then by all of the democracies. These beliefs had been in place since 1945. Although few of the democracies had supported the American Vietnam effort, they followed the greatest nation in the world in most other matters. The U.S. defeat left them — to say nothing of the United States itself — milling about in confusion. As they turned, the second crisis struck, in the form of an international economic failure. That depression has now been with us twenty years.

We have, however, become so accustomed to our political and business leaders addressing themselves only to limited manifestations of this crisis and always in a positive way — stimulating what they call a temporary recession or managing a Third World debt problem or waging a localized war against inflation or concentrating upon that portion of an economy which they have superficially stimulated to the point of explosion while the rest remains in profound decline — that we are never quite certain whether the depression is still with us or is on the point of disappearing. Nightly, it seems, we drop off to sleep with the vague expectation that all will be clear in the morning. Mysteriously, there is always a new explosion in the night and when we awake, the problem has been transformed into yet another limited manifestation.

This depression, of proportions as great if not greater than that of the 1930s, still engulfs us. None of our governments appear to have any idea of how to end it. How could they? The essence of rational leadership is control justified by expertise. To admit failure is to admit loss of control. Officially, therefore, we haven't had a depression since the 1930s. And since most experts — the economists, for example — are part of the system, instead of being commentators in any real, independent sense, they contribute to the denial of reality. In other words, there is a constant need in our civilization to prefer illusions over reality, a need to deny our perceptions.

Indeed, we haven't seen anything over the last twenty years which resembles the traditional profile of a depression. The reason is very simple. After the economic crisis of the 1930s, we created a multitude of control valves and safety nets in order to avoid any future general collapse — strict banking regulations, for example, social security programs and in some places national health care systems. These valves and nets have been remarkably successful, in spite of the strains and the mismanagement of the last two decades. However, because the rational system prevents anyone who accepts legal responsibility from taking enough distance to get a general view, many of our governments, desperate and misguided, have begun dismantling those valves and nets as a theoretical solution to the general crisis.

Worse still, tinkering with these instruments has become a substitute for addressing the problem itself. Thus financial deregulation is used to simulate growth through paper speculation. When this produces inflation, controls are applied to the real economy, producing unemployment. When this job problem becomes so bad that it must be attacked, the result is the lowering of employment standards. When this unstable job creation leads to new inflation, the result is high interest rates. And on around again, guided by the professional economists, who are in effect pursuing, step by step, an internal argument without any reference to historic reality. For example, in a single decade the idea of using public debt as an economic tool has moved from the heroic to the villainous. In the same period private debt went in the opposite direction, from the villainous to the heroic. This was possible only because economists kept their noses as close to each specific argument as possible and thus avoided invoking any serious comparisons and any reference to the real lessons of the preceding period.

In general terms all this means that management methods are being mistaken for solutions and so, as if in some sophisticated game, the problem is pushed on with a long rational stick from point to point around the field. As a result we are perpetually either on the edge of a recession (never in it, let alone in a depression, whatever the indicators say) or we are artificially flush and then manage to convince ourselves that we are flying high.

The accompanying political argument had been going on for a few years before it became clear that its vocabulary didn't apply to the problem. For example, during the 1970s and 1980s, economic policies said to be of the Left in the United States, Canada, England and Germany led to the defeat of existing governments and to the election of new governments said to be of the Right. At the same time, identical policies in France, Spain, Australia and Italy were said to be of the Right and led to the replacement of their governments by those said to be of the Left.

This general confusion further clouded the public's linear memory. For example, the American Right has been in power for twenty of the last twenty-four years. One of its central themes is law and order. The argument is that the American Left — the *liberals*, whatever that word means — is incapable of maintaining law and order. And yet for twenty years the levels of armed robbery, violent crime and murder have continued annually to grow to record highs — records both for the United States and in comparison to other Western countries. Still, the American Right persists in thinking of itself, and is thought of by its opponents on the Left, as the voice of law and order.

Self-evident contradictions of this sort surround us. We talk endlessly of the individual and of individualism, for example, when any sensible glance at major issues indicates that we live in an era of great conformism. Our societies turn upon democratic principles, yet the quasi totality of our leading citizens refuse to take part in that process and, instead, leave the exercise of political power to those for whom they have contempt. Our business leaders hector us in the name of capitalism, when most of them are no more than corporate employees, isolated from personal risk. We are obsessed by competition, yet the largest item of international trade is armaments — an artificial consumer good. We condemn arms dealers as immoral and sleazy figures, while ignoring the fact that our own senior civil servants and senior corporate leadership together are responsible for more than 90 percent of the arms traded. Never has there been such a sea of available information, and yet all organizations — public and private — work on the principle that information is secret unless specifically declared not to be. There is a conviction that governments have never been so strong and at the same time a sense that they are virtually powerless to effect change unless some superhuman effort is made. Or, to return to my first economic example, after a century of carefully building both self-respect among employees and job stability for them, our first reaction when faced by a depression is to move out of manufacturing into the service industries. We tell ourselves that the latter are the wave of the future — computer software, sophisticated consulting — when most of the jobs we actually create are at the low end of service — waiting on tables, serving in shops, part-time, unprotected, without long-term prospects. In other words, much of the job creation of the 1980s represented a defeat for our theoretically balanced and stable societies.

We tend to blame this Western schizophrenia on national interests or on ideological conflicts. The official Left would put most of our problems down to uncontrolled self-interest, as if they still had a clear idea of how to harness self-interest for the general good. The official Right would shrug its shoulders manfully, that is to say cynically, as if to imply that reality is tough. But manful cynicism is probably a disguised form of confused helplessness. And none of these contradictions have anything to do with reality.

If anything, what all this tells us is that, while not blind, we see without being able to perceive the differences between illusion and reality. And so when one of these differences — particularly the international variety, with all the accompanying mythological baggage—appears to be resolved, there is general euphoria, which then gradually subsides without our schizophrenia being altered. This persistent displacement of responsibility causes us to lose track of the West's profound unity and instead to swing violently between optimistic and pessimistic convictions of nationalism and internationalism.

It is true that at first glance the West seems to be nothing more than a vague chimera. What is anyone to make of seventeen-odd countries spread throughout three continents and divided by language, mythology and persistent tribal rivalries? It isn't even in a place which can accurately be called the West.

At second glance the binding ties between Europe, North America and Australasia can be seen in a series of fundamental shared experiences and convictions. From the Judeo-Christian imprint through the Reformation, the Renaissance, the Industrial Revolution, the democratic and the revolutionary crises, the West was formed by a series of trials which turned into basic assumptions. And all these were themselves built upon our real and mythological assumptions about Greece and Rome. It is that West which is grouped beneath the sign of reason. Not the great and disordered empires of China and Russia, which have rolled through history upon a whole other series of experiences and assumptions. Not Japan, which is a case unto itself. Not what we call the Third World, which has been both a beneficiary and a victim of our assumptions. And it is that West which has become addicted to a particular set of illusions in order to avoid coming to terms with its own reality.

We are now more than four and a half centuries into an era which our obsession with progress and our servility to structure have caused us to name and rename a dozen times, as if this flashing of theoretically fundamental concepts indicated real movement. The reality is that we have not moved beyond the basic ideas of the sixteenth century which, for want of any better description, should be called the concepts of reason. This Age of Reason will soon have been with us for 500 years. With each passing day more ideas, structures and beliefs are hung upon the fragile back of those few concepts.

And yet, even in their early days, they were not ideas of great breadth. What's more, from birth they were based upon an essential misunder-standing — that reason constituted a moral weapon, when in fact it was nothing more than a disinterested administrative method. That funda-mental error may explain reason's continuing force, because centuries of Western elites have been obliged to invent a moral direction where none existed.

Memory is always the enemy of structure. The latter flourishes upon method and is frustrated by content. Our need to deny the amorality of reason ensured that memory would be the first victim of the new struc-tures. We must constantly remind ourselves, therefore, that the ratio-nal idea has run as the central force through almost five centuries of Western crises. It has provided the most basic assumptions and there-fore created the most basic of divisions. Reason remains the sign of Western man's conscious self and therefore of his better self. Reason is still accepted as the light which leads the way across the treacherous ground of our baser instincts.

At first there was an easy conviction that all this was so — a convic-tion made all the more easy by the moral baggage reason had been carrying for a thousand years. In varying ways, to varying degrees, the Greeks had identified reason (*logos*) as one of the key human charac-teristics — the superior characteristic. Reason was virtue. Rational ac-tion led to the greatest good. Roman thinkers did nothing to undermine the conviction, nor did the Christian churches, which simply narrowed the meaning to justify their received truths. And when, in the sixteenth century, thinkers began to free us from this sterile Scholasticism, they turned for guidance back to Socrates, Aristotle and the Stoics in search of a freestanding, ethical approach.

The implication is that most people — particularly the philoso-phers — were more or less agreed on what actually constituted reason. This simply isn't so. There was and is no generally accepted, concrete definition. As so often with basic concepts, they slip away when you try to approach them. And the philosophers have kept themselves busy redefining as the centuries have gone by.

In truth the definitions didn't really matter, any more than mine might. More to the point is what our civilization understands or senses or feels reason to be. What are our expectations? What is the mythology surrounding the word?

One thing is clear: despite successive redefinitions by philosophers, the popular understanding and expectations have remained virtually unchanged. This stability seems to withstand even the real effects of reason when it is applied; to withstand them so effectively that it is difficult to imagine a more stubbornly optimistic concept, except perhaps that of life after death.

What's more, the renewed and intense concentration on the rational element which started in the seventeenth century had an unexpected effect. Reason began, abruptly, to separate itself from and to outdistance the other more or less recognized human characteristics — spirit, appetite, faith and emotion, but also intuition, will and, most important, experience. This gradual encroachment on the foreground continues today. It has reached a degree of imbalance so extreme that the mythological importance of reason obscures all else and has driven the other elements into the marginal frontiers of doubtful respectability.

The practical effect of such a mesmerizing and prolonged solo has been to turn the last half millennium into the Age of Reason. We habitually divide this period up under a multitude of other headings: the Enlightenment, for example, Romanticism, Neo-Classicism, Neo-Realism, Symbolism, Aestheticism, Nihilism and Modernism, to name just a few. But the differences between these periods, like the difference between the school born of Bacon versus the school born of Descartes, all blend into one another when we stand back far enough to get a good look. And so Descartes's deductive, abstract arguments which prove their conclusions mathematically melt into Locke's empirical, mechanical approach which melts into Marx's determinism. In other words, since the 1620s, if not the 1530s, we seem to have merely been fiddling with details or rather, shifting from side to side to disguise from ourselves the fact that we have taken in that long period but one clear step — away, that is, from the divine revelation and absolute power of church and state.

That very real struggle against superstition and arbitrary power was won with the use of reason and of scepticism. And it has taken all this time for reason and logic on the one hand, and scepticism on the other, to seep into the roots of Western society. After all, there was still an absolute monarch in Germany 75 years ago and in France 120 years ago; universal suffrage is in general only 50 years old; the end of official Catholic anti-Semitism less than that; the largest landowner in England is still a duke; and American segregation, a tacit but legally organized form of slavery, began to die 40 years ago, although it now looks as if black poverty amounts to much the same thing.

It can, of course, easily be argued that reason still has not been absorbed into the roots of Western society. Large sections of the southern United States and of northern cities like New York and Washing-

ton, of southern Italy and of the Midlands in England and even of
London, for example, have either never risen out of or have slipped back
into a condition which more properly belongs to the Third World. But
the evolution of whole civilizations is always full of contradictions which
do not change the fundamental truths.

Our ideological bickering of the last hundred years has added extremely little to the central line we have been following. Instead, a
series of grandiose and dark events — religious bloodbaths in Europe,
Napoleonic dictatorships and unlimited industrial competition, to name
three — overcame Western society and seemed to do so thanks to rational methods. The original easy conviction that reason was a moral
force was gradually converted into a desperate, protective assumption.
The twentieth century, which has seen the final victory of pure reason
in power, has also seen unprecedented unleashings of violence and of
power deformed. It is hard, for example, to avoid noticing that the
murder of six million Jews was a perfectly rational act.

And yet our civilization has been constructed precisely in order to
avoid such conclusions. We carefully — rationally in fact — assign
blame for our crimes to the irrational impulse. In this way we merely
shut our eyes to the central and fundamental misunderstanding: reason
is no more than structure. And structure is most easily controlled by
those who feel themselves to be free of the cumbersome weight represented by common sense and humanism. Structure suits best those
whose talents lie in manipulation and who have a taste for power in its
purer forms.

Thus the Age of Reason has turned out to be the Age of Structure; a
time when, in the absence of purpose, the drive for power as a value in
itself has become the principal indicator of social approval. And the
winning of power has become the measure of social merit.

Knowledge, of course, was to be the guarantor of reason's moral
force — knowledge, an invincible weapon in the hands of the individual, a weapon which would ensure that society was built upon considered and sensible actions. But in a world turned upon power through
structure, the disinterested consideration of knowledge simply couldn't
hold and was rapidly transformed into our obsession with expertise. The
old civilization of class was replaced by one of castes — a highly sophisticated version of corporatism. Knowledge became the currency of power
and as such was retained. This civilization of secretive experts was
quite naturally obsessed not by the encouragement of understanding but
by the providing of answers.

Our unquenchable thirst for answers has become one of the obvious
characteristics of the West in the second half of the twentieth century.
But what are answers when there is neither memory nor general understanding to give them meaning? This running together of the right

answer with the search for truth is perhaps the most poignant sign of our confusion.

It is a curious sort of confusion. Organized and calm on the surface, our lives are lived in an atmosphere of nervous, even frenetic agitation. Hordes of essential answers fly about us and disappear, abruptly meaningless. Successive absolute solutions are provided for major public problems and then slip away without our consciously registering their failure. Neither the public and corporate authorities nor the experts are held responsible for their own actions in any sensible manner because the fracturing of memory and understanding has created a profound chaos in the individual's sense of what responsibility is.

This is part of the deadening of language which the reign of structure and abstract power has wrought. The central concepts upon which we operate were long ago severed from their roots and changed into formal rhetoric. They have no meaning. They are used wildly or administratively as masks. And the more our language becomes a tool for limiting general discourse, the more our desire for answers becomes frenzied.

Yet there is no great need for answers. Solutions are the cheapest commodity of our day. They are the medicine-show tonic of the rational elites. And the structures which produce them are largely responsible for the inner panic which seems endemic to modern man.

Of course, we try very hard to see this century in a more positive way; not so much more successful, as more dramatic. Meaningful. We see ourselves as victims of the disorder which inevitably follows upon the breakdown of religious and social order. In such a vacuum the collective Western consciousness couldn't help but splinter. It follows that the succession of great, all-encompassing ages — Reason, Enlightenment, Romanticism — had to end with an explosion. The resulting shards inevitably produced a confused age in which innumerable ideologies fought it out for control of our minds and our bodies.

And, so the tale has it, Fascism, Nazism, Communism, Marxism, Socialism, Democracy and Capitalism, among others, began to manoeuvre their intellectual, military and economic armies around the West. Indeed, around the globe. By midcentury, Fascism and Nazism had been destroyed, thanks to a temporary alliance among the others. Now Communism and Marxism may be on the point of being eliminated in their turn. Capitalism and Democracy, with some Socialist tinges, reign almost supreme after a century of confused general battle. It has been the second Hundred Years' War.

Unfortunately, like the first, this one has been relatively meaningless. A wasteful and superficial diversion. For example, in realpolitik terms, the century ends much as it began. Japan is still dominant and rising in the East, Germany dominant and rising in Europe, the United States shaky but dominant in the Americas. Russia, China and Britain are, as they were, in continued decline, each held together by rubber bands of doubtful strength. And the middle powers have returned to their relative stability of 1900. Even France ends much as it began, the loss of empire being counterbalanced by the reestablishment of a central role on the Continent.

This war of ideologies may have been costly in every sense, but that doesn't make it meaningful. Men are perfectly capable of inventing concrete but stupid reasons to justify killing each other. Great battles such as Crécy and Agincourt demonstrated that perfectly during the first Hundred Years' War.

The vacuum which all this was aimed at filling was not, in reality, a vacuum. The structure and methodology of reason have been dominant everywhere during these struggles. In fact, there has been a great underlying unity throughout the West in the twentieth century: the superficial confusion, which we have mistaken for a vacuum, is simply the product of reason's innate amorality. The conversion of Western civilization to a methodology devoid of values — humanist, moral or aesthetic — couldn't have helped but launch us into unending, meaningless battles. More to the point, the struggles of the twentieth century could be characterized as perfectly unconscious, largely because the underlying force was a headless abstraction. Perhaps that explains our obsession with the strengthening of the individual consciousness. Humans have a tendency to personalize those civilizationwide problems which escape them.

In the same decade that saw the affirmation of the rational nation-state — thanks to such things as the American Civil War, the Second Reform Bill in Britain, the decentralization of the Austrian Empire into the Austro-Hungarian Dual Monarchy, the freeing of the serfs in Russia, the creation of Germany, Canada and Italy — Matthew Arnold evoked in "Dover Beach" a vision of the century to come:

> And we are here as on a darkling plain
> Swept with confused alarms of struggle and flight,
> Where ignorant armies clash by night.

In such a context it hardly seems worth delving into the rivalries between the contemporary camps. Neither Capitalism nor Socialism can pretend to be an ideology. They are merely methods for dividing ownership and income. What is most peculiar for such theoretically practical methodologies, which are also theoretically opposed to each other, is that neither of them has ever existed, except in a highly tentative form. And even then they are invariably mixed together. Their mutually exclusive vocabularies have more to do with basic similarities than with differences. Like immature brothers, they have imposed their sibling rivalry upon us. The reality is that they are subspecies of the larger group which includes Christianity, Nazism and Communism, if for no other reason than that all of them prosper through the cultivation of desire, as indeed does Islam. Of the great world myths, only Buddhism is centred on the reduction of desire in the individual.

None of the modern ideologies can be considered great mythology. Marx, for example, although a talented analyst, compulsively proposed inapplicable ideas and inaccurate conclusions. That these ideas have had considerable superficial success doesn't make them any the less silly. In the sixteenth century, the Inquisition was a great success, and was central to the original defining of reason. And yet it made no sense at all with its belief that the best way to question people was to stretch them until their joints separated or to smash their limbs with mallets. All of Europe accepted it and trembled. The elites, even the kings, dared not protest until the worst was over.

Marx was fortunate to have been born eighty years before Walt Disney. Disney also promised a child's paradise and, unlike Marx, delivered on his promise. This remark is not as specious as it appears. After all, one of the proofs that ideologies subsequent to the birth of reason have had little to add is that when they do gain power, their actions bear absolutely no relationship to their mythology. There has therefore never been a Communist state. They were merely old-fashioned, inefficient but authoritarian dictatorships. Critics make a great deal out of the heavy-handed, inefficient communist bureaucracies. But was there anything innately communist about them? What was there to differentiate them from dozens of other heavy-handed inefficient bureaucracies — the late Manchus, for example, the Ottomans or Byzantium? The absence of private property is often seen as an essentially Marxist characteristic. But most feudal societies used the same idea and structure; the sole difference being that the ultimate repository of power had changed costume. A king representing God, who stood for the general good, had been replaced by a Supreme Soviet representing the Communist Party, which stood for the general good.

Marxism became the dreamlike answer to a real need in Western society, but any one of a handful of other dreams might have done just as well. Walt Disney, for example, riding in the front lines of mythology, converted America to a vision of itself in which the citizen is a viewer, the beliefs are cinematic assertions and the leaders are character actors. And that is more relevant to real life than an imaginary ideology or system — for example, Capitalism.

After all, today's leading advocates of free enterprise and competition, the well-protected bureaucratic managers of publicly traded companies, are generally and with relative ease able to neutralize their real owners (the shareholders) and those really responsible (the directors). As for competition on the level playing field, a classic demonstration of how it works was provided by airline deregulation in the United States in the 1980s. The promised result was to be more airlines competing to fly to more places at cheaper prices. Instead, fewer airlines are now flying to fewer places at higher prices. Unregulated competition leads to oligopolies at best and monopolies at worst. And both lead to price-fixing. This reality is erased in some people's minds because of an imaginary symbiosis between Capitalism and Democracy, which is just about as silly an idea as that of a symbiosis between Socialism and Democracy. If given a chance, both will corrupt public officials and install corporatism.

The Right and the Left, like Fascism and Communism, have never been anything more than marginal dialects on the extremes of reason. They are the naive answers that one would expect from a central ideology which, in its very heart, believes in absolute solutions. And so, despite this confusion of false ideologies, the ethic of reason has continued to spread within our societies. Certain characteristics of that ethic, less apparent in the beginning, have seeped through into dominating positions. It has produced a system determined to apply a kind of clean, unemotional logic to every decision, and this to the point where the dictatorship of the absolute monarchs has been replaced by that of absolute reason. The development and control of intricate systems, for example, has become the key to power.

The judgmental side of Descartes has come to the fore. It is answers we want — simple, absolute answers where, in reality, there is great complexity. An obsession with the true versus the false leads us to artificial solutions as reassuring as the old certainty that the world was flat. An obsession with efficiency as a value in itself has driven large parts of our economies into chaos. Briefing books and flowcharts have in our time become the protocols of power, just as the king's waking-up ceremony at Versailles was in the eighteenth century. Reason now has a great deal in common with the last days of the ancien régime. Reason possesses, as did the monarchy, a perfectly constructed, perfectly integrated, perfectly self-justifying system. The system itself has become the justification for the society. No one remembered in the late eighteenth century that the Church and the kings had originally developed their system of power in order to bring stability to an anarchical continent. Equally, no one seems to remember today the original purpose of the elaborate technocratic systems which dominate our lives. They were adopted in order to battle against the established forces of unfettered whims and self-interest, which used power however it suited them.

Until a few years ago there was general agreement that whatever reason dictated was by definition good. Since the mid-sixties, however, there has been a growing general sense that our systems are not working. Multiple signs of this are easily identified, but they somehow resist fitting into a pattern. The depression. The swollen armaments industry. The breakdown of the legal system. The confusion over ownership and capitalism. Random examples from an endless list. We see signs of failure, but the system provides no vocabulary for describing this breakdown, unless we become irrational; and the vocabulary of unreason is that of darkness, so we quite properly avoid it.

This absence of intellectual mechanisms for questioning our own actions becomes clear when the expression of any unstructured doubt — for example, over the export of arms to potential enemies or the loss of shareholder power to managers or the loss of parliamentary power to the executive — is automatically categorized as naive or idealistic or bad for the economy or simply bad for jobs. And should we attempt to use sensible words to deal with these problems, they will be caught up immediately in the structures of the official arguments which accompany the official modern ideologies — arguments as sterile as the ideologies are irrelevant. Our society contains no method of serious self-criticism for the simple reason that it is now a self-justifying system which generates its own logic.

It is hardly surprising that there has never been such confidence as there is today within our leadership about their unity of outlook. No matter which way they turn, they find other elites to confirm the reflection of themselves and of one another. Virtually identical programs in business schools and schools of public affairs are turning out people trained in the science of systems management. The Harvard Business School case method is the most famous example of this general obsession with management by solutions, a system in which the logic will always provide support for the conclusions. In troubled times the citizenry search for the responsible parties. When their elites are so similar, this tends to turn into a search for scapegoats. In the United States, there is a tendency now to single out Harvard. And yet, precisely the same approach reappears throughout Western educational systems, whether in the training of lawyers or political scientists or, notably, in France, in the Enarques, the graduates of the school which trains key state employees. The Ecole Nationale d'Administration (ENA) specializes in the abstract, logical process. In a sense the training in all these schools is designed to develop not a talent for solving problems but a method for recognizing the solutions which will satisfy the system. After that the established internal logic will provide all the necessary justifications.

For a good half century now it has been easy, even superficially satisfying, to say of our society that Christianity is dead and the psychiatrist is the new priest. But that is true only if you take the gossip columnist's view of civilization, a view in which character and detail are all that count. In reality we are today in the midst of a theology of pure power — power born of structure, not of dynasty or arms. The new holy trinity is organization, technology and information. The new priest is the technocrat — the man who understands the organization, makes use of the technology and controls access to the information, which is a compendium of "facts."

He has become the essential middleman between the people and the divinity. Like the old Christian priest, he holds the key to the tabernacle out of which, from time to time, he produces and distributes the wafer — those minimal nibbles at the divinity which leave the supplicant hungry for more. The wafer is knowledge, understanding, access, the hint of power. And the tabernacle is what it always was: the hiding place of this knowledge, the place which makes secrecy one of the keys to modern power. Finally there is the matter of absolution from personal responsibility. All religions seem to need special-case facilities to deal with the uncontrollable realities of a world which refuses to respond to their official ideology. These facilities take the form of personal-access mythology which is strapped almost arbitrarily to the side of the power structure. We have replaced the old phenomenon of sainthood with that of Herodom. As with Christianity, this has a double function. It gives the "people" something emotive, in the form of something concrete, to concentrate on. And, immobilized as all large systems are by their abstract nature, the Saint/Hero mechanism provides a practical way for that system to actually get things done.

No member of this priesthood would call himself a technocrat, although that is what he is. Whether graduates of Harvard, ENA, the London Business School or any of the hundreds of other similar places, they are committeemen, sometimes called number crunchers, always detached from the practical context, inevitably assertive, manipulative; in fact, they are highly sophisticated grease jockeys, trained to make the engine of government and business run but unsuited by training or temperament to drive the car or to have any idea of where it could be steered if events were somehow to put them behind the wheel. They are addicts of pure power, quite simply divorced from the questions of morality which were the original justification for reason's strength.

They may or may not be decent people. This amoral quality of our leadership is essential to understanding the nature of our times. The vocabularies of Locke and Voltaire and Jefferson have led us to judge men upon a simple scale of good and evil. A man who uses power to do evil is in theory judged to have been conscious of his acts and to be as fit for punishment as a perpetrator of premeditated murder. But the technocrat is not trained on that level. He understands events within the logic of the system. The greatest good is the greatest logic or the greatest appearance of efficiency or responsibility for the greatest possible part of the structure. He is therefore unpremeditated when he does good or evil. On a bad day he is the perfect manslaughterer, on a good day the perfect unintentional saint. What's more, the people who succeed at this kind of training are those whom it suits best. They therefore reinforce this amoral quality. *Dans le royaume des coulisses, l'eunuque est roi.*

This form of education is not only applied to the training of business and government leaders. In fact, it is now central to almost every profession. If you examine the creation of an architect, for example, or an art historian or a professor of literature or a military officer, you will find the same obsession with details, with the accumulation of facts, with internal logic. The "social scientists" — the economists and political scientists in particular — consist of little more than these elements, because they do not have even the touchstones of real action to restrain them. The overall picture of the role of the architect or the officer is lost in the background, but the technocrat who sets out to build or to fight is convinced that he is equipped with the greatest good of all time: the understanding of a system for reasoning and the possession of the equipment which fulfills that system, thus providing the concrete manifestations of its logic.

Robert McNamara is one of the great figures of this technocracy. While secretary of defense under Kennedy and Johnson, then as president of the World Bank, he shaped the Vietnam War, was central to launching both the nuclear arms race and the commercialization of the arms business and was again central to creating the financial structure which led to the current Third World debt crisis.

No doubt he is also a decent man, but that personal detail is irrelevant; or rather, what is astonishing about our systems is that the personal decency, or lack of it, of our leaders should have so little effect upon the impact of their actions. The way in which McNamara approached the Vietnam War was identical to the way in which he attacked the problems of the Third World while at the World Bank. The pure logic which on paper would win the war was the same logic which he applied to the massive recycling of the money deposited in the West by oil-producing companies, which in turn led to the Third World debt problem.

Throughout all these disasters he acted as the quintessential man of reason while remaining true to the abstract nature of the technocrat. In fact, he is still determined to go on doing good and apparently has no understanding of what he has done. It wasn't what he intended to do. It wasn't what the charts and briefing books said would happen. As a decent man, he is no doubt baffled. Other, less intelligent, less decent technocrats would simply have rewritten the brief in order to demonstrate that their logic had always been proved correct.

It may seem odd that the focus here has abruptly moved from large questions to the dissection of an individual. But Robert McNamara is a symbol of the end of the Age of Reason and, as I pick my way through the maze of the last forty years, his is one of the names which inevitably keeps recurring. The key to this examination is the avoidance of arguments limited to single sectors. What is interesting about McNamara is not what he did to boost the arms business, but the comparison between that and what he did to help Third World countries. More interesting still is the comparison between him and another key figure at the other end of the Age of Reason.

Cardinal Richelieu, a contemporary of Descartes, held power in France as the King's chief minister from 1624 to 1642. In many ways he was the first modern statesman, the first individual to apply an integrated rational method to that new concept — the nation-state. A standard reading of Richelieu — accurate in its details — would portray him as a devious, convoluted autocrat, while the same sort of examination would show McNamara to be a decent, honest man in search of fairness and efficiency. The wider reality is that Richelieu, in laying the foundations of the first modern state, made it possible for personal restraint and social responsibility to play central roles, while McNamara was in large part responsible for four of the West's most important postwar disasters. Yet in the eyes of the elites he has emerged from all that as an unblemished leader of our modern times and an example to be imitated.

Nevertheless, McNamara is very much a child of the Cardinal. Set side by side at a certain distance, they can hardly be distinguished from one another. Concentrated examination reveals only one important difference — Richelieu forced his policies on France and Europe with the clear logic of a revolutionary using a new weapon, while McNamara asserted his with the confident blindness of an inbred — that is, an overbred — aristocrat.

This youthfulness of Richelieu, compared with McNamara's intellectual degeneracy, make them the signposts of the Age of Reason — one at its opening, the other at its end, but united in a single great rational family. As for the essentials, little has changed. We began the seventeenth century in the grip of what philosophers of that time called blind logic. We end the twentieth century in the hands of blind reason, a more sophisticated version of the earlier problem.

What has changed radically are the roles which those who want power must play. We have lost an unsatisfactory pyramidal system, which did have a few advantages — functioning in a relatively public manner, for example. In its place, the management of power by the rational structures is much more absolute.

This doesn't mean that all power lies with the technocrats. In fact, the absolutism and inaccessibility which they have represented from the very beginning of the Age of Reason were, and indeed remain, so unrealistic that by the end of the eighteenth century a whole new type of public figure had to be invented: individuals who could — as Mussolini would have put it — make the trains run on time. Napoleon was the first and is still the definitive model. These Heroes promised to deliver the rational state, but to do so in a populist manner. The road from Napoleon to Hitler is direct. Indeed, most contemporary politicians still base their personas on this Heroic model.

And so the breakdown of public figures over the last century has resolved itself into a large group on the rational side — technocrats, Heroes and false Heroes — with, on the other, a small group that resists the structural imperatives and stands for an embattled humanist tradition. Jefferson is still perhaps the greatest example of this school, but there were others. Pascal Paoli, the Corsican, creator of the first modern republic, was one of the most inspired cases and perhaps the most tragic.

This same phenomenon of technocrats and Heroes versus practical humanists plays itself out in every sector of our society. The conflict is endlessly repeated with the same imbalance and the same results. It is as true among the military and the businessmen as it is among writers and architects.

The more these conflicts are examined, the clearer it becomes that certain of our most important instincts — the democratic, the practical, the imaginative — are profound enemies of the dominant rational approach. This war between the reasonable and the rational is one which our civilization, as we have constituted it, is congenitally unable to resolve. If anything, the rise of more and more parodically Heroic leaders indicates that the system in place is desperately driving itself forward according to its own logic. And endemic to that logic is the denial of all internal contradictions, to say nothing of internal wars.

But what are Richelieu and McNamara other than isolated remains on a field of ruins? The great danger, when looking at our society, is that what we see encourages us to become obsessed by individual personalities, thus mistaking the participants for the cause. Perhaps that is why

I approach this seamless web almost in the manner of an archeologist, as if engaged in a dig for some forgotten civilization — the Age of Reason somehow become Unreason.

Rational mythology has grown so thick and become so misleading that our reality — the one in which we actually live — does indeed seem to be dead and buried. The ground above us is strewn with collapsed columns and broken pots which indicate, despite the reassuring stories of our elites, that something is wrong. But this debris, taken piece by piece, tells us little.

And so, like a man sensible of his ignorance, I have begun in the chapters which follow by clearing away the underbrush to lay bare the obscured overall pattern. This undergrowth is made up largely of myth and of ideas, presented as if they were fact. The pattern is, in reality, not very complex. It is merely the evolution of the Age of Reason. Not a philosophical outline but an existential unfolding. Not theoretical argument but events which dovetail one into the other; the events which join Richelieu to McNamara across hundreds of years.

One of the first things to emerge from this progression is a profile of the technocrats and the Heroes as they gradually become the guardians of the rational idea and then of that idea gone wrong. Given our general obsession with personality, I couldn't help but pause long enough to sketch out the typology of these modern elites and then to illustrate them with some of our recent leaders. There is a justification for this self-indulgence. It demonstrates the common methodology used by those who hold the levers of power in the West.

Late as we are in the twentieth century, it is no longer possible to go on pretending that the arrival of our elites in positions of power is somehow an accident. They are precisely the people whom our system seeks out: Robert McNamara and Ronald Reagan, Robert Armstrong and Brian Mulroney, Valéry Giscard d'Estaing and William Westmoreland, Jim Slater and Michael Milken, along with armies of faceless corporate presidents. These are the desired and chosen leaders. They are also the precise product which our education system sets out to produce.

Like all functioning elites, ours seek to perpetuate themselves for the general good. As always, this involves the creation of an educational system. The formation process appears, at first glance, to differ from country to country, but once the common basic assumptions are dusted off, these differences disappear. Education is the one place where lofty ideals and misty mythology cannot avoid meeting the realities of crude self-interest.

And so, having uncovered an historical outline, an elite typology and the basic reproductive habits of that elite, I then sought a single example which would be equally true for all nations, would be clean and neat in both its abstract conception and its practical application and would illustrate the amoral — in fact, the darkly comic — nature of the rational approach. By far the cleanest and neatest of examples is the international arms trade. What makes it doubly interesting is that leaders as varied as Kennedy, de Gaulle and Harold Wilson were seduced by its attractions. They were then tripped up between the intentions of the arms business and its reality — tripped up so badly that the greater their success, the more disastrous the long-term effects on their economies and on their foreign policies.

The next step was to turn to a series of specialized areas — the military, government and business — to see whether the same general characteristics existed. The military come first because when humans undertake change — whether in technology or organization — they usually begin on the battlefield. This may be depressing, but that doesn't make it any the less true. Not surprisingly, therefore, the first technocrats were the staff officers. And the unprecedented violence of this century is partly a reflection of the struggle for dominance by the staff officers over the field officers, partly the result of the former's disastrous approach to strategy.

The case of government is more complex. There has been a gradual, widespread improvement in social standards, thanks in good part to the work of large bureaucracies. But the conversion of the political class into an extension of the technocracy has been a disaster. Perhaps the most damaging part of our obsession with expertise and systems has been the restructuring of elected assemblies to make them more efficient. This equation of the idea of efficiency — a third-level subproduct of reason — with the process of democratic government shows just how far away we have slipped from our common sense. Efficient decision making is, after all, a characteristic proper to authoritarian governments. Napoleon was efficient. Hitler was efficient. Efficient democracy can only mean democracy castrated. In fact, the question which arises is whether the rational approach has not removed from democracy its single greatest strength — the ability to act in an unconventional manner. When you examine, for example, our twenty-year-old battle against inflation, you can't help but note that politicians who become devotees of technocratic logic also become prisoners of conventional solutions.

It follows that the theology of power, under which the technocracy prospers, marginalizes the whole idea of opposition and therefore that of sensible change. Opposition becomes a refusal to participate in the process. It is irrational. And this trivialization of those who criticize or say no from outside the power structure applies not only to politics but to all organizations.

These victories of reason made the rise of the Heroes inevitable. And the marginalization of the politicians forced them in turn to take on, at least superficially, an Heroic profile, since that was the only available approach which could win them the status they needed. The effect of this change on the politicians themselves was profound. It altered the emotional relationship they had with the public. As the role of the leader has been destabilized, so his internal drives have turned into a psychodrama far removed from public arguments over ideology and administration.

In the meantime the very success of the technocrats and the Heroes was rendering powerless the law, which was theoretically their preferred tool for change and improvement. From the beginning of the Age of Reason, the law had been intended to protect the individual from the unreasonable actions of others, especially those in power. This involved regulating the proper relationship between ownership and the individual. Or between the state, the individual and the corporation. Or between defined responsibilities and the people charged with carrying out those responsibilities. In other words law attempted to regulate the application of power.

But the nature of power has completely changed in our society. There has been a marriage between the state and the means of production, an integration of the elites into an interchangeable technocracy, a confusion over ownership and management in the corporations. These new structures make it almost impossible for the law to judge illegal that which is wrong.

The realities of contemporary capitalism are central to our problems. Here is a term which has travelled far from the old concepts that still account for the vocabulary we use to describe the use of private property. Curiously enough, the word *capitalist* and all the supporting notions still seem to refer to the ownership of the means of production and to the earning of money and power through the successful working of that production. But most Western corporations are controlled by managers, not owners — managers who are virtually interchangeable with military staff officers and government bureaucrats.

There are others, of course, who also claim the robes of capitalism. Small businessmen, for example, are large in numbers and do often conform to the original concept. But they have little power or influence in our society. Far more important in the nontechnocratic business community are what used to be called speculators: bankers, brokers, promoters and others who act as if capitalism has progressed from the slow and awkward ownership of the means of production to a higher level, at which money is quite simply made out of money. The nineteenth century saw these moneymen as marginal, irresponsible parasites living off the flesh of real capitalism. Their relationship to other citizens was roughly that of the Mafia today. And yet we now treat them as if they were pillars of our society — both socially and economically.

As for the professional managers, their arrival was supposed to remove some of the selfishness from our economies. Unlike real owners, the managers were expected to be free from the logic of uncontrolled greed. Instead these employees have inherited the mythology of capitalism without having to bear personal responsibility for any of the essential risks. They have been free to apply the theory of unfettered capitalism as if it were a perfectible abstraction, not a human reality.

The leaders of all these specialized areas don't just act upon the population, however. Like everyone else, they are also acted upon by general social phenomena. Even a brief look at three of these phenomena — the myth of the secret, the obsession with individualism and the idolizing of stars — can help to clarify the effect that reason has had on our lives.

The invention of the secret is perhaps the most damaging outgrowth of the power produced when control over knowledge was combined with the protective armour of specialization. Until recently very little was considered improper to know. Today the restricted lists are endless. And yet there can't be more than two or three real secrets in the entire world. Even the construction of an atomic bomb is now part of available knowledge. Nevertheless the imprisoning of information continues, undeterred by endless access-to-information legislation.

These restrictions have been counterbalanced over the last thirty years by an apparent explosion in individual freedoms. This breakdown of social order — rules of dress, sexual controls, speech patterns, family structures — has been seen as a great victory for the individual. On the other hand, it may simply be a reflection of the individual's frustration at being locked up inside a specialization. These acts of personal freedom are irrelevant to the exercise of power. So in lieu of taking a real part in the evolution of society, the individual struggles to appear as if no one has power over his personal evolution. Thus victories won for these individual liberties may actually be an acceptance of defeat by the individual.

For example, never have so few people been willing to speak out on important questions. Their fear is tied not to physical threats, but to standing apart from fellow experts or risking a career or entering an area of nonexpertise. Not since the etiquette-ridden courts of the eighteenth century has public debate been so locked into fixed positions, fixed formulas and fixed elites expert in rhetoric. The nobles of that time gave themselves over in frustration to a frivolous self-indulgence, which could be called courtly egotism. It is difficult to identify any real difference between that courtly egotism and the personal freedoms which so obsess us today.

The combination of a restrictive technology inside power with decorative personal freedoms outside made the rise of a new class inevitable.

It was first identified by the American sociologist C. Wright Mills in the 1950s. The celebrities. The stars. The people whose sole reason for being famous is their fame. Tennis players, aristocratic names, children of painters, movie stars. History has always been filled with famous mistresses and actors, but their fame was measured largely by the degree to which the rays of the monarch fell upon them. Today's celebrities have fame unrelated to power. And over the last forty years they have gradually occupied large sections of the press, of conversations, of dreams. In the public imagination they have replaced the men of power who, being technocrats, are of little general interest.

These celebrities serve an important public purpose. They distract in the way that monarchs once used their courts to distract. And now that they have some control over that public mythology, they are actually rising to occupy places of real power.

Finally, our imagination has been radically altered in two areas by the Age of Reason. The image, which was first scratched on stone walls, then painted, printed, photographed and projected, can now be conceived as a three-dimensional whole by a computer program. In other words, after thousands of years of progress, the image has achieved technical perfection. That progress had been central to our sense of our own immortality and the completion of it has had a profoundly destabilizing effect on our sense of what we are. On top of that the undermining of universal language, in large part by the dialects of expertise, has meant that we can't turn to the word to steady ourselves. Instead, the writers and their pens, having invented the Age of Reason, are now its primary prisoners and so are unable to ask the right questions, let alone to break down the imprisoning linguistic walls of their own creation.

Blind reason is the element which links everything together in this general survey. What is blind reason? Perhaps it is nothing more than a sophisticated form of logic — a more sophisticated, more profoundly integrated, better structured version of the blind logic from which the reformers of the seventeenth and eighteenth centuries were determined to escape. Their escape was to have been made, of course, on the back of reason. In other words, we have ended up today very much where we began nearly half a millennium ago.

The end of something often resembles the beginning. More often than not our nose-to-the-glass view makes us believe that the end we are living is in fact a new beginning. This confusion is typical of an old civilization's self-confidence — limited by circumstances and by an absence of memory — and in many ways resembling the sort often produced by senility. Our rational need to control understanding and therefore memory has simply accentuated the confusion.

The end, in any case, is that part of the human experience most often mistaken for something else. Everything is at its most sophisticated, most organized, most stable. The very sophistication of the organism marks the divorce of those ideas which were reasonably clear and simple when they were first embraced from the marvellous, remarkable structure which has been built over and around those same ideas in the course of living with them. That structure becomes the superficial celebration of the ideas, which it also invariably crushes. This simple truth is hidden from us by the reassuring sense of stability which the structure creates. But stability is the most fragile element in the human condition. Nothing seems more permanent than a long-established government about to lose power, nothing more invincible than a grand army on the morning of its annihilation.

The present condition of reason is clear when the Byzantine systems of today are compared to the clear statements of Francis Bacon in the early seventeenth century or, for example, of Voltaire a hundred years later in his *Philosophical Dictionary*: "It is obvious to the whole world that a service is better than an injury, that gentleness is preferable to anger. It only remains, therefore, to use our reason to discern the shades of goodness and badness."[1] These are the sort of words which lead us to associate reason with morality, common sense and, gradually with a personal freedom which we now know as democracy.

How is it, then, that neither Voltaire nor his friends noticed the intensive use of reason by Ignatius Loyola a century earlier, when he organized the Jesuits and almost single-handedly mounted the Counter-Reformation? Loyola was delighted to find a system that would serve the authority of the pope. And Bacon, lord chancellor of England, was neither a democrat nor particularly obsessed by morality. What he was was modern — the ideologue of modern science and as such the most important single influence on the Encyclopedists.[2] And even Voltaire and his friends, although they made the error of thinking that morality and common sense were the natural partners of reason, also saw these three in the context of authority. They wanted a strong but fair king. They thought reason would render authority fair. How did they make such an obvious mistake?

They were thinking on their feet in the heat of the action. They were responding to real needs, just as Loyola had taken charge when Catholicism was faced by a Protestant victory and Richelieu had devised the modern state as a way of defeating the warring nobles. Even William Blake, with the clarity of his mystical vision, said in *Jerusalem*, "I must create a system or be enslaved by another man's."

In the wake of the Encyclopedists came a raft of philosophers who adapted these basic ideas in order to suit the evolution of events. But all they did was construct an ever more elaborate structure over a falsehood. From its very beginning as an applied idea, reason has been as success-ful — if not more successful — at creating new degrees of barbarism and violence as it has been at imposing reasonable actions. As fast to invent a new breed of authoritarian leaders, whom we soon called absolute dic-tators, as it was to produce paragons of responsible democracy.

This is our Western inheritance. The rest of the world, however, is locked in a struggle with other problems and other forces. That doesn't mean we are not closely linked to them. We are all inseparably linked. And we must develop policies which take those links into account. But nor does this mean that we must analyze or reform our societies solely in the light of other worlds. To do so would be the equivalent of closing down our steel industries because someone else produces cheaper steel with child labour.

Our own evolution is the result of events which bear only a vague re-semblance to those that shaped Africa, Asia or the Soviet Union. The Chinese, for example, looked into formal logic well before we became obsessed with it and found it less important than other things. They delved into the market economy when we were still in the Dark Ages, and therefore they do not associate it in any way with the democratic ideology. Western confusion over this led us foolishly to confuse economic liber-alism in China during the 1980s with a desire for political liberalism.

Buddhism, Hinduism and Islam are religions still carried by strong belief, while Christianity in the West has been largely reduced to a social phenomenon. Olivier Germain-Thomas's comparison of the life inside an Indian temple with the cool emptiness of Chartres is particularly moving. "The cathedrals in my country are only memories of a culture, while in this temple everything speaks, everything is vibration, everything sings, everything is alive." And in Buddhism, the reason for thinking about the world is to escape from it, not to find an explanation for its origins.[3]

As the West has closed itself ever more tightly into the self-justifying logic of its own system, we have found it increasingly difficult to con-centrate on the single truths of our situation. Instead the last twenty years have seen the rapid passage of a multitude of political and eco-nomic fashions, each of which was supposed to get us out of our dol-drums and our internal contradictions. Most of them have involved key factors outside the West — not because of practical internationalism but as the result of a self-delusionary hope that external solutions would solve our internal problems. They have all been sophisticated versions of the great eighteenth-century financial fraud, the South Sea Bubble.

None have delivered and so, in the last decade, the fashions have come and gone with even greater speed.

Massive lending at home and in the Third World had no sooner failed than we were righteously preaching fiscal austerity on every street-corner of the globe. Financial deregulation had no sooner brought a wave of national and international mergers large enough to destabilize our economies than we discovered the truth of divestment and called it rationalization. Japan has swung in our imagination from representing the golden model of the future to incarnating the unfair devil at the root of our economic difficulties and then swung back again. A decade of wild hopes attached to Chinese liberalism no sooner lay dead in Tienanmen Square than we turned with emotional relief to Central Europe.

The promise of major changes and therefore of massive economic needs in the old Warsaw Pact quickly had us salivating. Here was the new and dreamed-of hinterland. Here were people who believed that our system was best.

But some of these countries have never been touched by the Western evolution; some have had marginal experiences; others have been cut off since 1939. Their imaginary expectations are at least half a century behind our real experiences. Quite apart from the economic and political anarchy which the current situation involves, they would have to deal with a whole series of other basic internal questions before any real integration into the Western structure could begin. Whatever the ongoing changes actually hold for those living in what we used to call the Soviet bloc, the Western reaction is inescapably one of relief. Here is another fashion to hypnotize us with gratifying imaginary promises. Here is room for another round of prolonged self-delusions. Here is another excuse not to address our own problems.

This book is therefore about the West, that falsely geographic idea which refers to only 750 million people in a handful of countries spread around the globe. They are the countries fully in the grip of the Age of Reason. One way or another, of course, to a greater or lesser extent, that age has penetrated everywhere on the planet. Our own problems are often mirrored in those penetrations. For example, while the technocratic leadership was presenting to us its promised solutions for the good management of democratic societies, the same management principles were being presented in South Africa, Algeria, Morocco, Tanzania, Vietnam and Kenya as the solution to their problems. How could technocracy have a complementary relationship with democratic societies, in which the individual weighs his freedom by the calm and regularity in which his community is managed, when it was also meant to be an intimate part of systems which eliminate or ignore democracy and individualism? How could a great leap forward in democratic management methods also be a great leap forward in efficient repression elsewhere? The answer could quite simply be that reason has nothing to do with democratic freedom or individualism or social justice.

To get at the unassailable, self-serving logic of the ancien régime, Voltaire and his friends made great use of scepticism. Once they had succeeded, this scepticism, this talent for criticism, remained in the air, a far easier tool than the vigilant common sense and morality which were intended to guide man's reason. And so a new sceptical logic was born, liberated from the weight of historical precedent and therefore even more self-serving than the logic which had gone before.

This scepticism became a trademark of the new elites and gradually turned to cynicism. Worst of all, as the complexities of the new systems increased, with their rewards of abstract power for those who succeeded, the new elites began to develop a contempt for the citizen. The citizen became someone to whom the elite referred as if to a separate species: "He wouldn't understand this." "She needn't know about that." "He will vote for any sort of politician if a nice package is put together." "She panics easily, so unpleasant news should be held back." The inability of governments to discuss in a coherent manner the political and economic difficulties in which we are mired today is a prime example of their contempt.

The attitudes of our elites remain even less positive when dealing with women. This has nothing to do with and has not been changed by a century of lobbying and struggling to integrate women into the mechanisms of power. The simple truth is that they were not part of the formulation and creation of the Age of Reason. In fact, women were the symbol of the irrational. Ever since the birth of the Age of Reason, women have been perceived by the new elites to be on the losing side.

Examples are legion. Richelieu can be found writing to his vacillating king about the necessity of developing "the masculine virtue of making decisions rationally."[4] Centuries later, the slow push for universal suffrage in Western democracies illustrated that nothing had changed. When the aristocracy loosened its exclusive control on society, it was in order to include the votes of the other property holders — the middle classes. When the property holders weakened, it was to include those who did not own property. They in turn weakened, bit by bit, in order to extend the most basic civil right to the various excluded minorities — members of dissident religions were among the last to be allowed onto many voting lists. And after them the vote was extended to nonmembers of the ruling tribe — blacks in the United States and Asians in Canada, for example.

Women were not even considered during this process. Fewer than seventy-five years ago an aristocratic, well-educated, property-owning woman was considered less fit to vote than a penniless, uneducated miner or the segregated son of a freed slave. It would therefore be a great error to assume that our society has had or has within it today the basic flexibility to allow real female participation. After all, it has been created over a period of nearly five centuries without them in mind.

As recently as 1945, when the French government decided to create its revolutionary rational school of state administration, ENA, the following could be found in the introduction to the enabling legislation:

> No doubt young women are suited to a large number of junior jobs offered by the civil service. There are even certain bureaucracies, notably Public Health and Social Security, where their presence in management positions appears desirable. But their ability to fill junior positions is not reason enough to allow entry to the civil service, which must be able to furnish the executive management of the important public services. The aptitude for commanding, the capacity to handle important affairs, the need for a certain level of comportment when dealing with grave political problems: these are all important elements to be considered and which are not generally found in women.[5]

The minister responsible for these words and for the creation of ENA was Michel Debré, who went on to become prime minister in 1958.

These examples are not intended to suggest that women have played no role inside the structures of power. There have been remarkable queens, heads of government and ministers, just as there have been scientists, painters, writers and so on. Today, more than ever, women are occupying positions of influence. However, in the past they have been the exceptions to the rule and were usually obliged to hold on to their power by deforming themselves into honorary men or into magnified archetypes of the female who manipulated men. It still is not clear that women can successfully become part of the established structures without accepting those deformations.

What follows in this book is about the realities of Western rational civilization. It is a male reality. Women might well want to change that, but it isn't clear that the best way to do so is to shore up the existing structures by going into them. Even if they do so, it is difficult to see why women would want to claim responsibility for what has gone before.

Throughout the West, we are led by elected and nonelected elites who do not believe in the public. They cooperate with the established representational systems of democracy. But they do not believe in the value of the public's contribution. Nor do they believe in the existence of a public moral code. What they do believe in are Heroic appeals, contractual agreements and administrative methods. This means that in dealing with the public, they find it easier to appeal to the lowest common denominator within each of us. That this often succeeds reinforces their contempt for a public apparently capable of nothing better. They do not take into account that the public, like any of its members, is in fact capable of the highest and the lowest. Citizens are limited in their public role by time and knowledge. Their days are filled with jobs and families. They have come to fear stepping beyond their areas of expertise. In spite of the complaining they may do, they harbour a remarkably durable trust in their elites. Those elites, they believe, are made up of people who have been trained and chosen to deliver the Age of Reason. The contempt with which the elites reward this trust is a betrayal of those they are pledged to serve. Or, to be more concrete, it is a betrayal of their legal employer.

Cynicism, ambition, rhetoric and the worship of power — these were the characteristics commonly found in the courts of the eighteenth century. They are the characteristics of courtiers, which is precisely what our modern and dispassionate elites have become. And courtliness is the characteristic they most encourage throughout the population. The new message of the eighteenth century wasn't complicated. It attempted simply to break the captive logic of arbitrary power and superstition with reason and scepticism. Now that same self-justifying logic has asserted itself within the new system. It took us four and a half centuries to break the power of divine revelation, only to replace it with the divine revelations of reason. We must therefore break again, this time with arbitrary logic and the superstition of knowledge.

But in this maze of logic, the unforgiving extremes function with the greatest of ease. The acquisitive, the cynical, the religious fanatics of raw competition, the exploiters of society — all of them find the tools of reason, as shaped by time, to their particular liking. And yet, to argue against reason means arguing as an idiot or as an entertainer who seeks only to amuse. The structures of argument have been co-opted so completely by those who work the system that when an individual reaches for the words and phrases which he senses will express his case, he finds that they are already in active use in the service of power. This now amounts to a virtual dictatorship of vocabulary. It isn't really surprising that a society based upon structure and logic should determine the answer to most questions by laying out the manner in which they are posed. Somehow we must do today what Voltaire once did — scratch away the veneer in order to get at the basic foundations. We must rediscover how to ask simple questions about ourselves.

Technology and knowledge advance with great speed. That is, or can be, good. Man, however, does not change. He is as he was the day the German theologian Dietrich Bonhoeffer decided to go on speaking out against Nazi anti-Semitism knowing that this could only lead him to a death camp. He is also as he was the day he cheered in the Roman circus, the day he crucified Christ, the day he slaughtered the unarmed Valdesians, the day he opened the first gas oven at Auschwitz, the day he tortured rebels in Malaysia, Algeria and Vietnam. In his last interview, the French historian Fernand Braudel ended by saying that although knowledge meant man had less excuse for his barbarism, he was nevertheless "profoundly barbaric."[6] There are no inherited characteristics to help us avoid repeating the actions of our parents or grandparents. We are born with the schizophrenia of good and evil within us, so that each generation must persevere in self-recognition and in self-control. In ceding to the automatic reassurance of our logic, we have abandoned once more those powers of recognition and of control. Darkness seems scarcely different from light, with the web of structure and logic woven thick across both. We must therefore cut away these layers of false protection if we wish to regain control of our common sense and morality.

3

The Rise of Reason

It is a general weakness of men delivering ideas that they are able to convince themselves their words represent a break with the past and a new beginning. In the early stages of a revolution, history is at its most malleable. Disorder and optimism combine to wipe out those truths artificially manufactured by the preceding regime. At the same time, they usually wipe out the memory of any inconvenient real events.

The men of the seventeenth and eighteenth centuries, for example, were not wrong to condemn darkness and superstition. They were writing close to a time when it had been common to feed a consecrated Host to a sick cow in order to drive out the demon; a time of saint worship and of church corruption.[1] And, of course, a time of willful political leadership.

If the philosophers of reason believed that nothing provokes violence so effectively as fear and that fear is the product of ignorance, it was because they had arrived on the scene after two hundred years of religious and civil wars. These had produced levels of civilian violence not achieved again until the twentieth century. The reasonable men of the eighteenth century wanted to cut the roots of this fear. Their strategy was to attack what Isaiah Berlin called the "dark mysteries and grotesque fairy tales which went by the names of theology, metaphysics and other brands of concealed dogma or superstition with which unscrupulous knaves had for so long befuddled the stupid and benighted multitudes whom they murdered, enslaved, oppressed and exploited."[2] It was quite natural that this assault on darkness and on the divine aspect of the absolute monarchs who presided over it should eventually have been called the Enlightenment. The fact that the leadership came from France added a particular excitement to the affair, given that the leading European example of absolutism and of royal divine right was the French king and his court. And the French intellectual opposition had grown into a veritable army of thinkers in all domains — philosophy, yes, but also agriculture, science, military organization and, of course, novel writing. The novelists were like deep-penetration patrols, striking out where least expected. By virtue of his devotion to the publication of the *Encyclopédie,* Diderot was the chief of staff of the operation, supported by faithful staff officers like d'Alembert. The strategist and champion of individual combat was Voltaire. He was constantly on the front lines of public debate, constantly inventing the phrases which might make change possible.

What these philosophes do not seem to have noticed, however, was that the very methods they were about to loose upon the world, in the name of reason, had been in ever-increasing practical use throughout the two preceding centuries of violence. In fact, these methods had been used by Richelieu 150 years earlier precisely to create the absolutist state against which the Enlightenment was now rebelling.

Perhaps Voltaire and his friends believed that the forces of reason had suffered from being scattered in a disordered way around the previous century, when they had been used for a variety of causes, both worthy and corrupt. What was needed was to capture them so that reason could devote knowledge to the development of morality and common sense. That was how the philosophes presented their crusade.

Of course, neither morality nor common sense were new issues. They had once been integrated into the medieval concept, had then been rescued by new thinkers and reintegrated into the concept of divine monarchies. And here they were, once again lost in the degenerate structures of an aging system, being rescued by yet another group of thinkers who proclaimed the supremacy of reason as the new solution to man's problems.

This eighteenth-century revolution in mythology was therefore not so much something new as it was the repackaging of disparate forces already at play. The most revolutionary effect of their consolidation was the replacement of the control of the old class structure by two new sorts of leadership — that of the technocrat and that of the Hero. This tendency has been leading the way ever since, even though there is still no popular or official or philosophical consensus that these two are the complementary heads of the rational power structure.

The technocrat began his existence as the ideal servant of the people — a man freed from both irrational ambition and self-interest. Then, with surprising rapidity, he evolved into one who used the system with a distant contempt for the people.

The Hero was a more complex phenomenon. He appeared unexpectedly out of the shadows of reason, drawn forward when the people showed uncontrollable impatience with the way they were being governed. This impatience may have been provoked by poor or selfish government, by the inability of the new technocracy actually to govern or even by leadership which somehow bored the populace. With the old royal-baronial rivalry gone, there was no fixed structure to take up the slack of unpopular government. The idea of elections was new and, even now, two centuries later, does not easily convert the people's desires into appropriate government. And so it was that, in those moments when there was maximum confusion, the Hero took to stepping forward out of the shadows and presenting himself as the exciting face of reason; the man who could deliver the people's needs and be loved by them; the man who could take over the difficult labour of reasoning on behalf of the tired and confused citizen.

Trapped between these technocrats and Heroes were the reasonable men who thought of themselves as true men of reason — men who held firmly to their common sense morality. But they were neither efficient enough nor exciting enough to hold their own in a squeeze between vicious structuralism and heroic logic. Many did, in fact, hold their own for a period of time — Pascal Paoli for twenty years in Corsica, Jefferson for even longer in the new United States, the first Pitt for several decades in England. Michel de L'Hospital almost succeeded in preventing the French wars of religion. The host of those who served the good cause, and still serve, in the way Diderot would have hoped they might, is legion. But they are not the ones who have defined the main line of the last four and a half centuries. They have been the exceptions to the rule, fighting a rearguard action in defence of humanism.

That main line has been obscured by two of our obsessions. One is an uncontrollable desire to give ourselves the impression that we have made yet another fresh start. We are constantly declaring new ages. The conversion of the original Age of Reason into the Enlightenment of the eighteenth century was only a first step. Had humanity turned a great corner in the process? Not according to most definitions of the Enlightenment; for example, as a "conviction that reason could achieve all knowledge, supplant organized religion and ensure progress towards happiness and perfection."[3]

The rational machine continued on from there, being redefined ad infinitum, notably by Kant, until at last Nietzsche theoretically rejected the concept itself. But Nietzsche's discovery that reason was subject to passion and to supermen came a full half century after the real superman had actually galloped onto the public stage and given a demonstration. Napoleon had ridden in on the back of reason, reorganized Europe in the name of reason and governed beneath the same principle. The subsequent effect was to bolster the rational approach, not to discourage it.

This tells us a great deal about our other obscuring obsession. We have great difficulty dealing with philosophy in the context of real events. These two categories seem to live on separate planets. For example, we are still convinced that violence is the product of fear and fear the product of ignorance. And yet, since the beginning of the Age of

Reason, there has been a parallel growth in both knowledge and violence, culminating in the slaughters of the twentieth century.

Does this mean that knowledge creates greater fear than does ignorance? Or that the rational system has distorted the value of knowledge? Or something else? One thing it does demonstrate is that the separation of philosophy from real events has encouraged the invention of mythological obscurantism. The constant launching of new philosophical ages is part of that invention.

Revolutions do not begin on dates, although we constantly search for that kind of reassuring touch point. An argument can be made that the assumptions and methods of applied reason were first developed by the Inquisition. In its revolutionary approach to what a question consists of, what constitutes an answer and what is truth, all the key elements of modern intellectual thought can be found.

The Inquisitors were the first to formalize the idea that to every question there is a right answer. The answer is known, but the question must be asked and correctly answered. Relativism, humanism, common sense and moral beliefs were all irrelevant to this process because they assume doubt. Since the Inquisitors knew the answer, doubt was impossible. Process, however, was essential for efficient governance and process required that questions be asked in order to produce the correct answer.

When the Inquisition was created in the thirteenth century no one, least of all Pope Gregory, understood what was being set in motion. Issuing a bull which made the persecution of heresy the special function of the Dominicans hardly seemed a revolutionary step. The Inquisitors' definition of truth was arrived at slowly, as was the process which permitted them to establish it. But as each detail of that process emerged, so the assumptions involved became clear.

Everything the Inquisition did — except the execution of the guilty — took place in secret. Public silence surrounded the work of the travelling Inquisitors. Unlike judges, magistrates, nobles and kings, who have always worn some symbolic costume, the Inquisitors wore the simplest, most anonymous black, like the proverbial accountant. And while their power permitted them to do their work on the basis of accusations and denunciations, what they really wanted were complete inquisitions. Being already in possession of the truth, they were interested in the rational demonstration of it by each victim. Perhaps the most telling detail was that each of these secret tribunals included a notary. His job was to record every word of every question and answer. These notarised manuscripts became the perpetual records of truth. But again, the purpose of such exactitude was to glorify the methodology, not the outcome. The notary was there to confirm the relationship between a priori truth and assembled fact. On the surface the Inquisitors were torturers and monsters. On a more profound level they were moral auditors.

If one is looking for an individual father of the Age of Reason, Niccolo Machiavelli is probably the right candidate. After all, he laid out in *The Prince* (1513) and in *The Discourses* (1519) a governing method which is with us to this day. The humanists of the Renaissance attacked him violently, as did the Encyclopedists in their time.

They recognized in Machiavelli their elder brother from the dark side. "A detestable political system which can be summed up in two words — the art of tyranny."[4] But this ex-senior civil servant of Florence, with a particular interest in military reorganization, remains nonetheless a man of our times: an ambitious individual, tainted but not swallowed by nationalism, constantly in search of an employer. Faced by the Medici princes after their destruction of the Florentine republican government, he wrote his books in good part in order to win favour with the new regime. He would have been a perfect recruit for the new class of intellectuals sought four and a half centuries later by Henry Kissinger — men who, by virtue of not belonging to or believing in any one concrete thing, could be considered independent. Of course, if viewed with the less trusting eye of an employer, that emotional and intellectual freedom could also be seen to offer the neutrality of a mercenary.

Machiavelli's message — that "new modes and orders," that is a new system and new ways, would reward the sharp-eyed sceptic — made him into the lasting symbol of the Age of Reason. Popular mythology insisted that he was the prophet of political immorality. In truth, he was indifferent to moral questions. He was a modern courtier in search of employment. Vitality, not Virtue, was the characteristic he sought in a political leader. At the centre of everything he wrote was the theme of political efficiency. To this day, men who find themselves burdened by the adjective *Machiavellian* also find their careers severely limited. And yet the question that might be asked is: Why do so few men carry the adjective? If you were to edit the sixteenth-century references out of *The Prince* and then to retitle it *Power and the Executive* or *Effective Government*, the book would immediately be adopted by all contemporary management courses aimed at training businessmen, civil servants and professional politicians. It would be considered an ideal manual for the preparation of the modern world leader.

Hard on Machiavelli's heels came the third act of the rise of reason — the schism in the Catholic church. Luther's *95 Theses* (1517), the Church of England (1531), Calvin's *Institutio Religionis Christianae* (1536) burst out like a single large explosion. The arbitrary nature of official Catholicism was probably responsible for lighting the fuse. But a growing awareness of the rational argument also made people believe that reform was possible. And an almost unconscious common sense populism pushed the instigators to translate the Bible into various vernaculars. That simple act of vulgarization destroyed the priests' monopoly over the word. It remains one of the most successful blows ever struck against manipulative secrecy.

The clarity of such early ideas as freedom of dissent, personal responsibility and individual freedom was soon drowned, however, in a sea of blood. As the massacres produced by these religious wars passed from the thousands to the hundreds of thousands to the millions, both sides seemed to lose sight of their purpose. In the end the Reformation clearly changed Europe. But the ambiguity inherent in the whole process was so great that the shape of the future was determined more by those who fought reform than by the reformers.

Ignatius Loyola was an unlikely leader for the Counter-Reformation and an even less likely formulator of modern rational methodology. A minor Spanish noble, ambitious and much given to both war and womanizing, he had a talent for playing the royal courts. These skills of the courtier were to be essential later in his life.

While he was in battle as a young man, a cannonball passed between his legs, smashing the bones and crippling him. His manic drive refused this situation. He forced upon himself a series of extremely risky operations in which the legs were rebroken and reset. The final result still wasn't pleasing to the eye. The operations had left a piece of bone protruding out of line on one leg, and so, in a last act of courtly egotism, he forced the doctors to begin all over again in order to saw off the distorting bone.[5]

This final folly of pleasure broke him, physically and mentally, and the resulting crisis brought on his passage towards God. His actual conversion was full of the sort of mysteries and meetings with the divine that one would expect from an important saint. Then, abruptly, the predictable became unpredictable. The classic road to salvation turned into a revolution.

No sooner was the initial miraculous part of the process over than he attached himself to a rigorously intellectual view of the Church. That intellectual abstraction was neatly tied up, thanks to his notarylike obsession with detail, law, procedure and, eventually, structure. This solidification process took only a few years. It began with Ignatius — alone on the roads of Spain, limping towards God (the operations had not been entirely successful), preaching and teaching in towns and villages, carried forward with the aid of love and what appeared to be a natural communion with the people; indeed, a natural communion with the earth itself. Suddenly, others began to follow him and his example. The Church could not ignore this little band, all dressed in simple black and out working their faith among the people.

At first observers imagined that these young men were renewing the example of Saint Francis of Assisi, that theirs also was a vow of poverty and simplicity. But the uniform of Ignatius's band was the result neither of humility nor of a spirituality which left them indifferent, let alone unconscious of, their physical well-being.

Ignatius went out among the people to reason with them. To draw them to God not through love but through logic. He had not dispensed with his fashionable appearance in order to bring man closer to God. Rather, his appearance had been consciously tailored to advance the cause of winning individuals back to the Church. He sought discretion by costuming himself in simplicity. Ignatius was in the process of becoming the first complete rational technocrat.

In those times any religious initiative was dangerous. Ignatius was regularly and anonymously denounced to the Inquisition. The Inquisition, with its mastery of fear, was indeed the guiding spirit of the new era, but others were learning from its methods and carrying them further. The Inquisitors were failing to keep up with their own concept — power through structure. It became obvious how badly they had fallen behind when the time came to deal with Loyola. In 1535, about to leave Paris with his followers, he heard by rumour that someone had denounced him and his book of religious *Exercises*. His life was therefore in danger. Without hesitation he went directly to the local Inquisitor and announced that he was leaving for Spain. If they were going to accuse him of heresy, they should decide quickly. The Inquisitor, caught off guard and probably wondering whether the young man's brazenness meant he had important friends, replied that the accusation wasn't important. On the other hand, he would be curious to see Loyola's book. In the Inquisition's long experience, the best way to catch a man was through his writings.

The Inquisitor read the *Exercises* on the spot, praised them and asked if he might keep a copy. In other words, he wanted to keep a copy to examine it carefully for heretical flaws. The little book might also be a potential sword which could be held over Loyola's head if he needed to be manipulated later on.

Ignatius agreed but insisted they indict him immediately in order that he might be tried and cleared. The Inquisitor reassured him that it wasn't necessary. That is, he wished to keep his options open. Ignatius went out, found a notary public and brought him back to document and witness the Inquisitor's praise for the *Exercises*, as well as his refusal to prosecute.[6] This small, private scene was of monumental importance. The first organization ever to be built upon reasoned terror had just been outmanoeuvred by the future creator of the second.

Only four years later Loyola had personally convinced the Pope to allow the official proclamation of his order. Its documents of creation began with a statement of the methodology to which it was devoted. This methodology contained the essence of all that the Age of Reason would later propose as its aim:

> Whomever wishes to be a Jesuit must absorb absolutely this thought; that he is a member of a Society, instituted very precisely in order to seek out as its principal end to procure the progress of men's souls in their lives and in the Christian doctrine. . . . Its ends are to be accomplished by reasoning with the public and by teaching.[7]

The message was clear. First you must belong to an organization, one which possesses a method. Entry to the organization will be limited by the method. Its members will therefore be a trained elite. Its power will rest upon precision, research and movement. The elite will use its methods to educate the people and through this education to sell a particular point of view. And its success will be measured. The word *progress,* from those early times until today, has been used as a synonym for the word *measurement.*

This cool, professional approach was, of course, the product of an experienced, battleworn, ex-professional soldier, who organized the Society as a religious army. The process had little to do with the blind faith and the arbitrary powers of the old Church. Suddenly, it became clear that the Jesuit order held the keys to the future: organization and party policy. Doctrine shrank to little more than a useful tool. The role of God became quite secondary. Instead, the new order forced the Catholic world to put the interests of the Church itself — the mother organization — in the front row. In so doing they gradually reduced the religious wars from a fanatical level of belief and emotion down to the practical level of political interests. Practical meant negotiable — suddenly impossible questions of religious principle were converted into territorial claims, alliances through royal marriages, and financial security or insecurity.

Loyola's election to the generalship of the Society was an illustration of his methods. He had no rivals. His leadership was accepted by everyone. The result of the members' vote was a foregone conclusion. And yet Loyola refused to accept it. He turned and manoeuvred and stalled for two weeks with a modesty which, given that this was the same man who had just outsmarted the Pope and the Vatican bureaucracy, can only have been false. He then forced his companions to vote a second time. The result, of course, was the same. At last he wandered out across Rome to see his confessor and to ask his advice. The poor man could hardly recommend that Loyola refuse. The entire Church leadership would have been furious with him. Loyola made his confessor commit his advice to paper and send it over to the Society. On the basis of this sealed recommendation, which was the closest thing a mortal could arrange to an order from God, the theoretically modest man finally accepted.

The Society was an immediate success. By the time Loyola died in 1556, seventeen years after its creation, there were one thousand members. By 1700 there were twenty-three thousand — the most powerful political force in the West. They were running most European governments from behind the scenes, to say nothing of running their colonies. Even the Pope came to fear them and so eventually their enemies got together just long enough to have the Society disbanded in 1723. Nevertheless, it was the Jesuits who had almost single-handedly stemmed the tide of the Reformation.

At all times Loyola had used a careful, reasoned approach, free from dogma. For example, he pushed for the introduction of the Inquisition into Rome, to block the rise of new heretical errors, but opposed its use in Germany, where the Church hadn't enough power to make it stick. In the same "political" way, Loyola was for capital punishment when dealing with heretics, but "this seems to be beyond what the present situation in Germany can bear."[8]

His instructions to Jesuits struggling there might have been written in the twentieth century: people infected with error should be eliminated from government and teaching positions; heretical books should be burned; whatever the books, if by a tainted author they should be burned so that people could not learn to like the author; synods should be convoked to unmask specific errors; it was forbidden to call an heretic an "evangelical."[9]

This last simple instruction is one of the most fascinating because it heralded the future dictatorship of vocabulary, which has become so important in the twentieth century. Loyola was the first to recognize the force which specific words carried. It was therefore essential to control those words. To capture them absolutely for the use of the Church. Better still, by treating these captured words as icons, they could be packaged in order to produce a politically useful meaning. Thus, in the past there had been all sorts of "evangelical" figures, some good, some bad. The word simply meant *bringing the good news*. In the future only those speaking for the Church could benefit from the word.

In this century words such as *capitalism* or *revolutionary* or *free* are used in the same way. The very act of getting the word *free* into the public domain on your side places the other side in a difficult position.

That is why politicians or businessmen, about to cut back on social benefits or to close factories, always invoke fairness as part of their justification, along with such concepts as justice, rationalization and efficiency. These mythological words come to replace thought. They are the modern equivalent of an intellectual void.

Almost immediately, the Society of Jesus began to produce an educated elite inside the lay population. No other education of that time could match what it offered. Those who sought success for their children couldn't help but consider a Jesuit school. And yet, from the very beginning, the Jesuits' success was mixed with outside criticism of their cynicism, ambition, political interference, and amoral intelligence — everything that an Enarque or a Harvard MBA might be accused of today.

At the base of this criticism lay one fundamental truth. Whatever good the Society did, it seemed unable to avoid either deforming policy or producing brilliant students who were also somehow deformed. The more brilliant the student, the more shocking this deformation seemed to be.

The origin of this flaw lay in the original premise of the Order. The Protestants were the first active, widespread messengers of reform. Loyola stole the method which had delivered their message and applied it to defend a cause that stood resolutely against reason. What at first sight appeared to be a fundamental contradiction turned out to be a great success. In fact, reason was stronger in his hands than it had been in those of the reformers. What he had created was a flexible, unfettered weapon, free of all obligation either to morality or to specific ideas.

This severing of method from any roots provided the Jesuits with superficial strengths which were in fact profound weaknesses. The resulting system was incapable of defending itself against the inevitable invasion of extraneous, contradictory and destructive ideas, both moral and intellectual. And so it wasn't surprising that before the sixteenth century was over, the Society of Jesus had been invaded by virulent cynicism.

No great skill is needed to trace the pattern emerging from these three events. The Inquisitors, Machiavelli and Loyola were all devoted to a priori truths and the service of established power. Their profession was administration. Two of them were courtiers and drew heavily on their military experience. Their methodology was unrelated to ideas or morality. Fear and secrecy were their favourite weapons. They favoured personal anonymity, public discretion, simple dress and power exercised from behind a facade. Out on the cutting edge of social and political reform, methodology was becoming a mercenary for hire.

The next step was decisive. Early in the 1600s, rational technocracy found its long-term partner — the nation-state. This passionate marriage took place under the authority of a theoretically absolute monarch — Louis XIII — and was engineered by a Cardinal.

Of course, when we look at those years, the tendency is to become mesmerized by the philosophical fireworks which filled them. Francis Bacon and René Descartes led the West in rejecting the medieval past and creating two opposing rational schools, one drawn from the new science, the other from mathematics.

Bacon went to great pains to lay out the difference between constructing an argument in order to produce an answer, which he rejected, and doing so in order to seek an answer. "The logic now in use serves rather to fix and give stability to the errors which have their foundation in commonly received notions, than to help the search after truth. So it does more harm than good."[10] With perfect, effortless simplicity, he showed the fundamental difference between thought and judgment. This clarity, once released, seemed to languish for a century and a half, until the Encyclopedists seized upon Bacon and John Locke as their principal inspiration.

On closer examination, however, Bacon's clarity and open spirit seem less obvious. His personal career had been that of a courtier, with highs and lows not unlike that of Machiavelli. He betrayed his patron the Earl of Essex, further advanced himself by agreeing in a particular case to a torture-confession procedure in the Inquisition tradition and used public power to great personal profit. He appears to have been more Machiavellian than Machiavelli. Bacon wrote a great deal about truth but rejected the supremacy of common law and therefore of Parliament. He considered natural law or reason to be supreme. This definition of the source of truth required an absolute monarch served by a wise adviser — himself. And when, in his novella *The New Atlantis*, Bacon set about imagining an ideal society, the result was a dictatorship of technocrats who sought knowledge and truth. They then hid both from the citizen. Knowledge and power were married to secrecy and chastity. This chastity or asexuality may at first seem to be an oddity particular to Bacon's rational vision, but it will gradually show itself to be part of the general pattern.

A great deal is made of the differences between English and French philosophy, with Bacon and Descartes used to illustrate the parting of the ways. Their technical arguments are certainly very different. But the intent and the result are virtually indistinguishable.

Descartes, of course, remains the demigod of rational thought. His *Discourse on Method* formalized an astonishing view of reason. He was educated by the Jesuits and seemed to take from that — among other things — a submissive respect for authority. He even took the initiative to withdraw one of his books from circulation rather than risk displeasure. His celebrated exploration of doubt gradually showed itself to be a conservative force which prevented sensible arguments for change from passing the impossible tests of rational truth.

Descartes (1596–1650) was an exact contemporary of Richelieu (1585–1642). It was the Cardinal who, without reference to the thinker, would go on to build permanently into the first real modern state and into its methods all of Descartes's deductive ideas. One could even argue that it is Descartes who is in debt to Richelieu and not the contrary. By the time Descartes's *Discourse on Method* appeared in 1637, Richelieu had already been Prime Minister for thirteen years. As early as 1627 the Cardinal had introduced his thirteen-point proposal for "a Rational Reorganization of Government." The degree to which he was creating our future can be seen in such details as his restructuring of the educational system in order to produce more graduates in the scientific, practical professions and fewer in the general arts.

For someone who held power four centuries ago, Richelieu was a remarkable combination of the best and the worst of the twentieth century. As an individual he was the classic example of a technocratic leader. He had a nervous, impatient temperament, which made him far more effective behind the scenes than in public. He often dealt with widespread opposition by singling out and destroying one enemy in the group while reassuring the others. He had a cynical view of human events which made him think that the mere application of his own intelligence could manipulate history and change its direction.

He was obsessed with detail and therefore with unending work. This work consisted to a great extent of placing himself at the centre of the flow of information in order to control or to collect it. By the end of his life he was manipulating an extraordinary system of agents and was the master of everyone's secrets. Secrecy was central to his methods. In his very first public act as a young, relatively unknown bishop at the Etats-Généraux in 1614, he proposed a two-part method for their deliberations: first, laying out the precise hours at which they would meet, and second, insisting upon the absolute secrecy of everything said and done. Precision, hard work and secrecy. If this does not seem a clear enough model for the technocrat, then one can add, for example, his vindictiveness. Twenty-eight years later, as he himself lay dying, swollen, in unbearable agony and fully conscious of the fact that he was within days of his own demise, he concentrated his mind upon the trial and condemnation to death of his great enemy, the Marquis de Cinq Mars. Of the thirteen judges who had just tried the young man, eleven voted for execution. What Richelieu insisted upon knowing — he had no legal right to — were the names of the two dissenters.[11] Had his own disease given him even a short reprieve, he no doubt would have insisted that only traitors could have believed that Cinq Mars wasn't a traitor.

Richelieu had another characteristic, a peculiar one, which is often found in people who are better at dealing with systems than with individuals. In public, he could force himself to be the essence of cool reason. In private, he was given to particularly personal and vicious attacks. Richelieu specialized in anonymous or ghosted pamphlets. There was, for example, his anonymous published attack on Louis XIII's favourite, the Duc de Luynes. According to the Cardinal, the man had six major vices. He was "incompetent, a coward, ambitious, greedy, an ingrate and a cheat."[12] Language, for Richelieu, was a means of hiding his actions and thoughts rather than of communicating them. To his taste for private malice should be added a weakness for intrigues, which often accompanies both an obsession with secrecy and the seeking of power through structure.

But where did he get these tastes for intrigue and manipulation, this sad view of society and of the citizen and indeed of himself? The Chinese castration of imperial advisers was a means of removing dynastic dreams from ambitious young men. Certainly Richelieu's methods remind one of the eunuch approach. And the idle speculator can't help but gaze back at Bacon's praise of asexuality among rational elites or for that matter, back further at Ignatius Loyola, creator of the rational system, and wonder about the exact height at which the cannonball passed between his legs and the exact damage it did on the way through. Reason seems to have created a system which, whatever its good points, is often felt to be castrating. Is there any reason, then, to be surprised if it attracts to positions of power individuals who are prone to an asexual view of the world?

The structure that Richelieu put into place was, of course, filled with worthwhile and progressive characteristics. He had set out to create an honest administration, including that most difficult of things, an honest tax collection system. He was hard on elites that opposed him but relatively eager to help the poor, even if they had supported his enemies. He sought to remove the willful, irrational element from royal government.

> Common sense leads each one of us to understand that man, having been endowed with reason, should do nothing except that which is reasonable, since otherwise he would be acting contrary to his nature . . . there is nothing in nature less compatible with reason than emotion.[13]

The trademark of the nation-state was to be centralization and it was Richelieu who devised how to make this process unstoppable. He did this largely to create an efficient, honest government but also to destroy the negative power of both the Church and the aristocracy. It is difficult now to realize just how revolutionary all this was. His nationalism was a new idea, scarcely understood, let alone accepted. He was struggling against the mainstream of power and against the general belief in aristocratic rights. In many ways the modern republic and its equivalent, the constitutional monarchy, are Richelieu's creations.

At the same time, all his actions — positive and negative — were accompanied by the use of fear, that essential tool of modern organization. "Punishments and rewards," he wrote,

> are the two most important instruments of government. . . . Power is the cause of fear. It is certain that of all the forces capable of producing results in public affairs, fear, if based upon both esteem and reverence, is the most effective, since it can drive everyone to do his duty.[14]

At one point in his career the Cardinal was forced out of office. Abruptly he became clumsy, even incompetent. He said and did the wrong things. He showed signs of uncontrollable paranoia. His skills seemed to be suited to being in power, not in opposition. But if the rational method had grown out of the defence of established power, then why would one expect a great technocrat to flower in opposition? The effective use of power excludes the idea of honourable opposition.

A list of Richelieu's characteristics and policies makes him appear absolutely modern, but he should also be seen as the first man to fulfill Machiavelli's dream. Not to become the perfect prince. Machiavelli's prince was only the necessary, practical focus of a political method, given the time and the place. Richelieu was rather the fulfillment of Machiavelli's personal dream — that of the employee who uses the cover of a prince in order to institute a new system. Louis XIII, despite his weak character and emotional instability, was the perfect marionette for Richelieu. Those who concentrated on the Cardinal's operatic day-to-day relationships with the King and the Queen Mother saw constant chopping and changing and minor intrigue. They missed what was really happening to France.

In the hands of a consummate technocrat, it was being transformed from a feudal kingdom into a nation. The absolute monarchy which followed, and which is habitually seen as the glorious swan song of the old ways, was in fact the first complete manifestation of the rationally administered nation-state.

Beneath the palace theatre of absolute monarchy ran the growing power of Richelieu's state, devoid of any real attachment to royal rights or to morality of any kind. Versailles was the modern state in disguise — an elaborate game of charades. It was only a matter of time, given the forces which Richelieu had set in motion, before the prince was replaced by something even more malleable — the constitutional democracy, in which governments came and went, while the cardinals, or their secular equivalents, remained.

In Buddhism there is a phrase — *the middle way* — which has always fascinated Westerners dissatisfied with the direction our society has taken. On closer examination that middle way turns out to be extremely arduous. But the phrase nevertheless expresses a reasonableness which is absent from our own rational absolutism. The tendency of eighteenth-century writers to set allegories in the East was tied to the idea that these people were more likely to be sensible.

Not that moderation has been absent from Western thought. Bacon strained after it in his search for openness of mind, as did Richelieu in his attempts to create fair institutions. And certainly Blaise Pascal laboured to cover up the still-warm tracks of Descartes by establishing the moral fibre of reason: "All our dignity, then, consists in thought. It is upon this that we must depend. . . . Let us labour, then, to think well: this is the foundation of morality."[15]

In a sense Molière was Pascal's alter ego. And Molière's enormous popularity might have given the impression that there was hope for reasonable action. But those who told straight truths to large audiences — as Molière did — came to play a specific role in societies where judgmental power dominated the state, learning, business and every other key area. They fulfilled the function of a Punch and Judy show. After the citizen had given his day, year, life to the real system — the one that had power — he went out to dream and to laugh in the theatre, where Molière knocked his superiors about.

Still, Pascal could not be totally ignored. He could be admired, which meant he needn't be listened to. He could become like an honoured saint, better than other mortals but impossible to follow. As opposed, for example, to Thomas Hobbes, who was making an enormous impact in England by proposing a mechanical and secular social contract which depended on an absolute monarch and, above all, on fear as the control device.

Someone like John Locke was far more attractive. He attacked the old powers and the unexplained, unexplainable established order. And that was welcomed. Yet at the same time he led the citizenry, with his contractualism, farther along the easy path opened up by Bacon and Descartes which eventually brought them to an obsession with proofs and therefore with facts.

Facts at that time were such rare nuggets that no one realized how they would multiply. Everyone believed them to be solid and inanimate — to be true facts. No one yet understood that life would become an uncomfortable, endless walk down a seashore laid thick with facts of all sizes and shapes. Boulders, pebbles, shards, perfect ovals. No one had begun to imagine that these facts were without any order, imposed or natural — that facts were as meaningful as raw vocabulary without grammar or sentences. A man could pick up any fact he wished and fling it into the sea and make it skip. A practiced, talented arm could make it skip three, perhaps four times, while a lesser limb might make a single plunk with the same concrete proof of some truth or other. Another man might build with these facts some sort of fortress on the shore.

As for Locke, he certainly did not think that facts would rapidly become the weapons, not only of good men but of evil men, not only of truth but of lies. Had he but looked back at Richelieu's career, he might have seen what was to come. At the age of twenty in Rome, Richelieu had argued a sermon before the Pope in order to prove a particular point. The very next day he was again before the Pope and argued the same sermon in order to prove the opposite point.[16]

Europe had hardly reached the supposed birth of modern reason, and yet hints of the force of the future blind logic were already in the air. There were those who saw what was happening and who warned eloquently. Jonathan Swift's trenchant words came too soon and were too harsh. With books like *Gulliver's Travels* (1726) he became popular but was immediately categorized as marginal and peculiar. And there was that unhappy professor, Giambattista Vico, who tried to advance his ideas in the very Catholic city of Naples. He used an historical approach to combat the Cartesian self-justifying abstractions. Rationalists tended later to categorize him as an obscure reactionary in order to discount what he was saying. But he wasn't seeking to defend the old order, and certainly not the worst of the old order. Rather, he was striving for the same inquisitiveness as Pascal, the same care in seeking out right and wrong. "Today," he wrote in 1708,

> only criticism and judgement are admired. The subject itself has been relegated to the last row. . . . They say that as men are capable of judgement, one need only teach them a thing and they will know if it is true. But who can be sure to have seen everything?[17]

As for the new methods of analysis, "It is impossible to deny anything they say unless you attack them from the beginning."[18]

Vico was perhaps the first to recognize the irresistible strength of the new and theoretically free methods of argument, which in fact were structured to make a particular answer inevitable. He and Montesquieu both condemned the loss of the "political vocation" as it had been preached by the Greeks and the Romans — a vocation in favour of the cult of truth, a vision of society as a moral whole.[19] It was Montesquieu, a jurist from the minor nobility of Bordeaux, who initiated early in the eighteenth century the admiration of French philosophers for English freedoms.

But if truth was becoming nothing more than a structured argument studded with useful, malleable facts, then what was left of the moral whole except Machiavellianism on the one hand and raw sentiment on the other? Common sense, which might also be called careful emotion or prudence, was squeezed out of the picture. Vico and Montesquieu sensed what would happen after the anchors of the old system had finally been cut away — technocracy would reign in a curious coalition with almost animal emotion. The perfectly normal human emotive needs, in the absence of a social context which could deal with them, would degenerate into sentiment. And it was that base sentiment, unleashed by the rational technocrat, which would turn into the cult of the Hero.

The Lisbon earthquake struck in 1755 and shattered the moral legitimacy of established power. It did to the psychic inviolability of Church and absolute monarchs what the Vietnam War later did to that of the United States. This catastrophe, which killed indiscriminately thousands of children, women and men, poor and rich, seemed somehow to require an immediate explanation. The people of Europe asked themselves a collective Why? The Church and the constituted authorities couldn't stop themselves from replying that God was punishing sinners.

Instinctively the citizenry found this answer ridiculous. Lisbon wasn't a particularly sinning town, certainly not in comparison to Madrid, Paris or London. And those children, women, poor. They could know nothing of important sins. The claim of divine retribution was so obviously ridiculous that, abruptly, people felt liberated from any obligation to believe anything the authorities said. In particular the Church discredited its power to give or to withhold moral sanction on the way people led their lives.

Of all the citizens, those belonging to the aristocracy were in the most complex position. It had been decades since they had believed unquestionably in the foundations of their own legitimacy. However, they profited from the maintenance of a pretence of belief. That pretence was quickly cut to ribbons by the philosophers of the Enlightenment who, being in full flood, pounced with all their acerbic wit on the official Lisbon story. None of this was immediately clear in any concrete or structural way, but the veil had been rent.

In that same year, an event occurred which made it possible to believe for the first time that reason was not a mere idea, that reason could govern men. Philosophers would no longer have to invent mythical Oriental nations, as Montesquieu and Voltaire had done, in order to illustrate their arguments. They could now simply refer to the republic in Corsica.[20]

History is particular in the events that it chooses to retain. Retention usually requires the continued existence of a solid group — an organized nation or a reasonably numerous people — that will integrate the event into its mythology and nurture it over the centuries. The Corsican republic has slipped out of general memory because there was no one off the Mediterranean island interested in remembering. The philosophical ideas that Pascal Paoli applied, when constructing his republic, were largely French. And it was the French who destroyed his republic: first Louis XV; then the Revolution; then, definitively, Bonaparte. Even on the island itself, integration into France meant that the importance of the Paoli republic would be, indeed had to be, played down by the authorities.

Corsica had belonged to Genoa since the sixteenth century. The Genoese had always concentrated their power in the island's ports and kept a loose hold on the mountainous interior, where most of the population lived. From time to time — and increasingly in the eighteenth century — the rival Corsican clans would agree on a common leader and then rise up in revolt. Paoli's father had led one of these liberation forces with great success. But the Genoese then asked the Austrians and the French to support them militarily and in 1738 the elder Paoli fled to Naples, taking his thirteen-year-old son with him. Pascal Paoli was therefore brought up in exile in Italy, where he memorized the classics, learned Italian, French and English, was trained as an army officer and read all the eighteenth-century philosophers.

In 1755 the clans again came together and, "by the general voice," elected the then thirty-year-old exile their leader and asked him to come home. Paoli came determined to apply the ideas of the philosophes to that piece of the real world. He transformed what had begun as yet another clan revolt into something so different that the island was soon liberated except for a few besieged ports. In desperation the Genoese again turned to France for help and Louis XV sent an expedition. (By chance the future revolutionary Mirabeau was among the French officers.) Paoli's army used guerrilla tactics to make mincemeat of these regulars, but Louis's response to defeat was simply to send a second, larger expedition in return for Genoa's title deed to the island.

This invasion stirred Rousseau to write: "I still find it hard to believe that France is willing to call down upon herself the censure of the world."[21] The first Pitt, who was later to support the American revolutionaries against his own king, spoke up in Corsica's defence, saying of Paoli that he was "one of those men who are no longer to be found but in the *Lives of Plutarch*."[22]

The second French force included a young major, Count de Guibert, the future inventor of modern military strategy. Now that their own territorial expansion was in question, the French applied themselves seriously and the imbalance of numbers and of available funds combined to weaken Paoli's army. Then a single major strategic error in 1769 led to a Corsican military rout halfway across a mountain river on the Ponte Nuovo.

The republic was dead. Paoli fled. His senior officers — including Napoleon Bonaparte's father — went home. And Paris began its standard absorption of newly conquered territories. This included an interdiction on the teaching of the Corsican language and a gathering up of the local young male elite to be educated as Frenchmen on the mainland.

Paoli, meanwhile, was on his way to exile in England. At that time most philosophers believed that the English enjoyed the greatest political freedom in Europe. And Paoli had the expectation of being welcomed there thanks to James Boswell, who had come to Corsica a few years before and written a book devoted to glowing descriptions of Paoli's republic.

As the defeated leader crossed Europe on his way to London, he was greeted as the great hero of political reason. Enormous crowds — often so thick that he couldn't leave the houses he was staying in — followed him everywhere. His likeness was sold on handkerchiefs. The kings of Europe sought him out as he passed and paid homage. When he reached England, John Wesley wrote: "Lord, show him what is Thy will concerning him and give him a kingdom that cannot be moved!"[23]

This was the period leading up to the American Revolution, and the colonials had only three foreign heroes — Pitt the Elder, John Wilkes and Paoli. Corsica played a key role in the rise of the republican ideal within the thirteen colonies. Ships and children were named after the martyred leader. When the Revolution came, the rebels used his name as a rallying cry during charges against the English troops. And in later years the old revolutionaries throughout the American republic raised their glass in his honour on the night of Paoli's birthday.

It is difficult to imagine today the impact that the Corsican republic made on Europe and America during its fourteen years in operation and then again during the French Revolution, when Paoli was called from exile in London across to Paris. There he was cheered by the entire National Assembly, from moderates to revolutionaries, as the first man to have fought the kings and governed under the sign of reason. All of them — Mirabeau, Danton, Robespierre — knew that in 1762, when Paoli's republic was only seven years old, Rousseau had written in *The Social Contract*:

There is one country still capable of legislation — the island of Corsica. The courage and constancy with which that brave people have recovered and defended their liberty deserves the reward of having some wise man teach them how to preserve it.[24]

Various philosophers imagined themselves in this role, but Paoli himself was obliged by circumstances to fill it. Without being an ideologue, he saw himself as the agent of reason. His great common sense permitted him to act in a reasonable manner while the absolutist forces — old and new — flew about. In the end he was defeated by both: the tail end of the absolute monarchy combined with the new, strident forces of nationalist reason.

The modern equivalent of Corsica's popularity among the intellectuals and young of eighteenth-century Europe and America is perhaps that of Alexander Dubček's Czechoslovakia or Salvador Allende's Chile in the 1960s. And yet the situation was quite different. Paoli was the forerunner of an absolutely new idea. He was the first leader to try and to succeed. And then he was crucified — first by the old interests, then by the new. He popularized the rule of reason and thus carried the idea for the first time beyond the intellectuals and out to the general population of Europe. In popular terms his impact was like that of John Kennedy. Later, in exile, he came to resemble Norodom Sihanouk, the wandering shadow of a small country destroyed by the large powers.

Behind all these reverberations lay Paoli's practical invention of the modern republic, by no means an ideal creation. He was dealing with a poor population still divided into clans. Their election of him was representative only in the sense of a clan-based election. At best it could be said that if ever there was a society which resembled Marx's unconscious democracy, it was the Corsica on which Paoli landed in 1755.

He attempted to carry his country directly from the middle ages to the Age of Reason, jumping over the age of the absolute monarchs in a way which made use of every modern ideal. First he appeared to be the model republican leader. He dressed in simple clothing and refused the moneys voted him by the Assemblies. He created a public school system and a university. Although a believer himself, he dismantled the political and economic power of the Church, instituted a fair legal system, encouraged local industries in what we would now call a social-democratic manner, and helped the Assembly to produce a model constitution, which encouraged decentralization and delegation. His enlightened ideas on a variety of subjects were reported to the world by Boswell and other visitors, as well as through his vast correspondence.

He admired politicians in their role as the servants of the people. He was a nationalist within the limits of public service and of a free state. He admired William Penn's peaceful colony, where the people were "happier than Alexander the Great after destroying multitudes at the conquest of Thebes."[25] He had a strong sense of virtue and a "faith in the people" which he followed all of his life. The Corsican Constitution of 1762 drew on the ad hoc body of existing laws and upon the principles of the Enlightenment. His opening speech to the elected Consulta in May of the same year was a model of reason in action:

> Your fellow citizens in electing you to represent them have placed their dearest interests in your hands . . . so examine your consciences, enlighten each other by frank discussion, and be convinced that the resolutions you will take together will become the law of the land, because what they represent will be the sincere expression of the will of the country.

It was Paoli who first wrote of free citizens ready to accept "only liberty or death" and who, on returning to his country after twenty-one years of exile in England, fell to the ground to kiss the earth, thus sealing the link between reason and the love of country — an equation which, more than any other of that time, has been deformed to serve the opposite purpose.

Paoli's republic, much more than the American, was the precursor of the French Revolution. In 1790 Mirabeau, in order to cleanse his own hands, which had been "dirtied" by participation in the military expedition sent by Louis XV to destroy the Corsican republic, moved that the Assembly invite Paoli back from exile in England. The French Constitution of 1790 was an imitation of the one Paoli had instituted a quarter of a century before, and so he came to Paris as a hero. A wild reception greeted his entry into the Assembly. The leaders filed one after the other to the podium to praise him. Robespierre set the tone: "You defended freedom when we did not even dare to hope for it."[26]

The excited and unstable tribunes of Paris sent him to Corsica to govern in their name and in that of reason. Paoli was welcomed home as the national saviour. As in 1755, he put all temptations of personal glory aside and got to work. But this was the last high point of his life. Having invented the first government of reason, he was about to be squeezed between the two forces that were set to dominate the West — the technocrats and the Heroes — the classic division of modern rational society. Paoli's honesty, his age and the smallness of Corsica in the centre of this hurricane, all limited his freedom of movement.

He set about carrying out his mandate, only to discover that as Paris writhed into ever-greater confusion and the revolutionaries set about destroying each other, it was virtually impossible not to fall foul of them. It was hard to know whether his distance from the capital was an advantage or a disadvantage. In any case he was soon under attack from the Assembly, which did everything it could to destabilize him.

The element most susceptible to destabilization was the new generation of young Corsican aristocrats who had grown up during the twenty
years of French rule. They were a curious group. Almost schizophrenic.
Educated in France and drawn into the Parisian orbit — with all that
implied of superficial urban superiority covering up the demons of a
provincial inferiority complex — they were nevertheless sons of clan
leaders and themselves Corsican nationalists who resented the French
conquest. Paoli was their spiritual father.

Now, with the Revolution in Paris, a new phenomenon — romantic
reason — was in full flood. Every young man began to see himself as a
potential Hero, created not by the Paolian ideal of the self-sacrificing
public servant but by the new dream of the unleashed ego. If a young
man felt endowed with enough courage to snatch personal glory, then
destiny and reason somehow empowered him to do so at the expense of
whoever was in the way. Betrayal of causes and homeland were nothing
when weighed against glory — the new word for personal advancement.
Voltaire had already written in his *Philosophical Dictionary*: "He who
burns with ambition to become aedile, tribune, praetor, consul, dictator, cries out that he loves his country and he loves only himself."[27] For
a young Corsican consumed by the fires of Heroic ambition there could
be no greater obstacle than Paoli, the living spirit of reasonable public
service.

The Bonaparte brothers led the way in this new worship of the Hero.
Paoli had every reason to believe in their loyalty. Not only had their
father been one of his best and closest officers, their mother had been
a famous patriot, following her husband through the mountains from
battlefield to battlefield during the campaign against Louis XV's expedition. She had been there, six months pregnant, on May 8, 1769, when
the Corsican republic suffered its great and last defeat at Ponte Nuovo.
With her husband, she managed to flee the catastrophe and to reach
their home in Ajaccio, where Bonaparte was born. Twenty years later,
the young man was serving in the French artillery, but he was still
fiercely loyal to the Corsican cause. Like Paoli, he had initially been
encouraged by the Revolution of 1789. Then, as the confusion and
jingoism in Paris turned against the interests of his island, Bonaparte
wrote to Paoli of his hatred for the French and of his feelings for the
poor Corsicans, "weighed down by chains even as they kissed, trem-
bling, the hand which oppressed them."[28]

In truth, however, the factionalism and subterfuge of a revolution
gone wrong were already drawing these young Corsican aristocrats into
the emotional turbulence. Who was pure? Who wasn't? Who a revolutionary? Who a traitor? What was liberty? What was the public good?
Who should hold power? Who should die? Abstract rational thought was
operating at full force and with an immediate impact on the real world.

Paoli refused to let Corsica slip into this violent dialectic. Instead he continued on a course of steady, calm reform. The Paris Assembly was at its most radical stage and was looking for diversions. They declared Paoli a criminal and threatened to invade Corsica. They also focused on the young future clan leaders living in Paris and convinced them that Paoli's moderation was antirevolutionary. A small group was sent home to provoke Heroic, revolutionary events. Paoli countered by calling together the Corsican Consulta — 1,000 strong. They declared the island an independent republic for the second time in forty years.

But when the old man discovered that a group of young Corsicans, including the Bonapartes, was actually plotting against him to win power in Paris, he despaired and sought a counterweight to France. Only one existed — England. He placed the Corsican Republic under British protection, then discovered that they were just as rapacious as the French. London sent a governor — a Sir Gilbert Elliot — who turned out to be a technocrat of limited talents. Vain, given to plotting and flattery, jealous of prerogatives, an administrator who stayed inside his palace, Elliot could not accept that the support the English had on the island came entirely from the people's confidence in Paoli. Instead he saw the old man as a rival and plotted with the English authorities to squeeze the Corsican out.

Elliot believed that his own inability to control the island could be reversed through administrative manipulation. The problem, he argued, was Paoli's age. The old man slowed events by his lengthy consultations with the Corsicans. And his desire to support a state built on the principles of reason, while opposing French imperialism, was an idea too complex to function with a world war raging about them. Elliot believed that if he could get rid of Paoli, he would control the man's administrative system and therefore the government and the island. It took some time before his mandarin skills could force the old man into his third exile. This was followed by a night or so during which Elliot was technically in absolute control. Then everything evaporated around him. One minute he was master of the island. The next it wasn't safe for him to leave his palace. Shortly after, the English were obliged to abandon the island.

On paper, of course, Elliot had not lost Corsica. He had decided to withdraw from it. If any blame was due, it was to Paoli. Had the old man left sooner, Elliot would not have had to withdraw at all. In fact, there were lots of people he could blame in his reports. And, in what would later become the tradition of the staff officer — promoted for losing battles — Elliot managed to have himself rewarded with the title Baron Minto of Minto. He put the national symbol of Corsica — a moor's head with a white bandeau — into his family coat of arms.

As for Bonaparte, he had fled back to France the moment his plotting was discovered and had since concentrated his ambitions there. In some ways, having no attachment to the country made him a perfect model for the Hero. The importance of a detached or mercenary approach had been a recurring theme in the writing of rationalist thinkers since Machiavelli.

The Bonaparte brothers were still leading the way in the practical creation and worship of the rational Hero. By being first, doing so as an organized family group and getting a solid hold on power for more than a decade, they were able to define Heroic action for the next two centuries. The only problem they had in creating this mythological aura stemmed from the fact that they had made their way by betraying the first great rational statesman, who had also been their father figure and that of Corsica. In other words, they had also betrayed their own country.

Napoleon's embarrassment could be seen in his studious avoidance of Corsica once he had got hold of power in Paris. He also pushed ahead with the integration of the island into the French structure. The extraordinary educational and mythological machinery centered in the French capital ensured that Paoli would be eliminated from or deformed in, every aspect of organized culture and government. Since the Revolution was to be presented as the expression of reason and Napoleon as its natural inheritor, Paoli had to be presented as the enemy of reason.

The official mythology, therefore, gradually balanced the idolatry of Bonaparte with its ridiculing of Paoli. This formula was finally perfected in the twentieth century, in Abel Gance's brilliant but totally inaccurate film deifying Bonaparte. The young man is presented as an idealistic, disinterested, virginal — indeed, physically beautiful — nationalist, who must deal with Paoli, a degenerate, corpulent, corrupt — indeed, syphilitic — old dictator. The fact that Paoli was scrupulously honest, died poor, led a monastic life and introduced democracy, while Bonaparte went on to political, military and financial excess through uncontrolled, egocentric ambition, disappears effortlessly beneath the full flood of organized cinematic mythology. Even the personal physiques of the two men were inverted by Gance. Paoli was a tall, aesthetic figure. It was Bonaparte, an extremely short man with an undescended testicle, who ran to fat. But none of that mattered. After all, the creation of the Hero had as little to do with reality as did the administrative effectiveness of Sir Gilbert Elliot, later known as Baron Minto.

Long before this disastrous period in Paoli's life, the example of his first republic had already been embraced in the American colonies. There, reason was given a second opportunity to prove itself. The colonials were far luckier than the Corsicans. London was a long way away. The power of the British Parliament tempered the power of the king. And the power of the colonials' friends within Parliament in turn weakened the war party. The colonies were also reasonably large and led not by one brilliant man but by a remarkable collection of men. Within this group were two who would replace Paoli in international mythology as the republican ideal.

It is fair to say that had the United States not produced Washington and Jefferson, its history would have been quite different. Without a calm first president, equipped with perfect honour and a limited ambition, and a third president who possessed in addition a genius that could both imagine the republic of reason and put it into effect, it is highly unlikely that the revolutionary excitement could have been channelled and the country put onto a reasonable track.

Not that the Revolution was entirely satisfactory. The resulting Constitution, as the late Supreme Court Justice Thurgood Marshall has pointed out, was "defective from the start."[29] Even after a civil war and momentous social transformations, the current system of government is still unable to deal with the terrible economic disparities, the violence and the growing, uneducated, nonvoting percentage of the population. Nevertheless, Washington and Jefferson managed to hold the republic in place long enough for emotions to cool and for the nation to get off the revolutionary roller coaster. The French experience shows what might have happened. Caught in full revolution with no great republican leaders, they were thrown, as if in an epileptic fit, from republic to dictator to king to republic to dictator to republic to dictator and back to the republic they have today.

Our standard view is that the violent change provoked by the French Revolution was much greater than that of the American. France's subsequent instability is supposed to be the result. But if we are talking about profound social changes, then the analysis is wrong. In France the real revolution had already taken place, gradually, over the preceding twenty years.

The rising intellectual and administrative class was already converted to reason. Most of the latter came from the aristocracy, albeit the minor aristocracy, which was more accurately a manifestation of a new upper middle class. Many of the modernizing administrative changes they sought had already been made or were in process by the time the Revolution broke out. The Ecole Royale des Ponts et Chaussées (the national civil engineering school) had been founded in 1776, followed by the national mining engineering school and the Ecole Normale Supérieure (for the training of professors). Even the greatest of all the national schools, the Polytechnique, was created in midrevolution by the middle-class elements who felt they were involved in a continuing process, rather than beginning something new. The army structure had already been modernized under Louis XVI to an extent that the British would not reach until late in the nineteenth century. The revolutionary army, which amazed everyone by beating the great Prussian army at Valmy in 1792, was in fact the re-formed royal army, commanded in large part by the products of that system — young, well-born, professional officers, who had been converted to the principles of rational management well before 1789.

As for the king's divine right — that official enemy of the Revolution — no one had actually believed in it for years. How could they? Most of the ruling elite hardly believed in God. They certainly didn't believe in an active, hands-on God.

The superficial forms, which Louis XIV had originally given the state, were now its only cement. Louis XIV had dressed and lived like a Sun King in order to give the aristocracy and the population a concrete emanation of his power. On the rungs which descended from his throne of grandeur, each aristocrat had a perch in declining order of visible magnificence. Louis sought to tie the aristocracy to this meaningless code in order to control them while he consolidated his own power. He was, after all, a man who enjoyed great simplicity, a man perfectly conscious of the difference between his appearance as Sun King and his reality as the functioning head of state. Particularly during the second half of his reign, he tended to escape from sight whenever possible, shed his extravagant costumes and, like an actor offstage, sit quietly in a small salon with his wife.

It took only a century for the sense of that division to be lost. Louis XVI and his entourage had actually come to believe in the reality of appearances. They believed that it was this masquerade, this publicity system, which made Louis king; that without it, he was nothing. What's more, if appearances were all that mattered, there was no reason to worry about his real incompetence when it came to doing his job. This reasoning may sound familiar, because it resembles the assumptions often made about political leadership today.

Again and again during the Revolution, Louis was incapacitated not so much by his own weak character or his drinking or his wife's stupidity as by his inability to differentiate between appearance and reality. This came to a head during his abortive escape attempt of 1791, which ended in recapture at Varennes. Confusion in his own mind between his royal dignity and the need to disguise himself caused him to reject several effective escape plans. He settled for the most cumbersome approach and disdained any proper disguise. Louis wore a pink wig, as if the whole business were a costume party rather than a desperate, real moment. A government structure in which the leader and his senior advisers are willing to risk the existence of the entire system over whether the leader should or should not wear a proper servant's wig for twelve hours is not simply a sclerotic system. By normal clinical standards it is already dead.

But why was the result of revolution so much more destabilizing in France than in the United States? The first answer has already been given — America was lucky in its revolutionary leaders. The second is that, unlike France, America did not try to become a republic in more than name. Washington's job description fitted Voltaire's of a benevolent monarch in almost every way except for the title. Third, it is not clear that the history of the United States has been any more stable than that of France. For example, the ongoing high levels of violence associated with American civilization are usually attributed to the frontier tradition. They could just as easily be attributed to the syndrome of solving social problems with force, which was produced by the Revolution.

The real answer, however, may be far more general. The threat or promise of change brings out the frail nature of mankind's psyche. And sudden change is an imposition of instability. The rational argument, from its modern beginnings, has tried to avoid dealing with this reality. The multitude of abstract social models — mathematical, scientific, mechanical, and market based — are all based on an optimistic assumption that a schematic reorganization of society will be good for the human race. Even the idea of man as a perfectable being is dependent on an idea of manipulation from outside or above. The technocrats and the Heroes are the two favoured types of rational manipulators.

But what the French and American revolutions should have told us is that human beings do not respond effectively to this sort of manipulation. And the more abstract it is, the more they resist or slide on to an emotional and political roller coaster. In that sense revolution is a sign of the failure of both those who lose power and those who gain it. It provokes an instability which the people and the new leaders seek to control as rapidly as possible. But once let loose, this instability takes on a momentum of its own — a momentum that provokes physical suffering and blood. The end result may be that certain problems are solved, but in the process the civilization is permanently scarred by the violence. The violent act usually fosters both increased levels of inflexible extremism and absolutism and yet more violence.

With this much hindsight, it is relatively easy to identify the long-term destabilizing effects of extreme social engineering. People living in the eighteenth and nineteenth centuries had a far harder time reading the signals flashing all around them in a confusing array. Those who sought the middle way — like Paoli and Jefferson — had to grope through the disorder as best they could, aided by their common sense.

An interesting example of this process was Edmund Burke — a great Whig; a careful, inquisitive thinker; and a supporter of Corsica, Irish independence and the American revolutionaries. With his "Address to the Electors of Bristol" he laid out one of the first reasonable proposals for a practical relationship between the voter and the elected. He also opposed slavery. He did make, however, one important "ideological" error in his career. He opposed the French Revolution. Some of his arguments against it were brilliant; others were patently wrong. France was not a country he knew a great deal about and so, out of ignorance, he praised the ancien régime. But his practical sense did help him to see what was disastrous about the Revolution. He pointed out that he was in favour of a "moral regulated liberty as well as any gentleman in France [but would not] stand forward and give praise [to an] object stripped of all concrete relations [so that it stood] in all the solitude of a metaphysical idea."[30]

This opposition caused him to be recategorized by the great flow of rationalist philosophers, including Jeremy Bentham and James Mill, as a reactionary, rather in the way earlier philosophers had categorized Vico. In a sense Burke suffered the intellectual equivalent of condemnation by the Inquisition or elimination for serious consideration by Cartesian logic or a Stalinist show trial.

Those who categorized him didn't like his stands in favour of Paoli and Washington any more than they liked his opposition to the French Revolution. In fact, it wasn't his stands they disliked, it was how and why he took them. It wasn't that he opposed reform or justice, which he didn't, but that he rejected the new logic. On most days Burke had a solid historical sense. He was able to see events as they were and to see where an approximate moral truth lay. He was a practical man who relied on common sense. He didn't use a priori arguments. He was therefore an enemy of the new age.

To rational thinkers his support of reform in certain areas seemed to contradict his conservatism in others. But Burke saw reform and the maintenance of stability as part of a balance or a compromise which reflected the real world. And the real world was filled with contradictions which could not be eliminated by the egotistical sweep of an abstract hand. In that sense, even at his most conservative, he was closer to the middle way than were the optimistic rationalists, who imagined whole populations sliced free of their limiting past and present, then flipped over to fry in a new, clean future with all the inanimate passivity of a Big Mac. This was the reality that Burke groped for when attacking the French Revolution: the more complete the idealistic future proposed, the more certain it was to require some overriding dissolution imposed either by the initiators or by those who would appear in extremis to establish authority in the resulting anarchical situation. In either case the effect would be to unleash a level of violence which, in this clean, new world liberated from experience and common sense, would be virtually unrestrainable.

Burke, of course, wasn't the only reformer to have doubts about the Revolution. Thomas Jefferson was the American ambassador to France from 1785 to 1789. He and Lafayette had been friends during the American Revolution. In 1789 Jefferson was the only experienced and successful revolutionary in Paris and so his house became a mecca for the newly elected Assembly members. They asked his advice and he soon began to tell them they were slipping off course, that matters were moving out of control, not just for the king but for the reformers and the revolutionaries. They were losing sight of the concrete wrongs which had provoked the whole business. Real opportunities to consolidate democratic political power and social justice were slipping by because everyone was getting caught up in enormous battles over such abstract things as the true nature of man and which were the absolute solutions to all problems. Mirabeau and Danton were distracted by these large ideas and their own personal petty corruption. Robespierre and Saint-Just were emerging as the reincarnations of the Inquisitors and Loyola disguised in the garb of revolutionary avenging angels.

Jefferson's own revolutionary origins and his record as a fair and honest president have in the long run put him beyond the sort of intellectual show trial that Burke suffered. In fact, Jefferson may be the sole example of a great man of reason able to keep himself above and beyond the judgmental scourge of the rational ideologues. He was thus highly successful both in his ideas and in his political execution. His faults are there to be counted, but he was arguably the greatest public figure the modern world has produced. Philosopher, writer, architect, farmer, inventor, revolutionary, politician, head of state; a man surrounded by friends and by love. He avoided intrigue. Did not believe in secrecy. Understood the difference between the primacy of peace and the extremity in which war is justified. He failed to convince his colleagues to deal with the slave question in the Declaration of Independence but wrote: "Nothing is more certainly written in the book of fate, than that these people are to be free." But if "it is left to force itself on, human nature must shudder at the prospect held up."[31] He had the true democrat's faith in the people as "the source of all authority."[32] He acted in a constant state of moral consciousness. "An honest heart being the first blessing, a knowing head is the second." "Though you cannot see, when you take one step, what will be the next," he wrote to a nephew, "yet follow truth, justice and plain dealing, and never fear their leading you out of the labyrinth, in the easiest manner possible. The knot which you thought a Gordian one, will untie itself before you. Nothing is so mistaken as the supposition that a person can extricate himself from a difficulty by intrigue, by chicanery, by dissimilation, by trimming, by an untruth, by an unjustice."[33]

His words ring today like those of a choirboy. But that reflects upon us, not upon the words. Jefferson dealt as he spoke. "No experiment can be more interesting than that we are now trying, and which we trust will end in establishing the fact, that man may be governed by reason and truth. Our first object should therefore be to leave open to him all the avenues to truth."[34] Yet all the time he knew that the violent origins of the United States had created a mythology which its people were obliged to be proud of, and that pride could not prevent such violence from becoming an historical weight. "The blood of the people is become an inheritance."[35] It was something that had to be slowly absorbed by the new system.

Nowhere does he suggest that being a genius or a Hero or a champion or, for that matter, being someone capable of producing right answers was necessary to the function of good government. His description of George Washington is a veritable eulogy to the qualities of not being the best:

> His mind was great and powerful, without being of the very first order; his penetration strong, though not so accurate as that of a Newton, Bacon or Locke; and as far as he saw, no judgement was ever sounder. It was slow in operation, being little aided by invention or imagination, but sure in conclusion. . . . Perhaps the strongest feature in his character was prudence. . . . His integrity was most pure, his justice the most inflexible I have ever known, no motives of interest or consanguinity, of friendship or hatred, being able to bias his decision. . . . He considered our new Constitution as an experiment on the practicability of republican government . . . and would lose the last drop of his blood in support of it.[36]

It isn't surprising that politicians of all sorts have tried to claim Jefferson as their own. They usually hang their claim not on his general philosophical, moral or political beliefs, but on some specific concept used by Jefferson to reflect a concrete need of his time. President Reagan was particularly adept at this hijacking of isolated moral precepts, which he then used to justify actions that would have horrified Jefferson. What these pillagers of words avoid, however, is the great common sense that Jefferson brought to reason and morality, as well as the historical view to which, like Burke, he managed to marry all three. But then the historical view implies a solid memory of how the past had unfolded and that in turn hampers the clean lines of freestanding rational solutions.

How different France's revolutionary experience might have been had it had either Washington or Jefferson to guide events. Instead the people, their hearts still racing with the excitement and anguish of revolt, were lost in a sea of superhuman ideas and expectations, while being led by brilliant but immature egotists who rapidly murdered each other. When these were replaced by a group of venal and rather ordinary politicians, the people felt more than disappointment. They slipped into a national depression and sought desperately for the promised answers. It was then they needed leaders capable of explaining that the true glory of freedom was something as boring as an honest politician. Or that the process of reason was slow and cumbersome. Or that restraint of the individual ego was central to the victory of reason.

Instead, out of the confusion, there appeared a full-blown male version of the base sentiment that Montesquieu and Giambattista Vico had warned of seventy-five years before. The anchor of the old system had been cut away by an abstract revolution. The rational thinkers and technocrats were unable to give the pitching ship a direction. And so, in the absence of any stable social context, the perfectly normal emotive needs of the population degenerated into sentiment. It took on concrete form as the cult of the Hero, the golden calf of reason. Bonaparte, disciple of Paoli, came fresh from the betrayal of both his mentor and his homeland. That he was a foreigner made him a more perfect Hero. He was there not to repair the anchor but to sail the ship away. In other words, the Hero turned out to be reason's magician, who replaced memory and history with himself.

Of course, Bonaparte made the impact he did because he had undeniable talents. He still stands as the great modern general. He had a passion for administrative and legal reorganization. He couldn't conquer a city without wanting, like a Roman emperor, to open an avenue through the centre and then build something grand at either end. In fact, almost everything he did was subject to the effects of uncontrolled ego. And from the moment of his coup d'état on the eighteenth Brumaire — when he panicked at the podium of the Assembly and his brother had to carry it through — the chasm between the myth of the rational Hero on the one hand and the reality of the man and his acts on the other never ceased to widen.

In that context, it is worth pointing out that of the first four modern republics, Bonaparte destroyed three: Corsica, Haiti, whose leader,

Toussaint L'Ouverture, was thrown into a damp, cold prison to die of exposure, and France. And he didn't get on with the fourth, the United States.

Bonaparte quickly revealed the face of the Hero, and from the very beginning it contained all the characteristics of blind reason. He was judgmental — impatient of unclear situations. Not long before his coup d'état, he said that what France needed was a "complete victory for one party. Ten thousand killed, from one side or the other. If not, we'll have to keep starting over." Along with his judgments came a contempt for the people. "What they need is glory, the gratifications of vanity."[37] Beyond that he exploited a vaguely democratic vocabulary he didn't believe in. The real message he took from the Revolution was the necessity for rational administration. "Once the happiness of the French people is based upon the best organic laws, all of Europe will become free."[38] In other words, reason equals structure equals happiness and that is freedom. Reason means contented efficiency. Bonaparte understood that the power given by efficient methods and rational argument was far more absolute than anything the kings had known. The only thing needed to make this combination irresistible was an emotive personality. Thus, emotional instability — known as charisma — combined with a talent for rational methods, became the recipe for the modern absolute dictator.

Outside the Assembly on eighteenth Brumaire, just after his coup, Bonaparte felt his courage coming back and so began to harangue his soldiers: "This state of things can't go on. In three years they will lead us back to despotism. We want a Republic based upon equality, morality, civil liberty and political tolerance. With good administration, all individuals will forget which faction they belong to and they will be able to be French."[39] In other words, he carried out a coup to prevent despotism. He promised various liberties at the very moment that he was suppressing liberty. He promised efficiency, again, as the magic potion to produce what he had once called "happiness" and now called "French." That reason could have led so fast to blind nationalism is astounding.

It followed that he should next shut down the new — and even the old — mechanisms of free speech. After all the Bourbon monarchy had been a fairly loose organization in its last years. Even Voltaire had come back to Paris and been cheered at the theatre with the Queen present. Napoleon wouldn't have tolerated Voltaire for two minutes. He reduced the Assembly to a mouthpiece. Writers fled into exile. He took Richelieu's idea of a spy network a step further by developing the first truly modern and effective secret police system under the control of Fouché. He recreated Louis XIV's diversionary social control system by crowning himself emperor and distributing grand titles which required grand uniforms. Then he cynically set about distributing more medals than any state had ever seen. He referred to them as baubles.

And all the time he continued working on his own Heroic mythology. At the heart of it lay his most brilliant and most deformed discovery — the emotional trick which would bond a disturbed population to the Hero. This trick involved a very simple concept: all Heroes have a tragic destiny. They are married to the people. They sacrifice themselves like a virgin on the altar of mystical service. Napoleon's secretary, Count Roederer, recorded that when the Hero moved into the Tuileries — the dark, damp, but royal palace — the following exchange took place:

> *Roederer:*   "How sad this place is, General!"
> *Bonaparte:*   "Yes, like greatness!"[40]

For years he went on repeating this sort of mystical trash. While Moscow burned, for example, he engaged his confidant, Count Narbonne, in romantic conversation:

> For myself, I love above all tragedy, great, sublime, the way Corneille wrote it. Great men are truer to life in plays than in reality. In plays you only see them in crises which test them, in the moments of supreme decision-making. No time is lost on all these preparatory details that the historians make the mistake of trying to weigh us down with. . . . Man suffers many miseries, fluctuations and doubts. All of that must disappear in the hero. He is the monumental statue on which no weaknesses show. He is that statue, *Persia* by Cellini. That sublime statue where one hardly suspects the ordinary lead or tin thrown into the mix in order to produce his demi-god.[41]

Suddenly it becomes clear why Bonaparte was the only real hate of Jefferson's life. Even Alexander Hamilton, who had some of the makings of a dangerous Hero, was treated as an opponent, not a monster. But in dealing with Hamilton, it was the American system that was in question and Jefferson must have believed he could bring out the best in it. Therefore Hamilton would fail. Bonaparte functioned in another system and Jefferson knew, from his time in Paris, that there were no reasonable leaders to oppose this Hero. The American's fury was provoked also by his inability to admit that the success of reason depended entirely upon the presence of the right men. The proof of how easily it could be deformed was the success of Bonaparte, who had already betrayed everything reason had to offer. He was a

> wretch who . . . had been the author of more misery and suffering to the world, than any being who ever lived before him. After destroying the liberties of his country, he has exhausted all its resources, physical and

moral, to indulge his own maniac ambition, his own tyrannical and over-bearing spirit. . . . What sufferings can atone . . . for the miseries he has already inflicted on his own generation, and on those yet to come, on whom he has rivetted the chains of despotism![42]

Jefferson wasn't simply provoked by the irreparable damage Bonaparte had done to the promise of reason. It was also that this damage had been done within the first decades of the system's existence, when it should still have been full of unsoiled vitality. In one letter he attempted to reassure himself by comparing his own career to Bonaparte's:

Having been, like him, entrusted with the happiness of my country, I feel the blessing of resembling him in no other point. I have not caused the death of five or ten millions of human beings, the devastation of other countries, the depopulation of my own, the exhaustion of all its resources, the destruction of its liberties, nor its foreign subjugation. All this he has done to render more illustrious the atrocities perpetrated for illustrating himself and his family with plundered diadems and sceptres. On the contrary, I have the consolation to reflect that during the period of my administration not a drop of the blood of a single fellow citizen was shed by the sword of war or of the law, and that after cherishing for eight years their peace and prosperity I laid down their trust of my own accord and in the midst of their blessings and importunities to continue it.[43]

Of course, other men in the United States, in France and in other countries have since tried to do as well as he. And there have been multitudes of talented and dedicated public servants, elected and employed. They have accomplished wonderful things in the handful of nations which make up the West. But the aberrant myth of the Hero, with his tragic destiny, has nevertheless rolled on, always ready to interpose itself when the public servants slip too deeply into the manipulation of systems and the public loses its sense of direction.

By the end of the nineteenth century, the world was filling up with Kaiser Wilhelms and General Boulangers and Cecil Rhodeses — half-baked Heroes egged on by half-baked philosophers, who suffered in many cases from mental instability. This marriage of brilliance with insanity, which Friedrich Nietzsche still incarnates, created a perfect match for the glorification of the unpalatable.

In 1912 Léon Bloy, then a well-known French writer, published *L'Ame de Napoléon*. "Napoleon is inexplicable and, no doubt, the most inexplicable of men, because he is, first and above all, He who comes before the ONE who must come and who is perhaps not far away."[44]

You might imagine that these rantings would have caused people to laugh or to brand him as a deranged personality and to put him out of their minds. Instead Bloy became popular as part of a strange, unforeseen phenomenon, which was increasingly successful at creating a link between the rational Hero and the pre-Christian roots of earth religion. What Bloy was saying may superficially sound like Christian imagery. In truth it had more to do with animism. What he was really dealing with was the phenomenon of the inexplicable and the inevitable, the oneness of things, in which everything, animate and inanimate, is alive and the Hero is us.

When the eighteenth-century philosophers killed God, they thought they were engaged in housekeeping — the evils of corrupt religion would be swept away, the decent aspects of Christian morality would be dusted off and neatly repackaged inside reason. Inadvertently they rendered that morality nonessential to their new society. Or rather they rendered it optional. The new essential element was structure. And so, while there was no room for a Léon Bloy in the official ranks of philosophy, by the late nineteenth century there was a growing desire in society to believe in something that went beyond arid structure and beyond the rather sad judgments of the new rational leaders, whether they be middle-class politicians or technocrats. Certainly Bloy's prophecy turned out to be perfectly accurate — Napoleon was indeed a precursor. "He who comes before the ONE." The unexpected element was perhaps that the ONE turned out to be not French, but the bastard son of an Austrian customs official.

Léon Bloy may have been less intelligent than Nietzsche, but he was certainly no crazier. And while Nietzsche built a perfect philosophical nest for the cult of the pre-Christian Hero in the very heart of modern reason, Bloy had the advantage of bringing it all down to mystical practicalities in a manner which would satisfy the middle-class Sunday-lunch convictions of the new twentieth-century Right wing.

What is more, Bloy certainly wasn't much crazier than Oswald Spengler, who began a justification of the first great Hero as follows: "The tragic in Napoleon's life, which still awaits discovery by a poet great enough to comprehend it and shape it."[45] Although Spengler wrote of the age of Heroes as if it were the end of our civilization, he also found the beginnings of the new civilization in yet another Hero, supposedly of a different kind, cutting a swath through Africa and building a new, virginal civilization in his own wake. Cecil Rhodes was to be "the first precursor of a Western type of Caesar."[46] In fact, all Spengler is saying about Rhodes is that it was easier to be a Hero in Africa, where there were no deep foundations of Western civilization to slow you up.

These writers are usually dealt with as three separate phenomena — Bloy, an eccentric marginal; Spengler, a flash in the pan, overobsessed by cycles and too egocentric to be able to influence the Nazis for the better; and Nietzsche, not tarred by the Nazis' use of his ideas because he was not himself an anti-Semite, racial nationalist or indeed a German nationalist. Thus Nietzsche alone remains unsullied enough to become a major inspiration for contemporary thinkers of all political varieties.

The truth is that when the technicalities are swept away, what remains is their deification of the Hero. All three accomplished this by marrying the earth-religion god-Hero to the modern Hero of reason. Nietzsche's brilliant analysis of the superman is merely a tarted-up version of Bloy's crude abasement of the individual worshipping at the feet of the megalomaniac dictator. And when an educated individual allows himself to be titillated by the sophisticated musings of Nietzsche, he is simply satisfying the need of modern rational man to feel what Bloy admitted was the excitement of being dominated. In the case of all three writers, the superman gains his power thanks to the death of God on the one hand and to being invincibly armed with the excalibur of reason on the other.

There is in the late twentieth century a general feeling that Hitler — and perhaps Stalin, although people in the West feel no personal need to take him into account — was an accident of history. He caught us off guard, but we recovered in time to meet this force of evil in combat. Now he is gone. A horrible aberration. It isn't surprising that no one wants to hold on to the memory of Hitler as an image of modern normalcy. But if this is still the Age of Reason and if Hitler is the great image of reason's dark side, then he is still very much with us.

As human beings we find it impossible to accept the idea that a man can do certain things unless he is crazy. We cannot accept that such evil is within us. That is a sign of man's unshakable optimism and even of his desire to be good. We have, therefore, placed the establishment, staffing and running of death camps in the category of a lunatic act. Of course, there was a strong current of lunacy in both the man and his regime. But these organized massacres were not part of that lunacy.

History is weighed down with repeated massacres of nations, cities, armies and religious, social and political groups. But those earlier massacres were always tied to some relatively concrete political, economic or social ambition — the seizure of private property or of territory, the increase of one group's power, the extinction of a rival group's beliefs, the erasing of financial debts, or the setting of an example. This was true even of Genghis Khan's Mongol armies. They often began their occupation of a newly won territory by massacring the entire population

of one city. This convinced other cities to cooperate with the occu-
pier — to pay any taxes, to accept slavery for their sons.

What Hitler organized was something quite different. It was the first
absolutely gratuitous massacre in the history of man. It wasn't lunacy
that made this possible, even if some of those who carried it out were
clinically insane. Nor was this the simple product of traditional anti-
Semitism. It was more like the profound panic of a world somehow
abandoned to a logic which had cut the imaginations of the perpetrators
free from any sense of what a man ought to do versus what he ought not
to. The Holocaust was the result of a perfectly rational argument —
given what reason had become — that was self-justifying and hermetically sealed. There is, therefore, nothing surprising about the fact that
the meeting called to decide on "the final solution," was a gathering
mainly of senior ministerial representatives. Technocrats. Nor is it
surprising that this Wansee Conference lasted only an hour — one
meeting among many for those present — and turned entirely on the
modalities for administering the solution. The systematic, scientific way
in which those modalities were subsequently carried out has been categorized as an adjunct of lunacy or shrugged off as part of a phenomenon
called the banality of evil. The massacre was indeed "managed," even
"well managed." It had the clean efficiency of a Harvard case study.
There was no practical reason for it. No property was gained, as it had
all been expropriated already. No territory was at stake. The killings
were a money-losing proposition — Nazi Germany was destroying a
slave population capable of great production at a time when Aryan males
had been sent away to fight. Judaism was not in any serious way a rival
religion, since it did not proselytize. The power of Germany was not
increased by their deaths. And no example was being set for other
groups. After all, the whole process was kept secret.

An act of pure logic carried out in a rational manner, the Holocaust
was a child of the marriage between the two key practitioners of reason — the Hero and the technocrat. To put it down to lunacy or to the
banalization of evil in modern technological society is to miss the point.
And while we might have hoped that the dark side of this marriage had
burnt itself out with the exposure and destruction of Hitler, the events
of the last forty years indicate that the opposite is true.

Not only is the Napoleonic dream stronger today in our imaginations
than it has ever been, but one can already feel the slow falling away of
moral opprobrium from our memory of Hitler. In another fifty years we
may well find ourselves weighed down by a second monstrous dream of
pure grandeur to match that of the Emperor. Two men who dared. Two
men who were adored. Two men who led with brilliance. Two men who
administered fairly and efficiently. Two men who were modest in their
own needs but surrounded by lesser beings who profited from their

situation and came between the Hero and his people. This last invocation is the "campaign bed syndrome" — the Hero wishes only to sleep on his metal folding bed in a tent, to fight for the people and to walk among them in simple garb. If he must wear a uniform, he will make it simple, without braid, without medals. He is the people's soldier. Only the necessities of Heroship oblige him to sacrifice himself by sleeping on gilded beds in palaces, dressing up in the morning and creating a splendid aura for the people to admire. Needless to say, the rapacious elites, from whom the Hero protects the people, benefit from this. And so there are two men who were betrayed by those who surrounded them but not by the people. Two men who were destroyed, as befits the tragic destiny of Heroes.

The idea that Hitler may be treated with honour one hundred years after his death shouldn't be surprising. Napoleon, who suffered equally ignominious defeat followed by exile, was returned to Paris in a coffin with Caesarean pomp only twenty-five years after being deposed. The two men were responsible for approximately the same number of deaths. And the Napoleonic dream — that of combining efficient administration with the brute force required to ensure that it is properly applied — lies today beneath the pillow of every ambitious colonel who drops off to sleep at night in the hope that the tooth fairy of power will slip in before he awakes. In a few more years all the witnesses capable of imagining what the Hitlerian regime actually did will be dead. All witnesses of all sorts will be dead. Then mythology will be free to do whatever it wishes. And what will mythology do with the murder of six million Jews? In the absence of witnesses, that abomination will become a tragic abstract flaw proper to the Heroes' tragic destiny, rather in the way that Napoleon's invasion of Russia is referred to as the single great error of his career. The rapidity with which this normalization process is advancing can be seen in the new boldness of the Holocaust revisionists.

We now assume that we have rejected all dreams of supreme leaders and of violent government. And yet the language of even the most insignificant minister of postal services is filled with Napoleonic images of strength and efficiency. The public appearances of political leaders are routinely organized as imitative Napoleonic triumphs. And our tolerance for both dictatorship and violence has never been greater. Our friends and allies around the world over the last forty years have included an astonishing collection of mass murderers, drug dealers and practitioners of widespread torture. Even the Khmer Rouge were reintegrated into the international community without great difficulty on the pretext of solving a relatively minor legal problem. We simply accept that the world will produce Heroes and that those Heroes will kill countless masses of people.

THE PURPOSE OF TORTURING IS TO GET ANSWERS.[47]

The posted declaration of the Khmer Rouge authorities at Phnom Penh's Tuol Sleng Prison, their principal interrogation centre, is a reminder of their Western rational education. Thousands died within its walls.

Their motto might have been posted in Latin at an Inquisition interrogation of the seventeenth century. Or in a Czechoslovakian prison of the 1950s. Or in any contemporary Western military intelligence service, although modern methodology now finds that psychological torture is more effective than physical. The very problems which theoretically set off the original desire for reason have now reappeared as the official tools of reason. What's more, actions such as "torturing . . . to get answers" do not seem to carry with them any real, lasting stigma.

Instead we concentrate our relatively abstract moralistic feelings on one or two chosen massacres, which graphically illustrate our horror — a civilian airliner downed by terrorists or a small, innocent village burned — as if our minds were unable to register and digest in a meaningful manner any more than that.

There is no point in attempting to model ourselves on a man like Jefferson, whose genius enabled him to apply fully both a personal and a general moral standard. He was fortunate to be the man he was, but to emulate him would be to make of Jefferson precisely that thing he most detested — a Hero. And in doing so we would be ceding to the dream that we ourselves might also rise to that Heroic level.

The public domain requires, therefore, not a multiplication, but an abstraction of morality. And moral standards, since they are personal and applied, cannot be abstracted. That hasn't prevented us from seeking solutions to our problems, and the modern solution has been to set standards through constitutions and laws. But again, constitutions and laws are abstractions and subject more than we can accept to the will of those who manage them. And they are either technocrats or Heroes.

4

The Rational Courtesan

To believe that any class will act in a gratuitous, disinterested manner over a period of several centuries would be misplaced optimism. The intellectual and practical creation of our rational civilization by a succession of courtiers can only have been an act of self-perpetuation and self-promotion.

That doesn't exclude idealism from their motives or real improvements in our condition from their acts. But their underlying approach was that of courtiers and, however admirable parts of our society may be, at heart it is a civilization of courtesanage.

We don't see this in ourselves because we have learned to describe in admirable and positive terms those characteristics which, stripped down, would have been appropriate in Versailles or the Forbidden City. And we concentrate on the conflicts between such sectors as bureaucrats and businessmen rather than admit that they all use the same methods. The very idea of the courtier has been relegated carefully to a past filled with absolute monarchies.

But there is nothing about courtiers which is proper to royal courts. They are characterized not by function, but by an approach towards gaining power. Only one important factor has changed over the centuries. In the past, when they succeeded in seizing real power, they were obliged to make a difficult choice. They could maintain their parasitic methods behind the screen of the old ruling class or they could transform themselves into a responsible ruling elite. The eunuchs behind the Manchus in the nineteenth century chose the parasitic route and gradually drained China of its energy and its direction. The Georgian eunuchs did the same thing in the seventeenth century when they controlled the Safavid dynasty of Persia. The Baghdad caliphs of the great Abbasid caliphate were so discredited by the power of their eunuchs in the tenth century that the military took over and left them as mere figureheads. Individual courtiers — even eunuchs — did occasionally transform themselves into true leaders. But a class of courtiers has never transformed itself into a responsible elite.

Rational society has refined that difficult choice between courtesan-age and leadership almost to the point of rendering it irrelevant. After all, our society was largely conceived by the courtiers, with their own private and elitist skills in mind. They dominate the very idea of modernism — particularly our wider sense of it — and therefore influence our denigration of other social forces as being retrograde or inefficient. For the first time in Western history, the courtiers don't need to change when they win power, because power has been designed in their image.

The modern technocrat and the royal courtier are virtually indistinguishable. Of course, superficial details have changed. The great accomplishment of the rational approach was to remove the need for external characteristics by creating an all-inclusive abstract method. For example, in many places castration was standard practice.

Picturesque though this absence of testicles may seem in such cases as the Chinese emperor's eunuchs or those of the Persian shah, it was only an incidental detail. Castration established the fact that by function, or lack of it, the courtier did not have dynastic pretensions. He was the emperor's man. More to the point, however, was the division between inner court and outer court, which was particularly clear in China. The eunuchs were in the inner court and thus served power and not the population. The notion of "inner" meant they served in a secretive and arbitrary manner. Their personal power could be increased to the extent that they were able to elaborate on the formal structures surrounding the emperor. Perhaps the most eloquent surviving illustration of this power is the maze of high walled lanes which carve up the Forbidden City in Peking. Each short section leads everywhere and nowhere and was part of the unlimited manipulation which the eunuch lived.

Life at Versailles turned less on geographical intricacy and more on a maze of rules and dress codes and minutely carved-up privileges. The man who tasted the king's food (his brother). The man who carried his hat. But which man with which hat for which level of ceremony? The right to enter here but not there. Presence at the waking-up ceremony. At the king's meal. Hunting with the king. Not permitted to hunt but permitted to follow the hunt. The permutations were endless. In Diderot's words, they were "artificial productions of the most sought after perfections."[1] And in the process religious policy was set and wars declared or not. In all of this Versailles resembled the court of the Baghdad caliphate seven hundred years before, when the powerful eunuchs were ranked by their responsibility for the caliph's personal property. The Bearer of the Inkwell, for example. At the top was the one who wrapped his head with a special crown.

The second Duc de Saint-Simon was the great diarist of Versailles and himself a consummate courtier. The first duke, his father, had begun life in the stables and a terrible social inferiority complex drove the son to waste his genius in working the palace corridors. Like most courtiers he was filled with contempt for others but incapable of the introspection which permits irony. And so he could describe another man, who might have been himself, as "one of those court insects that one is always surprised to see and to find everywhere and whose very existence is built on a fear of being consequential."[2]

A sharp tongue in itself is harmless enough. As harmless as the nightly gatherings early in the sixteenth century in northern Italy of a handful of aristocrats. They sat in a circle in the *sala delle veglie* of the Duchess of Urbino in order to determine the characteristics of the perfect courtier. One of them — the diplomat Baldesar Castiglione — later published the entire "debate" as *The Book of the Courtier* and this instant best-seller was felt to have captured all the elegance of the Renaissance. Here was the bible of civilized behaviour. And the participants were also men of consequence, who went on to become a bishop, an archbishop, a cardinal, a secretary to the pope, a doge of Genoa, a duke of Nemours, a prefect of Rome. They didn't manage to settle whether beauty or fine dancing or elegant clothes were or were not superior to using deception in the interests of the master or honesty or loyalty or personal courage for the sole purpose of distinguishing oneself. However, the mastery of reason was one of the few undoubted requirements: "Reason has such power that it always brings the sense to obey it and extends its rule by marvelous ways and means, provided ignorance does not seize upon what reason ought to possess."[3]

The reality behind all this chat was the Duchess's father-in-law, the first Duke of Urbino — one of the most battleworn mercenaries of his day. He operated in an Italy overcome by political violence and disorder. The Duchess was married to his only son, the second Duke, who was crippled and impotent. In effect, despite all the elegant talk about court life, the duchy was up for grabs and one of the Duchess's guests did indeed end up running the whole thing in the name of the pope. Of course, the charm of the Duchess of Urbino can't be denied, anymore than that of the Earl of Essex, so long as he stayed within close range of Elizabeth I's palaces. The moment she sent him off to deal with the real world in Ireland, his charm evaporated and the result was a military and political catastrophe.

Because everything in society was centered on the courts, so they seemed to harbour as much good as they did evil. Versailles permitted the King to protect Molière. Holbein's genius flourished in the shadow of Henry VIII. But the essence of the courts was power not creativity or elegance. A glance at Holbein's court drawings is enough to see that they depict the faces of manipulators, bullies and disciples of uncontrolled ambition, of cowardly violence and of betrayal.

What all this tells us about the modern variety of courtiers isn't very clear. McNamara, for example, may well be an evolved version of Richelieu. Or Giscard d'Estaing of Saint-Simon. But what really matters is that society has been restructured in order to convert these sorts of people into the mainstream of the social order. And that's why it is important to pause long enough to examine a handful of contemporary individuals in order to clarify what the modern courtier is like.

These individuals don't lead in the old political sense. They don't create policy in response to public needs. Nor do they function as forerunners of public need, formulating that which the public has not yet consciously formulated. Sometimes they are idealists, unconsciously dominated by their mechanical genius, like Robert McNamara or Michael Pitfield. Sometimes they are cynical opportunists, like Henry Kissinger, Harold Wilson or James Baker, playing the narrow field between the system and the politicians. Sometimes, as with Simon Reisman, the disequilibrium between apparently uncontrollable emotions and advanced technical skills seems to be so great that the resulting conflict carries public policy off course. There are also men who would like to have a moral or an ideological position but are dominated by a mechanical version of intellectual skills, like Jacques Chirac. Or men, like Valéry Giscard, of intelligence severely limited apart from the narrow mechanical skills necessary to carry them to the fore. Or men like Sir Robert Armstrong, of great intelligence, but all of it consumed by those same mechanical skills, so that they function brilliantly and with absolute self-confidence, although to no apparent purpose.

Taken together, they form a group, a class, a type, linked by a particular sort of intelligence involving their central talents as systems men. They are men who create and work principally within and through the systems of which they are emanations. Men who deal in power. Men given to the manipulation of facts and contemptuous of public debate. The differences between them are in part generational, in part a function of their surviving traits of individualism. And yet their unity is not simply a function of society's training. It does not come only from a shared form of education. Rather, they are outstanding examples of the sort of man who is attracted to contemporary systems and who does well within them.

The idea of innate human qualities was much debated in the first half of the Age of Reason, then submerged beneath the growing need to prove everything by means of what were coming to be known as facts. And yet it is their innate mechanical and logical talents which link our new men of power together. They have what can most easily be summarized as a talent for manipulation. The system merely rewards them for this. They invariably seem to be lacking in applied moral common sense — that quality which accounts for a straightforward respect of the individual — in other words, a sense of proportion in dealing with those individuals and an understanding of the value of content over form. In other words, they resemble seventeenth- or eighteenth-century courtiers or courtesans.

Only gender separates those two words. English, for some reason, makes a greater distinction than French or, indeed, Italian, from which the words arise. English differentiates between social action and sexual action, as if to say that selling your honour isn't so bad as selling your body. For the Italians and the French, both words refer to clever and obsequious behaviour at court; whether this involves the soul, the body, or the mind, something is being sold. And since the role of the courtier is actually that of the mythological female at her most untrustworthy and amoral — that is, seeking favour by flattery or behaviour — as opposed to the real female, it is far better to describe the modern technocrat as a courtesan and his methods as courtesanage.

Robert McNamara is the individual who most dramatically fills the role of the man of reason in flamboyant decline. He straddles our era like a colossus, and yet, in any public poll ranking identifiable names, he would be lucky to pick up 1 percent. He is a man who believes in the forces of light and of darkness. A man of honour. He resigned as Johnson's secretary of defense because he felt the Vietnam War was spinning out of control. As head of the World Bank, he attempted to save a desperate Third World by sending a flood of money in its direction. He believes that the application of reason, logic and efficiency will necessarily produce good. And yet his actions have resulted in uncontrollable disasters from which the West has still not recovered.

When Robert McNamara left the presidency of the Ford Motor Company to become John Kennedy's Secretary of Defense in 1961, he was seen to be bringing modern management methods from private industry to government. No one imagined that those methods would turn out to be as disastrous for private industry as for public policy.

McNamara immediately set about reorganizing the Pentagon and the American armed forces. That is, he set about rationalizing them. No doubt he discovered great inefficiency. No doubt he exposed antediluvian methods and situations. He also set in motion three separate processes, the first two of which — the application of rational business principles to officer training and to arms production — will be dealt with at greater length in later chapters.

The idea behind training officers as rational executives was to incorporate "a number of business practices and techniques designed to make the Pentagon bureaucracy more efficient."[4] These apparently worthwhile techniques did far more than that. They revolutionized the American officer corps by introducing, in the words of Richard Gabriel, "the habits, values and practices of the business community."[5] This, in turn, changed the motivation of officers from self-sacrifice to self-interest. The effect was to transform the professional officer into half bureaucrat, half executive. In the process everyone mislaid the basic given of membership in an officer corps: that each individual in order to do his duty is prepared to do the unacceptable — that is, to die. Getting killed, after all, is not logical, rational, efficient or what a businessman would perceive as being in his personal self-interest.

This restructuring initiated a long period during which the American armed forces have been incapable of winning. Or, to put it another way, capable only of losing. Richard Gabriel, who is becoming the sort of nagging teller of truths to the American army that Basil Liddell Hart was to the British after World War I, explains better than anyone how the army has become a bureaucratic organism incapable of fighting in anything other than a clumsy, heavy-handed manner. The need to overwhelm vastly inferior enemies with sheer mass confirms rather than disproves this.

The second process began by McNamara evolved naturally from the first. As an ex-automobile manufacturer, he noticed that armaments were expensive. Building upon the Henry Ford principle of production-line cost reduction, McNamara concluded that it would be rational to limit armament costs by producing larger runs of each weapon and selling the surplus abroad. Foreign sales would cover perhaps not all, but at least part of the Pentagon's upfront investment in R and D, as well as reducing the unit cost of each weapon the United States needed itself. America's allies, in buying these weapons, would also be repaying the United States for some of the protection it provided. Finally, the use of American weaponry throughout the West would ensure a unity of material, thus facilitating both common action and emergency operational supply needs. Efficiency, return on the dollar, morality and sensible military strategy were all wrapped up together in a neat package.

The United States also happened to be running a three-billion-dollar general trade deficit. Foreign arms sales would be a way to balance the situation.

Thanks to all this sensible reasoning, the International Logistics Negotiations Organization was created. Its name was a suitably obtuse management formula for the arms-dealing agency of the American government. Before long most other Western countries had followed suit and adopted the same management theories. We were on our way to developing the largest weapons market in the history of the world which, perhaps more significant, is now the largest market of any kind anywhere in the world economy.

The third area which McNamara set out to reorganize was American military strategy. It struck him as both immoral and irrational that Western defense was based on a nuclear deterrent which could only be used in a way that would destroy the earth. This strategy, known as Massive Response, was based upon an all-or-nothing view of nuclear war. If the weapons were to be used, they would be used massively to destroy absolutely the opposing side. Destroying the other side inevitably meant destroying oneself, either because the enemy managed to get off a similar counterattack before expiring or because the quantity of weapons unleashed by one side alone would be enough to make life impossible on earth.

In the absence of such a massive attack, there was no nuclear strategy, no organization; in fact, there were no nuclear weapons of a suitably limited size, equipped with suitably limited delivery systems, to permit any except cataclysmic use. The "rational" use of nuclear weapons was impossible. On the other hand, the door was theoretically open to some sort of accidental unleashing of the apocalypse. From McNamara's rational point of view, this meant that American nuclear superiority "did not translate into usable military power."[6]

He and the American government therefore proposed a new strategy to the NATO allies. It was called Flexible Response. This strategy consisted of neat, more or less parallel lines of in-depth defence, which began at the frontier separating NATO territory from the Soviet bloc. Response to Soviet armies attacking Western Europe would escalate as the lines were crossed, from an initial use of conventional weapons up to battlefield nuclear weapons. And if the various levels of tactical nuclear weapons failed to stop this advance, the West would resort to the old massive and definitive, cataclysmic intercontinental strategic bombs. The lesser responses were intended to work. Therefore the strategy of Flexible Response lessened the risk of a cataclysm.

Of course, no one else, apart from McNamara and the American government, saw it that way. For Europe the meaning was quite clear: Washington was no longer willing to fight for its allies. Europe would have to be destroyed before the United States made up its mind to intervene seriously.

McNamara simply hadn't focused on the fact that he had drawn his neat, in-depth lines of escalating military response across the real world of Western Europe. Were Düsseldorf, Amsterdam, Bonn, Strasbourg, Paris and Rome in zones one, two, three or four? The flexible, measured, rational response which McNamara was proposing — or rather, thanks to the controlling superiority of America's leadership, imposing — was, in fact, a plan for the death and destruction of the people of Western Europe.

The imposition of Flexible Response in 1961 utterly destroyed European confidence in American leadership. The Allies refused this strategy for NATO, but they knew their refusal was meaningless. "It is evident," de Gaulle said in 1963, "that no independence is possible for a country which does not have nuclear weapons, because without them it is forced to rely on a country that does and therefore to accept its policies."[7] However serious the debate within NATO from 1961 to 1967 pretended to be, Flexible Response was effectively the alliance's strategy from the moment the United States announced it. The Germans, who — being in the front line of the sacrificial lambs — were most opposed to the strategy, also gave up arguing first, out of fear that further protest would drive Washington into an even greater withdrawal from Europe.

As for the French, Flexible Response made inevitable both their own independent nuclear force and their withdrawal from NATO. When that time came, de Gaulle explained that they could not belong to a "Europe of which the strategy is, within NATO, the American strategy."[8]

The proliferation of nuclear weapons produced by McNamara's rational strategy went far beyond the French *force de frappe*. In order to meet the new flowchart gradations of a possible military engagement, nuclear weapons and delivery systems of all sorts and sizes had to be developed. And the Soviets had to match each of them.

The result, apart from an ever-larger number of nuclear weapons developed at great expense, was a far higher risk of nuclear war than under the old strategy. First, there was a higher possibility of error, given that there were now weapons of declining size put more or less in the hands of a whole range of officials and officers of declining rank. There were now, for example, field commanders involved in the use of battlefield nuclear weapons and therefore subject to the risk of error. Second, the moral threshold involved in firing a "small" nuclear device attached to a tank or a cannon is much lower than that involved in releasing an ICBM.

The secondary result of Europe's loss of confidence in America's willingness to respond decisively to all attacks was, of course, a drop in the Soviet fear of a U.S. nuclear reprisal. The risk of the Soviet Union being tempted by military action had therefore risen. This in turn fuelled new military spending on both sides. Finally, continued American military failures added further to the risk. "When a nation has a record of successful military operations," Gabriel points out, "the available options of its adversaries are often self-limiting."[9] The failures which so damaged America's credibility were, of course, the product of McNamara's rationalized army.

The practical effect of Flexible Response was exactly the opposite of its theoretical intention, except that it did translate nuclear weapons into a "usable military power," as McNamara put it, and that was the original rational impetus for his reform.

What could be more surprising, therefore, than to find the same McNamara resurfacing in the early 1980s with virginal ingenuity as an opponent of Flexible Response? There he was in 1984 signing an appeal by Western "statesmen" which called for the withdrawal of nuclear battlefield weapons. The document's title had a familiar ring to it — *Managing East-West Conflict*. In 1986 McNamara published an entire book devoted to the dismantling of nuclear arsenals. What we lack, he said, is "an agreed conceptual framework for the management of relations with the Soviet Union." Why? "The substantial raising of the nuclear threshold, as was envisioned when Flexible Response was first conceived, has not become reality." What went wrong? he asks. Things were too ad hoc, he replies. The current situation is the "unplanned — and to me unacceptable — result of the long series of incremental decisions taken by military and civilian leaders of East and West."[10]

At no point does he mention, or indeed appear conscious, that the present situation of nuclear proliferation and strategic uncertainty is largely of his own creation. Nor does he acknowledge that it was done precisely through the use of advanced planning and management as devised by himself. Nor does he seem to realize that he has travelled in a complete circle.

The movement of history is the great enemy of someone like McNamara. History is linear memory and, as such, beyond organization and indifferent to reason. The characteristic common to the modern man of reason is this loss of memory; lost or rather, denied as an uncontrollable element. And if it must be remembered, then that evocation of real events is always presented as either quaint or dangerous. The past, when it involves a failed system, disappears from the mind. The past is always ad hoc. The future is always optimistic, because it is available for unencumbered solutioneering. And the present lies helpless beneath his feet, just begging to be managed.

It isn't surprising, therefore, that anything which was not on Robert McNamara's flowchart is not his fault. And none of what has gone wrong appears to have had anything to do with his planning.

In 1991 he proposed that all nuclear weapons should be destroyed, except for a few hundred on either side. These would be monitored by effective mutual policing. But if there were only two hundred missiles on either side, a nuclear war would become a practical possibility simply because people would believe that it could be fought without destroying the world. Policing would be possible. But at such low levels of weaponry, a single, minor deceit by either side would radically alter the strategic balance. And that would make such a deceit very tempting. Today's horrifying mass of weaponry has the peculiar characteristic of making strategic advances almost meaningless. Two thousand weapons on one side versus 1,900 on the other, or even 2,000 versus 1,500 is strategically meaningless. But 300 versus 200 is of capital importance. Even 250 versus 200 would be decisive.

A reduction in the number of nuclear warheads is clearly a good and sensible objective. The last few years have seen some small steps in that direction. These have been presented as major reductions by politicians eager for easy credit. The reality is that they are minor. However, for as long as the reform-minded leadership survives in Moscow, these reductions will continue to grow.

But what would be the advantage to man of actually rendering nuclear war rational? That, of course, is not a question which a man like Robert McNamara could ask. Rational is good. There is nothing more to say. The untouchable simplicity of his advanced logic rarely takes the human factor into consideration. To do so would cause an unprofessional distortion in his conceptual framework.

McNamara resigned for moral reasons, after eight years as secretary of defense, and devoted himself between 1969 and 1981 to a task which suited his vision of public service. His attempt to turn the World Bank into a Western bridge to the Third World could be seen as a personal act of atonement for his years in the Pentagon. There are indications that, in a confused manner, he himself saw the situation that way. It was as if, by shouldering a personal and private blame modelled on the emotive mechanisms of Christian guilt, he was able to avoid questioning his own methods. But this decision to distance himself from a war of which he had come to disapprove was in itself an astonishing act. He had been the most important Vietnam hawk within the administration. He had fought a tough insider's battle to carry the case for war. He had done this in the face of the antiwar advice the President was getting from such people as George Ball, Senator Wayne Morse, Senator Richard Russell, Senator Mike Mansfield, Vice President Hubert Humphrey and Senator William Fulbright. What's more, President Johnson was inexperienced in international affairs and was himself rather soft on the war.

If the fighting was allowed to drag on until America began to rip itself apart, it was in large part because Secretary of Defense Robert McNamara had succeeded in making it his own war. And then, when things didn't work out, he admitted no error and gave no hint of an apology. He simply walked away. More astonishing still, he walked away in protest against a war out of control, as if by that simple act he had washed his hands of it all. He seemed to believe that in this way he had removed himself from the history of the war.

From the Pentagon to the World Bank was only a few city blocks. There he immediately set about trying to do "good." That attempt turned into an international disaster. His central idea was to increase the amount of money committed to the bank so that it could then help countries in need. In order to deliver this help properly, he restructured the bank's methods of evaluation.

This meant creating two new devices — the Country Program Paper and the annual Country Allocation Exercise. The first "set out a five-year lending program for the Bank's International Development Agency in a given country against a detailed statistical analysis by sector of the country's economy." The second "set targets for the staff for each country and each sector within each country."[11] A truism of all technocrats is that they do not delegate and they are wedded to centralization. McNamara, therefore, oversaw these devices.

In 1973 the oil crisis began the flow of rapidly printed money out of the United States and other Western countries to pay the OPEC producers, who in turn sent it for deposit to the safest places on earth — that is, back to the United States, Canada and Western Europe. This printing of money caused inflation. The payments to OPEC caused a trade imbalance. The returning investment from OPEC doubled this imbalance by creating a foreign debt.

The American economy, crippled by inflation, energy costs, and the resulting trade imbalance, was in no shape to make good use of these returning funds. The situation was difficult. McNamara intervened to make it catastrophic. He saw an opportunity, in the growing mountain of unusable bank deposits, to push the cycle around another time by sending whatever money he could out to the Third World. He cajoled the commercial banks into following suit on the grounds that this influx of capital would create Third World prosperity. That prosperity would create local growth on the Western model and the accompanying needs would push the Third World countries to purchase Western industrial material and consumer goods. This would bring the money back again to the West in the form of a stimulation to production thanks to foreign sales. The depression would thus be ended and the trade balance righted.

Unfortunately, nowhere on McNamara's charts and models were the right questions asked. Is it wise to push fragile agrarian, often tribal, economies down the route of an oil-based, industrial development when there is an energy crisis which has already flattened the far-stronger economies of the West? Do these nations have any energy sources of their own in order to avoid the oil import trap which has done so much harm in the West? Do these new countries have the basic infrastructure to respond rapidly to such artificially induced growth? Should these agrarian societies, lacking in urban middle-class structures, often poor in natural resources, be pushed down this road at all? Does it suit their established economy? Does it suit their society? Wouldn't it be wiser to concentrate on improving their agrarian structure? If they are going to widen the base of their economy, would they not do better to concentrate at first on development which satisfies internal needs, rather than to throw themselves into the expensive, high risk international world of import-export wars?

Most basic of all was the question: what will happen if these massive loans from the West do not provoke Third World prosperity, and the poor nations are therefore unable to repay their debt? No one asked. And no one asked the related question: what will happen if the American and other Western banks, as a result of such a Third World failure, were themselves unable to repay their debts — that is, to pay their depositors?

In fact, nobody even bothered to program debt figures into the World Bank's World Development Model until 1981. That was almost a decade too late. At first glance such an error seems criminally incompetent. At second glance it is perfectly understandable. Devoid of memory, anchored in the present, inescapably optimistic about the future, rational models always have great difficulty adjusting themselves to simple reality.

The practical effects of McNamara's management were as follows. His centralized, abstract methods destroyed collegiality, whether it be among bank staffs or between the bank and its borrowers or the bank and its clients. At the heart of these methods was "management by fear,"[12] a phrase which endlessly recurs as an effect of contemporary organization. His two program devices involved lengthy country and staff reports. These became self-justifying, both on the part of bank staff and of the borrowing countries. Once a five-year program had begun, the bank employee directly responsible became committed to it working. He had, after all, recommended it. That country and that program were his. He adjusted his paperwork to keep the money flowing. Borrowing countries learned to flood the bank with tons of statistics, graphs, and charts to fit every need and keep everyone happy.[13]

In the early 1980s, the Philippine economy, for example, was still getting glowing reports — "one of the best in the Third World." Everyone was too committed to say what they really thought. At a certain point the debt crisis became so great that the truth could not be avoided. It came out of the blue, in total contradiction to everything that for years had been written inside the bank.

But Third World statistics had been favourably falsified for so long that the true figures seemed as unreal as the old ones. And when the International Monetary Fund (IMF) began to address the growing world crisis by imposing economic remedies of an impossible severity, its attitude was the result of years of statistics which seemed to have no relationship to populations. People hadn't actually prospered when their economies were relaxed and statistically doing well, so why should they actually suffer when the IMF made the same economies meet draconian tests of tight financial management? It could be argued that it has been decades since real people were included as a component in our widely accepted definitions of what an economy is; only the theory of people has been included or the statistical reflection of people.

McNamara is no doubt morally outraged by today's situation. He is the most perfect example of a technocrat holding great power while crippled by a personality cleanly divided between mechanical brilliance at one extreme and childlike idealism at the other, with absolutely no thread of common sense to link the two together.

Robert McNamara may be an exceptional example of the rational phenomenon, but he is not an exception to the rule. He is the rule in its most advanced form. Others like him abound in other countries. Edward Heath, for example, had the same unmeasured eagerness, combined with a conviction that systems will do good. The process that McNamara began in the United States, Heath initiated in Britain. His Central Policy Review Staff brought in bright outsiders. He had a planning and priorities style, which sought out methods for policy analysis and review as well as checking for program effectiveness. He, also, seemed unable to link his belief in methods with the actual effect of their application in a real world.

The sight of Edward Heath being ripped apart by the coal miners, during the disastrous strike which destroyed his government, demonstrated the weakness of the new man of reason when he ventures outside the protective defences of the system. And, unlike McNamara, he had been elected to do what he did. So the voters made him pay for his flaws.

Heath's failure is usually dealt with by referring to his brittle character and his overly intellectualized view of how government worked. Neither comment is inaccurate. What is interesting about Heath is precisely his conviction that people and structures could be made to change radically by the simple act of showing them a better way to do things. It didn't really matter whether the ways he proposed were better. It was his absolute conviction that they were which marked him as an early version of the technocrat with political power.

Robert Armstrong, for a decade secretary of the British Cabinet and head of the Civil Service, is a far more classic example of the rational administrator. From his appointment in 1978 he carefully avoided the technocrat's inferiority in public affairs by staying out of sight while quite naturally combining enormous political power without public responsibility. By background and training he seemed very much an old-style bureaucrat, yet his methods were perfectly modern. He was obsessive about secrecy. He controlled information flows even within the government, thus excluding certain ministers. He was, by nature, a manipulator of men and of structures. As with McNamara, this leadership by manipulation led to a demoralization of the civil service. In descriptions of him, the word *courtier* seems to appear effortlessly. "It is the courtier's role to endure, to appease, to employ guile and stealth, to manipulate power — always behind the throne — in such abilities, Armstrong excelled."[14]

On issues that interested him personally, he prevented, as far as possible, proper debate between ministers. The information fed out served only his cause. He didn't appear to believe in anything except the excellence of his own positions, which were determined by the immediate interests of his job combined with a class attitude.

Only with the Westland Helicopter crisis in 1985 did he finally step over the protective barriers of administrative structure in an attempt to protect his employer by managing the public debate. Westland was the last British-owned helicopter manufacturer. An American company wanted to buy it. The Prime Minister and some cabinet ministers were in favour of this sale, while the Secretary of State for Defence preferred a European consortium. What followed was a battle that split the cabinet, the business community and the press. This climaxed with the improper leaking of privileged information which helped the Prime Minister's position. Armstrong was called upon to calm the resulting storm by carrying out an official enquiry into how this information had been leaked. In truth, it's difficult to see how he could not have known the answers before he began. He presented the results of his investigation to the Prime Minister as if she were a distant observer, when there is every indication that Mrs. Thatcher was as involved as anyone else. Finally, he allowed himself to be called before the Commons Select Committee on Defence. The others, who were deeply involved and technically responsible, refused to appear. This turned him, the chief civil servant, into the defender of, and spokesman for, the political authorities. He did this with a jesuitical splitting of hairs which obscured the truth behind gerunds.

Perhaps it was his success in manipulating his way through that mess, in order to maintain a veil of unjustified secrecy and thus to save the government, which made Mrs. Thatcher send him off to Australia. Again the issue was secrecy. Again the circumstances required an artificial view of reality. A disgruntled retired British secret agent living in New South Wales had written his memoirs and, in the process, had revealed some of Britain's security methods. By the time Armstrong reached Australia, the contents of the book were already known. There was therefore nothing to be accomplished. However, for the rational, logical minds of Mrs. Thatcher and apparently of her senior civil servant, this public knowledge was merely an intervention by reality. They seemed to believe that by means of a determined legal, technical, and manipulative intervention, reality would be put back in its amateurish place.

However, the moment Armstrong stepped out of his protective cocoon in London, he no longer made any sense. The official view was that he had failed in Australia because it was a rougher sort of place — less civilized, less liable to give him the deference he deserved. The reality was that the lawyers who badgered him owed him nothing. He had no control over them. No purchase. Nothing to offer or to threaten.

The technocrat outside his own system is like any child outside his own house. In a moment of frustration at his own helplessness, Armstrong let loose his famous phrase, "Economical with the truth." This can be interpreted in many ways, but twist it as you will, those four words remain the perfect epitaph for the rational courtesan.

Of course, there were far purer practitioners in equivalent positions in other countries. One of the most rational was Michael Pitfield, head of the Canadian civil service (clerk of the Privy Council) under Pierre Trudeau almost continually from 1974 to 1982. Pitfield's brilliance got him to university by the age of fourteen and into the most important nonelected government position at thirty-seven. His youth and close links to the prime minister marked him, unfairly, as a partisan appointment. But it was his abstract management style that kept this political reputation alive.

The bureaucracy and the politicians — not only those in opposition — felt that there was something seriously wrong with both his methods and his actions. Most of them were singularly ill-prepared to do battle with him, either because of Pitfield's intellectual superiority or because, like McNamara, he was constantly redefining the way things were done. His opponents were therefore unable to find solid and commonly recognized ground upon which they could fight him.

Pitfield believed in what he was doing. He had a moral conviction as to which was the right side of each major question and that side was invariably tied to decency, social justice and the protection of the weak. In all that he resembled McNamara. Even his appearance — that of a tall, gangly doctoral student — somehow resembled the American's severe air of an outdated but upright notary.

Pitfield was continually experimenting with the structure of government, attempting to raise efficiency, cause information to flow, force ministers to consider policy options in a rational manner. He experimented so well that the individual ministers were gradually drained of power and kept off balance by the young bureaucrats in his central Privy Council Office. They maintained an atmosphere in which the ministers were constantly frightened of losing their jobs and increasingly in the dark as to what was really going on in the Prime Minister's mind and therefore in the government of which they — and not the Privy Council boys — were the responsible officers. Pitfield was certainly the finest practitioner yet seen of that bizarre management method which consists of using massive quantities of information to create confusion which in turn creates ignorance and thus removes power from those who receive the information.

One of the last reorganizations involved unifying two key departments — External Affairs and Trade. The principle was sound: diplomacy and international commerce were two aspects of foreign policy and therefore ought to be coordinated. The document laying out how the new department would work was brilliant. It read like a coded medieval Masonic plot grafted onto a detective novel and was filled with intricate cross-references between the two sectors — physical, not intellectual cross-references. In order to do what the organization chart required, an official would have had to think not so much about what his job required of him, as about how to play permanent hopscotch across the board. No one could possibly have had any idea of what he was actually meant to be doing on a practical level. Just keeping up with where one was in the structure and where everyone else was and which parts of what you were responsible for would be a full-time job.

Pitfield's organization was the final nail in the coffin of Canadian foreign policy. His misunderstanding seemed to be that advanced organization would produce content. If anything, his structures were designed to define all possible activities and therefore, in their very concept, to discourage nondefined activity. In other words, they were designed to destroy content.

The public service in Canada had always been much admired by the public, who had seen in it a collection of men and women devoted to just that — public service. That is, to the protection of the public. Pitfield's inaccessible structures led to the inevitable distancing of the public servant from the public. His admiration for the cool approach and his centralization of the decision-making process added to this distance and laid the foundations for a situation in which the servant would have contempt for his master — that is, the civil servant for the public. As for the public, it responded with growing distrust and resentment, despite the fact that those same years saw a very real growth in social programs and in the protection of the citizen.

The growing atmosphere of distrust and of fear within the civil service was seized upon by the Conservative government which came to power in 1984. They actively used these elements to demoralize the bureaucracy, whom they perceived as the enemy, and to bully them into doing whatever was wanted. Their assumption — that the public service was already political and in favour of the opposing side — freed the new government to politicize it openly, bringing in a large number of partisan outsiders. Thus Pitfield's scientific and idealistic management of what had been, before his arrival, one of the most effective and popular bureaucracies in the developed world resulted in its reduction to a relatively unpopular political tool for whatever politicians arrived in power.

McNamara, Heath and Pitfield seem scarcely to be born of the same egg as a man like Henry Kissinger. Whatever they did, they believed they were doing in the service of the public good. It was their methods and their lack of common sense which played against them. Kissinger used the same methods, but in a consciously cynical way. In their case the means were intended to serve the end. In his case the means served him.

Lermontov, in his poem attacking the men who had destroyed Pushkin, described the classic courtesan at his worst:

> You, greedy crew that round the sceptre crawl,
> Butchers of freedom, genius, and renown!
> Hid by the bulwark of the law, and all —
> Law, truth and honour in your steps cast down!

It is a vision which leads temptingly to Henry Kissinger, perhaps the technocratic personality who most neatly fills the traditional role. When Kissinger was playing Iago to President Nixon's Richard III, all the elements proper to a royal drama were present. But Kissinger wasn't simply the paragon of something past. He also used the modern techniques with a determined and narrow genius.

What isn't clear is whether he ever believed that he would be serving the public interest. We don't know what went through his mind during his first months as President Nixon's National Security Council Advisor. Perhaps he underwent a sudden private revelation that he craved power and had the manipulative talents to gain it. Perhaps, in the adrenaline rush of that revelation, he forgot about the nature of public service.

In those early days he sounded like a prophet of the new way down the golden road to a rational heaven. He wanted men around him who had "addressed themselves to acquiring substantive knowledge" in order to give them an opportunity not only to solve problems but "to contribute to the definition of goals."[15] They were to make up a new class of intellectuals, separate from the lawyers, bureaucrats and businessmen normally found in government.

But the true indicators of what was to come lay in Kissinger's past. His practical, intellectual and political hero had always been Prince Metternich, the man who dominated Europe for thirty-four years after the destruction of Napoleon. Those people in the government, the Congress and the press who ought to have been examining this newcomer's motives simply accepted the Metternich background as a sign of Kissinger's intellectual superiority. None of them questioned why they should be effortlessly seduced into believing that Kissinger was a voice of the future when he based his actions upon those of the most retrograde, hard-line, antireform political leader of the nineteenth century.

After the defeat of Napoleon, Metternich outmanoeuvred everyone in Europe who wanted the sort of humane peace which could absorb the social and political reforms produced by the preceding twenty-five years of revolution. He broke the power of any leader tainted by liberalism or interested in the idea of a fair society. As far as he was concerned, there had never been a French Revolution, Italian republics, elected assemblies or a claim to human rights. He subverted whatever good intentions the various kings of Europe had. He ensured the conversion of Czar Alexander to unenlightened despotism, thus taking Russia off its Europeanization curve and launching it on the century-long trajectory which produced the explosion of 1917. Above all, he set out to defeat the design of the British Foreign Secretary, Castelreagh, for a European compromise, which, while protecting the monarchies and the form of the old order, was designed to integrate many of the reforms of the preceding quarter century. Metternich destroyed that compromise, and it was not attempted again until after 1945.

Having done all this, Metternich set about reconstructing the Europe of the absolute monarchs. The resulting long but unpleasant peace was his success, one that Kissinger greatly admired. The explosions of 1848 were the direct result, rendering inevitable the division of Europe into revolutionaries and conservatives. This artificial schism made it impossible to imagine reasonable, common sense solutions. All was to be a battle of extremes. Marx's convictions about the inescapable struggle of the classes made sense largely thanks to Metternich's Europe. Without stretching the point too far, the unprecedented European violence and bloodletting in the twentieth century were made inevitable by Metternich's successful application of modern cynicism in a retrograde cause. This cynicism fed upon the development of artificial divisions between political powers and upon their separation from the more practical interests of the population. Prince Metternich did for the nineteenth century what Ignatius Loyola had done for the sixteenth.

Only now, after two world wars and endless civil wars and revolutions, does Western Europe seem cleansed of his divisive spirit. As for

Henry Kissinger, he revised the whole approach and made his own contribution to the Metternich school of political action.

Kissinger believed that the best time to deal with a troublesome area was when a crisis took events out of control. The heat of events — preferably violent events — would melt the old political, social and economic constraints which had made the area resistant to change. As these old structures melted in the white heat, Henry Kissinger, "Asbestos Man," would dash into the inferno and construct a completely different building. As Kissinger presented it, he was creating new hope out of old prejudices.

The press was understandably attracted to a man who was not only not frightened by danger but who loved risk and rose happily to the demands of crisis after crisis. More than newsworthy, this sort of action provoked great excitement. He was a front-page editor's dream. Better still, he was a tabloid editor's dream, because he rejected as ineffective the slow, careful building of relationships and development of solutions which were intended to prevent situations getting out of control. Henry Kissinger dealt with events as headlines and was one himself.

But hot moments do not melt the structures created by time. History has an extremely solid frame built upon profound memory. The flames of crisis create smoke and obscurity. They destroy windows, partitions, even floors. But the structures remain. When they do change, it is either very slowly or as the result of an absolute cataclysm. And even then, memory somehow still resists. To be convinced of this, one has only to look at France, Germany, Japan and Austria rising out of the disaster of the last war. Solutions imposed artificially in times of trouble leave everyone dissatisfied when calm returns. They are felt as personal aggressions, imposed against the tide of history upon people temporarily too weak to resist. The moment those same people recover sufficiently to resist, they invariably do — and often with violence, as in 1848. Or indeed as the Central Europeans did in 1989.

There is something else even more flawed about Kissinger's white-heat approach. Rousseau wrote in the *Social Contract*:

> Usurpers always choose troubled times to enact, in the atmosphere of general panic, laws which the public would never adopt when passions were cool. One of the surest ways of distinguishing the work of a law giver from that of a tyrant is to note the moment he chooses to give a people its constitution. [16]

Kissinger's instincts for usurpation were revealed soon after his arrival in Washington. A great deal of time could be spent, and indeed has been by others, on his involvement in the Cambodian operation or on his wiretapping interests. But these are secondary to his sense of power —

that is, to his sense of how to gain power through the manipulation of structure.

He began as the National Security Council adviser to the president. That was not a position of remarkable power. It counted for nothing in comparison to the secretary of state, the secretary of defense, or the council itself. And yet, by the end of Kissinger's tenure, it was the most powerful foreign policy–defence position in the United States. He wasn't even a member of the cabinet, responsible for a department legally charged by the American system of government with the administration of foreign or defence policies. He was little more than a creature of the president. Somehow he had got hold of the power.

It wasn't his role as adviser which made this possible, although his talents for courtesanage were remarkable and helped him to deal with a president more susceptible than most to the courtly approach. Kissinger's rise to power lay in his ability to reorganize the structure of government so that the council and the secretaries of state and of defense all became adjuncts to the adviser. In doing so he accomplished something far more serious than any of the Watergate participants. He subverted the American system of government in order to put himself at its centre.

With President Nixon's acquiescence, he minimized the number of meetings the council held, thereby limiting opportunities for real debate in a forum where he was not in charge. Instead he chaired a subcommittee called the Review Group, which included deputy heads from the CIA, the Joint Chiefs of Staff, defense and the secretary of state. They, in turn, referred questions either to junior committees or to the full council.

This managerial power allowed him to control the evolution of all issues. In the absence of full council meetings, he became the voice of the President. The Review Group decided whether issues had been properly prepared by departments and were ready for the council. What's more, his staff inundated the departments with requests for studies and surveys so that they had the impression they were participating in the decision-making process. In reality they were being kept busy in order to keep them out of the way. And when the council did meet, the President had been prepared to such a point of formality that he often made prepared statements on issues, thus rendering impossible any informal disagreements from cabinet members. And yet, the council's very purpose was the informal discussion of key security issues which, by their importance, stretched beyond single departmental responsibilities. Add to this the enormous briefing books — constructed to support Kissinger's point of view, but couched in the unassailable guise of a sea of facts — as well as the council staff, ready with the slightest extra fact or figure, and you have the whole government apparatus unable to move other than as instructed by the president's adviser.

The stultifying effect on practical democracy of the briefing books is an extraordinary modern phenomenon. If facts are knowledge and knowledge is truth, then these binders give a peculiar form of absolute power to those who prepare them. Whoever controls the briefing books controls the debate. The books kill the function of cabinet government, which was intended to make use of collegial common sense. They are one of the central tools of our time, beloved of all technocrats and used as a weapon of power throughout Western society wherever group discussion once played a role — in cabinets, cabinet committees, interdepartmental committees, corporate boards of directors, executive committees, advisory committees, emergency committees and just plain committees.

Kissinger added to his organizational skills an advanced sense of how to place himself on the trajectory of information in order to become its messenger or its reinterpreter or simply in order to be able to stop it. His need to control the flow of information was tied to an obsession with secrecy and, of course, to a climate of fear which seeped into everyone's life as he ceaselessly manipulated everything within reach.

He had another characteristic often found in courtesans: radical character changes. In public he was, indeed remains, the master of noble logic. The wise statesman:

> Last week I had the privilege of meeting [Japanese] Prime Minister Nakasone. . . . I said it was quite striking how different the perceptions of security were in Asia from Europe. And he said something to me which he authorized me to quote. He said, "The difference is the difference between European paintings and Japanese paintings."[17]

In private, however, Kissinger could switch abruptly into a devotee of gutter attacks and ridicule. Thus he insisted off the record that Secretary of State William Rogers was a "fag"; that Secretary of Defense Melvin Laird was a megalomaniac; that Daniel Ellsberg, who leaked the Pentagon Papers, was sexually aberrant.[18] He apparently relished the collecting of FBI reports on the private lives of public figures and the gathering of wiretaps on anyone who was not helpful to his cause.

Kissinger's belief in his ability to control events made him the kind of man who inadvertently unleashes anarchistic events. He believed he could alter the course of history through his modernized application of the Metternich approach. Despite his apparent use of history, however, the disjointedness of his actions reveals his technocratic soul. For example, he decided that the Shah of Iran was America's man in the Mediterranean. He pushed the Shah, already on the road to modernization, to go faster and to arm against the Russians, against Middle East instability, against Libya's Colonel Qaddafi. Although oil rich, Iran had a large population. The Shah spent as he was encouraged to spend but was soon strapped for funds. Kissinger, in one of his moments of brilliant clarity, pushed the Shah to finance his arms, his roads, his modern marvels by raising the oil price. Just a bit. But the oil price rapidly revealed itself to be one of those anarchistic elements. Kissinger reacted along with others, by becoming an advocate of the inflationary route: through inflation America would drown out the impact of the oil price increases. His spokesmen were to be found in meetings around the world, hinting at this miraculous cure, if only everyone would print money and remain calm while inflation digits rose.[19] The floating currencies, the currency wars (which are still with us), the Shah ever farther out of his depth, indeed on the road to extinction — all these realities indicate that history continued along its established way after Kissinger had finished temporarily distorting its course.

When technocrats are in elective office, their weaknesses take on a different form. They may be masters of artificial self-resuscitation, but they rarely have the characteristics necessary to make themselves believable in the full public light.

Jacques Chirac, for example, although twice prime minister of France, has never been able to shake the image that he has not earned his position. The slightly strained, abstract manner in which he presents his thoughts makes people think he doesn't really think them. They sense that his ambition is not balanced by a belief in any particular idea which justifies him holding public positions.

Twenty years after the event, no one has forgotten the brilliant manipulations with which he swept his political colleagues aside in order to get Valéry Giscard into the presidential office and himself, for the first time, into the prime ministership. Sharklike images, of a man ready to betray his friends and his party in order to get ahead, reappear in the public's mind each time he moves into action. And yet he is a man, one senses, who would like to do the right thing. In normal times he administers with a certain straightforward effectiveness. But in any explosive moment, when a real moral sense is required to control the situation, he panics and inevitably chooses the wrong side.

For example, in the week separating the two rounds of voting in the 1988 presidential election, when the polls showed him running seriously behind, he exploded into a myriad of "statesmanlike" actions. He ordered a military attack on nationalists in New Caledonia. The local military advised against it, but the prime minister wished to demonstrate his firm hand. As a result nineteen people were unnecessarily mowed down, with no possibility of defending themselves, during an assault on a cave in which they were hiding. He then attempted to demonstrate his humanity and international skills by negotiating the release of French hostages in the Middle East. All he did, in fact, was give in to a number of the kidnappers' demands. It is generally felt that — in return for a few seconds on the evening news, which showed him at the airport welcoming the freed prisoners home — he endangered the lives of other hostages. And, of course, by giving in, he encouraged the kidnappers to continue kidnapping. Finally, in order to attract a small group of strong nationalist voters, he turned a commercial disagreement over fisheries with a close ally — Canada — into a major diplomatic, almost military, incident.

The French voters, filled with common sense, interpreted these three actions as concrete proof that this man was not presidential material. Not only did Chirac's mistakes cost him in the final round of voting, they also cost his party in the subsequent legislative elections. There should be no doubt about the public's ability to make the right choices when presented with clear alternatives. The point is that the new technocratic leadership usually manages to distort the nature and value of that choice.

Chirac's tendency to misfire spectacularly in public makes him appear to be the opposite of a man like Henry Kissinger. Not really. Both of them have technical skills. Both of them have great ambition. Both of them lack moral common sense. Kissinger fills this void with carefully measured cynicism.

Alone among the first generations of elected technocrats, Harold Wilson succeeded politically. Perhaps this was because he combined acting skills with the cynicism and the ambition of a Kissinger. And he knew how to mix them in the right quantities. Rather like Kissinger, he did not use his understanding of contemporary systems to carry on a modernization crusade. He merely sought power within them through the art of manipulation. After several years of governing the country, he had created an atmosphere of effortless acceptance — acceptance, that is, that nothing disinterested or medium term, let alone long term, was possible when it came to public affairs. Only the crisis of the hour counted — the latest wage dispute, the next run on the pound. A technocrat devoid of beliefs — even misguided beliefs — is little more than a card sharp, moving his attention from hand to hand. No action of Wilson's could be clearly identified as having involved wrongdoing, because the sense of what was right and normal had been lost.

In that atmosphere even the normally elastic standards of truth in politics had been strained. For example, he carried on a crusade against white Rhodesia by maintaining a British-government-controlled economic blockade. This also involved subjecting the world to idealistic rhetoric about racial justice and equality. At the same time he was fully aware that the British-government-controlled oil company was supplying energy to the Salisbury regime.

Even if the question of morality is put aside, can he really have imagined that the truth would not come out? In the context of the technocratic mind, truth, like history and events, is what suits the interests of the system or the game plan of the man in charge. Truth is an intellectual abstraction, and a man like Harold Wilson felt himself in control of the definitions.

This peculiar view of reality, being independent of both established practices and current events, was further illustrated by his attitude towards the press. He used the media in order to portray himself as a man of the people, but when it came to the exercise of journalistic freedom, he used the full weight of his prime ministerial power and of legal threats to keep the media from attacking him. If, during a television interview, he sensed that things were getting out of hand, he was perfectly capable of having the cameras stopped in order to threaten legal action of the most menacing kind against the producers and interviewers who, after all, had to earn a living.

Harold Wilson's long reign as prime minister was neither historic nor dramatic, except in the sense of theatre farce. There was a drama a day, but to no particular purpose. Instead the atmosphere surrounding government was seedy. He sought power, played the system like an ordinary fiddle in a provincial orchestra, and then went away to the House of Lords. Only the fact that the system had been played rather than the country governed makes him interesting.

A much more extraordinary example of the early elected technocrat was the man Jacques Chirac helped to make president of France — Valéry Giscard or Giscard d'Estaing, if one takes into account his father's purchase of someone else's name in order to give his family the appearance of an aristocratic background. As the most hopeless of the group, Giscard reveals a great deal about the technocrat and about power.

He is a man of limited intelligence from a highly ambitious nouveau riche family, which was Pétainist during the last war. Giscard was raised to fulfill the family's destiny. He graduated from ENA in 1954 in his late thirties and set about becoming an important man. The talent with which he was born was the ability to move numbers about — an accountant's talent — which he combined with enormous self-assurance. This self-assurance could be, and often was, put down to a class mannerism. In fact, it was the assurance of the technocrat, who begins all encounters by defining the meeting in his own terms. Giscard's unusual talent was his ability to define absolutely everything in his own terms — from the world and France to individual problems.

His abstract financial talents, when added to his family's concrete financial backing, helped to make him a young minister of finance. There he appeared to be the first of the new breed of modern men. His ministerial responsibilities were relatively easy because Western economies were benefitting from an extended period of expansion. On top of this, Charles de Gaulle was giving the government creative and directed leadership, helped along by a number of inventive ministers who were provoking real growth. Giscard's job was to be the government's stick-in-the-mud. It was a negative, passive role, devoid of creativity and of leadership requirements.

Everyone else in the cabinet being a bit wild, Giscard's passive negativism was useful. He played the same role for a decade in an increasingly stable situation. When Georges Pompidou replaced de Gaulle, the relationship remained unchanged.

It was only after Pompidou had died in office and Giscard had become a presidential candidate that his character began to reveal itself. He started his campaign with a little administrative trick to destroy his Gaullist rival — Jacques Chaban-Delmas. Somehow Chaban's tax return was leaked to the press. Giscard, of course, was minister of finance — the man responsible for tax returns. Chaban had done nothing wrong, but he hadn't paid much tax. The returns of rich people under current tax systems throughout the West are invariably a shock. Giscard's own would probably have been far more shocking, but the minister of finance didn't leak his own.

This tax return was central to Giscard's presentation of Chaban as a tired, corrupt, old figure of the Right, while presenting himself as a liberal, ready to build the future. Technocratic skills were then considered synonyms for open, liberal attitudes. In reality there was nothing whatsoever in Giscard's record as minister of finance to indicate that he was a liberal. He had always been the conservative voice in the sometimes Jacobin, sometimes Girondin, Gaullist governments. Chaban, on the other hand, had been the most radical, socially conscious prime minister of the Fifth Republic.

Giscard's betrayal of Chaban was accompanied by Chirac's. In order to advance himself, the young cabinet minister provoked division within the Gaullist party and then delivered his part of it to Giscard. As a result it seemed as if all the young technocrats were rallying to Giscard.

This wasn't true. If you looked around the French administration, you discovered that Giscard had few friends. He was a solitary, isolated, ambitious number cruncher. All the interesting men in the civil service — the thinkers, the policymakers, the doers — were for Chaban or for the Socialist candidate, François Mitterrand. Chirac was simply after power and he got it. Giscard, once elected, rewarded the young man's betrayal of his friends by making him prime minister.

The squeezing of Chaban by Giscard and Chirac was a classic battle between the new men of power at their worst and the old at their best. Chaban was no doubt a bit of a rogue. But he was also a Resistance hero, someone who had chosen the defeated side early in World War II, when it seemed to have no hope of recovering. Thus, he had opted not to seek power but to support the better values in society. Chaban, when named prime minister, had seized the reins of power and begun active reforms. And yet it was Giscard and Chirac who, in presenting themselves during the presidential elections as new, rational and efficient, argued that they were the men of reform. In truth they didn't really know what to do with the political power once they had it. But in the battle between the flawed reality of Chaban's good policies and the illusory image of Giscard's and Chirac's modernism, it was the illusory image which won.

The moment the 1974 election was over, Giscard began lurching from one ridiculous gesture to another. Garbagemen were invited for breakfast at the Elysée Palace. On the other hand, at official dinners, he and his wife insisted on being served first, as if they were royalty of the ancien régime. Two elderly women who had done a great deal of voluntary work for good causes were invited to the palace for tea. They were given tea on their own, alone in a large salon, then led to a grander room, where Giscard was waiting to greet them. He was seated upon a large chair, as if upon a throne, and greeted them sitting down. There is an endless supply of similar stories.

At the same time Giscard's economic judgments were hopeless. He was the first Western leader, long before Reagan and Thatcher, to try to strangle inflation with high interest rates, thus causing bankruptcies and unemployment. Again and again he went before the public and explained with his absolute self-assurance that the problems were specific and temporary, when they were in reality general and long term. He was the first of the Western leaders to generalize the technician's view that the public ought never to be told the real economic situation, that they were not capable of understanding or helping.

In fact he very rapidly ceded to the evidence of his own incompetence by changing prime ministers. Chirac's replacement was Raymond Barre, an economist. Thus, before half his seven-year term was up, Giscard surrendered control over the very area which he had convinced the public would make him a good president.

The people now sensed that they had made a fundamental error, but they couldn't quite understand what it was. Since the modern definition of intelligence was an apparent form of technocracy, they did not have the language to say that Giscard was stupid or, to put it politely, that he had a narrow, limited sort of intelligence. He was defeated in the next presidential election in good part because the public had decided that he was intelligent but silly (his social pretensions) and dishonest (the diamonds which he had accepted from President/Emperor Bokassa of the

Central African Republic). He was probably these things as well, but primarily his problem was a lack of usable intelligence. In 1991 his career came full circle when he took advantage of rising intolerance, over the number of nonwhite immigrants in France, to announce a policy which could be described as based on race. His father, the Pétainist, would have been proud.

Finally, James Baker and Simon Reisman — both of whom belong to this same class but are quite different in their methods. Their conflict ended in a victory for indirection and it highlighted which characteristics give the modern technocrat an advantage in the use of power and which, being confused with those of public man, in fact weaken him. Simon Reisman, a product of the depression, rose to become deputy minister of finance in Ottawa, resigned to become a lobbyist for major corporations, then returned to government to negotiate the United States–Canada trade pact in the late 1980s. There he came up against James Baker, who was then secretary of the treasury and whose career had been built in the shadow of George Bush. Baker is in many ways the inheritor of the Kissinger method. He, better than Kissinger, seems to understand the Metternich principles of control and management at all times. One of the things which makes him superior to Kissinger in these situations is that he knows how to restrain his own ego.

Reisman, on the other hand, suffered from the worst possible of the technocrats' flaws. Whatever the issue at stake, his ego strode before him. This made him a boisterous and bullying but ineffective negotiator. Earlier in his career Reisman's flaws had appeared to be strengths. While the old-style public servants had exercised a certain reserve, Reisman seemed to be permanently throwing tantrums and shouting at people. In this way he passed for a man eager to get things done. His constant bullying seemed to indicate intellectual superiority.

By the time there was enough evidence on which to doubt his intelligence and indeed to question his emotional equilibrium, the system already had him on the fast track. And a single success in the mid-sixties — the United States–Canada Automobile Pact — which he claimed was his own invention, became the concrete proof that he was a competent policymaker and administrator. In reality, he was a rabble-rouser for conventional wisdom, not intellectually strong enough to break away from the standard line of the economists.

Reisman was soon one of the pivotal deputy ministers and able to unleash fully his methods. With senior Japanese businessmen in his office, he is said to have phoned someone else and shouted down the line — "I've got these goddamned Japs in here who want a lower tariff!"

During a session with trade negotiators from the EEC in the late 1960s, Reisman suddenly began to bully them as he might his subordinates. When this didn't work, he swore at them. Within moments he had slipped into a screaming tantrum. The result was that Canada made enemies for nothing. The technocrat's power, after all, is limited to the system he dominates.[20]

While his energy and the fear he generated made his departments work, Reisman's obsession with power led him to undermine his effectiveness on the larger front. He constantly denigrated the other deputy ministers. Later, when he was at the summit of his powers, he managed to defeat a proposal for a guaranteed annual income, which an important part of the Cabinet favoured. Reisman boasted openly that he alone had blocked the people's elected representatives. When he resigned early in 1974 as deputy minister of finance, it was to create a lobbying company designed to serve precisely those interests he had been responsible for controlling as a public servant. The protests were so great that they led to strict new government regulations on civil servants and conflict of interest. These seemed to have little effect.

Reisman's reputation as a tough negotiator and his support for free trade with the United States persuaded the Canadian government to call on him to lead its team during the United States–Canada trade pact negotiations. Both sides knew that the results would alter profoundly North America's political and economic makeup. It was then that all his theoretical strengths revealed themselves as weaknesses.

He put together a relatively small team, cut off from well-organized support in the civil service. His aggressive leading from the front, in the manner of an old-fashioned cavalry general with quick spurs and a slow brain, undermined any hope of teamwork. All rested on his legendary powers as a tough negotiator. Washington played to this weakness by putting forward an unknown, quiet chief negotiator. Reisman saw this as an insult to his reputation and powers. He was drawn on to ever more egotistical, headline-oriented behaviour. Meanwhile, the American negotiator was quietly fronting for an enormous, invisible team in Washington, which was highly organized, highly professional, and walking away with the advantage on most key points. Out of sight and seemingly indifferent sat James Baker, perfectly in control.

Like Reisman, Kissinger and Chirac, Baker, without any accompanying moral purpose or devotion to ideas, is driven by a voracious taste for power and a profound hatred of losing. Unlike them, however, he is a master of the invisible manipulation which allows a systems man to make full use of the power he accumulates.

He mistrusts solutions offered in a loud voice and has no respect for those who offer them.[21] His negotiating methods are perfectly clear. In his own words:

The trick is getting them where you want them, on your terms. Then *you* have the options. Pull the trigger or don't. It doesn't matter once you've got them where you want them. The important thing is knowing that it's in your hands, that you can do whatever you determine is in your interest to do.[22]

That is Baker's description of how to kill a wild turkey. As Reisman stubbed out his cigar on the negotiating table and shouted and swore, the American secretary of the treasury can only have seen him as yet another bird, drawn to the feeding trough and prancing about nervously as the emotions associated with hunger are increasingly confused with those of danger. In the final, apparently desperate days of negotiation, Baker suddenly emerged, as if noticing for the first time that something was going on, and drew the confused Canadians into his office, where he fired the mortal shot. They died happily because they were concentrated on the trough when the bullet entered their collective brain.

Baker's first appearances as President Bush's secretary of state, however, were unimpressive. He and the President flung themselves into a series of foreign trips, which infuriated America's allies. Political observers began to mumble that he was no good outside the Washington system, where he had everyone under his spell. But Baker learns fast and within weeks he had withdrawn back into his old turkey-hunting stance. In no time at all he began to get the hang of international political games.

That he was capable of international manipulation on the Metternich level had been clear since his 1985 negotiation of the Plaza agreement, which was designed to deal with the then declining dollar. This required the unwilling cooperation of the President and of Donald Regan, who was both the ex-secretary of the treasury and the then presidential chief of staff. But it also required the cooperation of the other Western governments, who had a great deal to lose. Baker played them off against each other with such smooth and confident moves that they were never able to mount an organized counterargument. But a truly superior systems man can operate anywhere if he is careful to first get a handle on the structure into which he is venturing.

Baker quickly grasped the international mechanisms. He handled his home ground with great skill, slipping pieces of information into the public domain as he felt appropriate, but otherwise playing a hand which was often described as tight or disciplined. Quite simply, he functioned best in secret. He used the professionals of the State Department, but primarily as a source of information. He made policy in a closed circle which consisted of four advisers.

The problem was that he appeared to have no particular set of values. Therefore, to make policy in isolation is to do so without direction or

intent. And so his sophisticated methods were to little avail when applied against people who have an integrated view of what they want. In
the months preceding and following Iraq's occupation of Kuwait, Baker
was unable to make his skills work for him. In spite of unprecedented
support in the international community, including the Islamic countries, his initiatives were ineffective. A disinterested look at the diplomatic configuration suggests that all the elements were there for a
negotiated settlement, including enough time to put it together. Adequate time in an international crisis is a rare advantage for those who
want a settlement. And yet the end result was a war with an unsatisfactory conclusion.

These rapid and incomplete portraits of complex men are concentrated
on the common strains running through those who have been in charge
of the Western world for the last few decades. Modern men of power
come in many apparently different forms. But certain characteristics
link them. First, a great difficulty in coming to terms with the democratic process. The talents of the technocrat do not suit public debate or
an open relationship with the people. They become aloof in order to hide
contempt; or ridiculously friendly, as if the people were idiots or simply
confused. Their innate talents lead them in other directions. They are
masters of structure, of backstairs battles, of prestructuring or withholding information. They are merchants of knowledge, selling it in
return for power. They set enormous value upon secrecy.

Intentionally or otherwise, their methods induce fear among those
who must deal regularly with them. Almost without exception they are
bullies. Primarily this appears to be intellectual intimidation. Combined
with the use of secrecy and systems manipulation, it is used to frighten
people on the practical level of their incomes, pensions, and careers. In
many cases, this degenerates into nasty, personal, off-the-record attacks. Others will make them on-the-record as a shock tactic. It therefore isn't surprising that these men are rarely surrounded or helped by
friends. They are usually solitary beings, floating through the structures
of the state in the manner of McNamara and Giscard. Or they attach
themselves to a single public figure, a front man, as Kissinger did or
Pitfield or Baker.

In many ways they resemble the Chinese eunuchs at their worst. The
modern eunuch keeps his testicles, but seems to suffer from the same
effects of isolation. Perhaps castration is as much a state of mind as a
physical fact. The technocrats suffer from character defects which have
to do with their inability to maintain any links between reason, common
sense and morality. They believe themselves to be the inheritors of the

Age of Reason and therefore do not understand why their talents fail to produce the intended results. Their abstract view of the machinery of human society prevents them from understanding the natural flow of events and from remembering when they themselves have erred and why.

That is to say they don't seem to understand the historical process. Instead they seem actually to believe that their definitions of the world will become both real and permanent simply because they are the result of applied logic. When these formulae refuse to stick, the technocratic mind, rather than deal with failure, simply wipes the slate clean and writes a new definition. They are, in that sense, slaves of dogma. At the same time they tend to avoid the maintenance of linear memory. An accurate picture of recent events would prevent the constant reorganizations which they use as a means of erasing the past and justifying current actions.

Their talents have become the modern definition of intelligence. It is an extremely narrow definition and it eliminates a large part of both the human experience and the human character. Suffice it to say that under the current definition of intelligence, Socrates, Byron, Jefferson, Washington, Churchill, Dickens, Joseph Conrad, John A. Macdonald and Georges Clemenceau would have been unintelligent or eccentric or romantic or unreliable.

The technocrats are hedonists of power. Their obsession with structures and their inability or unwillingness to link these to the public good make this power an abstract force — a force that works, more often than not, at cross-purposes to the real needs of a painfully real world.

5

Voltaire's Children

Between the newly ordained Jesuit, the young Marxist, the fresh staff officer, Enarque or MBA, there is no appreciable difference. All five are dominated by method and each of their methods arises from a common source. Appearances suggest that there must be some serious differences among them, since they regularly do battle with each other on behalf of their countries or professions. The differences must lie, therefore, in the content which they subject to their universal method. Or perhaps their rivalry is the result of their respective interests which, if the ferocity of their battles tells us anything, differ greatly.

Yet when you examine these differences or the content involved or even their respective interests, you search in vain for any remarkable contradictions. All that separates them are the positions they occupy. They defend the structural interests assigned to them by their system. And even then, if you remove the screen of ideology, the ends they seek are pretty much of a kind.

At first glance this seems to be good news — proof that rational structures and the resulting education have broken down the barriers of narrow nationalism. Here are indications of an international order uniting all modern elites.

But has this rational education system produced the elites imagined by the philosophers of reason? Are they children Voltaire would recognize? Men like McNamara and Chirac are famous alumni, but are they really fair examples? The way to answer these questions is to compare the original intent of rational education with that of its contemporary descendant. If, for example, our elites seem to be trained with methods and intentions which betray Western civilization's declared values, perhaps it is because the original creators of those values misunderstood what they were dealing with. If we are producing elites which serve neither our needs nor our desires, perhaps the problem is that our expectations have always been ill founded. Perhaps these elites are the perfectly logical products of a rational society.

A unified Western elite, using a single system of reasoning, was precisely what Loyola set out to create in 1539. Thanks to his extraordinary invention, the Jesuits constituted the first international intellectual system. And yet, in the few years between the creation of the order and Loyola's death, the unfortunate reality of his invention clarified itself. The Jesuits rapidly became either the tools of local interests or simply replaced them. Within forty years the modern method, although remaining profoundly international, had linked itself inextricably to nationalism.

The second half of the twentieth century has marked the apotheosis of that original marriage. Systems dominate everywhere, as do the systems men. At the same time nationalism has never been so strong, so much an end in itself.

Americans have become obsessed by the state of the United States and with the American dream and why it doesn't seem to work. The Western Europeans have turned in upon themselves. The purpose of their supranational body is largely to deal with the disorder of nationalist forces elsewhere, including the growing nationalism of the United States. The Third World is made up of a hundred or so new nations, just starting down the long, complicated trail of the national dream. The Soviet abstraction has inadvertently loosed its multitude of nationalisms in a dangerous and unpredictable way. And five nations in Central Europe, which had struggled unsuccessfully through much of the nineteenth and early twentieth centuries to establish rational, tribal identities, are now desperately trying yet again to rev up their dreams. In other words, despite the internationalist rhetoric which is so fashionable, we are now at the beginning of the most nationalist era the world has known.

The simple fact of belonging to what the Romans would have called a tribe — although what we have today are increasingly intellectual and political constructions which simulate tribalism — now gives legitimacy and justifies action. The national unit has become the ultimate tool of the modern manager and of his system.

And yet these men and, increasingly, women are Voltaire's children. They are the product of his attack on a corrupt society propped up by superstition, elaborate formality and the use of unlimited power. He had concentrated his criticism on the old elites and called for new, rational leaders who could see through the facade of eighteenth-century society. His ideal man of reason knew. And what he knew, he processed through morality and common sense.

The technocrat of today knows something. But his means of processing uses neither morality nor common sense. The differences between the imagined modern man of reason and the real thing can be found in his very name — *technocrat*.

Technology is a relatively new word, combining the Greek *techne* (skill, métier) with *logos* (knowledge). The skill of knowledge. But the noun *technocrat* has a very different meaning. *Techne* is, in this case, attached to *kratos* (strength, power). The technocrat's skill lies in his exercise of power. The skill of power. His is an abstract profession involving only narrow bands of knowledge. He hires himself out as a mercenary to organizations that control wider bands of knowledge and create, serve or sell. In other words he hires himself out in order to assume other people's power.

Voltaire used to ridicule the elite of his day by pointing out that, apart from their titles and their money, they were pitifully ignorant. They simply bought knowledge and advice — whether financial, architectural, ministerial, artistic or military. The elite's ignorance was so profound that it made them incapable of leading. Voltaire was not arguing that in order to lead or to assume responsibility you must be the perfect Renaissance man. But there was a need for general and perhaps for in-depth knowledge in some direction. And on that foundation there was a need to be interested in the ideas and creations of one's time. To read, to think, to ask questions, and to talk in wide circles, well beyond any particular competence. To look upon society as an organic, living thing.

The technocrats of our day make the old aristocratic leaders seem profound and civilized by comparison. The technocrat has been actively — indeed, intensely — trained. But by any standard comprehensible within the tradition of Western civilization, he is virtually illiterate. One of the reasons that he is unable to recognize the necessary relationship between power and morality is that moral traditions are the product of civilization and he has little knowledge of his own civilization.

Literacy is only defined as the ability to read because the assumption of Western civilization is that man wishes to read in order to participate fully in that civilization. Literacy refers to civilization as a shared experience. One of the signs of a dying civilization is that its language breaks down into exclusive dialects which prevent communication. A growing, healthy civilization uses language as a daily tool to keep the machinery of society moving. The role of responsible, literate elites is to aid and abet that communication.

What then is to be thought of elites who seek above all to develop private dialects? Who seek to communicate as little as possible? Who actively discourage the general population from understanding them? They are proponents of illiteracy.

What is to be thought of doctors, earning several hundred thousand dollars a year, whose annual reading is at best made up of two or three formula thrillers? Whose political understanding is limited to a schematic view of Capitalism versus Socialism? Who, by virtue of their profession's internal class system, are increasingly rewarded and admired as their knowledge of medicine narrows? In the nineteenth century, doctors were at the centre of political, social and cultural change. Today, a doctor tends to reach her summit when her view of the human body consciously limits itself to a single organ. Is this woman not illiterate?

What of a full professor of English literature who views fiction as an exercise separate from society? Who encourages such ideas as deconstructionism, which render literature inaccessible except to the most intimately initiated? Who seeks to destroy the great populist tradition of literature as a weapon used in the forefront of social change? Who recognizes in modern literature only those forms incomprehensible to the outsider? Who recognizes as proper subjects for literature only subjects distant from the world of the citizen? And in the process, who becomes himself incapable of understanding the movements of the outer world? Is he any more literate than, say, a small farmer who cannot read but who has an immediate and real understanding of the world about him?

What of the banker or economist, called upon to make real decisions about the evolution of his society's economy in a time of instability and inflation, who either has never heard of John Law or has endeavoured to forget who he was and what he did? He probably thinks even less about the nineteenth-century railway "bubbles" or the crash of the 1880s. What does it mean when he talks seriously of the catastrophe which awaits if debts are forgiven, given that he doesn't know that the entire strength and civilization of Athens — upon which we still model Western civilization — was created through Solon's wiping out of all crippling loans? Or indeed that America's economic strength in the twentieth century was in great part the result of constant financial defaultings during the nineteenth?

None of this is illiteracy as we normally understand it. Nor is it functional illiteracy. Perhaps the right term is *willful illiteracy*. It isn't surprising that the modern manager has difficulty leading steadily in a specific direction over a long period of time. He has no idea where we are or where we've come from. What's more, he doesn't want to know, because that kind of knowledge hampers his kind of action.

Instead he has learned to disguise this inner void in ways which create a false impression of wisdom. Voltaire had a genius for deflating the credibility and thus destroying the legitimacy of established power. His weapon was words so simple that anyone could understand and repeat them. Genius, unfortunately, is something which can't be passed on. Voltaire did however introduce an auxiliary weapon which was perfectly transferable. Scepticism. It was a useful tool when applying common sense to the unexplainable mysteries of established power. Scepticism was something that most men of average intelligence could handle. It was to become the great shared tool of the new rational elites.

But it is virtually impossible to maintain healthy scepticism when power is in your hands. To do so would require living in a state of constant personal conflict between belief in your public responsibilities and self-doubt over your ability to discharge them. Instead the new elites rolled these two elements together into a world-weary version of scepticism, which is what we know as cynicism. It involves a restrained contempt for both themselves and the public. To this was attached the elite's assumption — often justified — that whatever was done would be in the public's best interests.

And therein lay the tragedy of the new elites. The heart of reason is logic, but Voltaire had imagined this logic well anchored in common sense. He had seen reason as logic used reasonably. Scepticism had seemed to be no more than a complementary device. But cynicism was quite another matter. It severed the lines holding logic to common sense and suddenly logic was again adrift, as it had been under the old regimes — free to be blindly self-justifying or violently efficient or whatever suited the unfolding argument.

At least one thing is clear about the modern elites. They are truly international. But the curious self-deceptions of contemporary nationalism include the pretence that this isn't so. It seems to suit the national unit to believe that all characteristics tied to leadership are proper to the genius of the unit. No doubt it also suits the elites. If they are a manifestation of the national tribe, they are legitimate elites. Thus, never is the Enarque of one country compared with the MBA of another or the Marxist of a third. And since being a "professional" is one of the central values of our time, everyone is careful not to compare professions. The staff officer is never compared to the Jesuit or to the technocrat or to the manager. And yet, five minutes of conversation with any one of the above could be transformed into a conversation with any of the others by the simple device of interchanging their "professional" vocabulary.

This obsession with the particularity of the various professional groups is so strong that even when people wish to criticize their elites they cannot. There is no language available for outsiders who wish to criticize intelligently. The references to each profession are almost exclusively internal. In many ways the differences between various languages today are less profound than the differences between the professional dialects within each language. Any reasonably diligent person can learn one or two extra tongues. But the dialect of the accountant, doctor, political scientist, economist, literary historian or bureaucrat is available only to those who become one. This self-protective, self-satisfied provincialism resembles, if anything, the dialect and mannerisms of declining aristocracies.

The eighteenth-century rationalists would not be happy about the human product of their educational initiatives. Nor, for that matter, would Ignatius Loyola. And yet the lines of evolution are clear.

Loyola's intellectual church army had a dramatic air about it during the disorders and violent times of the Counter-Reformation. But the heart of his concept was an extremely modern and undramatic military structure. It had nothing to do with either the knight-errant tradition or personal valor. Instead his concept used the professionalism of the mercenary armies which were so prevalent in his time. Loyola converted this into modern professionalism.

He gave the Jesuits a highly centralized and autocratic structure. The general was elected for life. He in turn had absolute power to appoint the next level of leadership, the provincials. But Loyola's model went far beyond military autocracy. He introduced two revolutionary elements — a new kind of education and accounting for oneself regularly to superiors. The institutionalization of the second prolonged the effects of the first throughout the Jesuits' life. Absolute obedience lay at the heart of both the education and the accounting. Loyola's definition of obedience included the following:

> More easily may we suffer ourselves to be surpassed by other religious Orders in fasting, watching and other austerities . . . but in true and perfect obedience and the abnegation of our will and judgement, I greatly desire that those who serve God in this society should be conspicuous.

Abnegation of will and judgment were at the core of the new method. They have travelled unaltered through the last four centuries and now determine the shape of our contemporary elites.

Loyola's new style of obedience was induced by rigorous training, which began with a two-year novitiate. One year would have been normal. The purpose of these twenty-four months was to dismantle a young man's will into its component parts in order to isolate within those parts anything undesirable. The idea was not to change the man's ideas or beliefs but simply to eliminate the troublesome elements. The training then went on to purify what was adaptable and useful and to cement it all back together with the structure of the Society.

Dismantle. Clean and disinfect. Reassemble with the glue of the Society — its structures, rules and habits. The final product was then costumed in the ideology of the Kingdom of God.[1]

Ten to fifteen years of intense training followed. Long periods of learning, of pure spiritual discipline, of teaching, and of being tested in action succeeded each other as the Society observed and gradually decided whether the candidate was suitable for full membership.

The whole process was carefully and discreetly controlled through private interviews between the superior and the candidate. These were "the Accountings of the conscience." As always with Loyola, concepts of morality were submitted to rules of measurement. The idea of subjecting a man's conscience to a profit-and-loss examination, in which fault and blame were consciously sought out, was revolutionary. The mutual understanding, which these accountings established between the new priest and the Society, as to the nature of real power, was then maintained through the regular writing of reports by each Jesuit to his superior. These reports dealt with his work but also with his fellow Jesuits. Thus, reporting on other priests was placed in the context of group interests.

No detail was too small to be communicated. Meals. Sleep habits. Loyola spoke, almost seriously, of counting and reporting fleabites. This appeared to be paternalism. It was gradually formalized as part of the system, part of the Jesuits' obedience or professionalism. Observers called it despotism of the soul. And certainly there was nowhere left for individual characteristics to hide. The best modern term for this process might be *depersonalization*.

At first glance Jesuit training seems to resemble our contemporary brainwashing or reeducation methods. Modern interrogations and indoctrinations do not use violence or even the threat of violence. They concentrate on dismantling and disinfecting the mind of the victim before reassembling it in a different pattern. As for the Jesuit accountings and reportings, they appear to be the originals of the twentieth century's systems of social control through anonymous informants — systems we tend to identify with repressive societies, secret services and ministries of the interior.

If this unprecedented training and shaping of individuals produced the dominant intellectual force in Europe, it was in part because the Jesuits provided the most complete education. Loyola and the other founders had at once begun to analyze the best existing universities — Catholic and Protestant. That done, they set up their own colleges based on the latest methods and knowledge. And then they observed and experimented for forty years until, in 1599, they finalized their official *Ratio Studiorum,* or "study plan." If the system and the message were removed, what remained was a remarkable education. Francis Bacon himself couldn't help admiring their work, once he had set aside the message. In no time at all they were educating not only future Jesuits but the elites of Europe. This infuriated other orders and the political authorities. Jesuit control over the intellect and emotions of future civil leadership was an integral part of the Society's complex politicking — a natural extension of their influence over governments.

It is no accident that Richelieu and Descartes came through their system, any more than Voltaire and Diderot. But resistance to both the implicit message it contained and to the Society's political manipulations began to grow. Moreover, once the *Ratio Studiorum* had been formalized, the whole system stopped evolving. It was as if a highly effective machine were functioning without reference to reality. This disconnection became obvious in 1755 after the Lisbon earthquake. It was a leading Jesuit— Gabriele Malagrida — who launched the argument that this massive and indiscriminate death and destruction was a judgment from God. Popular reaction was the exact opposite to what he had intended.

The practical manifestation of the Jesuits' failure to keep up with social evolution was that new rational schools began to appear in the eighteenth century — schools more clearly tied to national interests and to separate, concrete definitions of professionalism. They dropped the Society's message and a good part of its humanist education. They kept the astonishing methodology and applied it to such institutions as military staff colleges and engineering schools. By the middle of the nineteenth century, these were proliferating into administrative schools — first aimed at public service, then at business. As the obsession with professionalism grew, so the focus narrowed and the actual educational content shrank still further. The jesuitical concept of obedience also disappeared, but the new professionalism manifested itself by concentrating on such things as structure, accounting, reporting, manoeuvring and mastery of detail, all of which could be summarized as an unconscious and undirected version of Loyola's "abnegation of will and judgement."

To those on the outside, the most visible sign that someone had received Jesuit training was his ability to outargue anyone. This weapon of "argument" has also been adopted by our elites. The Jesuits called it "rhetoric." To outsiders it appeared to be a pompous style of formal address. Given our informal era, it seems to have been buried with the past. Its formality, however, was merely its public disguise. Rhetoric was more than modern. It was revolutionary. And it is still very much with us.

Rhetoric began to overwhelm the Jesuits even before Loyola died — not because he sought it, but because it was the logical and inevitable extension of his own system, which called for priests to reason with the people. Clearly, to "reason" did not mean to enter into dialogue or to discuss or to explore. It meant to convince. That is to say, to argue in a manner which controlled the exchange and automatically resulted in the victory of the initiator. By reason he meant a predefined argument in which the people's questions and answers would inescapably lead them to accept the pope's authority. Everything lay in the advance definition of the form of the interchange between the priest and the individual. Rhetoric was the science of that form. Elegant phrasing was merely the decoration of the argument and, as such, distracted individuals from how the nuts and bolts of their interchange had been rigorously denaturalized and predetermined.

This is precisely the method used today by the MBA or the Enarque. The modern technocrat attempts at all costs to initiate any dialogue. Thus he is able to set, in the first sentences of any exchange, the context of the theoretical discussion about to take place. In written arguments briefing books play the same role. The intended audience unthinkingly accepts the parameters laid out. It is then caught up in the coil of the resulting logic and kept busy rushing back and forth between the questions and answers which the predefined structure imposes. In the process it feels the satisfaction produced by simply keeping up or the despair of inferiority if it does not. There is no time for reflection or consideration of the basic parameters.

We have difficulty linking the Jesuits' intellectual approach with that of the technocrats because we believe that formal eloquence was central to rhetoric. Modern argument doesn't rely upon the modulated qualities of the voice. Nor does it attempt to seduce by pleasing. There is no artifice. We are not enhanced by its appearance. In fact, modern argument is usually ugly and boring. The awkward bones of facts and figures are there as signs of honesty and freedom. The charts and graphs lay out lines of inevitability, which always begin in the past and advance as a simple matter of historical fact calmly into the future. There is no appearance of guile.

But this awkward, boring surface is the new form of elegant phrasing. The facts, the figures, the historic events used to set the direction of lines on graphs are all arbitrarily chosen in order to produce a given solution. To this is added an insistence that the constant questioning involved in modern argument is proof of its Socratic origins. Again and again the schools which form the twentieth century's elites throughout the West refer to their Socratic heritage. The implication is that doubt is constantly raised in their search for truth. In reality the way they teach is the opposite of a Socratic dialogue. In the Athenian's case every answer raised a question. With the contemporary elites every question produces an answer. Socrates would have thrown the modern elites out of his academy.

Why, then, do they so insistently claim him as their godfather? First, no one can give greater legitimacy to intellectual honesty through openness to doubt than Socrates. Second, they who can claim to carry the torch of Athens can also claim to carry the light of Western civilization. In Western mythology the Athenian inheritance is a mandate to struggle for the rule of philosophy and law, the citizen state, justice and beauty. And, on top of all of that, Socrates is the Christ martyr of the Athenian myth.

Along with the false questioning, the boring awkwardness and the endless facts, the claimed Athenian inheritance is also there to distract us from the predetermined mechanics of technocratic arguments. Rhetoric still dominates our lives. Unchanged from the seventeenth century, it has merely reversed its style from elegance to ugliness.

This becomes more intriguing if you observe the way in which a technocrat deals with a discussion when he arrives on the scene after it has begun. By his standards this is an argument out of control, so he does not join in. What he does is find a way to abrogate the discussion so that it can begin again on his terms. The classic method is to make a violent, irrational entry, which often involves personal invective. The very rudeness of the attack will stop the discussion. The technocrat then picks one or two small points — the weakest — out of the argument and concentrates all his sarcasm upon them. Such a reductio ad absurdum catches everyone unawares and before they can recover he reintroduces the entire discussion in his own manner. This form of public debate made its entry into the twentieth century via the Heroes — Hitler, Mussolini, Stalin. After 1945 it was adopted by the new elites.

The Society of Jesus had been overtaken by the new lay professional schools and by their elites as early as the middle of the eighteenth century. The Jesuits had not, however, lost their influence on modern trends. After being disbanded from 1773 to 1814, the Society returned to support conservative forces throughout the West. In the process there were endless intellectual marriages between their educational system and that of the new lay schools. The French Field Marshal Foch, for example, carried the jesuitical approach into the staff college and thus helped to set the disastrous direction of twentieth-century warfare.

The Society also continued its political manipulations. In 1860 the Jesuits were central to the organization of the First Vatican Council. The final battles for Italian unity were under way and the new nation's gains were automatically the Church's temporal loss. The Jesuits' aim was to use the Vatican Council to institutionalize the infallibility of the pope. Their idea was to create an uncontrollable sort of power. They succeeded. The pope became legally infallible. He was then free to demand a certain kind of loyalty from his followers. But the use of legal structures so late in the nineteenth century to enforce unquestioning obedience merely provoked revolt. The pope's infallibility has hung around his neck like an albatross ever since.

At first glance this seems to demonstrate the old rhetoric's inability to produce the intended result. And yet, if one can just disregard the outer shell, what difference was there between winning agreement on the pope's infallibility and Henry Kissinger's Vietnam peace plan? They were both classroom victories — brilliant on paper. And both were swept away by the next real event to come along. They are both perfect case studies. The pope's Jesuit adviser and Henry Kissinger would have received the best possible marks for these solutions, had they been presented as a case study at Harvard's Kennedy School of Government.

But this is a dramatic comparison and there is no need to seek out, in this way, exceptional events. Loyola's methods are integrated into those of our contemporary elites and can be found in thousands of banal social details. A characteristic proper to rhetoric, for example, is that its science of decorating all arguments extends to the presentation of itself. Thus, in England, the London Business School claims that the central concept of its Masters Program "is that management can be taught as a unified body of essential knowledge which can be applied to an organization."[2] The statement deforms our understanding of what the school does by misrepresenting the word *knowledge*. There is no such thing as knowledge which is universally applicable to all organizations. Knowledge is concrete and particular. What they mean by "knowledge" is method. And the casual throwing in of the adjective *essential* is positive charlatanism. What do they mean by "essential"? If that were true, then the majority of businesses in England, which do not yet employ business school graduates, would be bankrupt.

In other words, the London Business School teaches manipulation. And part of that manipulation is to present the art of manipulation itself as truth — that is, as knowledge. The presentation also attempts to leave an impression of universality, of open-mindedness and flexibility. But what they are really talking about is the training of managers who can do anything, for anybody, anywhere. That is the description of a mercenary or a *condottiere*.

Jefferson wrote the American Declaration of Independence. On the document itself, he and the other men who signed it pledged to each other their "lives, fortunes and sacred honour." Jefferson spent the rest of his life advising young Americans on their education and attempting to render it rational, as he understood reason, given his own experiences. And yet if one thing is certain about the modern manager, he pledges to no one his fortune or his life. As for honour, it simply isn't part of the equation. Some of the titles of the books written by professors at the Harvard Business School give a better sense of the manager's education — *Power and Influence, The New Competitors, Competitive Advantage, Managing Human Assets, The Marketing Edge — Making Strategies Work.* These professors have a very specific view of values. Take, for example, the description of the course which the same school offers on Comparative Ideology. It deals with "the role of ideology in modern business": "Ideology is a crucial analytical concept and an indispensable management tool, whose importance stems from the intimate connection between ideology and economic performance."[3]

It isn't surprising that the school's first Alumni Achievement Award was given to Robert McNamara. But what lies at the core of the minds which produce these titles? They are, they say, "preparing people to practice management."[4] In other words, they see themselves as "practicing," like doctors or lawyers, members of a reasonably specialized group which combines applied knowledge with a code of professional ethics.

The school was created in 1908 and, in that same moment, was fused together with its method. As the founders saw it, "business administration was the newest profession."[5] Schools of commerce had been multiplying around the United States for more than half a century. However, the determining event came in 1895 when a gruff, difficult, upper-middle-class Protestant — Frederick Winslow Taylor — gave a speech to the American Society of Mechanical Engineers. This was the formal public beginning of Taylorism or Scientific Management. On a concrete level Taylor was proposing a new way to organize factories. Yet from the beginning he designed and explained this reorganization as part of a social revolution which rejected both the pessimistic view of the class struggle and the optimistic humanist view of such things as profit sharing.

Taylor replaced both with a rational, scientific system to which all employees would adhere. Their reward for unquestioning adherence would be more money. The whole system would turn on the rise of a managerial class. "As a general rule," Taylor said, "the more men you have working efficiently in the management . . . the greater will be your economy."[6]

The future deans of the Harvard Business School visited Taylor in 1908, were seduced and decided to design their program around this theory. Taylor and his disciples supported them by regularly coming to Harvard to lecture. In 1924 there were already six hundred students and the Harvard casebooks were being used in one hundred colleges.

Taylor believed his system would produce "a conflict free, high consumption utopia based on mass production."[7] Subjection to machines would destroy man's natural tendency towards evil. A reign of technocrats would replace the corrupt and inefficient political elites. Individual choice would be submerged beneath systems and discouraged by cash benefits. Depersonalization of production would be the key to success.

Directly or indirectly Taylorism has dominated business school methodology and changed business structures around the world. But it was also adopted in varying forms by both the Soviet and the Nazi regimes. Lenin structured his economic reforms on his version of Scientific Management. "We must," he said, "organize in Russia the study and teaching of the Taylor system and systematically try it out and adapt it to our purposes."[8] Trotsky militarized Scientific Management during the civil war, using it for example, in his transportation policy. Stalin turned it into a Communist truth. The first Soviet Five-Year Plan was drawn up with the help of leading Taylorist advisers imported from the United States. As a result some two-thirds of Soviet industry was built by Americans. And now, some seventy years later, the business consultant descendants of Taylor are being invited back to the shattered Soviet Union to advise on how to undo the mess for which their approach is in good part responsible. The same principles were adopted by Albert Speer in his economic organization of the Third Reich. With a few adaptations, Scientific Management was used to run military production, forced labour and racial genetics programs, which included such things as gassing polio victims and genocide.

Of course it would be foolish to deny that Taylorism played a major role in early-twentieth-century industrial advances. On the other hand, it always preached that technocratic leadership was the new morality. Its antidemocratic premises were justified by "the redemptive role of a technically trained, professional middle class."[9] No doubt its proponents would refuse responsibility for the Soviet and Nazi experiences by arguing that any system can go wrong if misused. However, the astonishing thing about Scientific Management is that it has never gone wrong by its own standards. It has simply been more or less controlled by different civilizations. And, in any case, it would be wrong to ascribe too much blame or credit to Taylor and his disciples. Absolutist theories such as his tend to appear to be freestanding when they have in fact picked up on already existing trends and simply articulated them.

In the United States the drive towards a dictatorship of the technocracy was and is limited only because other social forces are at play. Harvard's version of the whole business school method is therefore fascinating. University authorities say it is "field-based and empirical," not "isolated in a laboratory or in hypothetical models." They add, of course, that it is based upon the school's "distinctive and continually developing teaching method — the case method." But there lies a major contradiction. The case method is above all famous for bringing a detached, abstract approach to the conduct of business. Harvard insists that the case approach "sharpens the qualities of understanding, judgment, articulateness, human sensitivity and intuition, necessary to the successful practice of management. . . . It obliges the students to confront unruly, intractable reality."[10]

In other words, they train the technocrat to tame reality. And reality being what it is — that is, real — they must deform it in order to accomplish this. There is nothing empirical about the process because it begins with a solution and a predetermined argument into which the problems must fit in order to arrive at that solution.

The student who succeeds best at this game invariably has an aptitude for abstract structures combined with an aggressive personality. Intelligence in this situation consists of a combination of analytical skills, untutored ambition and banal materialism. Creativity — which leads to new products — is not rewarded. Imagination — which enables the businessman to develop markets and sell — is also absent. And there is no hint that the values of society might be taken into consideration. How could they be? The methodology Harvard teaches is freestanding. It is constructed to be free from memory, beliefs and nonmanipulable obligations. As the London Business School might put it, their methodology is a unified body of essential knowledge which can be applied to any organization.

Whether they succeed or fail in their battle with reality is of little importance. In the absence of memory, there is no long-term reflection on results. Instead, one moves rapidly to the next case. The interference of any "unprofessional" outsider in the application of their system presents the only great danger, because he might insist upon the use of memory.[11]

This training can't help but have an effect on students. What it seems to do is to encourage their natural tendencies. Thus, if they were, as most people are, equipped with an unbalanced distribution of talents, the Business School doesn't try to redress this in search of a healthy equilibrium. Instead, it actively seeks students who suffer from the appropriate imbalance and then sets out to exaggerate it. Imagination, creativity, moral balance, knowledge, common sense, a social view — all these things wither. Competitiveness, having an ever-ready answer, a talent for manipulating situations — all these things are encouraged to grow. As a result amorality also grows; as does extreme agressivity when they are questioned by outsiders; as does a confusion between the nature of good versus having a ready answer to all questions. Above all, what is encouraged is the growth of an undisciplined form of self-interest, in which winning is what counts.

Such sudden respectability for undisciplined self-interest is one of the most surprising developments of the last three decades. It seems to indicate just how confused our society has become. In two and a half thousand years of Western social history, one of the very few things that most societies have agreed upon is that individual restraint is central to any civilization. In an authoritarian society, this restraint is imposed in part from above. In a free society, the individual imposes it, in part, upon him- or herself. In the complexity of the real world, there is always a combination of imposed and self-imposed restraint. The late twentieth century is actually the first era in which the leading centres of elite education have either turned their backs on the question of restraint or have actually taught that it should be thrown off. In other words, for the first time in Western history, our most respected institutions are preaching social anarchy.

The effect on contemporary students of pushing them further into imbalance has been to create ever-increasing human problems. They do have within them, even if dormant or mutant, the elements of every human being. Increasingly these frustrated human elements play havoc with the carcass they occupy. The Harvard School responded with a new course — The Social Psychology of Management — aimed at the "problems of the family, the individual's emotional life and the tension between career goals and personal aspirations." The professor assigned to this course admitted that "we have been abstracting people out of management as if they didn't exist. . . . Students have been taught to be utilitarians and calculators. [As a result] often they are running away from the intimacy of family life and running away from themselves." He went on to draw a surprising conclusion: "The capacity for intimacy and nurturing is a characteristic of the most effective leaders. Not only is there a direct connection between the capacity to give and personal satisfaction, but also it seems to release more creativity."[12]

The basis for this assertion isn't clear. An enumeration of the private lives of leaders and creators, good or bad, might well consist of a litany of disasters. In any case, the professor's answer to the student's personality problems is that more happiness is required. He teaches his course by the case method, thus attempting to "abstract" an a priori definition of personal happiness into management in an attempt to counterbalance the absence of the human element, which had previously been abstracted out.

If one looks at the situation from the school's point of view, this attitude is perfectly understandable. The school needs to compensate for undermining both the individual's decency and his or her role as a citizen. If it can do this by co-opting the combined idylls of family and personal happiness, it will have maintained its system intact.

These characteristics are not at all particular to Harvard. When the British felt their business methods had fallen behind, they asked Lord Franks to carry out a study. In 1963 he recommended the creation of a business school and went on: "We have a great deal to learn from the successful practices of the leading American Business Schools and from their fruitful experimentation . . . in methods and curricula."[13] This study led to the creation of the London Business School, which uses the same admissions test as do most American business schools.[14]

The results of these methods, when applied in two very different societies, are almost identical. The schools were created to improve management. It was argued that this improvement would lead to real growth, a revivified industrial base and healthier economies. But where have these modern managers gone to practice their profession? Seventy-one percent of Harvard MBA graduates go into nonmanufacturing. The figures in England are almost identical. Worse still, more than 80 percent of graduates are not in line functions. More than 80 percent do not manage.[15] In both America and Britain they are in consulting, banking and property developing. They have joined the sectors which do not provide capital goods — the service industries. It could be argued that their desire to avoid real management and to concentrate on areas as superficial and as abstract as their own training is one of the causes of our industrial decline and of our unhealthy concentration on services.

At its most basic the idea that personal self-gratification is the right counterbalance to the overemphasis in business schools on competition and winning is also a problem of geography. Industry today has great difficulty recruiting the first-class rising managers, who don't want to go where industry is physically situated. They wish to stay in the great centres of postindustrial self-gratification — New York, London, Toronto and Paris, for example. Pittsburgh and Birmingham, Hamilton and Lille are not target towns for personal nurturing.

In England the new elites avoid industry on an even larger scale than elsewhere and head for the City or for West End jobs. Their refusal to live in the towns where industrial activity takes place can be identified as an important element in the decline of British industry. Throughout the West this is one of the reasons for the perceived panacea of service industry growth.

The creation of contemporary government elites has followed the same path as that of the new business elites. The phenomenon has different superficial characteristics, but the underlying theme is identical. In many countries the trend began with the growth of the social sciences, which forced the full array of real social questions into a falsely scientific straitjacket. The postwar schools of political science and economics are a prime example, with their reliance on abstract models, flowcharts and impenetrable specialist dialects. Apart from being indescribably boring, they have also been almost flawlessly wrong on every issue they have addressed. The experts in these fields have projected our societies in a multitude of directions over the last forty years. Each time they have been able to prove their case with quantitative arguments and graphs as artificial as a case laid out by a prospective MBA.

That is how we came to flip from the absolute public conviction that Keynesian economics are right to the absolute certainty that they are wrong. That is how monetarism abruptly became a cure-all. How the mixed economy dropped from being next only to God to become the devil's device. Inflation was a harmless economic tool. Moments later it was little better than the assassin of free men's hopes. Then we woke up to discover that an investment device called debt was an even greater evil. Evil only, however, for governments. The same men who asserted this also asserted that commercial debts of historic sizes were good things. And nationalizations of state corporations, which for years we had been told were central to rebuilding the West's economy after the depression of the thirties, suddenly became the source of our problems. The new truth was privatization and competitiveness.

Never in these abrupt flips was the best of the last system hailed and the worst of the new identified. Calm, practical sense was impossible. The social scientists carry truths and assert them. To resist is to be on the other side.

One of the most fascinating phenomena in the "professionalizing of governance" has been the rapid growth of the John F. Kennedy School of Government at Harvard. The Kennedy School has gradually applied to the public sector criteria identical to those already applied to the private sector by the Harvard Business School. They see themselves as "a Professional School of Government." "What is needed," they say, "is nothing less than the education of a new profession. This profession should include persons elected to public office, individuals appointed to executive positions and career civil servants." The idea takes on frightening dimensions when one realizes that this school does not distinguish between the public servant and the elected official. But there is no reason for surprise. These are merely updated reiterations of the need for a technocratic dictatorship, as proposed by Scientific Management. The myth of salvation through efficient management is now so strong that no one pays much attention to the premises upon which the new elites are being educated.

Efficiency. Professionalism. A belief in right answers, which can only be produced by professionals. All these concepts simply exclude the basic democratic assumptions. Members of this single professional class of politicians, appointed ministers and civil servants "should be distinguished for their analytic skills, managerial competence, ethical sensitivity and institutional sense."

So much lies in these words. For example, they must be distinguished not for their ethics or their sense of ethics, but for their ethical sensitivity. That is, their sensitivity to other people's ethics and their ability to manipulate them in the interests of management. The idea that society is based upon an ethical foundation, to which the leaders as well as the citizens are bound, is not entertained.

The more management is explained, the more it sounds like *raison d'état*. The idea of governments invoking the public interest, as a justification for taking unjust or illegal action, has been with us since the French satirist Mathurin Régnier coined the phrase in 1609. It has been inseparable from the rise of reason and of the nation state. Now *raison d'état* is being turned into a blanket principle which could be summarized as: The technocrat knows best. Without anyone actually saying so, the citizen is eliminated as a participant. He or she is there to be managed. These professional politicians and civil servants are to have no sense of ideas, of policy or of responsibility. "Problem solving" is to be their central skill. "Obtaining answers after asking the right questions will often depend on the decision-maker's ability to recognize opportunities to use formal quantitative methods to structure problems and draw information from the data."[16]

What they are attempting to do, probably without consciously understanding their own motives or actions, is to create a class into which entry will be limited by common standards. That class will control public affairs. An aristocracy of public affairs. A rational, management meritocracy. They will share an obligatory methodology which, like a court ritual, will exclude all citizens who are not properly admitted. This class will deal with public affairs in a professional language which will be as inaccessible to the public as court ritual and Jesuit rhetoric used to be. And all of this is to be done in the name of reason, for the good of the public.

Never have ideas of Left and Right seemed less relevant. People who believe themselves to be liberal reformers are proposing an apparently reasonable form of government by elites. Only at second glance does it become clear that this form subverts the democratic process. People who think of themselves as part of the conservative forces — those who, by accepting the term *conservative*, ought to be protecting established values — embrace the new methodology eagerly as a faster way to profit personally at society's expense.

The heavy-handed verbiage of the Kennedy School and its limited power in American government seem strangely primitive when compared to those of the greatest school of public servants — l'Ecole Nationale d'Administration.

The desire to create a strong, technically minded French elite had been in the air since Richelieu. The first Grandes Ecoles were begun under Louis XVI and the most important of the great engineering schools — the Polytechnique — appeared during the Revolution, a cre-

ation of the Convention. The first attempt to create an equivalent training centre for the bureaucracy came under the Second Republic, in
1848. It disappeared rapidly, with Louis-Napoléon's coup d'état, but in
1871 a Monsieur Boutiny created l'Ecole Libre des Sciences Politiques.
It was private and he was backed by bankers and industrialists. The
future bureaucratic and eventually political elites began to funnel
through Sciences Po, as it came to be known, and ten years later Jules
Ferry, a moderate, reforming government minister, tried to nationalize
it, with the support of its founder. Léon Blum, a Socialist, tried again
in 1936. Finally, it was de Gaulle, aided by Jeanneney and Capitant,
two left-wing Gaullists, who in a single act nationalized Sciences Po and
created ENA.

Each of these advances in the education of a public elite took place
during moments of revolution or of great reform immediately after a
revolution. The rich conservatives who founded Sciences Po, like the
solid bourgeois who created ENA, were republicans acting in the aftermath of terrible civil violence. These initiatives were the continuation of a long dream which carried the conviction that democracy and
equality would be advanced by a well-trained bureaucracy. The future
prime minister, Michel Debré, had been put in charge of writing the
law creating the school and then of organizing it. It isn't surprising that
in his official report he wrote of the need to "take up again the belief and
the hope of the republicans of 1848 in the value of public moral virtue,
taught and understood." To accomplish this he said that ENA must give
its students a taste for certain key skills — "a sense of what man is,
which gives life to all work; a sense of decision-making which, after
weighing the risks, allows one to decide; a sense of the imagination
required to create with originality."[17]

In the midst of this hymn to the rational, humane and republican
virtues of an administrative elite, Debré interrupted himself with a
burst of pessimistic clarity. What would happen, he asked, if "this new
elite developed a belief in their caste, a belief which would pervert the
civil service?" He quickly recovered and produced arguments to prove
this outcome impossible.

But that, after a period of enthusiastic creativity, is precisely what
has happened. Simon Nora, a recent director of ENA, described how he
had gone straight from the Resistance to become a student in the new
school. "Blowing up trains or going to l'ENA was about the same. In
both cases, we were a small band who knew better than the others what
was good for the country. And we weren't completely wrong. We were
the best looking, the most honest, the most intelligent, and we had
carried the flame of legitimacy."[18]

This little outburst of passion and mystique and ego makes a certain amount of sense. After all, the first generation of Enarques had proved themselves before getting their ultimate education. They arrived in the school with a practical determination to change their world for the better, because their shattering wartime experience had convinced them that it could and must be done. Then they went on to run the country. And given the great problems of the fifties and sixties, they ran it well. People assumed that the new rational training of ENA had made it possible for them to do this. In reality that training had merely polished human characters which had been irrationally formed in the crisis of war.

From 1950 on, that same training was being applied to unformed characters, which contained the usual raw ingredients of youth. These students arrived fresh from the classroom and the bosom of their families. The result was not the same. Each year's class varied with the fashion of its time, but in general the students graduated with an undirected personal ambition. In the hands of young men who knew nothing about the real world but were rapidly given real power, abstract organization became an overwhelming, self-evident and absolute truth for all situations.

Within forty years ENA, and with it the other Grandes Ecoles, had completely changed. In the words of Jean-Michel Gaillard, an Enarque himself and a former adviser to President Mitterrand: "Whatever their official reason for existence or supposed vocation, they are institutions without content, machines for choosing multi-purpose elites and creating men good for anything and nothing."[19] The Enarques alone now number some four thousand. They control absolutely the civil service, have more than thirty-seven elected deputies, range between twenty-five and forty percent of the cabinet positions and around a third of the positions in the ministers' private offices, have had one president of the Republic and seven of the last eleven prime ministers. They produced all of the leading candidates for the 1988 presidential election, except the incumbent. What is more, the annual graduating class has now been reduced from 160 to 90, which will not reduce their power, but increase the power of those who have already gone through the school, as well as future graduates. Given public uneasiness over the growing power of ENA, this has been presented as a measure to restrain its power. In fact, every political figure involved in making the decision was an Enarque.

That they have become the multipurpose empty carcasses described by Gaillard is beyond doubt. Everywhere in Paris they can be seen, instantly identifiable in their ill-fitting, sombre clothes, which continue the Jesuit tradition of physical anonymity befitting a man of power. Their unsmiling, busy expressions convey a certain weary superiority.

Their conversation is so certain, so full of banal phrases, that the listener hardly notices the structures leading to answers.

This depersonalized and asexual language is the very worst of French. And yet, when subjected to such noncommunicative verbal authority, the listener is discouraged from dissent by the emanating murmurs of *"raison d'état"* and "privileged information."

The school now seems to have accepted that its graduates will continue in the same pattern, although this acceptance came only after years of attempting to maintain the initial postwar drive towards disinterested public service. With the passing of the Resistance generation, that drive slipped away and in 1958 the school's program was completely reorganized. This was done to make it much more abstract and theoretical. The idea of the multipurpose civil servant made its official entry into state education. No matter what careers lay ahead of them, all candidates were to be judged on identical tests of culture and knowledge, then trained at the school in an identical manner. In 1965 there were further changes in the same direction.

This system created profound problems in the national bureaucracy. The candidates for ENA were becoming a type suited to the constricted criteria of the entrance exams. Most of them would graduate successfully and go on to invest the French state with their narrow approach. By 1971 the directors were obliged to admit that the knowledgeable, multipurpose graduate was an impossible abstraction. That idea was replaced by one which abandoned knowledge. It concentrated instead on molding the students to fit into a single system which would deal with all areas of government. The individual was to be unidimensional but equipped with a multipurpose method. In its own words, the school was after students capable of "a polyvalent point of view."[20] The genius of their administrative system would permit them to deal with everything from theatre to taxes.

They were now very close to the Harvard idea of management. And, indeed, Taylorism had had a great vogue in France early in the century, as it had everywhere in Europe except Britain. France, however, was the mother of rational structure, with an evolution stretching back to Richelieu, and so produced its own theories of Scientific Management. The inventor was Henri Fayol, and he and his disciples rivaled Taylorism in influence for several decades. Then, in 1925, the two groups formally merged into one and became part of the larger historic process which led to ENA and the Enarque problem.

In spite of the new polyvalent theory, most people sensed that the problem had not been resolved. The elite was ever stronger and ever less creative. It was self-serving and self-protecting. Nevertheless the process continued and in 1986 the new director of ENA, Roger Fauroux, declared: "We must build into the civil service the sense of efficiency, of return on investment and of performance."[21] In other words the founding intentions of the school — reform and public service — had been completely lost.

And yet, when the subjects dealt with at ENA are examined, the first impression is encouraging. The courses seem to address the problems of the real world. Even the instructions attached to the entry examinations seem reasonable. They call for reflection rather than memory work, and for the use of intellect to dominate the subject. Above all, the applicant is instructed to attack the subjects from the high ground in order to dominate them. By "domination" the Enarque means "control." This is what Harvard called "taming unruly reality." And "reflection," in this case, means taking the time to work out the answer expected by the examiners. The professors' comments on the previous year's entry exams are always printed up as a guide for new students. There the form which replies ought to take is laid out chapter and verse, sometimes down to the headings. It is a highly sophisticated game of intellectual painting by numbers.

The comic level to which this control descends can be seen in the section of the entry exams devoted to sporting events. These events are laid out in government decrees filled with such sentences as: "The order of testing the candidates in the different sports is left to the discretion of the jury in function of the requirements of the organization." The events include:

> Distance Covered in a Given Time: competition with a maximum of fifteen competitors on the starting line. When the signal of the end of the race is given, the competitors should continue their efforts to the next control post where the performance they have accomplished will be registered.[22]

The nonsporting management problems which the professors give these students, along with encouragement to use their imagination, are presented in the same prestructured, suffocating manner.

Harvard and ENA are the high points of a general state of affairs. Business schools and administrative schools have popped up all over the West and reproduced the same logical errors of answer-oriented, multipurpose elites. Few of their graduates have the sense of relative truths produced by exposure to a real society. Absolute truths based on detached abstraction reign supreme. These truths are endlessly defendable and interchangeable. The Harvard-ENA graduate is unlikely to understand either the irony or the relativity of truth in Voltaire's discussion of the wildly different sorts of circumcisions to be found around the world: "A Parisian is taken aback when he is told that the Hottentots cut off one testicle from their male children. The Hottentots are perhaps surprised that the Parisians keep two."[23]

The quality of, and investment in, these technocratic leadership schools continues to increase at a time when the quality of general education is in a steep dive. Given that the very idea of reason began as a conversation among middle- and upper-middle-class elites, who believed in the value of excellence, it isn't surprising that more popular forms of education have always been a secondary consideration.

Within the ethos of reason there was also the idea of encouraging generalized education. Education instilled knowledge. Knowledge dispelled superstition, thus making it possible to reason. A man capable of reasoning was fit to be a citizen. But this idea of creating citizens was vague. What did the elites want them for? The eighteenth-century philosophers believed, after all, in permanently established but benevolent authority. Educating the masses was intended only to improve the relationship between the top and the bottom of society. Not to change the nature of the relationship.

Like any elite holding great power, the technocrats are not particularly interested in the creation of subsidiary elites. Thus, while a fortune continues to be spent on state schools and universities, the entire system continues to decline. The intellectual muscle needed to give it direction is concentrated instead upon the continued refining of the education of the technocratic elite. Indeed, whatever may be quoted about the need for general education, there has always been an underlying contradiction in what the nation-state wished to teach the citizen. The masses, it was believed, could not be given more than a basic education: basic skills and — nowhere in elite education does this appear — a moral framework. In other words, they were to receive the nuts and bolts of a humanist formation.

But from the beginning, the men of reason complained about the interfering weight of humanism or what they called, when dealing with education, the humanities. In the sixteenth and seventeenth centuries, the humanities were the area where superstition and prejudice could most easily hide. To flush them out, the victory of science was required. And yet, when Richelieu complained that the humanities took up too much space, one senses that he was already concerned not about the dangers of superstition but about the threat represented by a humanist education when the state is attempting to create a useful elite. This sense of the humanities, as a time-consuming interference in useful education, resurfaces again and again over the centuries. Boutiny evoked it when he created Sciences Po in 1871. It is evoked today whenever education is discussed.

Not only have the humanities been singled out as the enemy of reason, but there has been a serious attempt to co-opt them by trans-forming each sector into a science. Thus architecture has become a quantitative, technological formation in which the details add up to the building. Even art history has been converted from a study of beauty and craft into a mathematical view of creativity. The new art historians are interested not so much in art or in history as in technical evolution. The social sciences, new creations of the mathematical obsession, are of course the principal example of the humanities deformed. The reduc-tion of politics, economics, social problems and the arts to mathematical visions and obscure, hermetically sealed vocabularies may well be looked upon by those who come after us as one of the greatest follies of our civilization.

The removal of the humanities from education has undermined com-mon sense and restraint and thus encouraged us to lurch from extreme to extreme in public policy. And yet there is still too much of the humanities in education to suit the technocratic elites. They blame the troubles of state-funded education on this.

In fact our elites no longer believe that it is possible to offer a general, universal education. Perhaps in Britain they never believed it, except in the most abstract way and in small idealist circles. Even the Labour Party leaders tend to send their children to private schools, while calling for improved state education. Yet when they are in power, it doesn't improve. In the United States large sections of the population were happily abandoned to illiteracy from the very beginning. Now new sec-tions are added to this lumpen proletariat with each passing year. Ev-erywhere one hears the elites saying to each other, in private: "Well, of course, they are not educable." There are endless statistics to confirm the already educated in their pessimism. Seventy-two million Americans are illiterate, the majority of them white. This doesn't include the functionally illiterate. One-quarter of American children live below the poverty level. Forty percent of children in public schools are from racial minorities. The whites who can afford to are slipping away into the private school system. Twice as many children are born to American teenagers as to those of any other democracy.[24] But if you begin to add such facts as that forty million Americans do not have access to medical care, you are also obliged to wonder if the problem lies not with the population but with the elites, their expectations and their own educa-tion.

If Harvard, to remain with the same example, is what it claims to be and its graduates are to be found everywhere, then why are they show-ing no signs of being able to deal with their society's terrifying problems? Were Montesquieu's proverbial Persian to look in upon American soci-ety today, the only possible conclusion he could draw would be that never has such a magnificent elite failed so miserably and done so with such little grace, insisting as it does upon blaming the lowest end of the social scale for much of what is wrong.

Outside the United States, the decline in general education has been marked but less frightening. The German and the French are among the finest surviving public education systems in the West. Of the 5 percent who do go to private schools, most seem to come from broken homes or from among the aristocratic remnants and the very rich, two groups which often prefer exclusivity to quality.

Nevertheless, in 1986, when the French National Institute of Educational Research carried out an interpretive survey of sixteen thousand students, 69 percent of the fifteen-year-olds were either illiterate or marginally so. That is to say, they were either unable to read the text given to them or were obliged to read it out loud, slowly, in order to convert it into an oral message. The government had announced not long before, with antihumanist, managerial clarity, that it wanted to improve public education to the extent of getting 80 percent of the students through the baccalaureate (the last test before university). The current level is 50 percent.

The survey concluded that what was wrong was the way students were being taught to read. "To read you must invent."[25] Literacy requires the participation of the imagination of the reader. They also discovered that for 53 percent of the students, comic books were their primary reading pleasure. Television and films no doubt take up whatever inventive time remains.

Throughout the West the reaction to this crisis has been a growing chorus, calling for a return to basic education in order to stop the decline. But as always in a rational society, this return to basics is proposed as a narrow and absolute solution to what is a general problem. There is no accompanying hint that something ought to be done about the disastrous divorce of the humanities from the systems which control our societies. Or about developing a common sense line linking general with elite education. Or about evaluating why the most complex and competitive higher education systems ever seen in the history of the world do not produce elites capable of addressing the problems of their society. In fact, the assumed contempt for anything other than highly specialized education continues to grow. A general university education is increasingly considered to be of very little value. And the call for a return to basics in the classroom probably has more to do with attempting to quiet growing public fury over ballooning illiteracy than with a serious desire to understand the problem. If anything, it resembles another reactive and prepackaged formula. Another management fad. On top of which it echoes eerily the old calls for the working classes to work harder, bathe once a week and go to church on Sunday.

Meanwhile the elites continue to try to improve themselves by fur-

ther eliminating the humanities. The result has been the gradual appearance of an evolved technocrat who almost inevitably has the
character of an intellectual bully. These aggressive men and women
have no talent for what might be called the public emotions. The remarkable form their education has given them is fundamentally empty,
except when filled with the content of whatever job they are currently
doing. And when they are attacked over their management of that job,
they have a tendency to freeze hard on their positions, unable to compromise because they don't have the roots with which to penetrate into
the matter. They often become stubborn, absolute defenders of things
they care nothing for. This psychological rootlessness causes them to
confuse power with such things as morality and understanding.

Even within the elites, however, there is a growing awareness that
something is wrong, that their systems do not produce the announced
result. The business community — stuck with ever-larger legions of
these seriously flawed human beings, who are often unable to deal with
the unstructured problems to which senior management exposes them —
have begun paying lip service to the reeducation of their executives in
midstream.

The Aspen Institute, the leading U.S. business seminar and thinking
centre, now holds a one-week course on the humanities.[26] It has a
darkly comic title: Can the Humanities Improve Management Effectiveness? and an appropriate course description:

> AT&T, one of the world's largest and most influential corporations, be-
> lieves that a study of the humanities is an important educational experi-
> ence in the executive development of middle managers. This course is
> open to upper-middle management personnel judged to be high achievers
> with potential for advancement into executive management positions.
> Primary objectives — to improve management effectiveness, to develop
> more competent and socially-acclimated managers, and to assist in the
> succession process of managers to executives. . . . It is focused on five
> areas: leadership, interpersonal relations, problem-solving/decision-
> making, tolerance for change and personal introspection.

And a whole week to do it in. False and rather sad little remedies such
as this are proliferating in an attempt to tack humanism, post facto, onto
rationally formed beings. That does at least indicate that our contemporary elites are beginning to wonder whether, despite their satchels of
degrees, they are in fact educated.

In keeping with their lack of historical baggage, they tend to read as
little as possible, avoiding in particular history, philosophy and fiction,
limiting themselves to escapist novels, newspapers and technical documents. They may read a few biographies, which have come to play the
same voyeuristic, wish-fulfillment role that accounts of saints' lives

played in earlier societies. At home they hang little or nothing on their walls. And, as they rise to the top, their preferred form of "official" culture tends to be nineteenth-century opera and classical ballet — both dead arts. The once populist and sometimes revolutionary operas are now ritual, as are the ballets which, in any case, were never taken to be much more than high-class circus entertainment. Fine ankles, bare thighs and high leaps. Ballet's origins were as light interludes within operas. With the disappearance of functioning royal courts late in the nineteenth century, the great opera houses gradually became one of the focuses for the new elites. These palaces of marble and gold leaf were perfect reflectors of legitimacy for a civilization in which that concept was confused. It remains confused and, wonderful though the music and the performers may be, they are little more than background.

In short, unlike the Victorian upper middle classes, our contemporary elites are rarely wedded to culture. They tend to absent themselves from the continuation of their civilization. They therefore have little sense of the reverberations of their actions. The loss of an historical view is perhaps the most serious of their flaws, because they cannot imagine an impact which goes beyond a case study. In this context their adoption of Socrates as godfather makes sense. They simply don't have the coordinates to realize how silly it is to claim that relationship.

What is more, the entire process, which has developed rational education from the original formula of Ignatius through to today's virtual monopoly of the technocrats over Western leadership, has unfolded without any consideration of the woman as a participant. Women are now participants in large numbers. But the system has shown no sign of adapting itself to this relatively new reality. If the rational civilization is a male idea, then it isn't surprising that education should be an area particularly lacking in flexibility. Certainly the first area requiring transformation is the education of our elites. Since that education can be seen to be a failure, women might do better to become the catalysts leading to radical change, rather than just another ambitious group competing for a percentage of the top places in schools not worth going to.

The methods of the technocrats have now become parodies of those used by the courtesans in the last years of the divine monarchies. In the Russian court of the seventeenth century, "intricate intrigues were mistaken for shrewdness,"[27] a deformation which would apply to most Western elites today. The methods now essential to power are pseudo-scientific versions of life at court. The courtesan approach hardly seems to be a positive thing for modern women to aspire to. But if they want to beat our contemporary elites at their own game, that is the inevitable route.

At the heart of our problem lies the belief in the idea of single, all-purpose elites using a single all-purpose methodology. We have developed this in search of a social cohesion based on reason. Certainly, there is an essential need to find common ground on which an integrated moral view can be built. Without that, society can't function. But a society which teaches the philosophy of administration and "problem solving," as if it were the summit of learning, and concentrates on the creation of elites — whose primary talent is administration — has lost not only its common sense and its sense of moral value but also its understanding of technical advance. Management cannot solve problems. Nor can it stir creativity of any sort. It can only manage what it is given. If asked to do more, it will deform whatever is put into its hands.

One sign of a healthy Western civilization is that within a relatively integrated moral outlook — for example, agreement on democratic principles — a myriad of ideas and methods are brought face to face. Through civilized conflict the society's assumed moral correctness is constantly tested. This tension — emotional, intellectual, moral — is what advances the society. These contradictions are what make democracy work, but they also create technological advance.

By concentrating on an integrated management method run by a single elite, we are giving power to people whose primary skill lies in the removal of contradictions or at least the appearance of contradictions. Managers are not profoundly disturbed by failure or error. But they are driven to nervous collapse by the public demonstration of contradictory solutions. Of course they aren't alone in this reaction. They are accompanied by that inevitable creation of technocratic civilization — the Hero. Heroes take the whole process a step farther because they are mere exploiters and deformers of the elite's devotion to absolute truths.

How can social values be weighed when decisions are made on the basis of preintegrated logic? The ENA examiners recommend to their students that they dominate problems by attacking from above. From above what? From above society? From above its beliefs, standards and moral traditions? What is taught is efficiency freed from social reality. The more spectacular the successful creation of such an elite, the more rudderless the society becomes.

It is difficult to imagine how this can be dealt with unless we break down our education to more practical levels, for example by dismantling the funneling nature of elite education.

Jefferson, founder and patron of the University of Virginia, never allowed his university to give degrees. He considered them pretentious, irrelevant to learning and unconnected to the preparation for responsibility. This wasn't idealism. It was the opinion of the most successful practitioner of reason. The purpose of universities has now been inverted. Learning has become a goal-oriented process aimed at winning a degree.

As Gaillard has pointed out, we needed or thought we needed these sorts of elites when our societies were still under challenge from within by the forces of arbitrary power. That is no longer the case.[28] And we can't use the continued existence of such power outside the West as an excuse to continue creating a false elite inside our society.

"It is very dangerous," Northrop Frye wrote, "to assume that only emotions can stampede the mind."[29] We have embraced the analytic approach so absolutely that counterweights, such as the linear historical view, have been stampeded into irrelevance. This wasn't what Jefferson or the philosophers of the eighteenth century expected would happen. Analysis was a means for hunting out falsehood and superstition. But a clear, practical line back into past experience was the foundation upon which the rational man was to base his abstract examination. The Encyclopedists went to great lengths to lay out what had come before them, precisely because the established powers of the church and the monarchy had cut those lines in order to produce absolute truths which justified their power. Jefferson, who thought a great deal about the practical shape of the future and did so with reasonable optimism, came back again and again to an analytical and scientific approach based upon a full and conscious assumption of the past. His advice to various young men turned constantly around the welding of optimistic analysis to a linear historic base as the best way to ensure change while limiting the risks involved. He used the University of Virginia as a place to put his principles into practice.[30]

This careful approach was swept away by the forces of pure reason. In its place we have an elite created and dependent upon the death of memory. Not simply our memory of the past, but of the recent past and even of the present. This could equally be called the end of relativity or of comparison. What remains is a cheapened memory — little more than nostalgia — which is methodically used for the purposes of patriotism and advertising. Real memory does not induce regret. It is no more a conservative force than analysis is a tool for change. Memory is part of a seamless web with the future, there to help us remember exactly what our civilization is constructed upon and therefore in what ways our actions ought to be shaped in order to serve our needs and our interests.

By throwing ourselves into the analytical arms of technocracy we have gained the illusion that every day is another day. Every intent can be freshly argued. But every day is not another day. Common sense tells us that it is both the day after yesterday and the day before tomorrow.

One of the principal effects of our elite education has been to cut us off from the self-evident.

And the social sciences, which have monopolized our memory in this century, with promises of exploring every corner of it — indeed of us — have succeeded simply in dividing and obscuring any sense of our civilization. By occupying most of the humanist domains, they have further undermined humanism.

In order to improve this situation, we would first have to remove the contempt for the public which is buried deep within our elite education. Jefferson said that "Men by their constitutions are naturally divided into two parties: 1. Those who fear and distrust the people, and wish to draw all powers from them into the hands of the higher classes. 2. Those who identify themselves with the people, have confidence in them, cherish and consider them as the most honest and safe, although not the most wise depository of the public interests."[31] For the words *higher classes* we must substitute *managerial classes* or *technocratic*. These people have used the public's confidence in their judgment in order to insist that wisdom is the primordial public quality. That all other qualities are subsidiary, even dangerous for the public interest. Thus honesty and safety become metaphors for naïveté. And wisdom is reduced to a single, narrow view — their own. In other words, our modern elites fall into Jefferson's first category. They fear and distrust the people.

The depressing state of public education follows quite naturally from that, as does the reaction of the elites, which is to make greater efforts to strengthen their own training structures. It is harder and harder to raise money to pay for public education, because more and more of those who would pay the necessary taxes educate their children elsewhere. And the more expensive private education becomes, the more the middle classes resent being taxed for public education. They, after all, cannot really afford the private system. But they sense that education is becoming increasingly elitist. And to deprive their children of that kind of training is to deprive them of future opportunities as adults. To pay for schools and universities they must make enormous financial sacrifices. Thus the middle class, who were the heart and soul of the democratic, broadly based nation-state, are being converted into enemies of that society.

The curious thing is that the creation of competent elites shouldn't be a problem. In societies as rich and textured as ours, that is something which can almost look after itself. If the society is healthy, it will find outlets at the required levels or it will create them. And the more varied and contradictory these outlets are, the better. How this can be done will differ from country to country. The same is true for general, basic education. There is no need to search for global solutions, apart from an absolute necessity to destroy the idea that such things exist. There is a need to dismantle the obsessional structure which imprisons us and to explode the vertical logic which dominates learning.

At the same time it isn't surprising that our democratic nation-states are finding it impossible to develop ideas which might get us out of our political and economic difficulties. To govern a democracy you require constant vibrations from the population. Between our superior, enclosed, contemptuous elites and our disintegrating system of public education, we have lost the unity which is needed to feel those vibrations.

One of the areas where most waits to be done is the integration of parents into the school system. The current elites are against this because they say it really doesn't work — the wrong parents come forward, they don't understand modern education, and they demand restrictive forms of education. The periodic removal of controversial authors from school curricula under parental pressure is invariably given as an example of the dangers inherent in letting the citizens participate. Thus, the essential liberal democratic instincts of our society are themselves used to discourage people from democratic participation. The people are dangerous and the elites know best.

But what are the roots of this unhealthy democratic influence? Is not the problem that, even where school boards do exist, most citizens don't participate in elections, thus leaving control to fringe groups? If everyone believed it was more important to vote for school boards than for presidents and prime ministers, then a normal cross-section of citizens would appear on those boards. The decline of our school systems reflects perfectly our general problems. The elites preach power, not participation. They preach control, not contribution. They preach gratification of the ego, not the unglamorous duty of service to a larger whole.

Power is generally perceived as something exercised at the highest levels. And the lower levels are best occupied by experts — by people who know best in their field, whether it be education or tax planning.

In countries where most of the middle and upper classes send their children to private schools, the situation is even worse. Those who hold the bulk of the powerful places in government and industry, and who are responsible for the central administration of the education system, know that whatever happens, it will not affect their children. The education they create for other people's children — the children of less important people — cannot possibly be the same as the education they would insist upon for their own. Again, in Britain and the United States, the two Western countries in which private schools account for most of the elite, the public system is in the worst shape. And in those countries you are bound to hear again and again from the mouths of their elites the private complaint that large sections of the population are uneducable.

Were Voltaire to reappear today, it is unlikely that rising technocrats anywhere would recognize in him their spiritual father, nor he in them his children. Perhaps there would be a repeat of the Dostoyevski story, in which Christ returns to Seville in the sixteenth century the day after an auto da fé, during which the Grand Inquisitor has had a hundred heretics burned at the stake, all at once with great pomp, in front of the royal court and the population. The cardinal recognizes the Son of God, has him arrested and threatens to burn him also unless he leaves town. In Voltaire's case our elites would immediately begin to marginalize him through logical arguments designed to prove that his positions all suffer from lack of professionalism.

The attack might well be led by the five Harvard professors who wrote *Managing Human Assets.*[32] They would prove irrefutably, with an "organigram," that whether Voltaire was right or wrong didn't matter. His presence was a danger to stability. Enarques and structuralists would be produced to prove that he was a fraud. If not, how could such an intelligent man so endanger the interests of the state of which he was a citizen? Political scientists, supported by a chorus of poststructural-ists, would come forward to point out that Voltaire had never under-stood his own words. They would provide a properly professional analysis of his texts.

The prosecution could do worse for its closing argument than call on Dr. Madsen Pirie, president of the British Adam Smith Institute. Dr. Pirie had a great influence on Mrs. Thatcher's government. The ratio-nalization (or destruction) of the National Health Service has been one of his great successes. He would probably argue that Voltaire was a flawed Voltairean because he was an unconscious presocialist. Dr. Pirie would prove, however, that he himself was a pure Voltairean and there-fore bound to condemn the master. He would do this with the absolute conviction of a former professor of logic, which is what he is.

That attack, of course, would delight Voltaire. Professors of logic were always his enemy. His defence might be that by creating elites obsessed with the intellectual process that is used to produce decisions, we have indeed eliminated prejudice and superstition from that process. But we have also put ourselves into the hands of men who have no relationship to the organisms they govern. That is, we have abandoned to chance such things as social responsibility, identification with the organism and belief in what the organism represents. These have all been removed from the decision-making process.

All three may carry with them the risk of irrational decision making. But without them, only the abstract remains, devoid of common sense and moral responsibility. Reason, when so abstracted, becomes a series of unrelated assertions bereft of memory. And the elites who apply such abstractions give themselves over to competitiveness — a state of being which is characterized by unfocused, uncontrolled ambition and a my-

opic obsession with profit. Voltaire once complained, in the wake of
some state executions brought on by condemnations for blasphemy, that
"every sensible man, every honourable man, must hold the Christian
sect in horror." If he were alive today he would probably extend that
horror to the Rational sect.

6

The Flowering of
Armaments

We are living in the midst of a permanent wartime economy. The most important capital good produced in the West today is weaponry. The most important sector in international trade is not oil or automobiles or airplanes. It is armaments.

Many people imagine that this rearmament process was limited in time and place to the United States and to the eight years of the Reagan administration. In fact it began twenty years earlier and was a generalized phenomenon. What's more, nothing in the current moves towards détente and demilitarization indicates that this will change. No production cutbacks or economic reorientations are even being considered which would have more than a token effect on the system.

By any standards — historic, economic, moral, or simply practical — in a healthy economy arms would not occupy first place unless that society were at war. Even then, such prominence would be viewed as an aberration to be put up with no longer than events required.

This explosion in armaments production provides the perfect demonstration of how the rational system works. These enormous industries are the result of conscious policies. They have involved prolonged cooperation between most of the key modern elites — politicians, bureaucrats, corporate managers, staff officers, scientists and economists. The creation of this arms-oriented economy has been perhaps the happiest moment in the life of the rational system. There has been a purity, a structural malleability, a cool, abstract intelligence about the whole thing which are unmuddied by the realities of uncontrollable populations and unpredictable economies.

It is precisely this abstraction which has made it impossible for the citizen to get a handle on the situation. Living as we do in a civilization that wallows in information, statistics mean nothing. They become the commas and semicolons of everyday speech. Since they are mostly used by technocrats to decorate their self-fulfilling arguments, the citizen has developed an unconscious defence. He shuts off his value-weighing perceptions the moment he hears a number. In such a situation, intellectual resistance is virtually impossible. Deafness is therefore a healthy reaction. Unfortunately, the discounting of all statistics means that even those capable of conveying a relative truth are lost.

For example, to say that annual international and national arms sales are worth some $900 billion has absolutely no impact.[1] First, the figure is obviously inaccurate. Accuracy at such levels is impossible. It does, however, offer an approximation. It indicates that arms sales are large, enormous, unimaginably big.

In fact, nobody, whether citizen or banker or minister, has any concrete idea of what $900 billion means. Money itself is an abstract idea. People are capable of imagining what small amounts might mean by simply comparing the figures to concrete equivalents. Some can imagine the real impact of far-higher numbers than other people can. Men in charge of large industrial concerns might be able to imagine accurately hundreds of millions of dollars. However, somewhere in the high hundreds of millions the phenomenon of understandable quantity ceases to exist.

Even Robert McNamara, who invented financial control systems for the car industry, the Defense Department and for Third World development, was unable to produce any method that could control the practical application of such figures. While in charge, he himself lost complete control of both defence and development finances. This is not to say that someone else might have done better. No banker or economist who worked on the creation of these systems was able to control their budgets. Cost overruns became, and continue to be, an inevitability whenever the figures rise above the levels of concrete imagination. However technically strict the budget control systems, everyone from the citizen to the controller has come to accept, on some unspoken level, that financial controls do not work.

The problem involved is not unlike imagining a physical exploit. Almost everyone can imagine what it is like to jump over a bar raised 1 meter high, because almost everyone has done it. Many of us can imagine how we might jump 2.43 meters, which is the current world record, had fate only given us such things as longer legs and better muscles. We can even imagine jumping another meter or so higher. But 10 meters is not an imaginable jump. It belongs to the world of comic books.

The American annual overall defence budget alone is more than $300 billion. What do all the world's defence budgets add up to? How many thousand billion? And even that figure would not include the defence-oriented or defence-reliant or defence-subsidized sectors of our economies. All estimates of military influence upon our industries are too low because the military programs are so deeply integrated into theoretically civil sectors that they cannot be separated out for honest calculation. In Sweden, for example, where fairly serious attempts are made to understand the phenomenon, it is felt that civil products with military applications are worth as much as purely military goods. We could, therefore, plausibly take the figures for national arms production around the world and simply double them. Needless to say, we have no idea what the immediate financial or structural effect would be if all of this direct and indirect investment were removed. How many apparently unrelated programs or industries would suffer or abruptly collapse?

It should be remembered that while education, social services and highway construction together add up to less than 15 percent of the 1988 U.S. federal budget, defence's $312 billion represents 33 percent. Moreover, it is generally estimated that one-quarter of the U.S. gross domestic product (GDP) is militarily oriented.

Given the thirty-year-old French government policy of protecting and developing defence industries, the military-dependent percentage of their GDP is probably even higher. This integrated strategy has been aimed at creating an alternative to American weaponry, while using military investment to finance French civil high technology. What's more, they export 40 percent of their military production. This doesn't make them an exception among nations. Britain exports 33 percent. Looked at another way, more than half the capital goods exported by France are armaments.[2]

But even these official figures are too low. Many sales of arms or of parts are kept secret for security reasons. They appear in no statistics. And no prices attached to arms sales could be called "hard" prices. They are disguised by heavy subsidies and artificial inflations or deflations which are determined by a multitude of trade-offs justified by everything from foreign policy and international commerce considerations to local employment and national security.

A classic example during the sixties and seventies was the pricing of the Mirage fighter — one of the most successful fighters ever built, if judged by the quantity sold. Among its attractions was a ridiculously low price. This was the result of endlessly variable calculations, which could include such factors as the deduction of the price of the jet engines. The French government would buy the engines from the builder, SNECMA, a state corporation, at a generous price, which was not made public and which provided the company with healthy books. The government would then sell the engines to the theoretically private airplane manufacturer Dassault at any price that was felt appropriate to win foreign sales. Again, the price would not be made public. As a result Dassault could go into a specific international negotiation with a bewildering margin for manoeuvre. If selling the plane to a nation suited French foreign policy, Dassault could undercut any competitor.

What, then, was the real cost of the Mirage? What percentage of the GDP did it really represent? Did the company — SNECMA or Dassault — really make a profit on the sale? If in the annual calculations of French arms production, foreign sales, trade balance, inflation figures, productivity levels, and so on, a jet engine was priced at a hidden figure of one hundred francs, were any of those calculations accurate? Where are the dividing lines between foreign aid, foreign military aid, employment policies and industrial development? And even if you could answer all those questions, you would still not have dealt with the indirect question of the real price of a jet sold to a poor African country that produces uranium, the supply of which you want to control in order to feed your civil and military nuclear industry. France, after all, produces no uranium, but has the world's third largest nuclear arsenal, as well as using nuclear power plants to satisfy more than 50 percent of its energy needs.

American figures are as soft as the French but are arrived at in different ways. The Pentagon, for example, has a special program for the distribution of "surplus" weapons to allies, mainly in the Third World, which could not otherwise afford sophisticated attack helicopters. Only the minor costs of "refurbishing" and shipping these weapons actually show up in official calculations.

Forty percent of all U.S. scientists are employed on defence-related projects. Shortly before the end of the Soviet Union, NATO said that the Soviet figure continued to be 75 percent of all scientists, and that 40 percent of Soviet industry was given over to military production. A 1987 Congressional Research Service report placed the Soviet Union first in weapon supplies to Third World countries ($60 billion from 1983 to 1986). SIPRI, the Swedish independent research institute, agreed with this. In the wake of the growing Soviet crisis, there is general agreement that the United States is now in first place. SIPRI puts the Soviets second, after the United States, in overall arms sales.[3] Washington maintains that SIPRI is an unfriendly source. At such levels the order isn't of great importance and the new official figures coming out of Moscow are probably about as accurate as Western figures on our own production.

Many experts think the real figures for arms sales are two, three, even four times higher than the $900 billion arrived at by adding up available statistics. There isn't much point in attempting to digest or understand such numbers. Their very unimaginability should be taken as a general summary of the state of affairs. We have maintained, and despite all economic difficulties continue to maintain, historic highs for military spending in a world technically at peace.

The cutbacks initiated by Gorbachev and Reagan captured the world's imagination. Certainly they were a good thing. Certainly they were moves in the right direction. But the truth is that they were peanuts on the mountain of military equipment and expenditure. The good news was so minor that its historical significance rivaled that of the Kellogg-Briand Pact. As for the current manic joy over military budget cutbacks around the globe, it should be noted that only the annual growth levels are being reduced. The budgets themselves remain at their historic highs. Even if cut by a staggering amount — say 25 percent — they would still be way above historic wartime levels. However, they will not be severely cut. The results of the Gulf War will include a general rearming in the Islamic world and a reevaluation of weaponry in both the West and the splintered Soviet Union. That reevaluation will lead to the highly publicized retiring of some older weapons systems, both nuclear and conventional. But it will also result in a wave of high-tech military modernization. The shattering of the twinned superpower status quo has created yet more optimism about serious cuts in arms production. However, it has also brought about an uncontrollable explosion in nationalism, which — accompanied by unsatisfied racial rivalries — is constantly fracturing nations into ever smaller units. This will probably produce an expanding, not a shrinking, weapons market.

Perhaps the unimaginable size of all this commerce and production explains why the politicians, the press and the public apply their moral indignation to flea-size military scandals which they can concretely imagine. The $20 to $30 million involved in the Iran-Contra arms affair must be seen in the light of an average new weapons contract, which would run around $300 to $400 million. Twenty million dollars in the arms business is so small an amount as to be invisible to the professionals. But the public loved Irangate because the sum involved was not only imaginable, it could even be picked apart with the tweezers of frustrated traditional moral indignation.

Meanwhile, every year, the Pentagon inexplicably loses — simply loses — about a billion dollars' worth of arms and equipment.[4] The budgets, the costs and the actual stocks are so large that they cannot be subjected to even the most sophisticated methods of accountancy. The numbers can be explained. They cannot, however, be reduced to a rational sequence. They are therefore so out of control that the loss of $1 billion is a mere statistical occurrence.

And so, while a nation looked under every mat, attempting to trace every penny of Irangate's $20 million, no one was held responsible for the loss of $1 billion. No one was fired. The admission of the loss produced a few mentions in a few papers and was promptly forgotten. Apart from incompetence and error the disappearance of $1 billion suggests a great leeway for fraud, given that the military is the single largest purchaser of goods and services in the United States.

At the same time as Irangate, the Pentagon Audit Committee was finishing a four-year investigation of corporate overcharging. They discovered that ninety-five contractors had lied about costs on 365 out of 774 contracts. The overcharge amounted to $788.9 million. Rockwell International Corporation on a single contract involving 340 bombs had overcharged by $7.4 million. While the nation agonized over Adnan Khashoggi's $12 million, federal investigators were finding it inexplicably difficult to bring themselves to lay contractor fraud charges in these 365 cases.[5]

The politicians who justify military expenditures claim that we are at peace. They talk of a peace bought through defence. Given their various political allegiances, they justify the costs in the name of Democracy, Capitalism, Socialism, Communism, the dictatorship of the proletariat or the struggle against the forces of colonialism. They also admit, with a shrug, that while defence budgets may be too high, they are also essential.

When out of power, those of the Left seize upon the arms business as a symbol of the military-industrial complex prophesied by that odd John and Jesus team — the American Marxist intellectual C. Wright Mills and the conservative administrator Dwight D. Eisenhower. When in power, the Left adopts the attitude of the Right, which on this subject tends to say the same things whether in office or out. Thus governments of the Left and Right both lament the situation as the inescapable result of having had to face enemies who care nothing for their people and so spend vast amounts on weaponry. Western governments have had no choice, they argue, but to follow suit. The various socialist governments of Britain, France and Germany have perfected this argument over the last three decades. Because of current events in the Soviet bloc, this rhetoric is now in limbo. It is already beginning to reemerge, however, in an appropriately amended form.

As for the great liberal centre, it remains relatively silent. Liberals know that much of the expansion in weapon production happened during their years in power. They know that they themselves applied the most rational modern methods available. The result was a rapid acceleration in arms spending. They feel that this must have been some terrible accident of history — the coincidence of the Vietnam War with a growth in inflation, followed hard by the oil crisis, for example. And yet their rational methods should have been able to deal with these relatively limited problems.

Liberals also know what a disaster it is to appear naive. They dare not, therefore, speak out against arms production. And yet they, more than others, sense the real problem.

Arms production and sales have nothing to do with the existence of a military-industrial complex. That term implies a well-thought-out organization with an intent — what the law would call forethought. But if the arms business is neither manageable nor accountable to its own experts, let alone to political figures, then it cannot be filled with fore-thought and intent.

The flowering of weaponry is the full expression of the genuine loss of purpose among the military, the administrators and the industrial elites of the West, all driven as much by their own confusion as by their unity of method. It is not surprising, therefore, that the politicians and the press, who feed off the elites in their search for subject matter, should have been unable to make more of the Iran affair than a trivial game of individual wrongdoing. They could have used this minute arms deal as an opportunity to lay bare the way the American and most Western economies work on a day-to-day basis. Irangate was not an exception. It was a common transaction. One of thousands. But in order to take such an approach, people would have to accept that the selling of arms, for the first time in modern Western history, is no longer a marginal business.

For the last two decades the world has been overwhelmed by economic crisis and confusion. Our governments prefer to talk about periodic recessions while desperately attempting to unblock the economy with everything from tight to loose money, from high tariffs and massive foreign lending to low tariffs, inflated currencies and unrepayable domestic debt. Their most successful attempted solution, however, if measured in jobs created and products sold, has been the gradual conversion of our ailing half social democratic, half capitalistic societies from peace-time to wartime economics.

This situation is the result of a long process which went into high speed during the early sixties, when a centre-left American government under Kennedy, a radical-conservative French government under de Gaulle and a socialist British government under Wilson each decided, for its own reasons, that the best way to finance indigenous weapons programs was to sell as many arms as possible abroad. It was all part of a new approach to government spending introduced by the first wave of apolitical technocrats. The underlying assumption was that a method which strengthened a nation's arms production would also increase its independence.

Charles de Gaulle was the first to start down this road. He came to power at the age of sixty-eight in an unstable political situation. In many ways the economy he inherited in 1958 was basically still in the nineteenth century. With his long-standing devotion to advanced military technology and his sense that he had only a limited time to work, de Gaulle set about modernizing military and civil France at breakneck speed.

A soldier with a vision, he had also suffered repeatedly at the hands of the sclerotic Napoleonic traditions of the army and its self-justifying general staff. He was also obliged to deal with an officer corps which had brought him to power and which therefore felt equally empowered to remove him.

Whatever he wanted to do to France as a whole, the military structure was the part he understood best. He therefore set about revolutionizing the entire economy through the military structure. This made far more sense than one might think. De Gaulle was convinced that the old army stood in the way of a new France. He believed, with the idealism of an eighteenth-century man of reason, that only a new technocratic officer class could drive out the mythology of the anti-democratic, antirepublican, antimechanized-warfare traditional officer corps.

He therefore promoted technical officers. The three principal generals of de Gaulle's years in office were all engineers — Polytechnicians — who immediately began to promote other technicians. Their percentage of the officer corps rose from twenty-five to fifty.

De Gaulle next started to feed credits through the army into the industrial sector. It was as a natural extension of this new military research and production that France began to sell arms abroad with greater aggressivity. Already in the late 1950s French foreign weapons sales were growing at 16 percent per year, while those of the rest of the world were at 10 percent.[6] This early growth was easy, given the tiny base from which the new government had begun.

In fact all appeared calm in the international arms market. The United States effortlessly dominated the scene by virtually giving away its weapons as a continuation of its Marshall Plan attitudes. Britain ran a comfortable second, thanks to the continued production of its war industries and to a virtual monopoly in its colonies and ex-colonies.

This situation exploded on February 6, 1961, when President Kennedy delivered a Special Message to Congress on America's general balance-of-payments crisis. The United States was three billion dollars on the wrong side. One of the central conclusions to which Kennedy — that is, McNamara and the new Department of Defense technicians — had come was that the United States could no longer afford to give away weapons. They had to be sold. More specifically, the United States had to sell many more weapons than it had been giving away. Kennedy presented this commercial reality in an idealistic package. He spoke of the need to defend democracy and the need for America's allies to undertake a drastic modernization of their military capabilities. The allies were to assume a greater burden in Western defence, but they were to do so with U.S. weapons, not their own. By buying in the United States, they would be compensating America for the heavy financial burden it bore as the defender of freedom. Kennedy was very specific. He went on to "urge the purchase of the new weapons and weapons systems by those of our allies who are financially capable of doing so." Rhetoric aside, the President was urging America's allies to subsidize the American economy by buying American arms. It was the perfect illustration of a phenomenon de Gaulle had described in his *War Memoirs*: "The United States approaches important matters with straightforward emotions which disguise complicated policies."

McNamara further confused the new policy with a backup explanation in the latest rational jargon. This official statement came in three parts, of which the first, although written in technocratic language, is well worth quoting:

> 1. To further the practice of co-operative logistics and standardization with our allies by integrating our supply systems to the maximum extent feasible and by helping to limit proliferation of different types of equipment.[7]

Like most of McNamara's policies, its real effect was the inverse of its announced or intended effect.

The frenzied proliferation of all weapons, including nuclear ones, over the last two decades, has its origins in this policy. The North Atlantic Council, the political arm of NATO, includes a committee — called the Military Agency for Standardization — to which each nation sends a representative. Its job is to discuss weapons and weapon systems with the idea of agreeing on a single standard for bullets, shells, rifles, tanks, fighters and so on. The theory is that all ammunition and parts should be interchangeable between the allies in times of crisis and that their common strategy is based upon a clear and practical understanding of the capabilities of one another's equipment. The unwritten principle is that this standardization will be reached through a trade-off between the various arms industries of the various allies. No one is to lose out by becoming a buyer who does not sell. If a Belgian rifle is chosen, then the tank will be German and the plane American. The reality, however, was that the standardization committee had always been a door through which the United States could supply its allies. With the new Kennedy-McNamara policy, it became a door through which the United States sold its weapons.

Just enough non-American weapons had always been adopted under the standardization system to keep the allies happy. Occasionally European orders were part of specific NATO policy. The post–World War II rapid industrialization of northern Italy by Agnelli/Fiat was largely driven by military orders. The impetus was a NATO conviction that prosperity would destroy the great power of the Communist party in that area, which it did. In general, however, cooperation, standardization and integration actually meant that the allies should buy American. What's more, the new sales policy came at the same time as America's new nuclear strategy of flexible response. One of the obvious consequences of this strategy, which the United States forced upon its allies, was that it required massive conventional rearmament by everyone. In other words Kennedy introduced a strategy requiring rearmament at the same time that he introduced a policy of selling weapons.

Finally the new arms commercialization policy was given a practical form. The Pentagon created the International Logistics Negotiations branch to look after selling weapons. Its first director, Henry Kuss, was the leading expert on arms supplies. He made no secret of what motor drove the policy. In a speech to a gathering of American arms manufacturers, he laid it out clearly:

> From the military point of view we stand to lose all of the major international relationships paid for with grant aid money unless we can establish professional military relationships through the sales media. . . .
> The solution to the balance of payments deficit is principally in more trade. All other solutions merely temporize the problem.[8]

Thanks to his efforts, American arms sales rose sharply. But this aggressive approach also focused the minds of the allies, particularly the French. It was one of the three preliminary causes for French disenchantment with NATO.[9] Those who sat on the NATO standardization committee at that time remember the constant battles between Washington and Paris; the former expecting everyone to buy American, the latter insisting on French sales to the alliance equal to French purchases.

General Pierre Gallois, one of France's most original military thinkers, wrote that if Europe were to accept America's policy, it would become no more than "a producer of consumer products. As for the rest, why not save money and use whatever the Americans produce. On the commercial front there is nothing wrong with this division of labour except that it would turn Western Europe into an under-developed continent. We would have to slowly close our engineering schools, our laboratories, our research bodies and begin training our youth to be salesmen and to working solely under foreign license."[10]

Curiously enough, this ironic vision of a comfortable decline is not far from that being seriously recommended by most Western economists, who now believe it to be an absolute truth that nations should get out of industries which can be run cheaper by other nations. Thus the United States should get out of steel in favour of Asia. And Canada should get out of agriculture in favour of the United States. Had Europe believed such an idea in the early sixties, it would now be an economic wasteland instead of the largest economic force in the world.

The French refused this option in 1961 and set about redesigning their entire economy in order to compete on all fronts but, above all, in order to produce the latest weaponry. The Fifth National Plan emphasized six sectors which would theoretically secure independence and progress. All six reflected Ministry of Defence policies — atomic energy, electronics, computers, aviation, rockets and satellites. In electronics, 50 percent of the products were for the military sector. The entire economy responded to this massive injection of R and D funds. And the remarkable integration of the national elites made the whole idea of a military-industrial complex irrelevant. The military engineering school — the Polytechnique — produced the army's technicians as well as many of the senior bureaucrats and corporate leaders. There could not be a complex when there was only one elite, one source of financing, and no strong legal division between politics, defence, and industry. No time was spent on conflict-of-interest questions. There was only one interest.

An American aeronautics corporation might have two thousand of its eight thousand engineers devoted to such jobs as analysis and control. This was necessary because the company would have to justify (not explain) every detail of a project to its own government, argue the merits of the product, win over politicians and demonstrate the quality of its management methods, its control over subcontractors and its cost controls. And it would have to do the same with foreign governments for all international sales. A French corporation would have almost no one working in these areas. The technocrats in their own government would handle most of this through the Ministerial Delegation for Armaments.

Such elite integration was only a foreshadowing of that same unity in other Western countries. Elsewhere the official public barriers between government, industry and army maintained the fiction that there were real levers of control over armaments policy. However, the unity in approach of the technocrats in all three sectors meant that they could effortlessly develop policy across the lines, without reference to the control levers. The public niceties could all be dealt with after the fact. Legal and legislative approval of administrative action came to resemble a ribbon-cutting ceremony.

The French elites were not at all unconscious of the fact that their economy was being remodelled through military priorities. They believed that only the army could afford the kind of investments necessary to keep high-tech industries on the cutting edge of creativity.

This particular argument has become a great favourite in the late twentieth century. It is used everywhere on the globe when there is a need to justify military financing. The reality is that military investment is merely a facet of government investment. Whether these funds are earmarked for military or civilian R and D is neither here nor there.

In any case, as early as the 1960s the French army was officially providing 30 percent of the nation's R and D investments. In reality, the percentage of total national R and D devoted to the military sector was closer to 70 percent.[11] This same phenomenon was slower to take effect in the United States, thanks to the relatively healthy state of general industry before 1973. By 1980, however, 40 percent of American R and D was for military programs. And by 1985 it represented 50 percent of university research. By 1988, 70 percent of government-supported R and D was military.

De Gaulle's point had been that only the state can judge what research "is most useful to the public interest."[12] Political leaders around the world came to agree with this idea. They seemed to have little choice, because the situation they discovered on arriving in office consisted of a seamless web uniting R and D and military equipment. There did not appear to be any other way to do research. The only question, then, was to find ways to pay for both this research and the resulting "need" for new military equipment. The answer, quite simply, was to export. The sale of two hundred fighters abroad would finance the fifty planes needed for the nation's air force.

This economic-political-military truism — that national independence could be accomplished through domestic arms production, provided it was financed through exports — was to become a new religion in the Western world. Technocrats everywhere — whether officers or administrators — explained to their employers the remarkable benefits which this cycle would bring to the home economy. And what were perceived as the American and French successes seemed all the more attractive when compared to the British failure.

London had not turned its attention to a national arms policy fast enough and so had frittered away its postwar advantages, losing even most of its ex-colonial markets. By 1966 Harold Wilson and his Defence Minister Denis Healey had decided in desperation to join the race. Both men came from the left wing of the Labour party. And, in another reminder of the irrelevance of both ideology and militarism in what was happening, two of the three men central to the creation and running of the British Defence Sales organization were plucked from the automobile industry, just as in the United States, Robert McNamara had come to Defense from Detroit. The growth in the arms market was an industrial-administrative undertaking, not a military one. It had to do with the production and sale of mechanized and computerized material. Most of the people involved were not thinking seriously about the nature of that material.

The new British Defence Sales group was able to stop the collapse of the U.K. markets and London held on to fourth place in the ever-expanding world market. By the late eighties, Britain was again rivalling France for third place.

But everyone else had caught on to the trend long before that. By the late sixties, the Swedes, the Swiss, the Belgians, the Germans and the Italians were travelling the world selling their arms. The end of colonialism meant the rise of new states. New states meant new armies in need of new weaponry. These young governments were eager to buy but short of cash. That turned out to be a simple technical problem. The same Western governments which sold them the weapons would finance their expenditures through aid programs or general bank loans or specific armament-financing agreements, all facilitated by subsidized low pricing.

In other words the sellers were not actually financing their own military needs through foreign sales, because they were also financing the buyers. According to their rational accounting system, a fighter sold abroad more or less paid for a fighter in the home air force. In reality the seller government was paying for both. The whole process was and is little more than an inflationary chain in which money, in the form of debt, must be printed to finance the production of nonproductive goods to be stored at home or in other countries.

After a decade of this overexcited world competition for markets, the general economic crisis of 1973 threw governments and businesses into a confusion from which they still have not emerged. None of them were clear as to what had happened. The technocrats could see that the growth machinery was seriously stalled for the first time since 1945. They flailed around blindly for remedies, all of which failed. Printing money. Not printing money. Heavy industrial investment. Hard-nosed refusals to invest in sick, heavy industries. No matter what they spent or didn't spend, taxed or didn't tax, the economic body wouldn't move.

The only sector which responded positively and promptly to government stimulation was the arms industry. Tax breaks aimed at a normal industrial sector or R and D subsidies or depreciation benefits or any other support which lies within the competence of a government, may well encourage companies to produce. But that doesn't create consumers to buy. In times of economic troubles, consumers do not leap at products. They limit their expenses.

The arms industry, however, was and is a perfectly artificial business, not subject to real market conditions. Armaments are the ideal consumer product, because even the consumer is artificial. That is to say the consumer is a government, not an individual.

Moving the financial chips around in a circle suddenly took on a new importance. Paying countries to buy your weapons was a way to stimulate your own immobile economy. Ordering weapons at home for your own forces accomplished the same thing. The more weapons your own industry built for home or abroad, the more money you had to print. But this didn't look like classic inflationary economics. Governments were printing complex debt papers, not old-fashioned debt notes. Besides, patriotism was involved as well as export encouragement programs. International trade-offs could no longer be seen as expenditures. They were now stimulants.

The production of so many weapons has indeed kept men working in difficult times. Counting only directly related industries, some 400,000 jobs are now involved in the United States and 750,000 in Europe. But, curiously enough, as the socioeconomic role of building weapons has grown, the actual question of whether the selling producer is well defended has slipped into the background. The primary arguments surrounding most arms projects today relate to jobs, industrial structure, trade balances and technological development. The arms manufacturers have understood this and act accordingly.

In 1981, for example, Rockwell International sold Congress on the B-1B bomber by telling them that it would be composed of systems built in forty-eight of the American states, a remarkable bit of political-industrial economics. In 1986 in Britain Plessy justified its sale of six AR-3D radar systems to Iran for £240 million by stating: "This contract represents two years of work for 1,500 of our workers." "The Iranians," they added, "have promised not to use this system against the Iraquis." No doubt they were buying it to track shooting stars. Caspar Weinberger, President Reagan's Secretary of Defense, at least knew how to be perfectly straightforward: "We must remember at least 350,000 jobs are at stake and will be lost if there are any drastic military cuts." All in all the building of weapons has become the most important source of make-work projects in the late twentieth century. Neoconservatives may condemn Franklin D. Roosevelt's WPA projects, but at least they kept the countryside clean and were reasonably cheap.

The idea that building weapons is a good way to create jobs and to earn foreign currency is so naive as to have a certain charm about it. Even to believe that military spending might help the economy is revolutionary. Throughout history, military spending has been considered a disaster for economies. The twentieth-century Western belief in the opposite is, in part, a curious offshoot of Keynesian economics, produced by the conviction that it took World War II to end the depression. One of the extra lunacies of current economics is that while Keynes is now considered bad, weapon production programs are still good.

In order to obscure this contradiction, economists came up with the theory of "the trickle-down effect." The investment, for example, of several billion dollars into a nongrowth area such as tanks, in the hope that there will be a trickle down of a hundred million dollars, into civil transport, is presented as an efficient form of industrial investment.

Those who defend this theory always cite a long list of successes. There is hardly a plane or a radio which is not derivative of something military. Fast trains. New metals. The entire nuclear energy sector. Digital electronics. Satellite communications. The list is endless. And there are no signs of a waning in the political conviction that this is the right way to do research. During his first presidential campaign, George Bush went out of his way to reply to his opponents' complaint that 70 percent of federal support for R and D goes to the defence establishment: "Critics ignore the importance of defense research to science and technology, manufacturing and trade — expanding the frontiers of our knowledge — and contributing to our prosperity."[13]

The interesting question, however, is not whether this system works but whether any other system works better. Why can't governments make their investments directly in those civil sectors which they have been hoping might receive a few drops of new knowledge from military research? If civilian R and D is what we are really after, then the trickle-down system is an astonishingly inefficient way of going about it.

None of this is to suggest that all weapons could simply disappear or even that they should. It is merely to point out that Western economic priorities have never been so back to front.

The new elites, whatever their particular professional training, share identical views on how things ought to be done. But their basic premise is wrong. It was not the building of weapons for World War II which ended the Great Depression. It was the need, after the war, to reconstruct a devastated Europe. So if we are really hoping to end our economic difficulties by military means, then we must get down to seriously blowing things up. The prolonged bombing of the Gulf War was a small start in that direction.

The truth is that the central role now held by weaponry in our economies has become a major barrier to real growth and therefore to recovery. The problem with arms — if the human and moral questions are set aside — is that they are not really capital goods. You cannot build or evolve or develop through armaments. You can only stockpile them. Or you can use them. Once only, in most cases. And only to destroy. But the economic motor of capital goods is supposed to be growth, not destruction. In short, whether stockpiled or used, weapons are the most extravagant of consumer goods.

There is nothing new about arms dealers and armament races. But the dealers were always tiny dots on the economic screen and the international arms business was scarcely larger. For example, the naval race leading up to World War I was thought to be cripplingly expensive. It consisted of a mere thirty-four British and Allied dreadnoughts against twenty German and Austrian ships of the same type.

Those expenditures caused enormous public debate. Shortly before the 1914 outbreak, the Liberal government in Britain almost tore itself to pieces over the division between the First Lord of the Admiralty Winston Churchill and Lloyd George, the Chancellor of the Exchequer. Churchill wanted an annual naval budget large enough to pay for more dreadnoughts and Lloyd George opposed him for social and economic reasons. The British drive to lessen their own financial burden had made them start pressuring their allies — the dominions — to build dreadnoughts of their own. "The "Empire ships" would, of course, fall under the imperial command of the Admiralty. These pressures divided the various dominions. To oppose London's wish was to be soft on the Germans, ungrateful to the mother country and secretly republican. This argument had already played a role in destroying the Canadian government of Wilfrid Laurier in 1911 and it almost broke up the succeeding government of Robert Borden. The conviction of those in favour of the ships was that they would prevent war; of those against, that they would cause it.

The 1950s, the early 1960s and the 1980s were filled with identical rhetoric regarding the Cold War. But there is a fundamental difference between pre-1914 or pre-1939 and today. No period of peace has ever supported the levels of arms spending that we have experienced over the last thirty years. No period of peace has ever devoted to arms such high percentages of general economic activity.

And yet one thing has remained unchanged. Today's arms dealers are still the marginal, minor figures they always were. Adnan Khashoggi, despite his fame, was the least important person in the Iranian affair. Dealers do not make deals. They run after deals, attempting to insert themselves in order to pick up a few stray thousands or millions. They are the hyenas of an industry controlled by the governments, without whom no important arms sale can be made. No more than 5 percent of the arms trade is handled by the dealers and most of that is at the instigation of the purchasing or selling governments.[14] But the moment Khashoggi's name appeared in the Iran scandal, journalists and elected officials ran to point him out as a source of evil. *Time* magazine, arbiter of American popular mythology, put him on its cover with the title

"Those Shadowy Arms Traders." Inside were complicated diagrams involving governments, presidents, ministers and generals; but always at the centre was Khashoggi. Again and again reference was made by every news body covering the scandal to Khashoggi's missing twelve million dollars. These days twelve million dollars will hardly buy you a tank.

It is the government's role as chief arms dealer which should always draw the eye. Perhaps people cannot focus on this because it blurs the immoral reputation of the arms business. In the past, believing that dealers were evil provided a cost-free vision of right and wrong which involved very little damage to the citizen's immediate self-interest. Nevertheless, this clarity did help people to measure the state of their nation's affairs.

Now, suddenly, such shadowy, immortal monsters as Basil Zaharoff, the most famous arms dealer of the early twentieth century, have been replaced by our own elected officials and our own honest employees — the civil servants. What is the citizen to think? Politicians may be popular or unpopular. Honest or dishonest. Effective or ineffective. But the very nature of the democratic process makes it impossible to see them as the incarnation of evil. The politician cannot be evil unless the people believe themselves to be evil. As for the bureaucrats, who are the actual "dealers," their function as government employees frees them from the traditional controls of public moral responsibility.

Besides, the success of politicians and bureaucrats in selling arms abroad theoretically lightens the defence load on the taxpayer and helps the balance of payments. "As for the moral question," Raymond Brown said, when he was head of the British government Defence Sales Department, "I just put it out of my mind."[15] His then French equivalent, the Ministerial Delegate for Armaments Hugues de l'Estoile, gave an even more standard reply to the same sort of question. "When I am criticized for being an arms dealer, I always think that when I sign a contract I can guarantee for instance 10,000 jobs over three years."[16] As for Henry Kuss, the American government dealer, he saw himself not as a seller of arms, but as a man charged with rationalization and coordination.

Arms production has become so much part of what is perceived as the national economic self-interest that to criticize it is to be unrealistic, idealistic, simplistic and so on. Commentators and public officials therefore practice a self-censorship which is as widespread on the Left as on the Right. In 1986 Britain squeezed out France for third place in the international arms sales race. *Libération*, which is more or less the newspaper of the intelligent French Left, responded with a long, anguished analysis of what had gone wrong. They concluded that "a few people with a rather romantic view of the world have regretted that

France's foreign policy is sometimes limited to that of an arms dealer. They forget that if we want to be powerful we must rely on our power; that is, our weapons — those we possess and those we sell."[17] In 1987 France retook third place.

The degree to which foreign policy has been deformed and the law rendered irrelevant by systems management is more obvious in the arms sector than in any other. This often takes on comic proportions. During the early 1980s, the United States did everything it could to discourage the Europeans from building a new-generation fighter instead of buying an American machine. Washington claimed the American plane would be cheaper and better. Their arguments failed and in 1985 the Europeans started two consortia. The larger one included interests in Britain, Spain, Germany and Italy and had plans to build eight hundred fighters.

Washington's reaction was to try to push its way into that group. Not because it wanted to buy the fighter. There are already five separate American corporations working on versions of Washington's new-generation plane. Eventually these five will have to fight each other, at great cost, for the American market. Washington wanted into the European consortium simply as a way of getting more work for its own factories.

Governments are so desperate to create investment and employment through the building of arms that Washington would probably have participated in a Soviet fighter project if invited. Moscow would certainly have participated in an American project. The proof is that, although China and the West were still in indirect conflict on a series of fronts, and potentially in direct conflict on others, Western countries have showed no hesitation in signing military contracts with Beijing. In return for the few subsidized millions theoretically gained, we helped China become a serious competitor to Western weapons in the world market.

One of the characteristics of this curious market is that everyone is constantly accusing everyone else of unfair competition through artificial pricing. In 1987 the European Airbus consortium won a major contract in the United States. This was a serious defeat for Boeing–Lockheed–McDonnell Douglas on their home turf. Washington tried to break the deal by accusing the Europeans of reducing the civilian airliner's sale price through hidden military investments. This accusation was sent in a diplomatic note, which is, after all, something more usually addressed to enemies than to allies. The senior partner in the consortium is France and its then prime minister, Jacques Chirac,

replied immediately that if Washington touched the contract there
would be a European embargo on all U.S. goods and, besides, "All
American aeronautical constructors are financed by the Pentagon and
NASA."[18] Washington backed down. Of course both sides were right.

In this century smaller wars have always been seen by large countries
as testing grounds for new equipment and new tactics. Nowadays, in a
world of heavy competition, producers examine every violent incident in
the forty-odd wars currently being fought around the globe, in the hope
that one of their own weapons will have sunk, shot down or blown up
something built by their competition.

The virtual destruction of the American frigate *Stark* in the Persian
Gulf in 1987 and, before that, of the destroyer HMS *Sheffield* in the Falklands may have hurt U.S. and U.K. naval sales but helped those of the
French Exocet missile. Such examples are used actively in sales campaigns. The world's press is fed with descriptions of these battles as an
indirect way of praising the national weapon. The purpose and implications of the war being fought are irrelevant to this commercial activity.

The Gulf War was the most extensive equipment trial since World
War II. On February 15, 1991, in the midst of the war, President Bush
took time out to travel to the Patriot Missile factory in Andover, Mas-
sachusetts. There he gave what was billed as a major speech, which was
beamed live around the globe. His central message to the assembled
workers and to the world was that Patriots were "a triumph for American technology" and "essential for technological growth." He put this
in the context of the need to push ahead with SDI. The sales pitch was
reiterated on March 6 in his postwar State of the Union Address: "They
did it using America's state-of-the-art technology. We saw the excellence embodied in the Patriot Missile and the patriots who made it
work." In fact, negotiations to sell tens of billions of dollars worth of
new arms to Middle Eastern allies were already underway.[19]

In this and other cases, the producer's own national interests may
easily become irrelevant. For example, Canadian and French state corporations were pushed to sell their nuclear reactors throughout the
Third World. No politically responsible figure asked himself whether
the inevitable resulting proliferation in nuclear weapons was really
worth the few hundred million paid for the reactors. A more specific
case was that of Henri Conze, chief arms salesman of the French
government in the late 1980s. Times were so tough that Dassault, the
French manufacturer of fighters, was obliged to lay off eight hundred
men in 1987. Conze commented: "The future is very uncertain, but
industrialists must not fall into depression. The markets do exist. [He
was referring to the oil-producing nations.] The problem is when the
clients will once again have the money to modernize their defences. . . .
Who can tell what the price of oil will be in a year?"[20]

In other words, a mature male of above-average intelligence, who is a senior civil servant, hopes that the price of oil will go back up so that Middle Eastern governments will be able to buy yet more fighters. The effect of such a price hike on his own nation would be disastrous, since France, like most of Europe, imports all its hydrocarbons. This example merely indicates the frenzy into which the arms business has driven people.

It is hardly surprising, therefore, that the fear, as *Libération* put it, of appearing "rather romantic" simply pushes those who do criticize the current lunacy to concentrate on the sensational and the marginal: dealers with Jacuzzis in their jumbo jets, the psychiatric problems of colonels, which official said what to a president of the United States at what time of which day in what room. In reality, even the traditional key questions — who lied, what law was broken, who knew — are now irrelevant. In the arms business, everyone lies and usually does so in "the national interest." After all, they are public servants or are subsidized by public servants. The laws are almost always broken, most often by those who make them or who are paid to uphold them.

It is hardly surprising that decent men should be pushed to such tactics. First, there is the sense of economic imperative. Second, there is the conviction that these operations are all taking place as part of a larger national plan, with technocrats of all sorts justifying everything, from the weapon itself to the need of the potential buyer. Third, the operations take place within cocoons of secrecy which encourage men to give way to childish fantasies of how the world can be made to work.

In 1987, for example, $22.4 billion were requested in the American defense budget for "Black Programs" shielded from public scrutiny by withholding the name or the function or the cost or all three.[21] If the official tactics of senior government employees involve the hiding of real costs, of real prices, of indirect subsidies, of real foreign policy considerations, it is only another very small step for them to become involved in unofficial kickbacks and sales to forbidden countries. Such things as falsified end-user permits and invisible money in numbered accounts are the characteristics not of illegal but of legal arms dealing. This "airport fiction" side to the business makes an endless list of dubious activities acceptable, when common sense should tell the participants that they are not.

That was how Britain came to ship $50 million worth of tank parts to Iran in contravention of its own public policy. A regulation forbade the sale of "lethal" equipment to Iran or Iraq if it would significantly help either side. Those who wrote the regulation then set about manipulating it. Are spare parts lethal? Are they significant?

Even Sweden, with its strict law forbidding arms exports to "zones of conflict" found in 1986 that senior officials had been doing just that for ten years. Hundreds of millions of dollars' worth of weapons had been sent to Iran. When an investigation began, a senior officer jumped in front of a train — or was pushed. No one is quite certain which.

Martin Ardbo, former president of the Nobel subsidiary which did the exporting, confessed: "We thought we lived under a system of double morality. They [the government and the War Equipment Inspectorate] wanted us to do it like this." Like everyone else involved, Ardbo thought that by breaking the law he was serving his country.[22]

Our elites believe these social distortions to be of passing importance, compared to the strategic self-reliance financed by foreign arms sales. The truth is the exact opposite. Each foreign sale of arms imposes new limitations on the seller's foreign policy.

For a start there are the enormous costs involved in tooling up — not simply to build a weapon but to build in the quantities and according to the intricate variables, required for international markets. These costs lock the seller in. He must go on selling to pay off his investment and to keep his work force employed. Such things as foreign policy objections to clients inevitably become less important. The financing of the weapons production system itself becomes a foreign policy imperative.

But the seller's hands are tied by more than the need to sell. Weapons systems need spare parts and ammunition. The producer guarantees himself a long-term income in this way, because spare parts and ammunition are like interest on a deposit. Unfortunately, they also create a long-term commitment to the buyer. The refusal at any time to supply spare parts would destroy a country's reputation.

If it came in the middle of a war, it could cause the client to lose. Uninvolved nations all over the world would take note that the seller was unreliable. The more specific the moral or political reasons for not selling, the more catastrophic the effect would be for the supplier in the international marketplace. This was one of the justifications used by the Nobel employees in the Swedish arms scandal. They said that to cut off arms to Iran would damage Sweden's reputation as a reliable supplier. They were probably right. An arms sale is therefore a foreign policy commitment. The more aggressive the international sales campaign, the more commercial success will deform foreign policy.

As for the sophisticated weapons systems Western producers want for themselves, these are so expensive that most must be built by vast international consortia. This can create stronger alliances. But no one could suggest that it does anything for national independence.

Finally, with each passing year, more countries set up or expand indigenous arms production and enter the international competition. It is now a buyer's market and so winning a large contract depends on the promise of general military support for the buyer or of financial support in areas unrelated to defence. In fact the seller is more likely to end up bolstering his client's foreign policy than strengthening his own.

As for the attempts by suppliers to influence their clients' foreign or internal policies, these have invariably been a disaster. In 1958, for example, France adopted the Belgian FN rifle as part of NATO's standardization program. The FN used the American 7.62 bullet. At a difficult moment in the Algerian War, America used its disapproval of colonial wars as a reason for cutting off the supply of bullets. The French were convinced that the real reason was Washington's interest in the gas fields discovered in southern Algeria. This incident helped push France towards withdrawal from NATO and into active concentration on domestic arms production.

The rapid decline of British international sales from second to fourth place began with Harold Wilson's imposition of an arms embargo on South Africa in 1964. France immediately took its place and sold, among other things, sixty-four Mirage fighters, seventy-five helicopters, and several nuclear plants. Less than two years later, Wilson created the Defence Sales Organization to stabilize plummeting sales. Black African states had been frightened off as much as anyone else by the British application of principles to commerce. But with the new Sales Organization in place, Britain began to compete amorally alongside everyone else and soon had won back international respect. As for France, it had to keep its mouth more or less shut on the subject of apartheid until the late 1980s, when its last arms commitment to South Africa was completed.

In 1967 France cut off arms to Israel in an attempt to stop the Six-Day War. Israel immediately changed and diversified suppliers, then concentrated on domestic arms production. After General Augusto Pinochet's coup, the West gradually cut off military supplies. Chile now has an important arms industry. In other words, in each case the client immediately changes suppliers; then, chastened by such a crisis of dependency, sets about building his own arms industry; then begins selling his own weapons abroad. Thus the net result of pressuring a client has been to create yet another competitor.

In 1960 only a few Third World countries were serious arms producers. Today, twenty-seven of them are out there competing. From 1950 to 1972 an average 86 percent of major weapon systems sold to the Third World came from the United States, the Soviet Union, France and Britain. Today eleven Third World countries sell fighter aircraft for export. Nine sell naval ships. Twenty-two have ballistic missile programs. Six of them are already selling nuclear-capable missiles. China sells three models, Israel two, Brazil three, India four.[23] Beating unemployment and balancing trade figures through arms exports has become a serious economic policy in Argentina, Brazil, China, Egypt, India, Indonesia, Israel, Mexico, North and South Korea, the Philippines and Taiwan, to name only the most successful.

Brazil, for example, sells half the world's armoured fighting vehicles. It makes more money from arms than from coffee. Its military exports are worth more than its total defence budget. The Brazilians would argue that their weapons policy has been a great success because their government created an armaments industry without having any need for weapons at home. It has taken the original U.S.–France–U.K. theory of foreign sales to finance domestic needs one step further.

A number of Third World countries are now selling arms just to make money, in the absence of any domestic needs. Pakistan has forty thousand people devoted to the arms industry; its largest pool of technicians and skilled workers.[24] This approach allows developing countries to beat the developed world at its own game.

That they should have converted so easily to Western industrial methods in this particular area at first seems surprising. The explanation may be that their elites were and continue to be trained in the West. Just as an earlier generation of colonials was trained, for example, in Marxism in Paris and London, which it then tried to apply at home, so those trained from the sixties on learned the same methodology as Western technocrats. The most important component in these new elites has been the soldier. These military men returned home with three obsessions: industrialization, rational management and high-tech weaponry. There have been military governments throughout the Third World, and even when they relinquish the presidencies to civilians, they leave army officers behind in key administrative posts.

Between 1950 and the beginning of the world economic crisis in 1973, the GDP of developing countries grew at 5 percent per year. Their arms budgets grew at 7 percent and their arms import budgets at 8 percent.[25] The 1973 crisis crippled their GDP growth. But the military influence within their governments insisted on a maintenance of arms budget growth. This was yet another factor driving them into domestic and export arms production. From the beginning they understood their chief competitive advantage — cheap labour. To this they could add the absence of domestic political interference in export policies. These advantages are even more striking today, so Third World producers will no doubt continue to expand, proliferating weapons and reducing still further the influence of the main Western producers.

The list of the economic, foreign policy and military disadvantages to the current arms-selling race is almost endless. Secrecy, for example, has always been a factor in assuring a nation's defence. If you had a good weapon, you denied knowledge of it to your enemy. That has gone out the window along with the idea of supplying only your true allies. Today the desperate need to beat the competition by vaunting your products and selling to all buyers has made a nonsense of strategic weapons development.

Defence department experts in all countries would deny this. They would point out that they maintain careful lists of strategic goods and monitor the countries to which sale of these goods is banned. But these lists are unenforced and unenforceable. They are public relations blather. Most of the contraventions go unnoticed or unannounced. Those that do become public scandals are usually examined with outrageous hypocrisy.

In 1983, for example, a Japanese corporation sold the Russians four American-built computer-controlled machine tools to make ship propellers. These tools were on the American strategic ban list. The Director of U.S. government arms sales protested violently. He claimed that Soviet submarines would now be undetectable. A billion dollars would therefore have to be spent in the United States on new detection systems. "When you strip it all away," he lamented, "these people did terrible damage for the sake of making just one more sale."[26]

But if these tools were so strategically important, what were they doing in the hands of a Japanese corporation in the first place? The reality is that in the second half of the 1980s, five thousand machine tools from the Western strategic materials list were sold illegally by various nationalities to the Soviet Union. On top of that America's European partners in COCOM, the NATO-related control arm for strategic goods, want the list cut right back or simply done away with.

Beyond the fantasy of the strategic lists, the situation is even more out of control. For example, Israel has long been selling 35 percent of its military exports to South Africa. Other major clients include Taiwan, Pinochet's Chile, and Iran. Anastasio Somoza's Nicaragua was an important purchaser. In 1983 Brazil sold planes to Nicaragua, thus endangering the Contadora regional peace initiative it had just signed. Vickers of Britain and FMC of the United States have developed an armoured personnel carrier with the Chinese, who immediately set about selling it to Iran. Iran, of course, is on the U.S. and U.K. embargo list. China also sold bombers to both Iran and Iraq, just as France actively sold arms to both India and Pakistan during their last war.

China has recently moved into fourth place in the selling of arms to the Third World.

The Iran-Iraq war provided the clearest illustration of foreign policy standards in the age of armaments economics. Almost everyone condemned the war. But fifty nations sold arms to one side or the other. Twenty-eight of the fifty — including Brazil and China — sold heavily to both. Soviet ground-to-ground missiles were popular with the two armies. Iran, owner of American F-14 fighters, and desperate for spare parts, negotiated with Hanoi to buy the stockpile of planes abandoned in Vietnam by the Americans. The idea was to cannibalize them. Iran did manage to keep ten of its F-14s in the air. The parts must have come from Hanoi, Chile or a U.S. ally. As for Iraq, its main suppliers (for some $50 billion) were the Soviet Union, France, Brazil, South Africa and China.[27]

Elsewhere, Poland and Rumania were selling ammunition to the Nicaraguan Contras, who paid these Communist suppliers with their American aid dollars. And, in a transaction so well-rounded that all participants must have felt free from any link between belief and action, the Chinese government sold $7 million worth of surface-to-air missiles and small arms to the Nicaraguan Contras between 1984 and 1985. This Contra purchase was financed by the government of Taiwan.[28]

All these lists and combinations and transactions fly in the face of common sense. They make nonsense of the idea of foreign policy.

One thing is clear. Our frenzy to save our economies by selling arms has backfired. Not only do we lend such large amounts to purchasers that all real benefit is removed, we also make bad loans. Most of the borrowing countries cannot even meet the interest payments.

Worse still, government financing for Western military industries is so favourable that our industrialists are hard put to choose nonmilitary goods. In France the government was guaranteeing loans up to 85 percent of the contract at an interest rate of less than 7 percent, when commercial rates were permanently over 10. In the United States, the Foreign Military Sales Program will give credits on 100 percent of the contract at 3 percent interest, reimbursable in thirty years.

And yet the result of too many weapons in too many places is a curious feeling in most Western countries that they are inadequately defended. They have been too busy arming both their actual enemies and all possible future enemies.

Since 1950 the flow of arms to — or more recently, within — the Third World has increased at an average rate of about 10 percent per year. In the case of nations who are potential clients but who are technically bankrupt, weaponry is one of the last budget areas subjected to economic restraint. Apparently the IMF doesn't push them to stop buying arms until every other program has been reduced to tattered remains. Poland, for example, a country which can't afford paper to print books, has celebrated its return to democracy by ordering fighters from the United States.

We are now caught in the midst of great economic and moral confusion. Public officials, appointed or elected, of the Left or of the Right, are terrified to speak out against a sector which, according to universally accepted dogma, stands between us and economic collapse. Many of them believe arms production to be a weight tied around our necks. But this is an heretical and therefore secret belief. As a result armaments dominate our economies in a silent, sullen manner, without the public knowing quite what to think.

The standard excuse for an unfortunate action is its necessity. Unfortunately the necessity in question is usually the result of earlier conscious actions. The action is, therefore, not a necessity but an inadvertently chosen result. In public affairs, this embarrassing fact is usually obscured behind the declarative phenomenon *raison d'état*, which voids the idea of responsible government.

And so, as if in a squirrel cage, we keep going around and around, using the same solutions to economic problems with the same results. In the last decade, we have been spared major resource supply problems. Oil prices have moved in our favour. In many countries the level of government services has been reduced and the welfare state partially dismantled. And yet the unemployment rate in Europe rose from 5.8 percent in 1980 to over 11 percent in 1987. Then it began to drop, but very slowly. Unemployment also fell in the United States, but that was largely due to the replacement of full-time employment, offering job security and social protections, by part-time employment based on unsecured labour. More often than not these new jobs involve working at or below the official poverty line. By the end of the 1980s, general unemployment figures were on their way back up throughout the West.

It cannot be proved that this economic state is even partly caused by a reliance on arms production. But it can be established, easily and clearly, that arms production is now the central motor controlling both the speed and the direction of Western R and D, as well as industrial production, high-technology production and employment creation programs.

A glance at the U.S. Commerce Department's figures on orders to American factories shows that month after month the movement is determined by success or failure in the arms business. November 1986, for example, was a good month in American industry, with an increase of 4.1 percent. However, without the military equipment orders, it would have been only 1.3 percent. April 1987 was a bad month. Orders increased only 0.2 percent. Nevertheless, without the military orders they would have declined 0.2 percent. Month after month, the experienced eye darts straight to the military figures to see how the whole economy is doing.

In that context the Strategic Defense Initiative (SDI) takes on an industrial rather than a military hue. Even the President's and the Secretary of Defense's launching of the program didn't sound particularly convincing on the military front. Instead they stuck to listless repetitions of old clichés drawn from centuries of nationalistic vocabulary — "Our activities in space, partially in response to Soviet actions, are predicated on the fact that we must have free access and use of space," Caspar Weinberger said.[29] Pitt the Younger might have sent the same warning to Napoleon: "Our activities on the seas, partially in response to the Emperor of France's actions, are predicated on the fact that we must have free access and use of the seas." Or, indeed, so might Winston Churchill on the same subject in 1914, or Woodrow Wilson on the same subject in 1917. Or Palmerston in 1854 might have thus addressed the Russian czar: "Our activities in the Bosporus, partially in response to Imperial Russia's actions, are predicated on the fact that we must have free access and use of the Bosporus." Or perhaps Britain addressing the Dowager Empress over access to China in the 1890s. Or the Roman Senate addressing Carthage over access to grain in North Africa. Or, indeed, anyone you like, because Weinberger's formula is the eternal standard justification for military action dictated by economic interests.

What the Secretary of Defense really meant was that ad hoc military spending was not having a sufficient impact to get the economy turning without the government relying on a lot of paper to heat up the machinery. And this flood of bonds and junk bonds was even trickier to control. And arms sales were lagging because of new competition from new producers. What was needed was a vast, new industrial strategy — so sophisticated that most of the new producers would be eliminated — to get the United States in particular and the West in general on the move again. Needless to say, that strategy would revolve around military questions. It would be a new version of the Kennedy-McNamara military-industrial initiative of 1961. In 1993 the new Clinton administration tried to strengthen the impression that it was getting a handle on the arms budget by dropping the term SDI — identified with Reagan and the grandiose idea. They reverted to the program's original, boring, bureaucratic name — Ballistic Missile Defense Organization. This was less likely to attract public attention. The actual budget remained unchanged. Indeed, the revised U.S.–France–

U.K. sales pitch, based upon the Gulf War experience, is that lesser arms from lesser countries are a waste of money. Only the leading edge of technology can win.

And yet, when Western economists look at Japan with envy and incomprehension, searching to understand that country's continued economic success, they come up with every answer except the most obvious — the absence of a dominant arms industry. This is not to suggest any particular Japanese wisdom. They were simply kept out of the business by the rules set after World War II. Later, in order to avoid ever slipping back into militarism, they legally limited their defence expenditure to 1 percent of GNP.

This rule has protected the Japanese from the mesmerizing logic of military-inspired R and D, military-directed industrial capacity and military sales export policies. One cannot automatically put their economic success down to this escape, but they are the only developed nation both to have consistently avoided the economic crisis and to have avoided military-based economics. At the very least this is one of the explanations for their success.

The current pressure the West is putting on Japan to assume a greater defence burden and, for that matter, to take part in SDI shows how little we have thought about the role of the arms industry. It isn't really clear why we want Japan involved, if the business is as profitable as we claim. The subconscious implication is that involvement will weaken the Japanese economy in the same way that ours has been weakened. What better way to deal with Japan's economic strength than to draw it into a self-destructive syndrome? On the other hand, given the effectiveness of Japanese production, we will soon be beaten at our own game. What would the West do with its enormous industrial commitment to the export of weapons if everyone started clamouring for Japanese tanks and fighters?

Our reliance upon military economics began as a conscious attempt by technocrats to treat the burden of military expense in the same way that we treat any commercial economic problem — that is, in terms of profit and loss. This approach, they felt, would also strengthen our foreign policies and reinforce our national independence.

But the central theme was economic. Modern weaponry, they argued, was too expensive to be viably produced for the needs of a single nation. It followed that we had to produce more and sell the surplus abroad. As General Michel Fourquet wrote, when head of French military sales, we must *"admit as the basic rule* that its industries *can only live by exporting."*[30] The emphasis is his.

Three decades later our respective independences have not been re-inforced. Our foreign policies have been distorted. And we are mired in an economic crisis which itself is now two decades old. Many ex-planations are given for our persistent problems. But can we avoid asking whether those industries, which have come to dominate our economies over the same period, are not at least partially responsible? Certainly arms production has been given enormous financial and economic support — more than enough to make any viable industry a success. And thirty years is a long trial period for any economic prop-osition.

If part of the responsibility for our economic confusion lies with the weapons industry, is the reason perhaps that arms are not capital goods? They cannot act as an economic motor to drive a fully rounded economy if there are no real costs, no real buyers, and no real return on invest-ment in the form of civil infrastructure. As for singing the praises of the trickle-down effect, this borders on the ridiculous. Why should we tie our industrial investment and development to a method which is both inefficient and reliant upon luck? It is a sign of how flawed the rational system is that we have accepted with docility an economic development strategy which by comparison makes a roll of the dice on the tables of Monte Carlo look like a sure thing. Nevertheless, this system has taken on the form of a squirrel cage. And no one seems to remember how we got in or know how to get us out.

Weapons cannot be transformed into banal economic material be-cause they are not banal economic material. The defence of a nation is one of the few sacred duties of a society, along with such things as the maintenance of justice. You do not sell justice. You do not sell legislative seats. You do not sell off the presidency or the prime min-istership. You do not sell officers' commissions. You do not sell the interests of your country. All of these things are basic to the modern democratic state. It goes without saying, therefore, that you do not sell your own defence.

Weapons are an integral part of a nation's defence. Every important strategist from Sun Tzu on makes clear that the best defence is the avoidance of war through superior leadership. Failing that, it is the fighting of a fast war with as little physical damage as possible. The wise nation or alliance, therefore, keeps its weapons to itself in order to maintain whatever advantages they may offer. It refrains absolutely from arming anyone else.

This armed circumspection helps a nation to avoid the sort of large, destructive wars which go on and on. Those are the conflicts which cause great confusion and dangerous instability in the international military balance.

What, then, of the argument that modern weapons are too expensive to be viable unless there are large production runs? And don't large production runs dictate the need to export? The logic is tempting, but only the most narrowly focused creative accountancy has made weapons appear to be a source of profit. Even in the model case of the old Mirage fighter, if you added in the real costs of R and D, of subsidies, of foreign loans, of industrial investment, of foreign policy initiatives, and of training, you would find that a colossal loss had been made. Wheels, however, had been spun. Money had moved around the world. Men had worked and fighters been produced.

For contemporary economists and administrators, the spinning of wheels may well provide the illusion of economic development. However, the sensible thing to do would be to remove weapons production from the economic sector and put it back where most of it used to be — in the public domain. Until 1914 the history of weaponry was dominated by royal and state arsenals and shipyards. In that context weapons can be treated with the financial disinterest they deserve. They are the unfortunate tools of statehood and the state should assume straightforward responsibility for them. The taxpayer is paying now anyway. So why not eliminate the enormous extra costs created by pretending that arms are capital goods produced in the marketplace for buyers?

The alienation of Western citizenries from their own defence has been one of the most confusing public dramas of the last quarter century. Why did the democracies abruptly decide that they were no longer capable of assuming the costs of their own defence? What had so radically changed in the history of nations? Or in economic principles?

Nothing fundamental had changed. However, a crowd of fresh and clever technocrats had arrived in the American public service from such places as the automobile industry at the same time that a new generation of technocrats took over key positions in France. Their confidence in their new administrative methods had made them believe they could turn weapons into capital goods and make a profit for the government out of national defence.

There is nothing so tempting as alchemy. Every man would like to believe that he has the talent to make gold out of base metal. And the rational approach does result in a sort of alchemy. Weapons are declared to be capital goods. An economic structure is built in order to solidify what is no more than an assertion. The economy is then run as though weapons had changed their fundamental character. It hardly seems to matter that the economy doesn't respond to this new truth. The system is complete and therefore from within seems able to survive any failure. We now have enormous infrastructures dependent on continued weapons sales and so, in the face of continuing economic difficulties, our elites go on repeating all the while that their system works: sales make jobs, sales earn foreign exchange, sales justify R and D, sales pay for weapons at home, sales are a proof of foreign influence. None of this is true, but it doesn't matter. Our elites are convinced that it must be true.

This is modern rhetoric in action. The rise of an armaments-dependent economy demonstrates with clarity how reason at its most sophisticated tends to work. The historic and intellectual evolution from Machiavelli, Bacon, Loyola and Richelieu through to McNamara is perfectly integrated. The resulting elite, which answers rather than asks questions and depends on systems, is at its most impressive. Secrecy, *raison d'état*, the marriage between reason and nationalism, between amorality and the disappearance of personal responsibility — all of these typically rational characteristics are present. In the absence of common sense mechanisms, we are unable to imagine how we might go about changing the situation.

PART II

Scenes from a System That Doesn't Work

Never has failure been so ardently defended as though it were success. Partly because there has been some success. Partly because a civilization which is no more than a system has neither memory nor shape.

Our inexhaustible supply of facts has unexpectedly made everything true and false. The power of expertise has obscured the causes of both success and failure.

Immediate answers and absolute truths are the daily bread of rational civilization. No attempt is made to identify recurring patterns for fear that memory may be reconstituted.

Absolute truths hide in our simplest habits. Standard social analysis begins with government, moves on to the military and then economics. But the Age of Reason has continued the traditional order in which governments follow the trumpets of war.

The Question of Killing

Fighting is the most ancient and consistent of the organized arts, unless you accept prostitution as the doyen. While civil society has been subjected to endless radical reforms, warfare has come through the ages with unchanged principles. More precisely, the principles of war have remained the same; the structures of warfare have changed radically.

Those structural changes were introduced in the eighteenth century with great hope. It seemed as if the professionalizing of the officer corps would remove warfare from its origins: in the mud, that is, wielding clubs. The new rational officer would ensure fast and efficient wars. Great military leaders had always maintained an essential balance between imagination and what might be called professionalism. Here professionalism means the ability to manage the physical realities of an army and of a situation. Imagination means strategy or the innate flexibility needed to make circumstances work in your favour, to surprise the enemy and, of course, to win. The innovations begun in the eighteenth century were intended to institutionalize the professionalism and the strategic skills of the great generals. The new officer corps would then be able to reduce the levels of death and destruction which were involved. The clarity of the process seemed to promise the disappearance of "unnecessary" wars. A cooler analysis of what warfare entailed was intended to eliminate the multitude of emotive factors — superstition, personal pride or ambition, social status — which often seemed to drag us unnecessarily over the line into general violence.

Instead that process has led us full circle, right back into the mud with greater frequency and greater violence than ever before. What's more, there are no signs that our disastrous experiences, such as 1914–18, lead to any important reforms. Rational warfare seems to be short on memory, filled with self-confidence and devoid of both purpose and direction. More to the point, the nature of professional armies has led to the permanent maintenance of armed forces at wartime levels with wartime quantities of weaponry. Reality being far more practical than

theory, the result of the rational approach has been the institutionalization of a permanent state of war.

This century and the nineteenth have sent out paradoxical signals
about the power of the military. Our rhetoric and our constitutions
declare the supremacy of the civil authorities. Our elections and ministerial systems appear to confirm this. And yet the twentieth century,
in particular, is driven by enormous and purely military adventures of a
kind and a quantity unknown under the absolute monarchs. This taste
for continuous adventure began with Napoleon and shows no signs of
going away. And the leading edge of science, administration and industry continues to be dominated by the armies. Rather than allow ourselves to be discouraged by this phenomenon, we have developed an
inverse ratio: as the importance of the military has increased, so we have
found fresh ways to pretend that nothing is happening.

The last two centuries have placed new destructive powers in the
hands of commanding officers. The most obvious is modern weaponry.
But far more important has been the transformation of military mythology from its traditional base of "glorious victory" into something far
more complicated, which twins aimless and stolid technocratic generalship with the elevation of one's own casualties to the status of a
sacrificial rite. This warping of war from a tool of last resort, theoretically aimed at improving a state's nonmilitary position, into a twin-
headed monster of abstract methodology and cathartic bloodletting, is
one of the most unexpected children of reason. In some ways it is linked
to the killing of God and his replacement by both the Hero and the
modern military planner.

Unfortunately, having mentally shoved war aside, civil leaders are
now badly prepared for dealing with its very real presence at the centre
of our lives. This rational daydreaming has left us mentally disarmed,
while the world is physically in battle. Perhaps that is why civil society
so rapidly buries or erases completely any accurate memory of past
violence, as if to pretend that the past is the past and the present quite
different. It is difficult to think of another era in which individuals have
so carefully turned their backs upon the evidence of their own continuing violence by treating each dark event as if it were somehow unexpected — or the last of its kind. And they have done so in the midst of
our millennium's most violent century.

Never has savagery so dogged Western civilization and yet, at the
same time, so actively played the role of catalyst for civil change. Whatever it is that our mythology of scientific discoveries and philosophical
arguments so actively pretend about the evolution of society, it is war
which has led the way and which continues to lead the way in the
twentieth century. Even our technocratic structures first appeared in
the modernization of Europe's armed forces. The first technocrat was

not produced by ENA or Sciences Po or Harvard. He marched out of a military school and his profession was that of a staff officer.

Man's perpetual optimism, encouraged by the rational amputation of memory, permits him to turn away from the evidence of past chronology in order to act as if the future will be one of civil initiative. Perhaps we need to believe that things will be different. But we also need to act in such a way that change is given a chance. And there our denial of reality does nothing to lessen the very real presence of war and of the military leadership it imposes upon us.

One of the great pretenses of the last half century is that we have been at peace. This vision of the world is not so much false as falsely focused. The West has been locked in the grip of a nuclear peace, the only alternative to which was massive, if not total, self-destruction. But the creation of nuclear weapons produced two separate levels of peace and war. For almost fifty years we have had nuclear peace, while gradually slipping into a new sort of conventional world war. However, by limiting our focus to the developed world, we have been able to pretend that there has also been a conventional peace. The result is a perfectly artificial view of what constitutes war.

In the nineteenth century, war was something which involved white people on both sides. If only one side involved whites, then this was picturesque adventure. As for nonwhites fighting each other, that was hardly real. Rather, it was tribal conflict and thought of as a curiosity, of interest principally to eccentrics. Even conflicts between colonial powers were felt to be marginal, unless they threatened to spread to home territory.

Thus an incident between Austria and Prussia involving a thousand or so dead was a war. The fight in the Sudan between the British and the Mahdi, involving far greater losses, was only an expedition. This approach allowed us to think of the last half of the nineteenth century as a period of enduring peace.

The same sort of thinking still serves us well in our determination to ignore the violence which surrounds the West. The eighteen developed nations are indeed at peace with one another. They even managed for almost half a century not to go to war with their principal rival, the Soviet Union. And now the collapse of first the Soviet bloc and then the Union itself has encouraged us to proclaim successive short-lived new dawns and new world orders. It is popularly assumed that the Cold War is over and that even the risk of a nuclear war lies behind us. Nothing, however, proves that either assumption is correct. We have no idea into what form — geographic, political or ideological — the Soviet Union will finally settle. The civil wars in the former Yugoslavia and several of the former Soviet republics may be temporary aberrations or the beginning of widespread disorder. The nuclear and conventional forces remain intact on both sides. The nations of Central Europe may or may not successfully adopt democratic systems and/or liberal economies. Perhaps in a decade all these things will be clear.

Meanwhile, unstable times heighten the risks of war and encourage military adventures. The West is now caught up with the rest of the world in a state of general instability worse than any since World War II. As a direct result military violence, which has been growing steadily outside the West over the last forty years, has accelerated like a malignant cancer. In other words, recent events have encouraged warfare without changing the contradiction of continuing nuclear peace accompanied by an ever-wider and less controllable conventional war.

There was a period in the 1950s and early 1960s when the breakup of the European colonial empires seemed to threaten our illusion of calm. But then a series of solutions was found to still the waters. Countries were created throughout the world on the eighteenth-century European model of the nation-state. United Nations peacekeeping forces were invented — not to solve conflicts but to freeze them in place as unending half conflicts, from the Middle East to Southeast Asia.

At that time the intervention of the UN secretary-general and of a peacekeeping force at least implied that the situation could be handled. Now there are so many wars that it would be physically impossible for the United Nations to intervene in more than a few which become fashionable in the West. The use of peacekeeping forces is rarely considered. In fact, there are so many conflicts today that even international political mediation is a luxury in short supply.

This toleration of high levels of violence in the world at large as a normal part of Western "peace" is not only to be found at the United Nations. Most world, Western, and regional organizations, such as the Organization of African Unity, accept that this is the way the world works. Not with a bang, but with a seething mass of whimpers.

When the current economic crisis began in 1973, there were a handful of conflicts spread around the globe. By 1980 there were thirty or so, and today there are more than forty. Most statistics agree that an average of one thousand soldiers are killed every day throughout the world.[1] If anything, this is a conservative figure, kept down by the impossibility of collecting statistics from many of the ongoing wars. What are the casualties in the Cambodian countryside? In Eritrea? In the Shan States of Burma? No one really knows. A thousand casualties a day is approximately the same as the average number of French soldiers killed daily during World War I.[2] That conflict lasted only five years. Our current levels of violence have been with us for more than a decade. Some five thousand civilians also die every day as a direct or indirect result of war. Three and a half million dead soldiers over the last decade and twenty million dead civilians. And these figures do not include periodic massive massacres, such as in Cambodia.

In other words, most of the world is at war. Only we, a small minority, are exempted. We are the exception, not the rule. And yet we are directly and indirectly involved in this violence, even if the deaths within our own borders are limited to those produced by a few terrorist attacks, some regional revolts such as Ireland and Corsica, and growing levels of organized civil violence. Forty murders a month from gang wars in Washington and another forty in Los Angeles cannot be dismissed as unrelated crimes of passion or of greed.

But they pale beside numbers such as one thousand and five thousand dead daily. These cause our minds to disconnect. The figures are too high. The dead in question are from other civilizations. They are not us. Periodically we manage to focus on one of these disasters for a short time. To manage this we usually need some Western angle — hostages, for example, or the involvement of a Western humanitarian group. From the fervent Christian antislaver, Gordon at Khartoum, to the modern crusading journalist behind the lines with the Mujaheddin or the young doctors of Médecins Sans Frontières, there is an unbroken line.

We did manage to focus, very late in the day and for a brief period of time, on the mass murder of the Cambodians and, for several blinks of the eye, on the war-related starvation of millions of Ethiopians. Of course, we did so as if these people themselves lived on two islands. Nowhere was there a hint of the surrounding peoples also caught up in the disaster — the Akkas, the Karens, the Thai border people or the Sudanese and the Somalis. These people were not seen to be at war or to be dying, both of which they were. Only the starving Ethiopians and the martyred Cambodians caught our eye. In 1991 the unsuccessful uprising of Iraqi Kurds dominated our imagination for a short time thanks to the presence of Western troops and journalists. Tragic photos were published along with figures of between five hundred and two thousand civilian deaths per day. But war-related civilian deaths have been at that level for a long time in Somalia and the Sudan without Western interest moving beyond occasional serious articles.

This ability to focus on one fashionable war at a time allows us to pretend, when the conflict ends, that the world is again at peace. For example, in August 1988 the Russians withdrew from Afghanistan and a cease-fire was announced between Iran and Iraq. Afghanistan had been a popular war because it showed the Soviets to be in trouble. The Iran-Iraq mutual massacre had been going on for years before Western naval intervention in the Gulf won it some general news coverage. By then the casualty levels had already fallen from their worst levels. Both wars ended and Western leaders and journalists proclaimed that the world was moving back from the brink of violence. This, they said, was the summer of peace.

Within a week three to five thousand people had been shot dead in Burma, followed by a fresh army coup; at least five thousand were massacred in Burundi; a series of bombs exploded in Ireland, killing civilians and military, after which IRA activists were shot dead in an ambush; the President of Pakistan was blown up along with a planeload of officials and generals, including the American ambassador; riots in Chile lead to a handful of deaths; there was a violent coup in Haiti; a major battle between the Moroccans and the Polisario guerrillas who are fighting for the independence of the most desolate part of the Sahara, the Rio d'Oro; and the Iraqi army, freed by the Iran-Iraq truce, turned its attention to the Kurdish province, where there was an active rebellion. One hundred thousand Kurdish refugees fled into Turkey. The rebel force was surrounded and eliminated. In the absence of a large Western presence, this earlier Kurdish massacre received little attention, despite the use of chemical weapons on civilians.

Even in Afghanistan, theoretically basking in a new peace, a series of rebel attacks killed dozens of people, which led to a renewal of the war. What we called the Afghani peace was no more than the removal of white soldiers from that war. This list accounts only for violence fashionable enough to be reported. It leaves out the daily casualty levels in a series of ongoing wars from Cambodia and the Philippines to Lebanon, other Kurdish districts, Namibia, Angola, most Central American countries, Colombia, and so on. Curiously enough, no politician or journalist announced at the end of the week that the summer of 1988 had not, after all, been that of peace.

Even the nuclear bomb has been subjected to this division of war into the "real" Western version versus the "imaginary" sort elsewhere. For decades now we have been obsessed — and rightly — by the nuclear race and the ever-more-complex generations of missiles, antimissile missiles and multiple warheads, to the point where we are now dealing with the nuclearization of outer space. The gradual easing of tensions between the East and the West over the last few years has therefore been greeted with enormous relief. But there has never been a very high risk that the Soviets or the Americans, French and British would actually use their weapons.

The practical wild cards are the other nuclear forces proliferating around the world — India, Pakistan, Israel, Egypt, China, South Africa, perhaps Libya. Even Iraq may still be within reach of producing nuclear weaponry. None of these forces will have very sophisticated delivery systems. They don't need them since their targets are neither Washington nor Moscow. Nor, unlike the nuclear forces of the West, are they locked into overmuscled, intricately interwoven balances with their enemies. They could, therefore, actually be used successfully — that is, without necessarily provoking a mutually suicidal exchange. In other words, the immense nuclear forces of the West are almost imaginary, while the real nuclear weapons lie beyond our control in an invisible world of perpetual war and heavy daily casualties.

Our myopia provides us with an artificial peace of mind. It also deprives us of the means needed for dealing with these forces struggling close all around, unless we are prepared to unleash the full force of our military machine. In other words our only strategy for winning is to raise the ante so dramatically that the aftereffects will be beyond evaluation. But wars which are so profoundly destabilizing that they result in more rather than less disorder cannot be considered victories. Our all-or-nothing methodology also obscures the fact that, whether we intervene militarily or not, these are our wars in the practical sense that they are being fought with our economies and our weapons in the context of the Western-inspired nation-state. In our imaginations we cannot see them, but they are there and no real barriers exist to isolate us from their violence.

Only the occasional terrorist attack on our own citizens seems brutal enough to force us to look about. But those rare moments of narrowly focussed consciousness last rarely more than a week. That terrorist attacks have grown in a decade from 175 a year to 1,000 does show that the waves of violence in the world outside the West are breaking ever higher upon our shores. Yet what are a thousand attacks or a thousand deaths a year but a piddling figure when compared with the six thousand soldiers and civilians killed elsewhere every day?

Were it not for television, we would be denied even the forty-eight hours of bathos produced by a bomb in Paris or London. When seven kilos of dynamite kill twenty people in an urban centre, the sound of the explosion cannot be heard two blocks away. When this happened in 1986 in the Quartier Latin in Paris, an area dense with cinemas, bars and restaurants, tens of thousands of people went on happily eating, drinking and queuing up for romantic or political films, perfectly unaware that a few metres away 150 people were sprawled dead, bleeding and contorted on the pavement. And since few of those out entertaining themselves would get home in time for the evening news, only people who were not there were made aware before the next morning that anything had happened.

Except for a few victims, modern terrorism is mainly a media event. People are not killed to set an example. They are killed in order to provide film footage and newspaper copy which will generalize the specific and thus have political impact. And yet these little spurts of blood do remind us of the unacceptable style of violence implicit in modern wars. Our perspective is therefore quite different from that of the seventeenth century, or even the eighteenth. Mirabeau, speaking in Avignon in the early days of the French Revolution, warned that the nature of "national wars" would change war itself. "Our age will be that of wars far more ambitious, far more barbarous than in the past." [3]

Today we tend to explain this barbarism by Clausewitz's dictum: "To introduce into the philosophy of war a principle of moderation would be an absurdity — war is an act of violence pushed to its utmost bounds." But Clausewitz was an innocent bystander. Violence had broken out of its traditional grounds well before he began writing. If anything he was arguing in reaction to the ravages of the Napoleonic Wars, which he had witnessed for twenty years. His idea of absolute war had to be ripped out of context by others in order for it to be presented as a recommendation. What he had actually written surrounded his absolute statement with other equally strong and contradictory declarations. It was a complicated argument designed to eliminate the original apparently unquestionable truth. Clausewitz's theory, as the British strategist Basil Liddell Hart pointed out, was "too abstract and involved for concrete-minded soldiers to follow."[4] And so they simplified him. And used him to justify their already advanced desire to engage in absolute war. Mirabeau had fully understood what was about to happen as the forces of reason seized hold of state power. The old mercenary wars had been followed by the aristocratic wars, all of them fought in ignorance of and indifference to the state of the population in general. And to the extent that war had gone beyond professional bounds to touch the civilian population, it rarely did so for any reason other than to satisfy the individual soldier's personal desires, which would be summarized as sex, food and money. These remained wars between elites. The national wars — those Mirabeau warned of — were meant to be struggles between populations. His error, and indeed ours, has been to focus on the rise of the citizen-based nation-state as the primary reason for the rise of absolute war. The nation-state has played a role, but primarily in the context of the new professional officer class, which saw strategy as an abstraction and war as an increasingly blunt instrument.

This officer class was created to do away with the arbitrary power — and amateurism — of the aristocratic soldier. The professional soldier was to be an employee of the state, thus ending the tradition in which the state was regularly the hostage of successful generals. An obedient professional officer would be the willing executor of the state's wars. Unfortunately, given the new definition of unlimited wars, this also meant that the military leadership would go on, obediently fighting, so long as there were weapons and live recruits. The officer was theoretically no longer an initiator of war, but that meant he was also no longer a restraining factor. He followed orders, while the key powers were passed to the political authority. The experience of the last century, however, has shown the civil authorities consistently unable to assume that responsibility with any greater success than the soldiers and monarchs who preceded them. The gratuitous military and civil massacres which have appeared in the twentieth century for the first time are part of this failure.

Two thousand five hundred years ago, the Chinese strategist Sun Tzu began his theory on warfare as follows: "War is a matter of vital importance to the state. It is mandatory that it be thoroughly studied."[5] And yet outside today's professional military circles and in the absence of a fashionable crisis, the subject is either unmentionable, evoked in a nostalgic, personality-oriented way or highly politicized into black and white positions. It is not something to be carefully considered by citizens as part of their lives. C. Wright Mills was perhaps the first to recognize the growing dichotomy between violence out of control and a public refusal to pay attention. In the mid-1950s, he wrote: "All over the world, the warlord is returning. All over the world, reality is defined in his terms."[6] Mills's ideological bias on the edge of Marxism caused him to misunderstand why this was happening, but he had correctly identified the trend.

Today, when public figures evoke the world's violence, they do so merely to serve immediate purposes. The Reagan administration, for example, used to repeat endlessly that there were forty-two wars in the world, all of them provoked by Soviet ambition. This violence became an argument for increased defence spending. But the reality is that most of these conflicts have never had anything to do with Capitalism or Communism or any other Western ideology. How Saharan nomads, for example, could be devoted to the dictatorship of the proletariat has never been clear, any more than how Buddhist peasant rice farmers could be attached to competitive individualism and the marketplace. This view of the world is so artificial that when our theoretically ideological partners in the Third World become inconvenient, we painlessly change sides, the way we have several times with China. With Ethiopia-Somalia. With Iraq. With Egypt. Even with Cambodia.

Our fairy-tale approach to international conflicts has convinced Westerners that neither they nor their political leaders have the understanding of the mechanisms of war necessary to control it. The result has been a curious low-grade, generalized hysteria. Some thinkers refer to this as a sublimated fear of imminent disaster. On the Right they blame it for the appearance of idealistic movements which offer simple sweeping solutions to complex problems — the Greens, for example, or the movement in favour of unilateral disarmament.[7] There have actually been limited outbreaks of apolitical hysteria. The bomb shelter craze in the United States was an early example.

More recently the West exploded into cheerleader enthusiasm when first Burma, then China, showed signs of change. Here was proof that democracy and capitalism could win without having to go to war. The neurotic nature of this joy could be seen in the sullen confusion which came over us when government troops moved in and opened fire. Rather than pause and attempt to deal with our confusion, we simply rushed on to a new set of emotional superlatives aimed at liberalization in Central Europe. And when that liberalization began to produce nationalist violence and economic collapse, we dashed off to save an absolute monarchy in Kuwait at a cost which might have solved Central Europe's immediate problems. Then we rushed back to give the Soviets voluminous, self-serving and empty-handed advice. The Iraq incident — whatever the merits of the specific issue — unfolded throughout the West to the sound of easy patriotism and hysterical hyperbole from the mouths of government leaders and generals. In this way public debate was effectively reduced to good versus evil and men versus boys. In other words, the level of sensible debate was held down at the level of nineteenth-century jingoism. The citizenry either remained passive or actually cooperated when faced by this approach, which demonstrated the level of confusion inside our complex system.

For example, on a completely separate matter, more than 70 percent of French citizens, when asked, reply that they are for the maintenance of their own nuclear force — the *force de frappe*. More than 70 percent also reply that they are against its use, even in extremis.[8] They seem to be hoping that the crises can be managed one by one. But this belief in management is precisely where the danger lies. With the sole exception of avoiding an actual nuclear war, we have been remarkably incompetent at managing modern military crises. Not only have we made little sense out of nuclear development, but our conventional armies seem constantly to be preparing for wars that they will never fight, while losing most of those they are actually sent to win.

If the Iraq incident is temporarily set aside, the American army hasn't won a war since 1945. With the exception of MacArthur's Inchon leap in Korea, it hasn't even won an important incident. The other two Western interventionist forces — the British and the French — have done little better. The British can claim one important success — Malaya in the 1950s — and the French a few African incidents. Even the chosen strategy of the professional armies — trying to overwhelm all enemies with sheer mass — has failed more often than it has succeeded. And the successes have been so messy that they have created as many problems as they have solved.

This failure of the largest, most extensively trained and best-armed military forces in the history of the world should cause the citizenry to pause to reconsider its assumptions about organized violence. For example, it isn't surprising in this context that modern state structures discourage voting citizens from developing a sense that their political responsibilities include a close and dispassionate control of military affairs. The vast majority of citizens, as well as most of their civil servants and cabinet ministers, do not believe that their own armies are relevant to their lives or to the life of their society. They neither feel responsible for the armies their taxes support nor do they hate them. Most people are simply indifferent.

But no civilization can afford to turn its back upon the mechanisms of violence. The failure of our armies to deal with the modern wars of small guerrilla forces doesn't mean that military organization in general is outdated. It means that our military organization is inappropriate. The refusal to address the question of force because we don't wish to use it merely leaves us naked before those who may wish to use it against us.

8

Learning How to
Organize Death

Nothing particularly new has been said about war since 500 B.C., when Sun Tzu wrote his little book of military instruction. This wasn't read by Westerners until it was translated into French in the second half of the eighteenth century. Immediately his approach began to have an influence on the new, rationalist French thinking about war.

Sun Tzu's genius was such that it still reduces even Bonaparte to nothing more than a general — a man, that is, who can solve problems only by fighting. For Sun Tzu "Those skilled in war subdue the enemy's army without battle. They capture his cities without assaulting them and overthrow his state without protracted operations. Your aim must be to take the opponent's country intact. This is the art of offensive strategy."[1] Clearly he was not talking about offensive strategy as later interpreted by our World War I commanders or, for that matter, by the men who conceived the 1991 Iraq campaign, which began with sixty days of intensive, general bombing and ended with the oil infrastructure aflame and racial disorder.

When Sun Tzu's words are fully digested, it becomes less surprising that numbers alone confer no advantage if an army is properly led. "We have not yet seen a clever operation that was prolonged. For there has never been a protracted war from which a country has benefited." The modern general, indeed the modern Hero, has been unable to swallow that part of the lesson. The greater their genius, the greater their victories, the more they go on fighting. One of Sun Tzu's early disciples wrote: "War is like fire; those who will not put aside weapons are consumed by them." His practical strategy is as fresh today as when he first laid it out in the courts of China. "What is of supreme importance in war is to attack the enemy's strategy. The next best is to disrupt his alliances. The next to attack his army. The worst policy is to attack cities." This brings to mind Mao's early strategy. More important still, it reminds us of the German and Allied strategic bombing of cities, which had no effect. It was used again disastrously in Vietnam and is still the centerpiece of nuclear strategy. Sometimes Sun Tzu's phrases reappear almost word for word in the theories of Liddell Hart and Mao, so that when his ideas are heard for the first time they are immediately familiar. "An army may be likened to water, for just as flowing water avoids the heights and hastens to the lowlands, so an army avoids strength and strikes weaknesses." "March by an indirect route and divert the enemy by enticing him with a bait." "Speed is the essence of war."[2]

His constant underlying message is that generalship has nothing to do with fixed rules and fixed lines. Rather it is based upon a few truths which, when applied by a competent leader, break down into a myriad of actions. "The primary colours are only five in number but their melodies are so numerous that one cannot hear them all."[3]

Given the ponderous bloodbaths of our century and the last half century of leaden nuclear and conventional strategies, one is tempted to dismiss Sun Tzu as an idealist. But the attentive observer discovers the echo — conscious or unconscious — of Sun Tzu in the actions and words of every great modern commander. Napoleon constantly harked back to those secrets of the art "which served me instead of the 100,000 men of which I was short. It is the man, not men, that counts." That quality enabled him to tie much larger armies in knots. "I was too weak to defend, so I attacked."[4] Liddell Hart, perhaps the greatest strategist of this century, found himself restating Sun Tzu's principles: "For the profoundest truth of war is that the issue of battles is usually decided in the minds of the opposing commanders, not in the bodies of their men."[5] He continually ridiculed the "official Clausewitz." To state "that war is a continuation of policy by other means has become a catch-phrase and is therefore dangerous. We can say with equal truth, war is the bankruptcy of policy."[6] And Charles de Gaulle, in his first great military essay, *Le Fil de l'épée,* wrote: "In war, apart from a few basic principles, there is no universal system, only circumstance and personalities."[7]

At the heart of Sun Tzu's theory were mental flexibility, physical mobility, speed and the minimalization of violence and destruction. The commander's complete yet unpredictable vision was an essential element. Success was defined as the resolution of the problem. A simplification permits the division of all subsequent generals into two categories. There are the descendants of Sun Tzu, who could be described as the competent. All the rest can be lumped into the other category — the mediocre, the incompetent, the bureaucratic, the stolid, the victims of circumstance and those who cause unnecessary deaths in their own or the other camp.

The first three Western generals to discover modern, mobile warfare demonstrated their superiority so absolutely that they set the pattern for all the creative commanders who followed. The Duke of Marlborough and Prince Eugene understood little of organization. They were pure soldiers, who rendered the established rules of Western warfare irrelevant by ignoring formal linear tactics. Instead they raced about Europe at the beginning of the eighteenth century in an ungentlemanlike manner, dragging their armies with them and surprising the forces of Louis XIV, who imagined them far away. Frederick the Great later made the same use of speed. But he also inherited one of the first bureaucratic states, on whose foundation he created a professional army devoid of amateurs and mercenaries. Despite his peculiar pseudophilosophical relationship with Voltaire, he was as absolute a monarch as could be and he used his bureaucracy to reinforce that power. He was the first model for the technocratic-based dictator of the twentieth century, while Marlborough and Prince Eugene were the models for the wild card, which in this century turned up soldiers like the American George Patton and the German Heinz Guderian, who led the tank charge through France in May 1940.

In the wake of these three men came the flood of reason. The desire of those who seized it for military purposes was admirable. They were disgusted by having to fight in unprofessional armies under the orders of unqualified aristocrats, who as often as not might be incontinent dukes or ignorant children. These apostles of reason had themselves been forced to struggle as young officers out on the battlefield, where they were literally crippled by the cumbersome official strategies and tactics of their time, while Frederick humiliated and decimated them. Rather than blunder on or sink into depression, they sensed that there was a better way. And that way was dependent upon the exploitation of man's reason.

The Marquis de Bourcet began the process by creating a staff college — the first in the world — in Grenoble, and by writing his *Principles of Mountain Warfare* in 1764. That administrative school was far more than the first staff college. It was the first modern administrative school of any sort. That is to say, the military began training technocrats almost a century before government administrators started down the same road and 150 years before the first business school appeared. As for Bourcet's *Principles of Mountain Warfare,* it was to have a great influence on Bonaparte, inspiring his most brilliant campaign — the Italian.

In rapid succession after Bourcet came three French generals — Saint-Germain, Gribeauval and Guibert. The Comte de Saint-Germain was a radical defence minister. He was in and out of power several times as he struggled against court intrigues and the opposition of the military establishment. Although an aristocrat himself, his aim was to change the French army from one based upon class to one led by a professional officer corps. Jean-Baptiste de Gribeauval was the first general to help Saint-Germain make this change possible. His creation of a modern artillery laid the foundation for Napoleon's artillery, the single element Bonaparte is often credited with creating himself. In reality he merely exploited with brilliance an inherited machine. And behind Gribeauval came the Comte de Guibert, who linked the idea of professionalism solidly to reason and to strategy. He published his *General Essay on Tactics* in 1773, and it immediately had an enormous impact. The purpose of his book was to show how mobile warfare could be fought. Twice he was called to serve beside Saint-Germain at the ministry. During these terms he laid the entire framework for the modern army which the revolutionaries and Bonaparte would exploit. During both he was under constant attack.

His first appointment lasted two years, by which time the fury of the military establishment was so great that he was sent off for ten years to do regimental duty. He used that decade of exile to think and to write. His ambition was to link his idea of good soldiering with that of moral service and he demonstrated that link in his "Eulogy to Chancellor Michel de l'Hospital." Hospital had been a beacon of honesty and service in the sixteenth century, when, as head of government, he had attempted to prevent the religious wars that were to dog France for two centuries. Guibert's eulogy to Hospital was, of course, a way of attacking the court of Louis XVI. The attack wasn't particularly subtle and its success was so immediate and so great that Guibert was made a member of the Académie Française.

This was the only period in the academy's history when it served change rather than established power. The ceremony which welcomed Guibert in was the most spectacular in living memory and somehow became a manifestation for the power which enlightened circles were beginning to feel in 1786. Overnight Guibert had become the star of Paris intellectual life and thanks to this impetus was called back into the ministry a year later. Again the courtiers blocked much of what he attempted to do.

His linking of both military professionalism and strategy with reason and morality created a great dilemma — one which is still with us. But, then, why should changes come onto the scene pure and unfettered? In fact there is a remarkable if curious unity to the events which first brought mobile warfare into modern Western history and then gave birth to two types of strategy. One was aimed at generals trying to manipulate large armies. The other was the negation of formal warfare and is now known as guerrilla warfare. Both of these strategies arose largely out of the struggle to defend and to destroy Pascal Paoli's republic in Corsica.

Corsican by birth, Bonaparte had been brought up in the shadow of men who had used guerrilla tactics to fight European armies. His own father had been one of Paoli's chief officers and had fought for the first Corsican republic right up to its destruction at Ponte Nuovo. Paoli's army had used the *macchia,* the island's rough, impenetrable hills, as their principal weapon, the way others would later use the jungle. This strategy was so surprising to the French army that they corrupted *macchia* into *maquis* as a generic term describing guerrilla warfare. However, the only French officer to draw any practical conclusions from the constant mauling of their large, classical force by the small and usually invisible Corsican army was the Comte de Guibert. His role as a young officer in the expedition had been to command a band of Corsican irregulars who fought for the French against Paoli's republic. In the battle of Ponte Nuovo Guibert commanded the troops that captured the bridge, thus deciding the fate of the island. In writing his *General Essay on Tactics* he was greatly influenced by this war, which, although won by the Europeans, was won only because the Corsicans had grown more confident with each battle they won and finally had given in to the false pride of trying to fight like Europeans. At Ponte Nuovo they had come down out of the *maquis* and exposed themselves to formal battle in the restrained conditions of static warfare.

Born a few months after Ponte Nuovo, Bonaparte was sent as a teenager to the mainland to become a French officer and was thus exposed to Guibert's new methods. He rediscovered in them the flexibilities and indirectness of his heritage; but the simple Corsican use of mobility had now been absorbed and reformed by a European professional. The endless movement which was to give Bonaparte his control of Europe was in fact Corsican guerrilla tactics, transformed and expanded by Guibert into a strategy fit for large armies and then applied by Bonaparte, a man who had since childhood breathed the tactics of absolute mobility. It was a natural marriage.

This unity of source went beyond Bonaparte and the French. During the second Paoli government, which declined into an unhappy dependence upon the English, there was one bright spot. London sent a young colonel called John Moore to train the Corsicans in formal warfare. Like Paoli, he fell foul of the intrigues and ambitions of Elliot, George III's technocratic representative. He was expelled from Corsica by Elliot in the same month as Paoli. But in the short period of his command, his ideas were overwhelmed and reformed by what he discovered on the spot. Having come to teach, Moore took away with him new ideas. It was he who began the reform of British fighting methods. He created the Light Brigade, whose flexibility laid the groundwork for the Peninsular Campaign. After Moore's death in 1809 at Corunna, his methods were taken up by the man who replaced him — Arthur Wellesley, who was to become the Duke of Wellington. What Wellington added to Moore's tactics and strategy were his own experiences of mobile warfare in colonial India. Thus the gradual evolution of the European war towards a reckoning between Bonaparte and Wellesley was in a way a reckoning between two blown-up and somewhat formalized interpretations of Corsican *maquis* warfare.

The interesting point is that, again and again, the advances of mobile warfare in Europe have been made possible by the infusion of foreign experiences through a small and marginal section of the various officer corps. The suffocating weight of first the courtiers, then the staff officers, has been such that without foreign air no creative methods have been possible. The military history of the last hundred years is filled with foreign infusions. Each time the weight of military bureaucracy has succeeded in neutralizing these changes.

The fate of Guibert's reforms is the primary example. He had used reason to organize a modern army capable of mobile strategy. He was trying to remove incompetence and mediocrity by introducing a structure which promoted only the real soldiers. But the lesson drawn by civil authorities thirty years later, after the Napoleonic adventure, was that the combination of professionalism with genius created dangerous men. Genius suddenly appeared to be the enemy of stability, even though the central justification for creating an army based upon the principles of reason was precisely to harness that genius in the service of the nation. Abruptly the authorities inverted the purpose of professionalism and used it as a structure designed to eliminate genius. That is, they removed professionalism's very reason for existence — the creation of soldiers who can win — and reduced it to a talent for bureaucratic organization.

This was perhaps the inevitable result of the rational idea developed by Machiavelli and Richelieu. They had seen the development of professional armies as a way to create apolitical officers. History until then had been filled with political soldiers who used every personal success as an excuse to challenge established authority. But Guibert and Saint-Germain came along at the end of almost a century of military obedience. Earlier, in his *General Essay on Tactics,* Guibert had written:

> If by chance, there appears in a nation a good general, the politics of the ministers and the intrigues of the courtesans will take care to keep him away from the soldiers in peacetime. They prefer entrusting their soldiers to mediocre men, who are incapable of training them, but rather are passive and docile before all of their whims and beneath all of their

systems. . . . Once war begins, only disaster can force them to turn back to the good general.[8]

The effect of rational reform was not to eliminate this problem, but to expand it, so that Guibert's attack on the ancien régime came to apply with even greater ease to the authorities responsible for the Crimean War, the First World War, the Second, the Indochinese, the Vietnamese and almost any other. And it applies today to the command of our Western armies.

Reason, unable to cope with genius, had wed itself to mediocrity. Guibert and the other creators of the modern army all imagined a professional staff which would make the successful undertaking of war technically and materially possible, thus freeing a separate level of professional commanders to fight the war. Instead the various national staffs began leapfrogging, one over the other, to ever greater size and power. This began after Napoleon's defeat of Prussia. The Prussians attributed much of his superiority to his Gribeauval–Saint-Germain–Guibert organization. They set about catching up, and this led to the German General Staff, whose moments of glory were 1870 and 1914. Not only defeated but humiliated in 1870, the French propelled themselves further into reliance on a military bureaucracy. Shortly before World War I they managed to produce a staff-command tandem not all that different from the German model. It was Foch's period as commander of the Ecole de Guerre Supérieure which fixed in place this link between staff and command. As for England, even the Crimean disaster wasn't enough to provoke a real desire for change. In the 1860s half the officers' commissions were still being purchased. And as late as 1898, Kitchener's defeat of the Mahdist forces in the Sudan seemed to confirm that everything was still all right.

The Sudanese campaign appeared at the time to be a victory of Western know-how and technology over fearless Muslims. Moreover, Kitchener had the aura and dash of a modern Hero. He was solitary, somehow mysterious and devout. His manner was that of a great commander. In reality he was devoid of strategical and practical battlefield skills. He was an engineer and spent two years pedantically building a defended railway towards the Mahdist capital at Khartoum. When he finally got there, the deciding Battle of Omdurman was, as a leading war correspondent said, "not a battle but an execution." Thanks to machine guns and dum-dum bullets (which explode on impact, thus converting marginal wounds into fatal hits), the Anglo-Egyptian force was able to kill 10,800 while losing only 48 men. This apparently brilliant victory obscured the slow and heavy-handed methods of the winner, to say nothing of the inferiority of the enemy army. The power of well-led guerrilla forces and the neutralizing effects of an equally large and pedantic force on the other side therefore both came as surprises over the next fifteen years.

The first shock came almost immediately, in South Africa, where the virtually criminal amateurism of the British provoked a movement towards reform. Their campaign was similar to that of the Americans in Vietnam, except that in the end the British didn't lose. Although massively outnumbering the Boers and equipped with the latest weaponry, they didn't know how to read maps, often didn't even have maps, didn't understand the nature of time or movement or circumstance; in fact, didn't understand anything except a line charge. What was needed, apparently, was thorough staff training. Whatever the American problem may have been in Vietnam, it wasn't lack of staff training. It was probably the opposite. The interesting point is that the incapacity of the two armies to operate against the enemy was identical. In any case, the effect of the Boer experience was to launch the British into a ten-year frenzy of staff training. And only a fool would deny that they were in desperate need of administrative training relating to movement and supplies, to say nothing of the development of shared means of communication and integrated methods of action.

But had the British looked a little closer at their difficulties in South Africa, they would have seen that their real problem had been not amateurism — although that had been a serious handicap — but a misunderstanding about the nature of battle. As the French General Gambiez wrote seventy years later: "The Boers, not having read Clausewitz, tried all the indirect methods."[9] That is to say, they used flexibility and common sense. They were eventually beaten by Kitchener, who again applied slow, heavy-handed methods which included concentration camps and a scorched earth policy. The English military, however, became fixated not on their strategic defeats but on the details of their amateurism. They decided to concentrate on organizing the efficient application of their classical and awkward strategies. Had they looked closer still at the evolution of the German and French staffs, they would have discovered clear signs that that kind of reform led not to greater professionalism but to a dangerous form of bureaucratic logic.

These trained British officers, led by the General Staff, were, in Liddell Hart's words, intended to provide "a collective substitute for genius, which no army can count on producing at need."[10] The positive side of such integrated and formal training was that it created a shared methodology and a shared vocabulary. Communications were facilitated. Mutual understanding was assured. To take one of the most hackneyed examples of the old versus the new, the charge of the Light Brigade during the Crimean War down the wrong valley as the result of a misunderstood instruction was unlikely to be repeated. Sir William Robertson, Chief of the Imperial General Staff during World War I, said afterwards that thanks to their shared methods of administration, he had been able to telegraph to commanders everywhere without fear of misunderstanding. [11]

But given the mediocrity of the command, as enforced by the staff system, these shared methods and this shared vocabulary had the effect of reinforcing their constant errors. Staff administration provides a collective means of action and eliminates either singular or collective questioning.

Robertson also said, with great satisfaction, that common methodology kept them from panicking in difficult moments. The control of emotions and the prevention of panic is always presented by technocrats as a sign of their professionalism. To this day one of the first ploys used by professionals, when caught in public debate with nonprofessionals, is to suggest that the amateurs have panicked and that it is ignorance which leads to panic.

But a reexamination of the argument of professional cool over amateur panic, which was first used to great effect during World War I, leads one to question its value. Wouldn't it have been better for the staffs of the various armies to have panicked, instead of duly carrying on their mutual and pointless murder of the men under their command? Is not the inability to panic a sign of stupidity or of some serious character flaw?

The ability not to panic has been turned into one of the great virtues of the last hundred years. Not only military, but all sectors of leadership are judged on this ability. Everywhere we hear businessmen, bankers, bureaucrats, politicians and generals calming us with expert tones; indicating that we may relax and follow their expert lead. The rational method has become the cool approach of the insider.

What is this air of superiority based upon? Where are the examples to prove that cool knowledge advances the cause of civilization? In reality the ability to panic has always been one of the great strengths of those in positions of command.

To panic doesn't necessarily mean to turn and run. Intelligence and a sense of dignity usually allow the maintenance of external composure. Self-doubt combined with dignity is central to competent leadership. A man or an organization, even a society, capable of profound, internal panic is able to recognize when he or it is on the wrong track and perhaps to identify the error by giving in to the need for complete reevaluation. Out of that reevaluation may come the right track.

The man of reason, as we currently understand him, is incapable of this panic. He carries about within himself such expertise and structure that he has absolute assurance. Thanks to his intellectual tools, he can always prove, even when surrounded by self-generated disaster, that he is right. If on the field of battle — military or civil — things do not work out, then the circumstances are at fault. The commander of reason is equipped with sufficient self-confidence to persist no matter how wrong he is. Sooner or later — he can prove it — reality will see the light.

The ability to respond to circumstances — Sun Tzu's key to strategy — is only possible, of course, if the leader is able to scramble his preconceptions. The internal strength required to let oneself panic lies at the heart of that ability. Not only has twentieth-century military training ignored that strength. It has concentrated actively on stamping out any signs of such individual intelligence in the professional officer.

Like a Neanderthal emerging from his cave into the light of day, the staff officer walked into the twentieth century bearing the club of death, its handle carved from reason. This handle enabled him to manipulate predigested arguments with self-serving vocabulary, and so to emerge from the war of 1914–18 with his reputation virtually unscathed. The protective mythology he created pinned blame for the war's disasters on an imaginary race of old-fashioned, conservative generals. In reality World War I had been conceived and, at the senior level, waged by the new men on every front except perhaps the Russian. It was the first battlefield encounter of the competing, fully developed modern staffs.

The most professional among them was the German. Senior command and administrative functions had been rolled together in Berlin and maintained in a perfectly abstract separation from the fighting officers. This extreme abstraction actually gave them an initial advantage. It meant they had a complete concept — the Schlieffen Plan, named after Field Marshal Alfred von Schlieffen, Chief of the General Staff from 1891 to 1906. The Plan had been waiting, perfect in every detail, for almost a decade before it was used. In other words, the German General Staff was, if anything, overprepared. When they threw their idea into motion, it rolled forward with great velocity as far as its logic could carry it. But when that perfect logic ran up against reality on the banks of the Marne, the whole machine stopped dead. The members of the General Staff had been guilty of the most basic military error. They had tried to change circumstance to meet their strategies, rather than the opposite.

The French army had the advantage of being marginally less organized than the German, as well as being filled with colonial officers who undermined the Paris staff approach. This meant there was just enough room for individual initiative to allow one colonial *maquis* fighter (General Joseph Gallieni, Governor of Paris, who had made his name during the conquest of Indochina and then annexed Madagascar thanks to a particularly original campaign) to push another (Joseph Joffre, who, although of mediocre talent, was an expert in movements) into doing something that was in neither the staff manuals nor the staff mentality. Gallieni and Joffre stopped the Germans by acting irrationally. You could even say they succeeded by panicking. Had the French army already been in the hands of Foch and his friends, the disorderly but brilliant manoeuvre now known as the Taxis of the Marne, would have been impossible. And the war would probably have been lost.

Although the British had begun to take staff training seriously long after the French, they caught up so quickly during World War I that all originality was virtually eliminated. In fact, the British staff were well served in the early part of the war by having a commander in chief — Kitchener — who had no staff training. The full contradiction between his Heroic, inspiring exterior and the reality of his plodding methods finally came to a head. While he managed to remain popular with the population at home, those in the know were filled with despair. As a result the two rising staff officers, Douglas Haig and William Robertson, would later be able to defend their own incompetence by recalling how things had been when Kitchener was in charge.

The war was hardly a year old before it became clear that the only sectors in which there was room for some originality were those distant from the European capitals. Like technocrats of all sorts, Staff generals don't like to travel far from the centres of power. Absence is one of the few effective weapons which can be used against them. It was hardly surprising, therefore, that the only interesting campaign of World War I took place in the Middle East, under General Edmund Allenby. Or that the most interesting campaign of World War II also took place on the same ground under General Claude Auchinleck and General Archibald Wavell; or, indeed, even farther away under General Slim in the Far East. In Europe, however, the full weight of staff solidarity during World War I ensured almost five years of slow, methodical battlefield encounters danced to the music of butchery.

The degree to which Kitchener was used as a scapegoat by the new men can be seen in the command statistics. When the war broke out in 1914, forty of the forty-five senior command positions in the British Expeditionary Force were occupied by Staff College graduates. Fourteen of those forty had actually been professors at the college. And four of the key figures — including Haig and Robertson — had commanded the college. From the firing of the first guns in August 1914, the strategic and administrative leadership was in the hands of men who were the very flower of modernity.

The philosophy of their school can best be understood by comparing two of its star graduates. Haig and Allenby both went as students to the Staff College in 1896. Both ended their careers as peers of the realm and as field marshals. But it was Haig who had had great power, having commanded in Europe, where he was ultimately second only to Foch and largely responsible for successive disastrous campaigns. Allenby, on the other hand, had won his Middle Eastern war quite handily. The staff dealt with this by presenting his campaigns as extraneous rather than essential.

Haig had all the characteristics of the worst staff officer. Allenby had many of the best. If the system had really worked reasonably and dispassionately, rewarding the best and weeding out the worst, their careers would have been inverted. In fact, had the system worked at all, Haig would never have been promoted beyond colonel.

Allenby (nicknamed "Bull") was strong-willed, but also outgoing and warm. He was thus able to deal with other officers and to inspire his men. Haig was shy, unable to make an impact on others and eager to keep apart. Only by aloofness or secrecy could he disguise his weaknesses and succeed via paperwork and manipulation. Even when finally named to command the British forces in Europe, he rarely left his headquarters. Allenby was widely read, a student of ornithology, passionate about music. His perception was great, and his interests stretched far beyond warfare. Haig had a one-track mind, "like a telescope,"[12] fixed on soldiering. He had no other interests. The result was that Allenby generaled with a certain humanity and with the common sense that comes of recognizing the world in which violent events are taking place. Haig, on the other hand, was a narrow general, absorbed by technique and not so much indifferent to the human element of soldiering as unaware of it. He worked long hours, but in spite of this effort and application, he was slow on the uptake and showed neither imagination nor understanding. In their place he had contacts. He worked very hard at getting to know people who could help his career, including the Prince of Wales. Haig was, in fact, the perfect early model of the technocrat.

Allenby, on the other hand, was the sort of man a technocrat distrusts. For example, although both men were strong-willed, Allenby was open to the opinions of others. Haig had his mind closed up within his own misplaced self-confidence. And while it would be foolish to say that Allenby was not ambitious, Haig was literally consumed by ambition.

This pattern of conflict, between successful staff officers and competent leaders, has continued to repeat itself as the century unfolds. The originality of the young Wavell was criticized in the years just before World War I by his Staff College commandant, William Robertson. And General J. F. C. Fuller, one of the fathers of the revolutionary tank strategy, had to try twice before getting into the Staff College. Once in, he was convinced that he would not graduate. Only the outbreak of World War I saved him from this humiliation. The commandant of the college at that point was Launcelot Kiggel, the man who later became Haig's chief of staff. More precisely, Kiggel was the man who first visited the Passchendaele swamp after having sent 250,000 of his own men to their death in it. The shock of actually seeing what had seemed so rational on a map at headquarters was too much for him. He broke into tears and cried: "God, God, did we really send men into that?"

Much of World War I was fought under the banner of Foch's offensive strategy. He was certainly more intelligent than Haig and was not a technocrat of the secretive sort. Foch even had a sort of charisma which came from an inflexible, undentable optimism. Describing in 1921 how he had commanded the Allies, Foch said: "The war demonstrated that in order to win we needed to have a goal, a plan and a method." He then stopped himself, went back, and rephrased the sentence: "The war demonstrated the need for the command to have a goal, a plan and a method."[13] In other words he specifically and consciously removed the sole element which mattered — fighting to win — and replaced it with concern over the power of the senior officer. In his mind war was not about victory but about administration. His three tools of command were bureaucratic and inflexible. He made a great deal of the need for a commander to have tenacity, but in his context it merely became a reinforcement for rigidity. All this is the exact opposite of the principles laid down by the great strategists from Sun Tzu to de Gaulle.

Foch was in many ways the father of the modern French staff college. He first went there as a professor in 1895. From 1908 to 1911 he commanded the school and set the general intellectual pattern for what would follow in the trenches. "A battle won," he said, "is a battle in which one does not admit one is beaten." "You must act, because only that will give results." His strategy of "attack, always attack" was a replacement for thinking. Foch had been educated by Jesuits and was a strong admirer of their methods. His devotion to the idea that war could be run from headquarters wasn't unlike that of Loyola, who, once elected superior general, stayed in Rome until his death sixteen years later.

That World War I was a strategic disaster is now commonly accepted. Blame, however, has not been clearly assigned. It was the staff who made all decisions. These were arrived at abstractly, on paper, and were communicated in writing to the field commanders. Field officers, who dared to warn headquarters that these orders would result in disaster, were religiously ignored. Headquarters felt it more important to preserve what they saw as the essential chain of command — the common language, common method, common panic-suppressing chain of command. If, however, the results of a battle proved that the field officer's warnings had been right, then that officer — providing he had survived the carnage — was usually fired.

General Ferry, French field commander in 1915, heard rumours of an impending gas attack — the first of the war — and warned his superiors, as well as the British and Canadians on his flanks. His headquarters was furious. They instructed him not to deal directly with the Allies, but to limit himself to the proper reporting procedure. They also said he was a fool to believe, let alone report, such rumours. After the gas attack he was fired.

Shortly before the Germans attacked Verdun, beginning the bloodiest battle of the war, rumours reached the Minister of War that the local defence system was defective. These rumours had come from officers who had been unable to get the attention of their commander, Joffre. Thanks to an enquiry from the Minister, the defects now had his attention. Joffre chose to ignore them. Instead, he demanded that the Minister reveal the source of the rumours. The officers responsible had, after all, disregarded hierarchy. The Minister provided their names. They were duly fired. The Germans attacked. The defence crumbled.

Meanwhile, the various staffs on all sides worked long hours, sending reports, computing statistics, developing plans for unseen battlefields and sending off orders for these carefully organized battles. Twenty-one million men were mobilized in 1914. By 1918, 68 million had been mobilized. All along the staff claimed that this was not enough. They destroyed ministers and governments by manipulating information to make it seem that there were never enough men. And yet 68 million men in uniform represented a triumph of organization. The world had never seen anything like it. In truth, the generals did not have enough live bodies to play the various roles in their battlefield scenarios. They could have used more; but then that is a characteristic of modern organization. It is absolute in its statements of need and infinite in its ability to expand. The generals of World War I never had enough men in exactly the same way that today's generals never have enough equipment.

Not only did the generals have no sense of movement, they had no understanding of why they fought the battles. Before Foch's Somme campaign, General Fayolle wrote: "The battle he is dreaming of has no point. Not even to break through."[14] One million two hundred and fifty thousand men died on both sides in that single campaign. Six and a half million shells were fired by the French alone.

The only way to understand such insane events is to understand the minds of the commanders. They genuinely believed that they were on the side of right and that right took the form of a structure. Their devotion to methodology made them crusaders in a great battle for the advancement of man. A disinterested outsider might have pointed out that they seemed to be lacking the one essential talent for a general — the ability to win. Only their sense of structure had got them where they were.

When war struck, these uniformed technocrats had been obliged to command. In the absence of what Sun Tzu called strategical sense, they avoided absolute disaster by simply throwing live bodies at the enemy. This wasn't the reaction of panicked men. They were perfectly serene in their belief that this was the right thing to do. They had prepared themselves for this approach well before 1914. As early as 1909, Haig had talked of a long war in which the enemy would gradually be worn down. Robertson, as commandant of the Staff College, discouraged original thinking, which he believed had "no connection with the rough and bloody work of masses of men trying to kill each other."[15] Only Foch had thought and written about strategy, yet he also believed in throwing unlimited herds of men at the enemy.

The sheer volume of pointless carnage during World War I drew an angry but confused response from normal people. So important and widespread a division between reality and appearance — between winning wars and commanding armies — had not been seen in Western society since the last decades of the divine-right monarchies. Even then the division had been far less shocking, far less complete. For a real comparison one has to go back to the worst days of Church corruption before the Reformation. Then a vocabulary of devotion and purity was used to sponsor a world of disbelief, physical pleasure and profit making. Once the Reformation began, the same vocabulary was used to justify an unending series of massacres on both sides.

Our contemporary division had been out in the open only since 1914. But the rational form has so deeply occupied our languages and other means of communication, through the tools of perfect logic, that reality is often reduced to a minor component. It is as if Galileo's equipment and knowledge had changed sides and were suddenly being used to marshal all his powers of observation, demonstration and argument to prove that the sun moved around the world. Reason, structure, calm and process are now the tools of established power and conventional wisdom. And in times of crisis, conventional wisdom becomes the absolute truth of ruling elites. It gives them the confidence to go on because it eliminates the need for thought or doubt, which in turn allows the elites to categorize any attempts at either as naïveté or treason. The average man, witness to a barbaric massacre, is left to scratch about in search of some new means of communication which will allow him to express the obvious.

The point, however, is not the indifference of professional armies to the lives of their soldiers. There is nothing personal in this indifference. It's simply that the staff approach tends naturally towards large, blunt methods. There is no profound difference between the way it uses men or explosives. The only change over the last eighty years has been a growing political cost tied to losing large quantities of men. The staffs have therefore shifted their emphasis to equipment and explosives without — as the Iraq episode demonstrated in 1991 — abandoning their devotion to the massing of men. The rational substitution for motivation and strategy is an unlimited quantity of firepower, machinery and men. Throwing massive quantities of one or more of these elements at the opposing side is meant to either overwhelm them or wear them down. This is not strategy. It is a return to mythological barbarism.

Firepower is perhaps the most interesting element of the three, because it is the approach preferred by most modern elites. Its attractiveness lies in its abstract and quantifiable nature. It removes the unpleasant need for physical contact and visible violence. The only difficulty is that massive shelling and bombing didn't work in World War I. They didn't work in World War II either. They failed in Indochina and Vietnam and were marginally relevant in Iraq. But technocrats tend to reject the idea of linear development. Memory is irrational. Each problem is proper unto its own argument. If someone were to point out that bombs had already been dropped in massive quantities in other places at other times and failed to have the desired effect, the technocrat-officer would simply explain that, until the moment at hand, the explosives had been wrongly used.

The apparent love World War I commanders bore for equipment wasn't without paradox. For example, they collected up masses of tanks during the war, between the wars and during the early stages of World War II. And then they blocked the intelligent use of those tanks. What concerned them was not how the tank might best be used but how it might best be controlled by the staff structures.

It could be argued that during the entire European campaign of World War I, there were only three examples of good and telling action. The blocking at the Marne inspired by Gallieni was one. Liddell Hart attributes two others to Churchill: the mobilization of the British fleet before war was declared, which began the starvation process that broke Germany five years later, and the landing of three thousand men in Belgium behind the Germans, who were racing towards Paris in 1914. The landing was accompanied by leaks of false information which inflated the figure to forty thousand. It caused the Germans to look over their shoulders and slow down. The next five years consisted of slugging imposed from headquarters.

The technocrat, however, lives by the fictional reorganization of circumstances. Field Marshal Sir Douglas Haig therefore undertook to complete the official version of history. After the peace he set up a friendly committee to report on staff organization during the war. Its report concluded: "The outstanding feature of the evidence brought before us has been the success of the work of the Staff throughout the war. This points indubitably to the soundness of the general principles on which the Staff is organized."[16]

It is difficult to assign any level of emotional value to this five-year reign of the staff officer. For example, between Haig, Foch and the German commander general Erich Ludendorff seventy-five years ago, and Pol Pot today, there is remarkably little difference. In common they have their self-righteousness, their obsession with secrecy, their ambition, their conviction of the justice of their mission, their readiness to sacrifice any number of men and their honest belief in the necessity of other people's deaths. There was a time when English admirals were hanged for losing battles. From 1914 on, Western nations instead took to hanging medals on the chests of incompetent commanders.

9

Persistent Continuity at the Heart of Power

It is generally assumed that from the point of view of military competence, things got better after 1918. That despite a bad start for the
Allies, both sides were better generalled in the Second World War than
in the First. That the Staffs were more or less kept under control.

And yet it took the same number of years to defeat a Germany which
began both far weaker than it had in 1914 and far weaker than the Allies
in 1939; a Germany weakened by the self-inflicted decimation of large
sections of its own population and numerically outnumbered by at least
three to one in 1940 and ten to one in 1943. Even after the Normandy
landings in 1944, when the Allies had absolute and permanent domination of the skies and the seas, as well as overwhelming advantages in
all forms of equipment, our generals still took almost a year to advance
ponderously across only one-third of Europe.[1]

The lesson our military professionals drew from the two world wars
was that there were worse things than being outgeneralled by the other
side. No matter how mediocre the leadership, an army equipped with
superior quantities of men, explosives and equipment would eventually
win if it had the tenacity and the political approval to keep pounding
away. Our generals seem incapable of unlearning this unfortunate lesson. And yet they have stumbled over the last half century through a
myriad of stalemates, losses and pyrrhic victories. In short, while they
eke out costly victories in full-scale wars, they are unable to adjust to
the small, unpredictable wars which have gradually spread around the
planet.

During World War II people were thankful that the commanders
showed some restraint in sending their troops off to be slaughtered.
Most of those generals had been junior officers in the trenches in the
previous war and so were sensitive to the question of casualties. However, this laudable self-control tells us nothing about the central point,
which was Germany's astonishing strength.

Perhaps the explanation is that while both sides suffered equally from the generalized bloodbath of World War I, it was rendered unbearable for the Germans by their defeat. That crisis temporarily broke the logic of the Age of Reason. Out of the fissure of shame and despair and dead beliefs emerged two sorts of men. One was the lunatic — the Nazi. The other was the pure officer, eager to use the forces of reason but by no means their prisoner. In normal times the lunatic would have been laughed at and the good soldier broken by the power of the staff. The Allies, on the other hand, were obliged actively to maintain the pretense that they had won the First World War and, therefore, that men like Foch and Haig had been good soldiers. Twenty years later the emotional and intellectual liberation-cum-anarchy provoked by Germany's defeat was matched on the battlefield against the imprisoning effects of the Allied victory. The result in 1940 was a perfect illustration of Sun Tzu's belief that wars are won in the minds of the commanders.

Nevertheless the strategic innovations which led to the German victory had begun in Britain with Basil Liddell Hart, who had been the first to write about a fast, deep-penetration tank strategy. He began in 1919 with an article in the *RUSI Journal*, drawing on the German use of tanks in their March 1918 offensive — itself a spark of desperate innovation produced by three and a half years of General Staff failure. Liddell Hart went on regularly trying to influence his government and the War Office. Within the British army soldiers like Fuller and Percy Hobart, already tank men, took up the same struggle, all to absolutely no avail.

In 1926 Liddell Hart toured the French army, spreading his ideas, and met Charles de Gaulle, who was then a young officer working for Marshal Pétain. De Gaulle began his own crusade for new tactics, but the imprisoning false mythology of the "victorious" army was even stronger in France than in Britain. The arrival after Foch's death of his staff man and bag carrier, General Maxime Weygand, as the chief of staff and the bearer of Foch's flame, assured that nothing new would be allowed to happen. A year later, the British tank men made a first breakthrough. They convinced the army to create an Experimental Armoured Force. However, the British staff soon managed to have the force disbanded.

Meanwhile, Hans von Seeckt, commander-in-chief of the Reichswehr, had begun immediately after the peace to create an army strategy in which "every action ought to be based on purpose." Although not a tank man, he made it possible for tank men to succeed. Defeat, however, had merely damaged the power of the Staff; not destroyed it. In 1926, von Seeckt was fired. In 1928, he fought back by publishing a book condemning conscript armies: "Mass becomes immobility. . . . Cannon fodder. . . . The whole future of warfare appears to me to be in the employment of mobile armies, relatively small but of high quality."[2]

All this time Heinz Guderian had been creeping up through the German tank regiments. At the time of the British Experimental Armoured Force, he was teaching tank tactics. By 1930 he was imitating British tactics with the use of dummy tanks, while waiting for the day when they would be properly equipped. In 1933 the British made another advance, with the creation of a Tank Brigade under Hobart. Had they continued on this road and convinced the French to do the same, 1940 could have been quite different. Instead the British military establishment did everything they could to limit Hobart's power. His brigade was reduced to the role of an experimental venture, as if tank strategy were still in its infancy. In 1934 de Gaulle made his own declaration in *Vers l'Armée de Métier*, rolling all the new ideas from Liddell Hart's 1919 strategy and Seeckt's mobile professionals into a single vision. What he said was brilliant, self-evident and violently opposed by the whole military establishment. In all probability it also came too late, because a year later the Germans created three panzer divisions, with Guderian commanding the second. By 1936 he was carrying out manoeuvres using Liddell Hart's and Hobart's exact methods; using their books and manuals, which he had personally arranged to have translated.

It would be a mistake to believe that the German General Staff played any positive role in this remarkably intelligent breakthrough. Once Seeckt had been fired, they reverted to standard staff attitudes and opposed the tank strategy. They were opposing not the tank itself, but, like the staffs in England and France, the proposed way of using it.

The reason for this general, fierce opposition was that Liddell Hart's tank strategy fulfilled exactly the principles laid out by Sun Tzu. It was a strategy of surprise, flexibility and originality. It gave the commander freedom to adapt to circumstances. It was the precise opposite of a staff plan. Where were the charts? Where were the *organigrams*? Where were the committees? And the committee decisions? Where were the balanced payoffs of the different corps interests? Where was the proper use of hierarchical power? The respect due to hierarchy?

Instead the staff generals were being asked simply to hand over this expensive equipment to a couple of relatively junior field commanders. And with no fixed instructions for use. Decisions were to be made on the ground, in the light of circumstance and at great speed, without consultation with HQ. Rather than laboriously plotted attacks in the Schlieffen Plan tradition, the tanks were simply to take off across field and forest looking for the best way through. All this was unacceptable to any rational staff officer. They therefore gave Guderian as much trouble as their British equivalents gave Hobart and the French gave de Gaulle.

It was Hitler who forced his own generals to allow the new strategy through. Hitler's genius lay in his use of the unexpected in order to paralyze opponents. That was what drew him to Guderian. He was able, as Liddell Hart pointed out, to demonstrate "the fallacy of orthodoxy."[3]

The reappearance of the word *genius* in the Hitlerian context reminds one how devoid it is of moral properties. It is a reminder of the lesson drawn by the established authorities of the day from the Napoleonic experience — that genius comes from the dark side of reason and should be destroyed. This logic, however, was and remains shortsighted. Genius, being free from moral value, comes on all sides of the spectrum. If you set out to destroy genius as something dangerous, then the more stable the society, the more successful that destruction will be. Only societies in disorder will be unable to do this. But stable societies are precisely those best able to guide genius onto safe moral ground. Unstable societies have always invited the worst in those with the genius to use power. Thus Fuller, Hobart and de Gaulle were destroyed, while Guderian, with Hitler's support, made his way through.

What Hitler lacked was the professional evenness to take proper and long-term advantage of the victories his genius would give him. He was, after all, certifiable. The General Staff could have given him that evenness, but instead they maintained a silent and sullen opposition. This was the result neither of class differences nor of some altruistic opposition to Nazism. It was the refusal of Hitler and his friends to respect established military structures or the powers attached to those structures which annoyed the generals. Thanks to their control of the administrative machinery, they were able to fire Erich von Manstein, the Chief of Staff to the Commander in Chief. It was Manstein who had created the general mechanized strategy which would win in 1940. To prevent him from having any role in its execution, the staff sent him off to command an infantry corps.

By the time the attack came in June 1940, they had even managed to half neutralize Guderian. He was limited to commanding a small part of the tanks. However, he more or less ignored orders and rushed ahead with what he had, as he had always said they should. The German General Staff had no choice but to run to catch up. Guderian not only beat an enemy far stronger and equipped with more tanks, he also did it with only a small portion of the available German tanks and while opposed by his own General Staff.

It was the friction between the staff's stolid, rational self-interest and Hitler's uneven genius which would fritter away over the next four years the clear victory Guderian had won for them all. In other words, Hitler was defeated by his own lunacy. He certainly was not defeated by the Allies.

After 1940 the Allied armies refused to use the liberty of thought defeat usually gives. Instead they settled down to amass enormous forces of men and armaments, just as they had in the previous war. Periodically an officer appeared who was capable of original thought. He was invariably fired as soon as this talent was demonstrated or shipped off to a theatre of war far from the heart of power.

Perhaps the most poignant case was that of the strategist Major General Eric Dorman-Smith, who created Wavell's victory of 40,000 men over 134,000 Italians in Egypt in October 1940. His approach "would have been laughed out of court had it been presented as a solution at the British Staff College."[4] Instead of being rewarded for this victory and snapped up as an invaluable adviser, he was left virtually unemployed. In 1942 Rommel was in Africa, had reversed the British advantage and was destroying all in his path. This time Dorman-Smith was advising Auchinleck and the two men set about stopping Rommel. In fact, they completely outgeneraled him and brought the German army to a halt. In the circumstances it was a remarkable victory.

However, their free-flowing methods — inspired rather than bureaucratic — had required a rapid reorganization of local British forces. This had affected military structures, which outraged the General Staff. The staff set about manoeuvring in the back rooms and corridors to get both men fired. The method they found was an expression of bureaucratic intelligence at its most sophisticated. They convinced Churchill that Auchinleck had been so successful that he ought immediately to attack Rommel again, in order to finish him off. They knew Auchinleck couldn't do this. The campaign had left his already inferior forces in no shape to take an immediate initiative. So when Churchill ordered him to attack, he — being an intelligent and responsible man — refused. As a result he was fired. It was some time before he was given another job. And that was even farther away from Europe, in India. As for Dorman-Smith, he was pursued by a vendetta which was, in Michael Elliott-Bateman's words, "a national disaster and a disgrace to the profession of arms."[5] The official line insisted that Dorman-Smith was "clever but quite unsound."[6] Expertise and stability are the two great arguments used by the modern man of reason to disguise his own incompetence. Perhaps the earliest example of this phenomenon came in the mid-eighteenth century, when George III's courtier-officers complained that General James Wolfe was mad. The King replied that he wished Wolfe would bite his other officers.

The most famous case during World War II was that of Air Vice-Marshal Sir Hugh Dowding. He foresaw the Battle of Britain and tried to prepare the Royal Air Force, despite opposition from the experts. They believed that massive bombing of Germany was the only thing worth preparing for. When the war came, he made the best of a bad situation and won the Battle of Britain. It was the only major air campaign won in the Western theatres of war and perhaps Britain's greatest victory of World War II. After all, losing it would have led to the invasion of England. The moment it was won, Dowding was fired — partly for being right, partly so that the strategic bombing experts could get on with flattening German and other European cities.

This insistent bombing of cities had so little to do with the idea of fighting wars to win them that it cannot simply be attributed to strategic incompetence. The Germans had already dropped as many bombs as they could on British cities without having any negative effect on either the Allied determination to fight or their military preparations. If anything, the more civilians the bombs killed, the more determined the citizenry became to fight. Why then, did the Allied command insist on a mirror repetition of what the Germans had done to Britain?

They must have believed their strategy would work. In this they were the inheritors of the Maginot Line mentality and of trench warfare strategy. Like Foch and Haig, they believed that their endless attacks would succeed. The men, equipment and explosives wasted in this way constitute one of the explanations for the war dragging on through 1945.

As for Dowding, his name was kept out of government publications about his victory and he was not made a marshal of the RAF. Gavin Stamp has pointed out that he was the only man since Nelson to have been called upon to save Britain, which he did.[7] His reward was the active enmity of the Air Force Staff, which, needless to say, focused only on the fact that he was a peculiar and difficult man.

Apart from odd, brief moments when Patton, the French general de Lattre de Tassigny and perhaps Montgomery managed to do what they wanted, originality — generalship in fact — was eliminated from the European theatre. Instead, the war was ploddingly completed by relatively competent but unimaginative linear warfare, not so different from that of the First War. Had the Germans not already been weakened by the Russians and heavily outnumbered, the fighting might have gone on for years. As in World War I, originality had a better chance the farther away it was from headquarters. In the Pacific, MacArthur proved that mobility could work, as he leapfrogged over island after island, leaving the Japanese intact but powerless behind him. And in Burma, Slim carried out a relatively original campaign.

Before that, Orde Wingate, although hampered by a truly unstable personality, made the first contemporary Western attempts at guerrilla warfare. His operations behind Japanese lines in the Burmese jungle were based on a strategy which owed a great deal to Sun Tzu and might later have been mistaken for that of Mao. "Pounce upon the enemy in the dark," Wingate wrote. "Smite him hip and thigh and vanish silently into the night."[8] As early as 1938, convinced that the God of Israel was calling him, he had given the Jews in Palestine the military framework which is still the basis of their strategy. His ongoing influence in Israel shows what effect he might have had had he not been killed on the opening day of his second Burmese operation. One of his strengths was that he was conscious of the struggle between talent and managerial professionalism and could therefore fight back. "The chief difference between a good and a bad leader," he said, "is that a good leader has an accurate imagination." And yet, even had he survived, the defenders of professional orthodoxy would no doubt have eventually destroyed him. One has only to look at what they did to his memory. Although Wingate never lost a battle — which the other generals in the East certainly did, often through pure incompetence — he was the only commander treated roughly in the *Official History of the Japanese War.*[9]

What drives this petty persecution of good generals is not only the recognition that their success illustrates the incompetence of the staff approach. It is also a realization that these successful methods cannot regularly be imitated. Wingate instilled the spirit of his methods into the situation in Palestine and so they have come down to us via Israeli successes. But when Western armies attempt to imitate those methods, they fail. No general staff can adapt itself to a method based upon fluidity — certainly not fluidity as Sun Tzu defined it. "And as water has no constant form, there are in war no constant conditions."[10] Wingate, it should be remembered, had been refused admission to the Staff College when he applied in 1936.

❦

The events of modern warfare have been part of a single, unbroken evolution. And yet the anonymity of the staff, as compared to our throwing up of unrelated Heroic leaders upon whom to focus, has obscured this unity. General Maxime Weygand is one of the few famous staff figures to have been a major player over fifty years of warfare. If for no other reason, his is one of the great names in the rise of modern military structures.

His career carried him through the searing experience of the Dreyfus affair at the turn of the century, World War I as Foch's personal chief of staff, the between-war period as chief of the General Staff, the second half of the 1940 campaign as the military commander who led France to a conclusive defeat, and the postwar period, from which he emerged unscathed. It could be said that he was the model modern officer: mediocre, imperturbably self-confident, sectarian and personally victorious in all the military disasters for which he was responsible.

After Foch's death in 1929, Weygand was his natural successor as spokesman for the staff, with all their new and rational ways. And yet from his youth he had belonged to the classic Right. Like most officers he had combined army loyalty with anti-Semitism in his opposition to Captain Dreyfus. But Weygand had gone further. He had contributed to the memorial for Colonel Henry, the officer who had lied and blamed a Jew in order to protect the officer corps. And when de Gaulle published his *Vers l'Armée de Métier* in 1934, Weygand — then chief of the General Staff — had seen it as an irrational attack upon a rational system by a man who was difficult to measure and therefore unstable and therefore dangerous. He did everything he could to silence de Gaulle.

A creature of the staff, Weygand had scarcely seen active service. He stood for reason, efficiency, systems management, class privilege, anti-Semitism and the interests of the system over the truth. De Gaulle stood for republicanism, open questioning of structures and indifference to systems, whether constitutional or administrative. He possessed a kind of piercing irrationality which shed light upon truth.

In June 1940, while everything collapsed, the system continued to be rational and Weygand to be loyal to it. Given command of the French forces late in the battle — but not too late — he must have sought within his training, experience, powers, command and imagination some way to stop the irrational dash of Guderian's tanks. He must have thrown his mind back to the words and actions of his mentor, Marshal Foch. And yet he found nothing. Absolutely nothing. On the other hand, he believed, like most of the conservative military technicians who served the state, that the collapse of existing structures would lead to a social explosion.

De Gaulle, by then junior minister of defence, came to him and asked what his plans were for a counter attack or a defensive campaign. Weygand had none. He was obsessed by the risks of a Communist coup if the army were beaten and its structure collapsed. He therefore proposed to save the army, and the officer corps' power over it, by surrendering while the military structure was still intact. De Gaulle saw the situation quite differently. The system, he felt, had either gone mad or rendered itself traitorous by refusing to fulfill its obligations to the nation. He therefore got on a plane to London in order to pull that system down.

Finally the subsequent Allied victory and the postwar trials in France destroyed the reputations of most senior officers who had collaborated with the Axis. Weygand, almost alone in this category, emerged intact. To this day, his name is left off the list of those who can be criticized. A permanent vagueness hangs over his actions and his reputation. It could be said that this vagueness is, in fact, an aura surrounding the beloved of the staff.

Only by the most extreme subservience to chauvinism have we been able to go on telling ourselves that the Allies did well in the Second World War. The military difficulties of the West since 1945 arise in good part from this generalized childish boosterism, which has allowed the military establishment to act as if everything is in order, as if their methods are the right ones. The same is true of the German staff, who were able to blame their defeat in 1945 on the lunacy of the Nazis. They can all say that while there may have been some bugs in the new management systems during the First War, these were worked out in the Second to such an extent that staff planning now indeed makes circumstances change. In other words, their methods have been consecrated as military truth.

The staffs and staff colleges of the Western world cannot help but have noticed, however, their own almost unbroken line of military failure since 1945. The image of Western armies floundering about over the last half century is fixed in everyone's mind. But it is fixed there as a series of unrelated events. The last colonial wars were seen as wars of disengagement. The British failures were seen separately from the French, from the Spanish, from the Portuguese. The postcolonial wars were something else again. And on their tail came the guerrilla wars and the terrorist wars. In all there have been some two hundred conflicts, from Indochina, Algeria and Yemen to Korea, Lebanon, Cuba and Angola.[11]

The less expert observer might well wonder what has actually been happening. Is it not that sophisticated, rational armies have simply failed to come to terms with less sophisticated, irrational armies, who use guerrilla and revolutionary warfare and who are led by less sophisticated and less rational people? The result, to be absolutely clear, is that unsophisticated, irrational armies regularly beat sophisticated, rational ones. Our experts seem to draw some satisfaction from this rather in the way the French knighthood maintained that the English had only managed to massacre and defeat them at Agincourt in 1415 because they used peasants armed with daggers and socially unacceptable longbows. In fact many of the great armies that have been beaten over the last three thousand years — carrying their civilizations down with them — have been beaten by armies which were, according to the logic of the losers, inferior and backward.

Those who beat us are not doing anything new. Their actions simply reflect the principles of flexible strategy, laid out in simple, clear language five hundred years before Christ. Our armies lose because they have forgotten that the purpose of their job is to win. Instead they concentrate on organization, on their own positions of power within that organization and on preparing for a particular sort of war which is theoretically suited to their organization. They think they are flexible because they have collected massive amounts of powerful and rapid equipment. Weaponry, however, is inanimate. It is dependent on the will and imagination of the commanders. And those commanders are slaves to methodology and structure.

Quite naturally we seek excuses for our litany of otherwise heavy-handed, ill-adapted operations. But these excuses are undermined by the simplicity of the victors' methods, as indeed they are by the positive results whenever a Western commander aligns himself with the basic principles of strategy. When MacArthur leapfrogged behind the Koreans to the Inchon landing, he specifically drew his inspiration from James Wolfe's surprise landing at Quebec City in 1759.[12] And when the British Commander, Gerald Templer, outmanoeuvred the Communists during the Malaya troubles in the 1950s, it could be said that he out–Sun Tzued Mao Tse-tung.

"The experts in defence conceal themselves as if beneath the earth; those skilled in attack move as if from the heavens."[13] Every guerrilla army has taken this phrase of Sun Tzu's and adapted the words to its own needs. Our military structure's inability to do so has led us farther and farther away from reasonable action — and this despite frequent attempts by thinking soldiers to explain the problem. Elliott-Bateman tried in 1967 in his book *Defeat in the East*. It was specifically aimed at clarifying the American difficulties in Vietnam, in light of France's difficulties during the preceding Indochina campaign. He made no impact.

It was as if the American staff officers had convinced themselves of a triple-edged logic. First, the French were poor, old-fashioned, under-armed and without the airpower to sustain strategic bombing. Second, the power of the American military system was such that the actual commanding officers were no more than ciphers of the structure. They were to be organized and directed to victory by technical remote control. Indeed, the physical distance and difference between the Pentagon and the Vietnamese jungle made the remoteness even more complete. Third, the role of the field commander was so limited that it could be entrusted to lesser minds. On a more cynical level, by giving command to less intelligent, less imaginative men, the Pentagon could control and manipulate them.

The result of this logic was that the greatest war machine in the history of the world was put into the hands of a series of commanders — culminating, so to speak, in William Westmoreland — who seemed to suffer from severe intellectual limitations. General Westmoreland would have been perfectly interchangeable with Field Marshal Sir Douglas Haig or Marshal Foch.

The military tended to blame its subsequent failure on some combination of the press, the people and the government. The essential truth, however, is that while equipped with large battalions and sophisticated machinery, it lost successive battles. One of the most disturbing evocations of this failure was the dissatisfaction of the soldiers with their leaders, which led to the killing or wounding of one thousand American officers and NCOs by their own men.[14] The officers and NCOs were largely professional, the men mainly draftees.

Defeat in Vietnam led to the creation of a fully professional army. And yet, when part of this new force was sent in 1983 to the small Caribbean island of Grenada to fight fifty Cuban soldiers and six hundred Cuban civilians, it required seven full battalions and a full week to "win" the engagement.[15] Heavy equipment losses were suffered in the process, as well as relatively high casualties, the majority inflicted on the soldiers by their own army. Slightly more medals — 8,633 — were awarded than the number of men involved in the operation. The only lesson drawn from Grenada seems to have been that quantity, however clumsy, can overcome a lack of quality. And so, seven years later, 25,000 men were sent into Panama. This use of an elephant to squash a fly couldn't help but produce serious civilian casualties. One would have expected that such dominance would at least have ensured the continuance of civil order. Instead it led to anarchy, including the destruction of large parts of Panama City, massive looting and economic collapse. The destabilization was such that Panama still shows few signs of recovery.

As to whether the American senior military leadership had reformed itself, one had only to watch General Maxwell Thurman in action. General Thurman was an intelligence officer in Vietnam, had a short tour of duty there in the artillery and spent most of the twenty years before the Panama operation in such staff areas as personnel, reorganization and training. In the midst of his heavy-handed Panamanian operation, this dry, bespectacled desk officer gave himself over to public statements reminiscent of a B movie. He seemed so unaware of how a real field commander might act that he tended to typecast people as good guys or thugs and to take on the mannerisms of a John Wayne character.

Despite protestations of superiority, the British did no better over the same period. They managed one clear victory — Malaya in the 1950s — versus a series of losses — Palestine, Cyprus, Aden. Even the Suez landing was executed heavy-handedly and with such lumbering slowness that unsympathetic countries were given time to apply enough political pressure to stop the operation.

The British did pull off a set-piece operation in the Falklands. It was without any strategic or tactical use. Indeed, thanks to the distance involved and Argentina's badly trained and ill-equipped army, the whole thing could be carried out as if nothing had changed since June 1944 and the Normandy landing.

That same British army remains unable to fulfill its real responsibilities in Ireland. The standard excuses are that what they do in Ireland isn't real warfare and that the government won't release the soldiers to do what is necessary to win. But a successful army is one which knows how to adapt itself to the limitations of each situation. The most important task given the British army over the last quarter century has been the maintenance of order within the realm and they have been unable to adapt their methods to that situation.

The French have developed a certain rapid-action skill for use in ex-colonies in Africa. But all the major operations undertaken by their army since 1945 have either been lost or won in such a heavy-handed way that the victory wasn't politically useful. Algeria is the prime example of a victory lost by the method of winning it. More recent operations — the Lebanese intervention, the Greenpeace Rainbow Warrior incident, the massacre in New Caledonia — have shown that the French are little better adapted to contemporary military realities than are the British or the Americans.

These examples are reminders that technological advance and rational action are not innately on the side of intelligent, liberal reform. Neither are they innately on the side of inhumanity and destructiveness. Above all they are indifferent to value and comfortable with mediocre men whose chief qualities are ambition, self-assurance and a talent to manipulate.

This situation continues to rely upon a fascinating intellectual trick. Reason refers to modernity, which relates to systems and to methods. Intelligence, on the other hand, refers primarily to application. Even pure research is a form of application because it seeks to do rather than to manage. Application, as seen by systems men, is nonsequential. It seeks to do, not to continue. Continuity here has nothing to do with memory and everything to do with systems. Being nonsequential, application is unreliable and therefore untrustworthy. Intelligence in a soldier always invokes the fear of Napoleon — the fear of a soldier who can fight.

In order to be trusted with men and equipment, an officer must therefore be modern but neither too intelligent nor too competent. That in the event of action he may have a tendency to lose both men and equipment is irrelevant. The creation of modern armies is only related to combat in an abstract manner. The ability to fight successfully, if called upon to do so, is therefore a secondary consideration.

The obsession of our military with management systems rather than winning led them quite naturally to replace strategy with technology. And this combination of method and machinery tended automatically towards large, absolute solutions. From Kitchener's pedantic Sudanese campaign, through the heavy bombing of the two world wars to the overkill of Grenada, Panama and Iraq, the same tendency repeated itself.

An interesting example of how this system can deform the simplest military action was played out on the fringes of the Vietnam War. Those geographic outer edges had a particular importance because the North Vietnamese used them to move men and equipment. The local complications involved hill tribes, marginal nationalist movements, opium production, hidden transport routes and difficult terrain, usually mountainous jungle. Each of these was a small-scale problem with large-scale implications. It quickly became apparent that Western systems couldn't act on such a small scale. They couldn't even plan to act on that level.

The officers who were detailed to deal with the frontier areas discovered that there were no global solutions. Nor any possibility for massive troop movements. Nor any use for large-scale investments aimed at re-settlement or education or militia training. On the other hand, there were endless opportunities for small, individualized projects, which could have an enormous effect in such small and delicate situations.

However, any requests they made for the funding of a project at, say, $25,000, would be rejected by the staff in Saigon or Washington. The army planning system couldn't deal with a concrete proposal relating to a small hill tribe.

A particularly telling example was the attempt to create Fortified Villages in Vietnam. This strategy had begun as one of the few successful Western post–World War II innovations, developed under General Gerald Templer during the Malaya troubles of the 1950s. The idea was to defend chosen villages in Communist-dominated areas and gradually to house the population from the outlying area inside the defences. They would then be safe from guerrilla threats, which usually came during the night. During the day they were within walking distance of their fields.

Peasants in Vietnam suffered from the identical problem. However, the American staff in Saigon felt they could improve upon the solution. They constructed completely new villages in safe areas. These could have complex defence systems built in from conception. The army then moved villagers out of Communist zones into these safe zones.

This version of the Fortified Village, being technology-dependent, was expensive and required quite a bit of administration but not much soldiering. The villages hardly had to be defended. Unfortunately, the Saigon staff had also defeated the whole purpose of the exercise. Instead of building confidence in the countryside, they had emptied it. Instead of protecting the peasants in their homes, they had kidnapped them and dropped them down somewhere strange, far from their fields. On paper it all looked perfect and was of a size and consequence proper to modern management methods. They were convinced they had greatly improved the original shoestring-budget British plan. Of course the whole program was a disaster.

These large ideas applied to little problems are the result of an obsession with efficiency. There are two ways to define this word. The first has to do with quality as measured by a cost-versus-value ratio. For example, how much did a meal cost compared to how good was it? The second revolves around the idea that larger production runs permit lower costs per item: thus a McDonald's hamburger may not be any good, but it is cheaper because there are more of them.

Most people like to believe that they are benefiting from the first ratio. Certainly the mythology of advertising rarely mentions large production runs but never stops talking about quality versus cost. The staff officer's view of efficiency is not unlike that of modern commerce, with its use of quality ads to sell mass-produced goods. Thus the Pentagon believes itself to be more efficient for having financed five-million-dollar hill-tribe training programs and for having rejected those at twenty-five thousand. The same view of efficiency applies to sending armies into battle. More men and more equipment is efficient. It will get the job done.

Officers in France and England will effortlessly volunteer that this squandering of resources is an American phenomenon — a product of U.S. prosperity. Comforting though that idea is for some, a glance at both world wars indicates that assembly-line warfare was invented by the German, French and English General Staffs. Not by the Pentagon or by Henry Ford.

This replacement of officers with strategical talents by those with a taste for quantity bears a curious resemblance to what happened in the armies of the European monarchies at the end of the eighteenth century. Guibert wrote about the unreformed French army of 1773: "We have created a uniform which obliges the soldier and the officer to spend three hours a day on their *toilette*, which has turned men of war into wig brushers, shiners and polishers."[16] But elaborate dress wasn't the real problem. Since the military leadership of the late eighteenth century was filled with courtesans who had no idea of how to fight a war, their unconscious hope was that soldiers would so completely identify with uniforms, regiments and a sense of belonging that they would willingly march out in an exposed straight line to be shot at. Weaponry has replaced uniforms as the *toilette* of our day. The unexpressed theory is that if soldiers are "well armed," they won't notice that no one has told them how to win wars.

The superiority of small, fast armies applies to armaments as well as to men. Napoleon, despite his reputation as an artillery officer in an era when artillery was changing war, wasn't particularly interested in the latest equipment. He refused to use either shrapnel or observation balloons. He liked to keep things simple so that he could move fast. He had a sense of what his soldiers could digest and dominate in weaponry. These weapons had to be a natural extension of the soldier, not the contrary. If dominated by his weaponry, the soldier would not be able to act naturally and with speed.

The devotion of contemporary armies to quantity and technological superiority has inverted this relationship. The officer and the soldier — in fact, entire armies — have become appendages of their weapons. Two incidents during a single week in the spring of 1987 and a third in the summer of 1988 poignantly demonstrated the dangers of a technology addiction.

The first disaster involved a U.S. frigate, the *Stark*. She was cruising in the Persian Gulf as part of an American decision to guarantee the passage of oil tankers between the opposing forces of Iran and Iraq. An Iraqi Mirage fighter approached her. The ship's crew had had the Mirage under surveillance for three minutes. The fighter then launched two Exocet missiles, which struck and severely damaged the ship. Thirty-seven sailors were killed. The Mirage flew away unhindered.

A public outcry followed. Why had the frigate not reacted before, during or after the incident? All crew members had been at their stations. The ship was equipped with an antimissile system which could deal with the Exocet.

The explanation was that the extremely sophisticated antimissile system had been turned off. The reason was that, if left on, it would fire automatically at any approaching aircraft. There were a lot of planes in the air over the Persian Gulf. Some were friendly. Others were civilian. In addition, the frigate had given the fighter two warnings. This took two minutes. The antimissile system takes ninety seconds to activate. It was therefore thirty seconds from activation when the first Exocet struck, knocking out the ship's electronic system. Just as they reestablished power, the second missile struck.

None of the above constituted an equipment failure or an error on the part of the crew. However, the bow superstructure blocks the ship's own antimissile sensors and weapons. Therefore, when a suspicious plane approaches, the frigate must turn its stern in that direction so that

the antimissile system can detect any oncoming missiles. By close calculation, it has been established that there were enough seconds available to turn the ship, detect the missile and fire. Just enough seconds.
What such a frigate is supposed to do if approached by two suspicious
planes coming from opposite directions is problematic.

Military authorities analyzed this incident. They established human
error. The Captain was therefore relieved of his command and left the
navy. But if one considers the complexity of the reactions required when
faced by the indicators, of which only a few of the dozens possible have
been given, another question arises. Did the Captain have a real opportunity to decide on action or only a theoretical opportunity? In the
abstract, despite the confused circumstances, he had a couple of seconds to turn his ship, examine the information and order the antimissile
missiles fired. In reality the remarkable equipment defending the *Stark*
provided a theoretical defence — not one which could easily be used
even by well-trained men in a practical wartime crisis.

A few days later a young West German citizen flew a single-engine
Cessna from Finland across the Russian border. He penetrated Soviet
air space, crossed all the defence lines, and flew 680 kilometers to
Moscow, where he circled Red Square, buzzed Lenin's Tomb, and
landed at the foot of the Kremlin wall. The Soviets gave no explanations, but Western experts suggested that the Soviet radar system could
not spot either low- or slow-flying aircraft, partially as a result of tall
trees obscuring the screen. Everyone agreed, however, that the fault lay
with humans, not with the system. A number of men were fired.

In July 1988, again in the Persian Gulf, the American cruiser *Vincennes* shot down an Iran Air Airbus, killing 290 civilian passengers.
After initially misleading excuses from the navy and American politicians, a thousand-page U.S. Navy report eventually put the blame on
the Operations Officer. He was therefore to receive a letter of repri-
mand which would not become part of his official personal file. But if he
was at fault, why was the punishment so light? And if he wasn't, then
why punish him at all? The answer seems to be that the navy preferred
blaming a man to blaming the machinery — machinery so complex that
it couldn't easily differentiate between a tiny fighter and an enormous
Airbus. Their chief desire was to avoid criticism of the ship's Aegis
protection system. The navy has invested $46 billion in this system in
order to equip fifty-six cruisers and destroyers.

Meanwhile, twenty thousand men on twenty-five gigantic American
ships in the Persian Gulf were immobilized, like dinosaurs, hardly able
to move because of mines laid by little wood scows, and unable to turn
on their electronic equipment for fear of destroying everything in sight,
including fellow ships and planes. Shortly after the *Stark* incident and
almost a year before that of the *Vincennes*, Admiral Carlisle Trost, Chief

of Naval Operations, reacted to criticism of this general situation by invoking the magic formula — the navy doesn't build small ships, because smaller ships would be far less cost effective.[17]

This problem of unmanageable machinery has been constant over the last decade. The Iran rescue mission was betrayed by helicopters that wouldn't work. The Grenada operation lost a good percentage of its equipment through malfunction. When the American marines in Beirut were withdrawn to ships, after the explosion of a car bomb in their compound killed 240 of them, the navy suddenly discovered that so long as the ships stayed in the harbour their radar system couldn't be turned on. At any rate no one could figure out how to make it work while the ships' engines were off. They had to place marines around the decks with hand-held missiles to watch for low-flying planes and speedboats.

Richard Gabriel, in his study of recent American military engagements, concluded that an obsession with state-of-the-art equipment was crippling the army. The TOW antitank missile fails to work 30 percent of the time; 35 percent of Sidewinder missiles malfunction; so do 25 percent of the Sparrows. The fact is that the natural impulses of technocrats and the imperatives of technology have become so detached from the society of man that no one can tell where research ends and use begins.

An ever-growing amount of military equipment has been prematurely ripped from the womb of research. It has been put into an apparently practical form without taking into account what human beings can actually do in a real situation. On paper Western armies have a remarkable arsenal. In reality much of it is useless in wartime situations, unless the enemy can be so overwhelmed as to be irrelevant as an opponent. Quite simply, it is too complicated to use.

Even the M-16 rifle carried by the American soldier is too "sophisticated" — a value-laden word that switches the responsibility for failure from the weapon to the soldier. In ideal circumstances, the M-16 is no doubt the best rifle in the world. In reality it jams easily. Guerrilla soldiers around the world, who are constantly fighting in difficult circumstances, are far happier to have a basic Kalashnikov in their hands, even though it can't do a quarter of the things promised by the M-16. Military planners will reply that guerrilla fighters are not as "sophisticated" as Western soldiers. In most cases this simply isn't true. The average Western soldier has a lot of training but not much experience. The average guerrilla fighter knows what he can and cannot manipulate during real use.

The Western problem is that weapons are now developed without taking into account the humans who will have to use them or the practical circumstances of their use. The contemporary staff general is so eager to get more of this complex weaponry that he often budgets for the maximum amount of equipment without leaving any reserve for spare parts or training.

As a result in 1985 the U.S. Air Force had 7,200 aircraft without the means to sustain them at military readiness. Nor did they have the bases in Europe capable of handling the equipment which would be deployed there in case of crisis. They didn't have the fuel, ammunition, repair facilities or control towers to make the equipment usable. All they had was the equipment.[18]

This frenzied desire to have the largest possible quantities of the latest and most complex equipment could be called the Armada complex. And while it is true that budgets in other Western armies limit this collector's folly, the Armada complex is nevertheless a generalized condition of the Western military.

The West's victory over Iraq would seem to have laid all worries about military leadership, strategical competence and impractical equipment to rest. With a single success the stigma of dozens of lost engagements and mismanaged wars had been wiped away. But nothing is worse than confidence based upon a false interpretation of events. And a war in which one side refuses to fight is not a victory for the other if there is a subsequent peace which leaves the loser with effective power. In place of soft self-reassurance, we would do better to ask ourselves exactly what this war demonstrated about Western armies.

First, there is the question of mobilization. We mobilized on the scale of a world war and yet were able to gather together, right on the battlefront, troops and equipment from around the world without military interference from the enemy. We did this at our ease over a period of months, thereby confirming that the opponent was so inferior as to warrant neither world war methods nor rhetoric.

Second, we carried out a lengthy, unopposed bombing campaign which official publicity told us was the first of its kind — accurate and effective thanks to the new "smart bombs." In reality, only 7 percent of the 88,500 bombs dropped were smart.[19] We have no information on how smart they actually were. Only the successes were shown to the public on videotape. We do know, however, despite repeated claims by General Schwarzkopf that "we have managed to neutralize the fixed launchers" of the Scud missiles, that half of them remained operational.[20] As for the other 93 percent of Allied bombs, they had the traditional 25 percent accuracy rate. In other words, this campaign was not so very different from the interminable barrages of World War I and the strategic bombings of World War II, both of which caused heavy casualties while failing to accomplish military objectives. In the Iraq campaign, some military as well as most civil infrastructures were destroyed. We actually have no idea whether this had a determining effect on the Iraqis' ability to fight the war. The aftermath demonstrates that their army was not seriously damaged. Even the short ground war was filled with indications that a heavy, prolonged, generalized bombing campaign did not have an important effect on the outcome. For example, entire regiments, which had not been targeted during the bombing, surrendered without firing a shot. It now appears that Saddam Hussein's army, with the exception of his Republican Guard, had from the beginning been unwilling to fight. Our military leaders have countered that they were forced to act as if the enemy would fight because they had no information to the contrary. In other words, Western intelligence networks were not functioning. An army cannot fight an intelligent war without accurate information about the enemy.

Third, it is not at all clear that our equipment functioned well. Because our armies were able to draw on total Western stocks without impunity, they were not subjected to the limited conditions of real war, such as incurring heavy risks in order to replace equipment. For all we know, Western armies may have suffered the 25 percent equipment failure rates that previous experience would suggest. Our forces had the luxury of overarming themselves to such an extent that even high levels of failure would have had little importance.

Fourth, the strategy for the ground invasion was almost standard. It benefited from the element of surprise only because the enemy, being so inferior, had no possibility of gathering information beyond its own borders. What was presented as a rapid and daring ground war was actually a predictable manoeuvre against an enemy waiting either to surrender or, in the case of the Republican Guards, to duck until hostilities were over.

The strategies of armies, equipment and leadership employed during this war were those we have been preparing over the last half century for a major land war in Europe. Received wisdom now has it that, with the collapse of the Warsaw bloc and the Soviet Union, the Cold War is over. However, the basic rivalries between East and West remain, along with their military infrastructures.

In order to evaluate the Iraq campaign, one has to imagine it taking place against a real opponent, most probably in Europe. For a start there would be no air superiority. Six weeks of strategic bombing would be returned by six weeks of the same from the other side. The gathering of troops and equipment not already on the battlefront would be virtually impossible because of the enemy's long-range strike capability. Without rapid attack both armies would be severely damaged. Once engaged they would be dependent upon immediately available supplies. And the strategic movement of any army in any direction would be picked up immediately by the opponent's satellites.

Two specific examples give a more realistic picture of our situation. The U.S. General Accounting Office completed a report in January 1991 which concluded that the American army was so badly equipped and trained to resist chemical warfare that more than 50 percent of exposed troops would die.[21] There is no reason to suppose that the other Allied armies were better prepared. The second example relates to the Patriot missile, hero of the technological war. It now appears that its performance did not conform to claims made during the war. One hundred and fifty-eight Patriots were needed to hit forty-seven Scud missiles. These hits did not destroy the warhead. Instead they struck the fuel rocket at a point when it was almost spent. As a result, the warhead was simply diverted to another site. In fact, Israeli casualties and damaged buildings rose several-fold once the Patriots began operating.[22]

President Bush insisted on comparing Saddam Hussein to Hitler and, during his postwar state of the union address, persisted in comparisons with the military struggles of the two world wars: "Twice before in this century, an entire world was convulsed by war." Aside from this rhetoric, so overstated as to insult our intelligence, the West's pedantic methods against Iraq would have been a disaster if used against a real enemy. And even as a strategy for liberating Kuwait it was inappropriate. The Iraqis were left the maximum amount of time to prepare the destruction of the local civil and oil industry infrastructure and then were defeated in a manner which ensured they could carry out that destruction. This real catastrophe was exacerbated by the Iraqi refusal to fight followed by their reassumption of power at home. Worse still, not only did this war not solve the problems which caused it, the result will be massive regional growth in armed forces and new weaponry. Iran, for example, is busy rearming. Nevertheless, for the first time in memory, the Pentagon did not sabotage its own army. This was the result of a personal decision by General Colin Powell, Chairman of the Joint Chiefs of Staff, simply to ignore the official Pentagon system. In other words, there has been no reform, only a one-time informal exception to the rules.

In many ways the victory over Iraq eerily echoes that of the British over the Mahdi in the Sudan in 1898. Kitchener, a superficially colourful commander who was in reality slow and predictable, followed up two years of battlefield preparation with an easy victory over an opponent unequipped with such things as machine guns. The Mahdis' casualties were high. Those of the British were very low. There was a dramatic cavalry charge, not unlike the recent tank charge, which hadn't much to do with the outcome of the war. However, it was very exciting. This victory caused the British to believe that they were on the right military track. As a result they bungled the South African War and undertook the massacre of 1914–18. Comparisons of this sort are never quite satisfactory. However, carefully used they can at least discourage easy triumphalism.

☁

The swollen officer corps of the West have progressed from the myth of modern organization to the myth of the modern manager. All the syndromes of bureaucratic life are to be found in their headquarters. A nine-to-five attitude. Group decisions to protect each individual. An inability to respond to information which indicates that the system is doing the wrong thing. Leadership rarely rewarded. Business management systems consciously applied to running armies. It is not an exaggeration to say that officers now know more about systems management than about fighting wars.

In these "entrepreneurial officer corps," Richard Gabriel has written, "competition and careerism make every officer look out for himself. . . . Personnel managers are actually in charge of the system and they have redesigned the system of military promotion and rewards to reward managerial bureaucrats."[23] Army promotion boards are controlled by staff officers who have little or no frontline experience.

It isn't surprising that Western military organizations are unable to adapt themselves to doing battle with fast, light armies that fight outside rational tradition. The managerial officer is unlikely to understand why these conflicts are taking place. Or what the motivations of the officers involved might be. Or how such wars are fought on a daily basis. These Third World mysteries, which have now spread to the former communist world, are beneath their complex skills.

When on the morning of April 25, 1980, the American Secretary of Defense was obliged to announce the disastrous failure of the hundred-odd men sent on the Iran rescue mission, some 35,000 staff officers and other ranks stood outside their offices in the Pentagon watching him on overhead corridor television monitors. Their expressions were wry, curious, mildly confused.[24] They were hearing about a world indifferent to their methods and systems — a real world they were often required to imagine on paper. Almost every American military operation of the last forty years had been debated beforehand at great length in the thousands of offices off those corridors. The preparation had sometimes been so long that the relevant circumstances had completely changed by the time the operation was carried out. The message of the Secretary of Defense to the staff was that their imagining of the reality in Iran had led to a disaster. It was immediately apparent to everyone in the Pentagon that there had been human error out there, outside, on the ground.

A few years later, when the U.S. interservice committee cranked out the plans for the Grenada invasion, a tiny role in the attack force was allotted to each service represented on the committee. Indeed, a role was given to each *section* of each service represented on the committee. The operation was almost as complex as the Normandy landings — so complex that the only reason it succeeded was the total absence of any but token resistance. A large number of the 8,633 medals awarded were given to people on the planning staff who took no part in the operation. This was not unusual. In 1970 in Vietnam, 522,905 medals were awarded — double the number of American military personnel in South Asia.[25]

But if all this is true of Western armed forces and their capabilities, what does it mean about the intricate web of nuclear weapons which now surrounds us? Quite probably a good part of the offensive machinery which is supposed to deliver the bombs doesn't work, and an even greater part of the defensive equipment. After all, everyone agrees that nuclear defence is far more complex than simply throwing bombs at the other side. It's unlikely that we shall get a chance to find out if all this is true. But the Star Wars proposition, when seen in this context, suddenly appears to have had nothing to do with nuclear warfare. It belongs in the category of the desk officer's dream: endless amounts of equipment incomprehensible to anyone except an expert and virtually inoperable in a real situation.

It is one of the great ironies of military history that victories are eventually and invariably claimed by courtesans, who cloak themselves in the verbiage of the victor. And since they don't themselves understand strategy, they have no difficulty in convincing themselves that they are really the inheritors of the victor's methods. Our Western general staffs probably believe that they are the inheritors of the rapid movement, deep penetration, highly mobile tank strategists who stand out as the military heroes of the last world war.

One example of this is the persistence with which they go on constructing ever more complicated helicopters. These machines have taken on a logic of their own, unrelated to their proven battle performance. Whatever new equipment is stuck onto them, helicopters have a fatal flaw — a soldier firing an ordinary rifle can still bring one down with a single shot. Helicopters have now been endlessly used in combat, almost always with heavy losses and little impact on the enemy. However, it has been decided that helicopters are the new tank. Their loss rate is therefore irrelevant.

Were Liddell Hart, Fuller, Guderian, de Gaulle, and Dorman-Smith, to say nothing of Wingate, to present at today's staff colleges a new version of their ideas — a version adapted to current circumstances — they would be laughed out of the room. And were they to attempt to influence strategic planning, the personnel directors would quickly ship them off to provincial postings.

Charles de Gaulle was one of the most surprising victims of the modern military's double addiction to management and technology. He was, after all, the only one of the great strategists to later gain real power. As President of the French Republic he had a chance to put into place the ideas he had first laid out in *Vers l'Armée de Métier* thirty years before. De Gaulle had come to power in 1958 when the army was in revolt against the civil authorities. This revolt ostensibly turned on the Algerian problem. In reality it was part of the larger question of the French army's inability to accept a republican and democratic system as the ultimate authority. In truth, the traditional officer class — that strange combination of gentry and staff — had gone on controlling the machinery in exactly the way it had since 1914.

As President of the Republic, de Gaulle wanted to create a high-technology army — the modern version of his old tank force. It would be run by a new generation of officers — technicians who would not come from the gentry or the staff and who would not have a private club approach to the army. They would become the first generation of truly apolitical officers in the history of the French republics. By their simple absence from the political process, they would ensure political stability. This, de Gaulle felt, would definitively solve the never-ending problem of civil-military relations in France.

These new officers were trained and promoted as fast as possible. The Chief of Staff, General Charles Ailleret, was himself a technician. He had been in charge of new weapon projects. He was officially the "father" of the French nuclear bomb. The old staff and the old officer corps resisted these changes as actively as the circumstances permitted. They feared that a high-tech, professional force would remove all need for them. They were particularly opposed to the nuclear force, which could be operated by a handful of men. The president would therefore have direct control over the military machine without any need for intervention by the central staff.

By the time de Gaulle left power in 1969, it was clear that he had won. It was also clear, however, that his victory had not turned out as expected. The new technocrat officers came from the lower-middle and middle classes. They found themselves caught up in the officer corps without the traditional, gentry-based officer mythology. Technocracy provided no emotional comfort. They were at sea in a role which had always belonged to others. Inevitably they reached out for the nearest, most obvious belief system and that was loyalty to the armed forces — an in-house loyalty cut off from wider social or class commitments.

The rise of an inward-looking, technocratic, staff-oriented officer corps, isolated from society as a whole, was by no means particular to France. It has been a general Western phenomenon and has become particularly worrying in the United States. There new officers are increasingly drawn from the children of senior NCOs. These young men have been brought up in the physical world of army camps and the emotional world of military mythology. They don't have the outside links of the old officer class. Nor do they have links to their own class, for the simple reason that the stable privileges of military life raise them above their origins, whether as privates, sergeants or officers.

On the outside, after all, public programs — educational, social and legal — have been collapsing throughout the United States. The sole major exception has been the world of the armed forces, where everyone is taken care of in what amounts to a society of socialist paternalism. For poor and lower-middle-class Americans, life on the inside is much better than life on the outside. The interests of an officer corps produced in this atmosphere are particular to the world they know.

In the case of France, President de Gaulle was able to see the shift in loyalty of the officer class even before he left power. The new officers were not responding to the challenge of his new strategies. They began instead to transform the simple, new nuclear force and the new conventional machinery into an ever-more-complex and stolid abstraction. They began to reinforce the old staff resistance to political power. They discovered that this was a way to apply pressure on the politicians for a constant stream of new equipment.

The tank strategy in particular, which had been so resisted by the old military authorities, was something they had now fallen in love with. That is to say they fell in love with the tank — a wonderful piece of heavy, complicated machinery which could be armed in a myriad of ways. It was only a matter of time before they adapted it to a static view of strategy not unlike trench warfare. As indeed all the Western armies have done.

And the nuclear strategies suffered the same fate. *Flexible response* was the opposite of flexible. This term, stolen from the vocabulary of sensible strategies, was deformed to mean "gradual response." And gradual response is precisely what was used in World War I — a fixed, in-depth defence which required masses of bombs, equipment and men, in endless variations of size and combinations.

That was why the Europeans recognized the implications immediately, when this strategy was first introduced by McNamara in the early 1960s. They understood that it meant the continent would have to be destroyed before the United States considered any serious action of its own. But their moment of clarity gradually slipped away as the staff planners became mesmerized by the endless choice of interlocking weaponry which flexible response offered them. It was only a matter of time before the very complexity of French nuclear strategy, along with the strategies of the other Western powers, had been turned into an updated version of the Maginot Line. The American MX missile system, in particular, with its limited quantity of special railway tracks moving weapons about in a fixed pattern, is a physical parody of the old Maginot Line construction. And the recently renamed SDI, even if it were actually doable, would be a massive expansion of the same sort of static defence.

The military's response to the recent agreements on nuclear weapons reduction in Europe illustrated this state of mind. They really didn't care so long as they were compensated with increased quantities of conventional weapons. At first this appears sensible; the collapse of the Warsaw Pact and the Soviet Union, when added to the childish enthusiasm of the West, have left the impression that everything is up for grabs east of the EEC. But if one listens very closely to the demands of our military for conventional equipment or to their concerns over possible conventional arms reduction, a curious impression emerges. They seem almost pleased at the idea of fewer nuclear bombs and increased reliance on tanks and artillery. There is a revival of the old staff officer displeasure at the rise of nuclear weapons, which removed power from their headquarters and gave it to politicians. On a continent now crowded with fragile new nations whose diplomatic and military relationships may not be stabilized for a decade or more, a return to tanks and cannon holds out the hope of a return to manageable weapons and old-fashioned, thump-the-enemy warfare.

This sort of suffocating bureaucratic structure, which sees war as weaponry, rather in the way many aristocrats once saw war as protocol and uniforms, has turned a straightforward and brutal reality into an abstraction. In the process the officer's concrete sense that he is fighting to win has been undermined. This in turn has clouded the justification for asking a soldier to risk his life. Wars nevertheless have continued to turn around death and so it was inevitable that something would appear to counterbalance the atmosphere of obscure abstraction. Something comforting. This took the form of an emotional outlet called bravery.

Courage or bravery has become a pillar of the nation-state's mythology. In an earlier era "service" and "chivalric form" had played important roles. At that time courage was simply a practical characteristic required in the soldiers of a winning army. It was no more important than intelligence, humanity, professionalism and personality.

But with the rise of the bureaucratic staff army, courage evolved into a compensation for not fighting to win. It became a measurement for that new phenomenon — the Hero. Each soldier, each officer, was an individual who could dream of his own glory by comparing his own courage to that of the Hero.

Courage had always been something every man could hope to possess. Now it broke down into three forms. The first was relatively rare — that act of bravery which brought victory measurably closer. Not romantically. Not abstractly. Not the proverbial machine-gun post knocked out. But significantly closer. And not victory in a clash or battle, but victory in a great battle or war. The second sort of courage was not so rare. It was that of the individual whom fate throws into an impossible situation. This has nothing to do with victory. It has everything to do with a single man and his fate. It is war as an existential act, quite apart from victory or defeat. The third kind has become tragically common. It is that quality which men summon up from within themselves to deal with the hopeless fate dealt them by incompetent commanders. This courage is a form of individual dignity which makes the pointlessness of that man's death acceptable to his family and to society. Unfortunately that same dignity also has the effect of camouflaging both the commander's incompetence and the military structure which caused the man's death.

When we talk of valour and courage in the nation-state, we are more often than not talking about this dignified suicide of the inadvertently condemned. As for the medals which accompany such a waste of life, they are a trick of military incompetence. In lieu of victory and/or life, the individual is given a medal. As the Grenada operation demonstrated, in the American army even pointless death has been so devalued that the flushing of a general's toilet may as easily earn a shiny bit of metal.

The pinning on of stars reaches its full cynical significance when sanctified valour and bereaved families are used to lend dignity to wars stupidly fought. The courageous and their families are drawn into a circular trap. The sacrificed soldier was valorous under the orders of a commander who has rewarded his effort. The battle was therefore worth fighting. Courage made it worthwhile. The basic rule of war — that it is fought to be won — has been forgotten.

Courage has become a proof of virtue and of celebrity value. The point of the brave soldier's fame, like that of the pie-eating-contest winner who is interviewed on television, is that he or she, for that moment and in his or her own way, is the Hero. This is little more than hopeless dreaming to compensate for hopeless leadership.

There is no example in history of a nation that is unable or unwilling to defend itself surviving for any length of time. That was why Sun Tzu began by invoking the essential nature of military action. Machiavelli, with his cold and cynical eye and his ability to infuriate the good men who wished reason to be a moral force, nevertheless caught the essence of the problem: "There is nothing proportionate between the armed and the unarmed."

The West has never been so armed and yet felt itself so little defended. There is no consensus, even among the civil and military leadership, on a circumstance in which our arms might be used to defend us successfully. Repeated questioning of our citizenry over the last few decades reveals that a majority of those who have been in the direct line of fire — the Europeans — felt themselves unable to imagine any action which would defend their lives, their families, their homes or their countries.

In such an atmosphere it is hardly surprising that the officer corps are also looked down upon. Or that the officers themselves are genuinely confused about their role. For example, captains of nuclear submarines, if called upon to fire their warheads, have no idea where the missiles are aimed. The geographic coordinates are on an electronic disc legible only by the submarine's computer. When questioned about this, officers tend to express relief that their destructive powers at the moment of firing would remain abstract. They would rather not know what city will be destroyed by their personal action.[26]

A nation nevertheless has to defend itself. To defend a free people can only be understood as a moral act. To defend them well must be better than to defend them badly. A good defence minimizes the risks of death and destruction.

Guibert's eighteenth-century idea, of marshaling reason to organize armies in order to remove mediocrity and allow the competent soldiers to command, must certainly have been both a good and a moral idea. And yet the direct result of his success was the unleashing of Napoleon and, with him, the unleashing of the godlike Hero archetype. The subsequent deformation of reason into a bureaucratic sea designed to drown Heroes seemed perfectly justified. The stifling of genius became the free man's ultimate protection.

But this protection applied only where free men lived. Elsewhere the forces of darkness were able to gather up this entwined myth of reason and the Hero. And when those forces attacked free men, we found ourselves defended by a sea of technicians. The military staffs, called upon to fight on our behalf, proved themselves as bloody as Napoleon. The difference was that their killing arose not from the application of unbridled ambition but from ambition unapplied except as an adjunct of administrative power. Their casualties were the result not of aggression but of disinterest and ineptitude.

Mediocrity kills as successfully as genius and so we are forced back to our original beliefs about the relationship between morality and defence. There are two kinds of morality in the world of arms. There is the most narrow, which is the honest relationship between an officer and his men. In this the technocrat fails and the good field officer may succeed. But the rampant Hero also succeeds in this domain by distorting the devotion owed him by his men.

The larger kind of morality is that between the officer and the state. Within the nascent democracies of the nineteenth century it was possible for ambitious men to distort reason to their personal service. Somehow, as Foch and Haig demonstrated, this weakness for distortion went on into the middle of the twentieth.

By now we no longer have the excuse of inexperience. We ought to feel comfortable enough with our way of life to believe ourselves capable of maintaining soldiers on their path of duty. "The enlightened ruler," Sun Tzu wrote, "is prudent and the good general warned against rash action. Thus the state is kept secure and the army preserved."[27] Surely it would be wiser today to hand our defence to those able to defend us in the belief that we are capable of controlling them. Better the risk of honest genius than the impossibility of controlling manipulative and unresponsive mediocrity.

But how could any state actually build a military system bound by skill and morality? The establishment of a common understanding between the population and their defenders is the obvious answer and no population could believe in such a unity so long as the staff control the armies. The list of what would have to change is impossibly long. It begins with the eradication of the idea that the modern officer is little different from the modern bureaucrat or businessman. The officer is not a manager. Not a committee man. Not one who works towards group decisions.

The essence of good strategy is what it has always been — insecurity and uncertainty. The staff officers seek security and certainty. They build carefully laid-out attack and defence schemes. Only the removal of their controlling hand can change this.

One of the simplest steps in the right direction would involve a radical reduction in the size of our officer corps. They are now so bloated that they contain a self-serving internal logic, only indirectly related to strategy and national interests. Reduction is something advocated by such outsiders as the great British military historian Michael Howard and, of course, Richard Gabriel. A lean officer corps is more likely to concentrate on its role. The staff obsession with quantities of complex equipment could also be dealt with if the officer corps were small enough to have direction. On an even more practical level, soldiers should evaluate soldiers. There is no role for personnel officers in the molding of an officer corps. Any more than there is for bureaucrats in uniform acting as back-room strategists.

To do this and much more would require our political leadership taking on real responsibility. The history of the last forty years has been that of politicians letting staff officers dictate the agenda. Instead of playing bureaucratic games over money and equipment, governments would find themselves having to control thinkers who are capable of action.

As for the real staff structure needed to service any modern army, we have had two centuries of experience with rational administration. We now know what works and what doesn't. The politicians and the soldiers could control the staff if an intensive effort were made and maintained. What we must continually remind ourselves is that the original intent in professionalizing and rationally managing our armies was to have fewer, faster, less destructive and more decisive wars. The result instead has been the institutionalization of semi-permanent warfare which grows continually larger, more destructive and increasingly indecisive.

Our problem is increasingly one of identifying reality in a world which finds refuge in military illusions. Thus we pretend that we are at peace when the world is at war. We believe our armies are weak when defence budgets are higher than nations theoretically at peace have ever supported. We have enshrined the values of the fast and mobile wars while constantly preparing for slow, static, frontal assaults. We accept and encourage the generalship of technocrats, somehow ignoring their now long record of losses and draws. Finally, by glorifying our occasional victories over much weaker opponents, we manage to forget that the history of warfare is made up mainly of large unimaginative armies being defeated by small, imaginative forces.

The reality which can be identified in all of this is that the greatest risk for democracy is not the emergence of a Napoleon but the failure to reduce the function of administrators to administration. The real challenge is to control soldiers whose job it is to maintain a strategy of uncertainty. Man is a great deal happier with certainty, even if its comfort is false and dangerous.

But if common sense were able to sweep from our minds the fears of a less stable past, this control would appear as the natural duty of responsible citizens and their governments. If the Napoleonic Hero could be exorcised, we would find the moral value in our own defence and therefore in our soldiers. A free man's defence depends upon his willingness to kill the Hero within himself in order to be able to reject it in others.

10

In the Service of the Greater Self

So long as there is a clear belief in the purpose of an organization, those responsible will find a sensible way to run it. But if the heart of belief is only in structure, then the whole body will gradually lose its sense of direction and then its ability to function. The arms business is a prime example of the loss of direction in Western governments and of their growing inability to do what their societies expect of them. It is as if the confusion among those who govern has become so great that they mistake frenetic activity for the carrying out of their functions.

Any search for the cause of this crisis must focus on our continuing inability to deal with the contradictions between democracy and rational administration — contradictions which have led to the emasculation of the former, whether it be in elected assemblies or in ministerial offices. But the problem is not so simple as is generally suggested. After all, it was a combination of democratic government and rational administration which radically improved the social balance over a period of some two centuries. In the process, however, this coalition lost any practical sense of why or how it was done. The result has been an inversion of roles. Administration has increasingly become the purpose and democratic leadership has felt obliged to follow. Methodology has replaced direction. Moral value has been attributed to such technical tools as efficiency and speed.

The result has been a decline of the democratic function into one of mere process and a growing frustration, if not anger, among elected representatives and their electors. Increasingly that frustration has been seized upon by organized interests — what in Mussolini's day would have been called corporate interests. The essence of Corporatism is that each group has its own purpose, organization and financial strength. These group interests negate democracy, which depends on the contribution of individual citizens. It was generally believed that the last world war had defeated Corporatism. But the growing democratic void has enabled organized interests to occupy more and more of the structures of Western political leadership in the name — astonishingly enough — of the individual voter, frustrated as he or she is by the rational state. Thus, beneath the guise of populist rhetoric, the democratic system has turned increasingly to the service of specific interests. It is a remarkable confidence trick in which the voters have begun voluntarily handing their gains of the last two centuries back over to the same small groups — or their modern equivalents — which for so long were the principal beneficiaries of a grossly inequitable civilization.

The difficulty in dealing with this problem in a sensible way stems, as so often in rational society, from the absolutism of the ideologies which have defined the parameters of the debate. Once Max Weber, writing early in this century, had turned bureaucracy into a self-contained value, the way was open for others to focus on the contrary as a justification for their opposition to an equitable society. The resulting false debate has led to a growing number of destructive aberrations in a civilization which wishes to remain democratic. For example, political leaders have been steadily erecting buffers between themselves and the governmental system.

The most disturbing of these walls is the proliferation of unelected advisers, who are now so numerous and powerful that they virtually constitute praetorian guards. Their job is to bolster the power of those in office by increasing their independence from both the people's elected representatives and the administrative system. But as history has repeatedly demonstrated, public power in the hands of the unregulated personal advisers of the heads of government has always led to abuse. The elimination of this was one of the driving forces in the rise of bureaucracy.

What follows here is an attempt to isolate some of the contradictions in democratic-rational government as a way of uncovering their cause. Is it, for example, the rise in public services which is responsible, as the contemporary Right argues, for the decline in effective democracy? Have the political and the bureaucratic classes profoundly changed because the alteration in their powers now attracts a different sort of candidate? Is there a natural alliance between the democratic and bureaucratic methods? Or a natural tension which must be consciously and constantly controlled? What is clear when these and other questions are asked is that the great national coalitions beneath the banner of democracy and reason have disintegrated and the only way to make sense of the remains is to ensure a practical divorce between ideas and methods, which in being mixed together have deformed our society.

After making enormous progress over the last century towards basic justice in many areas, the Western nations are now accepting a general slippage backwards. The OECD members carry 30 million unemployed almost helplessly, as if it were a characteristic of modern societies. Most of these people are chronically unemployed. What progress there has been in the creation of new employment — particularly in the United States — has often depended upon unsecured, poverty-level, part-time employment — in other words, upon a return to nineteenth-century unreformed capitalism. This situation has been accompanied by rising levels of illiteracy, unseen since before World War I, while state school systems decline.

Having, through enlightened social policies, rendered the European and much of the North American working class virtually obsolete, our societies made a terrible discovery. There is no point in eliminating working-class conditions and absorbing the members of that class unless you eliminate the need for a working class or radically upgrade the general attitude towards their contribution. Both solutions are dependent upon a reorganization of the economy. Rather than attempt such an integrated policy, we have simply created a whole new working class. In countries such as Germany, Sweden and France, this was done by encouraging massive immigration from Third World countries. The conditions surrounding this immigration ensured that the newcomers would remain working class in the old nineteenth-century sense — often without a vote, without citizenship, often even without access to ongoing social security or education.

In the United States, despite the disappearance of the worst sorts of public racism and the emergence of a small black middle class, including some highly successful politicians, the blacks have been confirmed in their sub-working-class role. This emerges from all the statistics on unemployment, health care, mortality rates, education, prison occupation and family status. For example, infant mortality among blacks is more than double that of whites and the gap is widening. To this racial problem has been added a second subworking class made up of Hispanics who will be, at thirty million, the largest ethnic group in the United States by the year 2000. A large number of these immigrants fuel a low-cost, low-employment-standards black market economy which escapes all social regulation. This in turn has placed great pressure on the economies of the southern states to remain or return to pre-Roosevelt conditions, which in turn has created an industrial drain from the northern states. As a further pressure on this lowest-common-denominator style of competition, America is gradually integrating its economy with that of Mexico, a country that operates at the cheap and rough levels of the Third World.

In Britain a similar approach has led to the creation of large pockets of new wealth and to equally large pockets of new poverty. This return to the old rich-poor society with a gap in the middle has been encouraged by a decline in universal state services — whether practical, such as transportation, or social, such as health care.

In other words, there has been a gradual undermining of the idea of a general social consensus. All of this has been fuelled by a slavish devotion to the rational certitude that there are absolute answers to all questions and problems. These absolute solutions have succeeded each other over the last twenty years in a jarring and disruptive way. At the same time the ability of governments to effect economic development has been severely handicapped by a growing reliance on service industries for growth — a sector dominated not by sophisticated items such as computer software but by consumer goods and personal consumer services. These sectors, it goes without saying, also flourish on labour which is part-time, low wage and insecure, thus creating a false sense of having solved part of the job-creation problem. This growth in services also leaves the Western economies dependent on the most unstable area of economic activity, which is the first to collapse in an economic crisis. Put another way, service industries are to the economy what the uncontrolled printing of money is to monetary stability. They are both forms of inflation.

These examples of a general decline stand out in contrast to state mechanisms which have never been so sophisticated. This sophistication has reached a level of complexity so great that the systems are, in truth, incomprehensible not only to the citizen, but to the most part of the political class. The latter, in a slothful loss of intellectual and practical self-discipline, have simply accepted that this is the way things must be. The resulting void in responsible leadership has allowed an hysterical brand of simplistic politics to rise and take power on the back of truisms, clichés and chauvinism, all of which fall below the intellectual level of Jenkins' Ear jingoism.[1]

When President Bush, in his inaugural address, warmed to the theme of a kinder, gentler America, he said: "We know what works: Freedom works. We know what's right: Freedom is right. We know how to secure a more just and prosperous life for man on earth: through free markets, free speech, free elections." No one laughed at his absurd ordering of these three freedoms. The men of reason in the other political party, in his own party, in the media and in the universities found nothing to say.

Every word and concept of the wars of democracy and justice has been appropriated by those who traditionally opposed both and who seek power to undo what has been done. The moral sense of the eighteenth century has not only been turned upside down, this has been done with its own vocabulary. Thus Bush could give primacy to free markets over free men, as if to say that the right to speculate in junk bonds is more important than the removal of slavery. And Jefferson, Reagan could say, was against big government. Therefore, the forty million Americans without health care were not a government concern. But what Jefferson was against was unnecessary government — organisms which no longer contributed anything. He saw political power as a limited deck of cards. Those who held office were to play their hand carefully and endlessly, picking up old cards and putting down new ones, as old problems were solved and new problems arose.[2] Those who seek and often gain power today use the vocabulary of the eighteenth century the way television evangelists use the Old Testament.

By mistaking method for content and structure for morality, we have created a fatal weapon which can be used against any fair society. No honest man can use a modern system to create and serve as well as a dishonest man can use it to destroy and to fill his pockets. The resulting moral confusion cannot simply be laid at the feet of those guilty of taking advantage of the situation. They and their attitudes are the product of a method of reasoning which is now geriatric. The rational elites, obsessed by structure, have become increasingly authoritarian in a modern, administrative way. The citizens feel insulted and isolated. They look for someone to throw stones on their behalf. Any old stone will do. The cruder the better to crush the self-assurance of the obscure men and their obscure methods. The New Right, with its parody of democratic values, has been a crude but devastating stone with which to punish the modern elites. The New Left, which will eventually succeed it, could easily turn out to be equally crude.

And yet none of this can be said without considering just how bad things were two centuries ago, even sixty years ago, and how relatively good they are now. We have taken to punishing our elites and condemning the way our society works because of real flaws, but flaws in what context?

Take public health, for example. In the late seventeenth century Paris was without a sanitary system — its streets were a gigantic latrine for five hundred thousand people. The terraces of the king's palace — the Tuileries — smelled so strong that no one dared go onto them except to relieve themselves.

At that point in history, the modern administrative structure was in its infancy, limited to little more than the *maîtres de requêtes*. An early form of ombudsmen, they were judges who listened to complaints and requests addressed to the king. Richelieu had not even begun his razing of city walls with the idea of making central administrative control possible.

One hundred and fifty years later, in 1844, very little had changed. Six hundred thousand of the 912,000 residents of Paris lived in slums.[3] At Montfaucon, in the north of the city, transporters of excrement, who had been collecting door-to-door during the night, dumped their loads into great swamps of the same matter. Men spent their lives living on these shores and wading out every day in search of small objects they might sell. At Lille, in the 1860s, in the working-class district of Saint-Sauveur, 95 percent of the children died before the age of five.

The famed Paris sewer system was created over a long period in the second half of the last century. The long delays were largely due to the virulent opposition of the property owners, who did not want to pay to install sanitary piping in their buildings. These people were the New Right of their day. The Prefect of Paris, Monsieur Poubelle, succeeded in forcing garbage cans on the property owners in 1887 only after a ferocious public battle. This governmental interference in the individual's right to throw his garbage into the street — which was, in reality, the property owner's right to leave his tenants no other option — made Poubelle into the "cryptosocialist" of the hour. In 1900 the owners were still fighting against the obligations both to put their buildings on the public sewer system and to cooperate in the collection of garbage. In 1904 in the eleventh arrondissement, a working-class district, only two thousand out of eleven thousand buildings had been piped into the sewer system. By 1910 a little over half the city's buildings were on the sewers and only half the cities in France had any sewers at all.

Photos of early-twentieth-century Marseilles show great piles of refuse and excrement down the centre of the streets. Cholera outbreaks were common and ravaged the population. In 1954 the last city without, St. Rémy de Provence, installed sewers.

It was the gradual creation of an effective bureaucracy which brought an end to all this filth and disease, and the public servants did so against the desires of the mass of the middle and upper classes. The free market opposed sanitation. The rich opposed it. The civilized opposed it. Most of the educated opposed it. That was why it took a century to finish what could have been done in ten years. Put in contemporary terms, the market economy angrily and persistently opposed clean public water, sanitation, garbage collection and improved public health because they appeared to be unprofitable enterprises which, in addition, put limits on the individual's freedoms. These are simple historic truths which have been forgotten today, thus permitting the fashionable belief that even public water services should be privatized in order that they might benefit from the free-market system.

It was the property owners, with their unbelievably narrow self-interest, who made Marx a man to follow. That there was not some sort of abrupt social revolution in Western Europe and America in the late nineteenth and early twentieth centuries was due almost entirely to the devotion and gradual success of the administrative class. In effect they saved the property, rights and privileges of those who opposed their reforms. And they did so, despite being poorly paid, only half supported by the politicians, and resented — as they are still today — by those who had to contribute from their pockets.

How then, if the battle fought and won was both just and popular, have the old elites been able to convince so many citizens that public servants and the services they offer are to be looked upon with contempt? In part the explanation has been a spreading realization among those elites who oppose universal services that reason is just a method. It was therefore only a matter of time before people who opposed such things as public sanitation learned how to use the relevant skills, as one might learn how to use a new weapon. More to the point, the men of reason, like Chinese mandarins, have always been for hire. And pools of large capital lying where they do, the bulk of new rational argument is now provided by corporate-sponsored think tanks and foundations. Two centuries after the Encyclopédistes, their victims are busy paying for their own version of the truth to be written.

Citizens are nevertheless surprised by the facility with which the rational mechanism is being used to do exactly the opposite of what the eighteenth-century philosophers intended. This inversion has been facilitated by a natural division between elected representatives and administrative elites. Their on-again, off-again cooperation lasted through much of the late nineteenth and early twentieth centuries. For the last quarter century, it has been definitively off. At the best of times it was a fragile alliance which involved temporarily putting aside opposing values and different origins.

The main line of reason was always the creation of a new man — one who would revolutionize the governing of all men, thanks to a new process. The result of this public-private revolution would be a fair society. Democratic control was not part of the process. And moral belief was there only indirectly, because many eighteenth-century philosophers were convinced their rational structures would finally release the full force of morality into the public place.

"I sincerely believe," Jefferson wrote in 1814, while Napoleon was still raging across Europe and everything seemed to have gone wrong, "in the general existence of a moral instinct. I think it is the brightest gem with which the human character is studded."[4] Almost thirty years before, in 1787, Jefferson had been American ambassador in Paris. In those last moments before the cataclysm, he was the only man of reason on the scene to have applied his ideas to a successful revolution. His house was constantly filled with French thinkers and politicians seeking advice. In that atmosphere, he wrote to a young American:

> Man was destined for society. His morality, therefore, was to be formed in this object. He was endowed with a sense of right and wrong, merely relative to this. . . . The moral sense, or conscience, is as much a part of man as his leg or arm. It is given to all human beings in a stronger or weaker degree, as force of members is given them in a greater or less degree. It may be strengthened by exercise.[5]

There is no suggestion here that reason and morality were linked. As for the new systems, both American and French, they were experiments, but the idea of representative government had been neither assumed nor sought. Reason was to provide a process thanks to which new, properly trained elites would be able to create a better society. The result would be a just form of authoritarian government. Men of power would be expected to exercise self-control. Failing that, the system itself would limit them.

Democracy was an unexpected participant that somehow crashed the events. While the origins of modern reason lay with men principally interested in the uses of power, many of them royal or papal advisers seeking more effective ways to rule, those of democracy stretched back to the freemen of tribal northern Europe living in extended families. Little is known of this period after the decline of Rome. From the beginning, however, the concept of an association among equals runs through the evolution of democracy. The early attempts to reach beyond kinship resulted in gilds in Scandinavia and Germany. These gatherings of freemen began with little more than banquets and the swearing of oaths, but quickly evolved into self-protection, self-help groups. By the eighth century they were widespread in England. The earliest surviving gild statutes date from the first part of the eleventh century. Members swore faithful brotherhood to each other. "If one misdo, let all bear it; let all share the same lot," was the way the Cambridge Gild put it.

By the tenth century one could see the next stage — representative assemblies — emerging slowly in England with the delegates to the local Courts of Shire and the Hundred. Elsewhere in Europe, somewhat the same process was underway. There was a representative Cortes in Aragon in 1133 and Castile in 1162.

All these free associations predated the emergence of the European kings as an important force. Gradually the rising monarchs set about seizing all power in order to hand bits of it back, as if it were theirs to dispense arbitrarily. In Europe the concept of freemen in free association came under constant attack from these kings. Charlemagne began in earnest the efforts to control the gilds. In England these basic structures were left in place. Magna Carta in 1215 is often thought of as a struggle between king and barons. These were indeed the two groups with military power, but the dispute had to do, as Magna Carta clearly states, with the status of "all free men." The document lays out their rights in great detail.

These conflicts between freemen and kings began well before the gilds evolved into craft gilds tied to specific trades. The professional associations didn't abandon the principles of the old gilds. They carried on the idea of freemen in free association and fleshed out the concept of obligation. From their beginnings in pagan northern Europe, gild associations had been linked to oaths or contracts which turned on the obligations of the individual to the group. As the freeman's rights slowly grew, so did his obligations. Implicit in this was the idea of merit. The freeman had both to maintain and to merit his place in the association. As the circle widened and representative assemblies grew, so did this idea of meritocracy. A man chosen as a delegate to the Court of Shires was theoretically the best available, not simply an elder or a man with high inherited rank. A master craftsman in a craft gild held his position because of his skills.

The conversion of northern Europe to Christianity came well after the gilds were in place, but it gave comfort to the idea of freemen in free associations. After all, the underlying theme which the priests brought was that all men were equal before God. However, the Church went on, like the monarchies, to develop elaborate pyramidal structures designed to control the population. But the basic Christian theme remained and with the Reformation it was rereleased in a strengthened form which harped on the moral and social obligations of men equal before God. This renewed message was to play a major role in the affirmation of democratic rights.

When, in the early eighteenth century, many French philosophers focused on England and discovered a "fair society," they interpreted what they saw as a victory of ordered statehood. But what they had taken to be ordered statehood in reality had more to do with highly evolved tribalism which, thanks to the isolation of island life, had not been driven off course by external forces.

Democracy emerged in various parts of the West as a product of common sense, hardly related to intellect at all. It remained and remains an organic product of society, along with man's moral sense. Neither are structural nor analytical. Neither rose out of reason. Nor did reason rise out of them. Only with time could it be seen that an innate moral sense and a practical meritocracy were somehow in profound contradiction with efficient, rational structures. The freeman or gild concept had been a primitive version of participation via citizenship. The rational concept was participation by membership in an elite.

That the idea of government by elected representatives benefited at all from the various revolutions of reason must have been as much a surprise to the revolutionaries as to the kings. In fact, the new elites resisted step by step not simply the widening of the right to vote but the very principle of democratic participation. The new rational elites spoke of justice but defined the right to participate in the process by narrow criteria, such as privileged knowledge or levels of property ownership. The practical effect of this was that the Americans didn't reach universal suffrage, even for white males, until 1860; almost a century after the revolution. The Swiss beat them by twelve years. Denmark came third in 1866; then Norway in 1898. Most of the other modern elites, including the British, succeeded in resisting universal male suffrage until 1918 or 1919 — that is, until the return of the mistreated and angry armies from the first modern rational war made further resistance impossible.

Contemporary language doesn't equip us to distinguish between meritocracy and expertise. The two ideas have been actively confused, although they are actually in profound opposition. Whatever its flaws, the underlying assumptions of meritocracy are open-ended and embracing. They presume generosity, even if this presumption is often betrayed. The underlying assumptions of expertise and specialized knowledge are, on the other hand, elitist. They presume superiority and the privileged possession of answers. They promote both social barriers and political exclusion. It was the popular belief that a meritocracy could be enlarged through the simple redefinition of citizenship, which created the ongoing pressure for increased democracy. And it was the naturally self-dividing, structuralist and elitist tendencies of the rational elites which resisted this pressure and continues to undermine democracy's accomplishments.

France was the one exception to the rule of a long, slow battle leading eventually to one man, one vote. Almost from the beginning of the republican idea in power (1792), universal male suffrage was one of the qualifying characteristics. As a result, it appeared and disappeared with each succeeding revolution and coup d'état. The underlying message, which the rational elites were able to reinforce by holding themselves back just enough to suggest disapproval of the democratic process without openly opposing it, was that democracy should be associated with instability and political self-interest. Under the Third and Fourth Republics, this disassociation grew to be the continuous background music of national life. Rational administration, on the other hand — whether provided by a dictatorship, a liberal authoritarian leadership, or a strong bureaucratic management — was to be associated with fair, efficient and responsive government. The two Napoleonic experiences and that of Louis Philippe were there as early reminders.

This essential conflict between the new elites and the democratic process has never been publicly clarified in any of the Western nations. From the late eighteenth century on, the elected representative has been the odd man out in a world in which knowledge and expertise were meant to be guarantors of truth. At first glance this does not appear to be the case. Repeated constitutions have declared the rule of the popular will and guaranteed decision-making powers to elected assemblies. In some countries — those of British origin and Italy and Germany, for example — parliaments have almost absolute legal power. In others — such as the United States and France — power is divided among an elected executive, courts and the assemblies. But those assemblies are nevertheless legally decisive in the decision-making process. In other words, the people's representative has been inserted into the middle of the governing process as the supreme arbiter between executive action and expert administration on the one hand and the people on the other.

But it was clear from the beginning that those burdened with the responsibilities of practical power — the executive, the administrative elites, the courts — found the elected representative annoying and gratuitous. Given a chance, they actually rendered him gratuitous. The Napoleonic movement was early proof of that, as the forces of efficient, competent and Heroic power swept away the slowly burgeoning responsibilities of the elected. There was little protest from the legal experts, engineers, scientists, soldiers or public servants as Napoleon removed the democratic powers of the people. Nor did they disassociate themselves from his obsession with educating and organizing new elites, which went hand in hand with his lack of interest in training the general population. An alliance between a populist authoritarian executive and an efficient body of experts eliminated the time wasted with elected bodies. With a few exceptions, such as Chateaubriand and Madame de Staël, even the intellectuals remained silent, because they had, after all, formulated the idea of the rational state.

And after each subsequent authoritarian coup d'état, the rational elites pressed forward again to serve men like Louis Philippe and Napoleon III. These regimes devoted themselves to developing commercial and industrial infrastructures, modernizing city centres and constructing transportation systems. In fairness to Louis Philippe's more middle-class regime, education was also reformed to take in a broader sweep of people. The emphasis was nevertheless elsewhere and Napoleon III's rebuilding of Paris, under his planner-Prefect, Baron Georges Haussmann, was a prime example of the new, authoritarian elite phenomenon. For seventeen years one hundred thousand workmen tore down the core of medieval Paris and replaced it with an infrastructure of grand, wide and straight avenues. Thousands of architects, engineers, government administrators, corporations, bankers and speculators were employed full-time. Slums were replaced with solid, handsome buildings. The new sewer and clean water systems were part of the improvements, thus bringing cholera epidemics to an end. In the process, 27,500 houses were destroyed and the evicted families left to fend for themselves. Theirs was a long-term, not a temporary problem, because the Haussmann buildings were designed not for them, but for the new middle-class elites who identified with the regime and profited from it. The poor fled towards unplanned, uncontrolled slums on the edges of the city. These turned into the red belt around Paris, a Communist stronghold for a century.[6]

It is important to notice that the benefits, powers and relevant state structures gained by the elites were neither removed nor diminished when democracy returned in 1871. That is a general rule which can be observed in action again and again, in country after country, over the last two centuries.

Imperial grandeur and the desire to modernize were behind the unprecedented eviction and rebuilding campaign in Paris. So was crude political power, as the wide boulevards and avenues — designed for cavalry charges and cannon shots — cut straight through the rabbit warrens where popular uprisings had been common and difficult to contain. Emile Zola described in his novels the misery of the city under the Second Empire, little more than a century ago. For example from *Money*, a scene set in 1867 in one of the northern slums crowded with the evicted:

> Overcome with fear, Madame Caroline focused on the courtyard, a wasteland broken up with potholes, which the accumulated garbage had turned into one large cesspool. They threw everything there, since there was no pit for the purpose. It was a single great dung heap, growing all the time, poisoning the air. . . . Unsure of her footing, she tried to avoid the debris of vegetables and bones, while examining the habitations on either side, sort of animal lairs, indescribable, a single story high, half falling down, dilapidated and not propped up with any sort of support. Some had only tar paper for roofs. Many had no door, so she could see the black hole of a cave within, out of which came a sickening breath of misery. Families of eight, ten people were squeezed into these charnel houses, often without a bed; the men, the women, the children jammed in, causing each other to rot, like soiled fruit, left from childhood to the most monstrous promiscuity.[7]

But the alliance between authoritarian power and rational elites was by no means limited to France. The Napoleonic movement — that of the first Napoleon — spread throughout Europe in similar form. Populist aspirations were used everywhere to overthrow tired regimes in Italy, Germany and so on. The new elites of Trieste and Udine welcomed the change as their French equivalents had. When the authoritarian reality became clear, they were not discouraged from collaboration, because the building, organizing and training were already underway. That the vast majority of Napoleon's Grand Army — the one that died in the snows of Russia — was not French should be taken as a sign of the quasi-religious status which modern organization had attained.

This governing alliance grew and spread throughout the nineteenth century. Flagrant signs of it were to be seen wherever an authoritarian executive had won out over representative democracy. Ridding himself of Bismarck in 1890, Kaiser Wilhelm II of Germany had effectively abrogated responsible government by 1897. For two more decades he was able to concentrate on the construction of an empire, an economy and a military force with the full cooperation of a highly advanced social and administrative structure. Mussolini came to power in 1922 by threatening violence against a weakened democracy. By 1928 he had eliminated Italian political parties. During the more than two decades of his dictatorship, the administrative and economic elites kept the machinery of the state running, pleased — as the Fascist cliché went — to be making the trains run on time. The same was true in Nazi Germany, as Albert Speer, Hitler's minister of armaments, so convincingly described in his memoirs. It's interesting to note the lengths to which he went in order to paint himself and therefore all other technocrats as the victims of the system: "Technology is depriving mankind more and more of self-responsibility."[8] In other words he was attempting to remove the element of moral choice from his actions. A great deal has been written about the collaboration of the French technical and bureaucratic leadership from 1940 to 1944. And, indeed, had Britain been occupied after 1940, there is nothing except local chauvinism to suggest that the reaction would have been different.

But in all these cases the principal motivation was not specific ideological commitment to the authoritarian government in question, nor was it a lack of courage. To belong to a national elite was to serve the state, and the state wraps into its mythology everything from civil servants, scientists and judges to bank presidents and industrialists. Only the oddballs are capable of opposition. Most leaders of the French resistance had shown signs of what a rational man would call "peculiar behaviour" long before 1939.

As for the elected man, in the eyes of the new experts everywhere, he was grasping, self-interested, temperamental and capable of appealing to the worst in the populace in order to prolong his mandate. This attitude was implicit from the beginning of the rational argument. Francis Bacon's reference to "depraved politics" or, a little later, Adam Smith's to "that insidious and crafty animal vulgarly called a statesman or politician" have turned into a truism among administrators and specialists of the twentieth century. And so, each time there has been a renewal of the Napoleonic-Expert alliance — and there have been many over the last 150 years — most experts have not seemed particularly upset by the arrangement.

Thanks to these incidents and to the emergency governing powers required in countries threatened by new Napoleonic figures, the administrative religion with its sects of speed and efficiency was given a great boost. It has continued to strengthen and spread so that state structures have gradually reduced the representatives and their parliaments back to what they were before the Age of Reason — consultative bodies which let off steam, but can't really get in the way on any regular basis. They do meet more regularly than in the seventeenth century and are treated with great formal honour, and in major crises they are sometimes called upon to play essential roles. But that has always been the case. The modern executive, like the king before him, must turn to parliament when the ship of state is in danger. The American Congress appears, at first glance, to be the exception to this decline, but its powers have always been intentionally more political than policy shaping, immediate than long term, negative than creative.

It isn't surprising in this historical context that rational structures, moral beliefs and representative government have been confused as one in people's minds. Nor that today, while structures reign supreme, man's sense of right and wrong is in frenzied confusion. And that democracy in the West, after a gradual rise over 150 years, is in sharp decline. Not that there are fewer elections or fewer politicians or less talk of politics. There has never been so much voting and campaigning and talking throughout the developed world. But the direct effect of citizen politics upon policy and administration seems extremely tenuous. Parliaments have become colourful circuses and to the extent that they attempt to exercise power, it is increasingly as the public arm of lobby groups.

None of this would have been possible had the people themselves not been seduced by the religion of reason. Once they had accepted that such things as expertise, administration and efficiency were irrefutable values, they couldn't help but look upon their own assemblies — chosen by their own vote — as old-fashioned, talkative and inefficient gatherings. These were no longer places where all good citizens would aspire to serve for a time. Instead, the people took to watching their ministers dash schizophrenically about, lost between their attempts to become both administrators and stars. As administrators, they assimilate themselves with their bureaucrats in order to prove that the result of the democratic process is rational action. From there they somersault over and ever deeper into the light show of personality politics. They learn to project their looks, the whiteness of their teeth, their sporting abilities, their love for their wives and their ability to create fully formed children. Elected to set policy and govern, they flip frenetically from attempts at bureaucratic administration to embarrassing and irrelevant displays of "personality." Whatever policymaking aim they do manage to bring to power seems to wither away with experience.

An example as straightforward as sanitation demonstrates that the triangular coalition of moral sense, democracy, and rational structure took a long time to establish itself against the selfish interests of arbitrary power. Decades of revolutions, coups, crippling strikes, civil violence and civil wars testify to the difficulty of this general advance. With each victory, the new structures built up their defences and stocked up their weapons for the next advance. Even so it wasn't until the massacres of 1914–18 had drained away all the self-assurance of the old beliefs and the Russian Revolution had struck fear into even the most retrograde minds that the politicians and civil servants were able to begin seriously putting in place their new utopia. From that point on everything moved very fast. So fast that no one noticed the coming apart of the triangular coalition.

The widespread popular sense that moral standards, democracy and rational action were a holy trinity remained clear so long as the civil servants constituted a different class from the politicians, with each bringing different skills to the process of reform. Men from a greater and greater variety of social origins had been finding their way into the political process on all sides of the spectrum, while bureaucracies throughout the Western world were filled with relatively similar men from the middle and upper-middle classes. This marked the civil service as a quieter, almost altruistic place from which to advance society. The politicians, on the other hand, came together in a wild marketplace of ideological and financial ambitions to hammer out what to do and how to convince the populace to accept it, without giving much thought as to how it would be done.

But these characteristics began to change rapidly. As the bureaucracies consolidated the power which went with responsible government and social initiatives, so they attracted much more ambitious people. And once the rational system was in place, it was bound to attract an increasing number of candidates who were less interested in policy ideas and more interested in structures — interested, that is, in managing them, controlling them, playing them and acquiring the substantial power which automatically came with them.

These systems had in a flash become as widespread as the church structures during the heyday of European Christianity. They offered a detailed regularity which reached the entire population in a way not seen since the Roman Empire. Children stood up all across certain countries at precisely the same moment to sing their national anthem. In some nations they did the same dictation or precise history lesson on the same day, hour and probably minute in every village, town and city. Taxes were evaluated on standard forms. Animals were slaughtered according to national standards. Provincial barriers were broken down and, with the exception of a few peculiar cases like Canada and Australia, were destroyed absolutely.

Illiteracy was on the retreat, social programs were being financed, and rotten meat was being kept off the market. By fairly objective standards, the Western world was becoming a better place to live. And the programs went on multiplying in the flood of reform, so long frustrated and now released to spill over borders from country to country.

But the very success of reform was gradually favouring bureaucrats with a talent for management and blocking the way for those who offered ideas and commitment. By the early 1960s, the managers were setting the pace. This did not appear to be a betrayal of the idea of rational government. Rather, it was a fulfillment. And the structure now stood on its own, virtually freed from political constraints by its very size, complexity and professionalism. There was no place for a moral sense in such a sophisticated organization. The general assumption — now two centuries old — was that to be rational was in itself to be moral. As for the democratic procedure, it seemed increasingly inefficient and unprofessional. To debate policy in a public, populist manner was somehow flashy, embarrassing, pretentious. Policy emerged best and logically from professional analysis. Amateurs invited the release of superficiality, misguided emotions and doubtful ambitions.

The servants of the state — relatively recent servants — now faced the same problem that had faced the Jesuits after Ignatius's death. They were sworn to our contemporary equivalents of poverty and humility. Indeed, if you wanted riches and fame, you went into business or politics. But the reality was that they now had power and worked with the powerful. As with the Jesuits, humility was bound to disappear in the flush of success. It wasn't long before senior civil servants were paid more than politicians. And in the case of state corporations, the senior positions had to pay at industry levels in order to get industry "quality." So bureaucrats, who were one step removed from the heart of power, were paid more than bureaucrats at the centre, who, in turn, were paid more than their political masters. As with the Jesuits, the order was rich and its members lived within the order. Not that the bureaucrats profited from the funds of others. But in the process of administering this enormous system the life of a senior bureaucrat could become that of a comfortable and sometimes a rich man. They travelled, ate, met and gave orders as, a few years before, only a rich man could have done.

At the same time a popular belief was growing that government bureaucracies did not deliver. Endless stories of inefficiency and indolence became part of public debate. There was the banal wrench for which the Pentagon paid thousands. And the English child sent by a state social worker back to parents known to have beaten her. The parents then beat her to death. In the subsequent inquiry, the social worker was exonerated thanks to the support of her Local Authority. And the five thousand Canadians registered for unemployment payments who, during a mail strike, did not appear in person to collect their cheques, thus revealing that the names were fraudulent. These tales of woe go from the tragic to the grandiose. For example, it was the British Exchequer, not its chancellor, which managed to keep Britain out of the European Monetary Snake when it was first set up.

Of course, the sum total of all the failures is small potatoes when compared to the size of the modern state. But each little snag acts as a red flag, alienating the population from their public servants and driving onward the search for ever more sophisticated structures which, theoretically, will eliminate all risk of failure.

Again and again new cabinet ministers, provoked by these institutional difficulties, throw themselves into the conquest of their departments. They set out to master the machine, to understand it, to make it function better, to make it responsive to the slightest public wish. They pore over organization charts, program commitments, hiring standards, reporting lines. They are determined to master the process by becoming part of it. And by the end of their long working day they are physically and mentally exhausted.

Needless to say the minister in question hasn't had a moment to think about policy and execution. The administrative game, however, is not without its attractions. In the absence of reflection there is an addictive level of excitement which fills the day. The minister comes to feel that he is running an important organization. He begins to identify with his extremely competent employees. He becomes what is known as a good minister — which now means someone who is good with his department. What he has actually become is an honorary deputy minister. A superfluous undersecretary.

This bureaucratization of ministers has become so prevalent that in France the bureaucrats have become the ministers, thus completing the unity of structure inherent in the rational approach. There is only one real government class, political and bureaucratic, and that is usually entered through the Ecole Nationale d'Administration.

The public everywhere, along with most of the politicians, have accepted the "administrative" criterion as the right one for judging their ministers. However, an hour spent with any contemporary officeholder will illustrate the effect that this system has on his ability to think. His desk is littered with the endless detail of briefing material. When he has read that, more will take its place. His signature is awaited on endless memos and letters. In each of these he takes personal responsibility for every gas pump in the country or whatever the subject may happen to be. Deputies, undersecretaries, assistant deputies, advisers, assistants run in constantly to seek his advice on an oil leak off the West Coast, or on a request for funds from the East Side Modern Dance Troupe, or how to cover up the escape from the country of a paroled criminal. Not only does a "good" minister have no mental or physical time for policy, he also becomes an apologist for his departmental employees.

Perhaps a minister should not attempt to know or to understand every detail of his employees' activities. Perhaps he should not administer his department. Perhaps he should not work long hours. Perhaps he should keep his distance from the work of his department and thus allow his employees to be judged upon their results. This would be hard on some civil servants, but it would also benefit the most capable. The minister might not have on the tip of his tongue the answer to every question. Would the world suffer for that? He might also have the time and be more often in the frame of mind, necessary to consider policy and to reflect upon its execution. In other words, it might be worth asking whether, since the politician and the bureaucrat have different responsibilities, they would not each do better if they did their own job and kept a certain distance from one another.

Instead, the co-opting of ministers by their departments has become standard procedure — so standard that the ministerial function has lost much of its power. With that power has gone the essential role of cabinet discussion and therefore, in both parliamentary and executive democracies, of cabinet power. And all of this has happened without the political class admitting publicly that there has been any change.

In response to this ministerial crippling, the politicians have developed two tools of government. The first is a web of ministerial-level inter-departmental committees. These are meant to increase information flow, discussion and efficiency. This is supposed to help policy debates break through the barriers of departmental bureaucracy. The second is the explosion in the number of direct advisers to the head of government. These advisers, usually brought in from outside, take on the policy responsibilities which are properly those of cabinet ministers. They have no line function. No legal responsibilities. They are simply the president or the prime minister's adviser on, say, foreign policy. Everyone knows that the adviser alone has constant access to the president on that subject. Everyone understands that ideas can be put forward and problems solved by dealing directly with the adviser and avoiding the relevant minister and his department.

Both the committees and the advisers have altered profoundly the nature of representative government. And yet they have come about without any public debate and, of course, without any constitutional change. We are now pretending to be legally governed one way, when we are in fact governed another.

The interdepartmental committees attempt to treat structural problems with yet more structure. There are cabinet committee systems, for example, which group ministers by subject into smaller sections. The idea is to bring together in a single room every aspect of an important policy development area. Intelligent and complete discussions should then be possible without the overbearing inflexibility of full cabinet meetings. And departmental rivalries should be eliminated. In most countries there are a good dozen of these committees focused on such sectors as economic development or security or social policy. There will also be a theoretically all-powerful inner committee called something like Priorities and Planning or the National Security Council. Many have their own permanent secretariats. This gives them the consistency necessary to duplicate the cabinet itself by simply cutting up the pie of government responsibility in a different way.

These committees were supposed to free ministers from their departmental bureaucratic restraints, thus enabling them to think and act. Instead, by moving policy from the general interests of the cabinet to the specialized interests of the committee, they have shifted debate from political, social and moral priorities to that of concentrated expertise. And expertise is the area in which deputy ministers always outshine ministers.

In Britain the minister arrives in the committee primed by his own civil servants, carrying under his arm his thick, departmental briefing books and accompanied by at least one of his own bureaucrats — the one most expert in the subject of the day. The expert is there to whisper in his ear. The results of this situation are so blatantly obvious that a highly popular comic television series, "Yes, Minister," has been built around the minister–civil servant relationship. In Canada the expert is actually permitted to join in the ministerial debate. The civil servants, in any case, have already had lower-level meetings with civil servants from the other participating departments to work out the matter at hand before the ministers even enter the committee room.

In this context of ministerial debate structured to focus primarily on expertise, the ministers are thus at a severe disadvantage. Policy has, in effect, been made to conform to administrative priorities. The decisions of these committees are then presented to full cabinet with a recommendation. There the concerned and, compared to their colleagues, more or less expert ministers will speak as a single voice to the unconcerned. Only a nonexpert minister prone to suicide would speak up in opposition to the committee's recommendation. All the facts will be marshaled on the other side. A nonexpert minister could invoke principle, moral instinct, or common sense, but all these are suspect when faced by rational truth. He would also be inviting massed opposition to his own policies in the future. Thus cabinet committee decisions, which are fundamentally bureaucratic, are preemptive strikes on the real decision-making powers of the full cabinet. They weaken still further ministerial government. The extent to which the various ministerial committee decisions are themselves determined by preemptive strikes from the civil service is illustrated by the fact that there are dozens and dozens of nonministerial interdepartmental committees preparing the decisions to be "taken" at the interministerial committees. The direction in which this restructuring leads can be seen in Britain, where the very existence of the committees is secret, as is membership on any or all of them. Thus the primary and essential level of governmental decision making has been totally removed from visibility.

The United States differs only in that the cabinet is not responsible to the electors. The inner cabinet role was taken by the National Security Council for the first time under President Kennedy and was first perverted by its servants when Henry Kissinger was the adviser or chief servant. The subcommittees of the council function much the way cabinet committees do. Again, if the adviser is strong, then the unofficial nature of this structure, like the British version, gives it even more of an administrative stranglehold on a theoretically political process.

Beyond these parallel structures, there have been endless cure-all committees guaranteed to bring unresponsive bureaucracies into line with political objectives. Planning, programming and budgeting systems have been succeeded by public expenditure surveys, to say nothing of policy analysis and review or management by objectives or zero-based budgeting or cash limits and expenditure envelopes.[9]

None of these committees, cabinet or otherwise, has succeeded in doing what it was set up to do. That is, none of them has given fresh impetus to government. They have simply weighted it down further. As Beaverbrook complained during World War II: "Committees are the enemy of production."

The other tool used by political leaders to motivate their stalled government structures is the personal adviser. These individuals occupy the space between the leader and the structure. Advisers are unelected and nonresponsible. They are neither the people's representatives nor the people's servants. They are a republican version of the king's men — a civilian version of the praetorian guard. They represent an attempt by the head of government to get around government structures.

The Western praetorian guard is most visible — which does not necessarily mean most powerful — in the United States, where, under president, after president the controversy surrounding their advisers has grown. Sometimes these disputes and scandals have had to do with initiatives taken or orders given without proper authority. Often they have to do with corruption. Or with adventures into the worlds of security and defence. When the President's chief of staff is incompetent — as Hamilton Jordan was under President Carter and Donald Regan under President Reagan — or touched by scandal — as H. R. Haldeman was under President Nixon or John Sununu under President Bush — their power does not necessarily immediately shrink away. They exist only through the president's image and so they must first be perceived by the president as a political liability. When that happens the entire entourage will turn on them in a self-protective reflex.

People now assume that one of the central focuses of our attention on the American republic has always been the president's staff. But this is incorrect. Cabinet members were still carrying out their full functions in the 1960s. The loss of power to the White House staff began in earnest under President Kennedy. He was obsessed by what he was convinced were the obstructionist powers of the civil service establishment and the stultifying effects of all formal meetings, particularly committee meetings. He therefore called the cabinet together as little as possible because he thought this "to be unnecessary and involve a waste of time . . . All these problems Cabinet Ministers deal with are very specialized."[10] The cabinet never met to discuss policy. Policy was dealt with in small gatherings at which he and his advisers dominated. Apart from a few cabinet secretaries like Robert McNamara, who was prized by the White House and in any case could hold his own with anyone, this meetingless system of government meant that all power lay with the President and his advisers. Put another way, denied any regular relationship with the President, the secretaries and their departments were powerless. Foreign policy was made by Kennedy with his National Security Adviser, McGeorge Bundy, a professor from Harvard. In effect, they prepared the way for Henry Kissinger's usurpation of constitutional power from the same position of National Security Adviser eight years later. Bundy and the White House staff undermined Dean Rusk, the Secretary of State, by making fun of him behind the scenes, particularly because he liked meetings.[11] This parallels exactly Kissinger's more vicious undermining of then Secretary of State William Rogers.

The Kennedy method succeeded in that it gave him the personal power he wanted. However it seems to have permanently damaged the power of the cabinet and under successive presidents less dominant than himself, it has given uncontrolled power to the presidential advisers. This imbalance went to an all-time extreme under President Nixon, when the combination of White House power and isolation turned government towards conspiratorial and criminal acts.

Jimmy Carter, during his run for the White House, wrote that he would reinstitute "Cabinet government to prevent the excesses of the past." Never would "members of the White House staff dominate or act in a superior position to the members of our cabinet."[12] But in the middle of his term he spent forty-eight hours firing or forcing the retirement of five out of twelve members of his cabinet. His principal reason was their inability to get along with his own personal advisers. The victims, including Michael Blumenthal at Treasury, Joseph Califano at Health, Education and Welfare, Brock Adams at Transportation and James Schlesinger at Energy, were among the most successful and most aggressive members of the cabinet. As presidential chief of staff, Hamilton Jordan immediately went on television to deny publicly that these changes were made to give greater power to the White House. "It is a question of competence," he explained. At the same time, Carter's National Security Adviser, Zbigniew Brzezinski, was widely admired for his successful battle to become the nation's chief foreign policy architect.[13] As for the presidency of Ronald Reagan, it took the praetorian guard phenomenon to its logical conclusion. An aging head of state endowed with a limited IQ and a short attention span inevitably allowed many of the powers of a monarchical position to slip into the hands of his staff and, in this case, of his wife.

While it is true that cabinet secretaries are the unelected nominees of the president, they are nevertheless publicly appointed, after congressional hearings, to oversee an area of public responsibility. They are thus charged and vetted by the people's representatives to ensure that the nation's interests are served. The president's personal advisers, even the national security adviser, do not have to pass through congressional hearings. They have no public responsibilities. They are not accountable to the state. In general they are merely the president's sycophants.

Of course, American presidents have always had personal advisers, hangers-on and courtesans. The constitutional role of a republican monarch with limited powers made this inevitable. However, it is the continuing difficulty successive presidents have faced in making modern government work which has turned the members of their court into a virtual praetorian guard. To suggest that this was a conscious choice on someone's part would be to simplify falsely where the realities of power, personality and governing ensure complication. The reality is that over the thirty-year period since Kennedy, presidents — who were equipped with very different levels and types of intelligence, political skill, self-confidence and political beliefs — have all been rapidly closed in behind a wall of personal servants.

Praetorian guards have always had one characteristic in common. Because they are themselves beyond the constitutional and political laws, they have no effective rules to regulate their behaviour towards each other, their leader or the outside world. In the place of rules there is the privilege of sweet-scented anarchy. The battle for survival inside any palace — in this case, the White House — therefore, dictates that each adviser constantly struggle for more personal power or be eliminated. The difficulties between Nancy Reagan and her husband's Chief of Staff, Donald Regan, may have had a certain gossipy drama about them, but they were little different from those waged by Hamilton Jordan under President Carter or Henry Kissinger and H. R. Haldeman under President Nixon. One of the truisms proper to the growing power of presidential advisers is that although brought in to help stimulate a frustrating government system, they invariably end up undermining it.

The tendency throughout the West is the same. Mrs. Thatcher's personal economic adviser, Professor Alan Walters, forcing the resignation of Chancellor of the Exchequer Nigel Lawson, in 1989, for example. Or there was her use of a civil servant, Bernard Ingham, as both head of government information services — an administrative position — and as her personal political spokesman. In 1990 she sent her foreign policy adviser, Charles Powell, a civil servant, to a small private lunch organized to persuade the owner of a sympathetic newspaper, the *Daily Telegraph*, that it ought to give the government greater support.[14]

Brian Mulroney has managed to confuse the political with the administrative in an indiscriminate manner. He puts political friends into the civil service policy bureau — the Privy Council Office — and public servants into his personal political office. This culminated with a senior civil servant, Derek Burney, becoming his private secretary — that is, his political chief of staff. President Mitterrand's bevy of advisers for a long time were a reserve pen for the new elites. They moved directly from the Elysée to senior bureaucratic and political jobs, as if they were above and beyond the constituted powers of the cabinet. Increasingly the American president uses his advisers in the same way. When he wants to strengthen his control over a cabinet department, he moves someone out of his praetorian guard into the ministerial position. President Nixon catapulted Henry Kissinger from National Security Adviser to Secretary of State. President Reagan converted his personal Chief of Staff, James Baker, into Secretary of the Treasury.

This appearance of praetorian guards around elected presidents and prime ministers tells us two things. First, these leaders do not believe they will get what they need from the state structures unless they have what amounts to personal strongmen to ensure it. Second, heads of government no longer believe it necessary to treat representative assemblies as their primary interlocutor or as the source of political legitimacy. In other words, our leaders are returning to a guarded version of the original Napoleonic–rational elites alliance.

The rational elites have pushed the cause of modernization and efficiency with such assurance and persistence that any failure must be blamed on having gone neither far nor fast enough. Their definition of governance has become the norm. In response the people's representatives have been trying desperately to recapture their place at the heart of public power by modernizing themselves. But how can a populist assembly render itself efficient?

The great difficulty for elected representatives is that their chief tool is the word. They need it to argue ideas and to decide on action. But in a rational system of government, the unstructured word is a waste of time. What counts are executive action and effective administration. Even the concept of leadership now turns on those same skills. As for the role of the assemblies, it is increasingly believed by the citizenry that "Talk is air. Debate accomplishes nothing. All they do is sit around and talk."

Much of the responsibility for the decline of the word, as Marshal McLuhan pointed out, can be laid at the feet of electronic technology. While in our real lives we are unable to escape the cage of systems, our senses have been freed to embrace nonlinear imagination in new ways. Seeing and hearing so much more now, we have less reason to talk. We may even find it increasingly difficult to give an order to our words, because the images we watch and the sounds we hear are more often integral than sequential.

For example, those who have grown up since the arrival of television tend to watch five or more programs at once, holding a remote-control device and flipping channels every few seconds. The viewers know the ritual of these programs and so have no need to watch the step-by-step unfolding of events. Instead, they switch from program to program, spreading themselves throughout the whole.

Television is only one of the means of immediate communication which surround us. Sounds and images are everywhere. In elevators, bus terminals, cinemas, airplanes. There is scarcely a moment of electronic silence in the day. What meaning can organized debate have in a civilization which is able to transmit images to receptors implanted on an individual's retina? Is it surprising, then, that senators, deputies, members and representatives feel trapped by the weight of classical debate — a means of group reflection whose parameters were more or less set in the city-state of Athens?

And yet they and we are wrong to assimilate the intellectual revolution, which electronics may be bringing, with the doctrine of the rational elites. The former is new and, like the brain or indeed like classical debate, easily escapes the chains of structure. The rational approach, on the other hand, is now severely dated by its dependence on complex structures to hold and direct the minds and emotions of the citizen.

Nevertheless technology and reason have somehow been thrown together in both modern philosophy and popular mythology as if they were children of the same family. And this has increased our pessimism about the democratic process.

Citizens once gave their elected members great support against the nonelected, or executive, authorities. Now the member stands in isolation between the public and those who govern. The technocrats have already converted their ministers to the essential nature of efficiency in government. The ministers arrive in Parliament, or before congressional committees, dressed up in their efficient clothes. The elected representatives have great difficulty resisting the assumption that ministers should be judged on their effectiveness rather than on their policies. The forces of expertise and power insist that running things properly is the essence of modernity.

Uninformed policy discussions are amateurish and a waste of time, and so such debates are now among the least important functions of an assembly. For some time ordinary members have been rising to speak to virtually empty Houses. However, until recently, the minister whose bill was under debate stayed in his place to hear what was said and to be ready to reply to pertinent attacks. In most assemblies the minister now usually stays away. Until recently when the leader of a party rose to speak, members of other parties came to listen, partially out of respect, partially out of interest. Now the other parties purposely empty the House, as if to deny the opposing leader any credibility.

In place of the debating of policy, some sort of Question Period has become the most important moment of the day. It is used mainly to ask ministers questions about specific administrative failures. This falls in with the now-received wisdom that a modern elected representative will give great importance to judging a minister on his efficiency. The resulting test of wills is potentially also the minister's moment of public glory. To perform well he must know about every bridge and way station. He must have a ready answer to explain why any incident mentioned is not the fault of his department — that is to say, of his bureaucrats.

The pressure to conform to this doctrine of structure and method being what it is, these assemblies have applied to themselves the same standards they apply to ministers. And so a gaze back over the last half century of parliamentary reform shows that, in every country, almost every reform was aimed at greater speed to ensure faster passage of more laws and smoother handling of government business.

But is the nature of civilization "speed"? Or is it "consideration"? Any animal can rush around a corral four times a day. Only a human being can consciously oblige himself to go slowly in order to consider whether he is doing the right thing, doing it the right way, or ought in fact to be doing something else. The conscious decision to move slowly is not in contradiction to speed. A human can also decide to stop for a time, or to go very fast for a specific reason, for a specific period of time. Speed and efficiency are not in themselves signs of intelligence or capability or correctness. They do not carry with them any moral value. They don't necessarily make any social contribution. The most horrifying, violent moments of the twentieth century have centred around regimes wedded to efficiency and to speed. On the limited administrative level of the delivery of services, these two characteristics can, of course, be useful, but they are not in themselves manifestations of civilization.

The principal effect of constant efficiency assaults on Western assemblies has been to discourage reflection, if not to make it actually impossible. These places have become little more than shunting yards for legislation on its way through. Such a change had to have an impact on how the public would see its elected representatives. Suddenly they appeared to play no visibly useful role.

It follows that the assemblies have gradually altered what they require of their members. Tradition had it that elected representatives arrived with interests — defence of local concerns, consideration of national policy, support of friends or party and personal ambition. The reality was that an average member might have one or two of these, while other members would have others. Even the most local of politicians was at least an imperfect representative of real people. And all together they would constitute the assembly's mind, which was a reflection of the people's. In that sense the public assembly was electronic from the beginning. It was nonlinear and irrational because, at a single seating, it represented the whole. And that dense mass of national representation was the only thing that could force the racing structures of government to stop or at least to slow up in order to consider the public interest with greater care.

Now that assemblies are no longer places to think or from which to rise to great heights, most members fall into one of two groups — the devotees of local politics on the one hand, and those who arrive, ready for power, on the other. As for seeking to serve in an elected opposition, the contemporary elites see little point in this. A man on the rise is almost embarrassed to find himself formally and publicly against the constituted authorities. In the rational state, power is everything. Only losers oppose. Only marginal outsiders are proud to be on the outside.

The arrival in force of a breed of politicians who respond to the narrow focus on power should not be taken as proof that politics are dominated by egotism or venality. Rather, it confirms that, in the minds of both the citizenry and the expert elites, the administrative process has melded into one with the decision-making process. As early as the 1950s, François Mitterrand set out his central rule for contemporary public life: "As for the politician, there is only one possible ambition: to govern."[15] He entered his first ministry in 1944 and was still in place nearly half a century later.

Curiously enough, the primary purpose of the democratic process was never intended to be the election of a government, although one way and another governments did come to reflect the makeup of the assembly. The essential element was the proper constituting of a chamber of public reflection — a sort of national club — which would produce decisions in the public interest and control the government. Now, in most countries, the constituting of an assembly is little more than a mathematical process which leads to the immediate conferral of absolute power on a government. The same mathematical process is repeated once every four or five or seven years. This is in effect an elective monarchy.

Most Westerners quite happily embrace the American mythology, according to which the United States is the country and system of the future. But the United States has been the future for more than two centuries. The first of the revolutionary democracies, like the first television or the first mass-produced car, is now the most old-fashioned. It isn't surprising, that to protect themselves against the abuses of an eighteenth-century monarchy, elective or otherwise, they had from the beginning created their system of checks and balances. These included two assemblies, a strong court and the electoral college, which still technically chooses the president.

The American presidency, at its best, could have been an element in the evolution towards a healthy democratic process. At its worst it was an elective monarchy, only marginally different from the kings it sought to replace; absolute monarchs, who were constantly being nipped at the heels by a sophisticated mob of special interests — some legally constituted but most from a great and varied pack of courtesans. The presidency has moved toward this worst-case scenario. And all the other democracies, caught in the logic of rational government, have slipped in the same direction. Just as the end of cycles somehow come to resemble their beginnings, so we now find ourselves faced by the problems of the mid-eighteenth century. The more evolved and careful forms of democracy seem out of place. The American model, on the other hand, seems perfectly adapted to this civilization of power worshiping, decision by courtesanage, limited public participation and high levels of personal corruption.

The amputation of the real power of representative assemblies amounts to a major change in our civilization's view of itself. Curiously enough for a people who have devoted so much of the last century to exploring the individual's inner self, we have been overtaken by this change in a largely unconscious manner. It is as if a central nerve or muscle had been surgically removed from the body of the civilization, resulting in something like a lobotomy.

The emasculation of the Roman Senate under Augustus inaugurated the disintegration of Roman society. Ahead lay prosperity and glory greater than the strict, simple, tough Romans had ever known or imagined. But all that glory was built on a declining civil body. The "bread and circuses" of the later empire are generally equated with imperial degeneracy and a drift by the rural population to the city, following the imperial decision to import rather than to bother growing wheat. This is true in the same way that the British Parliament's repeal of the Corn Laws combined with the importing of cheap Indian cotton brought on a short imperial flurry followed by collapse. Or that the contemporary American decision to manufacture as much as possible abroad with cheap labour, while concentrating on services at home, is undermining their own civilization. But the point is that, with the decline of Roman society's internal mechanisms, the emperors were obliged to distract their citizens from the fact that they had become irrelevant to their own civilization.

This is a very simple conundrum. Societies grow into systems. The systems require management and are therefore increasingly wielded, like a tool or a weapon, by those who have power. The rest of the population is still needed to do specific things. But the citizens are not needed to contribute to the form or direction of the society. The more "advanced" the civilization, the more irrelevant the citizen becomes.

We are not quite so advanced as that, but neither are we so far off. Our professional elites have spent the last half century arguing over management methods, as if these were the only proper areas of political interest. If we could bring ourselves to think of reason as merely one of several management techniques and as something separate from the democratic process, our understanding of the situation would be quite different. In truth, if there are solutions to our confusion over government, they lie in the democratic, not the management, process. And essential to this is the reactivation or destreamlining of the assemblies. The reestablishment of true popular gatherings is one of the few easy actions available to the citizen. All it would require is a realization in the public mind that the decision-making process — that is, the process of creating national policy — is profoundly different from the administrative process. The two have no characteristics in common. One is organic and reflective. The other is linear and structured. One attempts to waste time usefully in order to understand and to build consensus. The other aims at speed and delivery. One is done of the people. The other is done for the people.

A great deal would follow naturally from the reestablishment of this distinction. Citizens would take a greater interest in their assembly and this would give courage to the representatives. They, in turn, would feel strong enough to establish a more independent relationship with the government, even in the parliamentary context. This would remind the ministers that they themselves have been victimized and made to feel permanently inadequate by the imposed religion of administrative competence. Only the most insecure of public men could believe that there is real value in mastering briefing books, covering for administrative error and living in a world of banal secrets which any child could see aren't worth keeping. Instead, they could be delegating to their employees and concentrating on the development of real policies.

The most difficult part of the adjustment would be getting rid of that sense, intrinsic to rational systems, that everything public must run smoothly. For example, that nuclear accidents can only be incidents. Or that artificial public calm will prevent public panic, and that calming lies are therefore necessary. Or that policy must emerge mysteriously and fully formed from committees of ministers, whose very existence is often secret. Why should policy appear like a phoenix from the fire, as if it were the natural and inevitable product of a rational process? This phoenix is now so much a part of our lives that it has become as dull and as tasteless as a battery hen.

The proper debating of policy is not smooth. Words are not air. Talk is not a waste of time. Arguing is useful. And speed is irrelevant unless there is a war on. The political class would have to get rid of the fear of verbal disorder which the technocratic classes have instilled in them. In all probability a different sort of individual would then rise to public office.

This, however, is not the direction in which we are headed. Instead, the assemblies are becoming the boutiques of special-interest groups. Nine thousand lobbyists are now registered in Washington. Their job is not to sell the representative on their client's goods. It is to buy the representative's vote in return for local jobs, campaign contributions, promises of income on retirement, and, in the worst of cases, payments here and now. Had John Tower become the American secretary of defense in 1989, his confirmation would have been an accurate reflection of reality. The former Senator from Texas, a major armaments manufacturing state, was a former Chairman of the Armed Forces Committee, an ex-Senate lobbyist who earned $750,000 in a single year on commissions from arms manufacturers, and a close supporter of George Bush.[16] Had his nomination been confirmed, his title could quite properly have been changed from Secretary of Defense to Secretary of Procurement.

There is, as Jefferson said, nothing "so afflicting and fatal to every honest hope as the corruption of the legislature."[17] And, indeed, the world of experts — whether they are public servants, businessmen or professors — has used this visible corruption as evidence of how out of date democracy is.

The American Congress is so profoundly a part of the lobby system that, while persistent bad publicity meant the senators couldn't avoid voting against the confirmation of John Tower, neither could they attribute their vote to the real reason — his corruption. The debate began on a high note. Both senators and the press questioned whether a lobbyist for arms manufacturers ought to be the secretary of defense. The senators then shied away from the essential issue and instead focused in on whether Tower drank and fornicated too much to hold the job. The ex-senator's relationship with the corporations was not profoundly different from that of other senators. It was just that he had gone a little too far. He had drawn attention to himself and therefore to the general situation. He was sacrificed so that the others could continue. And yet there is little secret about what they do. The statistics are declared and published. Democratic Senator Lloyd Bentsen, for example, the former vice presidential candidate, got $8.3 million for the 1988 campaign from political action committees.[18] PACs are organized lobby groups. In 1993 President Clinton named him Secretary of the Treasury.

It was only around the turn of the century that the rise of professionalism and a growing belief in the extended rule of law identified public corruption as a specific evil to be eliminated. And most of it was rapidly eliminated. However, almost as fast, the structures and assumptions of the modern, rational state simply amended themselves in order to legalize, formalize and indeed structure all the old forms of public corruption right into their normal procedures.

There has always been corruption in public affairs. But never — not even in the worst decades of the eighteenth century —.was it legalized in such logical detail that corruption could spread quite openly throughout the entire system. In all probability one of the principal reasons for this new development has been the gradual loss of the elected assemblies' real power to the executive, the bureaucracy and the judiciary. With the assemblies denied the ability to serve the public interest properly, it was only a matter of time before they would find other interests to serve. For that matter, it was only a question of time before the great organized interests outside the democratic process noticed that the parliaments were profoundly idle, humiliated and discontent. Their meeting could not have been more natural.

The conversion or return of parliaments to lobbying centres has more to do with an elaborate void seeking a new role than with the venality of individual men. Now they have that new role and, with it, a new importance. At the same time they have abandoned all pretension of practical democratic leadership and left government in the hands of rational structure and of the executive branch.

In fairness, the requirement that lobbyists register in Washington may have seemed at first to be a way of limiting the influence of organized financial interests over the people's representatives. In reality it formalized the role of business inside the democratic process. And since there is always a temptation to make more money than legally permitted, this massive regularization of criminality has simply pushed the illegal activities closer to the heart of government structures. The savings and loan scandal is a prime example of this.

Of course, popular mythology has it that influence peddling is at its worst in the United States. But then nations have always comforted themselves by giving foreign origins to venereal diseases. The same is true for political corruption. The Canadian government, in its rush to become a mirror image of its southern neighbour, has now followed the disastrous American path of formalizing the lobbyist's role. The British, thanks to their abhorrence of formal structures, have been able to do the same thing without any question of principle being asked. Year by year the number of company directorships and consultancy contracts picked up by sitting British MPs, including ex-cabinet ministers, continues to grow. Only the most stringent adherence to hypocrisy allows people to avoid pointing out the obvious — that putting an MP on your board or giving him a contract is buying yourself a lobbyist in Westminster.[19] The difference between this and the old British "rotten borough" system is that MPs used to be bought before their election. Now they are usually not purchased until their market value can be established. In France the single administrative elite has occupied the three seats of power — bureaucratic, political and business. There is therefore no need for one elite to lobby the other. They are, like the Holy Trinity, alternately, and at their own bidding, three separate bodies or three in one, indivisible.

Indeed, civil servants throughout the West have now caught on to the financial possibilities inherent in their public role. As with the politicians, this often begins with small kindnesses from lobbyists — lunches, dinners, a case of wine at Christmas, invitations to the country on weekends or to shoot game in season. But in general the real plum comes with retirement, which is increasingly taken early so that the newly private citizen can lobby. The senior British civil servant, for example, now counts on getting directorships and even a chairmanship of a private corporation when he retires. As Anthony Sampson has put it, by his "mid-fifties he will be searching anxiously for directorships with which to round off — or to crown — his career."[20] How can this not be having an effect on his commitment to the public good during precisely those final years when he is in senior-enough positions to have an effect on policy? Can the secretary of cabinet or the permanent secretary at the treasury be consciously or unconsciously thinking only of the public's interests when he is already surreptitiously job hunting in private industry?

In short, public servants are cashing in on their years of employment by the state. It would seem, in fact, that their obsessions with modernization and efficiency have brought them voluntarily to the same view of public service to which many elected representatives have been indirectly driven by the emasculation of the assemblies.

But these are merely signs of the confusion within the system. Corruption of the public system follows quite naturally from the maze of private-industry fads which have been sweeping Western governments for the last three decades. Privatization, no-hiring, efficiency devices. In themselves these and others have been sometimes marginally helpful, sometimes marginally harmful. But the general introduction of industry standards into the public domain has had a disastrous effect on an already confused situation.

The imposition of short-term profit methods in an area which is only indirectly and in the long run profit-oriented could not possibly have worked. Expecting business methods and market forces to do the job of government, when business and the market fought desperately against every humane and social accomplishment of government over the last two centuries, makes no sense at all. The public interest and the profit motive may be made to cooperate through wise political leadership, but they are not interchangeable. They are nevertheless being treated as if they were. What this implies is that the public does not believe that the governmental structures work. But then the politicians and the public servants don't believe it either.

11

Three Short Excursions into the Unreasonable

I

The received wisdom about bureaucratic inefficiency is that governments are too big. Size has been identified as an evil. A promulgator of indolence, waste and confusion.

There is no historic proof for this. Both the Roman Empire and the Roman Church functioned perfectly well under those conditions. Gigantic trading companies have functioned smoothly since the Hanseatic League in the fourteenth century—and not primarily because of the profit motive, but because everyone was clear about what they were there to buy and sell. With a clear belief in the purpose of an organization, bodies of any size seem to find a reasonable way to operate. What, then, are the origins of our incorrect assumptions linking government size with inefficiency?

The explanation might well be the unidimensional style of modern structures. These structures do not appear to be simple. Often they seem incomprehensibly complex. That is only because the rational approach requires that everything be laid out in a logical manner. Large organizations often are not suited to this rigorously skeletal approach. Trying to force them into a logical outline has the effect of destroying their natural impetus and tying everyone up in relationships instead of letting them act.

Modern structure also assumes that all functions are alike; therefore, all functions may be modernized. By "modernized" is meant subjected to universal standards of organization and efficiency. This inevitably involves the measurement of production, of profitability, a belief that lean is efficient, a belief that employees weigh down production.

But some functions are profoundly manual or profoundly mechanical. To "modernize" their structure is to render them inefficient. And some functions are properly labour-intensive. To attempt to modernize them through leanness will simply make them ineffective. Some functions are not meant to be profitable. They exist to lay the groundwork for the

profitable functions of others. These non-profit functions of the state —
such as transportation and communications — make it possible for the
citizen and the economic structure to carry on their business. To the
extent that making either transportation or communications profitable
harms the state's basic infrastructure, the citizen's ability to operate at
full capacity is also harmed.

Nevertheless, the marketplace measurement of profitability has been
applied to the American, Canadian and English rail systems and to the
American and Canadian postal systems. This includes the assumption
that competition will improve service in communications, a devotion to
computerized methodology, arguments in favour of lean manpower, and
calculations of new investment versus possible financial returns. As a
result Canada, once owner of the most complex rail structure in the
world, is busy shutting it down, while the remaining trains are being
shaken apart on medieval railbeds. The United States, driven by the
same theories, destroyed its system before anyone else and is now trying
to put it back together. As for Britain, much of its population has no
choice but to use the trains. If they could avoid them, they would.

The more these systems decline, the more the economists and planners say that they can but go on declining. They assert that there are a
shrinking number of potential passengers and a lessening need for rail
transport. The reality is that the transport experts have decided rail
transport is outdated. Their investment in new equipment is therefore
almost negligible. In order to cover their losses, they raise the cost for
the passenger, while offering fewer and fewer services. They have created a self-fulfilling prophecy. The British, for example, invest one-
third of what the Germans spend per passenger kilometre. And they
compensate for the resulting decline in users by charging one-third
more per kilometre travelled.

The Germans, on the other hand, like the French, continue to treat
their rail system as a fundamental need, adhering to the nineteenth-
century idea of a national and eventually continental infrastructure,
which requires massive investment without any rational plan for a clear
financial return. As a result they have maintained a large staff at all
levels. They continue to take the old-fashioned view of customer service, of cleanliness, of maximum number — and therefore maximum
choices — in the use of trains, of good food and of reliability. They have
spent money and employed people to ensure that these goals are imple-
mented. They have developed the best technology in order to produce
the fastest trains in the world, capable of doing more than 260 kph.
They are building new railbeds to ensure that the passenger gets a
perfectly smooth ride. The result is that passenger service is growing.
The trains are full. In France property values in the countryside are
rising according to their proximity to fast-train (TGV) stations. Busi-

ness is attracted to provincial towns served by the TGV, thus helping decentralization. The balance of payments is helped by the money not spent on imported fuel for less fuel-efficient transport systems, such as cars and airplanes; and by the sale all over Europe of railway technology. The essence of this success is that the entire sector was treated as providing an essential public service, therefore worthy of the best high technology in the context of a labour-, maintenance- and investment-intensive industry in which making a profit was secondary.

The example of the postal systems is even more blatant. The more the United States and Canada modernize — or rationalize — their mail delivery, the less mail they can deliver at a slower rate to fewer places, with increasing irregularity and at both greater expense and higher cost to the user. Why? Because no systems analysis can justify mail deliveries six days a week. Nor delivery to rural areas. Systems analysis tells us not to deliver to private doors. It tells us to leave mail in grouped boxes, which the public must walk to, whatever their age and whatever the weather.

The British and the French have done none of these things. Instead they have continued to offer the fullest, fastest and most accessible services possible. Two deliveries a day in Paris — to even the most inaccessible door. Flawless delivery time. They have turned post offices into the most varied communication centres possible. By offering more and better services they have encouraged people to use the post office. The resulting customers make the whole process more and more viable.

Meanwhile, in Canada, in order to cut employment costs, post offices are being closed. The postal service is being franchised to variety stores as a sideline. These offer little more than stamps. They also cut the public off from their public servants in the post office.

The question of employment is particularly interesting. Humans deliver mail. If you reduce costs by reducing employment, you undermine the system's performance. This sets in motion the spin towards shrinking services. Systems analysis doesn't understand this because it is busy trying to make each element of government service profitable, without realizing that a public service is not a separate, private corporation but part of a whole which is the entire public structure. If the profitability of a service were to be measured accurately, it would have to take into account the effect of that service on the lives and businesses of the population.

It can't be denied that employees are expensive. Their wages and social costs must be borne by the post office, which is the state, which is by extension the taxpaying citizen. But unemployment is also expensive. The same state has to pay for the unemployed person by contributing to his or her social security. Keeping someone unemployed can easily be as expensive as employing them, since one must add to social security payments the cost of administering that service. The expert's answer is to apply artificial and narrow employment-cost calculations and therefore to dismantle such programs. But this creates chronic poverty, which, quite apart from the moral question it poses, also costs the state a great deal. Whatever surrounds the poor — property, consumption, education levels, law and order, health levels — declines to their level and creates new expenses for the government. And while employment has its costs, it also adds to productivity. Unemployment is entirely an economic negative. If the employment of a man or woman makes the mail system work better, for example, which in turn strengthens the communications networks, which in turn boosts commercial activity, then the cost of those jobs is in itself a profit.

North American post offices ought to be busy hiring more employees. They should be building more post offices to get closer to the public and installing new communications services in order to make themselves as useful as possible by keeping up with technology. They should be dreaming of armies of men and women carrying mail wherever the public wishes it. Instead they dream of a mechanized service in which the public receives as little as possible but comes to central depots to collect mail from a box.

As so often in the late twentieth century, words are used as nonsense. Economists repeat endlessly that the age of the service industry is upon us. But to serve, after all, means to provide services to another. And yet in the most basic services, which have traditionally been the responsibility of the state because they have been considered to be part of the musculature of the civil body, we now seek profit above all and, if possible, that the served should serve.

There is a whole series of governmental and paragovernmental services in which the assumptions of modern management are quite simply wrong. In education is it cheaper to keep a teacher unemployed or employed? All the costs must be calculated, not just salary. The cost to the state of that teacher's own education, for example. And the increased value to the future economy of the education given to a child in a class of twenty, or better still ten, rather than the current thirty or forty. And the cost to the state of rampant illiteracy. All the Western nations now admit that their universal education systems are not working. They are all searching for new grand remedies, most of which have to do with reforms in structure, method and content. But education — quantity and quality — is above all the result of teaching. And teaching requires teachers, the more the better. A national education strategy may sound reassuring, but without more bodies a strategy is just a strategy.

The same sort of arguments can be made about road building and maintenance, ferry services, health care, environmental costs, libraries, public transport and university-taught advanced technology. However, the current attitude towards general economic troubles is to tighten the belt. Printing money is indeed inflationary. But investing in areas which will not respond to the treatment of lean reorganization, because the profit they offer, while indirect, is essential, is just as real a form of efficiency and creativity.

The current idea of profit and loss completely misses this larger sense of what constitutes profitability. Worse, it doesn't admit that different types of organizations respond positively to fundamentally different management assumptions. The businessmen, who are now constantly being called in to advise governments, miss these differences.

And yet private corporations are often extremely flexible in their own attitudes towards efficiency. The criteria used by large corporations in their corporate acquisition policies, their debt policies, their remuneration policies for employed executives, their long-term planning policies would be considered scandalously inefficient, cavalier and amateurish if they were used by governments. That doesn't necessarily mean that the corporations are wrong. What it means is that they are insisting upon imaginary corporate standards of profitability and efficiency from government which they wouldn't dream of applying to themselves. As Maurice Strong — the environmentalist, businessman and Deputy Secretary General of the United Nations — has pointed out, the most successful international organizations are the multinationals. Why? Because they simply adapt their needs and standards to wherever they are functioning at that moment.[1] They have made an economic virtue out of size and, when it comes to organization, out of flexibility and imagination. They have, in effect, invented new ways to count. These are probably inappropriate to public management. What they demonstrate, however, is that government should not be a prisoner of pedestrian economic clichés relating to size, efficiency and value. Like the multinationals, government must invent new ways to count.

II

The remarkable ineffectiveness of our governments in managing international economic cooperation over the last twenty years as well as the unravelling of the revolutionary international accords and structures of the 1940s and 1950s, must be put down to the internal failure of national structures. The systems managers ground to a halt on their own territory, where they had all the levers in their own hands. Confused by their inexplicable failure, they pushed their problems out into the international sphere. There they were able to act with an irresponsibility which would have been impossible at home. The inequality of the players and the absence of strong structures and effective enforcement agencies permitted them to do what they wished in search of short-term gains. They had to destroy international stability and, in particular, international financial stability.

The United States, given its great natural strength, was able again and again to shift its problems over its borders. The 1961 launch of international arms consumption, largely in order to balance the trade deficit; the 1973 encouragement of a first oil price rise in order to help the Iranians pay for their pro-Western armament program; and the subsequent attempt to wipe out the enormous oil price increases through the use of general inflation were all the insane acts of rational men who had come to the end of their tether. These decisions were no worse than, for example, those of the Western Europeans to replace their old working class with a new lumpen proletariat of Third World labourers. The record is littered with economists and technocrats of the day — socialists, conservatives and liberals — explaining the brilliance of this plan. That it would lead to a racial crisis within twenty years was not in their briefing books. Nor were the results of the race to sell arms to the Third World, into which they leaped as fast as the United States. Nor are the consequences of an organized European overfishing policy in the Atlantic reserves — a policy which is still in effect.

The single most selfish and destructive Western economic act of the last forty years remains, however, the unilateral American decision in 1973 to break the postwar agreement on pegged currencies as an easy way to deal with its international deficit. At the time this was euphemistically called a conversion to floating currencies. Then as now there were experts who justified it with great flurries of figures. However, the reality was that it meant a return to international financial anarchy.

It was the ensuing chaos which made the European Monetary System (the Snake) a necessity. The import-export balance, the deficits, the inflation needs of the United States, whipped each of the European currencies up and down in an uncoordinated manner, wreaking havoc on their industrial production, competitiveness and trade. The wild fluctuations in currencies and commodities which the Nixon policies invited drew the business community's eye gradually away from solid industrial investment to the roulette wheel of paper manipulation and paper profits. This created a business atmosphere dominated by reorganizations, mergers, and takeovers, none of which contributed to new production. The whole process made real economic growth almost impossible to achieve.

In practical terms the 1973 decision destroyed the unity of the industrialized nations. By playing national problems ruthlessly against those of allies, Washington created three rival blocs. This meant that

Japan was freed to play its own game. As for the European Community, its members abruptly realized that their only real option was to succeed as a community. From a psychological point of view, the Europe of 1992 was born in the currency float and oil price rise of 1973. And with each unilateral economic or military initiative taken by increasingly nationalist American governments over the last two decades, there has been an almost immediate reaction to further strengthen European unity. When one watched the Community walk into the 1989 GATT meeting in Montreal with a single voice and walk out in protest against American demands, it was clear how far things had gone and how superficial, for example, the theoretically close links between Thatcher and Reagan really were.

The international monetary disorder did eventually force the creation of the Group of Five (G5), which subsequently became the G7. This committee of the seven leading industrial powers was a desperate attempt to limit the damage caused by the multilateral roller coaster and to forge at least minimum economic links among them.[2] The striving for a common European financial policy is another more limited attempt to do the same thing. But the small size of these groups, the tensions within them, and the informal nature of the G7's operations, indicate that few countries are willing to tie themselves down again so long as the inward-looking management structures, which each has now been obliged to impose upon itself at home, make the profit-loss results of any international agreement so unclear. As a result we are all still strapped into the great economic roller coaster, which continues its violent ride.

III

It is difficult to approach the question of substantive change in our society in a sensible manner. Those who enter public life, and are therefore responsible for dealing with change, have more often than not become obstacles to, rather than facilitators of, open debate. The modern politician, cut off from so much of the real action and driven by a highly honed but aimless desire for power, presents himself increasingly as a consumer good.

Among the early models of this product was the urbane British prime minister of the early 1960s, Harold Macmillan. Grandson of a crofter and beneficiary of a new fortune made by his family in publishing, he had married a duke's daughter, adjusted his manner upwards to conform with that of the ruling caste and worked hard to leave the impression — through world-weary diffidence and dry humour — that he was a lot smarter and a great deal more in control of events than he actually was. His successor, the Labour leader Harold Wilson, devoted himself to tuning his accent and manner downwards and was careful always to sound less intelligent than he was. He also kept a pipe in his mouth, unlit, as a sort of rumpled, populist symbol, which his manner of dressing confirmed. The prop became the man: a comfy, trustworthy fellow who smokes a pipe.

This image had nothing to do with the man. Son of an industrial chemist and himself a product of Oxford, he stayed on there to collaborate on the Beveridge report, which laid out the technical structure of a future welfare state. He was the wartime director of economics and statistics in the civil service and originator of the Labour blueprint to nationalize the coal industry. In other words, he was a state-of-the-art technocrat. What's more, once in power he fiercely controlled, wherever possible, media reports about himself. This was possible in large part thanks to his ready use of Lord Goodman, one of the country's leading legal figures.

Of course, politicians have always used props. This was part of a tradition which had more to do with theatrics than with camouflage. Churchill and Roosevelt were among the last major examples of the old cavalier approach. Capes, siren suits, bevies of wartime uniforms, outlandish cigarette holders, cigars and hats. Considering that one of them was more or less obese and the other a cripple, they used their bodies and their faces in a seemingly endless variety of ways. Their physical attitudes immediately conveyed to the public a political intent — glares, belligerence, laughter, fury. Their speech combined the patrician with the populist thanks to a direct and pared-down elegance which revealed the force of their propositions. All these mannerisms demonstrated the fact that both men were nonconformists in pursuit of change.

Their range of theatrics didn't have the same function as the single, fixed image does for the breed of politicians which arrived on the scene in force with Macmillan and Wilson. These new men were seeking a "role" in or behind which they could function for life. The image was for the vote. Thus disguised, the politician could serve whatever interests he thought appropriate. Those of the Churchill-Roosevelt school used their props to illustrate and sell their policies. The modern politicians use theirs to disguise their ideas and activities.

One consequence of this is that the politician now tends to wear a single sort of suit. The cameramen will discover him always, everywhere, looking like himself thanks to a simple, familiar image designed for the viewer. The only question is whether that image has been wisely chosen. Will it wear well as he ages and progresses in his career? Or will it reveal itself as too regional or tied to a period or a cause? The aim is to find an all-purpose image, smooth and meaningless, which can survive happily in all times and under all circumstances. With the growth in political public relations sophistication, most images now come in two parts: statesman and populist. Formal and informal. Giscard's single-breasted, gray suit versus his gray flannels with V-neck sweater. Reagan's presidential suit versus his cowboy outfit. Carter's off-the-rack single-breasted suit against his blue jeans. The politician who dares to present himself today through more than two images is extremely rare. The feeling is that more than two would confuse the public.

For an actual illustration of the situation, one need only compare the contemporary generation of politicians in France with President Mitterrand, a survivor from two generations before. Mitterrand has a fine-tuned presence, which turns on literacy and great intelligence, set against a background of mystery. His dark, extravagant hats and cloaks are intended to link him with Léon Blum, the first Socialist prime minister, who was a romantic figure in the first half of the century, a poet and a duelist before becoming a government leader. Mitterrand was in the Resistance, was involved in still unexplained incidents during the Algerian war and has written many political books in a romantic, civilized style. A psychiatrist might well say that these hats and cloaks are also symbols of the mystery in which Mitterrand has always wrapped himself in order to avoid being pinned down by short-term politics.

The new generation in France has neither mystery nor literacy. Efficiency is represented by a gray suit, so they wear one, thus blending in with the bureaucrats, who wear the same uniform. They are all conforming to the original Jesuit premise that simple dress should be worn not in humility but in the interests of anonymity. In place of mystery there is power and secrecy hidden behind the predictable diction and clothes of the specialist. Most of them still daren't smile in public for fear of confusing their image with that of an actor or a singer, which would prevent their being seen as statesmen.

Meanwhile, even Canada, which thought itself immune to packaging, has twice chosen, in Brian Mulroney, a politician delivered in a cellophane wrapper of frozen superficiality. He is to be found alternately singing "When Irish Eyes are Smiling" while publicly hugging his wife and children, or dropping into a grave, double-breasted whisper to play the man of state.

Of course, it is the United States which dominates the Western imagination and which has set the pace by producing bevies of constructa-kit presidential candidates, as if the goal were perfect presidential plastic. Robert Dole, Senate minority leader and a former vice presidential nominee, is an intelligent man who has done enough things in his life to prove that he exists as a real person. But he has a stormy character and this has worked very much to his disadvantage. As a result of being a wounded war hero, he has a withered arm. Physical deformities now tend to be seen as sinister rather than admirable. The world of images, like that of the Catholic priest or the absolute monarch, seems to require a minimum level of physical perfection. The

Catholic priest must be physically perfect because deformity implies some dark intervention not unrelated to cloven hooves. The king must be handsome and brave, so that his subjects may bask in his glory. The modern politician must be perfect, that is to say, perfectly inoffensive. He therefore concentrates on the removal of bumps which annoy. Dole was covered with them when he launched himself into the 1988 race for the Republican presidential nomination. He hired a consultant, Dorothy Sarnoff, to help redefine his image. During the campaign, Ms. Sarnoff volunteered the following to an interviewer when she was asked if Dole had changed: "Of course. I changed him. He was the best student I ever had. A nice, nice man. I took away his snide." Another adviser, John Sears, architect of Ronald Reagan's primary victories in 1980, added that, "Mere competence is not going to get you the nomination. If Bob Dole can convince people he has a vision that's credible and that's better than the other candidate's, he'll be nominated and elected."[3]

The word "vision" seems out of place in such a statement. But in Sears's mouth, vision becomes one with image, while still suggesting statesmanship and magnanimity. He uses "vision" to mean "image" the way some people use "the loved one" to mean the dead. A few words and an inoffensive smile. "A kinder, gentler America." No policies attached. No indication of how and when. Just a soft, bumpless label which reflects the mood of the day. Mr. Dole failed, but the interesting thing is that Ms. Sarnoff and Mr. Sears felt free to talk in such a way in public, for quotation, during the campaign.

The general term for this is *personality politics*, which means the exact opposite of what it says. It mainly involves creating personality where there isn't any or controlling and disguising personality where it is too real. And even then these manufactured personas may fail absolutely because they are ill chosen or incompetently exploited when dealing with the real world.

It is hardly surprising, therefore, that modern politicians avoid whenever possible unstructured encounters with reality. They attempt to limit their visibility in public and before the press to manufactured events, which are meant to provide facsimiles of reality.

Meaningless telephone-to-the-ear and miner-hat photos have grown into major industries for politicians and advisers. But these are only the still shots of a far-more-complicated business. What matters are complete manufactured events which have symbolic value and are both plotted and scripted. For example, George Bush began his presidency by walking down the hall to call on his Vice President. This event was officially announced before it happened and was intended to demonstrate that the President had full confidence in Dan Quayle, who was already being criticized as a lightweight. Nothing actually happened to

Mr. Bush in the hallway and nothing in particular was said in Mr. Quayle's office. No doubt the Vice President got up from behind his desk, came forward and shook the President's hand. It was a symbolic visit. The President had honoured the Vice President by going to him.

The lives of a dozen and a half elected presidents and prime ministers are blocked out with these sorts of representative simulations. Some of them are quite extraordinary. Mrs. Thatcher's appearance at the local funeral for the village victims of the Lockerbie air crash was intended to demonstrate her sympathy for the suffering of ordinary citizens. This came at a time when most citizens seemed to feel that she and her economic policies served only the rich. The de rigueur trip of every Western leader who visits Southeast Asia to the Cambodian border refugee camps indicates humanitarian concern, while the Cambodian troubles have stretched on for more than a decade in large part because the West has ambiguous attitudes towards the different players.

These and hundreds of other minor events are played out every day. They are the equivalent of royal movements — or rather of the protocol appropriate to Ruritanian royalty. But the actors in these cases are not fictional princes from a light romantic novel.

There is also a whole industry of pretend events which are not even symbolic. President Reagan's salutes are still the reigning example of these. As Commander in Chief, it was entirely proper for him to receive the salutes of the nation's soldiers. Why he, in civilian dress, should have saluted them back isn't at all clear. But for him to salute political gatherings and television cameras was worse than meaningless. To do this on his last appearance before a Republican Convention made a mockery of his responsibilities as Commander in Chief. The salute, after all, is one of the few symbolic gestures which does mean something. It represents the link of obedience between those who command and those who are willing to risk their lives if so ordered.

In the last days before President Bush's inauguration, the White House revealed the exact events which would take Ronald Reagan out of the presidency and out of town. After the inauguration, President Bush would accompany Mr. Reagan to a helicopter on the Capitol grounds. As Mr. Reagan entered the helicopter, he would turn at the last moment and salute President Bush. The press reported this planned scenario faithfully so that everyone would watch for it. Mr. Reagan's salute seemed to be a vague combination of John the Baptist christening Christ in the river Jordan and of General Douglas MacArthur — who was fired in 1951 from the Korean War command — closing his subsequent dramatic self-defence before a joint session of Congress with the line: "Old soldiers never die, they just fade away." Had President Bush not responded with a salute, the symbolism would have been debated all over

Washington. A calculated insult? A declaration of independence? A betrayal? The *Washington Post* was able to report the next day: "Mr. Reagan, on the steps of the helicopter, saluted Mr. Bush, who was on the steps of the Capitol. Mr. Bush then saluted back."[4]

But that week had been full of images and sounds which bore no relationship to reality. In President Reagan's farewell address he had insisted on the effect that his eight years of government had had on the world:

> And something else we learned: once you begin a great movement, there's no telling where it will end. We meant to change a nation, and instead, we changed a world. Countries across the globe are turning to free markets and free speech [note the order] — and turning away from the ideologies of the past. For them the Great Rediscovery of the 1980s has been that, lo and behold, the moral way of government is the practical way of government.[5]

Five days later, the American Department of Justice released the result of its internal investigation, which concluded that President Reagan's friend, Edwin Meese, while serving as U.S. chief legal officer, had breached federal ethics standards on numerous occasions. He had "engaged in conduct which should not be tolerated of any government employee, especially not the Attorney General."[6]

A few days later one of the worst financial scandals in modern French politics erupted, involving close friends of President Mitterrand and insider trading. The first to resign was the Minister of Finance's Chief of Staff. A few days later, the British government began lying to its public on a daily basis in order to cover up the scandal involving an epidemic of salmonella poisoning from eggs. The reason seemed to be fear of a collapse in the sale of eggs. That same week, the ongoing massive Mafia trials in Italy backfired with a series of acquittals which were followed by suggestions of improper interference in the judicial process from obscure powers, thus confirming that organized crime was more influential than ever in Italian business and government. In the same month a Swiss minister had to resign over political-financial charges, a political corruption story took on major proportions in Austria, and in Athens the Koskotas scandal exploded again, involving the corruption of a personal friend of the Greek Prime Minister, soon to fall himself. Meanwhile, ministers and senior officials in Japan continued to resign over a case of industry corrupting public officials. Those involved included ex-Prime Minister Nakasone, known as the most Americanized of the Japanese leaders. And a few weeks later, the American Senate confirmation hearings of ex-Senator Tower would begin, thus highlighting the growing legal, as opposed to illegal, corruption of the people's representatives. Within a year Reagan made a personal visit to Japan on behalf of a Japanese corporation. For the use of his immense prestige, he charged two million dollars. He had, after all, walked away from Washington with a 68 percent public approval rating.[7]

The only possible conclusion is that the American people believed his image and disbelieved events, believed a projected reality and disbelieved an observed one. When the Iran-Contra hearings seemed to show that the President didn't know what was going on around him, the aging actor strung together a series of symbolic acts in order to demonstrate that he was in charge. The scenario called for the President to go to the Pentagon, to walk through the corridors, to meet with the Chiefs of Staff, to consult with them, to walk on farther in order eventually to hold a press conference on the results of his consultation. Every step of the way, photo opportunities were organized. Images were created and transmitted.

There is no question that, as a product of the remarkable Hollywood B-movie mythmaking school and subsequently of television product advertising, Reagan was well trained to increase the already wide gap between illusion and reality in public debate. In fact, this is a talent which he seems always to have possessed. In his prepresidential memoirs, *Where's the Rest of Me*, he talks of his wartime experience making training movies for bomber pilots as if he had actually been a combatant. He doesn't actually say it, but that is the impression left.

Mr. Reagan's professionalism permitted him to create images which were particularly galling to honest and competent critics whose grasp on a catastrophic reality seemed to carry no public weight against his imaginary victories and reassuring images. There was some tendency on the part of the responsible practitioners of public debate — politicians, journalists and intellectuals — to conclude from this that there was a problem with the citizen, who seemed unable to grasp the obvious difference between reality and advertising. The problem may have been the public's, but it was created elsewhere and there was very little a citizen or even groups of citizens could do about it.

As for the press — the public's principal source of more-or-less detached information — they have never been in such a difficult situation. In terms of imagery, it is almost impossible for them to come up with pictures which reflect political realities. Public figures simply do not offer exposed flanks.

Even George Bush has little difficulty in presenting helpful images. The Iraq war provided him opportunities to simulate the grandiose and the historic. But not long after his inauguration, the following item was to be found in newspapers around the world — in this case the *London Times*:

President Bush went for a spontaneous two-mile walk through bitter cold in his little home town of Kennebunkport, Maine, with his wife Barbara and his dog, Millie, to buy razor blades at a local chemist shop. His press secretary was not given advance notice and had to dash to catch up with the President, who kept warm for his weekend walk in a furry hat.[8]

What was Bush doing? He was symbolically and spontaneously demonstrating that he is a regular kind of guy who doesn't have a swelled head. The contrived nature of the event makes it impossible to know whether this message is accurate. More to the point, it is difficult to see its relevance to Bush's official functions.

The relevant point is that those who hold power bombard the media with these segmented, artificial images which, although false, cannot be ignored because the actors really are the government. By filling the public place in this way, they have deformed, if not actually drowned, reality. It is almost impossible in such an atmosphere for the press to help the citizen take part in an open debate on public affairs. The government won't debate. Communications, in its mind, means controlled presentations of governmental policies through the intermediaries of imaginary personalities and false events.

12

The Art of the Secret

Everything in the West is secret unless there is a conscious decision to the contrary. Our civilization, which never stops declaiming about the inviolability of free speech, operates as if it distrusts nothing more. This taste for the hidden has not played an accidental role in the distortion of practical democracy. Both experts and Heroic leaders have found secrecy to be their natural ally. The word *secrecy* itself has become one of the most popular of the twentieth century and been elevated to the same verbal pantheon as *management*, *planning*, *systems* and *efficiency*. But *secrecy* alone among these is not a new obsession.

Sun Tzu was giving advice 500 years before Christ on its military uses. He made a great deal of the role it could play in winning wars fast and without heavy costs. The Chinese character he used to indicate the concept of secrecy represented "the space between two objects"; that is, the intent was to divide the enemy through the use of foreknowledge.[1] Sun Tzu was very precise about the whole business. He laid out five different sorts of secret agents, each with a specific use. For example, inside agents (enemy officials paid to betray), double agents (enemy spies paid to betray) and expendable agents (those deliberately given false information).

The key to all five uses lay in his idea of secrecy as a tool to be used specifically, in other words sparingly, to accomplish specific goals. Secrecy itself was not a general condition. Things were open by nature because there was nothing innately secret about them. Therefore the careful and limited use of restrained information and of deception could be very effective. Sun Tzu's insistence that, to be successful, secrecy must be a narrow means and not an end in itself was not an ideal intended for everyone. The means only worked if there was a justifiable end and a moral purpose guiding the way. "He who is not sage and wise, humane and just, cannot use secret agents." Or again, "only the enlightened sovereign and the worthy general who are able to use the most intelligent people as agents are certain to achieve great things." This is not idealistic moralizing. Sun Tzu was a practical man who constantly differentiated between the illusion of success and real success.

Our understanding of secrecy is very different. The rational revolution left us with the conviction that truth is a fact or a compendium of facts. This has grown into a way of life — an integral part of Western civilization which now turns on structures and expertise. Most individuals with some expertise or authority work within these structures and therefore have control over an element of modern truth. Their responsibility is to facilitate the functioning of their part of the system. Doing that successfully amounts to compliance. The only individual power available to them involves obstructing where they are employed to facilitate. Obstruction within complex structures takes the form of retention; most often, the retention of information or expertise.

Secrecy, therefore, is not at all what the security laws suggest — a specific matter which involves hiding sensitive bits of information in the national interest. And yet we are fascinated by state secrets. We imagine them to be of great importance. As they grow in numbers, so do the threat and excitement provided by our enemies, who attempt to discover these valuable truths. This is the musical comedy side of secrecy, because state security and spying are the least important aspects of the whole system. We can reasonably imagine most states having two or three specific worthwhile or valuable secrets. But all the rest are artificially held back. At the root of that withholding lies our real problem, which is that reason by its nature encourages every citizen to use secrecy as a tool of personal power.

This phenomenon is not endemic in Western society. Throughout the Middle Ages we were organized in such a direct manner — between the extremes of feudal contractual relations and those of brute force — that there was no room for the privacy or layered structures which would permit the development of secrecy into an important social weapon. Medieval society was a rude world in which all basic human acts were also public ones. It was a world which confused the necessary with the licentious. It was reason which introduced the idea that man was more hidden than apparent and, as always in the development of rational thought, Machiavelli was the pioneer in this area. The courtier, back-room manipulator and corridor manoeuvrer argued that there was much to conceal if a man wished to better his rivals.

Machiavelli was followed six years later by the well-meaning Erasmus, who became the most influential scholar and humanist of the northern Renaissance. These two men appeared to be headed in opposite directions. Erasmus was arguing, among other things, for Christianity to turn away from dogmatic theological disputes and back to the simple message of Christ. His critical approach undermined the truisms of medieval scholasticism and opened the way for the Enlightenment. And yet, he was also the father of middle class conventional morality.

Erasmus celebrated public discretion, which was intended to curb the licentious by curbing the public style of the individual:

> It is bad for your health to retain urine, but honest to release it secretly. Certain recommend to the young that they hold back a fart by tightening the muscles in their backside. Well! It is also bad to make oneself sick in trying to be polite. If you are able to leave the room, you must release the wind outside. If not, you must cough as in the old precept: use one noise to hide another.[2]

"Use one noise to hide another." This practice would become a trademark of the educated man.

Machiavelli and Erasmus were not so very far apart in their view of the individual. At the core of the new behaviour lay an approach which could be called either discretion or secrecy, whether bowels were being emptied or governments manipulated. This theme of the secret heart ran throughout the growth of reason. From what these and other philosophers were saying, the Inquisition was reconfirmed in its long-standing belief that all men were concealing something. Their rational conclusion had been that truth could be revealed by the simple act of posing questions. Questioning could, of course, be carried out without the crutch of torture. On the other hand, torture ensured an answer. And a truism of reason is that to every question there is an answer. The answer. Therefore, the true answer. Loyola, coming hard on the heels of Machiavelli, was more interested in structuring the questions in order to get the appropriate true answer. He mastered the technique of discretion — that is to say, deceit — in the service of God and went on to raise this deceit to the level of a fine art in the techniques of organization and argument.

Richelieu took these ideas and further developed them in the service of the nation-state. He made the possession of knowledge into his most valuable weapon — knowledge received before others received it; knowledge intercepted without the sender or the receiver knowing; knowledge held back, perhaps forever, perhaps for future use; knowledge used opportunely to defeat others or to convince the king; false knowledge, such as invented facts or manufactured quotes or slander or self-serving good news, spread in order to aid his cause. All this was built upon an unrivalled continentwide network of informers and spies. The art of purchasing informers was one of his great contributions to modern government. Ultimately the art of the secret, combined with the advanced role played by the courtesan, replaced intelligence with cunning as the most important characteristic for those who hoped to gain positions of public power.

One of the first men to recover from this obsession and to reapply common sense to public service was the British diplomat Sir William Temple, who was also Jonathan Swift's patron. Temple pointed out that the credit derived in negotiations from truthfulness was more useful than the suspicion aroused by cunning.[3] He used this approach while negotiating the marriage in 1677 of Princess Mary with William of Orange, who later became Mary II and William III. This arrangement had precisely the announced and the intended effect. First, it loosely allied Britain with those European nations which had embraced the Reformation, thus stabilizing the moderate religious position of Anglicanism. Second, it diverted England's dynastic quarrel away from the two opposing schools of absolutism and towards a more contractual and limited interpretation of monarchy. Much of the careful moderation which for the next two centuries was associated with and admired in British politics was derived from that arrangement.

This should be compared with Richelieu's brilliant, cunning, secret negotiation fifty years earlier of Spanish royal marriages for Henry IV's son and daughter. Richelieu wanted a reasonable settlement with the French Protestants and feared the Spanish Catholic influence inside France. He tried to neutralize that element by pairing the French royal children with the Spanish. And so in 1615, the future Louis XIII was married to Anne, the daughter of the Spanish King; and Elisabeth, Louis's sister, to the future Philip IV of Spain. On the surface this was meant to reassure the conservative forces in France and to unify Catholic Europe. In reality Richelieu believed that by this double stroke he would transform Madrid from a meddling enemy into a manipulable ally.

Somehow it never struck him that those two marriages and the children they produced would generate a logic of their own. Within a decade they had resulted in the exact opposite of what he intended. Instead of neutralizing the Catholics and bringing the Protestants into the mainstream, he had created a situation which led eventually to the revocation of the Edict of Nantes and the expulsion of the Protestant community. The profound confusion produced by this successful use of secrecy on a matter central to the state started France off on a schizophrenic course between state reform and religious power from which it has not yet entirely recovered. The separate school crisis during Mitterrand's first presidential term was in some ways still a distant echo of the confusion created by Richelieu's Spanish marriages. The government was trying in the early 1980s to strengthen state education by weakening the financing of private Catholic schools. Centuries of revolution and political reform had still not managed to separate clearly state and church and in the late twentieth century the government failed yet again.

The philosophers of the eighteenth century had attacked secrecy and

cunning, just as they had attacked Machiavelli and the Jesuits. But so
long as they equated open truth with reason, they were attaching themselves to a system which carried secrecy in its heart.

In 1787 Jefferson wrote to Madison from Paris:

> And say, finally, whether peace is best preserved by giving energy to the
> government, or information to the people. This last is the most certain,
> and the most legitimate engine of government. Educate and inform the
> whole mass of the people. Enable them to see that it is their interest to
> preserve peace and order, and they will preserve them.

This approach was meant to be opposed to that of Alexander Hamilton's
Federalists, who took a more expedient and elitist view. Jefferson reiterated his commitment to an open and straightforward approach in his
first Inaugural Address: "the diffusion of information and the arraign-
ment of all abuses at the bar of public reason." The Federalists had held
great power for twelve years and their methods had led to serious corruption and profiteering. The new President immediately wrote to his
Secretary of the Treasury:

> Our predecessors have endeavored by intricacies of system and shuffling
> the investigator to cover everything from detection. I hope that we shall
> go in the contrary direction, and by our honest and judicious reformations
> . . . bring things back to that simple and intelligible system on which
> they should have been organized at first.

What Jefferson missed was that reason itself had created the intri-
cacies of the system. Rational elitism, which gave power to those who
had earned it, benefited the self-serving moneyed class. This was an
adjunct of Alexander Hamilton's belief that the state could be stabilized
by cementing federal financial institutions to the rich, whose prosperity
would then depend, as James Flexner has put it, on federal authority.
It was this Hamiltonian spirit, so close to the European rational approach, which was to mark the government of the United States over
the long term: an enthronement of the Heroic; financial opportunism;
and an optimistic vision of what the possession of office could accomplish.[4] Power was needed in order to build perfect systems. The joint
worship of Heroism and power could be counted on to obscure the
machinations of self-interest and deform the intent of the public will.
Jefferson's own idealized devotion to an imaginary sort of reason prevented him from seeing that much of his own labour was actually driven
by honest common sense.

From the very beginning of responsible government it was clear what
rational systems would do with information, the release of which would

not be to their advantage. What no one could have imagined was that a system in which selected information was consciously kept back by those in power would gradually become a system in which only selected information was released. The point is worth reiterating. At the end of the eighteenth century, everything was public knowledge except that which was consciously held back. By the second half of the twentieth century, everything was privileged information except that which was consciously given out.

Had so many dangerous secrets come into being? Would it, for example, harm an Englishwoman or her nation to know the names and responsibilities of her own government's cabinet committees? Or to know which of her elected members are on them? Or ought a citizen to know whether radiation is dropping upon him? The citizen's life is filled with thousands of these unanswered questions.

It is not that there are more secrets today. The nature of a secret has simply changed. In its purest form it was and still is information which, in the wrong hands, could damage the state. But very few bits of information can do that. States can be damaged by such things as the exhaustion of specific resources or changes in technology. More often than not, the problems of a state relate to the refusal of local elites to do their job — that is, to provide competent leadership and to protect the interests of the population as a whole. This includes improperly managing resources, failing to adjust to changes in technology or simply losing interest in leadership and management. Exploiting the pleasures of power without assuming the accompanying responsibilities is the most common means by which established elites inadvertently destroy their own nations. But none of this has to do with secrets.

Periodically a secret can be useful. The place and time of a military attack, for example. Perhaps the size of a military formation at a certain moment in a certain place. But that kind of information doesn't stay secret for very long. Besides, the nature of a defence is not necessarily a secret, since knowledge of it may be a deterrent. As for knowledge of new weapons, this has rarely helped the other side. Military history, as we have seen, usually gives quick victories to the best commander, not to the largest army or to the best equipped or to those armed with secret weapons.

The reality of spies who betray secrets is nevertheless dramatic. Betrayal is a central theme in all civilizations. It is as disturbing on the personal level as on the public because it is always the result of a personal choice by the betrayer and is therefore felt personally by the betrayed, whether an individual or a population.

However, no equation links this deep sense of betrayal with the relative importance of specific secrets. Even a case as infamous as that of Julius and Ethel Rosenberg demonstrated this ambiguity. Americans and convinced Communists, they delivered nuclear secrets to the Soviets, for which they were arrested in 1950, put on trial, convicted and, after a worldwide controversy, executed. If everything said at that time about ideology, loyalty, patriotism and betrayal is put aside, what remains is the secret itself and an estimate of its value.

Nuclear fission was discovered late in 1938 in Germany by Otto Hahn, who split the atom at the Kaiser Wilhelm Institute. This was neither an isolated nor a secret discovery. It was part of a long-term process spread throughout the West and, within a month of Hahn's breakthrough, it was being openly debated at the Fifth Washington Conference on Theoretical Physics. Fear of Germany's head start pushed a number of scientists to press Allied governments to move faster. The most famous among them, Albert Einstein — also a friend of Hahn and a former director of the Kaiser Wilhelm Institute — was encouraged by other scientists to take the lead. He agreed to write to President Roosevelt, calling for a concerted scientific effort. The eventual result was the Manhattan Project, which produced the first atomic bomb.

This success was in part the result of an international concentration of scientists in the Allied camp. However, the Germans had also failed to exploit their head start, and for several reasons. The Nazis decided that the nuclear domain involved impure Jewish science. They had also lost a number of their key scientists, both Jewish and anti-Nazi. Finally, the practical outcome of nuclear research was still uncertain, and scientists are unlikely to make promises to governments which may well imprison or kill them if they fail to deliver the appropriate results. The race to produce the first bomb was therefore largely imaginary. Nor did secrecy play a useful role.

The Allies dropped the first nuclear bomb on Hiroshima on August 6, 1945; that is, six and a half years after the first breakthrough. Many of the scientists who developed the bomb advised against dropping it, because they said that very act of exploding the bomb would give the Soviets the few remaining facts they needed to catch up. But if the Soviets were that close, then the difference between dropping the bomb and simply explaining enough about it to create a sufficient fear would have been marginal. Four years after Hiroshima, the Soviet Union tested its first bomb. That was in 1949, the year before the Rosenbergs were arrested.

What difference, then, did their betrayal make? Six months? A year? Two years? It now seems unlikely that anything very useful was handed over. Certainly the Rosenberg secrets did not alter the outcome of a war or change the balance of power. And yet this was one of the most important betrayals of the century. No other military development could rival the nuclear bomb in importance.

As for civil secrets, they aren't really secrets at all. They have more to do with negotiating techniques than with security. Sir William Temple demonstrated that the best deal is one that makes sense and looks good out in the open. Secrecy is only useful in selling a bad deal, and those rarely hold after the fact except as complex deformations of reality.

There are no more secrets today than there were when Sun Tzu wrote. What we do have now is a worship of the idea of secrecy. The brief vogue of existentialism in the middle part of the twentieth century illustrates precisely what has happened. A philosophy which declares that people will be judged by their acts could not possibly survive in the West. We believe that people are what they know and can be judged by their power; that is, by what they control. In a society based not upon action but upon systems, our place within the system determines our importance.

The measurement of our power is based upon the knowledge which either passes through our position or is produced by it. One of the truly curious characteristics of this society is that the individual can most easily exercise power by retaining the knowledge which is in his hands. Thus, he blocks the flow of paper or of information or of instructions through his intersection to the next. And with only the smallest of efforts he can alter the information in a minor or a major way. Abruptly he converts himself from a link into a barrier and demonstrates, if only to himself, his own existence.

The principles of Erasmus and Richelieu have been carried to such a preposterous extreme that the encouragement of such retention has become a religion of constipation. It's worth pointing out in passing that when you go beyond the Judeo-Christian rational civilization, actual physical constipation ceases to be a cultural phenomenon. The most obvious reason is that toilet training outside the West tends to take positive, reassuring, even pleasant forms, as opposed to our controlling and disciplining approach to what we see as an unpleasant function.[5] In Buddhist and Confucian societies, the idea of power through retention also disappears. The concept of the secret still exists, but in a different mode and not as a central theme. Even the Islamic world, which rises out of the same religious roots as ours, has drawn different conclusions and gone off in another direction.

The first victim of the Western system, in which everything is secret unless there is a conscious decision to the contrary, is the citizen, who is after all also a creator of secrets. The simple mathematics of this system are that the individual can control a small slice of exclusive knowledge, while the rest will be hidden among the rest of the population. The generalized secret has introduced such a terrible uncertainty into our society that citizens' confidence in their own ability to judge public matters has been damaged. They constantly complain that they don't know enough to make up their minds. They have a feeling that the mass of information available would not be available if it were truly worth having. The result is a despondent mental anarchy which prevents them from actively using the considerable powers democratic society has won. They are convinced that essential information is being held back.

The reality is that more than enough information is available on most subjects and our difficulty is therefore making sense out of the shapeless sea of facts in which we often seem to be drowning. Governments use the weapon of quantity as often as the weapon of retention in order to sell their point of view. Factual attacks from the outside can be neutralized by a volley of governmental facts. Governments and large corporations always have more material than their critics. That is one of the privileges of power. They also have access to captive research institutes and bevies of "independent" professors, who are kept on contract to provide supportive studies and statements. How is the citizen to choose among so many "true" statements? The factual snow job is one of the great inventions of the late twentieth century.

Our curious obsession with secrets, in a world where the real problem is keeping one's head above the flood of facts, has encouraged a generalized fantasy life revolving around spies and plots, as if only the convoluted had value. In a way, the Le Carré-esque school is merely a continuation of the old obsessions with popish plots, Jewish conspiracies and Masonic cabals. When Joseph Conrad wrote the first spy novel, *The Secret Agent*, he made it clear just how petty, abasing and fundamentally irrelevant the whole business was. G. K. Chesterton made fun of secret agents and terrorists in *The Man Who Was Thursday*. And Graham Greene carried on this understanding that the secret services are filled with third-rate men chasing third-rate secrets.

But the public sees it all quite differently. Living in organizations in which knowledge is power, they must treat the secret as a cult. The fictional spy is thus a glorified reflection of the citizen — James Bond on a good day, George Smiley on a bad. The great fictional archetypes have always reflected the chief concerns of their society. The Lancelots and Quixotes carried dreams of physical valour and justice. Our archetypes struggle in mazes without exits. They often lose and never really win, because the nature of the battle isn't clear.

Most people, upon hearing the word *intelligence*, would think of the CIA before they would Einstein. This is not a minor matter of linguistic evolution. Intelligence, after all, was one of the central concepts of the rational revolution. In this new and better world, men were no longer to be rewarded for their bloodline or their physical strength. The Age of Reason was to be the age of men using their intelligence to improve society and the state of man. The rational vision of government was tied to this.

It is therefore astonishing that in English the word *intelligence* should gradually have come to stand for the manipulation of secrets. In nineteenth-century dictionaries, there is no hint of the new meaning, apart from the word *intelligencer*, meaning one who conveys information. But with the rise of modern war and the parallel rise of the staff officer, the cult of secrecy invaded the idea of intelligence. This first became obvious at about the time of World War I. After that its evolution went so fast that when the historian Asa Briggs edited a new encyclopedia in 1989, he gave two definitions of equal length to the word *intelligence* — one tied to the positive, optimistic gathering and use of knowledge; the other to the retentive, negative use of secrecy.[6] Exactly the same evolution can be found in French, in which the word *renseignement* was first tied to knowledge and to the imparting of information. Gradually it has come to imply the gathering of information in order to retain it.

The effect of this burgeoning secret world upon our society has been destructive. A single example is sufficient. The Pentagon has been and remains profoundly divided from within, not by rival ideas but by rival sections seeking increased power. One of the most effective weapons they have is to withhold information from each other. This has been a constant factor in the failure of such military expeditions as Grenada and the Iran hostage expedition. The responsible people are quite simply not told what they need to know. This leads to failure on the ground. The subsequent investigations and explanations are invariably secret, because public disclosure theoretically would not be in the public interest — that is, it would damage the careers of those involved. The problem of retention is so great that today 3.5 million Americans must be given various levels of security clearance in order to keep the system functioning at all. In 1989, a normal year, the U.S. government created 6.8 million new secrets.[7] In Britain, even the curators of public museums are bound by the Official Secrets Act. Talking to the public puts them technically in breach of it. Again in 1989, the Victoria and Albert Museum restructured the responsibilities of its curators. Many protested. The museum invoked the Official Secrets Act to prevent their airing their disagreement.[8]

Knowledge retention has become an integrated characteristic of modern structures and is central to their immobilization. The premise of a rational system is that by organizing and training in great detail it will be possible to determine events. Accustomed to being dominated by tyrants, nature and the unknown, man will suddenly have the power to use organization in order to become the active director of his own destiny. From the earliest example of professionals — the staff officers — onwards, the expectation was that structure would be used to change circumstances. But the circumstances of war turned out to be unpredictable and stubborn. Those of civil government, involving millions of citizens spread over great distances and carrying with them a variety of long-established interests, are even more surprising and immovable.

The modern manager has had great successes and great failures in his attempts to change circumstances. His structures fly over the heads of civilizations rather than interacting with them. The result is that the success rate is higher when dealing with radical changes. Coming out of revolutions, wars or economic disasters, the structuralists are able to impose whole new patterns. The disappearance of the kings and the arrival of democracy provided grounds for massive re-creation. The disasters of this century, created in large part by the rational approach, also created a need for massive societal change which, again, suited the creative side of large structures.

Now, however, the West is bunged up with these organizations and is attempting valiantly to make massive longer-term programs function on a day-to-day basis. When a new idea comes along, it either tends to be supported or opposed for structural reasons. And structures have a natural tendency to say no, because a new idea disturbs. Not in the old way, in which habit, lethargy and established interests always tended to say no. That sort of blockage was concrete and identifiable. Now new ideas are rejected because they disturb organization. In this way energetic new ministers filled with good ideas will be rapidly deflated and co-opted to the conviction that "new" is impractical.

The difficulty today is that government is constantly called upon to deal with real, practical problems — employment, pollution, inflation, productivity, financing of social services. At the same time there is a long list of critical items which for decades have escaped practical attention. Knowledge of the situation has been widespread for years. General agreement on the seriousness of the situation has reached the level of the popular cliché. And yet the entire established structure of official science, public administration and corporate management unconsciously ignores the situation or actually works to discredit what it knows to be true.

The massive destruction of forests by acid rain, and the crumbling of European cities because of leaded gasoline are two very simple examples. The solutions are practical and imaginable and have been for a long time. Instead the American government has persisted for years in asserting that there is no solid proof of a link between acid rain and the death of forests. The United States has glanced away from their own New England states and Canada towards the Midwestern industrial states, which said that smokestack modernization would bankrupt them. And so a five-year study was proposed to look into the matter. When popular pressure in the late 1980s — which the authorities identified as irrational panic — reached a dangerous level, the government offered a series of half measures. These were proposed not as part of an admission that the problem existed but as a political sop. The basic denial continued.

For years the authorities and the experts in Britain and France fought desperately against unleaded gasoline. They did everything they could to discredit the environmentalists — calling them ignorant, childishly emotional and subversive. When, in the late 1980s, it was no longer possible to go on ignoring the problems of lead pollution, the two governments set about arguing over the level of response necessary. This process lasted a year. At the EEC level, many of the members were worried about the increase in oil import costs that lead-free gasoline would involve. Their economists told them this would have an important impact on their balance of payments. In the end all the governments compromised in favour of a gradual lead-reduction program, which will cost each country thousands of times more in damage to buildings and health than it will in oil imports.

The destruction of buildings, damage to statuary and long-term illness, however, are not part of the annual balance of payments. In order to maintain the fiction that their compromise is the correct one, the majority of EEC governments have been ready to prosecute member governments, such as the Dutch, who are unwilling to wait for clean gas. The Dutch said their cities and countryside were dying. The EEC replied that the strong Dutch environmental control regulations constituted unfair competition barriers to the other community members. The very idea that environmentally sound regulations could constitute unfair trade barriers to environmentally unsound products is an indication of the Alice in Wonderland mentality among Western elites.

The point of these well-known examples is that, whatever the merits of each case, modern structure responds to its own errors by a refusal to admit error. It responds to failure by a denial of failure. The system could prove that it does work by simply responding to problems with an open mind, rapidly and positively, eager to find solutions. Instead it automatically goes into a defensive pose, throws out diversions intended to slow criticism, then spends time and money to prove factually that there is no problem. As a final ploy it will attempt to gain time for new ploys by agreeing to negotiate. If even this fails, the system will drop its own position, grasp that of the other side and treat the new position as if it were an absolute truth always known.

The explanation for such odd reactions to rather straightforward problems is that systems are constructed from an assumption of correctness. They are built backwards from this assumption. There is no room for error, except through some properly laid-out procedure. That is why the system is unable to simply assimilate all the obvious factors before coming to conclusions.

Thus acid rain may lead to the destruction of trees but it doesn't fall into the same process as the decline of the Rust Belt states. And leaded gasoline may harm agriculture and stone buildings, but it doesn't fall into the same process as trade balances or competition regulations. The officials in charge of all these procedures are decent people. It's just that there is no room for them to use their common sense. And from the structure's point of view, when there is an error, it is the error which is in the wrong.

The temptation to use secrecy is now so great that it has become one of the prime skills of the leading courtesans. Presidential and prime ministerial advisers specialize in this commerce. Sir Robert Armstrong was famous for his secret manipulations. Henry Kissinger revelled as much in the wiretapping of rivals as he did in his secret Chinese negotiations and his secret Cambodian operation. There is nothing wrong with a few overblown egos puffing themselves up with secret games, providing this affects no one else. The real problem with the system is that it encourages the private inversion of public policies without anyone else having enough information to protect the public interest.

During the 1960s and early 1970s, local hill tribes in Southeast Asia agreed to give their military services to the war against Communism in return for the use of U.S. planes. They wanted the Americans to transport opium for them out of the hills and into the hands of heroin wholesalers. The American officers in the field were not ideologues. They organized this deal because it solved their military problems in a difficult situation. Some officers on higher levels or in the security services must have known about it, because the process of transfer and replacement went on without any new officers expressing shock. Whenever hints of this organization leaked out, there was an automatic denial. When everything was eventually confirmed in a carefully documented book in 1972, the authorities were horrified.[9] Of course, they were horrified off the record. There was never an official admission of what had gone on. Nor was there any attempt to explain how officers sent "to fight for freedom" had become drug dealers to advance the good cause. The question is interesting on a human level, but it also reflects how much difficulty sophisticated structures using secrecy have in maintaining a policy direction, let alone a moral standard. That particular secret was worth keeping, from the point of view of those involved, because it contained a terrible and inexplicable truth.

The more typical situation today is quite different. Now that every pencil has become a national secret, the majority of the people in theoretically sensitive positions are very low on the salary scale. Many of them are simple computer operators. They probably realize that what they are handling is not earth-shattering, despite being classified as secret, top secret or whatever. They also know, as case after case in England, France and the United States has shown, that almost any old piece of information has a market value several times their own salary.

The Ronald W. Pelton case in 1986 was quintessential petty-larceny spying. Pelton, salary $24,500, a National Security Agency (NSA) technician, sold a banal bit of information to the Soviets for $35,000. He did this by telephoning to the Soviet Embassy from his office. In a high-security building all external calls are automatically recorded. The NSA security system was so overburdened by the simple process of digesting the information collected in this way that it was weeks before anyone focused on the call. Weeks again before they managed to identify the voice of the caller. Then Pelton was dragged into the public light as a traitor. *Traitor* is a grand word for a man of below-average intelligence, confused about his hopeless personal finances, who gives in to the temptation to make a few bucks out of banal information.[10]

Clearly the scale of crimes has lost all meaning. In the same period Edwin Meese, the Attorney General, walked away free having, as his own department concluded, engaged in conduct that should not be tolerated of any government employee, especially not the chief law officer of the United States. Meese was cleared on a technicality while Pelton was imprisoned on principle. And that is as it should be in a society where security and secrecy have little to do with content and everything to do with structure.

Petty-larceny spying is just a sidebar to this structural phenomenon. The computer maze which increasingly dominates all information, from the most banal to the most complex, is part of a seamless whole. While every individual may try to control his little package of knowledge, a determined gatherer of intelligence can penetrate almost anywhere. Between the civil and the military sectors there is no longer any real division. Governments may push the definition of restricted or secret information further and further outwards, but they cannot cut themselves off from the electronic structure which has become their means of contact with the outside. Increasingly the cases of military and industrial espionage which are uncovered turn on the impossibility of closing electronic doors. In other words, through our obsession with secrecy and retention, we uselessly obstruct the functioning of our society, while those who are actually in the business of gathering information illegally can do so without much difficulty.

These mountains of information which must be retained have made the fortune of people in the shredder business. Private companies now send fully equipped trucks, manned by security-cleared employees, from office building to office building. The men go in to gather bags jammed full of secrets. These they carry downstairs and outside to the parking lot, where all is shredded on the spot.

The individual, never without resources, has reacted in some countries by fighting for new laws which offer the citizen the right to know. But these laws merely confirm the principle that everything is secret unless specifically decided otherwise. The citizen will know only what he specifically asks. Indeed, the right-to-know laws encourage increased retention of information. They drive the experts to use greater cunning — to register their information in more disconnected ways, so that when it is fished out it will give away as little as possible of what else is in the water. In that sense the countries with right-to-know legislation are not as far as they think from places such as Britain, where the belief in secrecy still grows unchecked.

When Lord Stockton, chairman of the British publishing house Macmillan and son of Harold Macmillan, protested against the passage of a new, more inclusive Official Secrets Act in 1989, he said that now "the mechanisms of tyranny are inbuilt in our society."[11] He regretted that Britain had learned nothing from the more open approach of Canada and the United States. But the differences are more apparent than real. In 1983 Canada enacted an Access to Information Act which now draws more than ten thousand requests for information per year. And yet in his annual report of 1991, the Federal Information Commissioner appointed by Parliament accused the government of hiding information in a manner which bordered on being antidemocratic and of treating openness as "an alien culture."[12]

There are endless simple methods for any government to get around access-to-information legislation. The simplest is to formally classify the information in question at some level of secrecy. All Western governments now routinely classify planning documents, whether they relate to culture or fisheries, as secret. The most famous modern example of this was the Pentagon Papers.

In June 1971 seven thousand pages of American government documents and analyses covering the preceding quarter century of Vietnam policy-making were leaked to the *New York Times*. They were all classified secret. Many inside journalists and the paper's own lawyers were against publication. The lawyers felt so strongly about the need to respect the secrecy act that they walked out on the newspaper, which then went ahead and published in nine installments. President Nixon and the government structures did everything they could to stop them. A court order blocking publication was followed by "the most important press case in U.S. history," which finally ended in the Supreme Court with a victory for the *Times*. It is probable, given the current Justices of the Court, who are much more sympathetic to the desires of authority, that were the *Times* to plead a similar case today, it would lose. In 1989 Erwin Griswold, who as Solicitor General had presented the original case for the government, wrote that he had "never seen any trace of a threat to the national security from the publication" of the Papers.[13]

Access-to-information laws amount to little more than legislative manoeuvres that open or close peepholes. They do not change the basic assumptions of a rational society, which are: only through the control of knowledge can a man define his own existence; only by a judicious holding back of what he knows can he prove that he matters. Such massive retention has played a role in our society's inability to debate problems openly and to act upon them.

Take Mrs. Thatcher, for example. She is perhaps the most perfectly modern public leader yet to have appeared anywhere. Her ability to combine hectoring with an absolute assurance of holding truth made her the mistress of retention. It was often felt, even by her admirers, that she used the methods of a nanny, but why should that be surprising when nannies are responsible for toilet training and general social retention? The nanny may be outdated as a social institution, but she is perfectly adapted to the governing of modern democracies.

It was mesmerizing to watch Mrs. Thatcher pursuing escaped secrets around the world as if she could force them back under cover. A relatively harmless book called *Spy Catcher* — by a retired, second-level, ex-secret agent called Peter Wright — was published in 1987. She, the Prime Minister of a functioning democracy, chased this one-week tabloid wonder from country to country in an attempt to have seized and banned what had already been read by everyone who was interested.[14] Or again, following a television documentary on the shooting in Gibraltar of three IRA terrorists by the British SAS, she insisted that the journalists either did not know the facts or had ignored them. The television network felt obliged to carry out an inquiry. The resulting report by well-known Conservatives exonerated the journalists. She rejected the report and insisted that the program had been unfair. Her attitude was that only the responsible authorities can know enough to say what is the truth.

The point of these two almost-comical examples is that the official secrets acts of Western countries have gradually been brought into line with the sophistication of modern management structures. These laws are no longer simple mechanisms for punishing treason. They have been given real teeth — that is, whole new rows of teeth with a detailed administrative bite designed to match the massive but intricate growth of artificial secrets. The practical result is that governments now have greater legal control than ever before over the information which the public needs to clarify how they are governed.

Almost a century ago, on December 22, 1894, Captain Alfred Dreyfus, a junior officer in the central bureau of French military security, was court-martialed for treason and sent to prison on Devil's Island. The handwriting on a piece of paper found by a cleaning woman in a wastepaper basket in the German military attaché's office had mistakenly been identified as belonging to Dreyfus. The *bordereau*, as this scrap of paper was known, contained information of troop movements. The evidence against Dreyfus was contradictory; however, he was Jewish at a time of growing anti-Semitism and therefore made a convenient scapegoat.

The army did everything it could to cover up the weakness of its case and an officer called Major Henry fabricated additional false evidence. Nevertheless, information continued to leak out and late in 1897 the real culprit, Count Major Esterhazy, known to be a gambler, a womanizer and heavily in debt, was publicly identified. Emile Zola, the most popular novelist of the day and an outspoken advocate of social and political reform, chose that moment to enter the debate. With the question of guilt settled in everything except legal form, he felt able to concentrate on the horrifying use of Dreyfus as an excuse for anti-Semitism. "La vérité est en marche," he wrote, "et rien ne l'arrêtera." "Truth is on the march and nothing can stop it." Esterhazy was put on trial and, in a travesty of justice, acquitted.

The Dreyfusards were now doubly outraged. Zola wrote an intentionally libellous letter to the President of the Republic and published it in Georges Clemençeau's newspaper *L'Aurore* under the title "*J'Accuse.*" This forced a libel suit against Zola and put the Dreyfus case back into the courts. The novelist was sentenced to a year in prison and fined three thousand francs. However, he had fled to London before the trial was over and waited there for the boil to burst. His use of the courts had done the trick. He was able to go home eleven months later when Dreyfus was given a new trial. Though its outcome was still short of clear acquittal, the President of the Republic pardoned Dreyfus. He was reinstated in the army, promoted and went on to complete a respectable but rather ordinary career.

This was perhaps the most important political and legal battle over a question of secrecy and treason to take place in any modern Western nation. Its outcome eventually led to the breaking of military power and the strengthening of civil structures. The debate stretched on for almost a decade and divided the nation.

Were Captain Dreyfus to be convicted and imprisoned for treason today in Paris, London or Washington, his defenders wouldn't have a hope of reversing the verdict. The various official secrets acts would prevent them from taking up the case in a serious manner. In Britain, the mythological home of fair justice, Zola would today be silenced by the law from the moment of his first intervention. Were he to persist, he might well be tried himself in a secret court, this being a matter of state security. Were he to succeed in using the libel laws, he might well find himself bankrupted by both court costs and an order to pay several million pounds to the libelled parties. In fact, examining the Western countries one by one, there doesn't seem to be any case since that of Dreyfus, with the possible exception of the Pentagon Papers, in which popular forces were able to take on the state security laws over a major issue of unjustified secrecy and win.

Definitions are simple yet central reflections of society. They are the elements upon which everyone consciously or unconsciously agrees, the givens which precede all conversations and actions and laws.

Under the old regime of church and monarch, truth was defined as an absolute. The early men of reason disturbed the status quo by questioning that definition. They pointed out that it involved an arbitrary absolute. They didn't question the idea of an absolute truth. They concentrated on creating rational methods for discovering it. In that sense truth became relative for a time. "You have the right," Diderot wrote, "to expect that I shall search for the truth, but not that I should find it."[15]

The simple pleasure of this honest search removed the emphasis from the need to find truth, which depended, perhaps more than ever before in history, upon common sense. And even as the desire to find absolute truths regained momentum, it did so through a relative process. The mid-eighteenth-century English definitions of truth illustrate this.

Johnson defined it as "honesty, reality, faithfulness." Chambers, in his *Cyclopaedia: or Universal Dictionary*, which later inspired the Encyclopédistes, put it that truth was "a term used in opposition to falsehood and applied to propositions which answer or accord to the nature and reality of the thing." The basic French definition of truth in the nineteenth-century *Littré Dictionary* ran as follows: "A quality by which things appear to be what they are." Littré, like Johnson and Chambers, was trying to be reasonable.

Compare their careful restraint to Noah Webster's brand-new nineteenth-century definition: "Truth, conformity to fact or reality: exact accordance with that which is, or has been, or shall be." Or to the contemporary *Oxford* definition: "In accordance with fact or reality." Or the *American Heritage*: "Consistent with fact or reality." Or the *Petit Robert*: "Knowledge which conforms with reality. That to which the spirit can and must give its agreement." The "knowledge" in question, of course, is factual knowledge. The use of the word *must* summarizes the new attitude.[16]

Truth today is as much an absolute as it was in the fifteenth century. Then as now the greatest power is the one that enables the holding of truth. The heart of our absolutism is the "fact" which we must all accept as the guarantor of irrefutable veracity.

And now that truth is a fact, it is not surprising that facts have become like rabbits, "user friendly," prone to copulation, rapid multiplication and jumping about, to the point where the planet lies metres deep beneath their hopping mass. Nor is it surprising that as a result truth has become as arbitrary as paper money in an inflated economy. The same truth alters endlessly according to the choice of facts. That choice is in the hands of every expert, of every individual who controls a file or signs a letter. Finding themselves with the power of truth in their hands, is it surprising that they retain it? This is their personal version of the schoolboy's dream — of doing the one thing which even Merlin and Lancelot could not — pulling the sword from the stone.

Every man now has a weapon — secrecy — that can give him some protection against other men's absolute truths. It also gives him self-pride. Secrecy has become the device which tells man he is worth something.

The negative, retentive, constipating refusal to reveal, to act, to cooperate, is the key to rational man. Truth today is not so much fact as fact retained. This is not to say that we truly believe even the great spy scandals to be important. A few seconds of introspection are enough for anyone to fix the real role, for example, of Philby, Burgess and Maclean in the decline of Britain. They had none. Twenty years of regular betrayal at the highest levels were virtually irrelevant to a nation which was collapsing for concrete reasons.

And so we do not worship in any profoundly divine manner the spies of Le Carré or the athletics of Bond. Anymore than we are deeply scarred by actual spy scandals. They are the miserable little *faits divers* of our century.

On the other hand, their very lack of real importance has freed us to treat real and fictional spies as the romantic model of modern civilization. They have replaced the old models of courage and chivalry. Given that there are no real secrets, those betrayed by Philby are, to all intents and purposes, as important as those each citizen retains.

Our obsession with secrecy and plots is therefore not aimed at opening the curtains in order to let in light. Rather we are wallowing in the dream that our personal limited powers of retention belong in the same category as those which occupy the front pages of the press. There was a subliminal identifying shiver of pleasure when Robert Calvi was found hanging by the neck from London Bridge. When Senator Joe McCarthy pointed his finger, there was an unconscious sensation that he was pointing it at each of us. When Gouzenko came forward in disguise to spill the beans in public, individuals imagined themselves beneath the white hood, revealing all.[17] Colonel North's popularity stems only in part from the fact that he was attacked for defending a certain vision of the American dream. Just as important was his willingness to risk all by adopting the most secretive of methods.

We do not follow the trail of mystery in search of the truth, but in search of the confirmation that mystery exists. These imaginary secrets are titillating because all of us are bearers of fact and therefore control secrets.

13

The Secretive Knight

In defence of the technocrats' addiction to secrecy, it must be said that they have long found comfort in their view of science as the miraculous knight of reason. Science led the way in the battle against the forces of darkness. Discoveries were celebrated as if new territories had been won on the road to a place of eternal light where knowledge would reign. And yet these very real advances in the uncovering of nature's secrets seemed increasingly to create a world which escaped the control of society. New knowledge and new positive powers in the hands of man seemed inevitably to be matched with new inaccessible elites and a new sophistication in the arts of violence and destruction.

Science, the miraculous knight, has consistently resembled a splicing together of Merlin and Lancelot. The former was part prophet, part magician, born of a devil and a virtuous maiden, at one with the laws of nature and therefore able to exploit them. He secretly prepared Arthur to become the perfect king in his hour of destiny. In part because of his immortality, Merlin can be alternately a symbol of freedom or of enslavement. Lancelot, on the other hand, was the greatest of Arthur's knights, the model of chivalry, bravery and fidelity. But he also carried with him the secret of his adulterous love for the Queen, a betrayal which negated all of his qualities. He twice caught sight of the Grail. But his impurity caused him to fail at the last moment and eventually it was that impure secret which brought on the war that destroyed the Round Table and caused Arthur's death. And so the servant of the greater good inexplicably destroyed it, just as the miraculous Merlin, uncoverer of perfection, inexplicably was unable to understand the forces he was releasing.

The great Scientific Revolution in which we are still engulfed began in 1543 when Copernicus published *On the Revolution of the Celestial Spheres*, laying out a theory in which the earth revolved around the sun. From then on all progress seemed to be a victory against established authority and official ideas. Interestingly enough, the opposition to Copernicus was firmer among the leaders of the Reformation, beginning

with Martin Luther, than it was in Rome, where Pope Clement VII
gave approval for an earlier version of the *Revolution* to be published.
However, when Galileo published his *Dialogue on the Chief Systems* in
1632, clarifying and actually proving Copernicus's argument, he was
put on trial by the Inquisition and forced to recant.

It seemed clear from then on that scientists had embraced the ultimate virtue. They did not appeal in their arguments, as the twentieth-
century mathematician and humanist Jacob Bronowski has put it, to
race, politics, sex or age. They resisted "every form of persuasion but
the fact."[1] Truth was their guide in a world where everyone else was led
by interest. Francis Bacon's social model of a dictatorship led by scientists, as laid out in *New Atlantis*, must be seen in that context. His idea
of a nocturnal council of senior scientists, who would decide in secrecy
what to do with the new knowledge and how much to tell the population
at large, was the beginning of a debate which is still with us. As suited
the mind of a courtier, Bacon opted for secrecy and manipulation in the
best interests of the public.

But the more general view among scientists has always been that
secrecy has no place in their work. To the contrary, theirs is a permanent and open debate around the world — a "Republic of Science," as
Michael Polanyi put it. "In the free cooperation of independent scientists we shall find a highly simplified model of a free society."[2] Or as the
nuclear physicist Robert Oppenheimer wrote, "One thing we find
throughout the house: there are no locks; there are no shut doors;
wherever we go there are the signs and usually the words of welcome.
It is an open house, open to all comers."[3]

Of course, the situation is not quite so simple. The Republic of
Science does exist in the exalted sphere of pure research. Not only
secrecy has no role; neither does social interest. Virtue at this level is
the investigation and revelation of the laws of nature. The line between
this disinterested work and applied science is theoretically clear. In
practice it is confused. Many scientists find themselves on both sides.
Once across on the side of application, a whole other set of rules applies.
Application involves the interests of race, politics, sex and age, just for
a start. Nonscientific choices must be made. Secrecy becomes a tool of
the knowledge holder.

It is the confusion over how to deal with crossing the line from
theoretical to practical science which so troubles the scientists. If, once
across, they surrender all power over knowledge, they quickly find themselves forced by public and private authorities to do things which disturb
them for nonscientific reasons. The virtue found in theoretical work is
the disinterested purity of the laws of nature. However, human civilization is always "interested" and all choices surrounding scientific application eventually touch moral questions. A very different sort of

virtue is involved and the scientist is faced with the impossible task of satisfying both.

This contradiction has been gradually obscured by a third and arbitrary value: the virtue attached to all progress. In order to establish this, the inevitability attributed to theoretical science is arbitrarily extended to applied science, thus eliminating the possibility of making practical choices through public mechanisms. Common sense can tell us at any time that no application is inevitable. Or that civilization must decide what it wishes to do with a breakthrough of science. However, in the rush and disorder of the Scientific Revolution, very few choices have been made by society. Theoretical research may well be open and disinterested, but it also deals in areas obscure to the citizenry. That obscurity has somehow set the tone for all levels of scientific work, thus making any sensible intervention by the citizenry virtually impossible.

In spite of this there was a widespread feeling until the arrival of nuclear power that the force of science, in the words of André Malraux, "could not turn upon man."[4] The Western world abounded in paintings and statuary which celebrated the good wrought by science. One of the most absolute of these evocations is the 1899 statue of *Nature Uncovering Herself Before Science*, by the French artist Louis-Ernest Barrias. There she is in the great hall of *fêtes* in the Orsay Museum in Paris, a voluptuous, life-size woman sculpted out of marble, onyx, lapis lazuli and malachite. Her wonderful shoulders and breasts are bare. A scarab beetle at her waist holds together with its claws the drapery which hides the rest of her. The scarab is knowledge. No doubt the sculptor meant us to feel that, with a little coaxing, the beetle would release the cloth, revealing, as it slipped away, the most secret and intimate parts; that knowledge could and would reveal all secrets, if we befriended it. With the help of knowledge, men would penetrate the secrets of nature and the world.

And yet the beetle was in a position to play it either way. By simply using its little claws to keep the veils in place, knowledge would gain great power. Science, with the aid of the beetle, could explore every orifice of nature, giving itself orgasmic pleasure along the way, but deal out to the public only that information which suited it. Few men like to share a mistress, but they do like everyone to know that she is beautiful and gives pleasure.

Although the idealized nineteenth-century love affair between man and the secrets of science was passionate, very early on there were doubts about the innate goodness of such progress. Frankenstein's monster was the most popular example. Mary Shelley's story of the struggle between science and humanism was written in 1818. Frankenstein, the optimistic scientist, creates his ugly monster and educates him with Goethe, Plutarch, Milton. The monster, however, cannot live without love and so becomes a reluctant murderer. The drama ends in Antarctica, where Frankenstein dies and his monster wanders off alone into the snow in order to do the same. By midcentury the philosopher of art, John Ruskin, was writing of modern science such things as: "It gives lectures on Botany, of which the object is to show that there is no flower." Or again, "there was some excuse for your being a little proud when, about last sixth of April you knotted a copper wire all the way to Bombay, and flashed a message along it, and back — But what was the message, and what the answer? Is India the better for what you said to her?"[5]

Of course, it could be argued that Ruskin was responsible for much of the romantic overstatement which allowed many writers and creators to surrender in their ongoing battle for a public voice and retreat into private places and subjects. His basic contention, that progress was not of itself good, became the contention of many of the creative, unscientific minds. They assumed, following Ruskin, that if not of itself good, then progress must be of itself bad. And so they fled away to the safer ground of private questions, on which so much of the twentieth century's creativity has taken place.

But Ruskin was himself one of the great revolutionary theorists of art and architecture. He helped civilization to see in a new way and in so doing helped to release a fresh burst of creativity which spread from Dante Gabriel Rossetti, William Morris and the Pre-Raphaelites to George Eliot, Walt Whitman and Marcel Proust. The instinctive leaps in his theory resembled those of theoretical scientific research. A century later, Bronowski was examining the same question. Is there any difference between "the creative acts of the mind in art and in science"? He argued that the discoveries of science and works of art are both explorations — in fact, "are explosions, of a hidden likeness."[6] It was not this sort of creativity which bothered Ruskin, who was also an accomplished geologist, but the seeming impossibility of having any control over the direction and speed of subsequent applications. In truth, if there had been a divorce of science from art, it was an unwilling separation, forced by the absolute doctrine of structure and progress. Ruskin was astonishingly modern. His theories of beauty led him increasingly to political radicalism. His attacks on the mindlessness of applied science were tied into his attacks on social and economic structures which "actually promoted human suffering and the destruction of beauty, whether natural or man-made."[7]

As for the general public, by the middle of the twentieth century, its unquestioning confidence in the innate good of science had worn thin. What remained was a profound, inexpressible need to go on believing that science must be allowed to unfold, that nothing was more reprehensible than even a hint of resistance in the face of scientific progress.

Logic can multiply the smallest doubt at terrifying speed and to question is to doubt. To doubt is to fear. To fear is irrational. To be irrational is to embrace ignorance and emotional instability. And before you know it, you are a Luddite.

As a result, whatever fears are felt, our attitude towards science is that whether pure or applied, it is a single force which must be allowed to move forward. The word *forward* no longer makes any sense to us, but then many of our difficulties lie in these language traps. A civilization which moves massively in any direction without conscious self-control is in disordered flight as if pursued by enemy hordes. For example, over the last two decades we have become used to frightened groups who belong to what is called the Right, urging upon civilization a general flight into the past. At the same time the inaccessible, almost mystical religion of progress through science has enforced a flight forward into unknown futures.

As for the scientists, the vast majority of whom continue to believe in the inviolability of progress, they still do so with the driven purity of terrorists. Indeed, their devotion to the need for physical change reassures us that our society is not in confusion or bogged down. The few scientists who learn to doubt and dare to do so publicly, are usually discredited as being unstable by the majority of the scientific community.

From time to time, a scientific leader will find the right words with which to question our society's assumptions. The Nobel Prize–winning chemist, John Polanyi, calmly persists in a campaign for common sense to be applied to the development of knowledge. "The progress of science," he argues, "has its own logic, which you ignore at your peril."[8] He is not suggesting that attempts should be made to restrain pure science, but that society, with the aid of scientists, must develop mechanisms of choice which apply common sense, public interest and morality to the development of scientific breakthroughs.

The prime example of the seemingly uncontrollable relationship between research and development was the investigation which entered its final stage with Einstein's theory of relativity in 1905 and culminated with Otto Hahn's splitting of the atom in 1939. The first application was the atomic bomb. The scientists who produced that explosion felt themselves obliged to discuss, in secret, as the times required, the implications of their work. These discussions produced a report which was delivered by hand in June 1945, a month before the first atomic bomb test, to Henry Stimson, the American Secretary of War:

In the past, science has often been able to provide new methods of protection against new weapons of aggression. . . . But it cannot promise such efficient protection against the destructive use of nuclear power. The protection can come only from the political organization of the world. Among all the arguments calling for an efficient international organization for peace, the existence of nuclear weapons is the most compelling one.

[We] cannot hope to avoid a nuclear armament race either by keeping secret from the competing nations the basic scientific facts of nuclear power, or by cornering the raw materials required for such a race.

[T]he race for nuclear armaments will be on in earnest not later than the morning after our first demonstration of the existence of nuclear weapons.

The Franck Report was received and put away, to be ignored by the political and the administrative structure. The nuclear physicists who signed this document were in the unusual position of inventing a process whose full consequences were immediately foreseeable. Their call for common sense before the bomb was dropped can be seen as a cry of desperation. Because, from the moment of the explosion, a new profession could not help but be formalized — that of the scientists trained and employed to further develop the greatest weapon ever invented. That profession would have a structure linking it to the structures of the state. And the whole thing would be buoyed up by a self-justifying logic. Only in those last days before the explosion were the inventors both conscious and free; a combination which, as the Book of Genesis established some time ago, brings on expulsion from the garden of innocence and an admission of the evil within each individual.

In the Franck Report, the scientists were attempting to take responsibility for the unacceptable application of their inevitable invention. That is the optimistic interpretation. A more cynical view would be that they were declaring pure science to be an innocent participant in the whole affair and shifting responsibility for any application to the politicians. But it was the finest scientists of the century who in the first place had encouraged the politicians to build the bomb or had themselves agreed to build it. Einstein, Leo Szilard, Niels Bohr, James Franck, J. Robert Oppenheimer and dozens of others were involved. All considered themselves to be humanists, and many were pacifists. Their call in 1945 for nuclear restraint by the politicians was sincere, but was it honest?

Einstein, who wrote to President Roosevelt in 1939 encouraging him to build the bomb as fast as possible in order to stay ahead of the Germans, said after it was dropped, "If I knew they were going to do this, I would have become a shoemaker." If Einstein did not understand the process of development and did not help the public to understand it, what responsibility was he taking in his letter of 1939? To put it crudely, just because Einstein thought himself a nice guy doesn't mean he was.

The real problem is that during four hundred years of scientific revolution, the continual message has been that invention and change are virtues. Rational virtues. As for the dividing line between the inevitability of pure science and the choices theoretically presented by applied science, no attempt has ever been made to formalize the crossover point in coordination with the development of a public process of choice. Only the scientists have had any hope of identifying that line before, during or after it is crossed, as the Manhattan Project demonstrated. It would be unrealistic to imagine that the line could ever be perfectly clear. However, the "Republic of Science" could improve this situation if it recognized a second obligation, equal to that of open debate among experts — that is, an obligation to help the citizen understand the choices at stake. This would involve refusing the comforts of exclusive language and exclusive dialogues with the power structures. In other words, for the first time in modern history, to develop the idea that society, with the help of the scientist, has a brief to alter the progress of progress.

And yet, as John Polanyi points out, most scientists continue to remain silent because they regard themselves as too poorly informed to make a contribution outside their narrow fields. In a world of expertise and competing structures, they, the mythological experts, are indeed ignorant about the political and economic structures which administer society. When the occasional scientist does actually speak out, he is more often than not mercilessly martyrized.

The example of Oppenheimer is wired into the collective memory of the international scientific community like an illuminated cross that flashes on whenever they are tempted to convert their scientific expertise into public morality. Oppenheimer was the physicist chosen to direct the Manhattan Project. Neither before nor after Hiroshima did he doubt that it was "man's highest function to know and to understand the objective world and its laws."[9] However, he found the division between knowing and applying increasingly difficult to deal with. From the Franck Report on, he grew reluctant about further development of the bomb. He gradually applied what could be described as scientifically informed moral or humanist standards in order to put a brake on the nuclear military program, for whose future he was still partially responsible. As a result he was caught up in the net of McCarthyism and treated as part of the Communist scare. This led to his removal from positions of responsibility. Only then did he seriously carry his campaign for the moral application of scientific knowledge outside the circles of scientific and political power into the arena of public debate.

Our civilization detests the expert who gives in to generalized free speech. Public comment by an individual speaking outside his area of expertise, or even attempting to draw wider conclusions from his specific knowledge, is seen as a dangerous victory of emotion over professional competence. It interferes in the domains of others and it suggests that structures are inadequate. The words of a writer or of a journalist are relatively harmless. They come from the margins. But a proper expert, who is therefore a full participant in society, is attacking himself when he attacks others. As for critical public comment by an individual on his own area of expertise, that is almost worse. He is betraying the secrets of his *confrèrie*. Expertise and structure thus succeed in silencing most serious public debate.

In the world of science the modern secret finds its full worth. Knowing and understanding are the qualities of rational man which permit him to act. But the scientist retains that knowledge. He holds it back. Not in its details. Those are handed over to companies and governments. But he holds back any configuration of those details which would allow the citizen to understand. When faced by questioning from non-experts, the scientist invariably retreats behind veils of complication and specialization. Of course it is complicated. But there is no other profession in which the sense of obligation to convert the inner dialect into the language of man is so absolutely absent. Through this form of secrecy the scientist makes it impossible for the citizen to know and to understand and therefore to act, except in ignorance. At its best, thanks to solid common sense, human ignorance may still attain the level of decent humanism; at worst it is emotive and fearful. In any case, both humanism and emotion will be discounted by expertise.

The nuclear industry has become a microcosm of all the protective superiority and secrecy attached to scientific knowledge. In France, for example, the decision was taken by the administrative elites, in the late 1950s, to reduce oil imports by converting to nuclear energy. Some 70 percent of the country's needs are now satisfied by nuclear reactors. Soon the figure will be 80 percent, as twenty more plants are added to the existing forty and fast-breeder reactors come fully on stream. Between the introduction of the original plants and 1986, there was not a single nuclear accident in France. Its elites were thus able to boast at home and around the world of their system's superiority. Like the systems of other countries, it was being sold on the international market. The other builders of nuclear plants — the United States, Canada, the United Kingdom, Japan, the Soviet Union — had not had many accidents and most of those were described as mere technical incidents. In general this appeared to be a safe industry bringing much needed energy to those who lacked oil and coal. For decades it was unsullied in the public mind. This was the future of technology: clean, silent, invisible as opposed to the dirty, noisy, obtrusive methods of the nineteenth century. The sense of purity was such that the scientific myth of moral change for the good of mankind was given a whole new boost. The public good was here synonymous with applied knowledge. Young scientists around the world dreamed of joining the nuclear sector and doing good, not unlike the young men who once dreamed of following Saint Francis. They were not seeking great fortunes on the backs of others. They weren't becoming property developers or currency speculators or leveraged buyout manipulators. They were choosing public service, which if not so sacrificial as joining the early Franciscans was nevertheless neither selfish nor self-interested.

And what was true everywhere else was particularly true in France, where the industry's record was perfect. A national consensus, ever more solid, reflected the confidence of experience and, inevitably, the confidence born of necessity as the country became increasingly reliant on the nuclear grid. Nuclear scientists had once worked for a future dream. Now they defended a national system.

Then, in 1986, came the accident at Chernobyl. The leak had been so bad that it was first detected outside the Soviet Union when the alarm systems inside Swedish reactors went off as if there were a local disaster. All of Europe went on radiation alert. In the weeks that followed, it became clear that there had been massive contamination of food products across the continent. Milk and cheese were destroyed in most places. Italy destroyed its vegetables and kept children indoors. Contaminated animals were killed and burnt.

Curiously, France alone seemed to have been spared by the winds bearing clouds of radiation. Life went on. Milk, cheese, vegetables and animals were eaten. As citizens looked at the daily maps of radiation movements in their newspapers, they could not help but be confused by the Cartesian elegance with which the winds carried contamination to the north and to the south, leaving a neat hole in the middle large enough to accommodate France.

As it turned out, there had been no stupidity or political manipulation. The French nuclear scientists were simply so used to protecting their citizens from the moral dangers of knowledge improperly understood that they had extended the same protection to the Russians.

This protective impulse might be called the conspiracy against panic. Rational man's greatest fear remains that the citizen will fall back on his baser instincts and act rashly. Reason over passion. Reason over fear. Reason over panic. Above all, modern man must remain calm.

Interestingly enough, in those countries which dealt most openly with the dangers of the Chernobyl accident, the citizens took their right to panic to heart. They listened carefully to all warnings and advice. They did not eat what they were told was dangerous. They did not complain about lost crops. They kept their children indoors. No one ran amok in the streets. They used their common sense to panic with dignity.

And when, in France, the knowledge began to filter through that they had been treated like children, the citizens reacted with a certain anger. First, French lamb was rejected at foreign borders as toxic. France's experts blamed this on foreign ignorance. Then even French herbs were turned back from Japan. The international press began to concentrate on the refusal of Paris to admit that something serious had happened. Gradually the French citizen's confidence in the nuclear system was shaken. In the weeks that followed, the revelation of undeniable deceit forced a certain openness upon the experts.

Suddenly, nuclear reactors, safe for thirty years, began to have accidents — a half dozen in the next twelve months. Then accounts of earlier accidents began to leak out. On April 4, 1984, at Bugey, which lies in the intensely cultivated and heavily populated area between the Swiss border and Lyon, the official unpublished report had said — "An incident of this gravity has not been met with before on a heavy water reactor. : . . A supplementary failure . . . would therefore have led to a complete loss of electrical power, an unmeasurable situation. . . . The failure of the valves to close would have led to an additional degeneration of the incident towards a situation difficult to control."[10]

The scientist responsible for this report no doubt feels that the subsequent leaking and publication of his words was a betrayal. He would probably say that if read by untrained, uninvolved outsiders, the report could be used to create a narrow and sensationalist picture of the truth. As for the truth, that is a vast intricate thing which an outsider could not possibly understand.

The average person, if called upon to listen to this explanation, would sense beneath the scientist's words an anger beyond any rational explanation. The source of this fury is the scientist's, and above all the nuclear scientist's, belief that he is Merlin/Lancelot, the miraculous servant of the future. Suddenly, ordinary people everywhere are accusing him of endangering their lives.

The beloved child reacts to the questioning of his actions as though his motives — that is, his moral judgment — were being questioned. He responds with the weapons he most despises. He reacts with fear; with hatred of the outsider. He lashes out. He conceals. In fact, he does the very thing he keeps saying the ignorant public will do if they are not carefully handled: he panics. And having been nursed upon the abstract, he panics badly, without common sense or dignity. This makes it impossible for society to deal calmly with the problems which arise from his labours.

In 1987 constantly high levels of radioactive contamination were registered on a beach near the Dounreay nuclear plant in Scotland. These levels were confirmed by separate expert measurement. In fact, the responsible scientists did not deny the findings. However, the plant was scheduled for expansion. Studies and hearings were underway. The same responsible scientists refused to take the beach contamination levels into account in their studies of safety standards. One had nothing to do with the other.[11] It was as if they had been presented not with facts but with disloyal information which had inexplicably gone over to the side of darkness.

Repeated leaks at the nuclear plant of Pickering — in the suburbs of Toronto, surrounded by five million people — are consistently described as technical problems. In the post-Chernobyl period, a documented public report in Canada threw doubt on local nuclear safety standards. The Canadian government reacted by instructing its Crown-owned nuclear reactor development corporation to reexamine those standards. Instead the corporation explained at great length that reexamination was unnecessary because the public report was based upon unfounded fears. The refusal to entertain doubt seemed to be absolute.

The scientists within nuclear plants usually report incidents to their superiors. This is part of internal expert structures. For example, it is known that in 1986 there were 2,836 accidents in the 99 American nuclear plants. In 1987 there were 2,940 accidents in the then 105 nuclear plants.[12] The information blockage seems to come at the moment when the technical knowledge threatens to escape from the absolute control of the expert system.

Over twenty-eight years, reactor accidents at the enormous Du Pont Savannah River nuclear plant in South Carolina were reported by the plant to the regional office of the Atomic Energy Commission (AEC). This included a 1985 memorandum written by a scientist to his superiors summarizing thirty "reactor incidents of greatest significance." None of this was acted on. Nor was the information reported to the central offices of the AEC or to the Department of Energy. The information was kept secret. Those concerned pretended that nothing had happened. And yet they are not the sort of people normally thought of as belonging to the criminal element. They are quite probably good citizens. Loving parents who pay their taxes and take their children to Little League practice or piano lessons. When the information finally came out, the Energy Department put this secrecy down to a deeply rooted institutional practice going back to the Manhattan Project in 1942, when security was all-important.[13] But this hardly explains a decision not to report incidents to the Department of Energy. The

Department of Energy could hardly be called a foreign agency. Rather, this obsessive retention reflects a terrible confusion of expertise, self-worth and morality.

By treating the public as children likely to panic, the scientist can succeed in making them do just that. Witness the weeping and self-flagellation in British novelist Martin Amis's introduction to his book of short stories, *Einstein's Monsters*. Nuclear weapons "make me want to throw up, they make me feel sick to my stomach." In the case of a nuclear war, "I shall be obliged (and it's the last thing I'll feel like doing) to retrace that long mile home, through the firestorm, the remains of the thousand-miles-an-hour winds, the warped atoms, the grovelling dead. Then — God willing if I still have the strength, and, of course, if they are still alive — I must find my wife and children and I must kill them."[14] Amis's hysteria gives comfort to the scientist and to the authorities. The expert feels exonerated in his withholding of knowledge, although Amis slipped into this frenzy only because, after forty years of refusing to discuss nuclear power in a calm, open manner, the scientists have left the amateur no other style of argument.

Curiously enough, such attacks simply reinforce the scientist's view that, while nuclear weapons are a necessary evil dictated by the needs of uncivilized man, nuclear power is a good necessary to the well-being of man. And yet the risk of a catastrophe is far more likely to come from peaceful reactors than from bombs. The weapons, after all, are dormant. Someone must decide to use them. Common sense and simple humanity protect us. The reactors, however, are constantly exploding. That is how they produce energy. All that stands between man and the unleashing of this force is the effectiveness of the machinery containing the explosions and the competence of those responsible for administering the plants. One thing we do know is that neither mechanical nor human infallibility has ever existed. Passenger jets crash. High-speed, high-technology trains crash. Dams give way. Bridges fall down. And there were 2,940 nuclear accidents in the United States alone in 1987 in only 105 plants.

The late 1980s saw a breakthrough for sensible concerns over nuclear power. Britain, for example, has virtually abandoned the building of additional nuclear plants. But the way in which this happened shows that no progress has been made in bringing the secrets of science out into the open for public scrutiny. To the contrary. No public debate preceded the government's decision; not even debate among nuclear scientists. It was simply announced that the planned government privatization of electricity would not include the nuclear sector. Closer examination revealed that this was for two reasons. First, despite decades of promises to the contrary, nuclear power was still more expensive than old-fashioned energy sources. Second, the private sector was not interested in investing in such a risky sector. They were particularly disturbed by the risks and costs involved in dismantling old plants.

Nowhere was there a hint that the public should be concerned by those risks or costs. Instead, the Chairman of the Atomic Energy Authority repeated the standard arguments:"We have to demonstrate that nuclear power is not only safe but economic. There is no doubt that the public has been confused by press reports about the financial risk of nuclear power."[15]

In other words, neither the nuclear scientists nor the government and business elites admitted anything. Instead they stated that problems in the nuclear industry came from confusion in the public's mind — which is to say, from ignorance. One senses that what has happened in Britain constitutes only a temporary pause. The scientific community is still convinced that it must go on. It will, therefore, continue pushing inside the various systems until, one day, the British government will abruptly announce a new, improved program. This decision will seem to come out of nowhere and yet the program will be born fully formed. One of the arguments which will make continuation seem to be inevitable will be that most other Western nations have not paused. France and Canada are plunging onwards. The United States will begin again the moment there is a new energy crisis. Only Sweden appears to have made a definitive decision to denuclearize. In the spring of 1991 — the fifth anniversary of Chernobyl — the industry began a concerted international effort to sell the public on its new safety standards.[16]

The interesting questions in this debate are the simple ones the experts avoid. Why should the public submit itself to uncertain risks? What right do the scientists have to impose their timetable on the general population? Why are the scientists so panicked by the fear of moving carefully? Why do they feel obliged to flee so erratically into the future?

There is little difference between the nuclear scientist's moralistic prevention, through the retention of knowledge, of proper public debate and that of scientists in other areas. For example, every year there are two million cases of human poisoning through contact with applied pesticides. Forty thousand of these are mortal. Pesticides have poisoned water tables throughout the world. In 1987 the main rice-producing area in Italy was obliged to truck in drinking water for the farming families. Rice, of course, is grown in flooded fields. The farmers had poisoned their own water tables. The effect on the rice produced is another question, which the farmers themselves wouldn't want to discuss. In southern Europe there is an epidemic of microscopic red spiders which attack crops. These spiders are a side effect of advanced chemical antimildew treatments. A number of European studies have identified a sharp rise in terminal diseases among early-middle-aged farmers and have linked this to intensive chemical farming. The University of Guelph has tied the sharp rise in Parkinson's disease to an element in chemical fertilizers. There is also a sharp growth in human immunity to antibiotics. For example, in 1960 only 13 percent of staphylococcus infections were resistant to penicillin. In 1988 the figure was 91 percent. In part this has been traced back to overuse of these drugs, which has also led to epidemics of such diseases as meningitis and gonorrhea. Numerous tracing tests have also followed part of the problem back to the feeding of antibiotics to cows, sheep, pigs and chickens to prevent disease and stimulate growth. Fifty-five percent of American antibiotics are used on farm animals. In a phenomenon called "jumping genes," the bacteria are now developing defence mechanisms faster than the scientists can come up with new treatments. In a related development, the feeding of hormones to animals has been forbidden in Europe. This was a political victory over the local hormone experts, who deny any side effects, as do their colleagues in the United States. The appearance of salmonellosis inside fresh eggs was first seriously noted in the United States. In the nine years from 1979 to 1988, the recorded incidence multiplied sixfold. Dr. Douglas Archer, director of the Microbiology Division of the Food and Drug Administration's Center for Food Safety and Applied Nutrition, confirmed in December 1988 that the cause was the battery-hen advanced-production method. A month later a British cabinet minister, Edwina Currie, spoke publicly of this problem and was forced to resign.[17]

These random examples are relatively straightforward. The refusal of most organizations to admit that there is a problem when one does arise, let alone do anything about it, could simply be put down to corporate interests. Nothing is neater than to blame human greed. However, most of the corporations involved are run by managers, not owners. Many of these managers are scientists or engineers. Most are technocrats of one sort or another. And beyond them are gigantic reserves of expertise in universities, hospitals and institutes. The vast majority of these honourable scientists either cooperate with the problem-denial process or simply remain silent. They seem unable to step back from progress in order to disapprove specific advances.

Thus the pesticide poisonings are blamed on incorrect use by the farmers. Water-table contamination cannot be specifically linked to agriculture. When, in January 1989, it was revealed that the pesticide levels in water processed by four U.K. water authorities were above what Common Market health standards allowed, the reaction of the authorities and the government was childlike. They said the EEC level was too low. They said this was bad news for consumers, who would have to pay more if the strict regulations were complied with. There wasn't a hint of concern over possible health implications. The red spider epidemic is blamed on incorrect use of the antimildew products. And the spiders are seen as a technical incident which is being dealt with through the creation of additional chemical treatments. There is an absolute denial that chemical fertilizers cause any diseases or have any effects on such things as water systems. And yet the water in apparently pristine lakes in Canada can no longer be drunk unfiltered. The government warns against eating too many fish caught in these waters. Oysters and mussels from beds in unpolluted areas off Europe and North America suddenly poison people. The problem is rarely admitted to be local. The poison has been carried into the area by a current. Not a serious word is said about the millions of tons of agricultural runoff, which is one of the causes of the tragic change in all these waters. It is denied that antibiotics survive through the food cycle. Each example of tracing is treated as incidental. Rather than reexamine its liberal use of antibiotics, the scientific community flees forward, discovering cures for calamities which its previous cures have caused. Not only do the North American creators of hormones for animals deny there are any risks, they claim that the European ban is a ploy by protectionist governments against competitive foreign products. They are terrified that the European precedent will help antihormone pressure groups in the United States. The European hormone producers side with the Americans and have created a pressure group called European Enterprises for Animal Health. The name is a perfect example of the dictatorship of vocabulary carried to the point of nonsense. They have appropriated SPCA sentiments for the name of an organization devoted to the chemical fattening of animals for slaughter.

Annual analyses of the cost of organic grain farming versus chemical grain farming in the United States show that the organic system is now marginally cheaper. The production costs are the same, but the chemical farmer must pay for his expensive chemicals. Despite these facts, the scientific community remains united with the corporate structure in denigrating what they define as a nonscientific approach. Why something that works better, has no negative side effects and costs less should be eliminated on the basis of devotion to what is seen as modernity is not at all clear. The modern devotion to efficiency evaporates the moment the proposed method does not complement the methods in place. In 1989 a remarkable breakthrough was made. The American National Academy of Sciences announced the results of a long study which established that organic farming was as productive if not more productive than chemical farming. They are now recommending that forty years of government policies promoting "modern" agriculture be reversed. This revolutionary announcement was greeted with silence from the scientific community. Nor did this news roll across borders causing great discussion in the rice region of northern Italy or the intensive market garden area of southern France or in England, which prides itself on having the most modern, industrialized agriculture in Europe.

Again, the question which the scientific community shows little interest in asking or answering is why the public should be submitted to the risks without its understanding or consent. The thirty-five chemical products which go into the production and preservation of a modern apple may or may not present a risk to public health. But why was the use of these insecticides, artificial fertilizers, fungicides and preservatives rushed ahead with? Why was there no time to publicly consider whether this was the right road and whether the citizen wished to travel down it? The parliamentary systems demand that a government justify its actions in public. The scientific community has changed our life more in this century than any parliament, and yet it feels obliged to justify nothing.

As for the scandal in early 1989 over whether British eggs contained salmonella, the process involved might easily have been mistaken for satire. First, no reference was made by scientists, politicians or journalists to the fact that this is a problem in all Western countries in which advanced industrial methods are used to raise chickens. Second, the crisis immediately fell to the lowest level of nationalism — British eggs are good. Overnight every hen was waving a Union Jack as Mrs. Thatcher stood up for working chickens. Third, the Minister who dared to speak the truth was left in isolation by the scientific community, in order to give the impression that she was hysterical. That she had panicked. Fourth, having gotten rid of her, the responsible officials took partial measures — just enough to prevent panic — which confirmed that the Minister had been right all the time.

Attitudes towards science have seemed to be changing over the last few years. The sudden rise of the Green movement to a level of political importance imposed on the politicians, the bureaucrats, the businessmen and even on the scientists a more careful agenda. However, the victories being won for environmentalism are taking place almost exclusively in the political arena. This demonstrates the muscles democracy is capable of flexing. But there is a great distance between showing biceps and changing a society. For the latter, one must win over, change or destroy the system.

At this point neither the scientific community nor the bureaucrats nor the business managers have shown any major signs of responding to the new political signals. There has been a response which implies acquiescence. Environmentally sound paragraphs are now inserted, along with other motherhood issues, into the speeches of politicians and corporate leaders. Deprived of their exclusive vocabulary, environmentally oriented political parties such as the Greens have already begun to founder on the complexities of modern politics. And the few real changes to have been made are concentrated in narrow areas where there are political points to be scored.

The British government calls for environmental responsibility while attempting to keep the quality of municipal water at as low a level as legally possible. The American government is concerned about deforestation in Brazil while its own emissions of carbon dioxide are growing faster every year — faster than the world's growth rate. The Canadian government bangs on about the dangers of acid rain while closing its eyes to the equivalent of desertification through massive deforestation. And no existing structures have engaged in any sort of discussion with those who question the wisdom of following applied science blindly into the future. If one listens attentively, there is at best a sullen silence.

The problem is not Green or anti-Green any more than it is environmentalists versus capitalists. The problem is a whole approach to truth and knowledge retention and power which goes far beyond these movements. The Green approach deals with an important slice of the scientific problem, but only a slice. Environmental risks are a result of the problem but are not the problem itself.

If the scientific-administrative structure were somehow to be won over to the Greens, it would be just as secretive, retentive and sure of itself as ever. From the self-evident truths of nuclear energy as a beneficial social good, we would pass to the self-evident truth of generalized nondevelopment.

The psychological effect the rational approach produces in people stems in part from the confusing of such words as *modern* and *good*. These belong together as little as *back to nature* and *good*. The public knows that absolutes have no place in process, but our society offers us no tools for questioning or rejecting with common sense.

The comic level to which this descends can be seen in the mythology surrounding French wine. The romantic image of a plump old *vigneron*, working with his gnarled hands on the vines, is central to the pleasure of drinking wine. Along with it come other images which have to do with past glories — Henri IV drank only Nuits St. Georges; Chambertin was the favourite wine of Napoleon. And yet there is a professional and public conviction that wine produced other than with modern methodology would be undrinkable. If you say to a Frenchman, "this is organic wine," he will roll his eyes. But organic wine is simply wine made more or less as it was for Henri IV or Napoleon, that is, as it was before two late-nineteenth-century revolutions: the arrival of phylloxera, which wiped out the vineyards; and the introduction of the scientific sugaring of pressed grape juice, known as chaptalization. The organic producer macerates the grape juice longer with its skin and pips; the resulting wine is held longer in wood casks and kept longer in the bottle. Its stability, body and taste come from itself.

Modern wine tends to be filled with sulfur, chemical stabilizers, fungicides, beet sugar and alcohol additives. These elements, not grape alcohol, are the cause of most hangovers. Contemporary wine doesn't taste anything like Henri IV's Nuit St. Georges. It is forced, matures quicker and dies faster. Like nuclear reactors, modern wine is part of the secretive promise of our society.

14

Of Princes and Heroes

There is a curious conceit in the West that our leaders are the product of chance or accident. We therefore tend to complain in an oddly disinterested way about those we place in authority over us. Stranger still, when faced by public needs, problems or crises, we have a tendency to expect the almost-instantaneous appearance of leaders who are appropriate to the situation.

The reality is that leaders are rarely produced by either events or accidents. They tend rather to be the natural product of long-term structures and of a civilization's gradual evolution. The citizens' choices are often so limited by these trends that they find themselves obliged to fight wars under the leadership of social reformers, as was the case in Britain, France and the United States for most of World War I. Sixty years later the economic collapse of 1973 found the United States in the hands of a pure politician, devoid of financial common sense. France and Britain were then led by technocrats, whose tools were primarily administrative. Germany alone of the Western nations had a competent economist in place at the right moment and that for reasons unrelated to the immediate crisis.

These missed rendezvous are often used as evidence to support the modern truism that democracy is an unwieldy and ineffective way to govern. A more honest and accurate argument would be that democracy is increasingly crippled by the acceptance of rational methodology in the creation and selection of leaders. These leaders are then inappropriate to the democratic process and actually undermine it by working against its inherent needs. From our conversion to reason two types of leaders have emerged: the rational prince and the Hero.

The prince remains true to his origins. He was very much the creation of Machiavelli, and then of Loyola, Bacon, Descartes and Richelieu. Modern leaders are not eager to claim these ancestors. Nevertheless, it was Machiavelli's rational prince who multiplied and occupied the positions of administrative power so effectively that he was soon spreading out into politics. The politicians themselves then began to imitate the methods of their employees, thus obscuring the natural and profound enmity between democracy and rational management. As a result the development of the citizen's democratic reflexes was constantly sabotaged and the development of the idea of the democratic leader was alternately blocked and deformed.

The general frustration created by these obscure battles eventually produced a new type of leader — the Hero. He was a facile combination of the democratic and the rational approaches — simultaneously popular and efficient. He was popular thanks to the combining of the majesty proper to kings with the worship proper to God in order to twist public opinion into adulation. He was efficient because his power left him free to administer without social restraint.

Unfortunately this joint solution was a betrayal of both public opinion and public administration. All Heroes, it rapidly became clear, were the enemies of the public interest. And the key to their power was a talent for using effective violence against the citizenry when necessary. Even the Hero who used his power to do good was merely preparing the way for another who would do evil with greater ease. The perplexing question this raises is how a civilization, which emerged from the destruction of the absolute power of kings and churches, in the name of such things as liberty and equality, could have become devoted to such a cult.

Stranger still, it was clear from Napoleon on that only the rare individual could become a real Hero, capable of the superhuman feats and weaknesses which destroy the power and self-respect of the citizen. The continued growth of the Heroic option therefore meant the development of a third and more easily attainable leadership type — the falsely Heroic leader. These people might rise to power through violence, in imitation of the real Hero, or through the established methods of democratic society. But they would deform that process by using Heroic imagery and promises of Heroic efficiency.

The overall effect has been that our society now finds itself dominated by the occasional terrifying real Hero, scattered between bevies of false Heroes, most of whom have managed to use the electoral system, and a whole range of unelected rational princes, the leading examples of whom preside over our legal codes. None of these three categories is easily controlled, because their power is the fruit of a profound rejection of the democratic relationship.

Princes

On October 13, 1761, a thirty-year-old French Calvinist, Marc-Antoine Calas, hanged himself in his father's shop on the rue des Filatiers in

Toulouse.[1] In order to protect his son's reputation, Jean Calas, who was a leading textile merchant, tried to hide the suicide. The tensions between the town's Catholic majority and Protestant minority led to the growth of a rumour that Jean Calas had strangled his son after discovering that he was about to convert to Catholicism. The merchant was subsequently arrested and a protracted trial followed. He was condemned first by the municipal magistrate and later by the *Parlement* of Toulouse. On March 10, 1762, he was executed by being broken on the wheel, a method which involved stripping the victim naked and tying him with arms and legs spread-eagled to the flat of a large wagon wheel, which was laid on the ground. One or two men then set about smashing his joints and bones one by one with a metal bar. Having been made pliable, the arms and legs were then woven through the spokes. Finally the wheel was raised up to a vertical position and the victim left to die in agony. Calas died protesting his innocence. Such a condemnation also meant that his family lost their civil and property rights.

Twelve days later Calas's widow went to Voltaire and begged him for help. He was then sixty-eight years old and Europe's most popular playwright. Already one of the most famous men of his day, he was a leading gadfly in the continentwide agitation for political and social reform. A permanent threat of imprisonment in France hung over his head. He had recently fled the service of Frederick the Great of Prussia and settled at Ferney, an estate perched prudently on the French-Swiss border. From there he lashed out in all directions at those who caught his attention.

Voltaire's first reaction to Madame Calas's plea was that her husband had been guilty. His horror of organized religion made him believe the worst of all sects. However, he investigated the case and became convinced that a great injustice had been done. He wrote to his contacts in Paris — ministers, courtiers, parliamentarians — asking them to intervene. They weren't interested.

This was a turning point in Voltaire's life. Perhaps the most important. He had never had a great philosophical scheme. However, he passionately desired reform and his already long career had been made up in good part of looking for the right way to force the hand of governments. He had been a courtier and a royal adviser, a playwright and an historian. Three years before he had taken up a specific human rights cause, involving six brothers whose inheritance had been stolen by the Jesuits. He now took personal charge of the Calas case and began pouring out a torrent of words in all directions.

In the process Voltaire virtually invented the idea of public opinion and demonstrated how it could be marshalled for a good cause. Instead of arguing from a high plane as the other eighteenth-century philosophers habitually did, he came down to the realities of human life. As a result he developed the idea that specific, heart-rending cases could be converted into great battles which would set standards and force widespread reform.

More important, he concentrated on the law — on legal reform and on the fairness of its application. Of course, Voltaire wasn't the first man of letters to seek social reform through legal reform. Jonathan Swift had taken on endless cases in Dublin in the first half of the century. Voltaire, who was a great admirer of Swift, had spent three months in the same house with him more than thirty years before during his English exile. His later concentration on satirical political novels, pamphlets and poetic attacks owed a great deal to Swift. And Henry Fielding had begun his attacks on the law with a trilogy of plays in 1730. In 1749, by which time Fielding was a lawyer and a justice of the peace, he published *Tom Jones*, a novel that was in part a demonstration of the need for legal reform. Voltaire used the English model and English thinkers throughout most of his life as the political example to be followed.

However, the Calas case was something new. Within a year Voltaire had turned it into the talk of Europe. The misfortune of Jean Calas began to take on mythological proportions. Voltaire kept up his assault. It took two years to force a judicial review of the case. And on March 9, 1765, three and a half years after the execution, the forty appellate judges of the Town Hall of Toulouse unanimously exonerated Calas. Every man and woman in Europe could see and feel that justice had been done. The pattern had been set for the great populist legal battles, which in our century would produce the Dreyfus case and Watergate. As for Voltaire, he was no longer seen as a political gadfly. He was now the defender of Calas and therefore the defender of Justice. He went on to take up a stream of other cases over his last twenty years.

The rule of law had thus been fixed in the consciousness of the citizenry as the most reliable tool for controlling leaders and achieving both political and social justice. Only a few years before, the ideas of Montesquieu, a senior judge-turned-writer, had quite naturally been addressed to other members of the elites. Now even the complex and highly intellectual message of the *Encyclopédistes* had a populist reverberation they themselves didn't quite understand. Their arguments in favour of a strong monarchy bound by an inviolable legal code suddenly caused others to wonder why, since the legal codes were to be inviolable, the monarch had to be strong. That refrain had a longer history in England, but there it took on a new amplification when King George III's refusal to act in a law-abiding manner provoked American gentlemen — including landed gentry and city merchants — into revolutionary action.

It became clear during these and other debates that the new rational public man was meant to be first and foremost a lawmaker. This was to ensure the reign of Justice, which was generally understood to mean the exercise of authority in the maintenance of right.[2] The importance of lawmaking was confirmed by the Napoleonic experience, which demonstrated that, even when a Hero was in power, rule by law was to be second only to military glory. While Napoleon was busy conquering Europe and violating the citizen's most basic rights, he was also putting his name, with the accompaniment of great pomp, to a new revolutionary legal code. It has been central to his Heroic myth that he be given credit for writing, if not all, certainly a great part of the Napoleonic Code. He was described and depicted staying up for entire nights to dictate the new standards of justice. In reality most of the Code had been in preparation before his rise to power. A committee of great legal thinkers then gave it shape. Napoleon made some late drafting amendments and, to his credit, enacted the whole package. Whatever the historical truth, the idea had been established that, while Heroes might seize more arbitrary power than an absolute monarch, they did so on behalf of the citizen. That idea is still with us.

Implicit in the new, popular crusade for lawmaking was the question of form and style. The rule of law meant that the actual formulation of the laws must be clear. Without clarity there could be no general understanding among the citizenry; and without understanding, no sense of whether right had been maintained.

It has taken two centuries for that clarity gradually to disappear, while the law has grown to become a force in itself rather than an extension of representative decision making. The swelling mass of legislation processed by our assemblies has to do increasingly with administrative methods rather than the enunciation of policy. Most of the laws relate to technical aspects of the system's development. And the sheer weight of the laws makes actual governing almost impossible. With very few exceptions, neither the elected representatives nor the citizens understand the legal structure.

Over the last hundred years, our thin legal codes doubled their thickness, then tripled, then quadrupled. As justice took hold in detail, so it seemed to become more demanding, and so further legislation was required. Along the way something peculiar happened. Our languages gradually proved themselves incapable of absolute concepts. The propositions of justice laid out in the seventeenth and eighteenth centuries had seemed perfectly clear. The subsequent inability of legislators to write legal sentences which could capture these propositions was, at first, blamed on incomplete policy decisions. By the late 1950s, this excuse was wearing thin. Each new law, no matter how well drafted, failed to achieve the marriage of principle with application. Further laws were required to plug the holes which inexplicably appeared or to extend the regulation to areas inexplicably excluded. And each additional law created not fewer but more holes.

As the tapestry of the different Western legal systems grew in complexity, so each became less like a fireman's blanket and more like a crazy fisherman's net, which allowed all sorts of fish through — big and small, depending on such factors as intelligence, luck and money. Criminal law, for example, proved itself not too bad when it came to dealing with amateurs, pretty hopeless with small-time thieves and unable to touch the professionals. Tax laws soon had many major corporations paying less than any employee working on their assembly line, because the corporations could take advantage of hundreds of provisions related to tax loss, special investments, write-offs and shelters, while the employees had their taxes simply deducted at source.

The legal profession began expanding by leaps and bounds in order both to plug these multiplying holes and to exploit them. Today there are 350,000 lawyers in the United States; 25,000 in Washington alone, where they devote themselves to governmental structures. In France, the argumentative onus and inquisitory role in law is only partially entrusted to lawyers. *Magistrates, notaires* and the *Conseil d'Etat* — a bureaucratic corps devoted to cases which pit the public against the administration — account for a large percentage of legal activities. In spite of this, the number of lawyers has approximately doubled over the last twenty-five years from 10,000 to 20,000. There have been equivalent increases in most Western countries. Swelling national legal codes represent only a small part of their work. Administrative regulations are equally important, as are new areas in multinational law. For example, the law of the European Community is now as important as that of each member state.

Thus, in the growing maze of technicalities, a cat-and-mouse game began between opposing armies of lawyers, whether struggling over criminal cases, corporate takeovers, taxation policy, environmental standards or thousands of other personal, private and public issues. Only the sides they represented made them opponents. Their skills were the same. Their methods came from the same source. The sides, however, were not equal. Those writing the laws couldn't possibly keep up with those legally breaking them, because the legislator must obey his own rules. As for the mass of lawyers working against the public interest — whether for criminals, corporations or individuals with a personal agenda — they were restrained only by the technicalities and so kept a constant lead over the legislators.

The critical mass of laws and the intricate struggles surrounding them began ineluctably to transfer real power from the people's representatives to those who interpreted the legal code. When it came to creating policy, the interpretation of law gradually became as important as that of legislating it, then more important. Whatever the constitutions of the nations may say, the reality today is that judges and courts are more important legislators than the elected representatives.

This is the third element in the decline of the elected assemblies. Just as parts of the representative's power have gone to the executive and to the administration, so another part has gone to those who argue and apply the law. As the lawmakers have declined, the law itself has grown into a seamless structure. Like administration, it has become both a substitute for policy and a body on whose back policy can be made.

The fixation of most eighteenth-century thinkers on inviolable legal codes was produced by two factors: their desire to end the intolerable rule of arbitrary, absolute authority and their belief in some sort of social contract. Their assumption was that this contract would automatically encapsulate and defend acceptable social standards. John Locke's *Social Contract* had been published in 1690, just forty years before Voltaire's exile in England. For most people Locke seemed to have swept away the authoritarian origins of contractualism in the philosophy of Hobbes. Locke's approach was more flexible. And properly controlled authoritarianism didn't bother the proponents of reason. The rational, contractual approach to law seemed to them to provide guarantees for justice.

Even so, to a minority these dreams of justice, rendered absolute by the application of unfettered intelligence, seemed dangerously dissociated from the realities of human society. Rousseau, for example, reacted by attempting to reattach the new legal concepts to their roots — that is, to humanity. "I refer to morals, customs and, above all, belief: this feature, unknown to our political theorists, is the one on which the success of all other laws depends."[3] In the 1950s that idea was still being expressed by Learned Hand, the greatest American judge of his day and a constant advocate of social justice. Surrounded by the explosion of regulation, he wrote: "I often wonder whether we do not rest our hopes too much upon constitutions, upon laws and upon courts. These are false hopes; believe me, these are false hopes. Liberty lies in the hearts of men and women; when it dies there no constitution, no law, no court can save it."[4] This same ethos, balancing legal codes with a moral centre, had been perfectly expressed at the moment of America's creation, when Edmund Burke rose in the House of Commons to speak against his own country's opinion and state interest by seeking justice for the revolutionary cause. "It is not what a lawyer tells me I may do, but what humanity, reason and justice tell me I ought to do."[5]

Burke approached the American Revolution in exactly the same way that Voltaire had approached the Calas case. He sought justice in a specific case, believing that any victory over the details of evil would eventually defeat it in general. But as the web of legal statutes has grown, so the chase after specific justice has, like democratic consultation, become more of a release device than one which leads to general solutions. These focused quests, particularly when they are successful, now often result in even greater injustice. Watergate was an apparently successful quest for greater honesty in American presidents and their entourage. Instead it became a manual for the use of a subsequent presidency, which engaged in far greater dishonesty without the president or his popularity being touched.

The general reaction, to legal complexity and the resulting obscurity that encourages legalistic manipulation, has been a growing desire for freestanding laws — that is, laws rendered inviolable by a bill of rights. Where such bills already exist, as in the United States, the drive has been to strengthen them. This curious movement was created in part by the abdication of the confused and frustrated political classes. If a bill of rights would ensure the justice they no longer felt able to create themselves, then why not surrender some of their theoretical powers to a document which could? The perceived success of the American Bill of Rights lies at the origin of this argument, which has recently been successful in Canada and is steadily growing in England. Lord Scarman, for example, one of the nine Law Lords and Chairman of the Law Commission for seven years, eventually came out in favour of a British Bill of Rights: "When times are abnormally alive with fear and prejudice, the common law is at a disadvantage; it cannot resist the will, however frightened and prejudiced it may be, of parliament."[6]

But how successful has the American Bill of Rights actually been, and in comparison to what other system? Despite U.S. power and riches, no developed country suffers from greater economic and human rights disparities or has higher levels of criminal violence. Forty million Americans are without any access to health care. Racial slums are abandoned by the authorities. In Los Angeles 70,000 young belong to street gangs which murder some 380 of their own every year, as they have each year for the last decade.[7] A higher percentage of the national wealth is in the hands of a smaller percentage of the population than in any other Western country. There are 25,000 murders a year — a figure which grows to new record levels every twelve months. To this should be added 1.5 million violent crimes per year and 12.3 million property crimes.

Only the United States among the Western countries has permitted the return of vigilante groups to help in the maintenance of public order. There is no other way to describe the Guardian Angels who first gave themselves to the New York City subway system and are now patrolling a growing number of neighborhoods. For the constituted authorities to permit their presence, and the public to welcome it, is to concede that the legal system doesn't work at any level, from the policeman on his beat to the Supreme Court justice.

It was the Bill of Rights itself, as interpreted by the Supreme Court, which made slavery legal in the Dred Scott case of 1857. That same Bill of Rights negated the results of the Civil War by making de facto slavery legal in the form of Segregation thanks to the court's decision on *Plessy* v. *Ferguson* in 1896. Indeed, that same Bill of Rights ended de facto slavery with the *Brown* v. *School Board* decision in 1954, only after great internal debate among the judges. In 1905 the Court approved the exploitation of workers, women, children and immigrants, thanks to *Lochner* v. *New York*. It continues to find women unequal to men, in such cases as *Bradwell* v. *Illinois* or *Hoyt* v. *Florida*. In *Korematsu* v. *U.S.A.* it also approved the removal by the Executive of the constitutional rights of the American Japanese after Pearl Harbor.

This is not to say that legislatures are incapable of acting badly. Over the question of Japanese rights in 1941, the parliaments of both Britain and Canada were guilty in the same way as the American Supreme Court of racism combined with financial opportunism — that is to say, the removal of rights, internment and forced disposition of property. The point is, however, that the Bill of Rights gave no extra protection, nor did the wisdom of the judges.

Still more important, these policy questions central to morality and humanism, central to the very nature of the citizen, were decided by an appointed body. The elected representatives thus escaped all responsibility for decisions which were essential to the moral and physical well-being of their electors. Worse still, so did the citizen.

Our confidence in the courts, when cooly examined, turns out to be confidence in the judges. It is a confidence based upon a reassuring vision. "Unlike most others who pronounce in the public domain, judges appear to offer, and to deliver, clear and definitive answers. Justice according to law is a coin which, when tossed, does not rest on the rim. It comes down head or tails; it is clear who has won and who has lost. The judge gives his reasons, pronounces the result and withdraws to the chill and distant heights."[8] Lord McCluskey, the senior Scottish judge, gave this description in 1986. Judge Learned Hand put it that the judge's "authority and immunity depend upon the assumption that he speaks from the mouth of others, so he must present his authority by cloaking himself in the majesty of an overshadowing past."[9] Montesquieu was the senior judge in Bordeaux in the early eighteenth century. He described the situation in his limpid manner. "When I visit a country, I don't examine whether the laws are good, but whether they are executed, because there are good laws everywhere."[10] Or again, Lord McCluskey: "The judge hears both sides. He passes all the material over his own well-calibrated mind, satisfies himself how the law applies to the established facts, and pronounces judgement which determines the rights and liabilities of the litigants."[11]

All this makes the judge sound very much like someone we know. A mythological figure. A disinterested servant of power and justice. One who is indifferent to lobbying and independent from the opinion of the majority. Who tries to decide with the general good in mind.

He is, of course, the Prince. Machiavelli's Prince, but also every-man's ideal prince. He is the Goldfriend of Anglo-Saxon literature. He is Solomon and Henri IV, *le bon roi* and other just kings. He is, above all, the long-lost benevolent despot of the philosophers of reason. He is Frederick of Prussia, Catherine of Russia and Christina of Sweden as Descartes, Grimm, Voltaire and Diderot had hoped to mould them. He is the prince of reason.

❦

That being so, the judge is precisely what the descendants of reason — technocrats in all their forms — have always wanted. Perhaps more important, he is precisely the sort of individual that they have laboured to make our entire civilization feel it ought to want. And in a sense they are right. If we are to have a civilization of systems so complex and unending that they avoid all normal control devices, then we also need a tyrant, benevolent and fair, who will simply say, when the system gets out of hand — "That won't do. Stop it."

But what would be the point in accepting this sacrifice of democratic rights if the legal system and its control devices don't work? The evidence is strong that they don't. Judges have great difficulty in composing fair and clear judgments. The citizen is being squeezed out of his role as jurist. The system seems unable to judge fast enough to keep the system up to date. And worst of all, the law and its officers are capable only of prosecuting the crimes which hardly matter. The major crimes escape them entirely.

First there is the question of the judges' ability to judge fairly and clearly. The citizen might be reassured by the fact that Western courts have made a series of generous judgments over the last thirty years. However, that is a short period of time. And even in this new age of justice, their calls have been close. Between 1974 and 1984, 20 percent of the judgments of the American Supreme Court were by margins of 5 to 4. In 1987 Justice Lewis Powell retired. Of forty-one cases decided by 5 to 4 during his last term, he cast the majority vote thirty-three times. He was key to decisions on both abortion and affirmative action, although he did not always cast a reform vote. His successor is less generous in spirit. As a result, in early 1989 the Court began to reverse itself on affirmative action in a series of decisions such as *Wards Cove Packing* v. *Antonio*. Most of these Supreme Court votes were also by 5 to 4.[12] According to the late reforming justice, Thurgood Marshall, the legal interpretation of the Court has now come full circle, back to the situation before *Brown* v. *Board of Education* began the desegregation process.

In 1991 the political reversal of the Court majority was complete. Thurgood Marshall became so frustrated by yet another right-wing decision that he resigned. The case in question reversed by 6 votes to 3 earlier Supreme Court decisions on the admissibility of unrelated information in murder trials.[13] No doubt Justice Marshall, then aged eighty-two, was particularly distressed by the knowledge that the pattern of future decisions was established for the next two decades. He described the situation in his dissenting opinion:

> The real question then is whether today's majority has come forward with the type of extraordinary showing that this court has historically demanded before overruling one of its precedents. In my view, the majority clearly has not made any such showing. Indeed, the striking feature of the majority's opinion is its radical assertion that it need not even try.
>
> Renouncing this Court's historical commitment to a conception of "the judiciary as a source of impersonal and reasoned judgments" . . . the majority declares itself free to discard any principle of constitutional liberty which [it has previously] recognized or reaffirmed.

In a separate dissenting opinion, Justice John Paul Stevens wrote that "today's majority has obviously been moved by an argument that has strong political appeal but no proper place in a reasoned judicial opinion."

Both Justices thus invoked reason and, indeed, Thurgood Marshall opened his moving dissent with the charge that "power, not reason, is the new currency of this Court's decision-making." On one level this is perfectly accurate. However, if you take a longer, historical view, it was the rational conviction that justice can better be accomplished by judicial administration than by democratic politics which first opened the door to the use of executive power to deny justice by determining nominations solely on the basis of ideology. After all, a bill of rights, which can be manipulated for lengthy periods through the appointment for life of justices, removes the responsibility for specific political changes from the democratic process. And Chief Justice Rehnquist, in his majority ruling in the same 1991 case, quite happily said that adherence to the precedents set by the Court's previous decisions "is the preferred course," however, not when a decision is perceived as unworkable or "badly reasoned."

And that is where arguments about the nature of justice approach reality. President Reagan, his Attorney General, Edwin Meese — who escaped on a technicality from prosecution by the courts — and his supporters always saw the political return of the Right as happening in three stages: first the creation of an accepted philosophical position; then the winning of the presidency; and finally the "roll[ing] back, on all fronts, [of] the liberal conquest of the last half century."[14] That roll-back could only be accomplished in the Supreme Court, which is why the most important decisions of President Reagan's two terms were his court nominations. It took only eight years to rebalance the Supreme Court in favour of the Right. President Bush's nominations have created a large majority. A justice usually sits for at least ten to fifteen years. That is, two and a half to four presidential terms during which he is responsible to no one except his own interpretation of the law.

The justice is therefore a powerful policymaker. This is by no means limited to the United States. In Canada, which recently gave itself a bill of rights, the now retired Chief Justice of the Supreme Court, Brian Dickson, pointed out that he and his colleagues were now the "final arbiter" of many of the major social policy questions confronting society. Dickson added, "It is power unsought."[15] Indeed, two justices have already had to resign, unable to bear the strain of this new responsibility.

And yet the power of judges is seriously hampered. They may not choose problems for consideration. They must wait for them to come to the court. They and the nation may have to wait ten or twenty years for the definitive case in any area of concern to reach one of the supreme courts. It is thus a dangerously passive way to create policy. Perhaps more telling for the citizen is the reluctance of the judges to assume this responsibility. They are themselves exposed to public judgment when they themselves feel only partially responsible. They know that our society did not begin its modern period on an understanding that the judge would be prince. They feel used by the system, like reluctant Caesars, manipulated by their praetorian guard.

The citizen's role in the burgeoning legal process is limited to jury duty. This has been absolutely central to the Western idea of fair justice. However, it never goes beyond the first level of trial. Appeals court proceedings are the exclusive responsibility of judges. And as the power of the courts grows, so the role of the jury keeps on shrinking, particularly in the common-law countries. The administrators of our legal systems have been working for some time to narrow the public's role in the meting out of justice. They seem to feel that law has become too complicated for untrained jurists to understand. Juries are therefore now considered unnecessary in an increasing number of trial categories, particularly in Britain. And the powers of juries, where they do exist are increasingly limited. Even the principle of a unanimous verdict has been put aside whenever possible.

The idea of being judged by the unanimous decision of one's peers is one of the last areas in which humanism outweighs logic. The juror brings common sense to the court, a factor which is implied by the phrase *reasonable doubt*. That doubt provides the citizen far better protection than any bill of rights and yet it is slipping away without a murmur of protest from the public.

When, in 1972, the U.S. Supreme Court abandoned the fundamental principle of jury unanimity for state trials in their decision on *Apodaca* v. *Oregon*, Justice Thurgood Marshall wrote in dissent:

> Today the Court cuts the heart out of two of the most important and inseparable safeguards the Bill of Rights offers a criminal defendant: the right to submit his case to a jury and the right to proof beyond a reasonable doubt. . . . The skeleton of these safeguards remains, but the Court strips them of life and of meaning. . . . The Court asserts that when a jury votes nine to three for conviction, the doubts of the three do not impeach the verdict of the nine. [But] we know what has happened: the prosecutor has tried and failed to persuade these jurors of the defendant's guilt. In such circumstances, it does violence to language and to logic to say that the government has proved the defendant's guilt beyond a reasonable doubt.[16]

Put another way, our elites do not trust our judgment. The experts who have influence on law reform — whether inside the bureaucracy, the law societies, the courts or the influential law firms — will never put it that way in public. Instead they argue that the present system is awkward and old fashioned. The rational argument, as always, is for efficiency.

Perhaps these arguments would be acceptable if they carried with them a conviction that the result would be a wider application of greater justice. Even on the technical front, efficiency reforms have not solved any problems. The process of justice falls farther and farther behind the event which provokes it. Between the charging of an individual and the final resolution of the case, one, two, three, even four years may go by. If the charge is a serious one, the existence of everyone involved will slip into limbo. The delays now associated with justice send a signal to all citizens: they cannot rely on the legal system to protect them, because involvement with the courts will be a destructive, not a protective, experience.

Those responsible for law reform deny none of this. They say it is proof of the need for more drastic reforms. But their earlier changes have now been in place long enough to bear responsibility for a worsening situation. No doubt there is an urgent need for massive reform. But there is nothing to suggest that the "efficiency" sought by official law reform committees in every Western country can solve our legal problems. This sort of reform seems to be little more than tinkering. The more fundamental problem is that the statutes cannot deal with the agility and imagination attached to major crimes because our legal systems are designed to deal with specifics. And specifics for the intelligent are like obstacles on an obstacle course. The difficult spots are highlighted. You go around them.

Periodically, however, even the intelligent make mistakes. They become overconfident or overintelligent. They become carried away by a lax or corrupt political atmosphere or by an overheated economy. And so they get caught. From the public's point of view, these captures appear to be serious assaults by the legal system on corruption and criminality in the elites. In reality they are almost accidental events.

For example, the recent "assaults" on insider trading, involving such people as Michael Milken in the United States and Ernest Saunders, former chairman of the scandal-ridden British company, Guinness, merely remind businessmen that that is how all intelligent trading is done. This is an extension of the obstacle-course phenomenon in which, for example, new taxation regulations immediately cause an explosion in creative accounting until a way around is discovered.

The American Justice Department recently finished a three-year investigation of General Dynamics Corporation in search of evidence that the company had defrauded the government during the building of nuclear attack submarines. They succeeded in finding evidence that the company may have falsified information about submarine delivery schedules and cost overruns, but the Department lacked an identifiable party to charge. Since the Navy had acquiesced in General Dynamics activities, it would have had to be included in the charge. The Department of Justice was reluctant to charge the American Navy. This was the second incident over which the Department had considered charging General Dynamics. In 1986, while the investigation was going on, the company received eight billion dollars in further defence contracts.[17]

The possibility of intentional massive fraud, by a key defence contractor with the acquiescence of the American Navy, is of national importance and constitutes a major challenge to the maintenance of public justice. But these sorts of events, or rather nonevents, are considered so normal that they cause not a ripple in the sea of public debate. The General Dynamics case didn't even get onto the important pages of the newspapers, nor was it dealt with by the frontline journalists of national affairs. What other explanation can there be for such public indifference than that citizens no longer believe their legal system can work? And what the citizen will put up with rarely remains an urgent matter for the politicians and the press.

On the rare occasions when criminals belonging to the elites are brought to court, the circumstances always suggest that somehow a profound error has been made and that the accused, although perhaps guilty, really ought not to be there. In 1986 in the Plaza-Athénée Hotel in Paris, a rich American businessman fired five shots at the Vice President of the Franco-Arab Chamber of Commerce, seriously wounding him. Their argument was over a three-million-dollar commission owed to the American, Taj Jamil Pasha, for a turnkey factory contract in Germany. Jamil was released on bail of 800,000 francs ($160,000). He returned to France for the trial three years later. The judge treated him with great respect, referred to his career at the very heart of big business and freed him on payment of a fine of 42,000 francs ($8,000). He can return to France whenever he wishes. The preceding case in the same courtroom involved a young Moroccan accused of trying to hold up a hotel with a pellet gun. He asked for bail. It was his first encounter with the law and he had already been held without bail for nine months. His request was refused and he was taken back to prison.

The scene was not very different from that in London in 1988 when the well-known City banker, Roger Seelig, arrived in court to deny the twelve charges brought against him by the Metropolitan Police Fraud Squad in connection with the Guinness case. He was freed on bail of £500,000 paid by two successful businessmen, Sir Terence Conran and Paul Hamlyn. The general feeling in the business community about the charges arising out of the Guinness affair was that, whatever had happened, it had all been good business. The charges were therefore unfair. Seelig was preceded in court by a man accused of eating a £3.95 pizza with the intention of not paying. The accused was sentenced on the spot to £50 or seven days in jail. Having been short £3.95, he was unlikely to have 50. Seelig went on to do something quite unusual. He conducted his own defence. By early 1992, some four years later, the legal process had worn him down. The judge discharged the jury because of serious concern over Seelig's mental and emotional health, and he found himself free without any clear legal statement being made on his case.[18]

It could be argued that the poor have always gone to prison and the rich gone free. In the Jamil case the court reporter of *Le Monde* was reduced to quoting La Fontaine: "According to whether you are powerful or miserable . . ."[19] Equally, kings or law courts have traditionally reached out from time to time to punish a few of their elite who have become too big for their boots. Louis XIV made Fouquet, his Superintendent of Finance, into an example. Today's courts have chosen Boesky, Saunders and a few others. There is no question of justice being applied to all who may have transgressed. The courts can't handle the flow of petty criminals and murders. What would they do with half the business leadership of the eighteen developed countries?

This is not to suggest that the social disparities in Western society are now as great as they were in the seventeenth century. Or that justice is now as violent as it once was. Sentences were far more widespread and violent than ours but, on those occasions when aristocrats and burghers did come to trial, justice was often as violent for them as it was for peasants. The question here is whether the institutions of reason have improved the equality of justice. It could probably be argued, given the decline in the incidence of treason, religious conflicts and political divisions, that the ratio of convicts from the elites to those from the poorer classes is now lower than it was under the absolute monarchs.

Moreover, there have been profound changes in the nature of major crime over the last half century. It is a truism that the Italian mafia has a major role in Italian banking and business and in the largest political party, the Christian Democrats; that the offshore banking havens, such as Bermuda, the Turks and Caicos, the Bahamas and Hong Kong, which are used by most major multinationals to reduce their tax bills, are also used by organized crime to launder their income. Most major international banks have branches in these havens. That is merely a fact. It is a truism that American banks have been penetrated by organized crime, along with whole industrial sectors, particularly the entertainment industry — Hollywood and film distribution in particular. That is one of the explanations for the exorbitant costs involved in making American films. The charges of criminal activities against the Bank of Credit and Commerce International (BCCI) in 1991 should be seen as an exceptional occurrence brought on by the uncontrolled and extreme activities of the bank. The possibility of fifteen billion dollars in concealed losses and widespread involvement with secret service agencies was bound to attract attention eventually. The BCCI is, however, not an exception in its contempt for national laws. Its carelessness will provide a rare opportunity to examine relatively common banking procedures. The drug trade, once the family business of a few Sicilians, has now taken on gigantic multinational proportions, involving Chinese and Latin American organizations as well as the Italian. Drugs rate today as one of the largest international currency earners.

All this escapes our system of justice. The authorities are reduced to humiliating seizures of a few kilos here, a few kilos there. Occasionally, there is a "big" haul, which usually consists of a few hundred kilos — that is to say, of nothing. No more than 10 percent of the estimated annual drug trade has ever been seized. And when a theoretically important criminal figure is arrested, it is with the greatest difficulty that the government gets a conviction or a long sentence. The 25,000-man

American expedition to Panama, resulting in four hundred deaths and hundreds of millions of dollars worth of economic damage, was mounted in the name of justice to shut down a major cocaine network by over-throwing General Manuel Noriega. He was overthrown, a friendly government was installed, and the drug business went on undisturbed. As for Noriega, he and his lawyers spent the subsequent years running circles around, or rather through, American law. The end result was a conviction, but the process of appeal will drag it all on for several more years.

Drugs aside, our authorities have failed to understand how money moves and agreements are made. Our legal codes search for proof of misdemeanors in the forms of contracts and the physical exchange of goods for currency. Organized crime operates without contracts. Without paper. Without borders. Multinationals use contracts, but these may be in any jurisdiction, including offshore havens. Our legal codes and courts are virtually irrelevant when it comes to organized crime. But they are equally irrelevant when it comes to regulating multinational corporations. The point is not that there is a moral equivalence between drug cartels and multinationals, but that our laws are meaningless when it comes to international operations, whether criminal or corporate. When the scandal surrounding BCCI's operations exploded on July 5, 1991, one of the clients named, among the drug lords, dictators, terrorists and gun runners, was the CIA. Almost immediately, Richard Kerr, the Deputy Director of the CIA, confirmed that the Agency had transferred substantial amounts of money through the BCCI, that the bank had been "involved in illegal activities such as money-laundering, narcotics and terrorism," but that the CIA had used the bank "not in any illegal way."[20] This raised two questions. What does the CIA understand "legal" to mean? And, more to the point, given that this statement may well be accurate, what do the functioning elites of the West understand by legal activity, as opposed to legal theory? Kerr made his statement while speaking to a school civics forum.

The difficulties into which our legal systems seem to be slipping have provoked renewed debate over the nature of law. Curiously enough, most of our experts — both liberal and Right wing — have fallen back on the argument that law is rooted in contract; the contract of the individual with society and, on a more banal level, the endless contracts which make society function. Many of them argue, as does the American John Rawls, that the principles of justice are not evident in our common sense.[21] He therefore seeks an agreed social contract. This approach might make sense if there was some hope that these contracts, high and low, could be enforced and in a manner which reflected their social intent. If not, then in place of a common sense understanding of law and of social standards, all we have is a morass of meaningless technicalities open to exploitation by experts.

There are few areas which remain reasonably enforceable. Divorce and murder perhaps retain the greatest clarity. But once we leave the specific, we discover that the whole system turns — in spite of our continuing eighteenth-century obsession with absolute justice — on the assumption that the law will work because it is in some way an expression of the citizenry and the citizen therefore believes in it. The reality is, however, that the creator is increasingly the expert. And the citizens' roles as legislator and jurist have faded, so they no longer feel directly involved.

When contemporary legal wisdom speaks of law as contract, one is tempted to reply that the power of money — legal and illegal — thinks that contracts are a joke; both the contracts of the individual with society and those of the legal codes. They are playthings to be manipulated by professionals such as lawyers, who are trained to do so. These people use — or misuse — common sense and make the governments of the world look like children. Besides, at the heart of justice must be the citizens' belief in the laws they obey and their collaboration with the authorities. The actual statutes do not exist because everyone would act in a criminal manner without them. They are there to lay out general social standards and, above all, to deal with a small minority who have always rejected responsible behaviour. There is an assumption in any social contract that the constituted elites are protectors — for better or worse — of that social agreement. The idea that a civilization could function with its elites as the principal abusers of the contract is impossible. And yet that is precisely what we have.

In many ways, with its ineffectual complexity, law has become like court etiquette of the late eighteenth century. Each man goes through the motions of acquiescence. Then those with power of any sort go away and do something quite different. And the judges preside over these formalities like rational princes who have neither the paternalistic authority of an absolute monarch nor the populist authority of an elected leader to ensure that the social contract is respected.

Heroes

The sudden appearance of the Hero at the end of the eighteenth century came as a shock to a civilization in full and relatively optimistic mutation. Bonaparte seemed to materialize out of nowhere. Neither philosophers nor those in authority knew what to make of him. They didn't understand how he could be an invention of the rational revolution. And yet they could see him being admired and eventually worshipped as the natural son of reason: the liberator of peoples; the lawgiver; the administrative reformer; the patron of sciences; the modest ruler, always in simple uniforms, who made no dynastic claims for preferment and sought to create a meritocracy. In the future society they had imagined, however, none of these qualities fitted naturally together with military coups, dictatorship maintained by violence, permanent censorship of free speech and therefore of writing and thinking, the emasculation and eventually the destruction of responsible government, the glorification of an individual, military adventurism, and the institutionalization of profiteering for those in power. Somehow Napoleon had effortlessly introduced both of the above lists.

Perhaps it wasn't surprising that this new Hero escaped understanding. In fact, the implications of the Heroic phenomenon still have not fully sunk into the consciousness of Western society. We simply accept that our expert elites prefer dealing with judges and courts rather than politicians and parliaments. The people's representatives themselves have been so discouraged by their inability to keep up with the great search for absolute answers and the rush to efficiency and modernity that they have gradually given over many of their responsibilities — that is, the power of the people — to the various administrative elites and to the judges in particular. This loss of practical democratic power has pushed the politicians to bolster their position by concentrating on personal appeal. That is to say, they attempt to lead through personality, a phenomenon usually known as "personality politics." These phrases have a vaguely amusing ring about them. They are reassuring. They imply that nothing more is at stake than a bit of ego from inoffensive politicians. This is so misleading as to be false. Personality is a pleasant way of describing the Napoleonic method of managing the public and from his reign onwards, it developed into the principal public tool of the new Heroic dictators.

What is it then, precisely, that contemporary politicians in democratic societies are attempting to create by using this method? Not personalities. They are attempting to turn themselves into freestanding public objects which require no supporting walls or cables such as party, policy, beliefs or representative responsibilities. They wish to transform themselves into this freestanding monolith so that the public will come to them in admiration, without intermediaries or conditions. Not admiration of anything in particular, such as policy or action. Just a warm, imprecise admiration tied to personal characteristics — being tough, for example, or loving or caring or familiar or awe-inspiring. The politician attempts to create a sense of well-being or dependence in the citizenry.

In short, they wish to become Heroes. Not real Heroes, who claw their way to the top in the tradition of reason's first monster, Napoleon. They will settle for an imitation Heroship, in which they are worshipped for their appearance. Modern politicians are to Napoleon what Louis XVI was to Louis XIV. The sight of a Quayle or a Mulroney dressed up for the grand role does add comic relief to public life. "And yet," as Naphta pointed out in Thomas Mann's *The Magic Mountain*, "the insipid is not synonymous with the harmless."[22]

The popular success of such consciously constructed personalities may have something to do with the remarkable self-discipline they need to make themselves over in the heroic mode. Self-discipline has not been seen as a great virtue by citizens of the West over the last few decades. In the 1950s and 1960s, it was popularly assumed to be a preference of the Right, and this misapprehension remains in the political debate. But nothing could be less disciplined than the New Right, with its romantic mythologizing of freedom, equality and individualism in order to obscure such practical policies as the legalization of dishonest speculation through financial deregulation. The New Right is even more undisciplined than the liberal middle classes, which have redefined personal freedom as the privilege not to give of themselves when it comes to protecting or advancing the public good. Throughout the West they have gradually withdrawn from public life, claiming that politics is too damaging to their private lives. These lives tend now to be devoted to careerism, travel, holidays, sport, exercise and the caressing of a private state of mind which might be described as an obsession with their personal well-being. For both the New Right and the middle-class liberals, individualism has come to mean self-indulgence.

Such a childlike approach to the role of the citizen has allowed them to invert logic in a remarkable way. The public servant — police officer, soldier, tax collector, health authority — who is paid by the citizen, now becomes the enemy of the citizen. This transformation is, in part, the result of individuals feeling that they have lost control of the public mechanism. But what is self-discipline in public life if not working to ensure that one's beliefs have some effect? The tendency among Western elites is rather to evade paying taxes wherever legally possible and to pay the remainder resentfully, taking government services for granted, while grumbling about them and looking upon public servants and public services as money and time wasters. Thus our elites sink into precisely that childish, irresponsible mold which a technocratic society assumes is the real character of every citizen in a democracy.

Should we be surprised, then, that the dream of the Hero still roams so freely through the Western imagination? The Hero incarnates self-discipline. Like the suffering Christ, he is disciplined on behalf of the populace. So long as he is there to protect them, the citizenry may continue to be childish. The Hero has the mythological power to assume responsibility for our rational structures, while giving flight through his own personality to all our romantic fantasies.

The rational idea that society is perfectible can also give him the right to use violence. This chastising, punishing Hero first appeared during the French Revolution with the Jacobins under the leadership of Robespierre and Saint-Just. The immediate and effortless marriage which they accomplished between those avenging powers normally associated with the Old Testament God and the new high-rational expectations imposed on each citizen should have given an early warning of the dangers inherent in Heroic leadership. Instead the physical elimination of impure citizens has become a recurring theme. This sort of extremism had once been proper to the defence of religious doctrines. In the twentieth century, we have seen Heroic leadership on the Right and the Left justify the taking of lives on the basis of everything from racial purity to economic and social methodology. Only Heroes are strong enough to establish a virtuous society through bloodletting.

Whether paternalistic or avenging, the Heroic argument is that the public stage remains chronically empty. Therefore only extraordinary leadership can save the day. This is the standard justification for a coup d'état "in the public interest." Perhaps the earliest example of the rational coup was Oliver Cromwell's dismissal of the Rump Parliament in 1653 with the aid of his soldiers and a populist slogan — "You have sat too long here for any good you have been doing. Depart, I say, and let us have done with you. In the name of God, go." He, the virtuous leader, claimed to speak for the people better than the people's representatives. His actions brought about a political, economic and social revolution. However, because they were encased in strong Puritan themes and because the British monarchy was subsequently restored with most of its superficial trappings, the historic image of these events has been confused. It was left to Bonaparte, with his military investiture of the elected assembly on 18 Brumaire, to crystalize the idea of the Hero's virtuous obligation to carry out a public-interest coup against the people's representatives:

> What have you done with that France which I left you in full expression of its genius? I left you peace and I come back to find war! I left you with victories and I return to find defeat! I left you the millions of Italy and I return to find laws of pillage and the people in misery! What have you done with a hundred thousand Frenchmen I knew, my companions of glory? They are dead! This cannot go on.[23]

The modern false Hero tends not to lead troops into elected assemblies. However, he has retained all of the Hero's themes: the incompetence of the assembly, the chronically empty public stage, the need for extraordinary and virtuous leadership. Virtue is regularly redefined to reflect fashion. Sometimes it refers to honesty, sometimes to personal virtue, sometimes to devotion to the people's welfare. Over the last twenty years, it has tended to refer to the virtue of personal enrichment.

Politicians know that if they can only get up onto the public stage and stay on their feet, they will be able to give the impression that they are filling the stage by the very presence of their personality. Of course they will not be filling it and so the Heroic mythology of emptiness will stay in place, thus making their presence seem even more essential. This conundrum is to the twentieth century what the indivisibility of the Holy Trinity was to the Middle Ages or the nature of predestination to the Reformation. As always, the successful installation of an unsolvable paradox at the heart of public affairs means that those who hold power can find justification for almost any sort of action.

The very survival, in the heart of modern false Heroes, of the themes established by Cromwell and Bonaparte means that the social forces which originally produced this phenomenon are not dead. Just as one Hero once drew forth another and the emergence of Heroes prepared the way for false Heroes in their image, so the disappointment provoked by these superficial imitations may in turn encourage the emergence of another real one.

The popular mythologies of television, film, videos, novels, comics and advertising are now given over to unnamed strangers who ride into town or to little guys who become champions against all odds or to wise visitors from other civilizations or to solitary soldiers who defeat armies. Ronald Reagan struck gold with the repeated invocation of his own line from a movie about Notre Dame football coach Knute Rockne and his dying star player, George Gripp, Hero of the turf, whose last words to his teammates were that they should go out and score. "Win one for the Gipper!" caught the essence of our wistful obsession or belief that we are, in Léon Bloy's words, always waiting for HE who will come. That the language is insultingly hokey only makes the phenomenon worse. The obviously ridiculous has somehow become palatable.

Part of our difficulty in maintaining a sense of the dangers implicit in Heroes, whether true or false, comes from the separation of the heroic from the Hero. Rarely has there been such a complete divorce of a word from its meaning. Born as it is of courage, heroism turns on self-sacrifice and humility. It is a sacrifice which comes with no guarantee that the gesture will help anyone. And as the military example shows, only rarely does heroism bring victory. The hero's survival is an accident, because the essence of the heroic act is submission to unlimited risk. In other words the heroic act is perfectly irrational.

The rational Hero, on the other hand, is ego unchained; god on earth;

the golden calf; whether a general, a tennis player or a politician. He is the colossus whose shade eases the uncertainty of all those who gather below. He is the emanation of the dreams of those who crowd together at his feet. He is their unearned and unattainable expectation.

The Hero is thus the great destroyer of individualism. In this era, which we claim belongs to the individual, we dreamily watch and admire bevies of Heroes in all domains in a way no civilization has ever done. Settembrini, in *The Magic Mountain*, is perhaps the greatest evocation of the man of reason. He considers himself an individualist. But, as the questioning voice of the ordinary man in the novel points out, "to be that, one had to recognize the difference between morality and blessedness," which Settembrini certainly doesn't. [24] It was their inability to recognize that difference which caused the disciples of reason, while in the very process of creating the new moral individual, inadvertently also to create a new version of the "blessed one" they thought they had just finished striking down. In effect, they had combined the mythological powers of the knight, the monarch and the deity to produce a new earthly divinity.

For two centuries now we have been living with the rational Hero. Born fully formed in the person of Napoleon, he sprang out of the confusion which swept Europe at the end of the eighteenth century. Napoleon was finally dethroned in 1815 and died six years later in exile. Two decades after that first burial in Saint Helena, organized mythology caught up with the phenomenon. The German philosopher Hegel had already written of "world-historical figures" who break the established mold and change history. But it was the Scot Thomas Carlyle who laid out in 1841, the year of the triumphant return of Napoleon's body to Paris, a complete concept of the modern saviour in his book *On Heroes, Hero Worship and the Heroic in History*. His approach was fawning, indeed worshipful. And with phrases such as the "the strong just man," he successfully inserted this new invention of rational dictatorship into the age-old mythological structure of heroic leadership. Suddenly the likes of Napoleon were being represented as natural descendants of the earlier hunter, warrior, and martyr heroes, who had played a practical and often essential role in their simpler, more direct societies. It also followed that the new rational Hero was a necessary type of leader.

Generations of historians have quibbled over the details of what is the properly heroic role for modern leaders; but they have left in place the assumption that modern Heroes are part of a single evolution through history. As a result, for the last hundred and fifty years, every revolutionary, general and beer-hall conspirator has been able to invoke antecedents running from Julius Caesar and various barbarian tribal leaders — real and imaginary, such as Vercingetorix, Siguror and Siegfried — to chivalrous knights, Joan of Arc and frontier Indian fighters.

Seven years after Carlyle's malevolent contribution, the first major false Hero appeared. He was Napoleon's nephew. A physically awkward weakling and an incompetent conspirator, who tended to panic under stress, he had neither talent nor experience on the battlefield. He managed instead to wrap himself in his uncle's Caesarean aura and to pass himself off as a dashing and romantic leader during the presidential election of 1848. His principle contribution to the Heroic profile was a genius for public relations. Thus he replaced his uncle's practical skills with the illusion of those skills. It could be said that he invented the idea of the Hero as actor. In 1851, he used his power as President to carry out a coup d'état and a year later was Emperor, all this again in imitation of his uncle.

Napoleon III subsequently made a fool of himself on the battlefields of Italy, where he abruptly abandoned his Italian allies because the sight of blood had upset him. In 1870 he was decisively defeated by the Prussian army and crept away to exile in England. Nevertheless, the manner in which he had initially taken power, the subsequent eighteen years of highly visible grandeur and his squashing of practical democracy with massive programs of administrative reform and public works all combined to create the model for future false Heroes.

Napoleon III had been defeated by the genius of the Prussian Chancellor, Bismarck, and by a relatively new Prussian General Staff. Eighteen years later these servants found themselves serving a new Emperor, Wilhelm II, who was bombastic, of limited intelligence and filled with self-confidence. He was given to dramatic gestures, dressing up and stridency. His misfortune was that his royal powers were severely constrained by a reasonably buoyant democratic structure and impressive social institutions. He dreamed of stripping all that away to return to the absolute power of his ancestor Frederick the Great. However, Wilhelm didn't resemble Frederick, who had been an austere, withdrawn and almost monklike individual, endowed with military genius and boundless intellectual ambitions. Wilhelm's actual role model was the modern Hero, as defined by Napoleon and imitated by Napoleon III.

In their style, he solved his political problems by carrying out what amounted to a coup d'état from within. In 1890 he fired Bismarck, installed servile chancellors in his place and gradually destroyed all limits on his own personal power. He then reigned as he wished for a further twenty-eight years. Curiously enough, he was bolstered in his approach by Max Weber, the leading German thinker of the day, who opposed the Kaiser's methods but wrote continually about the revolutionary role played in history by charismatic Heroes. Only the disastrous reality of World War I was able to cut through the illusion of Wilhelm's leadership.

In the meantime other, lesser sorts of false Heroes had been popping up throughout the West. Comic-opera conquerors like General Boulanger. Mystical generals like Kitchener, whose aura disguised limited talents. A slow and therefore barbarous general like Ulysses Grant was able to gather the Caesarean mantle convincingly enough around himself to win the American presidency. Equally incompetent staff officers, such as Foch and Haig, later covered their bureaucratic methods with dashing attitudes, thus transporting the false Hero into the realm of absolute internal contradiction.

It was, however, only in the 1920s and 1930s, 115 years after Napoleon, that two false Heroes were able to perfect the imitation of the real. Of the two, Hitler was the more astonishing phenomenon. What our civilization has retained from that experience is not what it pretends to have retained. On the surface we remember Hitler as a monster and tell ourselves that men like him must never again come to power. In reality, however, we have noted that he was highly successful. A small, ugly, illegitimate, lower-class, failed painter rose to a glory not seen since Napoleon Bonaparte. And yet Hitler did not rise to power by defeating Germany's enemies. He wasn't even a particularly skilled conspirator. Instead, like Napoleon III, he combined a genius for public relations with the phenomena of secrecy and police power, which had been slowly developing since Machiavelli, Bacon, Loyola and Richelieu. Hitler took this science of obscure manipulation to new heights of professionalism, while disguising its shabbiness behind his public relations screen of Heroic glory and purity.

Here, truly, was the little guy who became a champion against all odds. He was the ultimate illusion. Here — if you put aside the specific events of his career, his racism, his violence, his mental instability — is the model which has been retained by the image makers of today and indeed by rational civilization. For example, if one compares the public style of contemporary political leaders with that of democratic politicians before World War II, they have very little in common. The old politics tended to be dowdy. It tended towards groups of men on podiums behind long tables engaging in lengthy political evenings. There was a reassuring middle- or lower-middle-class air about most of democracy. Even the rising forces of socialism adopted those conventions and concentrated on issues as opposed to leaders. At its best the style was slow and dreary. At its worst there was an atmosphere of smoky rooms, corruption and ward-heeling.

The contemporary political style only begins to make sense if it is compared to the Hitlerian method. We have become accustomed to the high, spartan podiums from which a single, dramatically lit leader speaks while surrounded by a darkness in which large crowds have been assembled. Modern political conventions or rallies are primarily derived from those of Nuremberg. We now accept as normal the spectacular and officially joyous celebrations, involving massed flags, music and projected images of the leader. In day-to-day life that individual is now routinely and alternately presented as a withdrawn, august figure or, at the other extreme, a man of the people engaged in direct populist encounters.

Between these two images lies the reality of democratic politics. And yet modern leaders carefully avoid being seen in protracted serious conversations or negotiations with lower-level public figures. Increasingly they avoid those encounters even behind the scenes. Lower-level officials are sent to represent the leader, who is held back for essential or scripted sessions. At public meetings forty years ago, leaders tended to sit out onstage along with the other speakers, waiting their turn. Now they are kept out of sight and marched in Heroically at the last and most dramatic moment. In their other role, as direct representatives of the people, they are shot, as if from a mystical cannon, directly into shopping malls or fish factories or barbecues where the hands of the people can be shaken.

This high-low imagery is tied to the conversion of the leader into some sort of sexual image. Various methods are used. For example, there is the prerational religious and monarchical equation of power with potency, which Napoleon used so effectively. There is also the suggestion — perfected by Hitler — of restraint or self-imposed purity to illustrate a personal sacrifice in the service of the public.

Some or all of these elements can be found in the political campaigns and governing methods of most contemporary politicians. It cannot be said that these are merely superficial deformities. The process of election and the government's ongoing relationship with the population are both central to the democratic system.

What then, are we to make of the modern Heroes who sincerely attempt to serve the public good? Perhaps the simple answer is that they are not modern Heroes but belong rather to a prerational tradition. This does not mean that their actions will be understood in a prerational manner. Instead they will find themselves in constant conflict with society's expectations of them. For example, even fanatically honest men have found it almost impossible to resist the deifying needs of our times.

Garibaldi was probably the most famous man of the mid-nineteenth century. Brilliant guerrilla fighter, champion of just causes around the world, the man who made united Italy a military and emotional reality, advocate of reforms which have only recently become realistic possibilities, he found himself constantly at the centre of change. He also felt constantly obliged to flee public affairs and take refuge in isolated places in order to resist the personal implications of his Heroic activities.[25]

The son of a fisherman in Nice, he began a confused naval career by serving various powers on the Mediterranean. This culminated with his participation in a republican mutiny against the King of Piedmont. Garibaldi was twenty-seven. His flight led to South America where, for twelve years, he joined and eventually led rebellions against Argentinian and Brazilian dictators. By 1848 he was back in Italy and began in earnest his struggle for Italian unity. He was neither a nationalist nor a patriot as we now understand those terms. He did not believe in the absolute virtue of nation-states or racial groups. He saw them only as interim tools for achieving social justice. By justice, Garibaldi meant such things as worker rights, racial equality, religious freedom, female emancipation and the abolition of capital punishment.

This meant that although he was struggling on the same side as King Victor Emmanuel of Piedmont and his prime minister, Count Camillo Cavour, Garibaldi didn't hesitate to attack them whenever they left the path of justice. His was above all a populist voice, raised to defend the interests of all people. On the other hand, each time his military genius gave him power, Garibaldi promptly handed it over to constituted authorities. The most famous example was his 1860 lightning conquest, at the head of one thousand red-shirted volunteers, of the large Bourbon kingdom that stretched from Naples to Sicily. No sooner had he made himself Dictator of the Two Sicilies than he handed the whole territory over to Piedmont in order to force the creation of a united Italy. He then withdrew from the public fray to his simple house, out on the island of Caprera, between Corsica and Sardinia, from which he emerged periodically over the next twenty-two years to fight for various reforms.

Garibaldi, whatever his eccentricities and impossibly elevated standards for public action, never took advantage of his military successes and the public's adulation in order to advance his personal interests or to seize power. It is sometimes argued that he was outmanoeuvred by venal politicians. But that is a point of view which primarily reflects the thinking of our civilization. We expect a Hero, however noble his cause, to seek power; in truth, we require him to want power. The reality is that, although Garibaldi raged against the politicians' manipulations, he refused to play their games and left them free room to manoeuvre. His refusals were not feints designed to strengthen his future position. Given the obsessions of our times, they simply increased his aura as a Hero approaching divinity.

And so Italy is filled with hundreds of thousands of relics left by the great man in his passage from town to town. In the municipal museum of Cremona, for example, like pieces of the Cross, a few objects under glass are tied together with a red ribbon. These include a splinter from a door in his house on Caprera, along with a piece of granite and dried flowers from his tomb. Beside this is another glass case, containing what appears to be the dried baby finger of a martyred saint. It is a cigar butt which the Hero had smoked in Cremona. The object is carefully labelled by hand:

> Avanzo d'un sigaro che G. Garibaldi
> fumara sul Torrazzo il 5 aprile
> del 1862, raccolto e donato al Museo
> da Giovanni Bergamaschi.

These relics lie about Italy like a promise that the Hero will return to earth. Thus, while Garibaldi resisted all the worst temptations of rational society, his example couldn't help but create the hope that another Hero would follow who would be the best of men. A leader who could carry the dreams of the people but also make them work. In other words, someone who could fill the mythological role of Carlyle's "strong, just man."

That Hero appeared forty years later in the person of Mussolini, who was Garibaldi's exact opposite. The expectation of rational society is that the Hero will assume power. Sooner or later someone with his own agenda comes along and does just that.

At the heart of the problem is our idea of the individual who is "the best." It is a concept which damages our general understanding of what civilization can accomplish. Attempts to do better or to widen our knowledge in the arts or science or elsewhere are often described as the pursuit of excellence. This is a practical, indeed a humanist approach towards civilization. The search for the best, on the other hand, is an abstract and arbitrary business, which has its origins in warrior societies and idol worship. The man who is the best in whatever domain, is in effect, Hero for a day.

A society which mistakes the worship of the best for the pursuit of excellence will have difficulty focusing on established precedent and established procedure. These are swept away in the emotion of the Heroic. And so, acts which are unacceptable in a democratic society — false heroics, for example, or the manipulation of institutions, even of the elected assembly — become mere transitory problems when a leader successfully assumes the cloak of the Hero. In the circumstances it seems to be a small price to pay. And so, before the advancing Hero and false Hero, the morality and social conventions of democratic society fade away.

There is nothing in official Western dogma which identifies the Heroes, false Heroes and Princes, particularly the princes of law, as important factors in our civilization. Laws, constitutions, open and free elections, responsible assemblies and governments — all these are intended to determine the rules by which we govern ourselves and are governed.

The control of the leader by the citizen is not, however, primarily dependent on laws and constitutions. These are theoretical expressions of a relationship. The reality of rational structures imposes a bureaucratic or an emotive relationship.

Citizens inevitably find themselves in a pyramidal relationship to the Prince. Structure and expertise guarantee the Prince superiority. The Hero, true or false, good or evil, governs thanks to an emotive trick, in which he is not chosen as an integrated, practical element in society, but is annointed as a mystical leader. The annointment may well take the form of a vote, but then Napoleon demonstrated from the very birth of the Hero that voting in an Heroic context will negate democratic common sense.

There is nothing original about a civilization which celebrates and maintains a fictional self-portrait for its own reassurance. Rome maintained the fiction of a republican citizenry defended by an all-powerful Senate long after the emperors were in control. Most European countries continue to think of themselves as the product of racial and cultural unity, when they are generally patchworks of conquered tribes and defeated minority cultures. The United States thinks of itself as the prophet of egalitarianism, when it is among the least egalitarian of the Western nations. None of this is of great importance so long as the state continues to function in a reasonable manner.

There is, however, a very immediate danger when a civilization is unable to recognize the nature of its leadership and to understand its origins. This invites unattainable expectations and a profound misunderstanding of the mechanisms by which orders are given and obeyed. The result is a tendency to swing erratically from manic and manipulable optimism to confused disappointment and pessimism, from adulation for those in office to contempt. In the absence of a commonly held sense of what constitutes the clear, fair and successful exercise of power, the desire for something mystical called leadership grows into a haunting and hypnotizing refrain. In the process the citizens lose their self-respect and sense of direction, thus acting in the immature manner that the Princes and Heroes expect of them.

15

The Hero and the Politics of Immortality

On Easter morning one man became the envy of the human race. It was not so much the rising as his advance knowledge that he would rise which made all so envious. This underlying myth of Western civilization remains central, even in a largely post-Christian era when such questions have slipped increasingly into the subconscious. Time, after all, is the essential human condition, and the knowledge that it will one day cease to pass is the essential human fear. It is not dying which upsets the individual but ceasing to exist. We assume that accepting death on Calvary, while difficult, was made easier by the knowledge that it was, after all, only a three-day affair.

For other men and women, death remains unacceptable because of the surrounding uncertainty. If only this uncertainty were removed, says an officer in *War and Peace*, his men would go into battle without fear. Even if the answer to the question were that after death there would be nothing, the fear would have lost its power. And this despite our uncertainty having been transformed into the certainty that we are, after all, in Martin Luther's words, "just so much excrement passing through the rectum of the world."

There is a general and pervasive pattern to the way men meet the problems of meaninglessness and uncertainty. They create ever-more-intricate societies to soften the blow of death by simulating a physical and social eternity on earth. Fighting against death, Camus said, amounts to claiming that life has a meaning. Unfortunately, it also reveals a fear that life does not have a meaning.

Men who thrust themselves into the leadership of these societies betray an exaggerated determination to deal with that anxiety. Unlike normal citizens, who carry on this struggle in the bosom of their families or of their limited communities — or within their own hearts — the public figure deals with death out on the public stage. While our equipment for seeking immortality consists of our families, beliefs and careers, the public man's equipment consists of us. That he wishes to live in this way tells us something about that man, and therefore about the direction in which he might try to lead society.

The argument that religions and indeed societies are no more than calming devices for anxiety-ridden mortals is a little too easy. On the other hand, the promise by Christianity, Islam, even Buddhism of some sort of life after death, must have calmed the populace and thus made governing easier. While rebellion or revolution are the reactions of the cornered animal, belief in any sort of afterlife removes this need.

In the West, of course, God has been dead for some time. What remains is religion as social belief, which is at best a moral code and at worst social etiquette. A real belief feels to the believer to be a natural state and does not respond to questioning. That is one of the reasons we have so much difficulty dealing with the Islamic world. They don't want to discuss fundamentals. They are not interested in a rational analysis. They believe the way we once believed. Not only do we find this incomprehensible and frustrating, we also find it troubling, because their certainty is a reflection of our own past.

We and our leaders have been surviving for a while now in societies which do not have any escape routes through belief from anxiety. This may be one of the explanations for the childish hysteria of the last few decades over economic management theories such as nationalization, privatization and free markets. The death of God was supposed to release mankind from absolute obsessions, so that we could give ourselves to rational analysis. Instead the new structures have simply taken the old absolute obsessions which were tied to the soul and applied them to our economic lives. For example, the free market may be a good, bad or insufficient idea, but, in any case, it is just a crude commercial code. Now it is regularly equated with or given credit for or even precedence over the freedom of man. But the freedom of man is a moral statement on the human condition, both in the practical and in the humanist sense. To equate it with a school of business is to betray a certain confusion. An unconscious unease.

We have, in effect, replaced beliefs with systems, and this has created a new kind of calming device which proposes eternity on earth. The web of Western rational society offers the individual a fixed place as an expert in a self-fulfilling and apparently eternal structure. The very lack of clarity, the lack of clear goals and conclusions, the very ease with which the structure weaves endlessly about us is what makes it resemble the eternal bed of nirvana. While many complain that they feel trapped in the maze of modern civilization, their complaints rise out of the emotional comfort of that stability.

The leader is the one static element in society. He is the one who, whatever the civilization, must deal with his personal insecurity through interplay with the people he leads. If there is any difference between running our society and running another, it is precisely the formlessness of ours. The maze may offer the reassurance of the eternal, but unlike earlier societies, rational structures make it almost impossible to give a sustained direction to the civilization. Seen as a whole, Western society is profoundly inefficient. Those who lead it cannot help feeling that it lacks an inner tension. They want to push it about. To reorganize. To make it respond to needs. They wish to lead, and to do so they feel they must put tension into the organism.

The leader carries all of our confusion with him as he attempts to climb above society in search of a clear view which would indicate the right direction. There, on his imaginary mountain, he stands alone, suffering the personal anxiety of freedom. He watches us dancing aimlessly below, half struggling with mortality in our comforting maze. He can see we have a certain reassurance, lost in our earthly eternity. But how is he to get his own reassurance if he cannot make all of us and the structure itself respond to his efforts?

Leaders have always suffered from these anguishes. Hadrian, trying to make sense out of a tired Roman Empire, or Pope Paul III, faced by the confused interests of the Church during the Reformation, must have felt the same. Today's leader, operating in the late Age of Reason, has a particular problem. There has never before been anything as complex as our society. The leader quite naturally feels that he somehow hasn't climbed high enough — a bit higher and he will finally be able to make out the pattern. But all the constraints on modern leadership, proper to the parliaments and the administration and the courts, are there precisely to prevent him from climbing too high.

The fear of failure will inevitably come over him, the fear that if society refuses to respond, his life will have no meaning. And the greater that fear, the more likely he is to mistake himself for a composer gazing down upon us as if we were random notes waiting to be composed. If he has great talent — even a narrow genius for military affairs or histrionics — he may create for a brief moment what he and the population believe is music — a sort of mystical sound which seems to rise out of eternity. The deeper he can penetrate into the animistic roots of any society, the more he may convince its citizens that this music will capture as much of the future as it has released of the past. And in that moment there will be a fusion between the populace and the leader. That fusion is like a Zen moment — instantaneous and eternal. Long after it is over, the individual will remember what it was like to be part of eternity. As for the particular Napoleon who composes the tune, he is — given the impossibility of using the word *god* in the modern world — a Hero.

But the individual, by giving himself to this moment and to the Hero, betrays himself utterly. These experiences of satisfaction through ecstasy seem inevitably to lead civilizations deep into a sea of injustice and often of blood. That is why justice is not about fulfillment or rising to heroic heights, but about restraint and careful attention.

The philosophers of the seventeenth and eighteenth centuries thought that the message of reason was precisely such restraint. But while they held back the satisfaction of the ego with one hand, they dealt out the explosion of egocentrism with the other in the form of the mythological Hero, the god of reason.

The Middle Ages had offered the leader and his subjects quite a different view of eternity, perhaps because of the plagues sweeping across Europe and the repeated breakdowns of order, with armies of mercenaries constantly on the move like human shadows of the black death. "No other [age] has laid so much stress . . . on the thought of death," Erik Erikson wrote. "An ever expiring call to *memento mori* resounded through life."[1] Death was placed before each person's eyes in a sustained and graphic manner which we cannot imagine.

To die was to escape out of a violent world of sin and temptation into the hands of God. The methods ensuring escape were clearly laid out, including detailed remission procedures if a rule were broken. Even methods which would put a man farther on the credit side were carefully elaborated for the simplest of minds to follow. They were like riders on an insurance policy for entrance to paradise. The growth of Indulgences eventually destroyed the credibility of this whole process, even for the most credulous of men. But in the earlier stages, they had believed.

These medieval attitudes contrast sharply with our own. We have fewer plagues but more wars and of a far bloodier nature. Our approach is to hide death. It is another of our new secrets. There is absolutely no general conviction that death is something to be faced. Instead we place our quest for eternity on the material level. Life is devoted to working, preparing, saving, driving ourselves towards something undefined. The process of our movement through the system gives us the sense of being somehow here forever.

Since our age is technological, most people add to their material obsession a devotion to defeating disease. In the background lurks the idea of immortality. If five years can be added to a life, why not ten? And if ten, why not . . . ? The culture surrounding old age has been changed to the point where its vocabulary is filled with the promise of a new youth. Phrases such as "the golden age" have emerged to obscure the realities of physical decline. Charles de Gaulle, as always out of step with the conventions of his time, said old age was a shipwreck. Of course, the individual must attempt both to survive and to make use of that survival. It is the obscuring of the inevitable process which is so new and so peculiar. Not only, it seems, should we not prepare our minds for termination, we should, as the moment approaches, create a whole new set of illusions in order to avoid the relevant thoughts.

The modern Hero's power comes from this obscuring of our mortal destiny. We live a half lie and that opens even the most sophisticated among us to the kind of elementary emotional manipulation which would have been laughed off the stage in a more direct civilization.

When President Reagan stated in 1982: "We have never interfered in the internal government of a country and have no intention of doing so, nor have ever had any thought of that kind," people did not break into titters of embarrassed laughter and say out loud, "Hey, we've done it 48 times in Central and South America alone!" Instead, they said to themselves, Yes, we are a good and freedom-loving people. The Grenada operation came shortly after. When the Socialist President Mitterrand converted France's electoral system to proportional representation in order to divide the Right — by enabling a neo-Fascist party to win seats in the Assembly — while claiming that he was doing this to strengthen democracy, very few people were outraged. After two years of social disarray as a direct result, he was reelected with a strong majority. When Brian Mulroney stated that President Reagan was his close and good friend and thus susceptible to his influence, people didn't howl with amusement and nudge him — "Brian, he has trouble remembering your name."

What is going through the minds of these leaders and citizens? Clearly there is some collusion. Neither side is lying, because the element of deception is missing. Self-deception, then? But the actions in these episodes don't have the ring of self-deception. They are too open and guileless.

Is there a flaw, then, in their memory patterns? Certainly the manner in which the Western individual remembers does seem to have changed. There are now two kinds of memory. One is related to structures. Each structure is self-fulfilling and self-perpetuating. The memories they produce are therefore internal, logical and unattached to the outer world. The other sort is eclectic: one-off memories. People. Places. Events. This is the memory of a McLuhanesque world in which there is no sentence structure and no order. The mind soars and dives, like a gull over a vast municipal garbage dump.

What is missing is linear memory — that is to say, the historical view. We may remember the event of two days ago, but cannot remember the passage of the two days. All words are neither true nor false without this linear pattern in the mind. They are merely words, well or badly said by people who are liked or disliked. Without an ordered memory, civilization is impossible. The weight of the words, their value and even the sentiments attached to them are lost.

The leader on the mountain, anguished by his own uncertainty, sees all of this. He feels the weightlessness of words. He notes the loss of memory. These two things together translate into a withering of the citizen's ability to judge clearly. This makes it more difficult than ever to govern well. On the other hand, it becomes far easier to compose dances of confusion and darkness. Dances of the Hero's ego.

The citizens are not without defences. Their common sense remains intact. They can simply refuse to respond to the worst forms of leadership. They can imprison the leader in a frustrated limbo by limiting their relationship to the level of parody. But in such an aura of confusion, society is always seconds away from not dancing at all or from dancing to the tune of a leader who has the full genius of the dark side.

As a child Adolf Hitler had wanted to be an architect. He carried a small museum of his adolescent architectural projects about with him — all the way, in fact, to the besieged bunker where he committed suicide. He spread the idea of architectural grandeur throughout his Reich.

But from the very beginning of his political ambitions, there was a destructive drive which people couldn't make any sense of. They attempted to explain his characteristics analytically, as if they were dealing with a normal person who suffered from specific flaws: he was anti-Semitic; he wasn't a democrat; he frenetically flipped between charm and fury. Because this was the very first unleashing of a Hero both complete and false, they didn't think to look upon him as a wholly imaginary being. The manner in which he was conceived, as a single deformed reflection of the German people, designed to exploit their desperation, escaped the parameters of established political thinking.

His destructive drive grew as the forties progressed, displacing his creative, "architectural" persona. Albert Speer, who had been in charge of the German war industry, tried some twenty years later to rehabilitate his own reputation by claiming that he himself had managed to delay the release of Hitler's destructiveness until the last days of the war. "He was deliberately attempting to let the people perish with himself. He no longer knew any moral boundaries: a man to whom the end of his own life meant the end of everything."[2] Speer's analysis was almost perfect. It wasn't defeat, however, which pushed Hitler to an apocalyptic vision of himself. The Final Solution had been decided in January 1942, long before the tide of the war had turned. And the massacre of the Slavs, to make room for Teutons on the lands east of Germany, was already under way. It was Hitler's success which allowed him to give in to his own sense of his powers or, rather, of his rights.

And when the tide did turn against him, that sense was simply aggravated.

To maintain the energy of the constructive Hero is a tiring business. Creativity is limited by time and by effort expended. It is constantly reliant on others. It is not so different from the Godlike act of creating children. This can be done, slowly, by animal methods involving nine months of natural development and a commitment to twenty years of training. The process is serial and limits the quantity. The satisfaction is greater for a woman than for a man, who contributes only a bit of liquid for a few seconds and can never even be certain that the drops involved were his own. For a dozen years Hitler harped on about the importance of architecture and pored over ambitious drawings. He had absolute power over planning and spending as well as having an architect, Speer, as his chief economic adviser. And yet only one of his great building projects was completed — a new Reichstag which was scarcely used.

Destruction is the other power of God, equal to creation in many ways. Above all, it is easier and faster. Between creating life and taking it away, the Hero invariably settles for the latter. It is, if nothing else, more immediately satisfying.

Hitler came to see himself as embodying all of the German civilization — not just the government, but the race, culture, history and mythology. Therefore, when he ceased to exist, all would cease. There would be no eternity after his departure. Erikson said of Hitler that he had "an almost pitiful fear . . . that he might be nothing. He had to challenge this possibility by being deliberately and totally anonymous (his actions in earlier life); and only out of this self-chosen nothingness could he become everything. Allness or nothingness, then, is the motto of such men."[3]

In this context, concepts of morality disappear. The Hero takes everything upon himself and removes any need for society's definitions of guilt or of the inviolable rights of individuals. Jean Genet, a convicted murderer-turned-existentialist philosopher and writer, carried this idea to its maniacal conclusion. In *The Thief's Journal*, he wrote: "Acts must be carried through to their completion. Whatever their point of departure, the end will be beautiful. It is because an action has not been completed that it is vile."[4]

It follows that actions are the only possible expression of the self. There is nothing beyond the self. And the more intense the act, the greater its beauty. The most beautiful act, therefore, is murder. It is indeed the greatest act. Having killed God, man must replace him. And there is no easier way for a man to prove himself God than by taking another man's life. "If there is a God," Nietzsche cries, "how can one tolerate not being God oneself?" And if there isn't, the same assumption of divinity is even more necessary. In theory, the Hero may choose between creating and destroying. In practice, destruction is the only realizable choice.

In Genet's play *The Balcony*, men come to a brothel where they can pretend to have the function they have always wished to have. This is the ultimate statement on rational structure and man's reduction to a functionary role. Dressed as judges, generals and bishops, the brothel's clients talk of "mirrors that glorify," of being "reflected ad infinitum." They are delighted to be the reflection of someone else's eternity. The main character in the play is the chief of police. He controls everything, but no one knows him. He is the rational man of power, operating efficiently behind the scenes with such tools as secrecy and manipulation. No one has ever come to the brothel asking to play him. His only desire is to be a source for other people's reflections. He lives for that day. And when it comes, he says, "I shall be not the hundred-thousandth-reflection-within a reflection in a mirror, but the One and Only, into whom a hundred thousand want to merge." He will then "go and rot in people's minds." While waiting for that day, he builds himself a fantastic tomb, hollowed out beneath a red marble mountain, with rooms and niches and, in the middle, a tiny diamond sentry box. He will bury himself there for eternity while the reflecting world revolves around him.[5]

Some seventeen hundred years ago, during the period which lasted from the loss of belief in Roman deities to the victory of Christianity, there was an explosion in the number of gods and spirits competing to fill the void. In the nineteenth century, while Christianity tried desperately to recover from the effective death of God, there was an explosion in the worship of an endless panoply of saints. The Hero has multiplied in our day with that same assurance disguising confusion. And our endless reaffirmations of individualism on closer examination reveal themselves to be little more than the terrible confusion of individuals seeking to find their reflections in role models. These political and military leaders, terrorists, capitalists, medal winners and stars are arranged about us in an unconscious hierarchy of Heroes who dominate our imaginations and hopes to an extent that we can never admit.

Even Genet's fanciful idea of an eternally reflecting tomb has already been constructed wherever a Hero has survived long enough to be succeeded by reflections. Generalissimo Franco had a shaft dug to the exact centre of an inaccessible mountain. There a seventy-metre-long granite gallery of cathedral proportions was hollowed out. It took thousands of civil war prisoners ten years to fulfill his dream. The whole mountain was surmounted by a five-hundred-foot-high steel cross. Franco lies exactly below the shaft, in the centre of the tomb. His friends from the civil war — his primary reflections — lie buried around him.

Napoleon's tomb in the Invalides is based on the same principle. Mere humans stand in the Church of the Dome on the austere white floor, bare of all seating and decoration, and look up at the most beautiful dome in France. Around them in a circle are chapels containing the tombs of Napoleonic and more recent French marshals. Directly below the dome, a great marble well has been hollowed out and lined with a dozen enormous statues of Victories. In the centre a massive, curving tomb of red porphyry holds the body of the original Hero. Like Egyptian pharaohs who lived forever, he is encased by several coffins — tin-sheeted iron inside mahogany inside two layers of lead inside ebony inside oak. And all those in the marble mass. He lies as if at the vortex of a cosmic cone ascending into heaven.

～

This is not so very different from the case of the twentieth century's three great stuffed men. The idea of publicly displaying these theoretically dead revolutionary leaders may or may not have been their idea. The cooperation of their immediate successors — that is to say, their immediate reflections — was in any case required and they did indeed arrange for the embalming and enthronement of their Heroes.

Are there particular godhead characteristics to be noted in their appearances? Lenin's shedding beard and ever-more-waxy complexion are hardly impressive. Mao's obesity is a serious impediment to credible immortality. When he comes into view, there is a momentary pause while the Peking crowds are caught between a giggle at the thought of the taxidermy involved and a respectful gesture appropriate to the Buddha. He lies, after all, at the centre of a great mausoleum, whose floor plan is copied exactly from that of a Buddhist temple. He lies where the Buddha ought to be sitting or lying. As for Ho Chi Minh, his asceticism was an example to all Heroes hopeful of preservation. The moment he comes into view — again, the layout is that of a temple — the Hanoi crowds are awestruck. His skin lies like prosciutto upon his bones, as if he had not died but been hung and slowly dried. He appears to be napping. His specially built mausoleum is the most impressive building in the otherwise dilapidated city.

There is a fourth Communist leader on display; perhaps the most evocative of the contemporary Heroes. Georgi Dimitrov may or may not have put a match to the Reichstag in 1933. He was put on trial for doing so and, although acquitted, became Hitler's excuse for shutting down the pretend world of democracy and entering into the eternal void of his own ego. Dimitrov survived prison during World War II and went on to become Stalin's reflection in Bulgaria during the late 1940s. He did for Bulgaria what Hitler did for Germany — he liquidated democracy. In 1949 he died.

Stalin offered the Bulgarians the use of his official embalmer, the one who had done Lenin. Mister Sbarsky, the taxidermist, was the first of a new priesthood, empowered to confer immortality. His work on Lenin was an historic act. His work in Sofia on Dimitrov confirmed a modern principle.

That principle first emerged late in the nineteenth century, when the well-preserved bodies of a number of early Catholic saints came to the attention of Rome's mythological machinery. Soon the bodies of other long-buried or even lost saints began popping up throughout Christendom. As if to counter the growing rumours of God's death, they were all put on display in churches. The sight of these demigods, miraculously preserved, as if ready for bodily assumption on the Day of Judgment, was intended to help win people back to the Christian idea of immortality. The Church didn't stop at that. It sensed that the technological twentieth century would turn upon concrete proofs and so set about stuffing and displaying newly dead saints.

There isn't much difference between Saint Vincent de Paul, suspended in glass over the altar of his church on the rue de Sèvres in Paris, and Lenin, Mao, Ho or Dimitrov. All five must have known that, as Heroes, something like external exhibition awaited them. However, Saint Clare, the friend and supporter of Saint Francis of Assisi, would have been horrified to think that — six hundred years after her death in modest simplicity and absolute acceptance of mortality — she would be dug up and put on show in the crypt of her church. Marble steps have been laid on top of her rough stone so that the public may climb down in glory to a double-barred grille on the other side of which she lies. A nun, whose face is hidden by a thick veil, repeats endlessly: *"E il corpo vero di Santa Chiara."* ("This is the true body of Saint Clare.") Clare would probably say — "So what!" — and make them rebury her body. She would be doubly horrified to discover that the chanting nun feels that she herself exists in part because Saint Clare's body is there. The nun would be upset if someone pointed out to her that she was acting like a Communist.

As for the four embalmed revolutionary Heroes, the spectacle they have become might embarrass them on an intellectual level. But we can be almost certain that it would give them great subconscious satisfaction; at least as much satisfaction as Napoleon and Franco would get from their own idolatrous display as Christian altars. All of these men operated in the age of the Hero and they are among the happy few to have become officially immortal. To become a Hero is to accept, if not desire, that the people will want your immortality. Of course, if they decide they no longer wish it, you may be abruptly mortalized and shoved underground forever or for a time. Lenin is now entering that dubious phase. By all the historic standards of earthly deification, the citizens who pass before such altars can see that their great man is a god. The message which the authorities intended to send, by laying out these men exactly as they have, is perfectly clear.

Beyond that, the public may or may not think that the Hero is a satisfactory guarantee of immortality. He is, however, a rare concrete indication of its possible existence. As a result the edge of death is theoretically softened for the millions of individuals who are exposed to these One-and-Only Heroes — on display or encased in marble — whose reflections they might wish to become.

The democratic process offers no equivalent softness. Participation by the citizen in a democracy is a down-to-earth business which has very little to do with grandeur and Heroism. But our complex rational systems draw individuals into fixed positions as experts. The reassurance felt by belonging in this way contradicts the very idea of participatory democracy. Political initiative therefore shifts over to the leaders and they in turn encourage the ever-more-passive individual to dream. Heroic leaders always encourage the people to dream, as if the capacity to dream were a positive political attribute. In truth, it has more to do with unleashing our fears, which then swell into the limitless realms of fantasy.

And yet, when we look at our own leaders, they don't resemble the Hitlerian Hero. These are not Napoleons marching across Europe. But the methods they use and their assumptions are those of the Hero. False Heroes, no doubt, but they manipulate the tools of power in a parody of greatness. Most of the time there are no public indications of this peculiarity. Then abruptly, during the 1991 Iraq war, they all slipped effortlessly into the bellicose overstatement of hard, bitter war leaders.

To dismiss this as inoffensive is to miss the point. Our rational structures are not carrying us slowly but surely towards balanced, open and straightforward leadership. Instead, they carry us ever deeper into a world where the assumptions of leadership may lean towards parody, but the parody in question is that of the Hero.

16

The Hijacking of Capitalism

When I use a word, it means just what I choose it to mean.
                                                    –Humpty Dumpty

Nowhere has the role of Lewis Carroll as linguistic architect of the twentieth century been more apparent than in the world of big business. Nouns, verbs and adjectives are flung about with great enthusiasm, anger and sincerity, leaving mythological trails so evident that not one of them needs to be explained. *Capitalism*, *free enterprise*, *risk*, *private ownership* — all these phrases and many more, when heard or read, produce a nod of instant understanding and either approval or disapproval.

Thanks to this clarity, we have been able to carry on an endless public debate over what form modern society should take. Should we release the creative/selfish forces of free enterprise? Or should we protect/coddle/free the citizen in the face of the challenges/dangers of risk?

These questions have been further simplified by a tendency to use interchangeably the phrases free world and free enterprise. George Bush, and Ronald Reagan before him, spoke of free markets and free men, in that order. While some Western leaders are more discreet in their wording, not many of them, even the socialists, would give much energy to disagreeing with the principle.

Such whirling about of rootless words has created the illusion of a real debate. And that illusion is so convincing that we rarely examine exactly who is arguing with such fervour in the name of capitalism. The curious thing is that very few of them are capitalists. Instead, there are bevies of corporate managers, financial managers, financial speculators and service providers. Still more curious, if you begin to question them, you discover that they are horrified by the personal commitment and personal risk which is central to capitalism. They are, in effect, the prophets and defenders of an economic system which they reject.

What we have done in the West is throw three elements together as if they were part of a natural family: democracy, reason and capitalism. But they are not even natural friends. The businessmen who speak so aggressively today in capitalism's defence are, in reality, the product of its defeat by reason. This product is by no means unidimensional, however. The speculators, for example, are a sign of reason's failure. The service providers seem inoffensive enough. All they do is fill a void in our economy. The danger lies in our believing that they are a new solution, rather than another sign of our problem. As for the managers in capitalists' clothing, they are not entirely a disaster. After all, during the period of their rise to power, we did establish some sort of general social compromise, shaky and uneven though it is.

However, the gap between the capitalist illusion and its reality is now so great that the practitioners and indeed the civil authorities have difficulty making economic decisions in a sensible manner. Their problem begins with the democracy = capitalism equation. Running democracy and capitalism together as a single idea is a wonderful Marxian joke. That is to say, in the tradition of the Marx Brothers. Neither history nor philosophy link free markets and free men. They have nothing more to do with each other than the accidents of time and place allow. In fact, free enterprise worked far better in its purer state, when it operated beneath friendly, authoritarian government structures. Unquestioned political stability suits the embracing of financial risk. Authoritarian governments can ally themselves to money without fear of conflict of interest. They can do things faster. Compromise less. Democracy, on the other hand, is subject to ongoing political and social compromise. It tends to want to curb activities of all sorts, business-related or not, in order to protect the maximum number of people.

Thus capitalism's moments of greatest glory were under the benign authority of early Victorian England, before universal male suffrage and before child labour laws, work safety regulations, the right to strike and contractual employment. It flowered under Louis Philippe, the businessman's King, who even dressed like a company president; and again under Emperor Napoleon III, who removed the universal male suffrage which had been established by the short-lived Second Republic. It did well under Kaiser Wilhelm II, who cut back on the liberal reforms of his father and of Bismarck. The last Russian czar presided over the greatest expansion of free enterprise the world has ever seen. And in the United States, capitalism was healthiest and happiest in the period before white male universal suffrage in 1860, and then again in the late nineteenth and early twentieth centuries, when large segments of the population were without a vote because of the waves of immigration. Even after becoming citizens, these newcomers remained politically docile during the long process of integrating their particular community into the mainstream of society. American capitalists were at their most dissatisfied from the early 1930s to the 1970s — the period when there was the most active participation by the citizenry in public affairs. In spite of a prolonged economic crisis, business interests have been happier during the last two decades than at any time since the day before the collapse of 1929. This happiness coincides with a decline in the percentage of voter participation to levels not seen since the arrival of male universal suffrage. Nor is this pattern limited to the West. The most vibrant new centres of capitalism to appear over the last few decades are Singapore, Taiwan, Thailand and Korea. All four are governed through sophisticated and cooperative authoritarian systems.

Widespread confusion between the freedoms proper to democracy and those proper to capitalism further confirms that business leaders no longer understand their own ideology. And yet the credo has been public knowledge for several centuries. Capitalism involves the use of capital, not simply its ownership. You cannot own an abstraction. Only the owning of something renders capital concrete. Property, for example. Or a factory. Gold for a long time seemed interchangeable with capital, but it was in reality a concrete good which came to be the measure of capital because it was portable.

However, the ownership of something thanks to the transferral of capital is not enough to make the owner a capitalist. After all, the ownership of inanimate objects, such as land or buildings or gold, existed long before capitalism. Those who increase their capital by trading in such commodities are merely speculating on the value of goods. To make money out of an increase in their value is not a capitalist act.

Capitalism is the ownership and use of the concrete but dynamic elements in a society — what is commonly known as the means of production. A capitalist is someone who produces more capital through the production of the means he owns. This necessitates the periodic reinvestment of part of the capital earned into the repair, modernization and expansion of the means. Capitalism is therefore the ownership of an abstraction called capital, rendered concrete by its ownership of the means of production, which through actual production creates new capital.

However, capitalism as conceived today tends to revolve around something called the profit motive, even though profit is neither a cause of capitalism nor at the heart of the capitalist action. Profit is a useful result of the process, nothing more. As for the ownership of the means of production, this has been superseded by their management. And yet, to manage is to administer, which is a bureaucratic function. Alternately, there is a growing reliance upon the use of capital itself to produce new capital. But that is speculation, not production. Much of the development of the means of production is now rejected as unprofitable and, frankly, beneath the dignity of the modern manager, who would rather leave such labour and factory-intensive "dirty" work to Third World societies. Finally, the contemporary idea of capitalism grandly presents "service" as its new sophisticated manifestation. But the selling of one's own skills is not a capitalist art. And most of the jobs being created by the service industries are — with the exception of the high-technology sector — descendants of the pre-eighteenth-century commerce in trade and services.

The service industries cannot even claim to be at the creative end of capitalism — that is, the front end, which converts abstract capital into production. Instead, they live off the results of capitalism. Politely put, they are the tertiary sector, which, in simple terms, means they are economic parasites. The consultants, public relations advisers, financial advisers from bankers to brokers and all the other expert mercenaries are new versions of the courtesans who hung around the kings and nobles. The Master of Royal Fireworks. The Concierge (official candlelighter). The Mistress of the Bedchamber. The moneylenders. Mixed into these service industries are those who speculate in goods. The property developer and the owner of large commerces are the most prominent examples. The property developer existed long before capitalism and will exist long after. He is usually linked to financial institutions, which deal in the abstractions of capital, or to those which administer inanimate goods, such as notaries or government departments. Donald Trump and Robert Campeau existed in the Middle Ages and in the nineteenth century without being considered capitalists. Solvent or bankrupt, they are not capitalists today.

On August 13, 1987, the New York Stock Exchange celebrated five straight years of strong growth. The Dow Jones Average had risen 245 percent since 1982. The London Stock Exchange 300 percent. The Toronto Stock Exchange 200 percent. The Paris Bourse 300 percent. And the Tokyo Exchange 1800 percent. In that same period real economic growth in nonfinancial — that is to say, capitalist — areas had been minimal. Unemployment, already high, had continued to rise to record levels in Europe, had dropped a bit in Canada and quite a bit in America. The American improvement had depended on a willingness to ignore the lowering of employment standards and the use of part-time labour to count as full-time labour. To put it bluntly, in the 1930s, women who took in washing to get by were not heralded as job-creation success stories, but our service-industry economy measures differently. In that same period the debt crisis put most Western banks into technical bankruptcy. The number of American banks to actually go bankrupt rose every year to a 1987 record of 208, the highest since 1933. Ten percent of the remaining banks (fifteen hundred out of fifteen thousand) were on the Federal Deposit Insurance Corporation's list of troubled institutions. A whole category of smaller financial institutions, the thrifts or savings and loans, were virtually bankrupt. Annual business bankruptcies continued to rise throughout the West, setting new records every year.

The only production sector to show serious growth was armaments; noncapital goods which do not themselves create further production. National debts continued to soar; currencies to fly up and down. The trade in real goods was so troubled that the GATT (General Agreement on Trade and Tariffs) talks were stalled and most nations were turning towards protective measures. And yet the stock markets continued their record rise.

The purpose of a stock market is to provide a regulated forum in which current owners of the means of production may either sell to new owners by putting their own shares on the market or expand their means of production by raising additional financing through the issuing of new shares. A rise in the market should be a sign of the rising value of the means of production, thanks to increased sales and new investment. Neither of these things happened between 1982 and 1987. And yet, enormous sums of capital poured into the market. Where did the money go? It seemed to disappear into some sort of paper-printing maze in which managers and speculators chased each other around in a directionless circle with nothing in mind except control of the management levers and the maximization — indeed, the artificial creation — of profits. It was perfectly appropriate that the American secretary of the treasury, the German minister of the economy and both the Canadian and the French ministers of finance during much of this period were ex-stockbrokers or ex-merchant bankers. And that the star, of what many people came to see as a generalized, irresponsible American corporate managerial style during the 1980s, was Ross Johnson, a particularly close friend of the Canadian prime minister.[1]

Modern capitalism could justify this general situation only by claiming that the maximization of profits is at the heart of the process. But if maximized profits really have become the justification for the existence of a capitalist economy, then services and financial speculation really are the new capitalist enterprises. And if that is the case, then capitalism, which was one of Western man's greatest innovations, has been debased today into a fancy version of old-fashioned speculation, in the tradition of the South Sea Bubble and the John Law inflationary bust. When Black Monday, the crash of October 19, 1987, came and nothing particularly dramatic happened to Western society, it did indeed seem that capitalism, in its modern form, had become so divorced from the means of production and obsessed with paper profits that it had also become irrelevant to the real economy.

Perplexed by the apparently unsolvable nature of various economic problems, the citizen turns to the capitalist in search of some explanation. The capitalist inevitably chides him for failing to use his initiative and for not working hard enough. This lecture is followed by the invocation of a personal moral rigour which turns on risk, competitiveness, market forces and individualism. Finally he refers the citizen to his government, as the party responsible for inflation, unemployment, stock-market crashes and restrictions on each man's freedom to act. The citizen turns to go as instructed, but as he does his eye is caught by something strange in the capitalist's appearance. This, he suddenly realizes, doesn't look like a man in command, an owner, a risk taker. He does indeed project assurance, but there is no fire in his eyes. He is too sure of himself to be really responsible. And his clothes are too uniform for an individualist. There is no edge of creativity about him, nor the wear and tear of having built an enterprise. His words are too much part of a universal patter on free enterprise and the profit motive. Suddenly, the citizen understands — this is not an owner of the means of production. This is an employee in drag.

He is chairman, president, chief executive officer, chief operating officer — he is anything he wants to call himself, but he doesn't own the place. He has been hired to do this job. He has a contract guaranteeing him employment under set conditions, cars, first-class travel, pension plans, holidays, club memberships. He is an MBA or an engineer who has a stock option for two thousand shares paid for by the company. Even those aren't his. They're just a legal way to save him years of tax on extra income. He'll sell the shares on retirement and walk away with the cash. And if, for some reason, he were fired, his contract would include a settlement provision to make him a reasonably rich man.

If the citizen were to insist on meeting the real capitalist — the owner — he might find himself being humoured by the chairman, who would insist that the owners are just stock speculators. Besides, there are 173,000 of them. If asked how, then, this modified capitalism can control and give direction to the managers, he might launch into a long explanation of the role played by his board of directors and his annual meetings. The citizen realizes immediately that the annual meeting is a toothless affair. Because of the impossibility of assembling the 173,000 shareholders, management will exercise the majority of the votes. As for the board of directors, the game is more subtle.

Most directors are nominated indirectly by the management. Most directors take on the job not because they wish to control the company, but because sitting on the board is prestigious. It gives them good contacts, extra power around town and extra income. They do not devote themselves to ensuring the company is making the right decisions. They just keep their eyes open for basic errors. More important, they watch for opportunities for themselves — not so much of the insider-dealing sort, but more subtle opportunities. Service contracts, for example, which might be given to other companies they are involved in.

And even if they did wish to be diligent, how would they do it? The management accompanies each resolution presented to the board with thick briefing books. These resemble the briefing books prepared for government cabinet committee meetings. These company briefs have been prepared by dozens, perhaps hundreds, of experts on the proposed matter. What is the director to say? Whatever it is, the management will have a reassuring answer. Four or five managers will be board members. If national assemblies, with the authority of universal suffrage, are unable to control governments despite the glare of public debate, and cabinets are unable to make government structure move, despite the prodding of parliaments, how could a few part-time directors succeed, when limited to private debate and deprived of even the organized support of the shareholders?

Besides, management works very hard to turn directors into captives. They are paid quite handsomely. The fees in the United States are now between thirty and fifty thousand dollars a year. And the more money the directors will take, the more the managers can pay themselves. There are also all sorts of perks. Meetings in agreeable places. The cost of bringing spouses thrown in. Presents from time to time. Access to the company's services, whatever they might be. Banking institutions almost routinely offer their directors access to Swiss or other offshore accounts. The offer is not illegal, but the director's use of it will unavoidably be. The director who takes up the offer thus forfeits any right to make trouble on the board. He becomes a member of the club. One of the boys. And the bank management has enough information on his private affairs to control him if necessary.

The assumption that board members exercise effective authority over corporations is one of the central fallacies of contemporary capitalism. The board of directors was never designed to be a control unit representing 173,000 shareholders. It was designed to be a gathering of all or most of the owners. As such, it was a body of real authority. One or more of the director-owners was almost certainly running the company. That sort of situation still exists, but it is limited almost exclusively to smaller corporations.

Free enterprise throughout the West is dominated by employees, more and more of them products of business school training or an equivalent. Like bureaucrats, they do not lean naturally towards the inventive approach — neither inventive investment, nor developing goods, nor winning markets by selling goods. They specialize in developing systems within which they can operate and in producing tight programs which are modelled upon the case study approach. They are invariably eager to change circumstance and to force it into a set pattern.

An individual who stands out, disagrees or takes risks is a danger to such systems and is effortlessly, unconsciously sidelined. The top management of large Western corporations and multinationals has been chosen by the system — because systems have an inbred logic — for their mediocrity. There are exceptions, of course. But there are exceptions to everything. André Malraux described the early stages of this phenomenon half a century ago in *Man's Fate*. Gisors, the Shanghai manager of a French-owned company, explained his position: "Modern capitalism is much more the strength of organization than that of power."[2]

These managers have no power of their own. They play the corridors the way eunuchs once played the maze of alleys in the Forbidden City. Their interest lies in career advancement and this can best be done by delivering immediate proofs of success. Their management style is therefore based upon rapid returns. The quarterly report syndrome is proper to this approach. There must be constant and immediate signs of success and these must be structured in order to encourage the stock market and to throw constant sops to the board of directors. Long-term planning, basic and long-term investment, both to improve the established production and to create new production, are the last thing they want.

There are managers who wish to stay with a company, in which case they are stolid and terrified of risk. There are managers who fly upwards from company to company, keeping one step ahead of their own activities. They need immediate results. Neither of these types is interested in the aggressive exploitation of the means of production. Neither sort is attracted to the production of things nor to their sale. Things are concrete. Managers, by nature, take what can only be called an intellectual approach. Reason is their sign. They can know and explain without touching. To touch is to slip down into a lower world. It is almost as if they fear the reality of capitalism; fear that the dark, satanic mills might take hold of them and squeeze out their illusions of grandeur, leaving them prisoners of the means of production for the rest of time. No doubt they sense accurately that the reality of the factory world is not easily susceptible to abstract manipulation.

A great deal has been said about the inflexibility of Western industry when faced by that of Japan or of Korea or of other new capitalist nations. In rather the same way that the staff officers, who ran World War I, blamed their disasters on the old army class, so the technocrats, symbols of the future, have managed to blame the failures of Western business on the old industrialists. But the old owner-managers of the West haven't been around for decades. At most there are a few pockets of survivors here and there. It is the technocrats, the MBAs in particular, who have been so lacking in flexibility that they have ceded much of the Western means of production to the other civilizations. And it is they who have taken the success of these other cultures as a proof that Western capitalism had to die and be reborn in a clean, urban, nonindustrial form.

The lesson they have drawn is clear: if lesser civilizations will assume the hands-on work, the more advanced West can concentrate on working with its brain. Thanks to the proliferation of business schools, this self-interested approach has almost instantaneously been converted into a philosophical rationale. Rosabeth Moss Kanter at the Harvard Business School writes as a leading thinker of the "post-entrepreneurial company," as if this were an intended and welcome result of business evolution. She sees companies marrying "the best of the creative, entrepreneurial approach with the discipline, focus and teamwork of an agile innovative corporation." She writes confidently of "the coming demise of bureaucracy and hierarchy."[3]

Kanter's critique of the big, old American corporations is in many ways accurate. But the changes she imagines are dependent on the fact that much of the entrepreneurial and unbeatable competition from the Third World owes its success to social injustice. This does not seem to have made an impact on the intellect of management thinkers or of managers in general. In their exciting role as capitalists they talk endlessly about the innate value of competition. To be competitive is their equivalent of morality. They treat competition as if it were a universal value enshrined within a single definition. Thus they miss the essential relativity of competition. Of course a nation which uses nineteenth-century social standards as a basis for industrial production will produce cheaper goods than one which uses middle-class standards. But even the rolling back of social policy sought by the New Right in the United States and Britain will not reduce production costs to Third World levels.

For example, heavy industries, such as steel, have been hard hit by Korean production. In 1979, the American industry employed 435,000 people. Ten years later, it employed 169,000.[4] Why is Korean steel so much cheaper? Before the recent worker protests, Koreans were putting in the longest average work week in the world — fifty-seven hours. In return they earned 10 percent of a Western salary. Since the Korean cost of living is quite high, the workers live in slum conditions. Unions have been virtually banned and strikes forbidden. The work conditions are reminiscent of nineteenth-century England. In 1986, 1,660 workers were killed on the job; 141,809 were injured.[5]

Given the modern manager's devotion to an international "standard" of competition, the effect of the marginal improvement in social conditions brought about in Korea by persistent and violent street demonstrations has been to weaken Korea's attractiveness as a capitalist producer. The citizen who listens to the modern rhetoric of free markets and free men would assume that a bit more social justice and democracy are good things. The cause of Western civilization has been advanced. The manager, however, sets aside rhetoric when it comes to specifics. From his point of view, Korea is now less competitive.

For those companies that wish to sell in the North American market, it is now far more competitive to produce goods by using the southern American States and northern Mexico in tandem. Social standards in the American South were never high, but they are now being reinstitutionalized at a low level by industrial investors in search of cheap, unsecured, and unprotected labour. A few hours farther south, across the border, is a massive assembly area called the Maquiladora zone. The southern American states function at half the wage levels of the north, of Canada and of Europe. The Maquiladora zone functions at mid-nineteenth-century levels of child labour laws and factory safety regulations. Wages are a tenth those of the developed world. Dangerous chemicals and explosives can be processed there without the expense of protection for the worker or the environment. A product manufactured between Tennessee and Mexico is now more competitive than one manufactured in Asia.

The effect of this tandem is to put downward competitive pressures on the northern United States; on Canada, now linked southward by a continental economic integration pact; and on other countries who wish to compete in these markets or to compete with their exports. The Maquiladora experiment has been so successful that corporations have pushed the American and Mexican governments towards a full-scale economic pact. The Mexicans hope that this will lead to an influx of capital, new jobs and an improved economy. But the interest of the investors is primarily in cheap, unsecured labour and unregulated industrial production standards.

Why would sophisticated, technocratic employees seek aggressively to destabilize the structures of their own countries in order to give comfort to the sort of social systems which their fathers rejected as criminal less than a century ago? And why would they or we entrust any part of our fundamental needs to unstable societies which have not yet gone through the economic and political turbulence which surrounds most industrial revolutions? No doubt the managers in government and industry looked at their flowcharts and thought there was no other way. It apparently did not occur to them to question the effects of this strategy on their own society.

368 Scenes from a System That Doesn't Work

They have been comforted by a seemingly endless parade of business school professors and economists who spend large parts of their lives on contract to corporations in one way or another. These men have provided an intellectual rationale for economic masochism. At the heart of their analyses one inevitably finds the marketplace. Any integrated view of society, social concerns, morality, democracy and indeed capitalism is necessarily pushed to the margins. This theoretical "marketplace" and the accompanying theoretical "competition," which is required by anyone who wishes to survive in it have both been defined by such people as Michael Porter in a manner which assumes the end of any evolved social contract. Porter is a professor at the Harvard Business School, the author of several books on competition and is having an important effect on business and government in several countries.[6]

The complexity of the financial formulas and mathematical models which he uses suggests that a sophisticated advance is being made in business methods. In reality, what Porter and many others are recommending is a return to savage economics. Beneath the patina of their highly professional approach is a deep pessimism about the ability of civilization to determine its course. It follows that we must passively subject ourselves to market forces and reserve all our sophistication for reacting to these brutal "natural" forces, rather than act to control or direct them, even if the result of such passivity is the destruction of our society.

Curiously enough, the arguments used by these economists and business school "thinkers" not only obscure the underlying economic effects, they are also extraneous to the corporate life of endless meetings, aimed more at gathering information to be used against those who know less than at actually doing something. There is only so much time and for an executive much of it goes to seducing protectors, inserting oneself into the system, building fortresses of additional structure and initiating plans to be fed out through the structure. The comedy of corporate life, unrelated as it is to corporate production, has been widely satirized.

The manager is willing and even eager to put the advances of Western society at risk because he is not anchored by reality. He doesn't own. He isn't really responsible. He doesn't like the concrete of capitalism. His world is an abstraction. Without the anchor of reality he has no idea of how far to go. A capitalist monster of the nineteenth century might or might not have been held back by the public consciousness that he was responsible for what he did. The more he acted against the perceived interests of his own society, the more his reputation suffered. To the extent that his ambition was to rise in society, he might eventually have reined himself in, in the Andrew Carnegie manner, and attempted to counterbalance his reputation by doing some good. The manager, on the other hand, deals in capitalist theories, not capitalism. (By abstract standards the Mexicans are more competitive than the Germans.) He presents this "truth" as an inevitability. There is a frigidity — or, again, an asexuality — in the way he insists that destiny is the slave of theory and he with it.

In many ways he resembles an eighteenth-century nouveau-riche bourgeois trying to pass himself off as an aristocrat. He goes further than any duke would go in his mannerisms, his clothes and his snobbery. The manager is the *bourgeois gentilhomme* of capitalism.

These peculiarities appear in even the most solid of corporations. Boeing, for example, is not only the largest constructor of planes, it has been probably the best. This quality was rewarded by great success, to the point where the company sold $30 billion worth of airplanes in 1988 and still had one thousand back orders. To meet this demand it went on a massive hiring binge, to the extent that some forty percent of the workers soon had less than two years' experience. There was enormous pressure on everyone to keep the assembly line going and going fast. The result was an abrupt drop in quality. Crossed wires on warning systems. Crossed wires on fire extinguisher systems. Thirty cases of backward plumbing. Engine-casing temperature sensors installed in reverse order. A disintegrating wing flap on a plane's first day of service. Metal fatigue disintegration of a 737 in flight. Disintegration of part of a 747 in flight. The U.S. aviation agency began reviewing Boeing's assembly procedures.[7]

Why did the executive employees of Boeing not realize that their production pace was too fast? Why do they still maintain that it is not too fast? A reasonable executive would conclude that the company would do less harm to its own reputation by limiting production than by turning out craft of a lesser quality. Why do they feel that speed and quantity are paramount? Why do they think that precision work can be exponentially multiplied? Driven by an abstract logic and obsessed by maximizing profits, they seem unable to pace themselves, even in one of the finest high technology corporations in the world. Neither the system nor the managers possess the restraint proper to common sense.

One of the most obvious innovations of the managed corporation has been the division of currency into two sorts — apparent money and real money. Apparent money belongs to the corporation but is used by the employees, directly or indirectly, for their personal lives. Real money actually comes out of the individual's pocket. Some people have only real money. Blue collar workers, for example. Or the self-employed. Or writers and painters, apart from the odd grant.

The executive classes of the West — particularly from industry, but increasingly from government — live large parts of their lives on apparent income. They eat, travel, phone and drive without even considering real cost, because that cost is limited only by their professional level. It is difficult to imagine a quality urban restaurant which does not earn at least half its income from apparent money. At lunchtime, the figure would be closer to 100 percent. City hotels would be empty without the corporate managers. The quality car market would shrivel away without the company car. Sports clubs would be bankrupt without company memberships. A whole category of more expensive air travel — Executive or Business Class — has been created for managers who have not quite reached the top. If there are any real capitalists on board — that is, those spending their own money to do business — they may well be in the cheap seats.

There is no way of calculating the costs to the corporations — and therefore to the shareholders who are, after all, the owners of the corporations — of this apparent money. The manager's official "perks" or expense accounts are a small part of the total. The rest are integrated into the self-justifying management method of the corporate structure. Apparent money does not double executive personnel costs. The figure is more likely to be three or four times the real salary level. In terms of financial costs to the shareholder, the industry manager is out of control. The more he profiteers from his company, the more he feels and indeed declares himself to be a capitalist. The further he moves up the corporate ladder, the more he spends apparent money in quantities which bear no relationship to the interests of the company or to the needs of the business he is doing. The size and contents of specific offices, for example, are only details of the size and architecture of corporate buildings. Does the decision to cover a new company headquarters with marble, for example, relate to corporate needs or to management's ego? The very shape of office towers is now routinely altered to pump up the executive's false sense of importance. Capitalists have corner offices. More and more office buildings are therefore built, at considerable extra cost, with zigzags in their facades. As a New York architect put it: "The more corner offices you can claim to have, the more marketable a building becomes."[8]

At this very moment tens of thousands of employees are flying above in corporate jets. This is as it should be if these private planes are helping them to do more and better business. The likelihood is that they aren't. There are rarely such imperatives of split-second timing in big business. In fact, there usually isn't much of a rush in the completion of big deals. They tend to be rather slow and complicated. There are certainly no real production requirements forcing the executive up into a Lear Jet. The commercial system is perfectly adequate for a corporate timetable. There are between 20,000 and 60,000 business aircraft in

North America. A small jet sells for between three and twenty million dollars. This does not include such costs as pilots, insurance, landing fees and fuel.

It is as if these men believed that moving faster, seeing more people and going to more meetings replaced the real process of industrial production. Perhaps their panicked rushing about is an attempt to simulate economic growth.

"Our attitudes towards growth are at the heart of the present dilemma of industrial society," the businessman and environmentalist, Maurice Strong, has written. "This is the disease which has spread through the body of modern technological societies."[9] Our obsession with profit has driven us to fall back on the idea that rapid growth is a characteristic of capitalism. It is true that the technological advances of the last century led to great growth. The gross world product has increased twenty-one times since 1900, the use of fossil fuels nearly thirtyfold, industrial production fifty times.[10] The resulting goods were consumed by both a dramatic rise in general standards of living and a population explosion — from 1.6 billion to 5 billion in eighty years. That most of the production came from the West further exaggerated the effects of this growth. We sold our products to the whole world in return for their cheap natural resources. These combined circumstances created a run of exceptional profits. And so in the subsequent era — our own — devoid as it is of linear memory, the business community began to treat fast growth and massive profits as basic characteristics of successful business, when it was, in reality, a short-lived anomaly.

The developing world's population continues to grow in a way which impoverishes rather than enriches them. The population level of the West has paused at saturation level. Our production needs can't help but pause as well. This is only a catastrophe if capitalism is treated as a machine which must produce constant and giant profits. Were we to return to more standard expectations, we would find it easier to accept modest returns.

The riches of the real capitalist — the owner-manager — came from his ownership and his reinvestment in that ownership. He devoted himself to production. He did not necessarily seek to increase his profit every year. Given low inflation rates, he was quite happy with a return of 5 to 7 percent. What he did seek was stable markets for his goods. Nothing returns to what it was, but it is important to understand the desire for solidity of the average real capitalist in order to judge better the frenetic and aimless leaping about of the modern manager and speculator.

These managers have now convinced themselves that profit is the essential nature of capitalism and that they are the new capitalists. From there to a disassociation of corporate profits and managerial income was but a step. Over the last decade, senior managers have gradually assumed all of the capitalists' robes and begun openly to pay themselves as if they were the owners. Thus, at a time of falling real incomes throughout the West and ongoing battles against wage increases from fear of renewed inflation, the senior management has been doubling and tripling its take home pay. In Britain in 1988 alone, top managers received a 31.5 percent increase. And that was after adjustment for inflation. At the middle level in the same year, the increase was 4.7 percent.[11] In 1990, in Britain again, the old and solid Prudential Corporation lost £300 million in a single venture and was forced for the first time in half a century to cut its reversionary bonuses to pensioners by 8 percent. At the same time, its chief executive received a 43 percent wage increase — £3000 additional per week. The equally respectable Norwich Union had an unprecedented loss of £148 million in the same year. This was matched by a 23 percent wage increase for the chief executive. At Rolls-Royce, the chairman, Lord Tombs, took a raise of 51 percent at a time when 34,000 of his workers were being threatened with dismissal unless they signed new contracts giving up their right to pay increases.[12] Company after company, throughout the West, is now paying its chief employee over a million dollars a year. Apparent income, involving perks, share schemes and management style, will multiply these sums several times. In other words, the manager has entered so deeply into his imaginary role as a capitalist that he mistakes his personal profit for that of his company and mistakes the shareholders' prosperity for his own.

For those who manage and do not own, there is nothing so disturbing as the sight of one who does. The company owner is a reminder of the manager's false pretences; a reminder that the latter has hijacked the occupation of the former, then deformed it to suit his own more comfortable needs.

The logic of the times has had something to do with what has happened to our economies, but the new elites — industrial and governmental — have also played a great role. They have created both market conditions and regulations which discourage private ownership and small businesses, while favouring the growth of large, anonymously owned companies. Those who do create companies find it difficult in the current atmosphere to grow beyond a certain size without ceding to the buy-out opportunities offered by the large corporations circling around them.

It isn't simply that the private ownership of larger companies has become structurally difficult. It has also become unfashionable. The hundreds of thousands of small businesses in which owners labour to make real money are looked upon by financial institutions, corporations and bureaucrats with superior bemusement. The world of big business is one of anonymity. The executive does not actually touch money. He exercises his profession. At that level, the owner finds himself isolated — treated as a rather simple oddball whose corporate structures are not complex enough. His desire to control his means of production in such a personal manner throws doubt on the stability of his ego. The important modern capitalist does not stand out. He blends into the structure. He is not an individualist. This fashion is so hypnotizing that owners dream of becoming rich and successful enough to sell their company to a corporation and so, at last, to become a senior executive — that is, an employee.

Vignerons in Burgundy have what comes close to being an ideal life. Their work covers almost every area of expertise. They must be highly sophisticated farmers, talented chemists, company managers, public relations spokesmen and efficient salesmen. They work indoors and out. They are tied to both local traditions and international commerce. Few producers have more than thirty hectares — that is, some sixty acres — of vineyards. With that they are millionaires, richer than most corporate presidents. Some years will be wonderful and others disastrous, but the stock of aging wine in their cellars will give them financial stability. It is one of the most agreeable, varied and remunerative small businesses in the world. And yet, in family after family, the children, on inheriting, rent out their vineyards on long leases and go off to become corporate employees, teachers or civil servants. To be employed, even with a lower potential income, is to be respectable. To work for oneself is looked down upon.

There lie two of the central characteristics of the modern capitalist. He wants to belong. He talks a great deal about his individualism, but nothing frightens him more than independent action. He is profoundly conformist. Second, he flees responsibility the way European aristocrats once fled their estates for the royal courts, as if it were beneath their dignity to actually run something.

❧

This flight from responsibility is also a flight from imagination. Imagination is at the heart of practical competition — that is, seeking to create both better products and new products. Attempting to sell the unknown is an area laden with risks. It is also one of the principal arguments used in favour of capitalism — that the buyer may choose and do so from the widest array of goods.

There is no denying that our economic system does try to produce the maximum quantity of goods. But it is not interested in exploiting the variety of tastes which exist in the population. Nor is it particularly interested in the quality of goods. The main desire of management is to minimize both risk and long-term investment. Central to this is a fervent belief in economies of scale. If the foibles of varying tastes were humoured, corporations would have to develop more and therefore smaller product lines. Instead they create blunt-edged products which can be aimed down the centre line of established taste, thus flooding the marketplace with enormous quantities of almost identical goods which are pitted against each other in areas of relatively established demand.

The battle of the marketplace cannot turn, then, on the public's comparison of products. Instead, it revolves around invisible organization strategies and visible packaging and publicity. This battle of quantity without variety can be seen in any sector, from high technology to basic manufacturing; from VCR systems, computers and cars to the simple selling of socks.

A visit to any sports store in Europe, North America or Australasia will produce the impression that dozens of distinctly different socks are on sale. A difference in price will indicate variation in quality. Packaging and labels will tell us that these socks are for tennis while those are for jogging. The colours and shapes of the packages will tell us that the contents are exciting. Images will suggest that the wearer already has or soon will have muscles. The labels will remind us of worldwide advertising linked to the fastest man or the richest champion.

But inside the packages, everyone will be selling one of two basic models. One will be short and destined for tennis, jogging and so on. The other will be long and destined for downhill or cross-country skiing and other winter sports. The weave of all the short socks will be virtually the same. The artificial content will be either 100 percent or approximately 30 percent. The long socks will have the same percentages but a heavier weave. The short socks will usually be white, perhaps with stripes around the top. There will be some colour choice in the long socks, perhaps because snow sports call for a contrast. Only in the odd, museumlike shops here or there, behind a modest facade, can proof be found that variety and quality exist. Without a hint of packaging, dozens of distinctly different sports socks — weaves, materials, colours, lengths — will appear. Interestingly enough, a price comparison with the mass-production shop will show that quality and originality are often cheaper than mass production. Economies of scale are somehow not necessarily economic when they hit the store counter. Is this because of the costs of packaging and of supporting a corporate structure, with its managers who do not actually contribute a great deal to the production of socks? Or is it a phenomenon of competition in a sphere artificially closed by the demands of mass production and mass distribution — what they used to call an oligopoly?

Socks are a simple example of how the marketplace offers greater and greater quantities of increasingly similar products. The electronics industry follows exactly the same pattern without a hint of embarrassment, perhaps because its products are the inventions of this era. In its case, the packaging will be the products' actual casing. In this way modern capitalism has inverted the purpose of practical competition. The drive to create different products which compete, thanks to various qualities, for the public's attention, has been replaced by the drive to differentiate virtually identical products in the public's eye through a competition between appearances.

In this atmosphere of homogenized quantity, integrated structure and glorified senior-level employees, it is only natural that smaller companies suffer. But the principal drive against them has come from within the management of the large corporations. Their own lack of interest in long-term investment, risk or, indeed, products is what pushes the managers to seek organizational ways of creating growth.

The most obvious solution is to buy the product-making capabilities of others. These mergers and acquisitions simulate growth by devouring someone else's creativity. And since large umbrella structures seem inevitably to smother, rather than kindle, originality in an acquired company, there is a continual need to acquire more and more. As with Dracula, there is never enough blood.

The current "free-market" mythology tells us that those are the breaks. Capitalism is tough. The weak die. The strong survive. The highest bidder wins and, anyway, small units are no longer profitable. What we are witnessing, according to our managerial capitalists, is a healthy weeding of our overgrown garden, a rationalization of the Western economy. Unfortunately, this hyperbole bears no relationship to what is actually happening.

The large corporations have in reality become the equivalent of deposit banks. They are perceived as centres of measurable value in troubled times, rather as gold once was. They own property and have such things as production capabilities, trained employees and established markets. This solidity attracts not only shareholder support but also that of governments. It is a support which comes regardless of efficiency and profits.

Among the tens of thousands of corporate bankruptcies since 1973, very few have involved large structures. It is the smaller, risk-oriented companies which have been going under. They had no layers of protective fat and so a decade of high interest rates destroyed them. Those who held their lifeline — the banks — did them few favours.

High interest rates did contribute to a temporary and superficial slowing of inflation, but they also changed the capitalist terrain so drastically as to make a normal economic recovery almost impossible. First, the message sent out via the inflation figures was totally inaccurate. Only a narrow slice of visible costs is measured in our tracking systems. The various consumer price indexes and other measuring devices do not cover what is really happening. Indeed, in many ways real inflation is higher now than it was in the seventies. As a result the balance created by monetarist policy is so artificial that the moment growth does increase, so does the measured inflation. Immediately, back up go the interest rates and down go growth and job creation. Using high interest rates to strangle narrowly defined inflation now resembles bleeding a patient to reduce his fever. It does temporarily do just that. But the patient's problem is not the fever. It is a serious infection which is producing the sweat and the high temperature. In ignorance of that, the doctor keeps on opening veins until the patient dies.

The effect of our anti-inflationary policies over the last two decades has been that while the smaller, lean and aggressive companies have been going bankrupt, the large, fat, lazy, directionless corporations have been getting through all right. The banks have lent them money at favoured rates. They themselves have been printing money on the public exchanges. And the governments continue to treat them as parapublic bodies. One can hardly blame the politicians, who are terrified by the idea of large corporations closing. The arrival of large groups on the unemployment market is a demonstrable sign of failure in economic management. What's more, when the managers lobby governments, they arrive as important contributors to the party in power. They also talk the same language as the civil servants whom they wish to influence.

And so it has all been a neat and tidy operation coordinated by managers in different private and public sectors. Capitalist creativity has been discouraged and financial manipulation encouraged. This starvation campaign has left the fat slightly thinner, having converted some of their flesh into cash. Now they are beefing themselves back up by picking over the carcasses of the young and lean. In 1984 alone, $140 billion were spent in the United States on mergers, acquisitions and leveraged buyouts. By 1988 this was almost $300 billion, with 3,310 companies involved. In the United Kingdom some £150 million a year was spent on corporate acquisitions before the crisis of 1973. This figure then rose steadily to £5 billion and has now jumped to £15 billion. The inevitable passing of the leveraged buyout as it first appeared does not represent a change in the situation, but rather the passing of a particular tool for speculation. For example, worldwide merger-acquisition transactions had risen to $375.9 billion in 1988, involving 5,634 deals. Then came the collapse in the speculative market. And yet the figures in 1989 were only marginally down, to $374.3 billion involving 5,222 deals.[13]

The public perception is that most of this activity is the work of speculators like T. Boone Pickens and the Junk Bond Kings. Not at all. The speculators are merely reflections of the managers. It was the management of big business which brought on the growth of the speculators in the first place. They were like blind pigs gorging themselves as they wandered aimlessly over the countryside. It was easy pickings. Popular imagery has the loyal management attempting to fight off the greedy speculators. Of course, in some cases this is true; but in most cases they fight because they fear their jobs are at stake. In general, however, management has stopped lobbying for controls on the speculators because they have joined forces with them.

What could be better, one wonders, than managers buying out their shareholders? They are at last becoming real capitalists. Owners of the means of production. Owner-managers. But that is not what is happening. Their ownership is based entirely on a debt load which is out of all proportion to the company's equity — often five to ten times equity. They have replaced a responsibly based ownership of shareholders with the sort of debt-based ownership which brought about the Great Depression. It is a world in which the managers of one large company take runs at the managers of another, usually somewhat smaller company. According to abstract theory, it is all a fair game. In fact, what the managers are doing is damaging the corporation which they now own by loading it up with debt in order to finance their takeover of it. The more productive the company, the more often it will be worth taking over. Many companies have been acquired twice in a decade, some three times. And each time the purchaser's costs are rolled yet again into the accounts of the purchased.

American corporate debt is now some $2.2 trillion. It has almost doubled in five years. Interest payments on this amount absorb 32 percent of America's total corporate cash flow. This figure does not include the $1.1 trillion of outstanding debt in the private financial sector — that is to say, the capital sums raised by financial institutions, mainly through corporate bonds and short-term corporate paper for their own use. Nor does it include the $1.17 trillion outstanding in the noncorporate sectors, most of which are in the service industries. In other words, a great deal more than 32 percent of corporate cash flow is absorbed by interest payments.

And yet business leaders have been mounting continual attacks on the government debt load, which absorbs only 15 percent of the annual tax receipts. In Britain the corporate sector spends some 11.5 percent of its income on interest payments. The government spends 10 percent.

Little of this corporate spending is investment in corporate production capabilities. It is simply the printing and spinning of paper money. In 1984, the same year that $140 billion was spent in the United States on mergers, acquisitions and leveraged buyouts, $78 billion worth of equity actually disappeared from the corporate world.[14]

The motive which drives the large corporations on to devour the small has nothing to do with capitalism. Their public relations departments will come up with self-congratulatory phrases, such as that of Philip Morris when it took over Kraft for $13.5 billion: "We believe the combination of Philip Morris and Kraft will create a U.S.–based food company that will compete more effectively in world food markets."[15] The reality is that these enormous financial deals are not related in any way to the use and development of the means of production. They are related to a general management structure in which ever-more-abstract financial methods give the impression of growth. The problem is not simply one of specific probusiness governments serving specific business interests. It is more a logical outcome of the management methods which have been developing for a century. As in other sectors, a perfectly rational system is far more easily abused by the dishonest than used by the honest. In this specific case, by allowing the uncontrolled development of financial manipulation, the authorities have released, for the first time since 1933, the full forces of irresponsible speculation.

The confirmation that this frenetic activity is illusory can be seen in the real growth statistics of Western economies. They have been shrinking since the 1960s and, during this last decade of deregulation, have continued to shrink. The simple truth is that the production of a tractor is the result of men who know about tractors actually producing them and then selling them to men who actually use them. Financial planning and management methods are, at best, marginal facilitators. The essential skills of capitalism are concrete. The rest, as they used to say, is fancy talk.

A part of that fancy talk has involved arguing that mergers would create diversification and diversification would provide stability in tough times. It would also widen the circle of experience within a single organization. The reality has been that the experience is not used. Instead management feels obliged to design ever larger structures which can deal with all this variety in a homogenized manner. Everything must fit in, and on paper it does. As a result the central managers know less and less about what the company actually does, while those with concrete experience and concrete responsibilities are squeezed into corporate models which have nothing to do with their production. Those who don't know, institutionalize their power; those who do know, live in fear of losing budgets and jobs.

Senior management and their doctrinal advisers in the business schools have noticed, unavoidably, that these methods are not working. Their response has been threefold. First, to shut down production in areas in which they cannot "compete." As pointed out, this involves turning whole production areas over to Third World countries. Second, to move into those Third World countries in order to take advantage of local social and employment standards — that is, to undermine the Western social consensus by relying on early industrial societies. Third, to reverse the process of the last twenty years by splitting their corporations into semiautonomous operations or by selling off chosen sectors. These semiautonomous operations give the managers all the tools of independence except the essential ones. As for the selling off of complete sectors, it simply brings most of those units full circle — that is, back to being smaller, specialized, independent companies. In the process, however, they have been saddled with two burdens of debt, each in the amount of the company's value. The first was imposed by the takeover company at the time of the original purchase. The second was imposed on the managers by that same owner who now wished to be bought out.

Finally, there is the fourth solution, which is to attempt to bring the magical production methods of the East to the West. The East in this case means Japan and it must be said for the Japanese option that it is at least constructive. It also has the exotic charm which always disarms adults when they express a desire to learn. Of course, in the 1960s and early 1970s the same Japanophiles now proposing the Eastern option were teaching their students, or declaring through business organizations, that the Japanese had not gone through a proper industrial revolution and instead had arbitrarily stuck industrial production methods on top of a medieval paternalistic social system. This was socially impossible. Therefore it would inevitably produce a revolution and then the whole edifice would come tumbling down.

Today Western economists and business philosophers call this piggybacking, of the industrial on top of the medieval, the Japanese Miracle. The religious image is suitable. It coincides with their own conversion on the road to stagnation. These are the voices of big solutions and so now they talk endlessly of production teams and worker participation and company loyalty. Why a Western white- or blue-collar worker should be interested in loyalty, participation and teamwork is not clear when the units they work for are disposed of by management or speculators with an indifference reminiscent of the slave trade. And if they are loyal and their teamwork does lead to success in the marketplace, their unit will probably be loaded down as fast as possible with debt in order to finance some other unrelated managerial manoeuvre.

There are indeed many ways to manufacture and sell an identical object and there have been endless discussions about participatory capitalism, right here in the West, going all the way back to 1799 when Robert Owen, a highly successful owner of cotton-spinning mills, bought the New Lanark mills in Scotland and organized a model community based on the principles of mutual cooperation. His work strengthened the cooperative movement which spread in many separate directions, for example, to Bismarckian Germany and much later to Gaullian France. According to the Swedish historian, Hakan Berggren, it also went by another route, via the Manchester school of liberalism, to inspire the Swedish idea of social democracy. There is, therefore, no need to look to Japan, which has indeed found a solution half medieval, half postindustrial and quite particular to their society.

What our thinkers miss is that the West's problem is not one of production methods. Of course, these problems do loom in the factories. Factories are concrete operations where problems cannot be disguised. But the problem itself is largely in the management structure and in the management. If they wish to look to the East, they should note that Japanese companies are scarcely organized at the top. In their system, most of our management would be out of a job for the simple reason that they are irrelevant to the research, creation and production of goods.

⁂

Doing away with themselves and their systems is not among the options being considered by management. Nevertheless, the refusal of the means of production to respond to abstract systems does present a problem. One of the solutions management has found is simply to decide that, as economies evolve towards higher levels of technique and education, so they will evolve away from production and into the heavenly spheres of service. The future of civilized man, therefore, lies in the service industries.

Before entertaining an idea so warm and attractive, it is worth opening a contemporary dictionary; for example, *Oxford*:

> Service: from the Latin *servitium* (slavery). The condition, status or occupation of a servant.

Beneath the word *service* and belonging to the same word family are *serviceable*, *servient*, *servile*, *servility*, *servitude*.

The philosopher of management would reply yes, precisely. In the future, civilized man, buying his less-sophisticated, messy goods — such as steel — from less-developed societies, will have at his beck and call the service industries of his own country. But the professor has confused his modifier. The primary servitude of a service industry is not to the public but to real industry; that is to say, to the industries which increasingly produce goods under the political controls of "lesser" civilizations.

What is this servitude? Quite simply, service industries only have a market as long as real industry continues to supply basic goods at an acceptable price and in a market where the public can afford to buy them. Those three criteria must be satisfied before the public can turn, with whatever remains in its pocket, to purchase service industry goods.

The present disorder in Korea shows just how delicate such a servitude can be. It also reminds us that such a relationship assumes our acceptance of and financial support for the social systems in that country. Even Akio Morita, the founder of Sony and thus the man who had led the way in humiliating Western managers, rejects the view that service industries are the wave of the future for developed economies. He believes that economic growth requires a flourishing industrial base that can produce real added value. [16]

Closing the dictionary and opening any history of civilizations, the curious reader might consider the characteristics of societies in decay. At the meeting point between their rise and their decline, societies — or rather the elites of societies — always discover that it is beneath their dignity to continue to do the concrete things which caused their rise. And so they set about organizing their lives in a manner diametrically opposed to that which created their civilization and therefore justified its existence. However, they invariably retain the original supporting vocabulary and mythology of their rise, as if these talismans will protect them.

In embracing the world of service industries, we abandon the foundations of a middle-class society devoted to the work ethic and driven by a flawed, often hypocritical, but nevertheless real belief in some sort of human equality. As if the name Karl Marx had never been heard, we throw ourselves into demonstrating the core of his analysis. While the substructure of a society is rotting away, the superstructure continues to prosper, living off the decay below. But when the substructure is finally gone, it is only a matter of time before the glorious surface crashes down under its own weight.

Businessmen and economists argue that it was essential to turn towards service industries because these were areas of new growth. Had they continued to concentrate on the traditional areas, then manpower savings through modernization would have created a permanent unemployment crisis. This is not entirely false. But then, neither is the portrait of our society, as one faced by an urgent choice over the direction to take, entirely true. Nor is the description of the service industries as the natural creators of new employment based on anything more than abstract logic.

The most interesting of the service areas — the high-technology industries — are the least labour-intensive sector in the economy. Seventy percent of the manufacturing costs of a semiconductor microchip is knowledge — that is, research, development and testing. Twelve percent is labour. In the case of prescription drugs, 15 percent is labour and 50 percent knowledge. What's more, these technologies are using less and less raw materials. Twenty-five to fifty kilos of fiberglass cable can transmit as many telephone messages as one ton of copper wire. And those fifty kilos of fiberglass cables require only 5 percent of the energy needed to produce one ton of copper wire.[17] There is nothing wrong with these savings. To the contrary, they suggest that we might be nearing the end of the terrifying multiplications of industrial activity whose effect on the earth is just beginning to show. The point is that the serious service industries are not going to be massive creators of solid employment. Indeed, they should not be put in the service category at all.

Inevitably though, the high-technology industries are invoked whenever the service sector is being worshipped. The suggestion is that computers, software and advanced communications are typical of our service-based future. The reality is that they belong to the manufacturing process, where they are essential in such areas as research, development, design, production and sales. As Akio Morita points out, these elements cannot be separated out to be kept in the developed world, while manufacturing is moved to the Third World.

Why, then, have Japanese corporations apparently gone the same way as those of the West by building factories in such places as Mexico and Thailand? The answer is that their overseas production is not the result of a decision to divide the industrial tasks. Japan consciously maintains a complete domestic structure. Foreign factories primarily reflect the success of their international sales drive. They may benefit from lower production costs abroad, but if domestic employment began to suffer, it is probable that overseas production would be cut back. The point is that the Japanese do not accept our revisionist idealizing of the tertiary sector.

The original idea of service industries included anyone who did not manufacture a product — that is to say, a capital good. Thus teaching and communications fell into the category. Many of these professions are now called public services, but if they form or help people, they are indeed making an indirect but essential contribution to production. In any case, it isn't these basic public service areas which are in expansion. Governments everywhere are trying to cut them back.

There are also services which are not considered industries because our obsession with profits seems to eliminate them from what we call the economy. In general these fall into the categories of charity and culture. As Maurice Strong puts it — "Most of the valid needs as yet unsatisfied are of a non-material nature."[18] Why anyone believes that these services ought to be in a volunteer structure is not terribly clear. Is getting meals to old people who live in isolation less important than making golf balls? Everyone will answer no. Why, then, treat the former as after-the-fact voluntary work and the latter as an essential industry? The answer is that our managerial elites have adopted the Andrew Carnegie conviction that "great inequalities between men are essential to competition and to capitalism."

The main category of service industries, in which most job creation takes place, is that which creates and satisfies artificial needs. This consumer industry explosion has generally been described as the inevitable product of a successful, rich and comfortable society, which already had all it needed. The next step was to create things it didn't need and to create actual services whose very attraction was that they were not necessary. These services and service objects, divorced as they are from utility, were free to grow, multiply, and build upon each other, creating their own self-contained justifications for existence. They could seize upon the minutest detail of clothing, hair, skin, sound, sight, housing, sport, food, transport, and build it up into a baroque cathedral of elements, style, complexity and apparent need.

There would be nothing particularly wrong with this if Western civilization, particularly that of the modern era, had self-indulgence as its goal. A glance at our history indicates the opposite. A glance at our contemporary situation indicates that while the area of greatest economic expansion is in the services of self-indulgence, growing percentages of the population are slipping back into pre-twentieth-century poverty.

And there lies the real paradox of modern capitalism. It is masterful at producing services people don't need and in large part probably don't want. It is brilliant at convincing people that they do need and want them. But it has difficulty turning itself to the production of those services which people really do need. Not only that, it often spends an enormous amount of time and effort convincing people that those services are either unrealistic, marginal or counterproductive. Never have our skills of organization been so developed, never have our desires for the accumulation of objects and comforts been so realizable, and never have events seemed so difficult to control. In other words, a rational economic structure finds it very difficult to give people what they really want because real human demand does not follow a fixed pattern. Giving people what they want is inefficient because it is irrational. On the other hand, it is efficient to give people what they do not want, because an artificial sales structure can ensure some rational buying patterns.

It is as if we are becoming what we originally set out to destroy. The elites of societies at such a highly evolved stage have invariably gathered into their hands sufficient real power to be able to betray the intrinsic line of their own society. They may utterly betray it while singing the sweetest lullaby to the contrary. While singing their hearts out for capitalism, competition and hard-won success, they may devote themselves to the employee's life, well paid and self-indulgent. The texture of our reigning mythologies is so thick that no one can see what is actually happening behind this intellectual and emotional camouflage.

Elites take criticism very badly. They immediately respond that the critic is on the side of the enemy — the Left, the foreign rival, the forces of Communism or any other handy ideology. But do the elites, with all their competence and power, actually believe that societies can be destroyed by anyone except those who lead them? The farmers, the factory workers, the ordinary civil servants, the lower- or even middle-level employees simply do not have the power to destroy or even to alter a society's direction. It is the elites who lead the way and the history of past civilizations is that the elites, at a certain point, cease to fulfill their obligations and begin to indulge themselves. The Roman farmer-soldier-citizens began importing wheat and hiring barbarians to fight for them. The European aristocrats abandoned their land and regiments and went to court, where they became well-dressed hangers-on and manipulators. And now our owner-producers are leaving ownership and factories and are becoming the hangers-on of urban comfort and excitement.

The modern manager is indeed an urban phenomenon. Preferably the city in question is New York, London, Paris, Toronto, Frankfurt, Milan. There he finds concrete daily proof of his own value by simply observing himself within the urban corporate structure. His hands are clean. He meets only people like himself. The industrial worker is a distant image, as dirty as the farm worker was in the memory of a noble landowner at the court of Louis XV.

The manager has no need to know such people or to go where they are. Often he has himself arrived from there, which heightens his desire not to go back. His Gucci shoes are proof that he has not just arrived from Essen or Baie-Comeau. What's more, he is also the prime believer in the advertising and the unnecessary services generated by his class. He buys the clothes, the cars, the makeup, the holidays, the sports equipment, the property, the pools, the tennis club memberships. Even armaments are built by the industrial managers for the consumption of the governmental managers.

Needless to say, none of these people want to live in Pittsburgh,

Hamilton, Leeds, Lille or anywhere except in the handful of great urban heavens. This drainage of the "undesirable" parts of nations has created enormous social and economic shifts. The only countershift has come from the managerial need to be served by a weekend haven, as well as by summer and winter holiday installations. Thus whole sections of the West are given over to pure consumption during short periods of time — Friday night to Sunday night or July and August, for example. The rest of the year they are virtually idle.

One of capitalism's greatest problems is that factories are less and less to be found in large urban centres. These companies cannot be well run by remote control. And the managerial class does not want to live where the factories can be found. Of course, some managers will live in these places, even good managers. But the pool from which they must be plucked is a birdbath compared to the ever-swelling sea of the urban managerial class. And if this class will not live in these places, then they are places which will continue to be drained of their activities. The conformism of our business elites is such that they will only go where they can find quantities of their own kind.

England has suffered more than any other country from this rush of talent towards a single city. The immediate and distant descendants of the men who actually made England — the Midlands industrial middle classes — are jammed into central London, trying to be merchant bankers, advertising executives and head-office managers.

The Midlands cities suffer from many things, but beneath their problems of equipment, labour and markets lies the simple fact that those who can afford to go to London do. There they devote themselves to being gentlemen — a word, like so many in this century, which implies one thing and means another. In this case it involves an education, accent and manner of dressing which suggests some sort of long-established social standing. In reality it means membership in the new managerial class, particularly devoted to service industries which pretend to produce but don't.

After fifteen years of general economic crisis and depression in the West, the business classes are larger and richer than they have ever been. The standards of living of the population as a whole have been declining, while that of the managerial class has continued to rise. There is a shrinking of the middle class in the United States, but that represents precisely the ejection of those in the old middle class who have not managed to convert to the newer, managerial-class model. Looking at the fate of the owners and managers of free enterprise over the last hundred years, it would be difficult to argue that they have suffered in the social democratic state. In fact, it would be impossible.

And yet it is worth thinking about the development over the last hundred years of social legislation, work codes, financial market standards, emission codes and taxation policies. Is there a single example in any Western country of business in general reacting positively to the creation of fairer standards? And, when what are called "probusiness" governments have come to power and proceeded to lower the legislated standards of corporate behaviour, is there a single example of business in general feeling that these standards have been lowered far enough? Is there a single example of management feeling that independent public comment on the way businesses conduct their business is fair? A single example of forestry replanting obligations being low enough? Of social security payments being low enough? Of allowable industrial emissions into the air or the water being high enough? Of workers' rights of any kind being restricted enough?

All this could be interpreted as the normal give-and-take of free societies. But societies do not grow and flower simply on the basis of guerrilla warfare. The idea contained in the concept of a "society," especially in a "democratic" or a "free society," is that the participants are in general agreement and are willing to cooperate. The business community, and in particular the managerial class today, seems to see itself as a privileged partner who may withhold cooperation at its sole discretion.

The labour movement often takes the same sort of attitude. But unions are just a creation of the business community. They are an exact reflection of the corporate mentality. If they are selfish, it is a selfishness proportionate to their employer's. A union can only react to situations it finds. So when someone like Arthur Scargill, head of the British miners' union, creates such disorder that it is clear he has quite another agenda than the settling of specific grievances, it may be true that he is out of control and dangerous. It is also true that he is the creation of long-term unsatisfactory attitudes among mine owners and managers. That he appears when that may no longer be the case merely demonstrates that history works slowly and that reflections may appear after the original mirror has been broken. Quite simply, the union leaders have learned a great deal from the management's noncooperative approach towards society.

There is a worrying self-satisfaction about the idea that capitalism is always the enemy of fairness. Is it true that the business classes have always stood united against reform and social cooperation? Clearly not, since the reform parties throughout the West were financed and sometimes led by members of those classes. Not only the British Liberal Party in its glory, but the Labour Party after it, was supported by men from the great Midlands industrial families. So were the Democratic

Party by the American equivalent, the French Radicals and even Socialists, the Canadian Liberals and so on.

Today few members of the business classes work within the reform parties. Fewer and fewer, in fact. These men appear to have moved increasingly to the sort of social refusal you would expect from a nineteenth-century robber baron. Their opposition to fair social standards is virulent. You have but to question them on visiting day at their child's private school or as they come out of their large houses with two or three cars in the drive.

Each will tell you in an excited manner about the destruction of initiative and the pulling down of free enterprise. No matter how pro-business the government in place, he will talk about Left-wing government policies. He will seem to have no inner vision of himself as a high-salaried and well-protected tenant of a business bureaucracy. Instead he has dressed himself up in his mind to play the role of Andrew Carnegie, the great capitalist, just the way Carnegie must have played himself. As the scene ends, he leaves you behind on his lawn and drives away in the company's Mercedes to his salaried penthouse corner office in heaven.

The question recurs: what makes him act this way? He himself doesn't seem to know. He has been handed the carcass of capitalist mythology and been left to do something with it. Rather than admit to himself the limitations of his own power, it is only natural that he should choose to dress himself up in the full regalia of the rampant capitalist. The real owner of real production facilities is the one far more likely today to be interested in social consensus. Without it, he has a great deal to lose.

The technocrat's refusal to be a cooperative partner in the establishment of public morality suits his temperament perfectly. He likes to create the context and set the rules before he agrees to play. In society this is impossible. The relationships are too complicated. He therefore switches into his natural mold, which is defensive, and uses his detached cleverness to manoeuvre his way through convention and law, cutting as close to the letter of permitted action as possible. The contemporary cliché has it that the Nietzschian Hero is a rebel against systems. But here it can be seen just how like Siamese twins the Hero-technocrat relationship is. "Morality is the herd instinct in the individual," Nietzsche wrote.[19] The Hero shows his amoral individualism by setting his personal moral agenda and imposing it. The corporate executive, being but an employee, demonstrates the same amoral individualism by defining the greatest good as the ability to manipulate systems.

When a fraud involving £215 million was discovered in the U.K. corporation ISC Technologies, the chairman of the parent company, Sir

Derek Alun-Jones, stated that the problem hadn't been picked up at first because £105 million of the total had been siphoned off through offshore companies. "Transactions with Panamanian, Liberian and Cayman Island companies are quite usual in business."[20] In other words, the company was quite used to the idea that the government and the citizenry could legally be denied corporate taxes through offshore mechanisms. Subsequently, certain managers had found a parallel way to remove money from the company. The difference was that the corporate cheat was legal. Moreover, this sort of legal cheat was so widespread as a way of doing business that it had become "quite usual." The illegal cheat was a rare, one-time affair.

It is this cleverness which a whole new generation of owners and managers, especially from the exploding service industries, has discovered and accepted as the norm for business attitudes. Their own service industries being so artificial, they have been able to grasp this cleverness and manipulate it into a means for making considerable amounts of money. There is very little distinction between avoiding the letter of the law and evading the law altogether. When a clever man is operating in the heat of the action, there is no difference at all.

Those on the Left, whose opposition to Capitalism is ritualistic, of course protested this sort of activity. Unfortunately, the battles they fight generally have little to do with the events taking place. At the 1978 World Socialist Congress, a resolution was passed which began:

> The Socialist International is fully aware of the growing importance of Multinational Corporations within the world economic order and of the urgent need to control the activities of these organizations. . . . Such controls can only be effective if better information systems on Multinationals are developed.[21]

But all the information was and is available. If anything, we know too much. In their desire to see the multinational as a premeditating monster, they were missing the very essence of the animal — that it has no particular direction or desires. It is moved only by the needs of its organization and by the narrow ambitions of its managers. The multinational is like a centipede, which moves across borders with the ease of a structured blob.

Because of this the employee of the multinational can be seen as the perfect international citizen. The adjective *anational* would probably be more appropriate. Already some economists are describing him as the harbinger of a future world in which all artificial barriers to the movement and commerce of man will have been swept away, taking with them the narrow, destructive selfishness of the nation-state. Who better to lead the way than the international manager, who has no ax to grind and just wants to do business?

The idea certainly has its attractions. However, the malleability of the multinational executive has its origins not in open-mindedness but in indifference. He is perfectly willing to agree with local politics if they agree with him. Equally, the moment they no longer suit his purposes, he feels free to subvert them. The power of his corporation will no doubt have permitted it to forge an important place in the local economy, often by buying up or smothering smaller national or regional competitors. To his own corporation's opposition to local policies the manager may well be able to add that of his company's friends — fellow multinationals, banks, international credit organizations and even other governments, particularly that of its home country. The issue at hand may be anything — taxation levels, pollution controls, employment standards, reinvestment policies, R & D obligations.

In annoying a multinational subsidiary, the local government will be creating for itself enemies that stretch far beyond the policy in question. And if that government holds firm, the manager and his corporate subsidiary may simply walk away to some other local situation which suits them better. What's more, the subsidiary may have created such local socio-economic tension that other multinationals will follow. They will leave behind an economic void which may contribute to the eventual fall of the recalcitrant government.

The manager and the organization to which he belongs are perfectly disinterested players. In their hands the idea of the public weal withers away. Social unity in any size community is based, after all, on the ability to accept *not* getting what you want. A desire to free man from the narrow-based interests of nationalism is no doubt a good thing, but freedom is also an agreement on how to share responsibilities. The nation-state is just one of man's many attempts to deal with that idea. Now organizations such as the EEC are attempting to widen the definition by establishing common standards among groups of nations. The multinational, with its anational managers, is an attempt to escape any responsibility, thus retaining the power to treat each community according to the corporation's interests.

And yet the multinational is not quite so indifferent as it pretends to be. Even a centipede has a general program in life. Even the most intricate system must satisfy itself. And the core of that system is in head office. It is the interests of the head-office managers which decide the general flow of investment and of capital. When head office is in New York, most of the board members will be American, as will most of the senior managers. They may buy and sell internationally, but they wake up on East Seventy-sixth Street. Their primary concerns are those which surround them. Their first political thoughts are for the country in which the corporation is based.

This will not stop them from playing off the policies of a nation in which they have a subsidiary against those of their own country. Their use of cheap Third World labour to force down Western standards is a typical example.

The end result, however, is not to give power to the subsidiary. Even when called upon by headquarters to appear threatening, the subsidiary is the passive element in an international structure. In the old colonial manner, local elites are hired to ensure local cooperation. The local authorities can but see themselves as the passive receivers of investments and jobs. You can always tell, from the form that economic discussions take, whether you are in a place which is at the centre of multinational structures or at the end of an extended loop. The further you are from the centre, the closer to the beginning of the discussion the word *jobs* will appear. Jobs are the passive element in industrial activity. They are received as the result of a process which begins elsewhere with such things as capital investment, R & D, industrial planning and markets.

The idea of Capitalism as a venture within society or between societies based upon cooperation and mutual profit is thus absent from the multinational model, and increasingly it is absent from the smaller managed corporations. Precisely that cooperation has made Japan's success possible. All the Japanese particular peculiarities, which we are now attempting to imitate, are merely consequences of that cooperation. That is why our efforts to imitate them resemble parody more than they do reorganization. You cannot have a Friedmanite view of market forces or a business school idea of business as structure and then expect to benefit from the cooperative methods proper to the Japanese or to the Swedes or even to the Koreans, to take three very different examples. The market approach and the cooperative approach are mutually destructive.

A few years ago, a full-page Gulf Oil advertisement appeared in many newspapers:

> PROFIT IS NOT A FOUR LETTER WORD. IT DOESN'T REPRESENT ILL-GOTTEN GAINS. PROFIT ISN'T THE RESULT OF RIPPING OFF THE CONSUMER. PROFIT IS WHAT A COMPANY WORKS WITH. IT'S THE MONEY WE USE TO FIND OR DEVELOP ENERGY.

Following the 1973 crisis, Western governments had desperately sought a way to deal with the economic catastrophe created by their dependence on OPEC oil. They finally decided to leave the corporate part of the price increase in the hands of the Western-based multinational companies responsible for transporting energy. These corporations could then reinvest their new riches at home or in stable countries outside OPEC, with the aim of discovering and developing a guaranteed energy supply for the West. Their reward for acting as good citizens was that they would make a big profit out of the reinvestment.

This was a leap of faith on the part of the citizenry and of their governments. They would have been perfectly justified in taxing away these massive windfall profits, which were bringing the Western economy to a halt. What is more, the lead-up to the crisis had been filled with events which indicated that the oil companies ought not to be trusted with the public interest.

For example, only months before the crisis, the Canadian oil companies (largely American owned) had told the government that national reserves were enough to last a century. They said this because they wanted permission to export across the border to the more profitable American market what reserves they actually did have. When the crisis came the declared national reserves turned out to be imaginary and Canada found itself a prisoner of both foreign supplies and the priorities of foreign oil companies. The managers had simply lied behind a screen of misleading statistics. It was not that they had been forced to choose between the interests of their shareholders and those of the citizens in their country of operation. Rather, they had chosen freely to make additional profits for their shareholders, which required endangering the fundamental well-being of the citizenry.

A second example affected the United States itself. In 1972 the companies agreed that some $4.50 a barrel would be enough to ensure adequate exploration and production for the domestic market.[22] That is to say, $4.50 would pay for exploration and ensure a healthy profit. A few months later, the crisis struck and OPEC raised the price, not to cover new costs but to increase profits. Abruptly the American companies discovered that they had underestimated the costs of exploration inside the United States. Instead of $4.50 a barrel, they could squeeze by with $10. Then it was $15. Then $20. In the case of each price increase, the justifying technical arguments were so watertight that no reference was made to the very recent cost-related lower price.

Some people assumed that the companies were making up for the hard struggles of earlier years by claiming their just reward. But most of these multinationals had been around for half a century. The days of risk were far behind them. They functioned more as oil banks, buying up the discoveries of the wildcatters, who risked their shirts on a daily basis. Between 1968 and 1972, the seven major U.S. oil companies had already accumulated net profits of $44 billion. In the same period, they had paid less than $2 billion in federal tax; an effective rate of 5 percent. When the crisis struck, they were already rich beyond the dreams of most corporations.

The Western governments decided, nevertheless, to entrust the companies with the gigantic new profits. In the first year of the crisis, their worldwide earnings increased 71 percent. Their net profits were $6.7 billion. They had paid $642 million in taxes. Texaco, for example, earned $1.3 billion after taxes. Exxon, $2.4 billion.[23] At this point, Western economies were plunging into the abyss.

The companies immediately began reinvesting their profits. But not in oil. Mobil bought Montgomery Ward, the department store chain — net worth $8.5 billion — and in the same period took out full-page ads:

WHY ARE YOU SO SUSPICIOUS OF LARGE CORPORATIONS?

Sun Oil bought the Stop-N-Go grocery chain. Shell went into plastics; Exxon into copper mining, while mounting a reassuring ad campaign:

YOU DON'T HAVE TO FEAR US.
PART OF THE PROBLEM OF THE LIBERALS'
DISLIKE APPEARS TO BE SNOBBERY PURE AND SIMPLE.

As the money rolling into their pockets further crippled the West, the corporations were able to buy companies at depressed prices. Insurance companies. Medical supply companies. Gulf tried to buy Ringling Brothers Barnum & Bailey Circus. Others discovered box manufacturing, timberland, general forest products, more department store chains. By the early 1980s, they had 25 percent of the listed resource chemical companies (copper, lead, zinc, silver, gold).

They had also taken over a majority of the largest American coal companies. Their first management initiative in this sector was to cut back production in order to get coal prices up. This was done in a nation already desperate for energy. By the end of the 1970s, they had fourteen of the twenty large coal reserves, two of the three top uranium producers, and three of the four large uranium reserves.[24]

Atlantic Richfield had a more concentrated strategy than the others. They bought up surface coal-mining reserves throughout the Midwest until they were the largest player. And then, without rushing to develop these resources, they began lobbying Washington to switch American energy dependence from oil to coal. Their argument was that domestic coal reserves were sufficient to provide long-term stability. They also argued that the market price for this coal would have to be the world price equivalent of an OPEC barrel of oil. They knew that surface coal is almost as cheap to mine as sand on a beach. So did everyone else in the energy sector. The potential profits were therefore unimaginable, even by oil crisis standards. The reason Atlantic Richfield was so eagerly lobbying Washington, instead of just going ahead and using its capitalist skills to mine and sell coal, had to do with physical infrastructure. There wasn't one for the distributing or burning of coal. What America needed in order to embrace the Atlantic Richfield strategy was coal pipelines and new coal-burning plants. Any innocent who had been listening to the free-market rhetoric of the oil companies would have imagined that Atlantic Richfield had already formed a syndicate with other coal-producing companies, so that they could all borrow against their future gigantic earnings in order to finance and construct this infrastructure. But that idea wasn't even entertained. Instead the entire infrastructure was to be built at public expense.

As for the windfall profits which the industry in general was receiving thanks to the oil price rise, some of them were indeed being reinvested in new energy development — not nearly enough, however, to eliminate the West's dependence on foreign oil. And so, like babes in the woods, governments and their citizens slipped towards the next oil crisis, which shook them more than the first.

These legal but dishonest actions by the oil companies are considered to be among the great exploits of modern capitalism. Their complex ruses were admired by other business sectors and raved over by stockbrokers and merchant bankers. At first glance it would seem that such an attitude was in direct contradiction of the principles of reason. After all, in the original *Encyclopédie*, Diderot began the entry on the "Morality of Richness": "The means for enriching oneself may be criminally immoral, although permitted by the law."[25]

Of all the integrated energy corporations involved, only one or two were owned or controlled by an individual or by an identifiable group of individuals. The mass of unnamed shareholders at no time pushed their companies to so betray the public trust and damage the fabric of the state. Like most stock market investors, they were in the passive position of watching their money grow or shrink. It was growing and so they were glad. They did not really consider the implications of that growth on their own society. The entire direct responsibility for carrying out what may have been the most irresponsible private economic act of the century lies with the managerial class, who are the flower of methodology and the children of reason.

17

The Miracle of the Loaves

Inflation has always meant flatulence. The seventeenth century expanded the meaning of the word, beyond the blowing up with and expelling of gas, to include such attitudinal derivatives as *bombast* and *pomposity*. It was only in the 1860s that *inflation* focused itself on economic phenomena.

This was not brought on by a revolution in the world of finance. Money has always been like a gas, which alternately rose and fell, poisoned and induced flowers, was opaque and then clear, sweet-smelling, then noxious. With hindsight, the nineteenth-century clarification that uncontrolled money was nothing more than uncontrolled farting therefore made perfect sense. From that moment on it became almost impossible to confuse inflation with growth.

And yet, that is precisely what businessmen, economists and bankers have insisted upon doing over the last thirty years. Just as our structures and elites prefer corporate manipulation to real production, so financial manipulation comes more naturally to them than the creation of new capital. The result has been the gradual conversion of our economies into myriad new forms of inflation, most of which are not measured by our many measuring institutes. Much of current economic argument turns upon levels of measured inflation which reflect the small potatoes of national economies. They do not reflect what is really happening. And so to all appearances, we do not inflate. Instead, behind an insistent discourse about sophisticated populations, postindustrial economies, postentrepreneurial corporations and service industries, we create offshore funds and uncontrollable offshore currencies, such as the Eurodollar, which grow according to their own logic. We run virtually uncontrolled money markets within our own borders. We permit highly leveraged buyouts. We allow takeovers to be financed by the privately initiated printing of money against the value of the target company's assets. We create false capital through the providing of imaginary services, particularly that of selling arms. We allow the uncontrolled printing of money through such devices as credit cards. We allow banks to service their bad debts through the issuing of new shares, thus permitting the public exchanges to be used not to increase capital through debt, but to cover disintegrating capital through more debt.

The list of monetary devices is endless. Most economists would protest that while these activities may or may not add to the atmosphere which creates inflation, they are not in themselves inflation. They think that if you want to know what is happening to the economy, you can limit yourself to the consumer price index or the GNP price index or other highly specific indexes.

But if these are sufficient, then why can we no longer have growth without an immediate explosion in measured inflation? The answer is that we are not experiencing real growth. And why do we have increasing prosperity at one end of society with increasing poverty at the other? Because the creation of wealth is now dependent on financial manipulation by a small percentage of the population and not on production by an integrated society. And why are we constantly being told that a fall in general standards of public service and/or standards of living is now essential to economic well-being? Because financial manipulation creates profits but adds nothing real to the economic wealth of the society. These abstract methods are so widespread and sophisticated that, as in the 1980s, they can create the impression of general prosperity when the reality is one of continued decay in both economic and social infrastructures. Our elites seem often to be the most perplexed by the inability of their systems to create real wealth. But, then, they are themselves the product of the rational system and not its creators. They therefore live in the profound expectation that their methods will work. Their isolation from reality is such that they believe their systems can produce growth where in the past only inflation has grown.

"We are money-makers, not thing-makers," Jim Slater, English merchant banker and the father of modern inflation, declared two decades ago, not long before he crashed, bringing down banks and corporations with him. Along with others like Sir Arnold Weinstock and Lord Stokes, he had declared himself to be a force of modernization and efficiency, a claim which had been accepted as truth by the British financial establishment.[1]

Slater had been trained as a company accountant. He had a natural talent for stock market manipulation. In 1964 he created Slater, Walker Securities and set about buying companies priced below the value of their property and parts, carving them up and selling off everything concrete until only a shell remained. He and his imitators had soon destroyed hundreds of integrated engineering and production corporations because these could easily be sold off for cash. And cash could then be played with. They were engaged in the dismantling of the British economy for personal profit and pleasure through inflationary financial manipulation. Slater claimed that he was releasing productive elements caught up in hidebound conglomerates. In fact, studies of industrial reorganization in that period show that there was no benefit to the "released" companies. Slater, Walker rose to fame in part by continual lending or investing of its own money in one or another of its own companies, thus manipulating their share values. Jim Slater — young, slim and engaging — was soon considered to be "the greatest financial wizard the City had ever known."[2] In 1969 he began to sell off his assets — to deconglomeratize. He announced that cash was the "optimum investment" and turned his attention to areas more directly related to cash — property speculation, financial management and investments in Hong Kong. This cash religion encouraged other banks to overextend themselves, pumped up property speculation and drove corporations to a point where 27.5 percent of their net cash flow was going out in interest payments. And yet that terrible figure was still 5 percent lower than the 32 percent currently being paid out by American corporations to cover their debts.

Nevertheless, it was an unheard-of level for the times and, when the first crash came in 1973, the unconventional inflation of the British economy meant that it was harder hit than most. Even Jim Slater's wizardry couldn't maintain the illusion of his own empire. He chopped and changed through 1974 and 1975, only to be left with almost valueless remains. His operations were subject to a multitude of investigations, all of which could easily have been carried out years before when he was apparently successful. In late 1975 he was forced out of his own company, a discredited man, and the pieces were picked up by another market player, Jimmy Goldsmith.

Some time passed before the British and other Western governments realized that they were failing to escape from their generalized state of depression. The habitual correctional devices weren't working. Their reaction to this failure resembled that of a manic depressive. That is, they began a long crusade against classic inflation; driving up interest rates and thus killing real investment; driving up unemployment and thus putting a strain on social services. This crusade went on and on. We are still on it. Somehow, no matter how Draconian the measures taken, we never manage to cut off the inflationary fat, clearing the way for healthy, noninflationary growth.

In absolute contradiction to this depressive anti-inflationary crusade, we went on a parallel, manic financial binge. Consciously or unconsciously, we began to lift restrictions and to lower standards throughout the financial sector, thus freeing the profound forces of inflation. Of course, no one was permitted to play directly with the traditional governmental inflationary control tool — money supply. This and the area of wage and price increases were roped off, so to speak, and kept under obsessional public scrutiny. Social justice, economic growth, the fear of nuclear war and various other themes retreated into the background as the West hovered over the monthly, weekly, sometimes daily, movements of inflationary charts. A tenth of a percentage movement up or down could cause a generalized shudder. Public life seemed to have been reduced to statistics. Elections were fought over fractions.

Meanwhile, every other potentially inflationary area was gradually being opened to marketplace manipulation. General economic activity was drawn towards the financial sector by this explosion in ever-less-regulated activities. Inventiveness concentrated itself on the creation of new, immeasurable financial abstractions — abstractions built upon abstractions — forms and levels of leverage which made the standards of 1929 seem almost responsible by comparison.

By the mid-1980s — even before the Big Bang — the annual value of transactions in the London financial market was $75 trillion a year. That is more than twenty-five times the total value of world trade, which was $2.84 trillion in 1988. Foreign exchange speculation in major world centres was $35 trillion a year — twelve times the total value of world trade. These transactions represent no concrete activity. They are multiplications of paper which have no beneficial effect on economic activity. Thus, the City in London may prosper and cohabit quite happily with general economic depression in the rest of Britain. The degree to which governments have become addicted to the easy pleasures of this speculation could be seen in Britain's reluctance to put the pound into the European Snake, and indeed into the European Monetary System, both of which are attempts to develop monetary stability in a large but realistically manageable geographic area.[3] The official British argument against participation has been that the Snake might limit the government's ability to set policies appropriate for competition at home and in the world. One of the unspoken reasons was that membership in the Snake might eventually limit the City's ability to speculate in currencies. The gradual conversion of the City to the Snake came as they realized that speculation would not be limited.

In this context the traditional definitions of bank exposure no longer mean very much. Writing in 1873, Walter Bagehot said of reserves: "The amount of that cash is so exceedingly small that a bystander almost trembles when he compares its minuteness with the immensity of the credit which rests upon it."[4] Bagehot's minuteness would seem enormous today. For example, in the mid-1980s, the American merchant bank Lehman Brothers had a capital base of $270 million. It had a daily exposure of $10 billion.

This floating speculation in bonds and securities is done by numbers men on computers. Convention calls them bankers, but they are merely technicians, whose training resembles that of a clerk and whose talents parallel that of a racetrack bookie. They have no experience away from their screens; no understanding of the industrial activity the illuminated numbers represent. Worse still, they have neither responsibility for nor a sense of the effect that their enormous transactions might have on society as a whole. As early as 1984 men such as this were trading $4.1 trillion in a single New York merchant bank, First Boston Corporation. That was more than the total American GNP.

The golden word which has permitted all of this is *deregulation*. The United States followed by the entire West, has raised this flag in the name of the spirit of initiative. There is no doubt that a half century of administrative structure building — aimed at repairing the injustice, instability and damages created by nineteenth- and early-twentieth-century free markets — had gone too far in certain areas. But the re-action to this overregulation has borne no relationship to the real problem at hand. The result has been the return of antisocial freedom: the freedom to act irresponsibly, to speculate and profiteer, not just over stocks but over money itself.

The problem does not lie only with specific fashions, which may be short-lived, from currency swaps, junk bonds, financial futures and options to stock index futures (which require a down payment of only 6 percent), leveraged buyouts and over-the-counter equities, whose real value is unclear and thus open to speculation and arbitrage. Nor are these fashions as short-lived as they sometimes appear. In an economy so distanced from reality, forms of speculation no longer disappear simply because they have been exposed as of dubious value. For example, junk bonds have gone on after their disasters of the late 1980s and now represent more than a quarter of all corporate bonds rated by Moody's. Nor are these dangerous phenomena limited to the United States. Japanese regulations permit leverage based on 5 percent. British corporate debt has risen from £10 billion just before the first crash in 1973 to £53 billion billion in 1988. One might suspect that this was a creation of the inflation-infected 1970s. But official inflation seemed neither to encourage nor to discourage corporate debt. Things got even further out of control during the 1980s. The whole process was fed by minor finance companies, which under stricter regulations would be considered marginal, if not criminal. With deregulation they became banks. And the large deposit banks, seeing the enormous paper profits made by these little speculators, leaped down into the gutter to play the same game. The overall picture is what Keynes would have called a Casino society.[5]

And that is now one of the determining activities of our economies. The truth is that annual growth in the U.S. economy after inflation has steadily shrunk as deregulation has proceeded: 4.2 percent during the 1960s, 3.1 percent during the crisis-ridden 1970s, and 2.1 percent during the theoretically prosperous 1980s. In Canada, despite its wide and solid social protection net, the number of people living in poverty grew in this period of deregulation from 14.7 percent in 1981 to 17.3 percent by 1985 and continues to grow.[6]

On Wall Street, on April 24, 1987, a rock band appeared on the floor of the American Stock Exchange to excite brokers with its music. The Hard Rock Café restaurant franchise was going public. The appearance of that band on the trading floor symbolized the service-industry mind, the role of hype in a deregulated marketplace and the idiotic joy which always appears in moments of economic anarchy.

What is consistently fascinating at such moments is the self-contained, self-absorption which comes over first traders, then businessmen, then the public and their government. Everyone starts to believe that what is happening is real. Speculation is transformed by a wand into investment and investment is safe. But most incredible of all is the abrupt illumination that money is something, when everyone knows perfectly well that it is just a notion, not even an abstraction, because we are unable to agree permanently what it is an abstraction of.

The best we have done is to find workable arrangements. This seems to work most successfully and for the longest period of time when there is some conservative relationship between real labour/resources/products and the quantity of money available. Within those limits a reasonable Keynesian and a reasonable monetarist are not very far apart. But people have difficulty remaining reasonable over abstractions. Instead they get so used to their arbitrary definition of the abstraction of money that they decide it is both real and absolute.

Our particular difficulties rise out of reason's natural preference for abstraction over reality. The result is quite revolutionary. We have formalized speculation into a rational system. And yet, if there is one lesson in history, it is that inflation and depression follow on the heels of an economy which gives itself over to speculation, particularly speculation on debt.

Contemporary monetarism, despite its narrow obsession with money supply and classic inflation, has produced the greatest debt levels of modern history, accompanied by onerous or impossible burdens of interest. Odder still, while the monetarists remain obsessed with the state's indebtedness, they are indifferent to unprecedented corporate and personal debt levels. In fact, the corporations are more strapped than governments by their interest payments. Interest, whether paid by governments or companies, is a basic form of inflation, but governments retain other mechanisms, such as law and regulation, for encouraging economic activity. While the British government is myopically paying out its debt, the British citizenry, for the first time in history, is spending more than it receives. Its debt load has doubled over the last six years. In the absence of real growth, corporations and individuals can only hope to repay these debts through continued inflation. Or they can default. The level of both corporate and personal bankruptcies continues to grow throughout the West, reaching historic levels each year. Now, in the early 1990s, it is three to four times higher than it was in the early seventies.

The Third World debt load is part of this same process. Rarely has there been a financial obligation more evocative of the inflationary spiral built by level upon level of debt. The process of its creation is worth repeating. The United States pushed the oil states — principally Iran — towards unnecessary consumption, much of it military. Iran pushed OPEC for oil price increases in order to pay for its consumption. The West then printed money to pay for the oil. The oil states had to send that money back to the West to pay for goods, in large part service-industry goods, particularly arms, and to deposit it in a safe place. The Western banks then owed this money to the producers, principally the Iranians and the Arabs. And as it was on deposit, they also owed them interest. The Western economies being stagnant, because of the oil price rise and the resulting paper money inflation, the banks found it handy to lend part of their enormous new deposits out to the Third World. The theory was that so much cash would speed development, thus creating a new market for unwanted Western goods. This didn't help the developing countries, however, because their economies had been paralysed by the same oil price increases, as well as by the decline in commodity prices caused by the collapse of Western economies. So the banks lent them more money to support the original loans. The more the West lent, the less the Third World could pay back. As it now stands, many of them cannot even service the debt without bankrupting themselves, causing civil disorder and destroying what little social stability they have.

Clearly the money is lost. However, our governments and banks have now spent a decade twisting and turning, forcing the debtors through stricter economic hoops than any Western country has imposed on itself. And when this produced no repayment, but instead exacerbated local poverty and suffering, our solution was to lend yet more money, thereby creating yet more unpayable debt. We then began forgiving a few hundred million here, writing down a few more there, rescheduling anything that seems on the verge of becoming what it actually is — a bad debt. One international conference has followed another as we have attempted to maintain the illusion of viable loans. When James Brady, the American secretary of the treasury, proposed an integrated plan for dealing with the situation, there was a sigh of relief in sensible quarters and anger in much of the banking community. But the Brady plan didn't even go halfway towards dealing with the problem. It was a quarter step in muffled boots. The publicity surrounding these debt-restructuring plans is such that people tend to imagine the problem is now being dealt with. In fact, the Third World debt did not shrink and indeed continues to grow.

The fear rational structures have of recognizing reality, calling it reality in open, public terms and dealing with it as reality is so deep set that even steps in the right direction must be disguised as something else. Were any citizens to settle down and listen to what our economic spokesmen are actually saying about the Third World debt, they would be astonished. The only possible conclusion they could draw is that our structures and/or our elites are mythomaniacs. That is, they are compulsive mythologizers. But this need to describe reality other than as it is — that is, to lie compulsively — is merely a facet of the rational conviction that man can and will change circumstances to suit his own plan. The more abstract our economies, the easier it is to believe that imaginary financial situations can be endlessly manipulated. There is, however, nothing in history to prove that this is so.

During the sixth century B.C., the people of Athens fell slowly into troubled times. The city was dominated by the Eupatridae, the aristocracy of birth, who controlled the government, owned most of the land and used its power to drive the poorer farmers into debt during bad seasons. The Eupatridae acted as bankers. When the farmers were unable to meet the interest payments on their debts, they were reduced to the state of serfs on what had been their own land. Some were sold into slavery. A serf or a slave was, needless to say, no longer an Athenian citizen. This debt situation spun further and further out of control.

Faced by an impossible division between rich and poor, resulting in economic instability and the risk of revolution, the desperate Athenians called Solon into public office and gave him full powers. Twenty years earlier, he had already served as archon — the annual chief ruler. He was also Athens's leading poet. He used his poetry to set examples and to create political drive. His message was constant: moderation and reform. He was as opposed to revolution as he was to tyranny. This sense of moderation is important to understand in light of what followed. Already the unpayable debts and the growing inequalities had pushed him to write:

Public evil enters the house of each man, the gates of his courtyard cannot keep it out, it leaps over the high wall; let him flee to a corner of his bed chamber, it will certainly find him out.

The atmosphere in which he took power was not so very different from the one we know today. The same manic-depressive mood lay over the society. The Draconian financial/legal policies of the depressive rulers were based on Draco's original legal code. The manic counter-weight revolved around the uncontrolled activities of the rich.

Solon's first act on taking power was to redeem all the forfeited land and to free all the enslaved citizens. This he did by fiat. That is to say, he legislated immediate default. The Athenians called it the "shaking off of burdens," but in practical terms what he had done amounted simply to ripping up the debt papers. In his own words, he had

> uprooted
> The mortgage stones that everywhere were planted
> And freed the fields that were enslaved before.

Having released both the people and the nation from their paper chains, he was able to reestablish the social balance. From there he went on to create a code of fair laws (in place of Draco's) and to lay the foundation for a democratic constitution. Athens immediately began its rise to glory, spewing out ideas, theatre, sculpture and architecture, democratic concepts and concrete riches. All this eventually became the foundation of Roman and indeed of Western civilization. Today we cannot move a step without some conscious or unconscious tribute to the genius of Solon and of Athens — a genius unleashed by defaulting on debts.

Henri IV was probably the greatest king of France. His road to the throne was long and expensive, winding as it did through a civil war which raged across the country. When he was finally upon it in 1600, the country lay in ruins and the government in debt to the amount of 348 million *livres* — a colossal sum for the time. Henri's chief minister was Sully, who to this day is considered one of the finest and most careful of public servants. He first refused to pay the interest on the debt. Then he negotiated the rates down from those originally agreed. He refused to meet the payment schedules. One way and another, he as good as defaulted. Within a decade he and Henri had rebuilt France.

In 1789 Jefferson wrote from Paris to James Madison about the principle of debt, applying common sense to reality. Today names such as Brazil or Peru could be substituted for that of eighteenth-century France.

Suppose that Louis the XIV and XV had contracted debts in the name of the French nation, to the amount of ten thousand milliards, and that the whole had been contracted in Holland. The interest of this sum would be five hundred milliards, which is the whole rent-roll or net proceeds of the territory of France. Must the present generation of men have retired from the territory in which nature produces them, and ceded it to the Dutch creditors? No, they have the same rights over the soil on which they were produced as the preceding generations had. They derive these rights not from them, but from nature. They then, and their soil are, by nature, clear of the debts of their predecessors.[7]

Throughout the nineteenth century, the loans which financed large American capital investment programs, mounted by private consortia, were continually defaulted on. The history of the American railroads is a history of default. More specifically, the history of American capitalism is one of default. This happened in a spectacular manner during the Panics of 1837, 1857, 1873, 1892–93 and 1907. None of this reneging happened in the civilized manner organized by a Solon or a Sully. Rather it involved a panic and a crash, which created massive bankruptcies, which in turn wiped out massive debts. Because of the disordered way in which each ripping up of obligations came, the result was always a short period of widespread depression before the cleansed economy took off again with renewed force. In the Panic of 1892–93 alone, four thousand banks and fourteen thousand commercial enterprises collapsed. In other words, the nonpayment of its debts was central to the construction of the United States. The difference between Henri IV and the American railway crashes is one of method, not content. The great depressions of the last hundred and fifty years can be seen as the default mechanisms of middle-class societies. Depressions free the citizens by making the paper worthless. The method was and is awkward and painful, particularly for the poor, but it destroys the paper chains and permits a new equilibrium to be built out of the pain and disorder of collapse.

One of the most surprising innovations of the late twentieth century has been not only the rationalization of speculation but, beyond that, the attachment of moral value, with vaguely religious origins, to the repayment of debts. This probably has something to do with the insertion of God as an official supporter of capitalism and democracy. There is a tendency to assume that the German thinker Max Weber made sense of all that in the early years of the twentieth century with such books as *The Protestant Ethic and the Spirit of Capitalism*. Weber described the rise of capitalism as both an initiator and then a product of the Reformation. The result was the bourgeois businessman who, "as long as he remained within the bounds of formal correctness, as long as his moral conduct was spotless and the use to which he put his wealth was not objectionable, could follow his pecuniary interests as he would and feel that he was fulfilling his duty in doing so." But Weber also pointed out that the success of capitalism led to an abandonment of Christian values and became "the pursuit of wealth, stripped of its religious and ethical meaning." He described the resulting high capitalism as a mundane passion resembling sport. What's more, he specifically exempted the "usurers, military contractors, traders in offices, tax farmers, large merchants and financial magnates"[8] from his Protestant-capitalist theory.

The simple truth is that the collecting of interest on debts contradicts the entire history of Christian doctrine. It is not a matter of fair versus unfair interest rates. To lend money for profit was and remains a basic venal sin. In this sin of usury it is the lender who is in the wrong. The borrower has weakened in a moment of need and the lender is exploiting his weakness. This theme has reappeared constantly throughout history to justify not only default but often the confiscation of the lender's goods and sometimes his life.

Christianity was by no means alone in its attachment of sin to lending. The moneylender was most definitely not on the fast Buddhist track to nirvana. Muslim lenders, at least in theory, were risking death. And it was clearly laid out in the Torah that Jews should not charge other Jews interest.[9]

European anti-Semitism was often rationalized by the immoral status of lending. But Jewish banking power was largely a self-fulfilling prophesy for Catholic states. In some cases Jews were forbidden any other occupation. By borrowing from individuals unprotected by the official racial or religious organization, it was all the easier for Christians to default. A little religious excitement would do the trick. Or a periodic pogrom. Or simply, in the case of kings, a refusal to pay, leaving the Jewish lender with no legal recourse. By organizing European society so that Christians could borrow from Jews, the Christians avoided contravening Catholic law. And the Jews, by lending to Christians, were not in contravention of their own religious laws. In other words, both sides were avoiding divine retribution by means of a technicality.

Of course, base anti-Semitism was attached to all this and it cannot be ignored. However, the list of unrepaid, jailed, exiled and hanged Catholic and Protestant lenders is so long that the default syndrome must also be looked at quite apart from religious and racial prejudice. The stark fact is that financiers have never had a respectable status in Western society; neither in its Christian nor its capitalist period. Bankers were never integrated as a class of worthy citizens along with burghers, merchants and capitalists. They were never considered to be making a contribution to the social fabric. Interest paid them was always believed to be money for nothing and therefore both immoral and inflationary in the most basic sense. They have always lived on the margins of the law and of society. From time to time individual bankers were swept up into the mainstream and won power and glory. But the moment they were no longer useful, they were flung back into the gutter.

Jacques Coeur, for example, rose through the tax-farm system in Bourges in central France early in the fifteenth century. Speculation made him still richer and he put himself in the service of King Charles VII. Gradually he combined his Europe-wide financial empire with official functions — Minister of Finance, Royal Counselor, diplomatic negotiator. He financed the King's conquest of Normandy in 1450–51. Eventually the King and the great nobles were deeply in debt to him. He was conveniently charged with the murder of the King's mistress, Agnès Sorel and imprisoned although cleared. He managed to escape to Rome.

In 1716 a Scottish monetary theorist was given permission to try out his paper money system in France. The government was heavily in debt and John Law's inflationary method promised to solve its problem. By 1718 he dominated the royal treasury and the financial markets through a spiraling international speculation which was built upon the imaginary development of a colony in Louisiana. The frenzy reached its apogee early in 1720, then collapsed, forcing Law to flee. He died penniless in Venice.

Very little changed over the years. In 1893 Emile Zola published his novel *Money*, in which he illustrated the methods of the financial markets and the moral opprobrium which fell upon the bankers of the day. His central character was a banker-promoter, Monsieur Saccard, who specialized in running up stocks which were issued on the basis of theoretical developments elsewhere — in this case, the Middle East. Because of the facility with which he makes money, he is the star of the financial world. As Zola points out: "what's the point in taking thirty years of your life to earn a miserable million francs, when in an hour, by a simple investment on the Exchange, you can put it in your pocket? . . . You become disgusted by honest savings, you even lose all sense of value."[10] Although Saccard's promotion eventually collapses, ruining hundreds of people, he simply begins again.

People like Zola's banker-promoter were often very rich, but no one really wanted to know them or know too much about them. They were speculators, marginal, nonproductive but always tempting. Our contemporary investment bankers — whom we celebrate as pillars of society and bastions of capitalism — are Monsieur Saccard's successors.

The emergence of the banker and speculator at the top of our list of worthy citizens is perfectly rational. When a well-tailored, responsible-sounding vice president of a deposit bank makes an appearance, this general social promotion of money lenders seems to make sense because he is an executive employee, a technocrat and an expert. The reassuring

sounds he makes cause the observer to forget the historic and indeed
actual implications of treating him with such awe.

It is far easier for the citizen to focus sensibly on those bankers who
are still kept on the margins of society. At the mention of the name
T. Boone Pickens, for example, the citizen can easily say to himself,
"Now this is a speculator." But this speculator is supported by the most
respectable New York investment banks — by precisely those well-
tailored, responsible-sounding bankers who produce awe and respect
wherever they go. And yet Pickens is, if anything, a more doubtful
figure than the Monsieur Saccard of Zola's story. The respectable bankers are embarrassed by his crudeness and yet annoyed to find themselves
mere followers in his financial games. The result is that they have taken
up his methods while being careful to remain clothed in their own
respectable appearance.

The new respectability of bankers has added weight to the argument
that paying debts is a moral obligation. And yet it is hard to forget that
whenever a society has defaulted on a crippling debt, its economy has
been the better for it — sometimes so much so that, as in the Athenian
or American case, the whole fabric of the society was catapulted into
growth and creativity.

The Third World debt crisis is a prime example of economic common
sense in conflict with structural morality. Since the early 1980s, people
as varied as the former New Zealand Conservative Prime Minister
Robert Muldoon and the British Socialist economist Lord Lever have
been calling for what amounts to a general default on the debt.[11] Their
point was that it would be far better to do it fast and to clear away the
paper chains than to go on constructing elaborate mazes of new paper,
which have all the disadvantages of a default and none of the advantages. The new paper syndrome simply drains the energies of both the
debtor and the lender countries for the sole purpose of protecting an
illusion.

No doubt the deed would already be done if our general deposit banks
had not attempted to hide their original error by throwing the money of
their small and medium depositors after that of the artificial oil profits.
Besides, the general rise of debt and deficits has created an unspoken
fear — that ripping up the Third World notes might destroy the sense
of moral obligation other debtors feel towards other debts. The Third
World's paper obligations are, after all, only the leading edge of a Western civilization dependent, as it has never been in the past, on debt
manipulation rather than industrial production for economic survival.
Right behind the nations of Africa and Asia are those of Central Europe,

to say nothing of the Western governments themselves, the corporate world and even the individual citizens, all of them more or less chained up by their paper obligations.

In fact, the sum which is destroying Third World societies isn't really very significant by Western standards. At $1.2 trillion, the entire Third World debt is less than the annual U.S. government budget. The London financial markets, it is worth repeating, do $75 trillion worth of transactions per year. If the paper were ripped up today, without any agreement among the parties, the banks would have a bad year, but they wouldn't go bankrupt. In fact, the smarter banks have already written down some of the amounts they are owed.

One of the things which stops us from doing it, with or without agreement, is the peculiar morality that public and private structures have arbitrarily welded onto the act of debt repayment. Tawney, in *Religion and the Rise of Capitalism*, pointed out that however badly medieval man did behave, he did so in a context which insisted upon his duty to alleviate the poverty of others and in full knowledge that the accumulation of riches was endangering his soul. The rise of the work ethic out of the Reformation changed all this, equating poverty with laziness and wealth with the idea of just rewards for hard work.[12] What followed was the unprecedented mistreatment of a large segment of society by a small segment. This social disorder was itself followed by the slow reintegration of the morality of social responsibility into Western society — that is, into the new nation-states. It was as if general common sense had extracted in extremis the best from the defunct medieval contract and then set about forcing it upon the new rational structures which were rapidly taking form.

Our current attitudes towards debt confirm that we have moved on to yet another stage. Now social morality is subordinated to the efficient functioning of the system. In this stage the social contract is subordinated to the financial contract. The idea of morality has been so deformed that it is used as a simile for the efficient functioning of systems and, therefore, as a simile for the respecting of contracted debts. The result is that we are unable to use our common sense to weigh the poverty and suffering created by the debt against the relatively limited impact on the system of a default.

And so, each time Mexico was considered unofficially bankrupt because of its inability to meet the interest payments on its debt, we felt obliged to offer a series of huge new loans. These were not designed to relaunch the Mexican economy. They were merely papers aimed at financing the Mexicans to pay the interest on the other papers which they already owed us. The advantage to Mexico was nil; to our banks, probably less than nil in the long term, because yet more unpayable debts were being created; to our society, certainly a lot less than nil, because it locked us further into a maze of artificial financial limits. And when a new Venezuelan government came to power in 1989 in an atmosphere of general hemispheric enthusiasm, the first Western act was to force an austerity program upon the President, with the intent of ensuring responsible debtor attitudes. When this program led to rioting and deaths, the reaction was twofold. First, American Secretary of the Treasury Brady proposed his quarter-step restructuring plan. The effect of this slow, negative process was to worsen the agony instead of resolving the problem. The Venezuelans themselves initiated a desperate conversion program. This involved giving ownership in parts of their national patrimony in return for cancelling the paper obligations. The program bears an eerie resemblance to Thomas Jefferson's "unnatural" scenario, in which insolvent debtor Frenchmen would have to abandon their country to lender Dutchmen.

Crises such as these are repeating themselves throughout the Third World. As the realization of the de facto default gradually sinks into the slow, slow minds of the financial and economist communities, a curious response emerges. The Third World, they say, should stop blaming the Western bankers for its problems. The real problem is the absence of capitalism in its countries. The real culprits are therefore governments of the Right and the Left that try to direct their national economies.

Of course, there is some truth in this. Throughout the Third World there is room for the releasing of responsible capitalism. But far more important are responsible agricultural programs which would encourage peasants to leave their hopeless urban slums and return to the land. In any case, responsible capitalism is not what most of the financiers and economists have in mind. Their imaginations are filled with the releasing of pent-up market forces. What they want is an industrial revolution which, like that of the West, must necessarily pass through the ugly, uncontrolled first period in which new industrial infrastructures are matched by social disruption and suffering — in other words, low wages, no job security and no environmental or safety regulations. No one puts it quite that way, but this is assumed in the argument.

However, there is no relationship between the unleashing of capitalism and the unpayable debts. There was a relationship in their creation. The original debts were incurred in an attempt to industrialize the Third World through the unleashing of capital. The World Bank and Robert McNamara led the way, followed enthusiastically by the banking and economist communities. But the attempt failed and the debts then became the barrier to future economic activity, particularly capitalist activity. The debts came to represent the victory of rational paper illusions over real activity. The problem is not the refusal of governments to unleash capitalist forces. The problem is the impossibility of breathing life into these countries so long as the unpayable debts remain in place.

By confusing the continued smooth functioning of systems on the one hand with moral values on the other, our society loses its ability to examine and judge whether each structure has any useful value. The practical effect of our hypnotized state is to leave moneylenders in charge of the economic and social agenda. The Third World debt is only a slice of this problem. The way we look at inflation and corporate financing is determined by the same confusion. Even government debt could be looked at in a different way and perhaps dealt with in a different manner if the nature of debt and of interest payments were examined dispassionately. If the importance of debt is reduced to its use as an abstract enabling device, then paper inflation, interest and repayment can be handled in a practical manner.

The hypnotic effect this uncontrolled paper economy has had can be seen in the world of corporate acquisitions. From the farthest margins of legality, a new kind of acquisitor advanced onto the respectable public stage in the early eighties. These men could be seen as a second generation of Jim Slaters. But when you examine a T. Boone Pickens, an Ivan Boesky, a Paul Bilzerian or a Henry Kravis, you realize that, while their technical skills are more sophisticated than those of the original corporate raiders, their intentions and social standards are actually far cruder. They seem to have evolved backwards, resembling, if anything, characters out of Zola. Their equivalents exist throughout the West, all united by a belief that capitalism is a paper transaction. They could be called the new inflationists. That society has accepted them so naturally seems to confirm our decision to normalize speculation as the leading edge of capitalism. And there can be no doubt that we have accepted. As early as 1983, for example, Pickens's epic run at Gulf Oil was backed by America's largest bank holding company, CitiCorp.[13]

That attempted takeover was played out like a parable of modern economics. On one side there was Gulf, the fifth largest American oil company, widely considered by the business community to be the perfect manager's operation. However, its return on capital for the preceding five years had been the lowest of the fourteen major U.S. oil companies; its dividend growth the slowest. And it had a lamentable record when it came to discovering new American oil. The lethargy of the directionless, self-justifying, risk-fearing managers had finally become so great that they had stumbled into financial trouble and woken themselves up, so to speak, by falling over. As a result they actually began making some personnel changes in order to give the appearance of trying harder.

Given the wide shareholder base and the company's repeated failures, we are led by the theory of free enterprise to expect that a responsible segment of the owners would rise up and replace the entire management with a new team. Instead Pickens arrived on the scene, having bought 13.2 percent of the company's shares, thanks to various forms of leverage. He was not an alternative to bad management. He was in the ball-and-chain business. What attracted him was that poor management had caused the share values to slide to the point where they stood at $40 versus the estimated $114 value of the company's assets. Mr. Pickens made no secret of what he intended to do if successful in getting control. He would sell off the company's oil and gas reserves — its only real assets — for a cash profit. In other words, he would strip the company.

Of course, this intention was dressed up in technocratic verbiage, in order to imply the opposite. The reserves were to be spun off into a "royalty trust." This would siphon off the company's earnings directly to the shareholder. The little shareholder would thus benefit from his investment. With a logic which would have confused Ignatius Loyola himself, it was explained that this removal of potential reinvestment capital would have the effect of increasing investment.

The reality was quite different from these imaginative explanations. Pickens had created a situation in which he couldn't lose. Either he would force his way onto the board of directors and from there force the company to sell off its assets, giving him a cash profit. Or, having already driven up the share prices by making the market expect a sell-off, he would force the management's friends to buy his 13.2 percent of the shares for roughly the same cash profit. In other words, either he destroyed the company or he further indebted it. In both cases, the money generated would be pure inflation.

What followed was a battle between a lethargic group of technocrats trying to save their jobs and a raider who wasn't interested in the industry or the company. His weapons were cash and the manipulation of the free enterprise system. The managers were armed with the full panoply of corporate and legal structures and regulations. The battle surged one way and then the other.

Just as Pickens appeared to be on the edge of victory, the Gulf management discovered a technicality capable of saving their day. If a majority of shareholders voted to move the company to Delaware, local laws would permit management to refuse Pickens a seat on the board. The struggle veered onto new ground — a proxy battle leading up to this vote. Managers are always at an advantage in the manipulation of invisible voters, and they were able to scrape together a narrow majority.

The company decamped to Delaware, though nothing actually moved. It was a paper operation.

In this battle between employed incompetence and irresponsible greed, there was no hint that the shareholders, the financial authorities, the large financial institutions or even the government had any sense that the free enterprise system was running off its rails. They all seemed to find the events quite normal. In fact, Pickens was backed by almost half the shareholders and by many of the most respectable financial institutions. His snatch-and-run technique was analyzed by all the public financial experts — from the *Wall Street Journal* to the *Financial Times* — as if it were a bonafide takeover attempt, rather than a simple stripping operation.

Only a few years before, these people had treated Pickens as a charlatan. What had changed their minds? Before Gulf, he had made a much-criticized snatch-and-run operation on the $4 billion oil company, Cities Service. This takeover bid had also "failed." However, the aim of the operation had been achieved — he and his backers made a large profit. Because the mainstream definition of contemporary capitalism centres on the word *profit*, that made him respectable.

Pickens is only one among hundreds of old-style sharks to have been welcomed into the mainstream of the American marketplace. Paul Bilzerian, for example, worth some $40 million, made a dozen or so runs at banal companies going innocently about their business before he was arrested. Hammermill Paper or Cluett Peabody and Company would look up from their desks and shop floors, startled by an unusual sound. Suddenly, out of the night, a madman would come charging in, a great sword over his head, the blade glinting with menace. Needless to say, they either fainted or paid up. Bilzerian didn't even bother to invent justifications, such as Pickens's insistence that he is standing up for the little shareholder. "If I were writing an article about myself," Bilzerian once said, "I'm not sure I'd write a positive story."[14]

Or consider the takeover of Beatrice, the consumer products giant. This unwieldy corporation was the creation of management men who had produced false growth through buyouts and diversification. In 1987 they, in turn, found themselves under attack from Kohlberg, Kravis, Roberts. Kravis used a tiny slice of equity — $40 million — to manipulate the purchase of Beatrice for $6.2 billion.[15] They then broke up the company and sold off pieces for about $3 billion. The whole process — from the $40 million investment to the $3 billion wrecking profit — took sixteen months. Not a penny of growth was involved. Kravis claimed that he had done the economy a service by taking production units away from administrators and selling them to doers. Of course, there is an element of truth in this; the kind of truth which is produced by logic out of control.

One group of technocrats — the management — had created a monstrous conglomerate, fomenting their sort of inflation in the process. Then a second group of technocrats — the takeover specialists — had come along to break it up, thus fomenting another. The purchasers of the units sold off by Kravis are now labouring under a whole new and unnecessary burden of debt — $6 billion worth.

This debt has been added to the American economy. It frees no one and involves no investment in new production. The Kravis argument is sophistry intended to cover the reality of a purchase based on valueless junk bonds and fast speculation. Quite apart from the buy-sell profit, the professional fees included $10 million to Drexel Burnham Lambert for junk bond financing; $45 million to Kohlberg, Kravis, Roberts for putting the deal together; $33 million to three banks — Kidder Peabody, Lazard and Salomon — for advice. None of these fees relates to economic activity. If our system allowed for prosecution on the basis of the spirit of the law or of the spirit of capitalism in a democracy, Henry Kravis would be a criminal. Instead his exploits are admired. This can only encourage others and make the producers of real goods feel that they are wasting their time.

Specific blame for this situation is laid by many people at the feet of men such as Donald Regan — who converted so much of the American public interest into a broker's dream world of commissions, commissions, commissions. This assignment of responsibility has the advantage of placing the problem in a specific country under a specific government. It is then possible to talk of Reaganism and the uncontrolled and irresponsible eighties. The reality is that the problems were not proper to the United States. Western economies, one after another, went down the same road. None of the highly educated elites — business management, government management or economists in general — rose in protest. As a matter of fact, those experts provided the rational structure and the vocabulary which gave the whole profiteering approach a socially acceptable appearance.

No doubt the result was not exactly as they had imagined it. Perhaps that is why the authorities, along with the general public, were reassured in a childlike way by the revelation that some of these transactions had actually been illegal. The Boesky revelations followed by those on Michael Milken brought forth a collective thrill. In Britain there was a heave of self-righteousness over the Guinness case. The President of the French Republic went on television to muse about the nature of money and joined in the theoretical public soul-searching over the insider trading of his friend Monsieur Pelat.

Abruptly there was a general feeling that things had changed; that a new more responsible era had begun with the new decade. But what was this feeling based upon, apart from wishful thinking and the easy pleasures of a few high-profile fraud cases? There has been virtually no reform of the laws and regulations relating to financial transactions. A great part of what is technically legal in the marketplace remains economically irresponsible. At 25 percent of all corporate bonds rated by Moodys, the junk bond is very much an economic tool of the nineties. When one of the most exciting and profitable new international financial markets is consecrated to swapping Third World debt among banks, it is clear that the investment houses have not rediscovered the virtues of financing new production. Kravis has left the bad publicity of the greedy eighties behind him and now offers a whole new approach to recycling his highly leveraged assets.

An ever-growing number of American banks are either going bankrupt or being artificially maintained in existence by the federal emergency bank insurance system, which is itself effectively bankrupt. Meanwhile, major new financial scandals appear at brief intervals. A series of linked stockbroker insolvency scandals erupted in Milan in 1991. Revelations of wrongdoing at the major American investment bank, Salomon Brothers, brought on legal charges and a major corporate shakeup. Warren Buffett, the "clean" financier brought in to repair the damage immediately volunteered that the temptations and the rules remain as they were in the American system. And the people who "attempt to behave badly . . . seem to be getting away with it." The British Serious Fraud Office began an international investigation of the large leisure company, Brent Walker. Among other problems, one billion pounds had mysteriously disappeared from their accounts in a matter of a few months. The result was 18 months of financial crisis followed by a major restructuring which involved 18 corporations. A series of Swedish finance companies collapsed in 1991, culminating with Gamlestaden. Weak regulations resulting in poorly secured loans were pinpointed by a government study.

The ex–New York mayoral candidate, Rudolph Giuliani, in his days as a U.S. attorney, instigated many of the fraud prosecutions of the late eighties. He believes that the financial community has "the ability to self-correct."[16] This implies that those under prosecution have deviated from general standards. That is incorrect. They are in the mainstream. The worst you could say about them is that they are swimming just ahead of the corporate average. In Britain Lord Roskill's Committee Report on Fraud Trails began as follows: "The public no longer believes that the legal system in England and Wales is capable of bringing the perpetrators of serious frauds expeditiously and effectively to book. . . . The public is right."[17]

In New York, the quantity of insider-trading violations has leapt up since deregulation. Even before Boesky, the SEC had brought seventy-seven enforcement actions between 1982 and 1985. That is the same quantity as between 1934 and 1981. It is not that men are more dishonest. It isn't simply that deregulation has returned us to the atmosphere of pre-1929, although it has. These are both results, not causes. As Robert Lekachman, then professor of economics at the City University of New York, said, "The market is no more crooked than ever, but it's still less honest than Monte Carlo, because there at least you know how much the house takes."[18] In a study of young men caught in the Boesky scandal, Carol Asher found them to be from middle-class backgrounds, with average BA's but a subsequent degree from one of the best business or law schools. They had above-average salaries and were on the promotion track. Their colleagues described them as "motivated," "bright," "conscientious," "determined," "intense," "eager," "entrepreneurial" and "very hard working."[19]

In other words, they neither needed to break the law nor were apparent lawbreaking types. They were simply part of an overall economic atmosphere in which the definition of smart had nothing to do with social standards, because society had canonized structure and the manipulation of it. They were like most people on Wall Street or in the City or the Bourse. Perhaps they had gone one step too far, even by the generally accepted standards.

The product of this atmosphere has been a general concern about the decline in ethics. Business schools have rushed to create courses on ethical behaviour. [20] But when the economic system has been abstracted from reality, there is nothing concrete upon which ethics can be judged. The result is a wild inflation in the definition of integrity. These flatulent ethics mirror our monetary inflation. An ethical decision taken under current business structures has no more reality than a real estate transaction in a Monopoly game.

Beyond these national and multinational manipulations of money and ethics, there is a whole parallel world which is entirely free from the need to manipulate because it isn't subject to any rules or standards. This twilight zone of finance — offshore, tax free, unregulated — is so imaginary that it could be considered pure inflation. And yet, the elements with which this zone plays are drawn from the real economies of nations.

The world of offshore funds, for example, takes us directly into the adventures of Zola's financier, Monsieur Saccard, selling the shares of his imaginary Middle East development on the Paris Bourse, and of the great English crash known as the South Sea Bubble. The South Sea Company was founded in 1711 with the idea of trading in slaves in

Spanish America. In 1720, despite mediocre growth, the company proposed assuming the British national debt. Parliament accepted and the company's shares soared from 128 to 1,000 and then collapsed. Apart from all the people ruined, a subsequent investigation revealed massive public corruption. It was the same year as John Law's fiasco in Paris.

Somehow the imposition of physical distance — of borders and of seas — between the investor and the investment has always given the investor a childlike confidence in his own judgment. Knowing that he cannot know what is really involved seems to make him more optimistic. Australian and Canadian mining stocks were sending shivers of almost erotic delight through the comfortable classes of Europe, such as the English gentry and the Parisian medical profession, as long ago as the mid-nineteenth century. With some spare time and some spare cash these same people still love to search desperately through their atlases for obscure settlements where gold or oil strikes have theoretically been made, while the shares run up and up. Before its spectacular bankruptcy, Dome Petroleum's mysterious Arctic strikes were the stuff of dreams in European country houses.[21]

But this distant wish fulfillment has taken on a whole new abstract charm in the late twentieth century. Offshore funds and the Eurodollar market, just to name two, are previously undiscovered universes. Even an atlas cannot tell you in which country these operations take place; nor a planetarium upon which sphere. They reside solely in the human imagination.

The Quantum Fund, managed by George Soros, is a good example of this new-universe imagination. Soros has even written a book on his methods called *The Alchemy of Finance*. There is no more inflationary idea than the turning of base metal into gold. This he has apparently done with his Fund valued in the billions of dollars. It is based in the Caribbean tax haven of Curaçao, thus escaping most Western disclosure requirements. He is among the most successful offshore money managers and revels in secrecy as he leaps from stocks to commodities to currency, and from country to country. One year gold is to be made in Finland, then perhaps in bananas, then in deutsche marks, then through the desperate middle European governments. The trick to his success seems to be the speed at which he moves and the essential customer confidence in his skills. They must have confidence because they cannot verify his actions. But is it confidence in his ability to choose investments, finance them with a complex undisclosed system of debt and realize profits in an unexplained manner? Or is it confidence in a dream which is the essence of inflationary riches?

Stocks and commodities have been wonderful sources of offshore manipulation, but nothing has been as exciting as currency speculation. During the last fifteen years of floating rates, all of our private financial institutions, plus the "entrepreneurial" money men, like Soros, have been able to devote themselves to playing the numbers. The competing interests of various nations have permitted the currency market speculators to play one economy off against another, thus running the currencies up and down, while leaping nimbly back and forth to make a profit on both sides. Soros fondly remembers making "the killing of a lifetime" in 1985 by getting himself on the right side of the dollar's decline. His Fund made a 122 percent return that year.

Finance ministers, who are meant to devote their time and energy to creating a solid financial base for national administration and growth, are instead forced to spend a good part of their lives outthinking the currency speculators. It is difficult for them to keep a step ahead because the speculators' abstract approach has nothing to do with capitalism, growth or investment. In fact, it doesn't have much to do with any economic factor. Currency speculation is the closest thing to a child's game that a grown man can play for a living. It is also the hardest activity for a single government to stop. And so the game of numerical abstractions goes on, unsettling incomes, production and stability. In the seventeenth century, Soros would have been hanged. Today, he is profiled in the *International Herald Tribune* and lauded for his talents.[22]

So many kinds of inflation have now been invented that we do not have the tools to measure them. We are still far from even admitting to ourselves that they *are* inflation. Instead we stick stubbornly to our classic measurements based upon narrow lists of concrete terms. But why should the measurement of inflation be based upon the sort of items which our society now says are marginal in such a sophisticated world? If we have turned our main drive towards the service industries, of which financial services are a part, then the nature of inflation has changed and we must examine what we really think it is.

For example, the credit card is a private means for printing currency which escapes any central bank control of the money supply. In the second half of the eighties, German credit cards multiplied approximately five times to some five million. From 1976 to 1988, the number of Visas and MasterCards in Britain went from 6.4 million to 24.5 million. For the single year 1987–88, British credit card spending grew 26 percent to some £8 billion. In France, there were 17.7 million cards by the end of 1988. In 1988 spending literally doubled in twelve months to 458 billion francs. The result of this evolution has been a massive growth in personal debt throughout the West. During the 1980s credit card spending multiplied seven times in Canada. In 1988 alone Canadian credit card debt grew from 10 to 12 billion dollars.[23]

Even in areas theoretically measured for inflation, the figures are deceptively low because they are not designed to reflect service economies. The increase in property costs, for example, will probably reflect only sales of new construction or rent increases in specific areas. Thus the 2 to 5 percent inflation figures which Western countries have been announcing do not include a full measurement of the tripling of most urban housing costs over the last ten years.[24]

Most consumer price index food lists are based on an assemblage of staples which hardly represent what people actually eat. The price of these staples moves far slower than the majority of foods, partly because they are staples and are not a growth area in consumption; and partly because the cost of staples is often indirectly controlled by general government programs, precisely because these areas do involve staples. Dairy, grain and egg production are typical of this phenomenon. Or again, barometers such as the GDP deflator measure the price of output produced entirely inside the country. They don't deal with imports. Even the illicit drug trade must be seen as an integral part of this swirling inflation. Estimates put it at some $300 billion a year. Enough, the Japanese deputy Finance Minister says, to "undermine the credibility of the financial system."[25] What, then, is one to think of the equally artificial arms market, three times larger than the drug market, with the added advantage of being both legal and secret? It appears nowhere in our monthly or annual inflation figures.

And what about the very straightforward question of interest rates? We seem to feel that levels are now higher than necessary, although tolerable when compared to those of the late 1970s. But current rates are actually very high when seen in the context of successful earlier economies. From 300 B.C. to A.D. 100, the Greeks charged between 6 and 9 percent. The Romans ranged from 6 to 8 percent between 500 B.C. and A.D. 100. As the Empire went into decline, the rates rose to 12 percent and after A.D. 300, went up still further. In the eighteenth century, British rates were around 6 percent; French 2 to 6 percent. In the nineteenth century, a period of strong growth, British rates were 4 to 5 percent; French, 3 to 6 percent; German, 4 percent; and American, 6 to 8 percent. And throughout most of the twentieth century, until 1973, rates were around 3 to 6 percent.[26]

For twenty years we have sometimes been below 10 percent, but more often above it. In general our rates for preferred customers are double historical averages. And the ability to print private money through credit cards has created a parallel interest rate which has been running between 15 and 22 percent. Third World loans and junk bonds almost all run at these levels. Common sense tells us that interest has nothing to do with real production or growth. It is an added nonproductive cost; that is, inflationary. Most of our economists remain convinced that high interest rates kill inflation, when the exact opposite is true.

Nor do any of our official methods of measurement reflect the explosion in service industry costs. The current economic religion preaches the essential nature of service expansion. On the other hand, those who measure inflation apparently consider much of the sector to be nonessential. Hotel rooms, restaurant costs, up-market clothes and luxury and semiluxury food costs have all been moving up on a regular basis at more than 10 percent a year. With the rise in two-job families, a whole series of services, which are still left out of most measures of inflation, have become necessary to many people, from prepared foods to laundry. These costs have almost all been rising at around 10 percent a year.

The art market explosion — with the participation of everyone from highly conservative pension funds to marginal speculators — is merely a smaller version of the junk bond phenomenon, as is the market in luxury illusions. One hesitates to mention Judy Garland's little red shoes from the *Wizard of Oz* being auctioned off for $165,000 or bottles of virtually dead nineteenth-century wine for tens of thousands or the van Goghs and Picassos sold for tens of millions. But these are part of a surprisingly large area in which objects of no value, or of a value which bears no reasonable relationship to the sums paid, have entered into the economy. Western civilization used to limit itself to one South Sea Bubble at a time. And when it burst we would settle down for a while, severely chastened. We now run thousands of bubbles concurrently and the inflationary cycle is so strong that when one pops, the paper money immediately inflates a new one.

The inflationary speculation of the financial sectors nevertheless dwarfs all the others. What is the difference between a Weimar banknote, a junk bond and a deposit bank preferred share floated to cover nonrecuperable loans? Nothing except appearance. All three are pure inflation. One indication of how far things have gone is the desire of business to see government intervene each time the situation gets out of hand. The willingness of governments to do so, despite a supposed devotion to market forces, shows that they realize just how dangerous the current system is. The irony of deregulation is that the more freedom business is given, the more dependent it becomes upon government as the saviour of last resort.

Financial marketplaces have never been capable of self-limitation except through catastrophe. One of our accomplishments was to regulate most of these explosions out of existence. Financial deregulation has reintroduced them. A well-trained city dog kept within set parameters can look after itself for a limited period in limited circumstances. An untrained dog shows more initiative but will inexplicably lick or bite children, run away, defecate on Persian rugs, demand endless scraps from the table and get run over. We have unleashed increasingly un-trained dogs in highly urban settings. The regulatory authorities are therefore forced to stay on permanent emergency footing in order to avoid catastrophes, while these animals wander freely across intersections and through houses.

Is it surprising, then, that inflation has dogged us for almost twenty years? Even the official sort, inaccurate and deceptively low, is constantly bubbling up, driven not by wages or wheat but by the multitude of inflationary elements we refuse to count. It is perfectly appropriate that the United Kingdom, the country that has most successfully reduced its national debt while sustaining for more than a decade a combination of extreme classic anti-inflationary policies with extreme deregulation, should today be the country least able to shake rising prices. The ability of governments in general to control their money supply as a means of controlling inflation is now virtually irrelevant. The money supply is as much in the hands of all these new indirect money printers as it is in those of any government mint. If the governments print, they are simply adding to the inflationary activities of private business. If, in an attempt to "strangle" inflation, they don't print, then they won't be able to pay their own bills.

The current situation, in which governments stand as the saviours of last resort — having abandoned many of their intermediate powers of guidance — actually breeds irresponsibility. And while government intervention late in the day prevents general calamities, it also maintains the fiction that the system is healthy. If the West were serious about inflation, it would have installed rigorous regulations to discourage the myriad new forms of speculation and accompanied this by interest rates of 5 percent or less. The effect would have been to discourage financial bubbles in the developed economies, while encouraging real investment in production, which translates into real growth.

Solon, in the very act of laying the foundations for Western civilization, identified the danger areas — "Public evil enters the house of each man." In a world of self-interest and self-delusion, he kept a measured view and a measured hand, treating debts with the same evenness that he treated justice. One of his aims was to demonstrate how each man might control the speculator within himself. Even-handed, careful, antirevolutionary, viewing all individual action as part of a whole, he was perhaps the first complete man of reason; an early version of Pascal Paoli or Thomas Jefferson. And to demonstrate the dangers of believing in one's own rational skills, he completed his task and then left Athens for ten years. In this way he avoided hero worship and the resulting temptation to hold on to power in the name of glory.

His simple precepts are useful when thinking about government debt, corporate debt, futures, junk bonds, money markets, offshore funds, the speculation in capital goods, interest rates, imaginary services and in general the increasing conversion of Western monetary structures into a type of financing which creates profits but not real wealth. These are abstractions upon abstractions upon the great abstraction itself — money. In Solon's clear and integral view, public evil has installed itself in every man's house. And it is comforting us with an inflation of self-delusion.

PART III

Surviving in Fantasy Land

The Individual in the World of Reason

Passivity is proper to domesticated animals.
It can be imperfectly imposed on humans by
threatening violence. It may be fully achieved
by an all-encompassing system which defines
existence.

"Consider your origins," Dante wrote.
"You were not made to live as brutes
But to follow virtue and knowledge."

Knowledge is neither information and expertise
nor an instruction manual. It is an investigation
of the human as a whole being in search of
doubt; an unlimited desire to understand.

The domesticated animal is unable to welcome
doubt, let alone assume it. Human strengths —
language, imagery, memory, character — are
therefore converted into burdens. These tools,
which promise virtue and knowledge, become
a fearful prison.

18

Images of Immortality

OR

THE VICTORY OF IDOLATRY

There are differences between the late-twentieth-century Western television viewer and the paleolithic inhabitant of Lascaux in the Dordogne. The former sits in a half darkened room, holding a remote control device. The latter was equipped with some sort of rudimentary torch while he stared at his cave drawings. These and other differences relate more to social organization than to the sensibility with which they see the images. If anything, the Lascaux viewers had a clearer, more conscious and more consciously integrated concept of what they were seeing than we do today. Not that the seventeen-thousand-year-old paintings of bulls, horses, deer, buffalo and men are simple or primitive. In fact, they are the products of accomplished craftsmen.

We cannot know precisely what the cave dwellers saw in their images or expected from what they saw. Our guesses are based largely on comparisons with isolated civilizations which maintained until recently a theoretically similar way of life dependent on hunting, gathering and stone implements. What we do know is that the phenomenon of the man-made image has always revolved around three interdependent forces — conscious or unconscious fear, which in turn is counterbalanced by some combination of magic and ritual. This is not particular to the West. And it is as true today as it was in the paleolithic era.

The list of fears which drive civilizations is endless. Fear of the unknown world outside the cave, outside the settlement, outside the country or world. Fear of being unable to survive because of hunger or enemies. Fear not of death, but of ceasing to exist — that is, fear that life is followed by a void.

The cave dwellers seem to have conceived their animal images as magic traps which might give them control over their prey, in the same way that Christians would thousands of years later conceive many images of Christ or the Virgin Mary as miraculous. If successfully communicated with, these statues and paintings seemed to give — indeed, in many places still seem to give — the supplicant some control over disease, poverty or death. Just as the ritual used in order to communicate with these images was key to Christian miracles, so the same must have been true for the Stone Age hunters who prepared to seek out their prey.

With time the relationship between fear, magic and ritual has changed. None of our fears was conquered as civilizations became first sedentary and then urban. But doubt and anxiety over the most obscure of fears — that of an external void — grew in importance. And while magic has gradually retreated back into our unconscious — which does not mean it has disappeared — ritual has grown to take its place. In this civilization, in which God is dead, there is no clear sense that the high levels of endemic social doubt or angst or fear are an inheritance of the lost Christian promise of eternal life. Nor is there a recognition that the vast structural web of our society and the endlessly predictable images of television and film are successors to religious ritual.

We have been confused in part by the rapid and revolutionary change in our official view of why images are created. Until the simultaneous beginnings of the Age of Reason and the Renaissance, this craft played a social, political and above all metaphysical or religious role. From the fifteenth century on — in the wake of the final technical breakthroughs which made it possible to paint a perfect image — the idea of art began quietly to separate itself from craft. By the eighteenth century the divorce was more or less formal, although there have been regular attempts to reunite the two. In the early nineteenth century, museums were created for the sole purpose of aesthetic enjoyment. The idea that art is its own reason for existence has now been so firmly established that few people would question it.

And yet it is improbable that the image, which has played a fundamentally religious or magical role for more than fifteen thousand years, could simply be freed of itself in the space of a few centuries to become a mere object of art. This is where the Western experience parts company with that of other civilizations. For the last two thousand years, Christianity has presented and fought for a monotheistic, anti-pagan, anti-idolatry dogma. Those who view Christianity from the outside have always been surprised by the aggressiveness of these claims, because the reality of our worship has always contradicted them.

The monotheistic argument, for example, was immediately negated by the division of God into a trinity. This idea of three in one or one in three was so complex that Christians themselves were constantly fighting over its meaning. The Virgin Mary was then given, to all intents and purposes, the status of a divinity, as were an increasing number of saints. In the opinion of everyone except the Christians, they had re-constituted a polytheistic religion.

The concept of the pagan was even more confusing. It indicated someone who did not worship "the true God." And yet the Muslims — who worshipped the same God as the Christians, used the same texts and adopted most of the same moral codes — were pagans, as were dozens of other sects who adopted minor doctrinal differences.

Finally, no civilization anywhere in the world has been so resolutely idolatrous as the Christian. The need to create and worship images designed in our own likeness is a constant in the history of the West. It is a virtually unaltered constant from the Greeks through the Romans to ourselves, with only marginal variations in the panoply of major and minor divinities. In spite of Christianity's Judaic origins, the Church managed so successfully to circumvent the Old Testament interdiction on image worship that only the images of other religions have been defined as idols. Six hundred years after Christ, Islam was provoked in large part by uncontrolled Christian idolatry. The Church responded by categorizing them as infidels — nonbelievers.

Some religious and social orders have avoided dependence on the image or even its use. From the West's point of view, Judaism is the prime example. Islam has been almost as successful, as have Shintoism, Confucianism and, for a long period of time, Buddhism. During the nineteenth century, Western colonial administrators were constantly coming across groups in Africa and Asia who avoided creating human likenesses and were highly suspicious of images. There was the stan-dard cliché about the native who was afraid to be photographed because he feared the photographer would capture his soul. The reaction of a Lascaux resident would no doubt have been the same.

This attitude actually makes very good sense. The native in question is an animist and does not believe in worshipping idols, but believes that everything, animate and inanimate, is alive. He is therefore an inte-grated part of the entire universe. He is unlikely to be frightened that death is a black hole leading to a void. Death simply returns him to the universe.

The particularity of Westerners has been their obsession with pre-senting gods, through images, not as devils or animals or abstractions, but as human beings. The painter's role has always stemmed from that basic metaphysical and social need. The gods live forever and we are created in their image. These repeated identifying mortal imitations do not simply reflect our dreams of immortality. The image, in idolatry as in animism, is a magic trap. In the West the painter's and sculptor's job has been to design the perfect trap for human immortality. As craftsmen their efforts were aimed for thousands of years at technical improvements. In the years around 1500, Raphael, Michelangelo and Leonardo made the final breakthroughs to the accurate representation of reality. There was, however, no accompanying metaphysical change. No heightened sense of magical power.

The Age of Reason has since witnessed a long and confused decline of the image as a source of general expectation; a decline accelerated by the inventions of the photograph and the motion picture, television and video. As expectations have dropped, confusion has grown. First, the confusion of a civilization without beliefs. Second, confusion over the significance of astonishingly perfected new images. As their technical power grows, the confusion they provoke also breeds distrust.

The result has been a growing chasm between the image and society. The craftsmen-artists have retreated onto a plane of their own. In their place as social participants we have two groups of image makers: the modern equivalent of the official artists, who receive approval from the museum experts; and the new ritualists, who produce electronic imitations of reality. What television and film have brought us is images realer than reality and yet, images separated from belief in a society which for the first time in almost two millennia does not believe.

The end of the Age of Reason is therefore a time in which the image is popularly felt to be false and yet also a time of idolatry, pure and simple. As electronic images have gradually slipped into a comfortable, highly structured and conservative formalism, our rational methods have been powerless to capitalize on what are, in fact, astonishing changes. A civilization of structure flees doubt. And so quite naturally, rational man has debased modern imagery into the lower ritual forms of a pagan religion.

Almost all civilizations have had an obsession with the possible relationship between immortality and the image, but most of them have limited the hypnotic effect of idolatrous self-reflection. The Christians took the full power of the divine image from earlier religions — those of the Greeks and the Romans — and integrated that pagan divinity into their own.[1] It is actually quite hard to blame the early Church fathers for doing this. They were devout men but socially and culturally unsophisticated, almost universally from lower- or, at most, middle-class backgrounds. Abruptly they found themselves thrust into the centre of affairs thanks to Constantine's Christian-inspired conquering of Rome in 312. The civilization they were expected to run was dominated by the cultured, ancient and sophisticated Roman aristocracy. Within a few years these simple priests were responsible for the theological anxieties of all the citizens of the greatest empire ever known. With so much power to be exercised, their honest simplicity, which had attracted Constantine in the first place, became a handicap.

How were they to capture the imaginations of such an enormous population, one which was devoted to a bizarre combination of rational Greek philosophy and baroque idolatry? The easy answer was to integrate both of these elements into Christianity. This solution took on the aspect of official policy when Damasus became Pope in 366. Rather than continue a failing effort to convert the Roman pagans to pure Christianity, he set about making the Church Roman. He brought in the ruling classes of the city, along with their Athenian philosophical background and their attachment to highly sophisticated imagery as a central characteristic of religion.

Only a half century later this approach was integrated into the intellectual mainstream of Christianity through the writings of Saint Augustine, who was then Bishop of Hippo in North Africa. On the subject of Christian art versus idolatry, he laid out a very fine difference between the two: "God is not the soul of all things but the maker of all souls."[2] As so often when complex distinctions are applied to simple moral questions, the effect was simply to provide justification for de facto idol worship. This approach was doubly and permanently locked in place by the arrival on the papal throne in 590 of the great Pope Gregory, who popularized and universalized the message of the Church through a simplification of the Christian message and the embrace of magic and miracles. This he did not by rejecting the sophisticated rational idolatry of the preceding two centuries but by building on its profound assumptions.

Finally, the devotion to magic and mysticism came to fruition in the middle of the seventh century when Eastern Christians, fleeing the Muslim explosion and its condemnation of idolatry, settled in Rome and took over the Church. Between 678 and 741, eleven of thirteen popes were Greek or Syrian. Refugees from the East. They brought their obsession with miraculous images and relics. Cartloads of saintly thigh bones and pieces of the Holy Cross arrived in Rome. It wasn't long before images decorated the inside of each church and became the central focus for the parishioners' anxieties. If there was any doubt over the Western approach, it was removed during the Iconoclastic struggle in the Eastern Empire from 726 to 843. Constantinople's attempts to eradicate the rampant use of images were constantly undermined by the Pope and the Church in Rome.[3]

This focus remained in place for a thousand years — until, that is, Christianity began to weaken beneath the pressure of a revived rationality. As the churches collapsed, the image was freed from their grasp.

But it was not freed from divinity. We killed God and replaced him with ourselves. In the process man himself inherited the full, divine power of the idolatrous Christian image.

The curious thing about the pagan heritage was its artificiality. Man had first to make the image, then believe in its powers. By comparison, the animistic native — who believes that there is life in everything and that he is an integrated part of that everything — holds an intellectually sound position. He is part of a concrete nirvana on earth. The Buddha added a wrinkle to this with his idea of a nonconcrete nirvana. Man, he said, would have difficulty leaving this earth, but if he succeeded it would be an eternal escape.

It's worth noting, in passing, the miraculous ability of Greek culture to stir in any civilization the deep, unconscious anxiety tied to fears of mortality, then pander to it with promises tied to idolatry. The Buddhists managed for centuries without statues of the Buddha. It was the passage of Alexander the Great through India that first tempted them down the ambiguous path of Buddha images — which are theoretically respected, not worshipped — in somewhat the same manner that statues of the Virgin were theoretically respected, not worshipped.

As for Mohammed, he brought a clear description of Paradise to the Koran:

> But for those that fear the majesty of their Lord
> there are two gardens planted with shady trees. Each
> is watered by a flowering spring. Each bears every kind
> of fruit in pairs. . . .
> They shall recline on couches lined with thick brocade
> and within their reach will hang the fruits of both
> gardens.
> They shall dwell with bashful virgins whom neither man
> nor jinnee will have touched before.
> Virgins as fair as corals and rubies. . . .
> And beside these there shall be two other gardens of
> darkest green. . . .
> Each planted with fruit trees, the palm and the
> pomegranate. . . .
> Which of your Lord's blessings would you deny?[4]

It isn't surprising that this clarity should have been accompanied by a general ban on images. God had passed on the full details of heaven through his Prophet. There was no room for humans to fiddle with his description.

Strangely enough, Christ had spoken to roughly the same sort of simple desert people some seven centuries earlier and done so almost entirely in parables. But at no time did he offer a hint of what heaven was like. He said a great deal about who would get there and how, but offered not a single word on the place itself. The faithful Christian who looked for hints found instead:

"Blessed are they which are persecuted for righteousness' sake: for theirs is the kingdom of heaven."
Or, "Whosoever therefore shall humble himself as this little child, the same is the greatest in the kingdom of heaven."
Or, "A rich man shall hardly enter into the kingdom of heaven."[5]

If Mohammed passed on a detailed description of heaven, while Christ didn't describe it at all, this can only have been intentional on both their parts. And yet we are talking about the same God, the same prophets and the same heaven. Any explanation for the divergence would be mere speculation. If we take Christ at his word, he seemed to be suggesting a heaven not unlike the Buddhist nirvana. But the Christian success in Europe was unrelated to this suggestion. Instead, the very vagueness of Christ's heaven left the West free to continue its pagan devotion to the melding of the mystic with the concrete.

It was through the image that this Western imagination had always revealed, and would continue to reveal, itself. Very little from the pre-Christian past needed to be changed. Even Christ's parables fitted neatly onto the foundations of Greek mythology and philosophy. The abstract simplicity of Christianity allowed its rapid assimilation into the image madness of Roman Europe. Christ's vague heaven was an apparently revolutionary new contribution. It formalized the nascent idea of immortality. But it was Roman Europe which converted that idea into a concrete image. And it was Europe — Greek, Roman and barbarian — which instilled magic into the immortal dream. Miraculous statues and paintings and objects were a gift from pagan Europe to Christ's lean religion. And from the bleeding statues of Christ and the healing images of the Virgin Mary, it was only one more step to the civil image as unconscious guarantor of human immortality.

The power of the pagan image — whether Christian or post-Christian — has little to do with believing and a great deal to do with the myths and archetypes of Western man. A fifth-generation urban atheist is today as much a prisoner of these expectations as a medieval peasant once was. If anything has changed at all, it is that with the Renaissance, the Reformation and the rise of reason, man finally learned how to produce not just images but the perfect images that he had always dreamed would carry great power. Faced by the impotence of this progress, he succumbed to confusion and to greater inner fear.

Long before that the Christian Church had set about developing Christ's heaven into a doctrinal, concrete reality. The Church paid painters to illustrate the official heaven. These craftsmen were initiated into a complex protocol which indicated precisely where everyone would sit or stand for eternity. They formalized the idea that Christians would lie on clouds. The Church set the record straight over the exact manner in which decomposed bodies would be recomposed to perfection on Judgment Day. Again, they commissioned thousands of painters to illustrate this.

As the old Roman aristocracy gradually disappeared, the role of illustration became more, not less, essential for both magical and practical reasons. Almost everyone, including the new and diverse, indeed fractured ruling classes, was illiterate. And while the priesthood could not read out to the public reassuring illustrative holy texts on heaven, as the Muslims could, they were able to bring the people into churches where eternity was demonstrated on all the walls.

When, in the Late Middle Ages, the Church began to use its definition of heaven as a corporate tool for fundraising via such things as indulgences, it damaged the credibility of its eternity. Subsequently, under attack for corruption, it began to slide away from its earlier commitment to a concrete description of heaven. The people in turn began to believe less. At first, with the Reformation, there was a move to create new Christian churches. But increasingly the Westerners reverted to a more properly pagan use of the image — a use which predates the conversion of Rome to Christ's cause. Today we are surrounded by millions of perfect, live images. The role they play is almost identical to that of the ancient idol: reassuring reflections whichever way man turns. What we have kept from the Christian period is the feeling that the painter and the image maker have the power to deliver a sense of eternity.

The slow, difficult technical progress towards the perfect capture of the image came in a disordered manner over several thousand years, with advances being made here and there or simultaneously in several places at once. The most intense scenes of this struggle took place in northern Italy from the thirteenth to the sixteenth century. In Siena, for example, each step of this creative explosion remains exposed on walls around the city like clues in an unfolding mystery.

Until the early 1500s, painters were obsessed with technical progress. They had always struggled with problems, such as perspective, in the unconscious expectation that if the perfect image could be created, something magical would happen. And so, even before rational man got hold of the idea of progress, it had been hopelessly confused between a technical process and a moral improvement.

This does not mean that the need to progress was always felt to be a simile for the quest, as in the quest for the Holy Grail. Rather, it was properly understood as an administrative process — an advance or a progress over controlled territory. Monarchs, for example, made a royal progress across their own kingdoms. Good might come of it, or bad, or nothing, depending on the king in question and on what he wanted at that time. The contradiction between what we now expect from progress and what we actually get is no worse than that suffered by the medieval gentry and peasantry as they dealt with the passage of a royal party. For that matter, our confusion is not greater than that of the medieval painter. All the time he was desperately seeking technical improvements, there was proof in his own work that his most powerful paintings were not necessarily the most perfect and, therefore, not the most advanced.

Duccio, for example, both progressed and was lost in the confusion created by progress. Between 1308 and 1318 he worked on the enormous front and rear of the *Maestà*, the altarpiece of the Cathedral of Siena. The *Maestà* consisted of countless small scenes on individual panels. Duccio completed each one before progressing to the next. In the process he made a series of technical discoveries unknown to any other painter. As he worked on a given panel, he was therefore obliged to notice that a few panels earlier he had made serious errors. These had not been errors at the time. It was only his own progress which made them into errors.

Doors, for example, had been placed incorrectly so that figures could not come through them. A few panels further on in the series, there is another door. This time the figures inside the room have been painted so that they could have come through the entrance.

All over the city of Siena, painters were grouped in the studios of different masters, learning from them, then going out on their own to add to what they had learned. One by one the technical secrets of the image were revealed. The final step of this progress can be glimpsed in the Piccolomini Library. There in 1505 Pinturicchio, began illustrating on the walls the glorious career of the Piccolomini family's pope, Pius II.

Pinturicchio had digested the technical lessons of those who came before him and had moved on to the point where the enormous mass of his images was so integrated by colour and detail and by the relation of the animate to the inanimate that the viewer could feel the details about to be swallowed up by the whole. Clearly the master was on the edge of creating the miraculous perfect image.

In the ninth mural, down on the lower left-hand side, Pinturicchio painted himself. And beside him is his student Raphael, who a few years later would solve the last technical mysteries of the image. He would make the breakthrough and take the flat, painted image as far as it could go.

Others will say it was Michelangelo or Leonardo who made the actual breakthrough. No doubt they did. So much time had passed, so much progress had been made, so many craftsmen had been thinking and working, that the last step could not help but be a mass effort. The question of perspective was solved and the perfect image created between 1405 and 1515, after thousands of years of craftsmen striving towards that moment.

Perhaps Raphael was most often given the credit because he was the most unidimensional figure of the three. He was the painter's painter — not a randy egomaniac, like Michelangelo, as famous for his life as for his painting; nor a scientist, strategist, inventor of weapons and machinery, like da Vinci, who also painted. Raphael resembled what the painter was to become in the Age of Reason: the invisible technocrat of images. With hindsight, he appears to have been the father of the "artist"; that is, of the man who painted to create beauty. But Raphael did not simply perfect the image. His greatest work was the frescoes in the Stanza della Segnatura, rooms in the papal apartments of Julius II. Their theme was the justification of the power of the Church through neo-Platonic philosophy. Julius was surrounded by thinkers who had updated this original betrayal of Christian dogma so that it still made sense — that is, could be justified — in the context of the humanist explosion of the Renaissance. But it was Raphael who had to turn this old internal contradiction into a unified image. The two most important frescoes were *The Dispute* and *The School of Athens*. It is not the detail of these scenes which makes them revolutionary, but that the thousands of years of search for the perfect image should have culminated in paintings which indisputably affirmed the marriage between the traditions of pagan idolatry and Christian immortality. With a vast flourish Raphael completed the pagan-Greco-Roman-Christian integration and closed the circle begun by Pope Damasus in the fourth century.

In any case, in twenty intensive years three men completed the miracle of the image. Paint became reality. The image became real, as real as paint would ever make it. The relationship between the viewed and the viewer was finally perfected. The viewer was integrated into the viewed. He came to the framed image in search of his eternal prison. He came as a willing virgin to Count Dracula, expecting the image to drink from him and to live forever.

This was a limited expectation in comparison to the Church's promise of Paradise. A bit of paint on a wall was, after all, a modest view of eternity, as modest as sleeping in a coffin during the day and coming out only at night. The image, like Dracula, was also the final reflection, unable to give out life, just as the count was invisible in a mirror.

So the viewer approached the perfect image in great expectation. He found a technical miracle. He found genius. He found emotion and beauty which seduced him in a way he had never been seduced before. But he did not find what he'd come for. This living reflection did not do to him what he had expected. Of course, like most metaphysical expectations, this one belonged in the realm of unformed yearning. There is never a blueprint for desire, and yet the perfecting of the image was one of the great disappointments of Western history.

For some twenty years after Raphael's discovery, craftsmen celebrated their triumph with an outpouring of genius.[6] But gradually the subconscious failure beneath this conscious success began to slow them and to darken their perspective. The viewer has only to watch Titian's opulence and sensuous joy gradually turn tragic. With no room left for progress, the image turned and dodged and circled back and buried itself like an animal chained to its own impossible promise, searching for some way to get beyond the mortality of the real.

The conscious mind does not look at a picture with all these thoughts to the fore. It looks instead for beauty, shock value or the reflection of something it knows. Human obsessions are not tied to practicality or proof or even to public argument. The impossibility tied to them is an attraction. And yet these obsessions almost always have practical secondary effects. They produce organizations, beliefs, objects and ways of behaviour. Society is in part the result of real needs such as military, economic and social. But it is at least equally the result of unobtainable obsessions.

So, while we may come to the image in search of Dracula, we find instead reflections of our reality — social conventions, for example, such as power relationships, established beliefs and patriotic emotions — or we may find images which reflect our expectations for justice or material comfort, or the picture may reinforce our prejudices. The painter reflects what society hopes he will reflect. If he inspires refusal or anxiety, then he is responding to something he senses in the social body.

When Romanticism began to flourish in the late eighteenth century and the ego began to grow until it dominated public life, people abruptly found Raphael far too modest a fellow to have been the father of the perfect image. So they tended to fall into line with the description of the technical breakthroughs which had been provided by Vasari in his *Lives of the Painters*, written shortly after the actual events. In other words, they transferred the credit to an irresponsible, antisocial individualist, Michelangelo — a veritable caricature of the artist in the twentieth century. If we were ever able to create a reasonable, open society, Leonardo would no doubt cease appearing to us as an overwhelming, almost forbidding, giant and the credit would be switched to him.

Though Michelangelo came to represent the artistic type of the future, he was very much part of a society in which the craftsman was an integrated element. The painter was a craftsman and a gild member. In Bruges the Flemish primitives of the fifteenth century belonged to the same craft gild as the harness-makers, glaziers and mirror makers. In Siena their carefully dated signatures were followed by such declarations as Thadeu Bartholi's "*Feait fieri agelella.*" "Made it proud." Their signature did not relate to ego, the way the modern painter's does. To the contrary, they signed as gild members, confirming their role as craftsmen and taking public responsibility for their contribution to the community. The image, after all, had a public function. It was accessible to every element in society. You needed neither money, rank nor literacy to look at a painting or a fresco.

As the painters inched closer to the perfect image, so society became ever more committed to having itself reflected. The donors of religious pictures had begun by having themselves painted discreetly into corners, often in little medallions. Gradually, they gathered the courage to insist on being integrated into the central structure of the image. Then abruptly, there they were, as large as everyone else in sculpture as well as painting. In St. Stephen's Cathedral in Vienna the pillars are decorated with life-size statues of saints and donors mixed together. It became increasingly common in paintings to find donors kneeling before Christ at the end of a row which began with the Apostles or the local saint. It wasn't long before the Apostles were gone and the image was devoted to Christ, Mary and the local lord. Or the town council. Or the king.

In paintings of the Apocalypse — that is, of Judgment Day — the local burghers or lords were portrayed safely on the side of the saved as Christ cast others down. The point of this was not to impress the local serfs or whatever with the remarkable connections of their masters. Nor was it to prove publicly the holiness of these people. The point was that Christ was immortal and they were beside him. The image was like a negative of life, waiting to be developed by death.

With ever-greater frequency, the painter dressed the Saviour, his family and the saints in the latest fashion of the town where the painting would hang. This was not the result of ignorance over how they might actually have dressed. There were accurate, well-known images of biblical dress — statues, mosaics and bas-reliefs. Nor was this an attempt to popularize Christianity. Nor to modernize it. The religion was perfectly accessible. Its message may have been distorted in various ways by churches; but the message of suffering on earth, of resurrection and of eternal life was perfectly clear.

If the Gabriel in Benedetto Bonfigli of Siena's *Annunciation* looked like a well-to-do dandy, his hair cut in the latest style with blond curls, then the idea was that a contemporary image could be as eternal as an angel. The three wise men in Pietro Perugino's painting of the *Offering* all resemble princes out of Botticelli's *Spring*. The reason is the same. And in Modena, there is an extraordinary transposition of ordinary citizens into biblical saints. This large group of life-size terra cotta figures by Guido Mazzoni and coloured by Bianchi Ferrari in 1509 is in the Church of San Giovanni. The figures are taking Christ off the cross. Each of them looks as if he has just walked off the streets of medieval Modena in order to give a hand with the body.

This dissolving of human actuality into the biblical promise of immortality goes beyond clothes and hair styles. In the Duomo in Orvieto, Fra Angelico and Signorelli painted an Apocalypse in which some of the figures step out of a fashion parade. But more important are the dead saved by the Resurrection and coming out of the ground. They are skeletons, becoming flesh as they rise, and chatting with each other. The painters' attention to corporal detail is libidinous. Needless to say, it is also highly secular. These rising dead are the people. This is an illustration of precisely how they will be reconstituted. The citizens of Orvieto could come to the Duomo and count the muscles, measure the breasts, check the eye colour. This is an image of themselves, resurrected in every detail for eternity. The point is made even more insistently in the Basilica of Santa Maria degli Angeli in Assisi, where the Maestro dell'Osservanza painted a *Martyrdom of Saint Bartholomew* in the early 1400s. On the left and right of the poor suffering saint, standing naked and bloodied, there is a line of Assisi burghers wearing fur-trimmed hats with long, wide tassels hanging down and flung elegantly over the opposite shoulder. These men are extremely well dressed for the fifteenth century. But they are inappropriately dressed for a martyrdom. The effect is that of a grotesque receiving line at a fashionable wedding. It is as if the sacred subject no longer matters, except by association. What matters is that the citizen is there, integrated with immortal people in an almost animate reflection.

All of this manoeuvring for the best spot on the wall abruptly lost its purpose once Raphael had created the perfect image and nothing magical had happened. The painters reacted by moving into overstatement. Even Titian's joyous outburst was an attempt to kick Raphael's reality into life through elaboration. More clouds, more people, more events. He was trying to take heaven by storm.

When this failed, many painters turned from the grandiose to the intimate and took a run at eroticism. Cranach the Elder's *Venus and Love* is a cool version of this move, with the lady, neither mythological nor goddesslike, standing naked except for a fashionable hat. The look in her eyes, coyly turned to the viewer, is clearly a sexual invitation aimed at any man willing to join her on the wall. This centrefold approach, to which *Playboy* owes a great deal, was so popular that towards the middle of the sixteenth century Cranach painted almost identical versions for admirers all over Europe. Bronzino's allegory *Venus, Cupid, Time and Folly* dropped any attempt at coolness. It is one of the most erotic scenes ever painted. The skin of the lady — its soft whiteness — is palpable. A thin, postpubescent Cupid has slipped an arm around and beneath one breast to take the other between his fingers while his lips brush hers. She has the essence of female nakedness, her body turned to the viewer, her thighs about to part, exuding a mixture of placidity and expectant energy. It is difficult to understand why the British authorities periodically set about seizing pornographic films, when something as explicit as this is hanging in the National Gallery.

From the body, painters turned back to society, but in a vague, uninvolved way. They began to redescribe the scenes they knew, this time with the full skills of perspective. They carried society with them in flights of fantasy, such as those of Fragonard, who attempted to make life better than it could ever have been with impossibly romantic colours in an edgeless, overflowing nature filled with opulent women and joyous couples. Or they used new gimmicks—like de la Tour's concentrated light and shadow — in an attempt to trick the image into animation. The English tried a naturalism which seemed to extinguish any barrier between the subject and the portrait. Gainsborough put *Mr. and Mrs. Andrews* under a tree with their fields behind. There they are as they really were — self-assured, boring and pompous. They are almost alive enough to drone on about their distant blood ties to a duke or their good shooting. Other painters began to fall into producing unapologetic propaganda. They leaped onto the new Hero bandwagon of the late eighteenth century and helped to pump up revolutionaries and generals.

The greatest Hero, Napoleon, had David, the greatest artistic Hero worshipper, at his side, along with a flock of other painters — Gros, Regnault and two of David's students, Ingres and Gérard. They were often called romantics because of a style which married the highly personal and the grandiose. When applied to Napoleon and his Empire, this revealed itself as a combination of base sentiment and idolatry. Their supportive relationship with those in power created the illusion that painters were still the community members they had always been — that David, in particular, was a modern version of the old burgher, gild member, craftsman of the Middle Ages. Not at all. He was a servant of power, not a constituent part. He made his own attitude towards Napoleon perfectly clear: "In the past altars would have been erected in the honour of such a man."[7] His paintings *were* those altars. In spite of his revolutionary politics, David developed no existence in his own right.

He developed instead into a worshipper. This demonstration of the painter as servant solidified the whole Beaux Arts approach, which locked "art" into a narrow technical process. This was in turn limited to a narrow choice of classical subjects. In return the painter might gain false respectability — not as a useful craftsman but as a delicate creator of beauty who needed protection from the real world.

There are many explanations for the gradual separation of the crafts-man from the artist and the accompanying loss by the painter of his role as a member of society. And yet it is hard to avoid noticing that the first signs of this division came on the heels of the perfection of the image. Throughout the Renaissance, the painter continued to think of himself as a craftsman. But the sense of his potential mystical powers, which society felt were dependent on his skills as a craftsman, began to evap-orate the moment Raphael broke the technical barrier. The painter suffered from an unspoken social rejection which provoked his slow decline into artistry.

The art historian R. G. Collingwood placed the beginning of the distinction between fine arts and useful arts in the eighteenth century.[8] Put another way, by the eighteenth century society was beginning con-sciously to doubt that art was useful.

The craftsman-become-artist reacted to his forced marginality the way social outcasts often do. He stood on his dignity. As he was not wanted, he became grand. As his social standing dropped, he became nonconformist, individualistic, irresponsible, moody, "bohemian." It was then that he switched his allegiance from Raphael to Michelangelo, an antisocial figure somewhat in the modern mold. But these new 'art-ists' were gradually slipping towards a definition of beauty which, in social terms, meant irrelevance. They were no longer called upon to reflect society, and so automatically, nor could they criticize or propose alternatives with any weight. As art withdrew from society, so it came to be a form of simple refusal or of anarchy.

And as the image lost its purpose, along with the potential for magic, so the artist began to slip away from it. Delacroix was among the first. In 1832 he escaped both physically and mentally from the Beaux Arts dictatorship by going to North Africa. He came back with rushing, disturbed, impressionistic images, particularly of horses in battle. In 1849 he began two enormous frescoes in St. Sulpice in Paris. Much of what is to come later in the century can be seen there in his Jacob wrestling with the Angel Gabriel. The light might have been by Monet. On the ground there is a hat van Gogh could have painted. The Im-pressionist slide quickly turned into a stampede, and early in the twen-tieth century the image had been rushed out of sight by abstraction. Forty years later, the perfected image reappeared in a series of new schools — realist, hyperrealist, natural-realist, magic-realist — as the artists made a strange attempt to create images more animate than those of the photographers and filmmakers of the twentieth century. The effect was surprising, but still the magic eluded them.

This flight from the image reflected a series of astonishing events. In 1839 the first photograph appeared. Delacroix was in full career. Gustave Moreau hadn't begun. Manet was seven. Cézanne was born with the photograph, Monet a year later. In 1845 the photographic plate was replaced by photographic film. Three years later Gauguin was born; van Gogh, eight years later; Toulouse-Lautrec not until 1864.

All of them came into a world awash with new, perfect images. From the technical point of view, almost any photograph was better than a Raphael or a Leonardo. And almost any idiot could produce one. In spite of this revolutionary change, the image itself still had not come alive. Instead it seemed to have retreated, yet again, just beyond the photographer's grasp. As the painters turned to abstraction, in denial of the image, or to surrealism, as if to mock it through the grotesque, it seemed as if, in their despair, they regretted even having believed that technical perfection was the secret to bringing it alive. And yet, there had always been painters whose power lay more in their mystical strengths than in their craftsmanship. And despite the twentieth century's romanticization of the creative process, these mystics were as far away from the modern idea of the artist as they were from the medieval profession of craftsman.

Even among the finest craftsmen, there was often an element of animist genius which overwhelmed and sometimes eliminated their skills. Duccio worked hard to eliminate his errors, but many remained. We can see these errors, but we can also see that the paintings are masterpieces — far greater, far more touching, more alive, than thousands of paintings by other very good painters who did not make any serious errors simply because they worked a few years later.

This is self-evident. But if the perfecting of the image was not essential to the quality or power of paintings, then the general and innate values of structure and expertise were actually in doubt even before the seventeenth and eighteenth centuries, when progress and reason blossomed as absolute, inviolable truths.

What is at stake in the case of painting is not simply whether a lack of perfection may succeed where perfection fails. If that were the case, it would be enough to note the superiority of Duccio, Carpaccio, and Pinturicchio's flawed work over the technically perfect canvases of, say, Veronese, Fragonard and Rubens. Nor is the point that genius — as it is now understood — may be more important than skill. In fact, genius as it appears in the mystical strain of painting is a refutation of genius as the modern West understands it.

This phenomenon isn't limited to a few oddball painters. Elements of mysticism can actually be found in even the most brilliant purveyors of skill and genius. What, for example, of Duccio and his doorway error in one of the *Maestà* panels? He solved that problem a few scenes later. With his new knowledge and improved skills, he could have gone back and corrected the doorway perspective. He didn't. Did he consciously decide that this incorrect image accomplished something he couldn't technically justify?

Look, for example, at the angels he painted throughout the *Maestà* panels. They seem familiar. Timeless. They are curiously old-fashioned in comparison to the rest, and yet they are also curiously modern. A fire shoots out from them, like a jet engine propelling their bodies forward. This could be seen as a silly, literal interpretation of how angels fly. Yet somehow it isn't silly. They seem almost to be out of another painting, if not out of another world. They reappear in the work of other painters in an equally strange manner. Perhaps it isn't so surprising to find precisely the same mystical, angelic energy a century later in the same city in the paintings of Soma di Pietra.

In Pinturicchio's frescoes illustrating the life of Pope Pius II, there is one scene in which all the cardinals are lined up before the Pope. They are crowned by the mass of their own hats, which sit like a gathered flock of snowy owls about to rush into flight straight at the viewer. They dance together on the men's heads, taking on peculiar angles and appearing to be three times bigger than the men who wear them. They are technically imperfect and yet the essence of the cardinals has been captured in their hats.

Until Raphael, the mystic strand was usually buried in the work of mainstream painters. Whenever it emerged it did so within images commissioned by the Church or the nobility or the town council or one of the gilds. Mysticism often appeared through the gap which remained between genius and incomplete skill. With Raphael that gap was filled. Over the next four centuries, the painters slipped away from society and the mystics gradually became a separable but minor strand in the background. The fact that they were irrational, antisocial in the conventional sense and therefore dangerous accentuated this marginality. Nevertheless, their paintings and objects continued to find a way to the public and to provoke reactions which society found disturbing.

Mysticism was seen as the last refuge of superstition. This was confirmed for rational man by the existence of relatively crude religious images which continued to exert an irrational influence over people. Often this was indeed little more than superstition, based, for example, on some theoretically miraculous event in the past. Here and there, however, there are images which have only to be looked at with an open mind to confirm that they do contain an active irrational force.

The crucifix which "spoke" to Saint Francis, telling him to "go repair my House which is falling into ruin" is a perfect example of this phenomenon. It is not the most beautiful of images. An unknown craftsman painted it around 1000 A.D. and the crucifix then hung in San Damiano, a small rural church. By the time Francis saw it, the church was run down, almost a ruin. He misunderstood the message, thinking it meant he was to rebuild the little stone building and not the Church of Rome.

There is still a force within this image. Of course, the religious circus which now engulfs Assisi gets in the way. No one will ever be able to look at the crucifix in the way Francis did — alone, in a run-down, rural church — that is to say, alone and at peace. Nevertheless, the force of the image can still be felt.

The changed position of the mystic strain after the breakthroughs of the Renaissance can be seen as early as the pictures of the German Grünewald. He used the new technical progress where it suited him and ignored it where it didn't. His *Resurrection* of 1515 for the Isenheim Altar seems to be one with painters of the past such as Uccello, but also with William Blake in the eighteenth century and Dali in ours. Christ rises in a spray of colours which resemble an unreal burst of electricity. The soldiers guarding his body tumble away in an inexplicable manner as he rises. A century later El Greco was fully engaged in deforming reality, for example, in *The Opening of the Fifth Seal*. The colours are seemingly uncontrolled. The bodies of the resurrected float in an imprecise and deformed manner. The picture is more an emotion than an image.

The purely mystical strain of painting spread as the power of reason prospered. In fact, Heinrich Füssli and William Blake worked while the waves of reason rolled high around them. In 1782, the year before Blake published his first book, *Poetical Sketches*, Füssli's painting *The Nightmare* caused a sensation across Europe. He portrayed a woman dressed, but collapsed erotically over the end of her bed, bent backwards in an impossible manner. A small shadowy monster is crouched on her breasts. A maddened horse peers in through dark curtains. Füssli's appeal to the nonrational made an enormous impact. William Blake's strange, disassociated figures conveyed that same sense of the uncontrollable. His angels, for example, appear awkward, naive, technically stilted, unbelievable. In a sense they are all of those things. They are very like the angels of Duccio and Soma di Pietra. They fly in the face of five centuries of technical progress. And yet they are almost alive. By a series of gestures, which we cannot identify intellectually as genius, Blake has almost brought it off. He has almost captured the image.

Goya was then in the full flood of his career. In his case, it seemed as if the Spanish royal family, who paid for so much of his work, didn't understand the forces he was releasing. His painting of the May 3, 1808, massacre of Spaniards by the occupying French forces was no doubt applauded by the nationalists, including the Spanish nobility. But those aren't simply Spanish peasants being executed. There is something wild and unearthly about them. They seem to be shouting at their executioners. It is an eternal cry of refusal — as much a cry of the Spanish Civil War, almost a century and a half later, as of any peasant uprising at any time in any country. It is more a mystical image of the human condition than the reflection of a single event.

Compare its rough, crazed feel to the perfect, lacquered pictures David was producing at the same time; works of skill and intelligence. They are moving, but moving in a singular way. They are remarkable political tools which assemble the viewer's emotions with a purpose in mind. Goya, meanwhile, was painting explosions. The viewer has only to look in order to feel a ripping apart within himself. Perhaps that is a description of the eternal — a formless, perpetual explosion.

Füssli, Blake and Goya were succeeded by men like Gustave Moreau, who began before the Impressionists and outlasted a number of them. The unnatural staginess of the mystical is there in his *Oedipus and the Sphinx* or in *Prometheus*, along with aggressive, inexplicable colours, which might have been by Grünewald. The subjects are classical but the feeling is barbaric. Mysticism was moving back towards centre stage, in part because the other painted images were collapsing under the weight of the photo and of the cinematograph, which arrived in 1896. But it was also propelled by a presentiment of ending — of death, in fact — which grew as the twentieth century began.

A turn-of-the-century group of painters in Vienna led the way in this dark prophesy. Every stroke of Egon Schiele's brush seemed to animate death, again like a Grünewald crucifixion. His 1913 portrait of *Heinrich Benesch and his Son*, for example, is a prophesy of the slaughter which will begin a year later and last for five years. The self-assured father's powerful hand is on the shoulder of his veallike son, leading him to death. The father thinks he sees but does not. The son sees, but feigns blindness. All of this is conveyed irrationally through the limitations of a theoretically conventional family portrait.

Once World War I had begun, an even deeper pessimism took hold. All the Blakean signs returned in the person of Magritte, who had the polished but telltale, awkward, almost gauche style which kept saying to the viewer — "Look what you've done! You fool! What will you do now?"

So much of what was happening to the image in the last thirty years of the nineteenth century and the first forty of this century was apparently new. Certainly these changes seemed to carry the optimism of newness and of great excitement. Invention was felt everywhere. Barriers were being crossed. Not only was the image finding new forms at the time, but those pictures still have the shock of newness when seen today.

And yet all the revelry of that period was less a celebration than a shattering. The Cubists, the Surrealists, the Expressionists, the frenzies of obscure lines, the slabs of raw paint or raw steel, the lumps of stone — what was it all, except a dance of death? Brilliant, overwhelming and evocative of man's discomfort with his own rational civilization. But the dance of what death? On one level, of the image. More important, it was the death of a certain expectation from the image. In terms of art history, each of these schools deserves great attention. In terms of civilization's relationship to art, they were part of a single demonstration that the image was no longer a pillar of society, as it had been in the Middle Ages; nor a constructive critic, as it had often been during the romantic rise of the ego; nor even a servant of power. The new image neither reflected nor criticized the rational, structured world that man was creating. Instead it exploded in turmoil, off on a separate plane, as if it had no place in this new world. For the first time in history, the image was refusing society.

As for the painters, it wasn't surprising that they had been jumping so high for so many years. Cubism was pulled out of a hat in 1907, eleven years after the cinematograph was invented and just as it was gathering steam. Surrealism was officially founded in 1924, three years after Charlie Chaplin's first feature, *The Kid*, revolutionized the moving image. Dali joined the Surrealists in Paris in 1929, and Picasso began his distorted nudes in 1930, both hard on the heels of Mickey Mouse's first appearance in 1928. In that year, Mr. Mouse's film, *Steamboat Bill*, made him the most famous cartoon character in the world. He — a mere image — rapidly became the most famous individual in the world. Period. According to polls, he still is. *Guernica* and the great Surrealist Exhibit in London came in 1936, the same year that television was introduced, also in London. This was six years after talking movies, five after both Donald Duck and Chaplin's masterpiece, *City Lights*, and one year after the first comic book. Snow White made her appearance in 1937 and in 1939 the first American television broadcast took place in New York.

Run as fast as the most remarkable painters of the twentieth century could, the image was constantly outstripping them. They were hindered in this race by their own gradual withdrawal into specialization on an "artistic" plane, separate from society. This act of self-categorization also brought them into the range of a new breed of art historians. As the painters ran desperately to catch up with technology, they were being pecked all over by flocks of curators, art critics, dealers and technocratic art historians, all of whom were multiplying with such rapidity that they have now become a prevalent species.

The earlier generations of art patrons and historians had often been obsessive people, desiring to touch, to feel, to hold, to stare, to attempt some mystical relationships with the image. The specialists tend now to be pariahs of art, trained and graded by the specific criteria essential to contemporary education and, if anything, frightened by the potential power of the image. Their relationship to creativity is rarely one of love or obsession. They are salaried to it. They seem more comfortable with analysis, as if a dozen or so photographs of a masterpiece, taken under perfectly controlled conditions in neutral isolation, would best satisfy them. They could then destroy the original and limit the public's understanding to their own photo-based analysis of the measurable elements. You cannot be an expert in genius or in the mystical. Genius and the mystical therefore frighten them.

And since these experts controlled the major galleries, it was not long before they were able to apply their standards to the Western definition of what was art. New generations of painters — cut off from the reverberations which their predecessors had felt, thanks to their integration into society — instead found that the only sustained reverberations came from the experts. In the ensuing confusion, many painters began producing directly for the museums — that is, for the technocrats of art.

That is now the dominant theme in Western painting. On the surface, it appears as if painters have turned away from egocentrism in order to reintegrate themselves into a world of public walls and public images, not unlike the gild craftsmen of the Middle Ages. But the resemblance is only superficial. Carpaccio, for example, painted public walls under contract from the constituted authorities. Those authorities were social, political and religious. They were not artistic authorities. His illustrations addressed that society's emotional and mythological needs, not his own and not those of image experts. Curiously enough, his integration into the social fabric, and the integration of his images into the public dream, gave him the personal freedom to release his full genius and mystical powers. The post-Raphael painter worked from the increasingly awkward position of the outsider but found his energy in the reverberations which he felt as a recently freed social critic. The second half of the twentieth century has seen painters gradually lose contact with that source of energy, as their link to society has been reduced largely to emanations from a socially irrelevant group of art experts. This constitutes a modern reestablishment of the Beaux Arts dictatorship.

Only the painters capable of dragging the mystical power out of themselves seem able to work productively within the breakdown of our society. They move untouched among the forces released by that breakdown. They seem unaffected by the fashions and standards dictated by the art experts. Today's confusion doesn't bother them. Instead of being disconcerted by our loss of centre, they seek ways of describing it. The secret, they have found, is to harness the violent, rampant forces released by that loss of centre. Theirs is an animist approach.

It is hardly surprising that Blake's images and words are more popular today than they have ever been. Nor is it surprising that the Englishman, Francis Bacon, was among the dominant modern painters. He said that he admired the craft of the Egyptians, "who were attempting to defeat death." He denied that he was trying to do the same, because he didn't believe in an afterworld. But that isn't the point. So much has moved in this century from the unconscious to the conscious. Almost alone, death and dreams of eternity have disappeared into the deep unconscious. "I am a realist," Bacon said. "I try to trap realism."[9]

No one has trapped the violence and self-destruction of our time so completely as he has. Those truncated, deformed bodies are as eternally alive in his canvases as the reconstituted dead are in Fra Angelico's *Resurrection*. In fact, their shapes, disproportionate mouths and eyes and heads broken up like jigsaw puzzles, express the reality of how many people see or feel themselves. In a society as determined as ours to replace social and moral cohesion with unaffective structure and technical progress, these violent, magic images of mortality are among the few available reminders of reality.

For most painters, however, the century has brought an ever-growing pessimism over the power of their craft. If they were disillusioned in the early sixteenth century by the limited effects of the perfect painted image, they were doubly wounded by the arrival of the photograph. Photographers have gone on developing their technology and the public has expectantly followed.

The moving picture had given them greater hope that the power of the image lay in that direction, as did sound, then colour. From 1948 on there was large-scale television broadcasting in the United States. "I Love Lucy" began in 1951. The first CinemaScope movie was shown in 1953. The film chosen for this experiment with a wide screen was appropriately *The Robe*, a story tied to Christ's immortality. Walt Disney established his regular television slot in 1954. The last few years have contributed halls with wraparound sound and most recently, computer-generated images of people and objects which appear to be real but can take any form, melt, divide and do endless things which in reality are impossible.

No doubt the commercial holograph is next. Films will then have the density of stage plays without losing the reality of the screen and of location shooting. In 1981 the director John Waters produced a "scratch and sniff" film called *Polyester*. Viewers carried a numbered card into the hall. From time to time a number would flash on the screen; the public would scratch that section of the card; and the hall would fill with an appropriate smell ranging from dirty running shoes to roses. The only technically producible element missing will soon be modulated viewer emotions. Huxley described in *Brave New World* in 1932, just after the arrival of the talking movie, how this could be done with carefully modulated intoxicating spray. The result was "An All-Super-Singing, Synthetic-Talking, Coloured, Stereoscopic Feely. With Synchronized Scent-Organ Accompaniment."[10] There is no reason to think that we won't go that far.

We seem to be nearing the end of the process in which the rough, pictorial lines first scratched and painted on cave walls have come to fruition. The final result is already known. We have captured the perfect image and it is dead. Worse still, it is not exactly dead. We have created images beyond reality. Images not alive and yet more real than those which are alive with flesh and blood. We can so easily create these hyperrealist animations that masses of them are permanently available. And being perfect imitations, they are truly believable. Even the creator of a TV movie or a rock video can capture a form more perfect than any accomplished by the genius of Raphael.

On the other hand, heavy restrictions are placed on these creators by the nature of the electronic image. Marshall McLuhan talked of television having to adapt to process rather than to packaged product.[11] Decades later there is still no wide understanding of just how accurate this statement was. Both the public and the critics are increasingly fixated on how terrible the product is and convinced that corporations or financial interests or individuals are the guilty parties.

But television has revealed itself to be a more interesting control device than most people imagine. It isn't particularly effective at exercising control over the viewer. It is too obvious as a propaganda or manipulation device. On the other hand, the electronic system — the machinery — does exercise a powerful control over those who are employed to make it work. The product needs of a broadcast channel or network are both unlimited in quantity and very limited in scope and variety. Those whose profession it is to produce cannot avoid altering their view of life in order to satisfy this insatiable but extremely specific hunger.

Beyond the lens, there is the fullness of the real world — disorderly, unexpected, filled with endless layers of expectation, understanding and misunderstanding. Its very size and uncontrollability has always made the viewer seek a focused interpretation in the creative image. Until the invention of the photograph, the painter's freeze-frame of reality sought both eternity and universality. Even a still life of a pear sought to capture something enormous through the specific. The viewer seeks that same eternal universality in the unfrozen frames of television.

The essential nature of television, however, relates not to the viewer's need for a reflective moment but to the system's to fill airtime. The sheer quantity of material required and the speed with which it must be created, eliminates the possibility of searching for true reflections. The system rewards productivity, not creativity. It does not forbid or eliminate creativity. Not rewarding it is enough to minimize such efforts.

When television began only a few decades ago, its employees set out with both optimism and some idealism. The movie director Norman Jewison talks about the creative talent originally gathered together in television. Through the 1950s these people worked with originality and skill to convert reality into interesting reflections. Live theatre was experimented with in new ways thanks to television's power to deliver instantaneous images to the public. The situation comedies had a fresh, sometimes crazed feeling, as radio and vaudeville traditions were adapted to the little screen. Newsmen like Edward R. Murrow seemed to have found an opening for presenting real events in a way that was partially freed from the old propaganda methods.

The conventional view is that, as the system grew, so did the potential profits. Packagers were brought in to produce the pablum we know today. And advertisers came to understand their power to discourage any political edge. Both these factors are very real. But scenarios which require arch villains are rarely accurate. Was there really a handful of individuals strong enough to wrestle down a phenomenon like television with the intention of castrating it? If so, why did a similar decline take place on publicly owned channels around the world — even in countries where there was no competition from privately owned networks? British television, public and private, looks good when compared to the American wasteland. But this is only an effect of comparison.

The ability of machinery to suck up programming at the speed of sound, then spew it out into an endlessly expandable void can only have helped exhaust the creative. But it was the way the programs sank into nowhere which discouraged the talented. Their images were not sitting in bookstores and libraries or hanging in galleries, museums or on the walls of houses or being projected in cinemas. They were simply beamed to an invisible audience, past whose eyes they might or might not flash, depending upon an arbitrary turning of dials or pushing of remote-control buttons. Surveys repeatedly show that for every person who watches a program, two or three other viewers glance at bits of it.

It is often said of the television-generation viewers — which now includes most people in the West under forty — that they have never been alone. That idea is typical of a civilization which denigrates accurate memory. Until the middle of the nineteenth century people were never alone. Families were grouped together in poverty or in riches. Even servants were integrated into the lives of their employers. Sex, for the poor, was a relatively public event, since families rarely had more than one or two rooms. In some societies couples were formally allotted moments alone for copulation. The basket weavers of Valabrego, a few miles from Avignon, lived in large, single-roomed group dwellings. They had a formal rotation system which left each couple alone for thirty minutes on Saturday. This was still going on in the 1940s. In the countryside of Europe and the poorer areas of North America, privacy became a dominant theme only after World War II.

To say that the television generation has never been alone, simply because it is in the constant presence of an animation machine, is certainly to treat the image as reality. It could more accurately be argued that people have never been so alone or so silent. For the first time in history, people are not gathering in families or larger groups to sing or play instruments or games. Television has removed the need for self-entertainment.

Nevertheless, it is the needs of the television structure, and not of the viewing public, which have forced the production emphasis from content to process. As the system has evolved, the creators have come to understand so perfectly the needs of the machinery that they have learned to avoid the temptations of reality. This is as true of news as it is of drama and sitcom.

A real event is not necessarily a television event. First, it must be visual and the camera must be there. This puts things such as trade disputes at a disadvantage and favours those *faits divers* which leave traces — plane disasters or oil spills, for example. It also favours personalized political stories over policy questions. The case of an unfaithful or drunken politician can be dealt with like drama. A politician who favours arms spending or arms control is boring on television. Judge Clarence Thomas's confirmation hearings were of little interest on television so long as they dealt with his legal opinions. Concrete debate over his sexual habits made perfect viewing. The rise of CNN (Cable News Network) canonizes the television view of reality as concrete, action-packed visuals. Wars make good television, providing the action is accessible and prolonged. The Middle East, for example, is an ideal setting for television war. Cameras can be permanently on the spot, and a fixed scenario of weekly car bombs, riots and shelling ensures that the television structure will have ongoing material.

This perpetual motion machine works effortlessly if the flood of images illustrates situations the viewer already understands. That is one of the explanations for the system's concentration on two or three wars when there are forty or so going on around the world. The others are eliminated because they are less accessible on a long-term basis. Or because the action is less predictable and regular. Or because the issue involved does not fit easily into the West's over-explained, childlike scenarios of Left versus Right or black versus white. Or because the need for endless images makes television structures unwilling to undertake the endless verbal explanations and nonvisual updates which would be required for the other thirty-seven wars to be regularly presented.

McLuhan pointed out that we are "poised between two ages — one of detribalization and one of retribalization."[12] One of the main forces on the side of retribalization is television and, indeed, the motion picture. Television has revealed itself to be the most provincial of the communication systems. The frenetic need for moving images includes the need that these images speak a language understood by the viewer.

Thus the American president speaking English is virtually absent from French and German television, as are the French president and the German chancellor speaking their languages on American television. Audiences most often see foreign heads of state walking or getting in and out of planes. They are reduced to minor dramatic actions because television requires motion. A journalist will explain in a voice-over why these inoffensive, irrelevant images are being shown.

The whole world does appear ready to devour an unlimited quantity of third-rate, dubbed U.S. sitcoms. But these do nothing to increase international understanding. Programs like "Dynasty" simply reinforced local, single-syllable ideas of the United States. "Dallas" increased international understanding of Americans to the same extent that the Charlie Chan movies contributed to an understanding of the Chinese, or Maurice Chevalier to an understanding of the French.

As for public affairs programming — often compared to newspaper or magazine or even radio journalism — it is rarely identified correctly as a descendant of the painted image. Television reporting is only related to traditional journalism because of their shared subject matter. The confusion is increased by the enormous efforts which are made by a small number of people, usually on publicly owned networks, to force the image into an uncomfortable and temporary marriage with information and interpretation. This requires a constant struggle to slow the images and to force unexpected questions onto a system which prefers expected answers. This is quality television and wherever it is found, it makes an impact. But the moment the people involved in production release their hold on the machinery, it rushes ahead without any memory of the real journalistic experience. Inevitably, they are forced to let go.

Journalism attempts to deal with a wild, undisciplined world. Television seeks the smooth image which provides continuity and reassurance. The more successfully a public affairs program introduces this roughness, the greater the pressure to discontinue the program or change its personnel. This is often put down to the specificity of advertisers on private television or to government financing of public television. But why, then, is it that print journalism prospers happily when the news is rough and disturbing? After all, the same sort of people own newspapers and television networks. The same companies advertise in both places.

The answer is that television and film have nothing to do with the history of language and everything to do with images and what we now call the history of art. The evening news on television does not belong in the same area of understanding as the daily newspaper or political history or political philosophy. Rather, the newscaster — whether it be a local talking head recounting three-alarm fires or Walter Cronkite, Richard Dimbleby, Christine Ochrent or Dan Rather — belongs in the same column as Saint Francis performing miracles through the images painted of him by Giotto and Bonaparte crossing the Alps in glory thanks to David's brush. As always with the image, it is the technical structure which dominates, unless the individual genius of the creator can rise above what is rationally possible. On television, it is impossible. There production is a group activity in which the creators themselves are a minority.

When the viewer settles down to watch the news or a sitcom, he or she is watching an image which arrives by unbroken line from Giotto and Duccio and Raphael, with all the expectations and promises that stretch back to the figures on the walls of the caves. And so Indiana Jones and "Dallas" 's J.R. — one of the few international figures of television — both must carry a little responsibility for the failure of the perfected image to deliver immortality.

～

For the first time in history, there is a sense that images are false, that the image is a social enemy and not a beneficial prolongation of man and of his society. The image in search of reflected immortality was formerly part of society. Now we sense that the flood of animated images is not made up of reflections but rather of manipulative tools promoting a false view of ourselves. Of course, we have always suffered from a relatively false view of ourselves and the creators of images have always played a role in this. But since the completion of technical progress during the Renaissance, the image has been slipping away from its magical role towards one of propaganda.

This sense that we are viewing false images is tied in part to our disappointed expectations when confronted by the millions of perfect animations which now fill the world. We have become a society confused by its own contradictions. On the one hand, we no longer believe in the religion which was central to almost two thousand years of our development. On the other hand, we have retained an official moral code which is the product of those Judeo-Christian beliefs. We try to attribute that code to a secular and rational truth. And yet the structure created by reason is tearing that same moral code apart. The new, smooth images of television and video are driven by their own logic and yet are a central part of the structure which is challenging the moral code.

In fact, Western society is without belief for the first time since the decline of active devotion in the official religion of the Roman Empire. Our situation is unprecedented. There is no example in the last two thousand years of any civilization surviving without belief for even fifty years. There is nothing in our traditions or our mythology to deal with it. Even in our animist archetypes there is no comfort to be found, because Western man has never been so divorced from all sense of himself as an integral part of the physical earth. The abstract structures which dominate Western civilization reject anything which hints at either the physical or the ethereal.

As an immediate result we have been overcome by frenetic, narrowly focused beliefs. The strangest social and economic fashions have taken on the full aura of religious belief for short periods of time. We have devoted ourselves to economic growth at all costs. And to uncontrolled consumption. We have given ourselves over to abstract ideas such as capitalism or socialism, market economies or nationalizations. Things as lowly as an energy source — nuclear — have been vested with seemingly divine properties. We have fallen into drug epidemics and sexual anarchy. There has been a deification of personal ambition.

We know that this century is the most violent ever achieved by man. We tend to blame this on the invention of new weapons of mass destruction. But weapons are inanimate objects. And men have often shown themselves capable of remarkable self-control, even when weapons are at hand and victory is sure. In this century we have opted not to control ourselves. Inexplicable violence is almost always the sign of deep fears being released and there can be no deeper fear than that of mortality unchained. With the disappearance of faith and the evaporation of all magic from the image, man's fear of mortality has been freed to roam in a manner not seen for two millennia.

The signs of this fear are everywhere. An unprecedented worship of the past has won over the elites of every developed country. This has nothing to do with memory. No one is now looking at the past in order to compare it with the present or to seek guidance for the future. Our obsession with the past is unrelated to our actions in the present.

Thus, the growing number of work-free hours, a sign of the West's economic evolution, are in good part devoted to mooning over the ruins, images and architecture of the past; this in a century theoretically turned towards the new. Fewer people than ever seek to integrate the new into their personal lives, except when it comes to practicalities like the kitchen, the bathroom and the car, or to electronic entertainment. What we really want are old houses, old furniture, old paintings, old silver. The superficial details of modern middle- and upper-middle-class single-family dwellings are largely pastiches of nineteenth- and eighteenth-century decoration, inside and out. A hundred or two hundred years ago men sought to buy and to visit the new. If they visited the old, it was not in search of some vague communication with the past, but in search of inspiration for the new. Jefferson marvelled at the proportions of the Roman Maison Carrée in Nîmes and went on to use its principles in the construction of the University of Virginia. On the same trip he examined agricultural methodology and scientific research. The modern visitor to the Maison Carrée is obsessed by its mythological past and its proximity to a quaint Provençal market.

Almost no one travels today to see the future. Even the most basic package tour, repeated endlessly, is devoted to an unending worship of the past. The churches and palaces of Europe have not been so full in a century — filled not by worshippers and nobles but by people who move through these great rooms in a vague, unfocused manner as if they expected to come across the trace of some lost promise.

This endless wandering is treated as the superficial product of a prosperous society. But why then do we millions move so insistently around the globe as if it were a Disneyland linked by jet engines instead of toy trains? What is it we see in the palaces and churches and ruins? Certainly not any reality, either historic or actual. Most of us move through these disaffected caverns knowing little or nothing about the societies which used them or about the contemporary societies which rose out of them. The buses shuttling millions of responsible adults from Versailles to the Eiffel Tower to the Louvre pass, as if blindfolded, through a highly modern city which contains one of the most successful state-of-the-art communications systems and the most powerful administrative elite in the world. We are driven on by a confusion as well as an angst which has become one of the trademarks of the twentieth century. This would have amazed the average citizen of fifteenth-century Siena.

One of the things we seek in the relics of the past is a manifestation of certainty. We apparently find hints of that reassurance which progress has lost us in the great monuments and in the optimistic images of the past.

At the same time, we remain confused over whether our fear of modern images is over- or understated. Certainly these images are out of control. Certainly they are more enemy than friend, as they trivialize beliefs and deify the superficial, while pushing forward public figures who are more image than content. But already our common sense has permitted us to reduce our historic receptivity to images in general. Rather than take television as truth, we have codified its content into iconographic forms. We can denigrate the situation comedies, police series and family sagas that make up the dramatic arm of television, just as we can categorize the news, analysis and current affairs programs that make up this information arm, as formula programming. But these are reassuring and misleading reactions.

The most accurate context in which to place television programming is that of general religious ritual. Unlike court etiquette or specific types of drama, religious ritual is designed to satisfy everyone. Like "Leave it to Beaver" or any other sitcom, religions at their very heart are classless. Like television, they eschew surprise, particularly creative surprise. Instead they flourish on the repetition of known formulas. People are drawn to television as they are to religions by the knowledge that they will find there what they already know. Reassurance is consistency and consistency is repetition.

Television — both drama and public affairs — consists largely of stylized popular mythology in which there are certain obligatory characters who must say and do certain things in a particular order. After watching the first minute of any television drama, most viewers could lay out the scenario that will follow, including the conclusion. Given the first line of banter in most scenes, a regular viewer could probably rhyme off the next three or four lines. Nothing can be more formal, stylized and dogmatic than a third-rate situation comedy or a television news report on famine in Africa. There is more flexibility in a Catholic mass or in classic Chinese opera.

On television fixed, standard, facial expressions are required during and after the standard ritualistic events. The manner in which the cameras shoot is part of established practice. These were first limited by the studio size and by the cost of equipment, but now the three basic camera shots, developed for sitcoms, have become part of television's stylized repetition. The camerawork in turn dictates when and where the characters may move within each scene. As in the endless church paintings of the Resurrection or the Day of Judgment or Heaven, everyone has a designated role and place. The approved gestures and sounds of television have now so impregnated our society that even when a neophyte politician or an untrained member of the public is interviewed, he or she falls almost effortlessly into the standard patterns of reply.

Television has become the daily religious service of the modern world.

Indeed, Christ's parables have been used as the basis for the continual moralizing which television drama delivers. Every half hour- or hour-long segment requires at least one moral lesson in order to drive the ritual onward. Television public affairs is no different. Each report from a journalist outside the studio must be constructed in parable form in order to pose a moral dilemma if the story is not complete, or to deliver a moral point if it is. This necessity to moralize demonstrates just how little public affairs television is related to print journalism and how much it is part of imagery.

The fact that reality bears little resemblance to what the screen shows is known on some level by the viewer. He or she understands that, beyond the television set, out on the streets, the world will be very different from the prescripted moralizing and the easy police drama killings. This is understood in the same way believing Christians once understood that outside the Church, in which they had just eaten the flesh of Christ, they would find disordered, filthy streets smelling of sewerage.

This ability to understand is by no means infallible. When societies are at the end of a line of evolution, there is often confusion as to which is reality and which ritual. The result can be disastrous. One of the most famous incidents of this sort was Marie Antoinette's "Let them eat brioche!" Out it snapped, fast and witty from her lips, a bon mot filled with subtlety. She didn't mention cake. That would have been a common, heavy-handed joke. In response to the people chanting for bread in the courtyard beneath the salons of Versailles, she recommended that they try the finest of bread — white, light, filled with eggs and butter. Most of the people below wouldn't even have known what brioche was. But then, she wasn't talking to them. Hers was a clever quip delivered, with a turn of her head away from the windows and their view of reality, back to the admiring courtesans who participated with her in the rituals of palace life. It is easy to imagine the progress of these few words, repeated eagerly at first, with the shared, sophisticated understanding of the participants, and then sullenly among some of the servants walking out of the room, along the endless corridors, repeating it to other servants, and on down the stairs, along more corridors, until abruptly it was out in the courtyard and being passed among the population, who took it up in confusion, then with disbelief that their Queen could have such contempt for them. Finally, it was repeated with horror and fury as they understood its implications. Marie Antoinette and her companions had lost all sense of what constituted reality. They had no sense of the limitations of court ritual.

In the same way we see politicians today who take the ritual of television at face value — with its facile and constant emotions — tears, love, hatred, all held together by a lobotomized Christian morality. They mistake these stylized emotions for the real thing. One of the first to do this was President Lyndon Johnson who, in all innocence, showed his fresh gallbladder scar to an informal gathering of journalists. Within hours the image was before the public. What could have been more banal? And yet, in a system of predetermined movement, this shocked profoundly. That is to say, Lyndon Johnson did something surprising. And surprise does not reassure, particularly from the head of state. Surprise breeds insecurity. Since then other politicians have cried on air or made personal confessions. On television people cry and confess every minute. But not really. Only ritualistically. During the American presidential primaries of 1972, when the front-runner, Senator Edmund Muskie, cried on television, he destroyed his campaign. When Prime Minister Bob Hawke of Australia did the same thing in the late 1980s, it almost finished him. If a real public figure cries on television, it affects the public in the same way that a priest could affect his parishioners by filling the communion plate with slices of real flesh, not wafers.

Like all ritual, television is also beyond the obligations of linear participation. When McLuhan originally wrote about television, he imagined that watching would require active participation from the viewer. We now know that passive will do. Viewers participate by knowing the ritual. They don't actually have to be present or paying attention all the time.

The television generations have a tendency to "watch" two, three, four or more programs at once. This is not because the programs are vacuous. It is because the viewer already knows the content and is more or less indifferent to it. What attracts him is participation in the eternal ritual of these programs. And while past generations could only wander in and out of one mass at a time, today we can participate in two, three, ten, thirty, forty rituals at once by simply pushing a remote-control device. An hour or so of doing this is enough to reveal that these are not forty rituals. They are forty variations on the same reflection. This is not formula programming but ritualistic repetition. The serious channel switcher can achieve a sort of electronic nirvana, in which all structures disappear and only a totally familiar void envelopes him.

Even reruns are satisfying supports for this system. The eating of Christ's flesh is clearly a more exciting moment in the mass than the preparatory prayers. In the same way, viewers wait to see Lucille Ball, in the old series, "I Love Lucy," go through the prescribed television movements for the nth time. During the peak Christmas viewing period in 1989, one of her reruns on U.S. television beat almost every new program and stood sixth in the national Nielsen viewer ratings.

Of course, here and there programs struggle against all this. And there are individuals who not only have a great understanding of how electronic media work but who struggle to use their talents in order to make the programs do unexpected things. In most countries this amounts to a few hours a week. Those programs have an impact out of all proportion, not only because what they offer is better, but because all ritual delights in occasional nonconformism.

Television falls into the same category as most modern, highly sophisticated systems. It is labour-intensive and pays well. In order to feed the insatiable hunger of airtime, it draws masses of people with creative talents into its structures. Those people might have made a contribution to the search for accurate and real reflections of man's state. Instead they have been sucked into the imaginary royal court of television ritual. Their situation resembles that of the eighteenth-century European aristocracy, who were drawn off their land, away from regional responsibilities as well as public and military service, in all of which they were desperately needed, and into the glittering orbit of the royal courts which turned upon apparently essential ritual. As a result, though they were no longer free to create trouble for the monarch, neither were they available to contribute to the well-being of their societies.

Ritual always carries with it a directness and immediacy. The wafer is the flesh of God's son. A man's presence in the royal bedchamber at a certain hour makes him important. The colour of a man's jacket or the shape of his shoes makes him a gentleman or a noble. Ritual creates a sense of heightened reality through the abstraction of concrete elements. Television ritual has taken a major step beyond this. Its images are not abstractions of reality. They are in themselves more real than ordinary reality. Television's images of death are more convincing than an actual death. In a sense, if televised death is more believable than real death, then television has succeeded in capturing the eternal image.

The degree to which electronic death has taken over our images of mortality can be seen in the general disappointment when a real death is televised. In the 1970s a CBC film crew went into a palliative care unit in Winnipeg and recorded, with his permission, a man's slow decline to death. An enormous audience zoomed in with anticipation on his last moments as his final breaths eased in and out. And when he died, he did it so quietly that the electronic sight and sound machinery didn't pick up any change. The audience had to be told that he was now dead. There were and are far more believable deaths ten times a night on television and in every movie house. For each of those deaths, the lighting would be right, the camera in the best spot in order to catch the tiniest expression, the sound perfect, the colour remarkable. The process from life to death would be clearly delineated. These would be believable deaths. A few of them would be remarkable cathartic experiences. In an average week of French television in 1988, there were 670 murders, fifteen rapes and twenty-seven torture scenes.[13] Television in most countries would be in the same range.

We have always been exposed to quantities of violent images. Paintings — with their decaying, decapitated and martyred bodies — were even more explicit. Their explosive effect on a world without the photograph or the film is now difficult for us to imagine. The public areas — churches, town halls, squares and palaces — were filled with painted and sculpted violence. People lived in public spaces in a way we no longer do. The difference between these images and those of film, television and video is not the genius or the emotive quality of one or the other. It is the perfection to the point of banality of the latter. And they are believable. Even the most pedestrian animated drama can produce what are, in effect, beautiful murders.

Societies have always organized themselves on the basis of self-restraint and generally accepted rules of action. The electronic image seems to have slipped through these nets of restraint and of ordered action simply because it appeared so suddenly and in such an unexpected manner. Society could force the medium to restrain itself. Perhaps what has confused people is that day after day, in almost every program, the images persistently throw basic Western moral mythology together with uncontrolled violence. The latter negates absolutely the former.

This confusion can be seen in the American public's reaction to the coverage of the Vietnam War. It is often said that the public lost its enthusiasm for the war because of the violence shown them by news cameras; specifically because of the images which showed GIs and Vietnamese children dying. In reality they didn't see many deaths and very few scenes of unleashed violence. The viewers were far more put off by the way this war upset their ritual and mythology. GIs were meant to be patriotic winners on the side of good. The nationalist adaption of Christ's parables is very clear about this stylized role.

But it was clear to any television viewer that these young men, constantly being interviewed on various battlefields, were *not* winning. They seemed confused about what they were doing there, confused about American mythology in relationship to this conflict, confused about what the side of good consisted of. Above all, they didn't sound or look like Heroes.

The viewers, including the politicians, blamed the journalists for these images; that is, they blamed the messenger. Behind the angry accusations of bias and unpatriotic attitudes, there was a real confusion over how the ritual images had been turned on their head so as to breed insecurity with unsettling scenes. A sensible answer might have been that the war was complicated while ritualistic dramas are not. They are simple. The moral roles within them are carefully delineated. As a participant you are either in the right or in the wrong. As a viewer you automatically identify with the characters who are in the right. And you constantly hope that those who are in the wrong will repent or at least indicate regret before they die. The television viewer's participation is both intense and passive; intense precisely because the ritual deals with basic assumptions, thanks to which the viewer may remain passive. He is dependent on the continued functioning in good order of the system. The viewer can change nothing. And so, because the images coming out of Vietnam were disturbing the established iconography, mythologies and rituals, the public exercised its power. It seized its remote control device and turned the war off.

With the real war over, both television and cinema were freed to return to ritual images. In no time at all they had rejuggled the Vietnam conflict so that the GI could once again become a Hero. The Vietnamese, having been identified during ten years of war as the aggressed-against little guys, could not suddenly become the villains. Instead, the image people reached into basic mythology and identified individual American officers, sergeants or corporals as the specific villains. Thus the American GI was fighting for right on behalf of the American people. However, a small group of un-American Americans betrayed the cause. They fitted into an iconography which can be traced from Benedict Arnold through to the "Communist agents" of the 1950s. Oliver Stone's film *Platoon* is a perfect example of this. He even provided two sergeants — one good, one evil — in order to clarify the "fact" that American sergeants are good; unfortunately, one in particular was evil. It is an Old Testament approach, dependent on the myth of the fallen angel as the exception to the rule. It also handily clears everyone else of responsibility. *Platoon* was part of the same process as the *Rambo* movies. However, the pure *Rambo* approach at least carries the honesty of a blatant lie. The Stone version is sophisticated distortion aimed at reestablishing an electronic moral parable.

The 1991 military campaign in Iraq demonstrated just how well the authorities had learned their lesson. They did not simply restrict access of journalists and, above all, television to the real war. They carefully chose appropriate images for release. That is, they designed the war's appearance. From the point of view of the electronic age, this visual management has rightly been compared to the war in Vietnam. But from the point of view of the public's access to independent information, the Iraq war had historic significance. For example, the citizen had far less access in 1991 to what was actually happening on the battlefields than it had had during the American Civil War, the Crimean War or the Boer War. As with Vietnam, knowledge about the conduct of these earlier wars had an important impact on political events at home. Fear of the modern image, the cumbersome nature of the electronic eye and the sophistication of modern management methods have all encouraged the authorities to remove an imperfect but nevertheless established democratic right.

The electronic media, like most modern structures, specialize in cut-and-paste jobs intended to rationalize reality — that is, to force reality into an abstract form. It isn't surprising that so much anxiety runs through our societies. People feel attached to the uncontrollable images and yet are drowning in them. Their fear swells while technology continues to progress, leaving man behind as a mere viewer.

It is as if these reflections — of death more convincing than death, of violence more terrifying than violence, of women more beautiful than women, of men stronger than men — are all Godlike and unbearable. In coming alive, they seem to have captured a monopoly on believable exaggeration and thus filled the normal space of the human imagination with graphic animations which leave room for little else. The internal fear from which we now suffer resembles that of a caveman with the image prowling about outside in place of our imagination.

It is as if ritual has been refined to its ultimate form. In the past it was limited in the West not only by the imperfections of the static image but by the presence of God. The official school, established by Saint Augustine, had God as the original creative force behind these images. But the practical reality of belief had him as an idolatrous force, filling an endless quantity of images and statues with some part of his power, so that he could be found at the centre of all reflections. The sacrifices, the martyrdoms, even beauty and love had meaning only in that divine context. Now the death of God combined with the perfection of the image has brought us to a whole new state of expectation. We are the image. We are the viewer and the viewed. There is no other distracting presence. And that image has all the Godly powers. It kills at will. Kills effortlessly. Kills beautifully. It dispenses morality. Judges endlessly. The electronic image is man as God and the ritual involved leads us not to a mysterious Holy Trinity but back to ourselves. In the absence of a clear understanding that we are now the only source, these images cannot help but return to the expression of magic and fear proper to idolatrous societies. This in turn facilitates the use of the electronic image as propaganda by whoever can control some part of it.

The electronic perfection of the image has been the final step in Western man's search for a pure idolatry. The process — which began with Pope Damasus integrating the rational and pagan foundations of Rome into the Christian church and which took another major step with Raphael's completion of the perfect static image while portraying the Athenian principles for a Renaissance pope — has now come to an end. Man's consuming inner fear is a reflection of that finality. It is as if we and our image were turning in an eternal circle staring warily and meaninglessly at each other.

❧

The first sign of an aggressive human reaction to this capture of our visual imagination came with the abrupt appearance and growth of comic strips. Forty-five years after the invention of the photographic plate, thirty-nine after the photographic film and five after the invention of photogravure, this awkward, naive, unsophisticated, voluntarily in-exact form of imagery popped up in England. The British "Ally Slopes" of 1884 evolved into the first American newspaper strip — "The Yellow Kid" — in 1896. It led to the phrase *yellow journalism*. The success of "The Yellow Kid" led to a proliferation of comic strips — "Krazy Kat" in 1913, "Little Orphan Annie" in 1924, "Tintin" and "Tarzan" in 1929, then hundreds of others.

A reasonable projection would have been that, as the cinema pro-gressed, these crude, manual, moving stories would have made less and less sense. The arrival of talkies in 1927 should have ended the matter once and for all. Instead, one year later Mickey Mouse made his first appearance in an animated cartoon. The success of this movie made no sense at all. Why would anyone watch an obviously unbelievable-looking mouse when there were images of real filmed people? And yet Mickey became more popular than any movie star. In 1935, the first full-length comic book appeared and started an explosive new growth in these crude pictures.

As the electronic images of real people improved to the point of perfection, so the cartoon increasingly became a release mechanism for the visual imagination or, rather, for the human need to exaggerate. That Mickey Mouse is still the most famous man in the world merely confirms that Disney was more important for the image than Picasso or any other modern painter. They have all had to struggle against the prison of the perfect image. Disney actually released the image from prison.

The return of William Blake to a position of great influence gave an indication of what was happening. Blake had combined the mystical with the narrative by using figures not unlike the cartoon figures of today. At the same time, he was the first to show that the immortal image was seated deeper in our imagination than in reality.

The second cartoon revolution rose in a Europe recovering from World War II. Perhaps the violent lunacy which had swept back and forth across the continent for six years released the necessary emotions. In any case the Belgians, French and Spaniards began to produce hard-bound book-length comic strip novellas known as *Bande Dessinée* (*BD*).

Luky Luke, an off-the-wall cowboy, became the new Mickey Mouse. Astérix, a warrior of ancient Gaul, evolved into a familiar Freudian repository of the French character. Marshall McLuhan, in a letter to the historian Harold Innis, noted in 1951 that "the comic book has been seen as a degenerate literary form instead of a nascent pictorial and dramatic form."[14] The medium has exploded out of this nascent state with an energy even he could not have imagined.

Then, in the 1960s, came a third explosion. Uncontrolled bouts of imagination produced cartoon novels filled with violence, exaggeration, sex and speed. A whole frustrated, irrational dream seemed to be bursting onto these pages, as if in reply to the perfect, predictable images of television and films. RanXerox, for example, is a robot man who punches out eyes and pulls off hands. He also makes love for hours on end.[15] But there is irony in his character and the books contain a cold, fearful vision of what we are becoming. The painter Bilal is the hero of many *BD* creators. In 1986 he published a cartoon novel called *La Femme Piège*.[16] This *Woman Trap* lives in a future world, sordid, in decline. The future that Bilal draws is dated only a few years ahead of us. London and Berlin are morgues fought over by bizarre revolutionary armies. The woman has blue hair, blue lips and kills men. Men with birds' heads are somehow linked to Egyptian mythology. Time is precise but in constant movement back and forth. There is a general and profound sense of fear which none of our electronic images could produce. This overflowing of fears and repressed imaginations along with open criticism of the status quo, which television faithfully respects, increasingly through the 1970s and 1980s began to appear in such monthlies as *Metal*, *Hurlant*, *Pilote*, *Heavy Metal*, *Hara Kiri*, *Charlie Hebdo*, and most recently the American magazine *Raw*, edited by Art Spiegelman.

When sixteen thousand French teenagers were interviewed in 1986 on the question of literacy, they were asked about their reading preferences.[17] More than one preference was permitted. The first nine were as follows:

1. Comic books (*Bande Dessinée*)	53 percent
2. Adventure or historical novels	40 percent
3. Police or spy novels	38 percent
4. Science fiction	30 percent
5. Magazines or reviews for teenagers (these contain comics)	26 percent
6. Fairy tales and legends	19 percent
7. Love stories	18 percent
8. Reporting, exploitation, travel	18 percent
9. Classical novels	18 percent

A more interesting question would have been what their visual preferences were, after putting comic books on the same list as paintings, television, video and film. Once a year some two hundred thousand people come to a *BD* gathering in Angoulême. And the two television series which imitate comic book mythology — *Star Trek* and *Dr. Who* — are the focus of equally popular annual conventions. It is hard to imagine any living painter or group of painters effortlessly drawing such crowds or causing the real excitement these fairs do. Certainly the gathering of film industry professionals at Cannes does not bear comparison. Nor does its television equivalent.

In North America, newspapers have maintained their daily quota of strip cartoons. These were once limited to the comics page for children and to the editorial page for adults. Gradually, strip cartoons which are social, political and simply entertaining have spread to other pages. Jules Feiffer and Garry Trudeau among others have gone from there to hardback annuals. Whole sections of bookstores are now filled with these cartoon volumes.

It was only a matter of time before American book-length original cartoons began appearing in hardback. The first to make an impact was Art Spiegelman's *Maus*.[18] Using simple, almost crude black-and-white drawings, Spiegelman managed to find a new way to reopen the healing wounds of public sensibility over the Holocaust. The Jews in his book are portrayed as mice, the Germans as cats. At the same time translations of *BD* began to appear. One of the constant themes in these dramatic comics is that Western society is in decline and that its peoples are gripped by an inner fear. Each image appears to refute the false hyperrealism and reassuring moralization of television and the cinema.

In the midst of this evolution, a number of painters turned to the cartoon. Andy Warhol and Roy Lichtenstein, for example, played with these images, but only within the context and vocabulary of official art. The effect on the art experts was shock. They concluded that these painters were revolutionaries. But Warhol and Lichtenstein were more like court painters who sought to attract attention by parading around the palace without their wigs. They were still addressing themselves to the court and its courtiers and still doing so within its structures.

This is quite different from the cartoonists, who, if anything, more closely resemble the craftsmen/painters who preceded Raphael. They deal with reality and address society as a whole. While the Warhols and Lichtensteins engage in sophisticated, amusing, shocking imitations of reality, the cartoonists actually seek new reflections of reality.

The official artists do amuse the court of critics, experts and social followers. In a way they are more conservative and patronizing than the official artists of the late nineteenth century. Take Lichtenstein, for example, who was pushed to paint blown-up versions of comic strips when, in 1960, one of his sons pointed to a Mickey Mouse comic book and said, "I bet you can't paint as good as that." He painted an outsized picture of Donald Duck. In 1962 he caused a sensation in the art world with his cartoon-based show at the Castelli gallery in New York. In November 1963 Lichtenstein said, "My work is different from comic strips — but I wouldn't call it a transformation. . . . What I do is form, whereas the comic strip is not formed in the sense I'm using the word; the comics have shapes, but there has been no effort to make them intensely unified."[19] This may sound surprisingly pretentious from the mouth of the leading pop artist, but Lichtenstein, after all, for a good part of his life was a university professor of art. On the other hand, copying comic strips made him rich and famous. This process had to turn, however, on one shared assumption — that Lichtenstein was an artist, while the cartoonists were not.

There could be no clearer example of how completely the craft and art functions have been separated by Western society. In hijacking the secondary idea of personal artistic merit, the artist himself loses track not simply of the technical craft so essential to earlier painters, but of the real relationship between the painter's image and the public. Lichtenstein ripped off the true public images — the comics — while denigrating them and thus amusing his fellow experts. Like most people caught up in the abstract reality of ritual, they assumed quite naturally that the cartoon was just an amusing tool to be manipulated by their talents. There really isn't much difference between Marie Antoinette's bon mot over bread and brioche and Warhol's soup cans. They are both expressions of clever artificiality, not of intelligent relevance.

What the artistic profession — with all its training schools for analysis and production, its museums and its experts devoted to judgment — missed was that the cartoonists have been seizing many of the tools of imagination which they have been laying down and which the perfect images of television have been unable to use. The cartoonist, almost alone, was still playing with the old conundrum of the image, society and immortality. What appeared to the rational, professional mind to be escapism was an attempt to go beyond the apparent reality which seems to have imprisoned our imagination. While Lichtenstein was mindlessly exploiting the images created by others, they, the others, were moving on, finding new images. While Warhol strove so desperately to shock with other people's ideas, a cartoonist called Chester Brown was drawing *BD*, in which the president of the United States was a talking penis attached to the body of an anemic small-time criminal.[20] No doubt some post-Warhol professional will eventually do an "artistic version" of this image.

In *Le Procès-verbal*, a novel by the French writer Le Clézio, the hero says: "I am in the cartoon of my choice."[21] A short time later, rational society locks him up and tells him that he is insane. To a remarkable degree, the visual side of the humanist tradition is now in the hands of the cartoonist, as is the quest for the immortal image. The art experts with their client artists are increasingly the allies of the television sit-com and of imprisoned reality. It is hardly surprising in a society which seems to be in decline, but worships structure too much to do anything about it, that imagination should be treated as an enemy and not as a friend of the people.

The next chapter of this struggle began in earnest in 1991 with the appearance of the film *Terminator II*. Through the use of computer programming, cartoon figures were created which appear to be real filmed people. This was the culmination of a decade of increasingly bold experiments: real babies with computer-designed mouths superimposed to make them talk; real heads combined with computer-designed bodies as in the film *Tron*. However, with *Terminator II* it has become possible on screen to cut in half the head of a real person, Arnold Schwarzeneg-ger, for example, and then put it back together again. In other words, the ritualistic images of the electronic world can now simulate that freedom of visual imagination which had taken refuge in the cartoon. It is as if the entire magical line of imagery had been occupied by the official school of ritual. Man-made imagery revolves, as it always has, around the forces of fear, magic and ritual. A radical change in the relationship between the last two cannot help but lead to a growth in the first. The more sophisticated the controlling images become, the more likely it is that individuals will seek reassurance in increased levels of fear. It is as if the last known refuge of visual imagination and fantasy had been occupied by the forces of structure.

19

Life in a Box –
Specialization and
the Individual

Surely we live in the paradise of the individual. Proof enough lies all around us. The uniforms of class and function are dropping away. Libel and security laws aside, any man or woman may say what he or she wishes on any subject without fear of going to jail. We may dress as we wish; wear our hair short or long; engage in uncountable marital, sexual and sports activities, almost all of which are available to all people irrespective of background. Only a few bastions equipped with a peculiar combination of class and cost can resist parts of this general, populist flow. We may read information of all sorts and persuasions or travel around the world for almost nothing, just to see for ourselves what once we had to learn from narrow public sources, which usually passed on their own unverifiable prejudices.

And yet, what is real individualism in the contemporary secular state? If it is self-gratification, then this is a golden era. If it has to do with personal public commitment, then we are witnessing the death of the individual and living in an age of unparalleled conformism. Specialization and professionalism have provided the great innovations in social structure during the Age of Reason. But they have not created the bonds necessary for public cooperation. Instead they have served to build defensive cells in which the individual is locked.

Much of modern individualism has been confined to superficial and personal matters. Our dentist, for example, leans over us, his skin tanned from a trip to some southern island, his teeth perfectly white, his shirt open two buttons to reveal a gold chain, his hair permed into perfect curls, his second or third wife waiting at home for their evening out in a nouvelle cuisine restaurant. On his tongue there is talk of wine vintages, tennis and squash. No doubt his car has some fast form and has been imported from another country. Or it has a tough town-and-country appearance, which indicates that he owns a weekend place. Can this possibly be the same blacksmith who pulled teeth in his spare time a few centuries ago? Or the lugubrious, black-suited pain inflictor satirized in Daumier's drawings? Or even the figure of fun joked about by Wilde? Or by Shaw? "Wretched, bankrupt ivory snatcher . . . gum architect. It's your business to hurt people."[1] No. This is modern man: the individualist in quest of inner peace and happiness.

The dominant mythology of the West to all intents and purposes remains the American dream. "Life, liberty and the pursuit of happiness." Life and liberty having been assured, the contemporary middle-class individual concentrates on the pursuit of happiness. Now we may divorce with facility or, for that matter, not marry at all but live in couples outside religious and civil law. No longer respecting hypocritical public decorum, we can see naked bodies entwined on the advertising pages of mainstream magazines, as well as in various stages of copulation in mainstream films. By simply reaching a little higher on any magazine rack, we can buy concentrated sex images. For that matter, we can walk through a door in any city and pay a small sum to see females or males or both acting out live intercourse.

Less than fifty years ago, an actress was considered "not good enough" to marry a middle-class son. His family would have cut him off if he tried. She was considered little more than a prostitute. Clothed while on stage or film, once off she removed them too easily. Now middle-class parents are thrilled if their daughter goes to acting school. They don't seem to mind if she later appears on the screen, naked or in sex scenes, provided this exposure takes place in a serious movie.

Equally, an army officer would have refused an accountant as his son-in-law less than half a century ago. Now he would welcome him into the family. Knowing how not to contribute to the financing of the public weal has become a generally accepted virtue of individualism.

This widespread freedom of choice is the product of reason's victory over arbitrary social values. The individual has been allowed out of his socially constructed cage. That, at least, is the contemporary myth. What is not clear, however, is what that liberation has to do with the fulfillment of individualism. The lessons of history seem relatively clear. Societies on the rise are simple, unadorned and relatively uncompromising. Those on the decline are given to open-mindedness, self-indulgence and the baroque. The Romans of the republic and early empire were farmers with well-defined duties and a simple way of life. The early Americans were good country gentlemen, unadorned except for their imaginations and their willingness to work. The leadership of such societies generally reflects these unpretentious characteristics. George Washington is the most famous modern example. Even in his own time he was presented as a latter-day Cincinnatus, the early Roman leader who served selflessly and then gave up power to return to his fields. But long before Washington there had been men like Henri IV — the first of the great modern kings — who in the early 1600s swept away protocol, ornament and grandeur. This he extended to refusing to bathe. It was Henri who wrote to his mistress — "Don't bathe. I'm coming home." These nascent, healthy societies are invariably imbued with a self-righteousness which is often tied to religious and moral inflexibility. And their mythologies of simplicity and goodness invariably turn a blind eye to political realities. The Romans and Americans, for example, were driven by military expansion and a slave-based economy. Nevertheless, such people tend to succeed and with success comes a comfort which in turn allows for greater ornament and self-indulgence. Who could blame them? And if that is degeneracy, well, societies are made to come and go. One can only hope that they will be allowed to go gently by the new tribe, which will inevitably appear to fill the void left by the old one's loss of ambition and self-restraint.

It doesn't take much effort to argue that we in the West show all these signs of indolent degeneracy and are therefore prime candidates for replacement. However, it is not clear that what we now think of as individualism is entirely an expression of self-satisfied self-indulgence. After all, our idea of the individual was formed by several centuries of struggle between the arbitrary powers of Church and State on the one hand and the disciples of reason on the other. The product — the citizen of the late twentieth century — bears little resemblance to the degenerate Roman or the degenerate eighteenth-century European aristocrat. Surely the dentist just described, with his harmless indulgences, is not our equivalent of a Neronic pleasure seeker. Surely the modern citizen's devotion to the virtues of superficial individualism is not of great importance. These pleasures are mere artifice.

The real state of individual development in our society can be seen in the way the citizen operates when faced by the structures of power. For example, an individual's willingness not to conform can best be measured when nonconformism threatens his life or that of his family, friends or other citizens. Fortunately we don't have many opportunities for that sort of test. On the other hand, we are measured every day by our responses to questions which have to do with such things as personal income, careers and public policy. A civilization which claims to have been constructed upon the foundation of the participating individual citizen will stand or fall on our detailed reaction to these questions.

Thomas Mann set out the two sides of this argument perfectly in *The Magic Mountain*. To be an individualist, "one had at least to recognize the difference between morality and blessedness."[2] An individual is someone who takes upon himself an understanding of what is moral and who monitors his own conduct. A man who depends upon blessedness is one who relies upon God and his representatives to define morality and to enforce it. He is a child of God — a ward who would not dream of claiming personal responsibility. The individual is more like a child who has grown up and left home. More dramatically put, man killed God in order to replace him. Either that or, having killed God, man was obliged to fill the resulting void. In either case he assumed the powers of moral judgment previously limited to divinities.

But none of the individual freedoms so prized by the dentist seem relevant to the citizen assuming God's role of judgment; that is, the role previously played by God's personal representatives on earth — the churches and the divine monarchs. The powers involved are practical and real. The only question is who will seize them. He who does so determines the shape of the life that others will enjoy or endure. The supreme act of individualism in a rational society should be for each citizen, in concert with the others, to seize those powers in order to exercise them for the common good. The supreme abrogation of individualism is for the citizen to be out buying a BMW while someone else is exercising his or her power of judgment. Those rights and privileges so cherished by the dentist seem to indicate a charming state of blessedness normally associated with earlier societies governed through divinity-directed mechanisms.

Just how confused we are over what we mean by individualism can most easily be seen by looking at the West from the outside. Buddhist societies are horrified by a great deal in the West, but the element which horrifies them most is our obsession with ourselves as a subject of unending interest. By their standards nothing could be unhealthier than a guilt-ridden, self-obsessed, proselytizing white male or female, selling God or democracy or liberalism or capitalism with insistent superior modesty. It is clear to the Buddhist that this individual understands neither herself nor his place. He is ill at ease in his role; *mal dans sa peau*; a hypocrite taking out her frustrations on the world.

As for the contemporary liberated Westerner, who thinks himself relaxed, friendly, open, in tune with himself and eager to be in tune with others — he comes across as even more revolting. He suffers from the same confused superiority as his guilt-ridden predecessor but has further confused himself by pretending that he doesn't feel superior. While the Westerner does not see or consciously understand this, the outsider sees it immediately. The Westerner's inability to mind his own business shows a lack of civilization. Among his most unacceptable characteristics is a determination to reveal what he thinks of as himself — his marriages, divorces and children; his feelings and loves. The European likes to think of that as an American characteristic, but the difference between the continents is merely one of degrees. Any man or woman produced by the Judeo-Christian tradition is dying to confess — unasked, if necessary. What the Buddhist seeks in the individual is, first, that he understands he is part of a whole and therefore of limited interest as a part and, second, to the extent that he tries to deal with the problem of his personal existence, he does so in a private manner. The individual who appears to sail upon calm waters is a man of quality. Any storms he battles within are his own business.

Of what, then, does Western individualism consist? There was a vision, in the nineteenth century, of the individualist as one who acted alone. He had to do so within the constraints of a well-organized society. Even the most anti-restraint of thinkers — John Stuart Mill — put it that "the liberty of the individual must be thus far limited. he must not make himself a nuisance to other people."[3]

But if the constraints of nineteenth-century Western civilization did put him in danger of causing a nuisance, he could simply go, or be sent, to the frontiers of North and South America or to Australasia. There he could give almost free rein to his individual liberty by engaging in a concretely existential life. If that sort of freedom was too extreme, there were still the endless sectors of the empires, where a man could go without cutting his ties to his own society while still freeing himself to varying degrees from that society's constraints. Those who wished maximum freedom could have themselves sent to the very edges of the empires — as factors of the Hudson's Bay Company or district commissioners in the southern Sudan, for example — where there would not be another Westerner within weeks of travel. Rimbaud fled Paris and poetry for an isolated Abyssinian trading post, where his chief business was rifles and slaves. This personal freedom killed him, as it did many others. In his case the weapon was disease, which was a more common danger for such people than violence. Those who wished to be at a nuisance-free distance and yet avoid too much individuality might go to a frontier regiment like the Rajputs in northern India or to the Legion in Algeria. There they would be released from the control of British and French society but restrained by regimental structure.

Even without leaving the West, a man eager for individual action could find room for manoeuvre within the rough structures which stretched beyond nineteenth-century middle-class society. In the slums, hospitals or factories, men from suffocating backgrounds could struggle against evil or good as if they were at war. By the 1920s, the worst of these rough patches were gone and the individual's scope of action was seriously limited. In a stable, middle-class society, restraint was highly prized. Curiously enough, this meant that, with even the smallest unrestrained act, a man could make a nuisance of himself and thus appear to be an individual.

That is one explanation for the rise of artistic individualism — a form of existentialism which did not necessarily mean leaving your country, although it often did involve moving to the margins of society. The prototypes were Byron and Shelley, who fled in marital disorder across Europe, calling for political revolution along the way. Lermontov was another early model — exiled to the Caucasus, where he fought frontier wars, wrote against the central powers he hated and engaged in private duels. Victor Hugo was a later and grander example, leaving France in protest and refusing to return as long as Louis-Napoléon was on the throne. These acts required a certain courage, a certain conviction, a degree of personal inner resolve. In many cases they approached the individualism of the frontiersman.

But today's individualism can't really be compared to all this existential activity. Is there a relationship between the frontiersman and the self-pampering modern dentist? Between the French Legionnaire and the downhill-skiing Porsche driver? Between the responsible citizen of a secular democracy and the executive cocaine sniffer? All these people were and are engaged in a form of defiance. But there does not appear to be much room for comparison. The phenomena belong to separate worlds.

The "individual" is an old idea. But "individualism," as it began to take form in the early nineteenth century, was a new expression of great hope. Since ordinary people still retained a memory of the positive side of the Middle Ages — of the gilds with their mixture of craftsmanship and social responsibility — it was as if the new individualists were assuming the old responsibilities of the citizen. The memory of the responsible, professional gild member carried within it a still-older memory — that of the citizen in the Greek city-state. The Athenian citizen — the idealized individual — had remained a semimythological role model for the citizen throughout Western history.

In fact, this continuity was an illusion. It had been destroyed when the power of the gilds and of the burghers and their towns was swept away by the wars of religion and replaced by the rise of the kings with their absolute, national powers. What survived was the idea of professionalism. The kingdoms of Europe were full of officially accredited professionals. However, their role was legitimized not by their competence but by an irrational power structure — a pyramid with God and the king at the top.

That is why the idea of professionalism, as it reappeared in the armies of conquering reason, was so intimately linked to the idea that men existed in their own right, not thanks to the licence of some arbitrary power. This applied as much to army officers and public servants as it did to traders and manufacturers. The contribution that they made to society via their professionalism was an assertion of their possession of reason. And to possess reason was to be a responsible individual.

The rise of the professional was therefore intimately linked— throughout the Industrial Revolution, the accompanying explosion of inventions and the growth of the middle classes — with Western man's assertion that he was a responsible individual. He was responsible to the degree that he was competent. Thus the value of individualism was pegged to the soaring value of specialization. By becoming better at what he did, each man believed that he was increasing his control over his own existence. He was building his personal empire of responsibility. This was both the measure of his worth and the sum of his contribution to society as a whole.

The assumption seemed to be that this new professionalism would lead to bodies of expertise joining together in a sort of populist meritocracy. The first large-scale manifestation of this idea came in the 1920s, in a horribly twisted form, with the rise of corporatism, which then turned into Fascism. This should have been interpreted as confirmation that the historic line from Athens and the gilds was nothing more than myth. The events of the 1920s and 1930s were not isolated incidents. Corporatism reappeared in the 1960s in such places as the British union movement, the American business group known as the Round Table and its imitative Canadian equivalent, the Business Council on National Issues. The last two can claim to have set much of their countries' contemporary economic and social agendas. The banding together of citizens into interest groups becomes corporatist, that is to say dangerous, only when the interest group loses its specific focus and seeks to override the democratic system. In the case of the British unions and the North American business councils, their every intervention into public affairs has been intended to undermine the democratic participation of individual citizens.

These three examples are part of a growing trend. They also demonstrate one of the ways in which the real effect of increasing professionalism has been to isolate the individual. The professional did indeed find that he could build his personal empire; but curiously enough, the more expert he became, the more his empire shrank. As this happened the individual found himself in an increasingly contradictory position. On the one hand, because he was a virtually all-powerful retainer of information, expertise and responsibility over a tiny area, his cooperation was essential to others who, although within his general discipline, were themselves experts in other tiny areas. Obviously the cooperation of the whole group, with each other and with society as a whole, was also essential to the general population. On the other hand, as these tiny areas of absolute responsibility proliferated, each individual was more securely locked in his confining cell of expertise. Inevitably he became increasingly powerless in society as a whole. The philosophers of the seventeenth and eighteenth centuries had thought they were building the foundations for a civilization of Renaissance individuals. The result has been the exact opposite.

While our mythology suggests that society is like a tree with the ripening fruits of professional individualism growing thick upon it, a more accurate image would show a maze of corridors, blocked by endless locked doors, each one leading in or out of a small cell.

This confusion is hardly surprising. Although the roots of our problem go back four centuries, it was not until the middle of the nineteenth century that all the relevant terms which describe the situation came into being or, pushed by changing structures, took on their current meanings. *To specialize*, for example, was an old verb which had traditionally been used in the way we now use *to highlight*. Only in 1855 did it come to rest on its modern meaning — to make narrower and more intensive. As part of this change, the word *specialization* had been coined in 1843 by John Stuart Mill and *specialist* by Herbert Spencer in 1856.[4]

The realization that knowledge and expertise, as applied by rational societies, undermined the individual instead of reinforcing him, began to dawn on people the moment this professional ethic formally entered the language. Spontaneously, yet more new words began to appear in order to provide a language for protest. *Individualisme*, the most important of these, appeared first in French, then in English. At its heart was a refusal of the burgeoning vocabulary that surrounded and imprisoned the professional. Individualism was created around the principle of a self-centred feeling or conduct. In other words, the conviction grew that the only way to develop individual qualities was to reject society.

The words of Charles Bonnet, who first identified the modern individual with his invention of the term *individualité* in 1760, show to what extent the purpose of individualism in a rational society was from the very beginning, social refusal and self-indulgence: "I am a being who feels and is intelligent; it is in the nature of all feeling and intelligent beings to wish to feel or to exist agreeably, and to wish to love oneself."[5]

In other words, if participating in society involves the emasculation of the individual, then individualism has no option but to base itself on the abdication of responsibility. Faced by the power of a whole civilization bound up in structure, the true individual flees. He refuses the rational dream of a world in which each man is an expert and therefore only part of a man. What he resents is not so much that he has been turned into a cell in the social body. Rather, he finds it unacceptable that each cell has little knowledge of the whole and therefore little influence over its workings. Judge Learned Hand, then a Harvard graduating student, spoke of this modern malaise to his classmates on their convocation day in 1893:

> Civilization implies specialization, specialization is forgetfulness of total values and the establishment of false ones, that is Philistinism. A savage can never fall into this condition, his values are all real, he supplies his own wants and finds them proceeding from himself, not from an estimate of those of others. We must in practice be specialists; the division of labour ordains us to know something of one subject and little of others; it forces Philistinism down our throats whether we like it or not.[6]

Hand spent his life on the bench attempting to bring his assumption of morality and common sense to bear on his judgments. He wanted to link his own specialization to the outer world. For that he was respected and treated as the greatest magistrate in America. He was not, however, named to the Supreme Court. It could be argued that, despite the best will in the world from those who are in what we call positions of responsibility, the system invariably manages not to reward those who succeed in communicating between boxes without respecting established structure.

While Judge Hand and a few other exceptional men have appealed to the citizen to reach beyond the limitations that society imposes, it is hardly realistic to expect each citizen to maintain such a level of individualism. The problem is the same as that created by the exceptional public standards which Jefferson set. In the best of all possible worlds, every man and woman will try to attain them. But to pretend that we shall all succeed would be pure hypocrisy.

The more understandable and common reaction of the citizen-expert is defensive. He attempts to turn his prison cell into a fortress by raising and thickening the walls. This padded box may be a cell, but it is also a link within some larger process and is therefore essential. He alone understands and controls the workings of his own box. His power as an individual consists of the ability to withhold his knowledge of cooperation. In other words, "information" is the currency of a society built upon systems. Once a man has given out his information, he has spent his capital. He therefore doles it out with care. He trades his information for that of others. When threatened, he refuses cooperation — for example, by exaggerating difficulties or inventing them or moving slowly or offering misleading information. The only real power of expertise lies in retention. The more self-confident the individual, the less likely he has been to choose an isolated and well-defended box. Even so, as Marshall McLuhan put it: "The expert, as such, is full of insecurity. That is why he specializes in order to obtain some degree of confidence."[7]

One of the specialist's most successful discoveries was that he could easily defend his territory by the simple development of a specialized language incomprehensible to nonexperts. The explosion in terminology over the last fifty years has left the languages of the West reeling. There is a general mistaken belief that these words have come largely from the English-language pool. This has permitted many people to attribute the breakdown of general communications in their societies to the imperial domination of English or, inversely, to the inability of such languages as German, French and Spanish to modernize.

But the expert-inspired explosion in vocabulary has happened to an equal degree in every Western language. The social sciences alone have flooded French, German, Italian, and, of course, English, with countless dialects. Subject after subject and profession after profession have now had the general understanding of their functions ripped out of the public's hands by the experts.

The example of philosophy actually verges on comedy. Socrates, Descartes, Bacon, Locke and Voltaire did not write in a specialized dialect. They wrote in basic Greek, French and English and they wrote for the general reader of their day. Their language is clear, eloquent and often both moving and amusing. The contemporary philosopher does not write in the basic language of our day. He is not accessible to the public. Stranger still, even the contemporary interpreter of earlier philosophy writes in inaccessible dialect. This means that almost anyone with a decent pre-university-level education can still pick up Bacon or Descartes, Voltaire or Locke and read them with both ease and pleasure. Yet even a university graduate is hard pressed to make his way through interpretations of these same thinkers by leading contemporary intellectuals such as Stuart Hampshire. Why, then, would anyone bother trying to read these modern obscurings of the original clarity? The answer is that contemporary universities use these interpretations as the expert's road into the original. The dead philosophers are thus treated as if they were amateurs, in need of expert explanation and protection.

The new specialized terminology amounts to a serious attack on language as a tool of common understanding. Certainly today, the walls between the boxes of expertise continue to grow thicker. The dialects of political science and sociology, for example, are increasingly incomprehensible to each other, even though they are examining identical areas. It is doubtful whether they have any separate existence one from the other. In fact, it is doubtful whether either of them exists at all as a real subject of expertise. However, they have occupied traditional areas of popular concern and set about walling off these areas from each other and, of course, from the public. The wall between these two false sciences and that of the economists is thicker still. The architect and the art historian each uses a dialect so distant that the lack of common systems of argument suggests they are separated from each other, to say nothing of from the economist, not by a dialectical difference but by different languages. And yet St. Peter's was built by painters.

An expert in one language, a German anthropologist, for example, is in many ways better equipped to communicate with the equivalent French anthropologist than with a German MBA. At first glance this might suggest that some wonderful international language is developing. Not at all. These new dialects are not healthy additions to any of our languages. They are rhetoric used to obscure understanding. If ever international integration raises the specter of specialist competition, they will obscure their language further in order to prevent that kind of communication.

The expert argues that none of this is so. He claims that his expanded language has paralleled an expanded understanding in his area. But this understanding is limited precisely to fellow experts in that area. Ten geographers who think the world is flat will tend to reinforce each other's errors. If they have a private dialect in which to do this, it becomes impossible for outsiders to disagree with them. Only a sailor can set them straight. The last person they want to meet is someone who, freed from the constraints of expertise, has sailed around the world.

The purpose of language is communication. It has no other reason for existence. A great civilization is one in which there is a rich texture and breadth and ease to that communication. When language begins to prevent communication, that civilization has entered into serious degeneracy.

The primary instigators of obstruction are the very people who should have been devoted to the increasing of communications — the professors. They have turned their universities into temples of expertise, pandering to modern society's weakness for exclusivity. Maurice Strong has gone so far as to say that "the inter-disciplinary, linear, synthesis abilities are better outside of universities than in." The American historian William Polk believes that universities should now be called multiversities, because their training is at the heart of what divides society rather than seeking to unite it.[8] They — the custodians of the Western, intellectual tradition — now devote themselves to the prevention of integrated thought. Because professors both train society's youth and catalogue current events — whether political, artistic or financial — they have become the official guardians of the boxes in which the educated live.

This obsession with expertise is such that the discussion of public affairs on a reasonable level is now almost impossible. If an engineer who builds bridges doesn't want interference from outside his domain, and a nuclear engineer feels the same about his responsibilities, then neither is likely to question the other's judgment. They know precisely how questions from any nonexpert would be treated by an expert — the same way they themselves would.

Their standard procedure when faced by outside questioning is to avoid answering and instead to discourage, even to frighten off the questioner, by implying that he is uninformed, inaccurate, superficial and, invariably, overexcited. If the questioner has some hierarchical power, the expert may feel obliged to answer with greater care. For example, he may release a minimum amount of information in heavy dialect and accompany it with apologies for the complexity, thus suggesting that the questioner is not competent to understand anything more. And if the questioner must be answered but need not be respected — a journalist, for example, or a politician — the expert may release a flood of incomprehensible data, thus drowning out debate while pretending to be cooperative. And even if someone does manage to penetrate the confusion of material, he will be obliged to argue against the expert in a context of such complexity that the public, to whom he is supposed to be communicating understanding, will quickly lose interest. In other words, by drawing the persistent outsider into his box, the expert will have rendered him powerless.

The contempt for the citizen which all of this self-defence through exclusivity shows is muted by the fact that the expert is himself a citizen. He or she considers it his right to treat his own area of expertise as exclusive territory. That, he believes, is what makes him an individual.

What is more, he knows that only the greater middle classes are divided up and isolated in boxes of specialization. The mass of the citizenry is not. He also knows that the mass, although no longer a lumpen proletariat or even an old-fashioned working class, is nevertheless caught up in work and family. These tens of millions of people maintain a tradition of belief in the good intentions of their rational elites. This is the result, in part, of the simple reality that most people do not have the time to seriously question their experts. Even if they find the time, they are not equipped with either the obscure vocabulary or an understanding of the obscure structures necessary to do so successfully. And even if they do persist, the rhetorical replies of expertise can only be taken as reassurance.

The experts exploit this trust with the active cynicism of frightened men. What frightens them is, in part, their own loss of individualism as a result of being caught up in the structures of rational society. The mass of the population, while not directly imprisoned by these structures, is entirely dependent upon the resulting manner in which society runs. There is also a relatively small percentage of the population that is rich enough to stay on the outside, along with the less powerful and the less educated. To the extent that they need or want things from society, even they are dependent. But it is the great middle classes who are trapped entirely within — the upper middle, middle middle, and lower middle. They are the functioning elite and yet must work for their living. They are the great creation of the Age of Reason and even where they do not constitute a majority, they dominate Western society. They are prisoners of their own expertise and as a result have been slipping into an ever more inarticulate state when it comes to their role as individual citizens.

During working hours a man's obligations to his employment function force him to restrain his views on this, his area of expertise. He is also silent on other people's areas of expertise. After all, the aim of structure is smooth functioning, not public criticism. And the expert's desire not to be criticized by those outside his box restrains him in turn from criticizing them. When he leaves his office/function at the end of the day, he is theoretically free. In reality, were he to engage in independent public comment on his area of expertise, while on his own time, he would find himself in serious trouble with the system that employs him. Such comment would be considered a form of treason. In many cases, his contractual employment conditions specifically prevent him from off-hours independent involvement in his area of expertise. His employer has the exclusive use of his knowledge. In effect, the employed expert has no individual rights over his own competence, except that of changing employers. This could hardly be considered an important right, particularly since any attempts to speak out as an individual expert will saddle him with a reputation as a difficult individual, making it virtually impossible to find employment elsewhere.

What we have, then, is an educated, reasonably prosperous, responsibly employed middle class that is virtually censored or self-censored when it comes to most of the responsibilities of the individual citizen. The obvious exception to this is the right to cast a secret ballot. On the other hand, the breakdown of society's traditional limitations — including most integrated religious and social beliefs — leaves all the members of this enormous middle class at liberty to use their free time however they wish, providing they don't interfere with the functioning of the system. They are also absolutely free to spend their money on whatever they want, again providing they do not challenge structures.

The obvious solution for the middle classes has been to deal with the terrible frustrations of their silent, controlled, boxed-up real lives by spending their spare time and money as steam-release devices — that is, to compensate for a relevant straitjacket with irrelevant freedoms. This is what we now call individualism — an immersion in the imaginary waters of self-gratification.

But for today's middle classes, more than frustration is at stake. Their need is also to forget that the individual's real powers have been castrated by his or her own expertise. This amnesia can only be produced by pretending that superficial expressions of individualism mean something.

Under the old despotic regimes, substantive nonconformism was treated as an attack on the interests of the regime. It was a capital crime. In the democratic nations of the twentieth century there aren't many capital crimes. Instead, substantive nonconformity is treated as irresponsible and unprofessional — forms of conduct in which no responsible citizen would wish to engage. To do so would be to endanger a safe position inside a box. But the middle-class male and now the middle-class female are products of an educational and social system which tells them that a successful life requires the penetration of an expert's box and the occupation of as much space as possible within and for as long a period of time as possible. Sensibly enough, few would risk losing that. This fear of acting in an irresponsible manner has struck a death blow to public debate among educated citizens.

Superficial nonconformism, on the other hand, leaves our rational structures indifferent. Questions of moral action and of physical appearance are increasingly irrelevant; they are categorized either as justified self-expression or conversely as suitable subjects for agitated public debate. In either case they are harmless vents. With this victory of nonsubstantive nonconformism, the citizen-expert becomes a schizophrenic— docile, diligent and controlling within his box; once out of it, as relaxed and original as possible, sometimes argumentative, sometimes fun loving and inevitably in search of happiness. At least, that is the theory.

The word *happiness* abounded in the early discourses on reason. Perhaps the most important invocations of it came in the American Declaration of Independence. We know what the author meant when he wrote "that [all men] are endowed by their Creator with certain unalienable rights, that among these are life, liberty and the pursuit of happiness." These are ideas which Jefferson expanded on again and again over the next forty-five years.

And he was not alone. Rarely has a word spread with greater speed from philosopher to philosopher. As God slowly died, crucified on the structural cross of the rational state, so *happiness* rose to become one of the new deities in a civilization that was converting to unconscious secular polytheism.

But today's meaning of the word *happiness* bears no relationship to Jefferson's. Or to that of the other rational leaders. Their happiness was primarily a pursuit of basic material comfort — although not in the modern, gratuitous sense. For them, "material" referred to the practical establishment of a well-organized, prosperous society. Jefferson was writing for men still struggling against an untamed continent — men with a clear memory of the material want and religious oppression they had escaped in Europe. His Declaration implied that, by establishing stable and organized well-being, they would also be creating rational contentment. Happiness was a simile for weal — as in *the public weal*, as in *le bien public*.

The sources from which he and others drew when they wrote of happiness were perfectly clear. There was Montesquieu, for example, with his *Lettres Persanes* in 1721, "Every man is capable of helping another man, but he must resemble the gods if he is to contribute to the happiness of a whole society." A quarter century before the American Revolution, Voltaire in his poem on the 1755 Lisbon earthquake, one of the turning points in Western beliefs, wrote, "And you will create out of this fatal chaos of disaster for every man a general happiness."[9] As tens of thousands lay dying, it is unlikely that he was referring to a future filled with powdered wigs and court balls, any more than with hot tubs and squash courts. The point of Voltaire's argument was not the individual's inalienable right to wear jeans.

Jefferson was still dwelling on the subject almost a half century after writing the Declaration of Independence. In 1823 he wrote to Coray, one of the great experts on ancient Greece and a promoter of modern Greek liberty: "The equal rights of man, and the happiness of every individual, are now acknowledged to be the only legitimate objects of government."

For "happiness" we might exchange "general well-being," meaning material sufficiency, freedom from despotic control and the right to such things as education. He goes on to say that "'the only device" by which equal rights and happiness can be "secured [is] government by the people, acting not in person, but by representatives chosen by themselves."[10] Happiness was a material and moral need, not a perpetual Victorian Christmas in the company of one's analyst. In 1825 Noah Webster published his first American dictionary. His definition of happiness began: "the agreeable sensations which spring from the enjoyment of good." Clearly, this is not a reference to the padded, form-fitting knee pads for the sensitive gardener which are called HAPPINEES.[11]

And yet the HAPPINEES company is closer to today's meaning than is anything written by Jefferson or Voltaire. Witness the arguments of Charles Murray, the influential American economist of the New Right. In the context of a discussion on "the pursuit of happiness and good government," he uses the need for happiness as an argument to decrease the role of government. "Up to now [success in social policy] has been to lift people above the poverty level or to increase equality. What we are really after [today] is an approach that will enable people to pursue happiness."[12] The word has been changed so dramatically from the intentions of Montesquieu and Jefferson that it now means exactly the opposite. Murray's vision of happiness is identical to that of an aging courtesan in the late eighteenth century. Today happiness has more to do with personality than with the state of man. In fact, the pursuit of happiness has become an escape from the state of man, just as individualism has abandoned power and left it to be gathered up by the structures of modern society, while the individual retreats into the indulgent pleasures of personality. The first desire of modern individualism is to give an impression of choice and of daring. Thus men and women hope truly to express themselves through such soft notions as life-style and self-fulfillment. This personal indulgence is impregnated by myths and verbiage and even clothing which hark back to the great romantic rebels of the last two centuries.

Almost all the early rebel models — Goethe, Byron, Constant, Lermontov — are still on active service. The mystics — from Blake to Nietzsche — have never been so busy. And their more or less existential descendants offer a full range of emotive refusals, from Rimbaud, Lawrence of Arabia, D'Annunzio, Eva Perón, Garbo and Hemingway to Boris Vian, James Dean, Che Guevara, Gérard Philipe and Marilyn Monroe. Each of them supports a variation on our different individualist styles. Most died young, thereby preserving their physical beauty. They were also, therefore, martyrs in some way, thus establishing their credentials as uncompromising individuals. Some lived longer and, as a result, were forced into alcoholism, withdrawal or eventual suicide.

These romantic victims — the Heroes of individualism — exude an ethos of rebellion. And yet, when you look at the contemporary lifestyles which are built on that rebellious mythology, you discover that they are profoundly conformist.

Take, as a minor example, an advertisement designed to sell a watch called Rado. The ad shows a tall, elegant man in a dark suit, staring confidently and seductively out at the reader.[13] Around him are life-size, white plaster casts of other men. They are like a background of ghosts. The text reads:

YOU DON'T FIT THE MOLD. WHY SHOULD YOUR WATCH? YOU DIDN'T GET WHERE YOU ARE BY FOLLOWING THE CROWD. NEITHER DID WE.

You examine the photo. The real man doesn't look particularly interesting. He looks exactly like the plaster molds, as if they were taken from his body. You examine the blowup of the watch. It looks perfectly all right; like any old good, solid timepiece. You would have trouble picking it out in a crowd of watches. The point is not that the ad contains a lie or uses false advertising. It's just that the words are in direct contradiction to the image. And the contradiction is not hidden. It is both obvious and essential to the advertisement.

No mistake has been made. Nor is this an exception. Nor a gimmick. It simply reflects individualism as a dream versus conformism as a reality. We have taken that ability of little boys — to lie in bed pretending we are pirates — and we have turned it into a formal part of adult society.

The modern intellectual tends to dismiss advertising and popular culture as either self-evident cynical manipulation or as simply irrelevant in comparison to such important ideas as the market economy or Marxism or democracy. But in this society you cannot dismiss what people wear, what they eat, what they do with their time or what they spend billions of dollars on. Advertising has grown from marginal hucksterism into the most sustained and cash-rich form of communication.

For decades there has been an all-out war between two soft drinks of almost identical taste — Coca-Cola and Pepsi-Cola. Hundreds of millions have been sunk into financing this war. More important, billions have been spent by the public on one or the other of the products. Both drinks lay claim to the same properties — youth, freedom, physical exploits, having fun and getting girls or, conversely, getting boys. In many parts of the Third World, they also possess the properties necessary to help political freedom defeat dictatorship. Coke, in particular, has become a minor idol which promises freedom, money and escape to big-time individualism in the West.

Clearly we are not talking about soft drinks. We are dealing here with what people want to believe about themselves. After all, you can scarcely claim to possess freedom of spirit and existential individualism on the grounds that you consume the same soft drink as three billion other people. This is conformism, not nonconformism.

The same could be said about the millions of McDonald's hamburgers eaten daily around the world. Clearly, this modern success story has nothing to do with selling the best hamburger. One look at the thin, grayish patties is enough to eliminate that possibility. One taste confirms that the meat is almost indistinguishable from the soft, innocuous bun and gooey ketchup. Sweetness seems to run each of these elements together. This is not a good hamburger. For that matter, McDonald's isn't even about people choosing the hamburger they like best. The corporation's approach has never seemed to involve winning the public through the mechanism of choice. Mac McDonald himself made it clear that he was removing freedom of choice: "if you gave people a choice, there would be chaos."[14]

And yet at some level, conscious or unconscious, people are convinced that by going to McDonald's they are demonstrating a sort of individualism — an individualism which turns its back on middle-class social convention by going out and eating a Big Mac. They don't have to dress up or eat decent, let alone good, food or, indeed, eat off plates or clear the table or wash dishes or deal with some snooty waiter or make conversation or sit up straight or sit still. They don't even have to sit down. Eating a McDonald's and drinking a Coke is an act of nonconformity and tens of millions of people are doing exactly that every day.

Blue jeans epitomize this idea of nonconforming individualism through absolute and massive conformity. The history of denim trousers is impeccable. Not only were they originally worn as tough work clothes, but the last of the Western mythological individualists — the cowboys — adopted them as their working uniform. The coarse cloth and the dark blue colour accurately reflect traditional, basic working-class apparel, so that somehow jeans stand as the frontier individualist's answer to the class-action approach of socialism or Communism. The moment a few of the martyred modern Heroes — James Dean, for example — began to wear them, they were effortlessly transformed into the uniform of rebellious middle-class youth.

Jeans became a symbol of nonconformity. To wear them was not to wear suits and ties and dresses; not to work in offices or fight in armies. To wear jeans was to rebel. And when that rebellion petered out in the early seventies, jeans as a revolutionary symbol survived. The beleaguered elites had already recognized that simply by slipping into these magic pants, they too could appear nonconformist. Suddenly everyone — prime ministers, cabinet secretaries and ministers, company presidents, opera stars — was walking around in jeans. Jimmy Carter was the first American president to join in by using them as a symbol of his personality. Jacques Chirac, conservative, tough technocrat and twice prime minister of France, was photographed for *Paris-Match* as he lounged outside his château in jeans. It was as if he had only two outfits: the serial gray suit and serial jeans.

The fact that by then more people were wearing jeans than suits seemed to have no effect on the mythology attached to one or the other. The rich, with their sense of irony — or lack of it — began to wear denim with mink. Or denim to drive their Rolls. Somehow it was less elitist if the owner of a hundred-thousand-dollar car drove it in twenty-dollar, working-class trousers.

At some point these innocuous trousers passed from being the great symbol of nonconformism to the greatest available symbol of faceless

484   *Surviving in Fantasy Land*

conformity. The suit and tie had never achieved such levels of uniformity. They had only been required for certain economic and social functions. And the suits themselves had differed from class to class and country to country. But blue jeans became the symbol of absolute conformity, irrespective of class and country. They also became a paradise for the advertiser, who could appeal to any dream of nonconformity, any dream at all, and still sell the same old goods.

The Italian Forenza jeans, for example, advertise theirs as "BASHED DAMAGED and otherwise made to look beautiful." The photo shows a beautiful, delicate girl dressed in worn, faded, shapeless jeans. The traditional image from which this borrows is no longer the cowboy, but the hobo or the garbageman from the days before municipal uniforms were issued. The large French bank, Banque Nationale de Paris, offers a special account to children — a "Jeans Savings Account." What could be more conforming than a savings account? In a wonderful deformation of thirty years of social history, they advertise this account with a photo of a young boy dressed above the waist as an executive and below the waist in jeans. There are Calvin Klein jeans sold via campaigns which target homosexuals. Esprit jeans advertises with separate photos of two young women. One is agreeably dumpy. The other is serenely Bergmanesque. Beneath the dumpy girl are the words "Cara Schanche, Berkeley, California, Age: 23, English Literature Student, Part-time Waitress, Anti-Racism Activist, Beginning Windsurfer, Friend of Dalai Lama." Beneath the photo of the leaner woman are the words "Ariel O'Donnell, San Francisco, Age: 21, Waitress/Bartender, Non-professional AIDS Educator, Cyclist, Art Restoration Student, Anglophile, Neo-Feminist." The two descriptions assemble an eclectic collection of fashionable, humanitarian and original activities in order to create an impression of individualism. There are also Buffalo jeans for sadomasochists. Since the Buffalo ads involve such things as bound women in denim, the buyer has the choice of identifying either with the girl delighting in punishment or with the invisible knot-expert punisher who is presumably male and presumably also wearing jeans. As for the original Levi's jeans, inside these a man or a woman can settle for being a plain individualist, without intellectual or psychiatric labels.

Even the silliest phenomena take on relevance when they reach such economic and social proportions. The sellers of life-styles have thought a great deal about the conformity-nonconformity contradiction in their products. Esprit jeans have turned this problem into a sublime new interpretation of individualism. Their advertisements have included the following philosophical statement:

Because denim and jean wear are such social equalizers today you don't necessarily need silks and satins to be elegant. Elegance is now, curiously enough, anti-fashion and anti-luxury. This new elegance has become a de-classification process that puts what you can do — your style and abilities — far ahead of what you can afford. Now you don't have to be rich to be elegant.

Rarely has the modern idea of nonconformity through aggressive conformity been better expressed. One only regrets the absence of an industrial award for sophistry.

This confusion is not, of course, limited to jeans. Even charity has become fashion. The standard phrase "the charity of your choice" has increasingly become the charity of the year. Tragic causes now sweep rapidly across nations and continents, capturing universal attention for a few weeks or months.

While the plight of the boat people was tearing at the heartstrings of the West, people could think of nothing else. That problem was not solved. Nor did the flow of refugees stop. But neither can such massive waves of emotion hover endlessly over a single tragedy. Fashion and style are always on the move. To pause is to invite choice. And choice, as Mac McDonald pointed out, produces confusion. So we moved relentlessly on, leaving the boat people in our wake in order to worry ourselves deeply over the plight of the starving Ethiopians. They are still starving, but we shifted focus to the AIDS victims, as star-studded benefits caught our attention. This was briefly interrupted by massive concern for the Kurdish people, who have been suffering for a century and continue to suffer. Our conforming generosity has already moved on.

Tourism has become perhaps the most popular means for individuals to give themselves the sensation that they have stepped outside the norm, while continuing to move within it. The international circuit of airplanes, hotels, ruins, folk dances, exotic foods and native clothes has indeed created a planetary Disneyland of sanitized exoticism. In Hawaii the Hyatt Regency Waikoloa has been built on a moonscape of black lava rock at a cost of $360 million.[15] This luxury hotel of 1,241 rooms is, in fact, devoted to the existential act. Once the guests have been taken to their rooms by boat, with a captain pretending to steer them through the lagoon while the hull is actually running on wheels in an underwater groove, they may pay for a safari to shoot boar or pheasants, to go formula car racing, to dine in a former palace, to helicopter into a volcano's mouth or simply to a secluded point for a champagne picnic, to swim (by appointment) with the hotel's dolphins or indeed to do almost anything exotic they have ever dreamed of.

The hotel owners have correctly identified a widespread and desperate need of people to experience unstructured excitement at almost any cost, providing it is organized and the responsibility is taken by the organizer. This may at first appear to be a fantasy land, but it is also the inevitable marriage between Disneyland and Jean Genet's bordello in *The Balcony*. It is the logical child of the Club Meds, spas and package tours. It is also the perfect metaphor for modern individualism.

One of the few radical things the modern middle-class male or female can do without reference to social structure is alter his or her own body. A recent study indicates that 54 percent of American men and 75 percent of women are obsessed with their physical appearance.[16] More to the point, they are ready to change it radically, as various studies and polls indicate. For example:

Would Change	Men (percentage)	Women (percentage)
Weight	56	78
Hair	36	35
Height	34	28
Hide signs of aging	27	48
Nose	19	21
Teeth	36	37
Legs	—	34
Bust	—	32
Feet	—	18

Given the money and the time, they can easily change seven of the above nine elements. Many of them already have. We are dealing here not with simple middle-class hysteria and self-indulgence. To change your own body, particularly to change fixed features by lopping off noses, planting balding scalps or sucking out cellulite, is to engage in a supremely individualistic act. The fact that it will neither satisfy the individual nor have any important effect on the attitudes of others is not particularly relevant. What is fascinating is the degree to which the human has turned in upon himself in search of some individual power.

The act of altering the fixed character of our body (as opposed to disguising it) belongs to the same family of action as suicide. There is a school of thought which considers suicide the supreme individual act. To decide on a button nose in place of something aquiline is obviously a less extreme statement, but it leads in the same direction. It is also a spin-off of the technical advances of reason. The same doctor who, thanks to a century of medical advances, can now reconstruct a burnt face or erase a harelip will probably be rewarded with a great deal more money if he chooses instead to satisfy the endless dreams of altered bodies.

The human, like the rat, will adapt to any circumstance and always responds to experiment. For the first time in history, we are able to experiment with our own bodies. Equally, for the first time in history, sex has been separated from its function, thanks to a myriad of birth control methods. This has made copulation another safe area for the individual to express his independence outside the structure. The explosion in venereal diseases, including AIDS, is a separate issue. After all, sexual experiments have no effect on administrative systems, apart from extra financial costs. Even the most extreme experiment — the change of sex — can take place without a person's career necessarily being adversely affected. What is interesting about the sexual explosion is not that society permits so much, but that so many human expectations and so much human energy should have been crowded into this area in search of a satisfaction denied in the public domain.

And for all of our romantic and erotic concentration, it isn't clear, by any means, that there are more orgasms per capita today than three hundred or six hundred years ago. After all, most people used to marry in their early-to-midteens and so got an early start when the sex drive is usually at its maximum. Also, rational society has bred an emotional-physical condition called stress, which has become one of the principal characteristics of people who occupy what are called positions of responsibility. That is, people who occupy boxes within structures. It could be argued that stress is caused neither by work nor by imaginary responsibility, but first by the loss of control over one's own actions, which comes from becoming part of the structure, and second from the strain of creating and maintaining a defence of secrecy around oneself, and third from the constant strain of trying to imagine what the secretive people in the adjoining boxes will do next. Studies show that stress is one of the main causes of impotence. Given the size of the modern middle classes and their entrapment within structures, it's fair to ask whether there isn't more talk about sex than there are orgasms.

A few things are certain. The variety of sexual partners has grown in comparison to the nineteenth and early twentieth centuries, but probably not in comparison to the seventeenth and eighteenth. Public references to sex have certainly increased. Above all, however, it is the dream which has grown — the dream of potency, of copulation, of mastery, of passion and, of course, of love, of possession, of eternal idylls. These have swelled in the imagination, in conversation and in public images as if there were no limit to the percentage of available space they might take up.

Only so much can be done with real sexual organs. And, apart from the probability that more women get more out of the act today than used to be the norm, the death of God didn't change those organs. Nor did the Reformation. Nor the conversion of the Roman Empire. But the imagination, once focused in that direction, has endless possibilities. A great deal of our imagination used to be consumed by our involvement in religious and social structures. Most of that is free today to concentrate on individual self-gratification. This does not mean that the romantic dream is new, any more than fantasies of sexual satisfaction or even pornography are new. They have always been around. But not in such quantities.

It wasn't until Pompeii was excavated in the eighteenth century and the licentious paintings in it uncovered that the idea of pornography began to gather impetus. The word itself did not appear until the mid-nineteenth century.[17] In English, *pornographer* appeared in 1850, *pornography* in 1864 and *pornographic* in 1880 — that is, simultaneously with the words *specialization* and *specialist*, as well as *individualism* and *individualist*. In the fifteenth century, there had been an Italian satirist who verged on the edge of pornography called Pietro Aretino. Cleland had published his more titillating than explicit *Fanny Hill* in 1748. Restif de La Bretonne had wandered through the low life of eighteenth-century Paris, churning out racy novels. And Casanova's eighteenth-century memoirs began appearing in the marketplace in 1826, almost three decades after his death. But all four men were pioneers. There was not much actual pornography around until the nineteenth century.

Abruptly the full imagination was focused on the sexual act, the sizes involved, its sounds, effects, quantities and importance. Specialist literature blossomed. *The Lustful Turk* (1828), *Rosa Fielding, or, A Victim of Lust* (1876), *The Amatory Experiences of a Surgeon* (1881) and late in the century an astonishing eleven-volume memoir, *The Secret Life*.[18] These and a flood of other books rose until they forced open the doors of legal restraint in the twentieth century. The moment sex was formally recognized in the public domain as an unrestricted private act, it was clear that the interests of the power structure and those of the individual had been separated. This should be hailed as a victory for private rights. But it could also be identified as the moment when the public structures realized that power could be maintained without regulating private behaviour.

In the Middle Ages man dreamed endlessly about turning base metals into gold and paintings into eternal images. But the energy he has put into imagining the orgasm during the last hundred years overshadows these other dreams. If Marx were functioning today, he would have been hard put to avoid saying that imaginary sex is the opiate of the people.

All around us there are illustrations of both soft and hard pornography: suggestive advertising, serious films and novels with obligatory carnal scenes, how-to books for better sex or more love or longer love and sexual fulfillment, books on finding the right partner through an evaluation of physical types or by colour charts or celestial analysis. Popular mythology has it that in the new, careful age of AIDS all of this is passé. But any cursory survey of films, magazines and books suggests that, as the fear of real sex grows, so does the use of suggestive images.

The idea underlying such endless discussion and dreaming about the physical act is that sexual expertise confers worldliness and is therefore part of becoming an affirmed individual. This is a curious suggestion. After all, large parts of the Third World are filled with teenage girls and boys who are great professional experts in sex. And their expertise is taken as proof of their lack of independence. What's more, outside the Western middle classes, sexual relationships have much more to do with a lack of individual affirmation than the contrary. History tells us that it is, above all, an area for manipulation and control. The middle-class Westerner can argue that the sexual revolution has ended this, but from there to believing that sexual independence is a leading indicator in the affirmation of the individual owes more to romantic comedy than to the real world. Perhaps the oddest part of our notion is the idea that sexual experience or expertise brings worldliness. Sex is many things — a need, a desire, an emotion, a release — but it has nothing to do with worldly sophistication, character building or even existential action.

Sex, in general, is more of an obstacle than anything else for those who wish to free themselves and act as individuals. It can not be a coincidence that most of the martyred existential heroes, in whom rational society has invested its dream of individualism, appear to have been asexual or to have led disastrous sex lives. At first glance this doesn't seem to fit with our sexual obsession. But then we aren't dealing with a successful affirmation of responsible individualism in the real world. We are creating private dreams which compensate for the fracturing of the individual and the castration of his or her power in public life.

Marshall McLuhan was convinced that one of the explanations for the rise of violence in our society was "the loss of private identity which has come rather suddenly upon Western man. [It] has produced a deep anger at this rip-off of his private self." The rip-off he was referring to has nothing to do with private enterprise versus government or the private self versus government or the private self versus private enterprise. Rather it is the product of a general structural phenomenon which affects every area.

But does the anger which McLuhan describes come from the loss of private identity or from that of public identity? He seemed to believe it came from the latter. "There are thus two kinds of violence relating to the same situation: first, the kind that comes from the unimportance of everybody; and second, the kind that comes from the impulse to restore one's private meaning by acts of violence."[19] The first example refers to the loss of a public identity — that is, the loss of real individual powers. The second fits the category of obsessional sex dreams and material self-gratification. Violence is an attempt to make a public statement with private means. It has always been a sign of frustration over public impotence.

Personal crimes have been rising steadily throughout the West. Sexual abuse of children, rape, wife beating — all seem to be on the increase. Only a small part of this is due to more effective reporting systems.

A recent poll of American university males revealed that 51 percent would rape a woman if they thought they could get away with it.[20] There are a number of possible explanations. One is that the average middle-class, twenty-year-old male has already had his personality fractured and recompacted in preparation for his insertion into the structure. He is constantly told that he is lucky to be free and privileged. He is surrounded by images and words which encourage him to believe himself masterly in matters of the body and capable of great seductive acts. He knows in his heart that he is unlikely to be either masterly or a Casanova. On top of that, he now also knows that the woman's expectations should be satisfied. In truth, he does not even believe himself capable of handling his own. No wonder rape looms as a simple expression of a private, unfettered individuality. Most banal of all, it becomes a way to avenge himself upon the system.

There is little to envy in the woman's position either. For perhaps the first time in history, she has a general sense of herself as an individual apart from men. This self-confidence gives her drive and makes her want to succeed. As a result she is eager to join the system. She does not have a clear idea of what it will do to her. Her focus is on her own past and on what men did to women — not on the male structure and what it does to men. Her enthusiasm makes her work harder and usually do a better job than the equivalent male. As a result the talented female tends to become an effective defender of the system which has so emasculated the male and which, therefore, was indirectly responsible for his resistance to strengthening the role of women.

At the same time the younger woman increasingly looks upon the younger male as an ally. Like him she has been exposed to the endless rhetoric about a new deal between the sexes. And there are concrete signs of improvement to support that rhetoric. But what is actually taking place is a meeting between a scarred, starved and brutalized male veteran of rational warfare and an untried, idealistic, gung-ho female volunteer.

～

The rapist's anger is part of the same problem as that of the face-lift and the suicide. His violence is directed against someone else, but in committing it he risks himself. And risking the self is the last cry of the individual. In that sense he is not very different from the Western political terrorist. They both destroy and, having risked themselves, expect to be destroyed in turn.

A first wave of nihilists, anarchists and revolutionaries appeared in the second half of the nineteenth century. When Archduke Franz-Ferdinand and his wife were shot in 1914, there had already been, since 1900, a bevy of political assassinations in the West — four kings, one queen, a crown prince, a Russian grand duke, three presidents and six prime ministers.

The literature and gossip of the day were filled with talk of these young men — more often than not, middle class and educated — who felt obliged to kill and almost inevitably to die themselves. When Archduke Ferdinand drove down the quai in Sarajevo, a team of six assassins were waiting, spread out over a distance of 350 metres in the crowd. Almost all of them were under-age students. All carried bombs and pistols and, equally important, cyanide to kill themselves immediately after firing. The first lost his nerve as the procession went by; as did the second. The third threw a bomb which wounded twelve people but missed the Archduke. In the ensuing chaos, the last three fled. It was only much later in the day that an accident of fate or stupidity caused the Archduke's car to turn off the official route, where it became blocked by the crowds on a side street. Gavrilo Princip, one of the three assassins who had fled, was moping in a café with his girlfriend when the limousine ground to a halt outside. He leapt to his feet, rushed out, put his hand over his eyes, turned his head away, and fired two shots in the general direction of Ferdinand and his wife. Both were fatal. He then tried to swallow his cyanide but got only enough down to make himself sick. He was captured, tried, and, being too young to hang, was imprisoned. He died of consumption and gangrene in an Austrian jail in 1917.

Princip was from a simple background, of limited intelligence, physically weak, ugly and short. He seems to have concentrated all his resentments in his nationalism. The terrorist group he belonged to was painfully amateurish. Their adventures involved carrying the weapons and bombs across country by train in a clunking suitcase, which was then discovered in Sarajevo by a hotel maid cleaning under one of their beds. Their incompetence, however, was matched by that of the local military commander. Finally, Ferdinand's self-pride and his image of himself as a generous reformer led him to refuse adequate protection.

The most interesting of the six terrorists was also the youngest, Vaso Čubrilović. Second in the line of assassins on the quai, he had lost his nerve at the last moment, panicked no doubt by the first assassin's failure to throw his bomb. Čubrilović in turn failed to throw his or to fire his pistol in spite of a clear target. He was later identified, captured, tried and, being a teenager, was jailed rather than executed. After the war, he was freed. He went on to become a revolutionary leader, an associate of Tito and an historian. He survived the guerrilla fighting of World War II to become one of Tito's ministers. In the late 1980s, he was still alive — the last of the six men who had, in a sense, brought the old world and its civilization to an end.

During a conversation in Belgrade in 1987, I asked him what he felt about the unprecedented violence which had been released by the assassination of Ferdinand. This tiny man in his nineties, shrunken, almost translucent in a heavy, dark ministerial suit, brushed the question aside: "I am an historian. There are no ifs in history. Only what happened. What didn't happen. The assassination was a reflection of our situation. Peace was impossible."[21]

He went on to describe politics as being dominated by three types — the rare great leader; the idealist who fails; and the opportunistic or narrowly motivated men who dominate. Čubrilović and his five young friends on the quai fell into the category of failed idealists. He saw Tito as a rare, great leader. But the satisfaction he felt over the creation of Yugoslavia seemed to have been largely wiped away by the rise to power of the third type — the technocrats and opportunists. For him such people represented the inevitable complications of living in society. That is, as a terrorist turned politician and minister, he looked upon these tens of thousands of successful administrators as the result of having built a country. Already he could sense the fabric of Yugoslavia pulling apart, because those who now held power had no agenda except structure. And yet, behind his considered reflections on seventy years of history, he spoke as if he had never recovered from that instant as a young terrorist on the quai in Sarajevo, when he had neither fired at the Archduke nor killed himself and so had failed to seize the great moment of his own individualism.

The terrorist is certainly the closest thing to an individual that this century has produced. Whatever organization he may belong to, in a single moment he must act, both alone and in an absolute manner. The politics of the West cause us to dwell on those terrorists who rise out of the Third World. Far more interesting, from our point of view, are those who rise out of the Western middle classes and thus completely cut their ties with the tattered remnants of Christian society. More to the point, they cut their ties with reason and with the structure it has created. Their supremely irrational act is not aimed so much at changing the world as it is at freeing themselves from it.

There were great debates among pre–World War I terrorists over what to do if innocent people strayed into the line of fire between themselves and a presidential target or if a wife and child unexpectedly went along for the ride in the carriage of their father, the prince — the carriage into which a bomb was to be thrown. Should the terrorists fire away and lob the bombs and damn the details in the name of justice? Or should they spare the innocent, thus inevitably sparing the guilty also? The very fact that they were asking such questions indicates that their principal concern was not the effect this assassination might have on the world, but rather the effect it would have on their own moral status. Whether they themselves died was not of great importance. What counted was properly defining their true nature as moral individuals before seriously thinking about killing and being killed.

André Malraux opened *Man's Fate* with an image of the terrorist as the quintessential seeker of autonomy from mankind. In complete darkness a young terrorist creeps through the bedroom of his victim, who is sleeping on his back under a mosquito net. The terrorist plunges his knife through the netting and deep into the man's chest, pinning him to the mattress. The man wakes in panic and agony. He struggles or convulses around the blade, which is held down by the terrorist's full weight. During this struggle the terrorist feels the human spirit of the victim rising through the wound, up the shaft of the knife, and into his own hands, arms and body. He is like Dracula, drinking strength from the blood or life force of his victim. The question of the fight for social justice, which brought him into the room to kill, has disappeared. It is a supremely egotistical act.

The Oswalds, Baader-Meinhoffs and Actions Directs of the last few decades are very like this young terrorist. If anything, they have been even less effective as social or political revolutionaries than the early terrorists. Max Frérot, the leading killer of Action Direct, is a good example of this. By 1986 everyone else in his revolutionary group had been captured. Frerot alone was left to wander, somehow untouchable, through the denseness of Paris and Lyon and other French cities. His ability to bomb and to shoot was heightened by this isolation.

The lone, unattached assassin is almost invisible in a structured society. Thus Frérot could go on killing. But each savage act seemed less oriented than the last. Random action is the sign of a smart terrorist. But his acts appeared to be the fruit of random thinking. Why was he killing these people? What were his aims? His strategy was not convincing on even the most basic level of social destabilization. The impression left was more that of a lonely man desperate to complete his individuality through a final act of self-immolation. And so his attacks were not more and more pertinent to his cause, but more and more daring, with himself increasingly at risk. If there were any doubt about whether his motivations were political or personal, the discovery of the remarkably indiscreet diary he kept, setting down names, places, dates and detailed descriptions of his operations, eliminated the political. In the end he failed even as a martyr. He was simply captured and has now been integrated back into the structure through the application of legal and bureaucratic rules. That is a far worse punishment than whatever sentence he may serve.

As an old man Malraux argued that terrorists had changed during his lifetime. "They have become quite logical people, while the terrorists I knew were closer to the Russian nihilists; that is to say, basically metaphysicians."[22] But have they changed or have they simply, like any nihilist, adapted to the society in which they operate? The revolutionaries of the late nineteenth century and early twentieth, like those of today, sought to destroy structure and reason. But in the nineteenth century this violent refusal by "individualists" to cooperate was more intuitive than carefully thought out. They had only early indications of what the forces of structure and reason contained and of the effect they would eventually have on society.

Today the situation is clear from their point of view: if you wish to destroy structure and reason, you must operate with logic and science. But if you are unfortunate enough to personally survive these killing attacks, then, like Gavrilo Princip, you are little better than a failed metaphysician. Whether they chain you up in an Austrian jail until you rot to death or commit you to a model modern prison for reeducation is irrelevant. In both cases you have ceased to exist as an individual, ceased to exist more completely than if you had never attempted to break away in order to assert your existence.

Look, for example, at the assassins of the cabinet minister Pierre Laporte in Montreal in 1970. So long as they held him captive, their own faces unknown, they were more than individuals. They were potential gods, holding in their hands the power of life or death. The moment they used that power in the purest existential way by killing him, and then were captured and put on trial — the whole configuration changed. The strangling of a plump, aging male cannot be, with hindsight, an Heroic act, particularly when the terrorists are young and strong. Now, decades later, they seem an even more motley, pitiful crew, like accidental leftovers of a cataclysmic but pointless act.

From the point of view of the terrorist, the only importance of the godly act is its effect on the one who carries it out. That effect — the establishment of perfect individualism — is only activated if he completes the act by committing suicide. If his victim dies and he lives, he is no more consequential a man than someone who kills in a hit-and-run accident and is then charged with manslaughter.

Few people aspire to acts of individualism sanctified by violence. The more common approaches to self-definition are less risky. The acquisition of material wealth, for example. The theory is that the greater a person's wealth, the more freedom he will have to act as he wishes. He becomes an individual by purchasing his freedom. However, the system usually requires an enormous and prolonged sacrifice of personal freedom — that is, a structured career — before delivering this material independence. The limitations involved are daily, yearly; in fact, they usually last a good thirty years. The whole idea of individualism as a function of wealth therefore rests upon a catch-22. That's why the middle-class Westerner has dressed material goods and personal pleasures in the mythological cloak of individualism. These are the small rewards he or she receives during decades of sacrifice. This is also one of the explanations for the importance that retirement has taken on in Western society. It isn't simply that we are going to live longer. The prison of the system leaves us to conclude that the reward of freedom lies ahead, always ahead.

Yet few of us seem convinced by the liberating powers of wealth or by the promise of a freer future once we have ceased sacrificing our lives. Instead, every social measuring device indicates that the level of personal anxiety and stress has been steadily rising. We seek relief through a growing array of irrational devices. The old religions have seen at least a superficial revival. People have also turned to psychiatrists, gurus, fundamentalist churches, Zen Buddhism, mind-emptying exercises, yoga and a growing selection of social drugs, both prescribable and illegal.

There can be no doubt that the road which Zen Buddhism offers out of the prison of reason is far superior to alternatives such as self-actualization (the combination of more money and increased spirituality), bioenergetics, colour therapy, getting in touch with your anima, massage to release emotional trauma fossilized in the body or Iyengar Yoga.[23] But none of these, including Zen, offer either practical reforms or revolutionary changes for the society we live in. Instead they offer temporary escape routes. After all, no matter what happens, sixty million Frenchmen or Englishmen are not going to become Zen Buddhists or even seek truth through an analyst. Instead, the fractured individual offers himself or herself periodic tranquilizers to take the mind off the realities of the imprisoning system.

In total contradiction to all this, the citizen expects his political leaders to take no tranquilizers. The explanation for this projected puritanism may lie in our Judeo-Christian origins. If we are obliged to suffer the profound and invisible travails of life, then a sacrificial lamb must be found who will visibly suffer. Or perhaps it is our revenge on the system. Political leaders are theoretically in charge of it and since we cannot punish abstract structures, why not punish those who appear to run them? Or perhaps we are attempting to give some importance to the crumbs that we now call individualism by refusing them to those we elect. Or perhaps it is sheer hypocrisy — by refusing to those who lead us the sort of life we claim for ourselves, we avoid the embarrassment of a mirror image in the public place.

In any case, these leaders quickly learn that, in return for whatever latitude they can develop in policy-making by manipulating the system, they must conform absolutely to a personal, public image which is extraordinarily strict and narrow. They look out from their presidential or prime ministerial or ministerial offices at a population which may say whatever it wishes on private matters, divorce as often as choice and finances permit, sleep with as many people of the opposite sex, the same sex, or both, as desire can realize, use drugs, dress up to their heart's content, collect expensive wines and eat in showy restaurants, just for starters. These acts may all be meaningless and superficial, but they are the modern version of happiness. And this happiness is specifically prohibited to the public figure.

He or she is expected to be heterosexual, married, faithful to wife or husband, modest in dress and speech, restrained in drink, a pure abstainer from drugs, driver of a nondescript sort of car. He or she should not be seen to waste money on fancy food. A public that finds personal sustenance from an unending dream of luxury is pleased to learn that its leader comes home from the office, so to speak, and just loves to relax by going into the kitchen and scrambling some eggs for the family. Needless to say, such an icon must incarnate an unending list of Boy-Scout or Girl-Guide qualities, from not having cheated at school to never swearing.

In a society whose structures are amoral and whose citizens are theoretically liberated, the political leader has become the repository, or rather the depository, of the old middle-class values. Of course, no one really fulfills any of these conditions. Anyone who did would probably be incapable of doing the job. Instead, they must deform their character sufficiently to give a false public impression of what it is. Falsification becomes an essential talent for the elected, and eagerness to be duped a characteristic for the citizen. This also suggests that only people with severely deformed characters will be able to rise to high office. The system can't help but reward those whose prime talents are acting and punish those who are straightforward.

In 1987 President Reagan twice failed to nominate successfully a justice to the Supreme Court. The second candidate — Professor Douglas Ginsburg of the Harvard Law School — was accused, during the confirmation hearings, of having taken a few puffs of marijuana in his distant past. This simply meant that he had acted in conformity with the majority of his generation. But by virtue of the position for which he was nominated, this banal and common event became a heinous weakness. Professor Ginsburg was abruptly reduced to defending himself with such infantile statements as: "To the best of my recollection, once as a college student in the 60's, and then on a few occasions in the 70's, I used marijuana. That is the only drug I ever used. I have not used it since. *It was a mistake and I regret it.*"[24]

What the Professor meant was that smoking marijuana had been a mistake in the context of getting this job. If the citizenry sincerely expected Douglas Ginsburg to regret his past puffs, they would have to regret sincerely their own past and present licentiousness. Clearly they don't. There was no sign during the Ginsburg confirmation of nationwide regret. The same hypocrisy was demonstrated over such things as Willy Brandt's girlfriends, Lyndon Johnson's swearing, Cecil Parkinson's pregnant mistress and Roy Jenkins's taste for Bordeaux.

There was a time when the populace had little choice but to bask in the reflection of the mythological free and easy lives led by their kings and nobles. Now those who have replaced the kings must bask in the shadow of the theoretically nonconformist lives led by a good part of their population. That, at any rate, is the theory. The reality is elsewhere.

This is an age of great conformity. It is difficult to find another period of such absolute conformism in the history of Western civilization. The citizens are so completely locked inside their boxes of expertise that they are effectively excluded from open public debate. We have disguised this truth by redefining individualism as an agreeable devotion to style and personal emotions. We project ourselves, as if in a romantic dream, against a backdrop of martyred existential outsiders. And in the absence of practical levers of power, we have convinced ourselves that these images are real. Film, television and magazines have given these outsiders a concrete form. We know them. We know them well, these blond men who lead the Bedouin against the Turks, these actresses who sleep with presidents and die, these poets who run off to deal in slaves in Ethiopia, these beauties who marry dictators and speak for the poor. We have seen them a thousand times on the screen. We know what they wear. We know the definition of their chest muscles, the depth of their cleavage. We know the sound of their voices.

Unfortunately, they bear no resemblance to the real outsiders from whom these images are freely drawn. The real men were more often short, without well-defined muscles, often running to fat like Bon-aparte; the real women sallow and confused behind makeup and furs. They most definitely were not wearing jeans. But, in any case, we don't actually want to meet the real outsider, determined as we are to hide from our own conformism. We wish to dream about him or her as if dreaming about ourselves. Their presence would make that impossible.

Our paradise of the individual is dependent upon carefully main-tained illusions. So long as real power remains in the rational structures of our society, only dreaming allows the citizen to remain sane. Even if there were a real and generalized desire among the population to drift away like Rimbaud, it wouldn't work. Ethiopia has enough trouble supporting its own population and the slave trade has been in difficulty for decades.

20

The Stars

Marie Antoinette was the first modern star. She was never really Queen of France. That was merely her role. She played queen. She never saw it as a position which, although held by right, involved responsibility or obligation.

Such irresponsibility seems natural today and we tend to confuse her starlike grandeur with that of other kings or queens. Louis XIV, after all, played a role. Elizabeth I was perhaps the finest star who ever performed. But Louis XIV, a simple man, played grandeur in order to solidify his power and to weaken that of the threatening nobility. Elizabeth turned herself into an overdressed, overjewelled, overmade-up virgin in order to protect herself from the power of men and therefore to exercise power herself.

Marie Antoinette was something quite new. Something revolutionary. There were hints of this in her miniature play farm, hidden out in the gardens of Versailles. The palace itself was a stage set, but her *Fermette* was more like the prototype for the movie star's Los Angeles estate or Michael Jackson's private zoo. Perfect little farm buildings. A few delightful animals of the finest breeding. Servants within hailing distance and the greatest palace in the world only a few hundred yards away. The *Fermette* was the original Disneyland: a place where the greatest queen in the world and her courtesans could dress up as milkmaids and farmers, then play at milking cows in a romantic idyll of simplicity.

The birth of the modern star came late at night, on June 20, 1791, when Marie Antoinette, Louis XVI, their son and daughter, governess and two maids escaped from the Tuileries Palace in the centre of Paris. The Constituent Assembly, as it saw things, had been holding them for their own and the nation's good in this immense and gilded prison, like peacocks in a cage. The ensuing chase is now known as the escape to Varennes, a small town near the German border and scene of the dramatic climax.

The Queen directed the whole escape and, of course, starred in it. The producer was a Swedish count, Axel de Fersen, who was Marie

Antoinette's greatest admirer and probably her lover. His original plan had had the King fleeing alone and disguised as a woman. Louis felt this masquerade lacked dignity and the Queen rejected it, in large part because it involved leaving her behind. The second plan had the King being whisked away, again alone, in a fast coach to rejoin the rebel army of nobles in exile. The Queen objected again. Her script involved something much more grandiose — the escape of the entire family in one fell swoop.

The royal family plus governess could only fit into a large, slow coach — a *berline* — which the Queen had piled high with luggage until it was capable of doing a mere ten kilometres per hour. A cabriolet followed at a respectful distance, carrying the minimum pair of maids.

The governess was to play a Russian baroness called Madame de Korff; the royal children, her son and daughter; the Queen, their governess; and the King, the baroness's valet. Marie Antoinette drew upon the palace wardrobe to get herself up as a maid. She didn't actually disguise herself. She played a maid the way she played a milkmaid at the *Fermette* or the way Garbo later played a queen or Dietrich a whore. No one was meant to mistake them for their roles. They were themselves — stars. Louis didn't even try to play the valet. He plunked a pink wig on his head and treated the whole thing as farce. His domineering Queen encouraged this approach.

The escape began on schedule, thanks to Fersen, who got them secretly out of the palace in separate small coaches and personally drove the Queen to the outskirts of Paris, where they all climbed into the *berline*. There Fersen left them and Marie Antoinette took over. The coach soon slowed to a leisurely minimum speed. They began to fall behind schedule and thus missed the cavalry detachments which were to provide protection in each town. The Queen and King stuck their heads out the windows as they rolled through hamlets. They were recognized. They greeted their subjects with waves. The escape turned into a theatrical royal progress, while the day slipped by into darkness. Around midnight, as they rolled out of a small place called Sainte-Menehould, the local municipal council, controlled by radicals, called an emergency meeting and decided to send their postman, a Monsieur Drouet, on to the next town by fast horse. There he overtook the royal coach, stirred up some sleeping citizens to block the bridge leading out of Varennes, and forced the royal family to climb down from their *berline*. The border and freedom were only a few kilometres away.

They were quickly surrounded by a growing crowd of ordinary citizens, hostile, admiring, curious. The mayor, a local tradesman, pushed through the melee and invited them to take refuge in his house. Having got them there, he was overwhelmed by the presence in his tiny living room of all four Bourbons. He didn't know whether to abase himself or arrest them. And so he did neither. Outside the confusion was growing. The postman was waking every radical in town and posting them around the *berline* or on the flimsy barricade blocking the bridge. Suddenly one of the lost cavalry escorts rode into town and forced its way through to the mayor's house. Their commanding officer informed the royal family that, provided they left immediately, it would be possible to fight their way out. It was clear that if they stayed, captivity would be the best they could hope for. Given the relationship between the weak King and his strong-willed wife, the decision was hers.

In this astonishingly clear existential moment, Marie Antoinette found herself unable to tell the difference between reality and appearances. Rather than risk a real action which could save the lives of her family, she withdrew into her self-image of the divinely appointed monarch against whom no one could act. She chose to ignore reality and to continue her established role. Outside the radicals were fraternizing with the King's cavalry. Within the hour his soldiers had changed sides. All was lost. The Queen's farce was over.

To understand how revolutionary an approach to power the Queen's had been, we need only look back a little over a century to the middle of the 1600s when the idea of a powerful woman was even less acceptable. Marie de Médicis, widow of Henri IV and Queen of France, had the same intellectual limitations as Marie Antoinette. Worse, she was highly emotional and very fat. Twice she was imprisoned. Twice she escaped, but not by dressing herself up in a pretended disguise and parading in full daylight across France. Instead, she wore only essentials and scaled down palace walls from upper floors in the dark of night, hiked through forests and mud and waded across dangerous rivers. The difference between the two queens was that, although Marie de Médicis saw her position as a privilege, she understood that it was dependent on her ability to assume the attached responsibilities. Even those queens and kings who had no intention of doing good understood that they had a job which involved real activity.

What made Marie Antoinette so modern was that she consecrated the division between power and fame. Until then the latter had been not so much wed to as bred from the former. Whoever had power, whether king or duke, pope or bishop, automatically had fame. At its worst this was the characteristic of a society in which the have-nots envy those who have. But it was also the manifestation of a general human need to imagine ourselves as taller, stronger, richer, better lovers or more important than we are. This has less to do with envy than with a need to dream. And that need must be focused on dreams which have been realized or at least appear to have been.

Of course, kings were never as wise, strong, beautiful or potent as fame described them, but the mystery surrounding a monarch made up for most personal limitations. To the degree that popular illusions were actually betrayed by cruelty or poor leadership or degeneracy, these men of power simply became the dark shadows of the public's imagination. And if the king was uninspiring, they could always focus on the court.

Life in the courts of Europe was, by all accounts, detestable. These were places filled with hypocrisy and ambition. Saint-Simon and Casanova chronicled the machinations in their diaries and memoirs. Swift railed against the cabals of Queen Anne's acolytes. Molière ridiculed the courtier's life. In the shadows of monarchs, men whose talents lay in currying favour invariably rose. A royal court also included a full cast of mythological figures — courageous knights, beautiful and pure virgin princesses, wise counsellors, poets, artists, the finest cooks, the finest horsemen and, of course, actresses, schemers, prelates, social climbers and reformers. There was something for the imagination of every citizen — good roles and evil roles. Even the most banal orgasm could take on a certain importance, thanks to titles and reputations but, above all, because this celebrity grew out of legitimate power. Court gazettes were the *People, Paris-Match, Der Spiegel* of their day and they spread the details of court life throughout the population.

By the second half of the eighteenth century, however, Thomas Jefferson, American ambassador in Paris, was able to look at Marie Antoinette with a clarity which would have been impossible only a few years before, when the vapours of royal mythology still clouded everyone's vision: "Some smartness of fancy, but no sound sense, was proud, disdainful of restraint, indignant at all obstacles to her will, eager in the pursuit of pleasure, and firm enough to hold to her desires, or perish in their wreck."[1] But surely this is the description of some Hollywood star, Faye Dunaway, for example. "Beset by rumors of being impossible, she is sticking to her self-image of a star on a grand scale."[2] Or of Madonna, alternately swathed in silk or arching a bared mount of Venus towards the camera. Or of this century's greatest star, Wallis Simpson, Duchess of Windsor, who was able to take hold of the last important king in the West and turn him into something resembling Louis XVI in a pink wig, fleeing endlessly about the world as if in a lumbering *berline* with too much luggage. Mrs. Simpson confirmed that fame in the twentieth century had been surgically separated from responsibility.

Between Marie Antoinette's innovation and Mrs. Simpson's demonstration of perfect modern stardom, there was a century and a half of confusion while the kings and their courts disintegrated. The new rational society abandoned fame as a social and human weakness unworthy of attention. But to abandon is to unleash and stardom immediately began to take on a momentum of its own. What had seemed at first to be a sensible division between responsibility and adulation was quickly deformed. Fame, by definition, occupies the public stage. It therefore could not help but come between the citizen and those who held public responsibilities.

In the process it splintered into three broad categories. There was the Heroic, which at first seemed to be a natural descendant of the old royal stardom because it benefitted the new breed of dictators, revolutionaries, soldiers and politicians. In reality this Napoleonic fame had to do with individualism gone wrong and it evolved quite naturally into a variety of modern Heroes from Hitler and tennis stars to terrorists and Olympic medallists. The second category involved the vulgar fame which had surrounded the demimondaines, actors, gamblers and other marginal courtiers of the old regimes. This has expanded effortlessly to produce our grab bag of contemporary celebrities, including again the sports stars, but also the actors, the aimless rich, the fashionable criminals, the money manipulators — in fact anyone who can momentarily catch society's attention.

Finally, the remaining segment of fame went to the philosophers, poets and the newly arrived novelists — that is, to the messengers of reason who had effectively destroyed the power of God and his churches, along with that of the absolute monarchs and their aristocracies. The new breed of soldiers, dictators, revolutionaries and politicians benefitted from these deaths, but they did not themselves do the killing.

The actual beheading of kings and restructuring of governments were secondary events in comparison to the undermining of the population's belief in and their acceptance of the rights of church and monarchy. The messengers of reason had devoted themselves throughout the seventeenth and eighteenth centuries to questioning and attacking this power. More important still, they imagined the alternatives. From the early eighteenth century to the middle of the nineteenth, they were busy inventing the phrases, the arguments, the very words necessary to describe an alternate society.

It is not surprising, therefore, that the single most famous man of his time was Voltaire. No king or queen or minister, let alone any soldier or actor, was as well known as this little man with a sharp tongue and no teeth. And with the sole exception of Napoleon, the most famous figures of the nineteenth century were men like Byron, Goethe, Tolstoy, Hugo and Balzac.

Napoleon, the original Hero, dominated the Western imagination for the first twenty years of the century, and in the process seduced the two most famous writers of his time — Byron indirectly and Goethe in a

single conversation on October 2, 1808. The Emperor had just conquered Prussia and, in a world of romantic symbols, had carried off the
sword of Frederick the Great. Now, at the height of his glory, he had
summoned the princes of Europe to Erfurt to witness his seduction of
the Russian Czar. In the midst of it all, he invited Goethe to breakfast.
Napoleon sat and ate. The writer, along with Talleyrand and various
generals, stood. Later, outside, Goethe refused to discuss what had been
said, as if to indicate that it would have been beneath either of them to
repeat the contents of their conversation.

In an atmosphere of rising German nationalism, Goethe's silence was
taken as a consecration of the Heroic sword by the romantic pen. The
two great men had had a private conversation. That fact alone constituted instant mythology. In any case, Talleyrand could be counted on to
leak the useful phrases. For example, the Emperor had apparently
stopped his military and political discussions with government leaders in
order to insist that he had read Goethe's novel, *The Sorrows of Young
Werther*, seven times. He then offered the author a detailed literary
criticism of the book.

This encounter seemed to reconfirm the importance of the word in a
world in which a visitor from the moon would have guessed that the
sword reigned supreme. In reality it was an early warning that the
writer's use of fame to influence power was going to be reduced to mere
notoriety. The new military and political Heroes were going to take over
the job of feeding the citizen with dreams. From the Napoleonic era on,
the structures of the new society began slowly to fence writers in. The
experts were gaining power and they looked upon these messengers of
reason with ambivalence. It was thanks to the writers, after all, that
mere managers were now in charge. On the other hand, those managers
could hardly forget that the written word had destroyed their predecessors.

The rising systems inevitably came between the writers' fame and
their freedom to use it in the real world. By the end of the nineteenth
century, that fame was being redefined as notoriety or celebrity and the
writers were withdrawing to a marginal position as specialists themselves or as notoriously unbalanced outsiders with a faculty for criticism
of the society in which they hardly participated. And so while Voltaire
was the most famous man of the eighteenth century, the most famous of
the twentieth is Mickey Mouse. Even in Shaoshan, Mao Tse-tung's
hometown, souvenir stands sell Mao and Mickey buttons side by side.

Fame, celebrity and stardom have become the daily bread of the late
twentieth century. We dismiss them as sources of superficial distraction
while courting them assiduously as the keys to success and power. This
phenomenon has grown to the point at which it has now gone full
circle — back to the essential role which fame played in the era of

absolute monarchs. The difference is that fame was then limited to functional categories. Today it is open ended and is used as much to shield the activities of the system as it is to subvert it. Perhaps most astonishing, in our vain search for rational alternatives to the rational impasse, it is the stars who are providing one of the few salable options. That in itself indicates just how badly the system has stumbled.

Never have public power and fame been so officially divorced from each other as they are today. This separation was intended to be a healthy advance proper to democracies. It is hard not to agree that the wielders of political and economic power should be no more than that. They may have money, expertise or responsibilities, but they should have none of the old trappings and adulation which were once their unwarranted rewards. Anyway, they now tend to be narrow, boring people who don't deserve to be the focus of our fantasies and dreams.

In the early 1950s, however, C. Wright Mills began writing about a new class which consisted entirely of famous people: "But what are the celebrities? The celebrities are the Names that need no further identification."[3] These people seemed to have fame without power. They certainly had it without responsibility. Mills had correctly identified the phenomenon, but he did not identify the role this class would soon play. All he noted was that the new fame of the celebrities served to disguise the new anonymity of those who held real power.

Was this class a creation of the population at large and made necessary by boredom in the absence of a royal court? Did the populace want to be distracted from its frustration at no longer understanding the power systems over which it theoretically had greater control than ever before in history? Or was it those now holding power who encouraged the growth of the celebrity class as a sort of magician's trick, in which the public's eyes are held mesmerized by the flashing of silk handkerchiefs, while the white pigeon of real power is slipped on and off stage?

Whatever the explanation, our rational, secular societies found it necessary to invent not only Heroes who undermine and destroy us, but celebrities and stars in such massive quantities that they obscure the meaning and purpose of everything we theoretically believe in. That the imaginary exploits of the stars should become our civilization's source of mythology is at first incomprehensible. That they should be seriously treated as offering social direction is a form of dark parody. And that they should become more popular than those who hold public responsibilities automatically changes the profile of those who will seek public office. Not since the emperor Nero wove acting, sports and political power into one disastrous formula by competing and winning at Olympus in both chariot racing and musical recital has the superficial been so profoundly confused with the public interest.

The result has been the compounding of our civilization's confused sense of direction. Devotion to rational structures and to the conviction that they automatically contain a worthy direction has left us as incapacitated by the rise of the stars as we were by the rise of the Hero. In attempts to give some meaning to the stars and their fame, we have taken to celebrating competition as a self-evident value. Or we carefully attribute mythological values where none exist. Or we measure the popularity of individuals, as if measurement conveyed value and was somehow related to the democratic process. Most peculiar of all, we assign a complex, internal class rating to the world of the stars, thus conforming to the old belief that any group which has internal standards is by definition real. Finally, we attribute so many real characteristics to their perfectly imaginary world that we begin to believe they are themselves real. It is hardly surprising that those who seek political power imitate the stars. Either that, or the machinery of public notoriety will give power to the stars themselves.

Among the first to point out the West's growing cult of competition was Learned Hand. In 1922 he warned the students of Bryn Mawr College:

> In competition there lies latent a fatal antimony. Men take their color from one another, catching a reflection from sources that themselves send out no light; they are chameleons surrounded by others of their species, mysteriously acquiring hue from a colorless environment. Such is the defeat which inevitably attends a community organized upon fame as a universal motive.[4]

Somehow, we have convinced ourselves that to be the best is to be something. The fastest runner. The greatest inventor. The best high C. The most beers in a half hour. The best chess player. The skater who turns the most times while in the air. The highest marks at school. At university. At dart throwing. The term *excellence* is used as if we were seeking content, when above all we seek a measurable result: a classification system or class system, with a king of the best at the top.

How fast this phenomenon has been growing can be seen in C. Wright Mills's words, written thirty years after Hand's:

> The professional celebrity, male or female, is the crowning result of the star system of a society that makes a fetish of competition. In America, this system is carried to the point where a man who can knock a small

white ball into a series of holes in the ground with more efficiency and skill than anyone else thereby gains social access to the President of the United States.[5]

The theory is that competition draws each individual along, bringing out of him or her the best he or she has to offer. Competition and the resulting fame are thought to be among the great achievements of our rational meritocracy. They promise both self-improvement and participation.

The reality is almost the opposite. In a world devoted to measuring the best, most of us aren't even in the competition. Human dignity being what it is, we eliminate ourselves from the competition in order to avoid giving other people the power to eliminate us. Not only does a society obsessed by competition not draw people out, it actually encourages them to hide what talents they have, by convincing them that they are insufficient. The common complaint that we have become spectator societies is the direct result of an overemphasis on competition.

The whole area of amateur sports has become symptomatic of the competitive atmosphere. The athletes are subject to unbearable pressures and lead abnormal lives which require everything from shaved bodies and forced diets to steroids. The whole process is tarred by a nationalism so cheap that it should more accurately be called jingoism. As the runner Bruce Kidd pointed out at the inquiry into Ben Johnson's illegal use of steroids, the various government-financing programs for amateur athletes turn them into professionals and force them to resort to drugs in order to keep on the road to stardom. What follows, if they are successful, is the commercialization of that stardom through corporate endorsements. And yet the phenomenon still has more to do with jingoism than with money. After all, the Communist countries were the leaders in this process.

What we have been witnessing is the growth of perfectly innocent, even banal, physical pastimes into something which makes governments, nations and international communications systems vibrate with excitement. Clearly what excites them is not sportsmanship, widely based participation or a profound or sustained interest in how many millimetres higher the high-jump bar has moved. These millimetres will be forgotten by most people within minutes of the end of the event. Few spectators will even register the figures when they are announced. Rather they are attracted by the event's ability to produce bevies of immediate stars who are tied to facile national emotions. These stars become not role models for the young — few would pretend they could ever jump so high — but dream models. They become the modern knights of the Round Table.

The confusion in both the public's and the competitors' minds as to what is happening on the field can be seen in the gradual adoption by these stars of military and political mannerisms. Witness, for example, Tommie Smith and John Carlos, two black American medal winners in the 1968 Olympics. Up on the podium, with their national anthem playing and the crowd applauding, they suddenly raised their clenched, black-gloved fists on behalf of the militant Black Power movement in the United States. They were suspended from the games, but almost immediately this most aggressive of political and military gestures seemed completely at home on the sports field. Every overexcited tennis star was soon throwing up one or two clenched fists and emitting animallike shouts of victory whenever he or she hit the ball well. Witness also Sylvester Stallone playing the boxer Rocky Balboa for the first time in 1976 and mimicking this gesture to great commercial effect at the same time that it was catching on as a symbol of the antiapartheid movement.

The raised arm with clenched fist has always been a symbol of violent combat. It carries a mixed meaning of victory and of defiance in defeat. It entered our conscious memory via two concurrent phenomena: the Roman legions whose raised open hand was later adopted by the Fascists and the Nazis; and the underclass of gladiators in the Circus addressing Caesar—"Those who are about to die salute you."

The first hint of how this salute would be transformed during the Age of Reason came in Michelangelo's Sistine Chapel. We see God creating the stars and the planets, his arm raised and an index finger pointed aggressively with terrifying power. The finger, the arm, God's face, all are charged with energy and a kind of anger, as if lightning is about to flash out from beneath his fingernail. Two frescoes down, God is busy creating man. Again, the arm is raised with enormous energy. His finger touches that of Adam, who is so passive and groggy that he has to support his own arm on his knee to keep his receiving finger in place. On the end wall Christ is dealing with the responsibilities of Judgment Day. The Saviour, who apparently had a weight-lifting background, has raised his arm above the saints and the assembled multitudes — not in calm illumination or Solomonic wisdom — but with threatening force, as if a single sweep of his hand will send everyone packing to hell. What makes these images so new is precisely this personalized energy and anger. The Holy Trinity is no longer raising its arm as an abstract symbol of authority. This is God as man-God the modern individual. And while such realism made him look terrifying, it also showed him in a fatally weakened form. If all God used to create man was physical energy, then man could have done it himself with the help of a few afternoons in the gym, an army to back him up, some ideology for comfort and a good PR campaign to drown out awkward questions.

This same gesture of individual arm-raising superiority entered popular mythology with David's painting *Le Serment des Horaces* in 1785. He portrayed three muscular Roman boys with their arms raised in what would eventually become the Nazi salute. Four years later the French Revolution got seriously under way when the legislators revolted against their king. David immediately immortalized them in the *Serment de Jeu de Paume* and incorporated the Horatii boys' republican gesture. This monumental unfinished picture was much copied and spread the notion that men showed their freedom by standing together in groups with their arms raised in joy and rebellion. But these were not the gestures of individuals. Nor was individualism being celebrated in David's endless portraits of Napoleon, who apparently spent his waking hours with one arm in the air and the other in the breast of his jacket.

The emergence of the ordinary citizen as an individual with his fist held up in defiance came in 1814, when Goya painted the massacre of simple Spanish nationalists by Napoleonic troops in Madrid in his *May 3, 1808*. This is not only the essential modern painting. It is the essential statement of modern man's view of himself. And it had the same electrifying effect on the Western imagination as Picasso's *Guernica* did more than a century later. On the right Goya placed the firing squad, rifles aimed, caught in the image a second before the triggers are pulled. On the left are the blood-soaked bodies of those already executed. In the centre, before the rifles, is a group of men, each trying to deal with the last second of his life. Four are painted in great detail. The dominant figure has both arms up in a gesture of acceptance and defiance. He is half a classical religious martyr and half the modern revolutionary individual. Most revolutionary, however, are the other three condemned men, pressed one behind the other. At the front there is a priest, bowed over, his hands clasped desperately in prayer. Behind and above him is a man staring straight out at the rifle barrels with his left arm in a tensed, upward motion, the fist clenched in fear and anger. Behind him is the third with his right hand clenched and raised in unambiguous defiance. This is the birth of the man-as-god image.[6]

From that moment the individual increasingly assumed a triumphalist public attitude, which usually ran ahead of his real accomplishments. These images became weapons in the struggle for further advances against arbitrary authority. Delacroix seized the revolution of 1830 as inspiration for his *Liberty Guiding the People*.[7] There on the barricades, leading the citizenry, is an Heroic woman with the flag raised in one hand and a rifle in the other. By 1836 in *La Marseillaise* — Rude's bas-relief on the Arc de Triomphe — this same symbol of the individual's power had become more ferocious than Michelangelo's God would ever have dared to be. Her shout and her extended arms, one straight up and the other bent upwards with force, are filled with violence. Lenin was quite naturally portrayed in similar stances, although with the cooler, more abstract air of an intellectual in a middle-class suit. And then the Fascists and the Nazis officially adopted the gesture, throwing into doubt four centuries of the individual's iconography.

It wasn't until 1937 and Picasso's *Guernica* that this doubt was clearly portrayed. There, on the right side of the catastrophic violence, is a woman raising both arms in imitation of the central figure in Goya's *May 3, 1808*. She is screaming. There is anger and defiance, but also fear and confusion. A great painter just couldn't help noticing that the man-god wasn't doing quite as well as his triumphal imagery had promised. Out in the real world, savage Heroes were parading around with their arms held high. And the stars had already begun both their ascent and their coopting of the free man's imagery.

Curiously enough, most people feigned surprise at the raised fists of the two black medal winners in the 1968 Olympics. And yet, the idea that a sports figure should raise an arm on behalf of a cause lasted scarcely a day. Soon everyone was doing it on behalf of themselves — competitors, winners, Heroes, stars. War cries came next. Suddenly, the entire military and nationalist vocabulary was wide open for any use. Competition became a metaphor for violence and war.

At Wimbledon in 1987 Jimmy Connors could be seen with one arm raised straight up, holding the tennis racket like a rifle or a flag, and the other arm in a tensed upward motion with the fist clenched. He was shouting. The various, admiring newspaper headlines included "CONNORS IN FULL CRY BATTLES BACK TO VICTORY."[8] His attitude and position is an exact imitation of Rude's *Marseillaise*.

Star tennis matches everywhere are now advertised as "a battle to the finish" or "a match of the titans." Even the most staid of sports have given in to military symbolism. At the end of the American PGA golf tournament in 1989, both the male winner — Curtis Strange — and the female — Laura Davies — had their clenched fists in the air. "Guts, it's something you're born with," Mr. Strange declared to explain his success.[9]

Tennis, however, is the most interesting of the competitive sports, first because it turns on the proverbial two-man "combat," and second, because it is a middle-class sport. The Orwellian prophesy of the lumpen proletariat in *1984* transferring their political frustrations to the football field comes to mind. But the stands at Flushing, Wimbledon and the Paris Open are filled with company presidents, politicians, the rich and the famous. Those not there in person are glued to their television sets. There is occasional light disapproval of a player's "bad behaviour." But in general this audience loves the raised fists, the war cries, the battle leaps. That is what they come for. Roland Barthes once wrote of the mythological role that professional wrestling plays for part of the population. Tennis has become the professional wrestling of the middle classes. It does not matter that unlike wrestling, the matches are not fixed.

"Used well," Aldous Huxley wrote, "[sport] can teach endurance and courage, a sense of fair play and a respect for rules, coordinated effort and the subordination of personal interests to those of the group. Used badly, it can encourage personal vanity and group vanity, greedy desire for victory and hatred of rivals, an intolerant esprit de corps and contempt for people."[10] In other words, the line between physical exercise and war is erased.

By 1974 the violence in Canadian hockey was so out of hand that Toronto lawyer William McMurtry was asked to head a governmental inquiry into its causes. During the hearings, he questioned Clarence Campbell, then president of the National Hockey League, which also controls the amateur leagues and, of course, has an enormous influence on the young, for this is the great national sport. When asked to define the purpose of the NHL, Mr. Campbell was remarkably honest; but then he belonged to an older generation, not trained in the technique of managing information. "It is the business of conducting the sport in a manner that will induce or be conducive to the support of it at the box office. . . . Show business, we are in the entertainment business and that can never be ignored. We must put on a spectacle that will attract people."[11]

Hollywood has produced a constant flood of sports films illustrating the spirit of our times. They emphasize untrained, undersize, underprivileged Heroes who overcome all barriers to become champions. Inevitably, in their moment of triumph, they raise a clenched fist. The background music comes in the style that Beethoven created for Napoleon. The most surprising of these film Heroes is Sylvester Stallone. He alternates between portraying underdog sports figures and underdog military figures. From a dramatic point of view, there is no difference. By choosing sports with intense physical contact, such as boxing, Stallone further confuses the two areas. In fact, it is unlikely that Jimmy Connors or other sports stars have been consciously copying Goya or Rude. If there is any image locked in their imagination, it is probably that of Stallone as Rocky Balboa raising his arms in triumph. Rocky's movements are those of a High Renaissance figure — God as portrayed by Michelangelo. Stallone has explained that he studies the paintings of the Renaissance in order to capture these movements. In other words, what began as the raised arm of God, then of kings, only to be stolen by the citizenry as a symbol of its freedom and individualism, from whom it was snatched by the usurping Heroes, has been stolen again, this time by the stars, who use it as a symbol of their Godlike role.

What is it that links Sylvester Stallone, the Olympic movement, non-Olympic sports, the desperate need of everything second-rate to call itself world class, and the organization of most human activities into measurable races? Competition. What matters is the fact that we compete, not why we do so. The resulting champions will be our stars and give the impression that they are leading us somewhere.

This allows the technocratic classes — particularly in business — to enshrine the act of competition as the religion of individualism, while avoiding more complicated questions — such as long-term commitments or social responsibility. Every MBA is able to see himself as a champion player in some Olympic sport or as a star who always comes through in his own movie. For example, the Lannick Group, an executive recruiting firm, runs a glossy ad headlined:

COMPETITION
SOMETIMES THE COMPETITION IS FIERCE. SOMETIMES IT'S NOT EASY TO STAND OUT. AND, SOMETIMES IT TAKES A LITTLE MORE THAN TALENT TO LEAP AHEAD OF THE REST.[12]

The ad is illustrated with a mass of suited businessmen, carrying briefcases, leaping like a school of salmon up a raging torrent. The recruiters at Lannick obviously don't fish or they would have realized that salmon fight their way up rivers because of unconscious genetic conformism. And they do so in order to lay their eggs. Most then die.

In some ways we have been forced to believe that the stars represent something, because the rational structures, with their enormous accumulations of power, produce no mythology. It is left to the celebrities to provide the aura for our everyday life.

This food for the imagination has to include grandeur, strength and success but also failure and suffering — in other words, the properties of prerational royal leadership. Everything about the king was widely known. His mistresses, his sexual prowess or problems, his obsessions, his tastes, what he ate, how he spent his days — all were discussed and debated. The king embodied power, but also suffering; an inevitable combination in a Christian society and one from which post-Christian societies have not escaped.

At the heart of the star's reputation there is always, therefore, tragic weakness. When, in 1988, the details of John Lennon's life were revealed in a long biography, general delight could be felt throughout the West. His loneliness, drug problems and impotency were examined and debated, in search of the truth.[13] That he remained the most famous of the Beatles was partly due to his talent but largely to his fleeing from the public scene to hide himself. Eventually it was tied to his being assassinated. Late in his career he had laid out his Christ role with various gestures, including lyrics which declared that "they" were going to "crucify" him.

Great flaws and suffering are essential to the ideal star, but the highest level is inevitably reserved for the martyrs. Monroe, Dean and Lennon are there by virtue of this ultimate act. Dalida, the French singer-star killed herself in 1987, after failing in an earlier attempt. She had already buried three husbands, each of whom had killed himself more or less for her. Her death came up first on all the news broadcasts and the leading politicians of the day went to her funeral. The citizen was therefore obliged to consider this event seriously. She had said, "I serve a minor art, but it is nevertheless a servitude which implies going to the end of oneself." Both the Socialist President of the Republic and the Conservative Prime Minister had been happy to be photographed with her on their arm. A friend of Dalida's was widely quoted after her death as saying: "Far into the night, she confided in me her fascination for the void of nothingness."[14]

Not all the star mythology rises out of the martyred Christ tradition. Ralph Lauren, the fashion designer, has built a commercial empire on the premise that he sells class and leadership. His flagship shop in New York has been decorated to resemble the mansion of a rich man. A false family crest has been engraved on the street door. The clothes themselves neither shock nor offer beauty. They promise upper-middle-class respectability. The ads portray polo grounds, shooting parties and country weekends.

This predictable marketing technique becomes interesting when third parties begin to treat it all as truth. In 1987, for example, *Esquire* magazine put Lauren on their cover. The theme was contemporary leadership. To help sell the issue they reproduced the cover in a full-page *New York Times* ad. The photograph shows Lauren in denim uniform, with semibomber jacket. One leg is raised up on an out-of-sight rock or chair. A thumb is hooked confidently in a pocket. The U.S. military cap on his head has gold braid. His eyes, behind dark glasses, stare straight at you and there is the cool smile of a commander on his face. The iconography is halfway between Douglas MacArthur and a navy fighter pilot. The headline is:

RALPH LAUREN ON LEADERSHIP

Beneath, they have reproduced his handwritten message:

A LEADER HAS THE VISION AND CONVICTION THAT A DREAM CAN BE ACHIEVED. HE INSPIRES THE POWER AND ENERGY TO GET IT DONE.

Beneath that, the magazine has printed its own message:

> LEADERSHIP ATTRACTS LEADERSHIP. LEADERS ARE THE DIFFERENCE BETWEEN SUC-
> CESS AND MEDIOCRITY. WHERE DO YOU FIND THEM? IN THE ONE PLACE WHERE
> STYLE AND SUBSTANCE MEET. IN ESQUIRE.[15]

The healthy reaction to this would be a knowing smile, accompanied
by the reflection that Lauren does good PR. But in the back of one's
mind is the real image of an American B-movie actor as president. The
point is not that the stars might take power, but that there has been a
divorce of real power from its presentation. If Lauren were any of the
things he is dressed up to resemble, then his words would be real,
whatever we thought of them. But he is not a leader. He does not, as far
as we know, have vision or conviction. Nor does he inspire power and
energy. What he does do is successfully sell clothes on the basis of false
snobbery. "So the world has come down to this," Joseph Roth wrote,
"that it admired and reverenced a dressmaker!"[16]

Such mythomania is by no means limited to fashion designers. Take
the most popular American talk-show host, Oprah Winfrey. In a 1989
cover story in the *New York Times Magazine*, this young woman, who is
watched every day by eleven to sixteen million people, was quoted as
saying:

> Everybody's greatness is relative to what the Universe put them here to
> do. I always knew that I was born for greatness. . . . I'm not God. I keep
> telling Shirley MacLaine, "You can't go around telling people you are
> God." It's a very difficult concept to accept.[17]

The journalist writing this profile does express incredulity as best she
can, but the social circumstances don't really permit incredulity, any
more than the French opponents of Napoleon were able to express
clearly their reasons. Self-confidence and the winds of the time ride in
Winfrey's favour.

She and Lauren are insignificant in comparison to the celebrity martyrs who neither claim nor propose anything, but have simply been
themselves. Elvis Presley has taken on a power of immortality which
rivals that of stuffed Heroes like Lenin. The Presley house — an imitation antebellum manor with columns, crystal chandeliers and gilded
mirrors — has assumed all the forms of a Christian place of pilgrim-
age.[18] Half a million people come every year to Graceland. More than
visit Washington's Mount Vernon or Jefferson's Monticello. Like Saint
Francis's cloak or Napoleon's hats, Elvis's jumpsuits are modeled on
mannequins escalating in size to illustrate his tragic decline into obesity
and despair. His wedding clothes are there, marking the moment when

every adoring girl lost him, and conversely, the moment when his calvary began. His five-foot wedding cake sits like a monument to the death
of several million romantic dreams. Behind the house, in Meditation
Garden, there is his grave at which to worship. This disappearance of
the body into the ground — as opposed to being stuffed and on display — has actually strengthened his myth. The supernatural sightings
of Elvis, as if he had risen from the dead, continue to increase.

Not many stars can rise to the religious level of incarnating mythology. Most, like Lauren and Winfrey, must state their message, thus
moving closer to the writers, philosophers and politicians. The singer
David Bowie, for example, offered moral and philosophical direction in a
1987 interview:

> *Question:* During the 1970s you bragged about your bisexuality. Today
> you live with your son, Zowie, in Switzerland, near Lausanne. You
> seem to have renounced your extravagant life.
> *Bowie:* I've changed a lot since leaving the United States in 1976. I lost
> track of who I was. There I lived a life of stereotyped decadence. I
> came back to Europe and decided to consolidate my role as a father.
> Living with my son, I've grown up. I've matured.
> *Question:* You once said: "I want to go through life as Superman. . . ."
> *Bowie:* My God! I must have been dead drunk. I must have read too
> much Nietzsche.
> *Question:* What is the greatest risk you've ever taken?
> *Bowie:* Using drugs. It's a risk I would recommend to no one.[19]

Most of those who actually hold power have never read Nietzsche and
have no idea how to say anything sensible about drugs. But that merely
accentuates how divided power and fame have become. And most stars
haven't read Nietzsche either. Their mythological messages are aimlessly created by the vagaries of personal taste and commercial opportunity. The rock star George Michael slips from music called "I Want
Your Sex" to music called "Faith." Given time, he will probably work
his way through every social and moral position, from human rights to
reincarnation.

One practical effect of a popular mythology dominated by stars is that
civilization finds it increasingly difficult to express and maintain any
prolonged moral judgment. Only short-lived moral impulses seem possible. They tend to appear suddenly, urgently, command our attention
and then disappear just as suddenly. The result is not fewer but more
moral convictions. They are well intentioned and rootless and so are
washed away by the next wave of concern or indignation. The practical
effect is to relativize all public events and questions of principle. In a
single issue of a magazine, for example, it is possible to publicize, as if
their fame alone made them compatible, any combination of real and

star personalities. The June 3, 1988, issue of *Paris-Match* is not unusual.[20] It begins with a meeting between the Pope and a well-known
writer, Maria-Antonietta Macciocchi, who had just given up Communism for the Church. She writes: "I had met Mao, De Gaulle, Ho Chi
Minh, and once, deep inside Qum, the holy city of Iran, I was received
by the terrible Khomeini. But I had never been so disturbed [as by the
Pope]."

This article was followed by a photo-interview with the latest sex
starlet, Beatrice Dalle, who was shown both nude and half dressed,
tucked into the corner of a room, mouth open and eyes orgasmic, as if
waiting to be leapt upon. She is quoted saying such things as: "Me
scandalous? Never!" Or, "They always offer me roles as a sex animal
and yet I am the reincarnation of the Virgin Mary." This was followed
by an interview with George Michael:

Question: Is it difficult to be a sex symbol?
Michael: It has its ups and downs.

The family celebration of Jacqueline Kennedy's daughter's law degree
was next, offering a brief glimpse of the mythological widow. After
Jackie came Jean-Marie Le Pen, leader of the extreme right wing in
France. He was then locked in a political battle for control of Marseille.
His popularity, as always, was dependent on his ability to fan racist
flames over the number of Third World immigrants in the city. But his
large and engaging smile was indistinguishable from that of Mrs.
Kennedy, George Michael, Beatrice Dalle or indeed the Pope, whose
second appearance in that issue had to do with his trip to South America.

Fame, not popularity, is central to the measurement of stardom. The
famous belong together — rock stars, popes, racists and saints. If their
position cannot be measured by the disembodied means of competition,
it can be gauged by weighing their emotional impact on the public. In
that sense fame has become the ultimate competition. This does not
resemble winning elections, because that would imply some sort of
resulting responsibility. Notoriety must be supported by the bearer but
does not of itself involve any obligation.

The astonishing thing, indeed, is just how forgotten or ignored the
individuals who wield real power, well or badly, now are. In the wake
of the first Ethiopian famine, a national poll asked French teenagers to
name the people who had done most to help those in the Third World.[21]
Of the twelve names given, seven were stars'. And more than 65 percent

of those questioned volunteered a star's name. Four of the five most often cited were singers or comedians. The foremost choice, named by 27 percent, was the singer Daniel Balavoine, who had already been killed in a motorcycle accident. Their third choice, the comedian Coluche — also dead in a motorcycle accident — was named by 11 percent. The singers France Gall and Bob Geldof came next. The only nonstar at the top was Mother Teresa, named by 15 percent. She, who plays the role of a medieval saint, is a star in the old sense of the word; an accidental leftover from another period of history. Balavoine and Coluche had done more than their share of good works, but what earned them such high ratings was that their deaths made them martyrs of a sort. Martyrs to what? To fame? To youth? It isn't very clear.

Meanwhile a mere 3 percent named the Red Cross. Taken all together the money raised by all eight stars, including Mother Teresa and Bob Geldof, does not add up to one day's worth of the help given by the Red Cross. That organization has its flaws, but its low public esteem is the result of being intentionally careful and modest. The Red Cross is not a celebrity. At least, however, it appeared on the list. The Western governments and their ministers, who do not spend nearly enough on aid programs, but who nevertheless spend more than anyone else, were not even mentioned.

This deformed scale of fame is now reflected in the amount of money stars make. Forty years ago, the pyramid of high earners would have been little changed from a century before. The landowners and the businessmen — capitalists, bankers, traders and property developers — would have been at the top of the list. Today most of the remaining capitalists and the sea of corporate managers are well below the stars. *Forbes* magazine's study of the top forty earners in the American entertainment business shows that their incomes range from a low of two million dollars to a high of eighty. The top ten each earn more than twenty million dollars a year. Eighteen of the forty are singers, nine are actors, and only six come from television. (Television, being ritualistic, doesn't tend to create freestanding celebrities. Three of the six are talk-show hosts.) And while only one novelist and one director are on the list, there are two cartoonists, three boxers and two out of the nine actors — Arnold Schwarzenegger and Sylvester Stallone — made their money by pretending to be boxers or by exhibiting their muscles in one way or another. This is part of the confusion between stardom, competition and the myth of the knight-crusader or duellist.

Almost no one in corporate America earns enough to make even the bottom of this list. Many company presidents earn $1 or $2 million. Oprah Winfrey earns $80. Madonna earns $63. With the exception of Chrysler's Lee Iacocca, also a celebrity, almost none makes above $10 million, let alone $20 or $50, in hard cash, although their incomes are heavily padded with such things as stock options. One of the cartoonists on the list is Charles Schultz, who draws *Peanuts*. His personal annual income is more than $30 million. His personal corporate sales in Japan alone are about $350 million.

When in 1987 Frenchwomen were asked to choose three famous women who would make them turn about to stare with admiration if passed in the street, fifty of the sixty-one named were stars. Four were politicians. The Princess of Wales was the only representative of the royal families who once defined the meaning of fame. What's more, she and the politicians were down at the bottom of the list. The stars were all at the top. The actress Catherine Deneuve was mentioned by almost three times more people than the politician Simone Veil, who was then the most famous French female public figure. For the last decade Deneuve has been more convincing as a public role-model-cum-princess than any public figure who actually does something. Mother Teresa didn't make the list.

The self-generation of internal class distinctions, containing protocol and etiquette, has always been a sign that a newly developed group is becoming part of organized society. The disordered but growing array of stars throughout the Western world were given their social foundation and structure in 1937 when Wallis Simpson, an American double-divorcée and the daughter of a superior boardinghouse keeper, married Edward VIII, the King-Emperor of England, Scotland, Wales, Canada, Australia, New Zealand, South Africa, India, etc. The resulting and unprecedented scandal threatened the government, forced his abdication and has fed the creation of thousands of books, films, novels and plays. It was not simply that Mrs. Simpson linked America and Europe. Or that her simple family was joined to the best family in the world. Or even that, in popular mythology, this couple represented the victory of romance over rank and obligation. Above all, Mrs. Simpson's conquest abruptly demonstrated that the only thing holding the King back from complete fame was his attachment to the real world. Once that was done away with, he became an autonomous star. He became the man in the world most famous for simply existing as himself.

The wanderings of this sad couple from continent to continent and party to party constituted a sort of royal progress of the King and Queen of Stardom. Everywhere they went, they conveyed legitimacy on actors, singers and the nouveaux riches by the simple act of greeting them and then dancing and dining with them — sharing their lives, in fact. The nouveaux riches, for the first time in history, were seeking social advancement, not through traditional established society but through the new class of stars. It was a fresh direction for new money and one of the signs that the fading royal courts and the rather boring modern ruling class of technocrats had lost their public lustre. If the modern equivalent of a French Collector of Salt Taxes could no longer dream of becoming a duke, received in splendour at court, well then, he'd dream of becoming a star who entertained the Duke and Duchess of Windsor.

The enduring impact of the Windsors on the star class and on public mythology was like that of Louis XIV and Queen Victoria on their respective aristocracies and societies. In 1987 the Duchess's jewels were sold at auction by Sotheby's, long after her husband's death and more than a decade after her own disappearance into senility. Bids came in from all the leading celebrities of our day, including Jacqueline Onassis, one of the two most famous women since the Duchess herself. The stars wanted to buy a bit of the legitimacy these pearls and diamonds carried.[22] Valued at $7 million, they sold for $50 million.

Elizabeth Taylor bid $623,000 by telephone for a diamond clip of Prince of Wales feathers. The moment it reached her, she went off to Malcolm Forbes's party of the year, with the clip on for everyone to see. Fashion designer Calvin Klein paid $1.3 million for three pieces. He told the press he was going to give them immediately to his wife: "The best presents just happen." Joan Collins was rumoured to have bought a sapphire brooch for $374,000. The publicity-hungry divorce lawyer Marvin Mitchelson paid $605,000 for an amethyst-and-turquoise necklace. He announced this to the press and dedicated his purchase to the memory of his mother. And just in case there was any doubt about whether people were paying for jewels or for souvenirs of legitimacy, a pearl-and-diamond choker, which was announced as imitation jewelry and therefore had no value, sold for $51,000.

As for the public — who once lived vicariously through the court gazettes and now followed the lives of the stars — they were able to participate in the auction thanks to a well-known direct-mail firm, the Franklin Mint, which bid successfully for a bracelet. Its full-page advertisement for the unlimited number of copies they made of this object was dominated by a photo of Mrs. Simpson at her most catlike, along with a superimposed photo of the bracelet. The copy began as follows:

THE DUCHESS. THE JEWELRY.

FOR THE WOMAN WHO KNOWS WHAT SHE WANTS AND GETS IT. MAKE YOUR OWN STATEMENT. WITH THE PANTHER BRACELET MADE FAMOUS BY ONE OF HISTORY'S MOST TALKED-ABOUT WOMEN. WALLIS SIMPSON, THE WOMAN WHO STOLE THE HEART OF THE KING OF ENGLAND AND REFUSED TO GIVE IT BACK.

RECENTLY IN GENEVA, SWITZERLAND, THIS BRACELET WAS PART OF THE AUCTION OF THE CENTURY. A SALE THAT NETTED IN EXCESS OF FIFTY MILLION DOLLARS. BIDDERS COMPETING FOR THE LEGENDARY JEWELRY OF THE DUCHESS OF WINDSOR INCLUDED THE RICH AND FAMOUS. FROM ELIZABETH TAYLOR TO JACQUELINE ONASSIS.

The price for this piece of the Duchess was $195 plus relevant state sales tax. Allowing for inflation, this was probably the price of a decent-size piece of the cross in the nineteenth century.

As for the desire of the new rich to become stars rather than aristocrats, this has pushed them to behaviour more ridiculous than the sort of things Molière and Shakespeare used to mock. The West is now filled with magazines whose only role is to play to their pretentions. Among the fattest, glossiest and most cynical is *Town & Country*, which feeds the ambitions of the moneyed by asking them to appear in the magazine. This in turn draws in local advertising. These relatively conventional people do not appear on horseback dressed for the hunt or in long dresses beneath their second-rate Monets just to show off their money. *Town & Country* permits them to appear as stars for whom posing in magazines is perfectly normal.

The attraction of stardom is so great that the most established among the rich, who may actually belong to the old aristocracy or gentry, cannot resist its attractions. The ruler of the Fiat empire, Gianni Agnelli, as well as his friends, inexplicably seem to feel obliged to give long interviews in which his private life is discussed in detail — his infidelities, his dreams and his problems with his son.[23]

Even violence is not excluded from the celebrity class structure. The crowds applauding outside the courtrooms in which William Kennedy Smith, Michael Milken and Claus von Bulow were tried demonstrate that there is fashionable crime versus unfashionable crime. Fashionable murder versus unfashionable murder.

The most interesting practitioner of real violence is the bullfighter. He is free from competition and receives the adulation of the crowd without in any way becoming a star. He fights not another man but an animal. And the purpose of that struggle is not that one will win and the other lose. Bullfighting is neither sport nor theatre. It is a public ceremony that the Aztecs would have understood or the Old Testament Jews or any Christian who can bring himself to admit that his religion is based upon the ritualistic celebration of human sacrifice.

The bullfighter is the opposite of an individual, to say nothing of a star. People are interested in stars because on some level they would like to be one. People don't go to bullfights in order to dream of themselves as the conquering toreador. The bullfighter's greatness increases with the degree to which he risks his life while nevertheless mastering the bull. The extent of risk is the degree to which he offers himself in sacrifice on behalf of the crowd. The higher the risk, the finer the ritual he must use. And in surviving, as he usually but not always does, the matador nevertheless offers a blood sacrifice to the people. In almost every civilization the bull rises out of the deep caverns of man's unconscious as a symbol of physical, sexual power. So what the crowd shares, if deprived of the actual death of a man, is the interposed sacrifice of our vital strength. It is a religious ceremony caught in evolution exactly halfway between the original offering up of a man on the altar and the more recent compromise of settling for some bread and wine.

At the *Féria* in Nîmes in 1987, Paco Ojeda was given an ear for the particularly brilliant but dangerous way he had dealt with a bull. Ojeda is one of the great matadors of our time — an emotional figure who can move a crowd in seconds with unexpected actions. A casual observer might think that the crowd was reacting to him as they would to a star. But when the fight in Nîmes was over and he began his triumphant walk around the ring, with the ear held up in one hand, someone threw him, among the shower of bouquets, a tiny circle of violets wrapped up tight in two leaves. Ojeda handed the ear to someone else and instead grasped the violets in his hand and held up the delicate spot of blue as he finished his circle, with the crowd on its feet. We are now used to the sports figure throwing up his fist at the first opportunity in an overstated pretense of physical daring. Ojeda, having truly risked his life, withdrew immediately into understatement, almost as if to say that he had given enough. This withdrawal, this modesty, merely increased the passion of the crowd. Interestingly enough, despite their popularity and fame, most bullfighters remain on the edges of society.

The common merchants of violence, on the other hand, are often true celebrities. Arms dealers, who used to be kept on the outside, with perhaps the exception of Basil Zaharoff, are now easily swept up by the world of stars. They bring with them a little air of mystery, of state secrets, of exciting corruption at the highest levels. Adnan Khashoggi, the Saudi Arabian dealer, moves from one celebrity party to another, giving interviews on his yacht, plane or in one of his houses. His daughter, Nabila, poses for fashion pictures standing on the wing of his jet. He throws bowling balls for the cameras in his private alley. His conversation slips from descriptions of his next yacht — "If the Sultan of Brunei buys the *Nabila I*, . . . I'll start building the *Nabila II*. It will be equipped with a submarine that can hold six people as well as a camera to film the sea bottom. Each cabin will have its own screen" — to future wars and economic packages which combine schools with tanks — "If the moderates take power in Iran and the result is peace with Iraq, then both nations will need to rebuild. That is a market of 170 billion dollars. If I get a tenth of that market, it'll be 17 billion!"[24]

Khashoggi illustrates how star societies remove moral judgment from more than just popular magazines. Even in the real world, all the famous are equal. The drawing cards at fashionable parties in London or New York may well be convicted criminals or people awaiting trial or acquitted. No tennis player, princess or movie star — not even a boxer — can rival the celebrity impact of a certain kind of murderer or fraud. Sydney Biddle Barrows, known as the Mayflower Madam, is an example. The product of a good family, she ran a brothel in New York until arrested and tried, with great publicity. Now she lives off her notoriety as a convicted criminal. Michele Sindona, the head of the Banco Ambrosiana, who died mysteriously in jail, was a favourite of Italian society after his bank collapsed and charges swirled around him. So is Licio Gelli, head of the influence-peddling masonic group P2, who escaped from a Swiss jail. The Kray brothers, a gang of professional thieves and killers, had a great vogue in London. In 1989, at the Royal Academy's monumental show celebrating the one-hundredth anniversary of the photograph, in a section called Figures of Style was the actor Michael Caine. Next to him was a portrait of the three Kray brothers. The fashion photographer David Bailey took both photos. The brothers were dressed in white shirts and ties with pocket handkerchiefs. They might have been a rock group were it not for the menacing air, which they consciously offered and Bailey consciously captured. Ronald Biggs, the "great train robber," has been a popular hero from the moment of his extravagant crime. Claus von Bulow, first convicted and then acquitted of attempting to murder his very rich wife, has been an increasingly sought-after guest ever since a warrant was issued for his arrest.

Reinaldo Herrera, an editor at *Vanity Fair*, has said that he relies on von Bulow to create dinner-party chemistry. He dreams of having both Jean Harris and Ivan Boesky as his guests. "They would add spice to the evening, because she was convicted of murder and he pleaded guilty to robbing nearly the world. But most normal houses don't have these great names at their fingertips."[25] Adnan Khashoggi's social star seemed to rise after he was arrested in Switzerland and extradited to the United States. He was freed on $10 million bail, obliged to wear an unremovable electronic monitoring bracelet on his wrist and limited to travel in the New York area, at the mercy of hostesses. While he sat in a Swiss jail, his daughter was at a ball given by Baron Hubert von Pantz in Paris. The other guests included the brother of President Mitterrand, the dress designer Enrico Coveri, the father and stepmother of the Princess of Wales, Henry Ford's widow, and Duke and Duchess de la Rochefoucauld and the Prince and Princess von Thurn und Taxis.

It is easy to understand the shiver of delight that bored people gain from dining with a well-spoken, well-dressed murderer or thief, but what is the attraction of a miserable fraud artist like Ivan Boesky? Quite simply, stars carry the king's fame without his responsibility. As a result, they don't like authority. So what could be more attractive than someone who has been making a fool of the state structure? The message seems to be that Jean Genet was right — the greatest good is a free-floating, completed act, unattached to the needs of the public weal.

And the greatest act is to kill or rob someone or, failing that, to rob public institutions.

This devotion to self-interest defines the modern celebrity. In one of those periodic epic events which mark their times, Princess Gloria von Thurn und Taxis threw a party in June 1986 at home in Bavaria, to celebrate her husband's sixtieth birthday. The Prince, who has since died, was one of the world's richest aristocrats. His party went on for three days of festivities, including a ball for 250. His house is larger than most palaces and is run by several hundred servants in uniforms whose style predates the French Revolution. Gloria, a young woman who loves being a star, chose the eighteenth century as the party's theme.

The guest list featured the celebrities of the world, who flew in from all directions. Adnan Khashoggi came dressed as an Oriental prince, his wife as Madame de Pompadour; they were accompanied by a pair of bare-chested Nubian slaves. Malcolm Forbes flew in on his plane — the *Capitalist Tool* — wearing a kilt. Alfred Taubman, a real estate tycoon who, as the owner of Sotheby's, presides over a board of confidence-giving aristocrats, but who personally turned the sale of Wallis Simpson's jewels into a financial and publicity triumph, arrived as a French king. Enrico Coveri, the accessories designer, whom success has turned into a dress designer, came as Don Giovanni. The correspondent for *Vanity Fair* thought about coming as Voltaire, although he worried that it might be too pretentious. Princess Gloria reassured him: "But that's what the eighteenth century was all about — pretentiousness."[26]

The Princess came as none other than Marie Antoinette. Beyond and above her magnificent dress and two-foot-high pink wig, she wore a pearl tiara which had belonged to, indeed been worn by, Marie Antoinette. But why would one of the richest princesses of our day choose to identify herself with, of all queens, the one who was most hated by her subjects, disliked by most of the aristocracy and in a singularly incompetent manner managed to lose her crown? Princess Gloria had found a guiding light. The last Queen of France was indeed the first modern star.

In a sense we have come full circle. The stars appear more real than those individuals who have real power. Those who have power increasingly feel obliged to imitate the stars. To be real is not enough. They must appear to be real.

Signs of this confusion began in 1956 when a movie actress married a semibankrupt but reigning prince. Monaco could no more have been considered a real place then than now. It was not independent in any political sense except for its right to welcome tax avoiders. Grace Kelly quickly demonstrated that she could turn her husband's principality into a going concern if three aspects of the burgeoning Western star society were linked together: gambling, tax evasion and courtesanage — which in this case meant that by associating with a famous celebrity you became a star yourself. Courtesanage was her personal contribution and she bolstered it by drawing her friends — principally singers and actors — into a revolving court of stars. Thirty years later her two daughters have become the perfect incarnations of second-generation celebrity. They are the combined reflection of an empty title, gambling, movie acting and international money. All four things were in themselves already reflections of a reality. And so the daughters are reflections of reflections. Stephanie, the second daughter, is a sometime swimsuit designer and singer of disco tunes. She paused in the midst of a 1987 radio interview to reflect upon her duties "in my role as princess and rock star," as if they were one and the same thing.

The first act of the stars' reign had begun with the Windsors in 1937. The second opened with the wedding of Grace, the princess–movie queen in 1956. Fifteen hundred journalists covered the event. Grace's wedding dress, with thousands of pearls sewn on the veil, was a creation of MGM Studios' most famous designer. The marriage attracted more international attention than Elizabeth II's coronation three years earlier. (On some level, conscious or unconscious, the tendency of the British royal family to convert themselves into twentieth-century stars probably dates from the Monaco wedding.) Grace and her wedding party sailed across the Atlantic to her wedding. As they steamed into Monaco's harbour, where her mythological prince and the court waited, Grace was placed on the bow of the liner. Then thousands of red and white carnations were showered upon her from the seaplane of Aristotle Onassis, who more or less controlled the local economy.[27]

For the next two decades, Grace and Rainier were given more sustained international attention than the royalty of any real country. This attention reflected neither power, title nor blood. They were ideal stars, linking the mythology of the old courts with that of the modern studios.

As for Aristotle Onassis, he more than any other illustrated the desire of crude money holders to become stars themselves by grabbing the coattails of those who were already. He was not out to buy respectability or titles or a place at court, but raw fame. He had begun by combining a mistress, Maria Callas, the most famous opera diva of her day, with control of Rainier's toy principality. He then dropped both and moved on to marry the widow of the most famous martyr of the second half of the twentieth century.

The Kennedy family provided the third act in the confusing consecration of the star. The young president's term of office seemed to signal a return to the eighteenth-century court system in which power and glamour were combined. But his martyrdom consigned the imagery of Camelot to the domain of the imagination. When Onassis married Mrs. Kennedy, the moral was clear: fame, not power, was the source of modern myth.

Twenty-five years after Kennedy was slain in Dallas, his niece, the host of a CBS Television news show, married Arnold Schwarzenegger. A former Mr. Universe and a B-movie star, he is one of the richest and most famous Americans of our time. The bride's maid of honour was King Arthur's daughter. The best man was a weight lifter. The guests, apart from the Kennedys, included NBC anchorman Tom Brokaw, tennis star Arthur Ashe, singer Andy Williams, TV news host–star Barbara Walters and Andy Warhol. That is far closer to the composition of a modern royal wedding than the *dépassé* event organized around Prince Charles and Lady Diana. It was perfectly natural, a year later, that President Bush should summon the image of *Conan the Barbarian* and *The Terminator* to the White House in order to name him chairman of the President's Council on Physical Fitness. The screen killer commented: "President Bush is very much committed not only to have this a kinder and gentler nation, but also a very fit nation."[28] Of course, Schwarzenegger had used steroids to build up his body.

In such an atmosphere it is hardly surprising that politicians should have begun turning themselves into stars. C. Wright Mills caught the shift long before the trend was clear. He demonstrated the growing confusion between celebrity and image and image and reality by reproducing a 1954 *New York Times* description of President Eisenhower's weekly television appearance:

> Last night's "information talk" by President Eisenhower was much his most successful television appearance. . . . The President and his television consultant, Robert Montgomery, apparently found a "format" that enabled General Eisenhower to achieve relaxation and immeasurably greater freedom of movement. The result was the attainment of television's most desired quality — naturalness. . . . As he neared the end of his talk and wanted to employ added emphasis, the General alternately knotted his hands or tapped the fingers of one on the palm of the other. Because they were intuitive his actions had the stamp of reality.[29]

The General was on his way to becoming an actor. If this was necessary for the victorious ex-commander of the forces of freedom, then it was essential for an ordinary politician.

For example, in 1954, the fixed movie-star smile was only a few years away from becoming the iconic symbol of success. One can easily trace the spread of this affectation from country to country. France, despite its well-established celebrity system, was one of the last to give in. The integrated, almost separate, political elite was partially responsible for the delay. In iconographic terms, the smile for the French was a symbol of intellectual deficiency and freedom from responsibility. Singers and actors smiled. But if a writer or a politician dared to show his teeth, he would not be taken seriously. Examine author photos from before the mid-seventies. In order to hold a pen, you had to keep your lips together. The same was true of election posters. Suddenly, in the late seventies, a few politicians began to clench their teeth in order to bare them by carefully drawing both upper and lower lips back into a fixed position, slightly curved upwards at each end. This awkward expression bore no relationship to personality or policy. But for the cameras it conveyed an image of the star. Overnight the smile became so important that François Mitterrand, who had already been in politics for forty years and was then a presidential candidate, had his incisors filed down, thus permitting him to flash his teeth without looking like a vampire.

The spread of the smile throughout the democracies was an important sign. The aim of public figures holding power in the nineteenth and early twentieth centuries had been to differentiate themselves from the preceding kings and their courts, who had gradually become identified more with their fame than with their power. Kings were glamorous; they smiled. The new rational democrats were sober and they did not smile. Clenched lips were a symbol of their devotion to public service, while the stars inherited the glamour and the public smile of kings. A century and a half later, the people's representatives suddenly seemed to tire of their sober, responsible appearance. And although they still held power, there can be no doubt who they were imitating.

Public figures began to embrace all the characteristics of the star, most of which are by definition superficial, if not venal. A few months after the 1984 American presidential election, Geraldine Ferraro, the first and therefore historic woman vice presidential candidate, cashed in on her celebrity through Pepsi-Cola ads. And for the cover of a glossy magazine in 1989, Canadian Finance Minister Michael Wilson posed in a dinner jacket. He was being tickled under the chin by a television personality in a black strapless evening gown. She was lying on a high bench, almost at his shoulder level, with her cleavage aimed at the camera and her lips puckered, as if posing for a *Playboy* centrefold. This cover story was about what to give people for Christmas. Wilson wanted cognac, a cashmere coat, an expensive pen and a nine-thousand-dollar laptop computer. The article appeared just as he was introducing a new sales tax which would cut seriously into the finances of lower-income citizens.[30]

Most Europeans would claim that these are signs of North American decay. In reality they are part of a general evolution which takes different forms in different countries. For example, there is the ascension of the pure star within the hierarchy of general news stories. No country could be more serious about its ideas and political analysis than France, but when four of its stars died in the mid-eighties, each death was treated as an event of primary importance. To be precise, each was the first item on all television and radio news broadcasts. And these were not simply announcements. The national evening news on each channel gave a lengthy analysis of their careers. These included personal statements from the President of the Republic, the Prime Minister and most of the major political leaders of the day. They commented on the national contributions made by the comedian, Coluche, killed on a motorbike in his forties; the impersonator Thierry Le Luron dead of AIDS in his thirties; the singer Dalida a suicide in her fifties; and the actress Simone Signoret dead of cancer after a long career.

A decade earlier, the same deaths would have been mentioned last on the news broadcasts, as thirty-second kickers. All four were given privately organized quasi-state funerals. Great war leaders and ex-prime ministers had died during the seventies and eighties, but they were sent off with nothing to match the pomp given Thierry Le Luron at La Madeleine. In the front row were Prime Minister Jacques Chirac, with his wife; the wife of President Mitterrand, the Minister of Culture François Leotard and the ex-Prime Minister and party leader Raymond Barre, with his wife. Valéry Giscard, the former President of the Republic, was not there, but he wrote a two-page essay on Le Luron for *Paris-Match*.

When the most famous star of the century, Sarah Bernhardt, died in 1923, there had been some front-page articles in the serious press and reports on inside pages over a period of three days. The President of the Republic had his aide-de-camp present a calling card at the undertakers'. Otherwise she was celebrated by the world of actors and playwrights. When Gérard Philipe, perhaps the most important French actor of the forties and fifties, died tragically young, at thirty-seven, in 1959, there were boxes on page one of most papers, referring to articles inside. No elected official commented. When the great singer Edith Piaf died in 1963, the pattern was the same.

When Yves Montand, actor and singer, died in 1991, French radio and television news broadcasts were given over in entirety or almost entirely to him. The President, the Prime Minister and all the leaders of the opposition made formal statements. Three of the serious national dailies gave him their entire front page. The others gave half. Constitutional reform was squeezed to the inside pages. The bombardment of Dubrovnik was eliminated. All but one of the serious weeklies gave him their cover, often including special inserts of thirty to forty pages.[31]

This same phenomenon can be seen in Britain through the gradual rise of the stars within the Queen's system of Honours. She distributes these upon the advice of her government. At first glance, this showering of medals and titles on singers, dressmakers and football players seems to show a welcome egalitarianism. But what is the actual purpose of honours? They were designed to reward services to the Crown and subsequently to the state and the public weal. In general this meant rewarding civil or military services. Of course, the rich have always been able to buy themselves some level of honour, either by filling the coffers of a political party or by financing some area of genuine public need, from poorhouses and training centres to concert halls and art galleries.

But most stars don't even pretend to have served the public weal. And the responsibility for giving these honours lies with those who hold formal positions of power. They decorate the stars in order to be identified with people more famous and more popular than they themselves are. In that sense the system of honours has been completely deformed, because instead of rewarding services, the established authorities are exploiting the fame of the stars.

This confusion between reality and fame can be seen in the way news is delivered to the public. The managers of the news distribution systems receive information which can be broken down into three categories. The first consists of the truth as presented by politicians, governments, government departments, private corporations and any other sort of organization or lobby group. Irrespective of their policies or interests, they all present their truth within the framework of contemporary argument.

These announcements are constituted either in the context of emotion, because jingoism and motherhood are impervious to argument, or of information, because information consists of facts and facts are the irrefutable basis of truth. There is not much that journalists can do with this rhetoric except run excerpts back-to-back with the equally rhetorical criticisms produced by rival politicians, opposition parties and unions. Faced by such impenetrable informational onslaughts, the public tends to withdraw into the passivity of a receptacle, just as the journalists tend toward the passivity of a conduit. Both are endlessly waiting for practical opportunities to bring the manipulators to ground.

Personal scandals are one of the few remaining areas in which this can be done. The journalists must catch the public figure on some minor moral point — a cabinet minister gets his secretary pregnant, a president accepts diamonds from an emperor-dictator who may also be a cannibal, another president suggests that underlings break into the opposition's headquarters. The citizen can latch onto this concrete scandal in lieu of serious public debate over major issues. The politicians protest that these are minor offenses. But they avoid mentioning their own systematic intellectual dishonesty on what they would consider major matters.

The second category of information consists of *faits divers* — murders, rapes, assassinations, kidnappings, highjackings, flash floods and blizzards. There is no real difference between the old three-alarm-fire story and a coup d'état. Both turn on immediate, concrete violence. Both make good news because they are easy to describe or show. The difficulty is that they come without warning and don't last long.

Finally, there is news of the celebrities. Celebrities must appear to do something on a regular basis or they may cease to be famous. They are reliable regular suppliers of information and thus of employment for journalists. This favours an increase in the coverage of pure stars, an encouragement for politicians to act like stars and an opening for stars into public life. After all, if appearances are what the news structure needs, the professional stars are professional appearers, while the politicians can never be more than talented amateurs.

The combination of these three news categories further confuses the line between responsible public life and stardom. It also encourages politicians and businessmen to present the real world of real events by concentrating on its celebritylike edges. A minister takes a group of journalists off to a mine, for example. He puts on a miner's hat, goes below earth, is filmed and photographed, then reemerges to make a rhetorical statement on mining policy. In other words the minister combines category one — rational propaganda — with category three — acting in a skit. A mining disaster would be even better for a minister who knows how to take advantage of a category-two *faits divers*. Flying over forest fires or earthquakes, visiting hospitals filled with victims, going to funerals after disasters — these are all part of a parabolesque deformation of public affairs in which elected officials act out an imaginary leading role.

It was only a matter of time before the journalists themselves became stars. For example, all electronic programming — whether news, public affairs or cultural — requires a host. The viewer or listener has access to public questions and to public figures only through this intermediary figure. The viewer's loyalty is therefore to the host, not his or her guests.

The host was there last week as the people's intermediary. He or she will be there next week, while the interviewee is often limited to a thirty-second clip. Sometimes he has ten minutes. Occasionally fifteen. Exceptionally thirty. These time slots are, of course, gross, not net. They include the host's introduction, questions, comments and conclusion. The most important personality on any electronic media show is, therefore, not the president of the United States. Not the pope. Not even Jane Fonda or Michael Jackson. And if the viewer does not identify principally with that host, well then, he will shortly switch channels in search of another intermediary.

The single most important television event of the Bush-Dukakis presidential campaign was not their two-part debate, but Bush's appearance on the CBS Evening News, hosted by Dan Rather. Rather challenged Bush over his involvement in the Iran-Contra affair. The then Vice President refused to deal with the questions. Instead, he attacked Rather, accusing him of dirty tactics. This confrontation revealed nothing about past policy; instead, it was Bush's ability to take on the host which surprised and impressed everyone. Bush managed to do the impossible: he threw doubt on the host's motives and competence. The ability to tarnish an established star proved that he had the makings of a star himself. Rather protested afterwards that the personality clash had been irrelevant; what mattered was the Vice President's refusal to answer his questions. But his protests rang hollow because he himself is one of the leading beneficiaries of a system that rewards celebrity over content.

All the same, television public affairs programming does allow the public to see men of power, to hear them reply under questioning, to witness company presidents and politicians being investigated. But what is the meaning of these questions and investigations if we have now come full circle, back to the eighteenth-century confusion of fame with power, so that all we can see is an illusion of reality?

Most television examinations of public affairs, for example, are reduced to parables, in a curious continuation of the Christian tradition. The Christian parable, however, attempted to effect social change by questioning and disturbing. The television parable is self-fulfilling and reassuring. Television interviews of public persons are little different from those with Madonna or Catherine Deneuve. The politician is examined through personal strengths and flaws. Of course, serious problems such as the West Bank, Lebanon, acid rain or arms control are repeatedly invoked, but in an unsustained manner, as if names were being dropped. This is the natural product of a system which has no faculty for continuity beyond personality. As a result the celebrity, Dan

Rather, failed in his attempt to sustain an argument on a concrete subject when the public person, George Bush, responded in the mode of a star by sticking to personality. Politicians often charge that the media refuse to deal with questions seriously. It is clear that the politicians have learned their lesson from the media. Now they themselves refuse.

During the 1950s and 60s, years of relative optimism, there was a great movement of technocrats towards politics in the belief that society needed to unite administration and political leadership in rational hands. One after another, men and women like Wilson, Trudeau, Heath, Carter, Giscard, Schmidt, Chirac and Thatcher won power. This was apparently the apotheosis of rational man, who had ceased serving out-moded politicians and himself become the new leader.

Within a few years most of them were considered failures. Some were defeated because they simply could not communicate. The few who survived did so on the strength of their personalities.

The subsequent counterwave of politicians did not question or reject the complex rational structures. They simply tried to instill confidence by proposing painfully simple solutions. This rise of mediocrity to the level of a public virtue produced leaders who were not intelligent but who had a certain talent as performers. They knew how to appear decisive or knowledgeable or in command. Some, like Margaret Thatcher, were actually technocrats, though she disguised this by addressing the world in a strident and highly personal manner. With unmatched ferocity she attacked inflation for a full decade, at the end of which inflation was higher in England than in all those "soft on social-ism" European countries who had hardly bothered to attack it. Her star qualities were so great that no one seemed to notice; any more than they noticed that her ferocity had not been matched by originality or inge-nuity. Her anti-inflationary weapons had been limited to the standard methods which had already been used unsuccessfully by technocrats such as Valéry Giscard, for whom she theoretically had contempt. But then, reality had not been at stake in her battle, only a theatrical version of it.

In the United States the system turned to a B-movie actor. America's intelligentsia have attempted to treat this event as an accident. An oddity. But it was precisely his qualities as a mediocre star of limited intelligence which brought Ronald Reagan to power and kept him there. Before seeking the presidency, Reagan wrote his autobiography: *Where's the Rest of Me?* This is a line from *King's Row*, a film in which his character wakes up in hospital to discover that his legs have been am-putated. Instead of being required reading in American universities, this book is out of print. And yet in it Reagan explains how, for the first time in the Age of Reason, a pure star was able to rise to the summit of power.

One of his basic principles was that leadership in a confused era is primarily a matter of clear perspective. He seems to have understood this as early as his first public appearance, when he was scarcely twenty. He was calling a football game live for radio:

> "We are speaking to you from high atop the Memorial Stadium of the University of Iowa, looking down from the west on the south forty yard line." Reagan the autobiographer goes on to comment: "I've always believed in the *teller who* locates himself, so the audience can see the game through his eyes."[32]

This is a principle which contradicts everything rational men believe and do. They provide answers and then prove them to the listener, who can not help but feel this is an aggression upon his dignity. Reagan may have insulted the intelligence of the people, but he did not question their dignity. He merely placed himself in a chosen position vis-à-vis reality, told people where he thought he was and then described in simple but mythological terms what he saw. If you accepted that he was where he said he was, it was difficult to reject the description that followed. He placed himself in such a manner that he spoke as if he were the people's eyes.

Actors understand that what all of us want is to believe. The plausibility of drama has always turned on our willing suspension of disbelief. It is not the unwilling suspension. The individual wants to believe. We can hardly be blamed for that.

The rational elites can deny this with answers and arguments, but the truth can be seen in the growing number of below-average politicians who occupy the positions of power from which clear descriptions can emanate. The illusion they create is double that of an actor like Reagan. In search of real power, they must pretend to be people who pretend to be real. They adjust their convictions with the arbitrariness of those who rely upon pollsters. They describe these temporary visions with memorized formulas. The stock phrases roll off their tongues. And they behave as much as possible like B-movie actors. In other words, after a period in which technocrats attempted to become stars and stars to become politicians, the political void has been occupied by the force of mediocrity, which can easily master enough of the star techniques to produce inoffensive personalities and enough of the rational vocabulary to create the sounds of competence.

George Bush, a technocrat and a longtime insider, has honed his vocabulary to disguise most signs of intelligence by speaking mainly in simple, show-business-style phrases. Even Barbara Bush falls victim to this need. In June 1989 it was rumoured that she was displeased with Lee Atwater, then the Republican National Committee Chairman. Mrs. Bush is always described as an old-fashioned, Eastern Seaboard, family-oriented, no-nonsense person — the very opposite of a star. And yet she had her press secretary inform the press that she had "telephoned [Mr. Atwater] to say, 'I love you.' " The first lady obviously has a better sense of the B-movie approach than Mrs. Reagan did. Not only does she resort easily to the sort of gushing celebrity overstatement which eliminates the possibility of a reply. She also finds it normal to intervene in a matter of national politics by simply evoking a hit song: "I Just Called to Say I Love You," by Stevie Wonder. It was an approach worthy of Ronald Reagan, who regularly used film scenarios and film dialogue in political speeches, as if they were real and in order to invoke a sympathetic, unconscious memory. As with President Reagan, her celebrity approach worked. The rumours died.

Mrs. Bush aside, the presence of such people in positions of power raises the question of what power has become if they can hold it. Has power itself become an illusion in a world where Lee Iacocca is thought to be a capitalist, Brian Mulroney a head of government, Ralph Lauren a leader, David Bowie a moral beacon, Bob Geldof the saviour of Ethiopia and Catherine Deneuve the symbol of womanhood? This confusion is quite genuine. The actor Tom Cruise earned $16 million between 1986 and 1987; that is to say, more than all but one or two American corporate presidents in the same period. In 1986, when he was twenty-three, Cruise said of his film *Top Gun*, which was about fighter pilots: "A top gun instructor once told me that there are only four occupations worthy of a man: actor, rock star, jet fighter pilot or president of the United States."[33] He was already an actor and had just played a fighter pilot in a film seen by more people than vote for the president of the United States. They did more than go out to vote for him. They went out and paid to see him. Since playing the role of a fighter pilot seems to weigh as heavily in mythological terms as actually being one, and since he had already received adulation beyond that reserved for a president, it may be fair to say that at twenty-three Tom Cruise had already held two and a half of the four occupations worthy of a man and would soon be on the cover of *Time* magazine.

Of course, this could all be dismissed as movie hype. What makes it real is that those who have power treat the stars seriously — frequent them, laud them, imitate them. What is more, the technocrats and the modern stars resemble each other, perhaps not surprisingly since both are products of rational society. Neither one seeks conversation or is really capable of it. Both thrive on staged proceedings. The actor, like the modern man of reason, must have his place determined and his lines memorized before he goes on stage.

Nothing is more terrifying to such people than someone who thinks in public — that is, someone who questions himself openly. The public itself has been soothed to such an extent by scripted debates imbued with theoretically "right" answers that it no longer seems to respond positively to arguments which create doubt. Real doubt creates real fear.

In the mid-1980s the heir to the British throne began to pose questions in public about social conditions, architecture and the lives people led. He also gave concrete demonstrations of open-ended thinking and self-doubt. He went away to an isolated Scottish island where he did menial farm chores in order to clear his mind and to contemplate.

The public reaction ranged from the shrill to the silently embarrassed. What they were all thinking was: Can a man who acts in this way become our king? He is a "legitimate" star. Fame, after all, is what the royal family saved from its original power = fame equation. On the other hand, he and his family are the central working mythology of the nation. And mythology should not think. In fact, theoretically it cannot.

What makes the Prince's admission of musing so interesting is that he represents a direct line back to the absolute monarchs. Not that he is refuting his constitutional position. But his comments are part of a long evolution, rather in the way that one monk during the Middle Ages might have written comments on a predecessor's manuscript. Here is the direct descendant of the original holders of both absolute power and absolute fame making a comment on the difficulties of public thought in the rational era.

Willy Brandt attempted the same thing with limited success when he was in power, as did Olaf Palme of Sweden. When Pierre Mendès-France tried, he was shut out of office for the next quarter century. Pierre Trudeau mused several times in public about difficult problems and possible solutions.[34] He was attacked from all sides as irresponsible. De Gaulle found a sensible compromise, given the times. He reserved his public thinking for the printed page and on those pages he allowed himself to ask fundamental questions. But when he spoke, it was either with reason or with emotion — that is to say, with answers or with mythology. He divided himself between the man of letters, who knows how to live with doubt, and the man of state, who is the epitome of certainty. The brilliance of this approach could be seen in the frustration and sometimes fury of the opposing elites.

The truism today is that mythological figures and men of power should not think in public. They should limit themselves to affirming truths. Stars, after all, are rarely equipped to engage in public debate. They would abhor the idea that the proper way to deal with confusion in society is to increase that confusion by asking uncomfortable questions until the source of the difficulties is exposed.

If the public personae of those who hold power are carefully examined in an historical context, the original connection between power and glamour can be seen to involve two very distinct sorts of fame. The first is that of useless celebrity, which abounded in the old royal courts and was of such concern to the courtiers. This fame remains today what it always was, dependent on but extraneous to a man's real functions, like icing on a cake. Theoretically harmless, in reality this decoration cloaks the public figure in a protective aura.

The second kind of fame is that which should be attached to the acceptance of public responsibility. The purpose of such notoriety is to make the public servant visible to the citizen so that we may judge him. If he holds power in order to serve us, then we must see him clearly and understand what he is doing. Fame, in that sense, is an obligation to be perfectly visible and therefore transparent.

Public figures today tend automatically to favour the first sort of fame — that of the courtiers and stars — in order to win and hold power. At the same time they obscure the manner in which they actually govern, while harping on about the prying of the media and the loss of their own privacy. In other words, they act like stars but insist that their personal lives are a private matter. This is patent hypocrisy. If you want to be a star, your sex life, indeed your orgasms, are of primary public interest, just as they were under the reign of the absolute monarchs.

The real problem is that public figures are now famous for all the wrong reasons while being allowed too much privacy in the areas that matter. If they ceased acting like stars, their private lives would cease to be of interest. Full light on their lives as public servants, however, would create the kind of celebrity which no star could bear. If the searching lights of stardom were turned on public officers for the right reasons, the public would come to expect something quite different from its leaders. It would begin to make sense to proceed through questioning and confusion, instead of through the formalized intractability necessary to stars.

21

The Faithful Witness

It is hardly surprising that those who hold power should attempt to control the words and language people use. Determining how individuals communicate is the best chance rulers have to control what they think. Clumsy men try to do this through violence and fear. Heavy-handed men running heavy-handed systems attempt the same thing through police-enforced censorship. The more sophisticated the elites, the more they concentrate on creating integrated intellectual systems which control expression through the communications structures. These systems require only the discreet use of censorship and uniformed men. In other words, those who take power will always try to change the established language. And those who hold power will try to control it. Governments produced by the most banal of electoral victories, like those produced by the crudest of coups d'état, will always feel obliged to dress themselves up linguistically in some way.

At stake are not simply particular temporary arguments but the entire baggage of a civilization. What a language says about a society's history will create mythology, direct the individual's imagination and limit or justify whatever those in power wish to do. We can recount our own history in a myriad of ways, twisting the origins and characteristics of the individual, the passage of kings, the sequence of wars, the evolution of architecture, the relationship between rich and poor, between men and women to suit whatever is currently at stake. But anyone attempting a disinterested look will notice that each major change in structure is either preceded or rapidly followed by some revolution in language. For the last half century, we have been lost in a jungle of social sciences which claim to have released man from the intellectual manipulations of the past, thanks to the application of disinterested rational analysis. And yet a calm look at any specific subject they have touched reveals that their objectivity has been just another interested manipulation of language.

The wordsmith — prophet, singer, poet, essayist, novelist — has always been either the catalyst of change or, inversely, the servant of established power. He breaks up the old formulas of wisdom or truth and thus frees the human imagination so that individuals can begin thinking of themselves and their society in new ways, which the writer must then express in new language. He may also put himself at the service of the new powers in order to build linguistic cages in which that freed imagination may be locked.

The breakup of the old Western linguistic order began in the fourteenth century, when men like Dante, Petrarch and Chaucer created remarkable social reflections by infusing their local languages with the genius of great poetry. They intentionally set these vulgar tongues in opposition to the Latin of the official religious and intellectual order. This breakup turned into what might be better described as a breakout in the sixteenth and seventeenth centuries, with first the dramatization of reality led by Shakespeare and Molière, then the insidious informality of the essay, which with Michel de Montaigne and Abraham Cowley began questioning the theoretical truths of their time, and finally the birth of a rough and undignified means of communication — the novel. In the hands of a one-armed old soldier like Cervantes and a troublemaking doctor like Rabelais, these simple prose stories created entire models of civilization for every man's imagination — models which reflected reality and not the official portrait of the world order. Finally, in the eighteenth and nineteenth centuries, this novel form came to full strength, poking its reflecting eye into the smallest corners of the established order. From Swift and Voltaire to Goethe, Dickens, Tolstoy and Zola, it mocked and dissected everything from the grand mythologies to the methods of industrial production and the ambitions of a small-town doctor's wife.

The novel was not a product or a creature of reason. It was the most irrational means of communication, subject to no stylistic order or ideological form. It was to intellectual order what animism is to religion — devoid of organized precedence or dependence on social structure. For the purposes of the novelist, everything was alive and therefore worthy of interest and doubt. At its best the novel became a vehicle for humanistic honesty. However, like democracy, it rose in tandem with the forces of reason. The endless specifics of reform made them allies to such a degree that the novel became the dominant linguistic form of the rational revolution.

In that process novelists became famous people and important factors in the process of social evolution. They wrote about every aspect of civilization and, if they had examined a problem seriously and then written well about it in their fiction, they could make an impact on the condition of the peasantry, public education, the morality of empire building or indeed on what women thought about men and men about women.

Most citizens still see our contemporary wordsmiths as an independent voice given more to criticizing the established powers than to praising them. And yet it is hard to think of another era when such a large percentage of the wordsmiths have been so cut off from general society and when language has been so powerless to communicate to the citizens the essence of what is happening around us and to us. The workings of power have never been so shielded by professional verbal obscurantism. The mechanisms of waste disposal management, opera houses, universities, hospitals, of everything to do with science, medicine, agriculture, museums and a thousand other sectors are protected by the breakdown of clear, universal language.

Strangely, writers seem unwilling or unable to attack effectively this professional obscurantism. In fact, the majority actively participate in it. They claim independence from established authority, but accept and even encourage the elitist structures that literature has developed over the last half century. As indignant individuals they rightly criticize power, but as writers they tend to encourage, through their own use of specialized literary forms, the Byzantine layering of language which divides and confuses our society. They have saved from the writer's inheritance his desire to speak out in the name of justice, but many have forgotten that this involves doing so first via their writing. In their rush to become part of rational society, which means to become respected professionals in their own right, they have forgotten that the single most important task of the wordsmith is to maintain the common language as a weapon whose clarity will protect society against the obscurities of power. The professional, by definition, is in society. He has his assigned territory over which his expertise gives him control. The writer is meant to be the faithful witness of everyman and should therefore be neither within society nor without. He must be of society — the constant link between all men.

Novelists had the power to make the new middle-class citizenry dream of freedom. They created a force which could pierce the shield of authority. That force consisted of ideas, situations and emotions clearly communicated. They used this to collapse the credibility of Church dogma and to lay out a path which the nascent democratic regimes could follow. They defined and posted and defended on a continuous basis the standards expected from a responsible citizen. They became the voice of the citizen against the ubiquitous *raison d'état*, which reappeared endlessly to justify everything from unjust laws and the use of child labour to incompetent generalship and inhuman conditions on warships. In places such as Russia, the novelist's was a loud voice widely and constantly heard, leading the way from the Napoleonic Wars to the Revolution of 1917. Throughout the West these storytellers, along with the poets and the essayists, baited and attacked and mocked again and again those with power and the systems they ran. The themes they popularized have gradually turned into the laws which, for all their flaws, have improved the state of man.

Emotion — so out of favour today in the management of public affairs — was one of the strengths novels used to neutralize the most convincing explanations of state interest and of financial necessity. A great novelist could keep his head up and his words flowing even in the passionate gales produced by the supermen Heroes, who increasingly seized power and wreaked general havoc. Elsewhere in society brilliant and decent men of reason were silenced by these Heroes. Reason, they discovered, eliminated the emotional force necessary to fight back. The novelist could be saved from this trap by his need to communicate with everyman, but also by the need to animate characters who were as real as real men and women. The novelist preached reason but was himself dependent upon common sense, constantly balancing intellect with emotion. He served our imagination through his devotion to clarity and universality. Those wordsmiths who in some way served established power almost always preached complexity and the obscurity of superior language.

With success and influence the novelists kept on multiplying until there were more of them than anyone could have imagined. And so, in the last years of the twentieth century, the citizen stares out expectantly into the vast scribbling crowd in search of the new Tolstoy, Zola's successor, Goethe reborn, Conrad or Lorca, and he does indeed find great writers and great novels. But above all he finds changed expectations, as the writing community is increasingly dominated by intractable purveyors of novels too opaque for any public beyond the semiprofessional reader, bevies of approving or disapproving professors of literature, multiplying hordes produced by creative-writing schools, esoteric sects producing high art of the sort which used to belong in the world of the vanity press and scores of hands rushing out detailed confessions of their personal loves and anxieties. Where the dangerous wordsmith and his weapon — the word — once led, a grand army of introspection, style and literary analysis now holds sway.

It is easy to bemoan a society in which the creative word no longer carries great weight in the large and small arguments of the day. But, citizens rightly ask — What does this person know to merit our ears? Even those writers, great and otherwise, who address the real world in their fiction, find that they are tarred by the broad brush of literature's withdrawal into professionalism and specialization. Perhaps this slide away from reality is simply part of an inevitable decline into dotage. After all, over the last seven hundred years the great centre stage of public communications has been held by a series of quite different dramatic forms. Thus the ballad gave way to the poem; and the poem more or less to the play and to the essay; and both of these to the novel. Now the electronic image is in the process of squeezing the novel out of the limelight. None of these forms ever quite disappears. But they do slip off the centre stage, out of the public's view and into the wings. There they hang about like dissatisfied old troupers, still convinced they could do it better than the newcomers. Yet history has little sympathy for the wordsmith as a delicate flower. And neither fatigue nor intellectual gentility are strong arguments for passivity.

The evolution of language can be reduced to a series of breakouts in the direction of that clarity which allows ideas to be delivered and understanding promoted. Those are the moments when writers explode the established arguments and light up the obscurities of power. Nothing is more terrifying to those in authority, whether their power is over a country, a factory or a child. They quickly launch hunts to recapture this wild language and, once successful, force it back into appropriate order. Two factors are constant: in its moments of freedom, language seeks clarity and communication; when imprisoned, the word instead becomes a complex and obscure shield for those who master it.

Over the last two and a half millennia, Western language has managed three escapes from the prison of established and appropriate order. The first occurred in the city-state of Athens, the second through the person of a young man who preached as the Messiah. The third started out audaciously with the genius of Dante and grew in strength despite constant opposition until it reached a maximum of freedom in the novel. That language now seems perilously close to being recaptured by the forces of order.

It was clear from the beginning of the Athenian escape that the resulting freed language would be the servant of the individual and not of established power. When Solon was called upon to save Athens from its financial, legal and political crisis in 594 B.C., he was already the greatest poet of his time and an experienced political figure. The reforms he brought about in turn laid the foundations for the city's greatness. More important still, he fixed firmly into the Western imagination a conviction that moderation and honesty were the essence of public affairs. His main weapon was the word and he proved that it could be a force for restraint, rather than an incitement to extremes, as so much of our history has seemed to show. He established not that writers should govern or preach but that their words should carefully reflect the reality of their times in the context of what was possible for men to understand and to act upon.

This freeing of language in 594 B.C. was an unexpected opportunity made possible by a crisis so great that the structures of established power were helpless. Solon may have been the leading populist poet of the day, but his greatest enemy was also poetry. The genius of Homer had provided the justifying texts for the old order.[1] *The Iliad* and *The Odyssey*, with their official gods and Heroes, had a stranglehold on imagination and power. Acceptance that humanity's affairs were decided on both the large and the personal scales at the level of divinities left no room for either individual responsibility or initiative. In fact, it invited the arbitrary and chaotic rule of Heroic leaders. Once the Athenian crisis had been dealt with and Solon had modestly withdrawn from power, his constitution was overthrown by the conservative forces. He had provided an alternate model for government, but not the more important thing — an alternate model for civilization and the individual.

Over the next two and a half centuries the struggle he had initiated swayed back and forth. Pericles made political advances which were superficially impressive but fragmentary on the level of the imagination. The invasion of wandering sophists — experts on various subjects who had great success selling their advice — demonstrated how confused the population was. These sophists bore an astonishing resemblance to our social scientists and technocrats. Then, in the years around 400 B.C., Socrates and Plato resolved at least the issue of language. Socrates' persistent attacks on doubtful knowledge were often aimed at the poets. He was attacking not only the Homeric dictatorship but also the old school of conservative poets-playwrights. By persisting with his loud, often rude questions and refusing to write a word himself, he undermined their control of the language. By questioning everyone in a simple, popular tongue, he was giving power to that part of the language not controlled by established forms.

In the end they formally accused him of heresy and of corrupting the minds of the young and, by a vote of 280 to 221, condemned him to death. This unjust and unwise victory backfired and brought about the undoing of the old order of the imagination. Plato, one of Socrates' students, was profoundly marked both by the trial and the subsequent legally imposed suicide. He felt driven to lay out a fundamentally secular and balanced way of organizing society. Whatever their flaws *The Republic* and other texts provided a complete alternate model for civilization and the individual. This illumination of nonarbitrary human relationships was so successful that every succeeding Western society has felt obliged to take it into account, as often to gain control over the individual's mind as to release it. Perhaps the most ironic claim of lineage has come in the last century from our own technocracy.

The Athenian breakout of language pitted moral standards and free thought — which were at first embedded in simple language and then in philosophy — against the highly evolved beauty of poetry which demanded unquestioning consent from the individual. The second out-break again began with simple language, again unwritten but this time preached. Christ's populist prose was inevitably pitted against sophisticated religions — first Judaism and then the heroic and divine panoply of Roman gods.

The few simple words he uttered seemed to have a universal and inherently uncontrollable strength such that their influence grew despite the obscurity of his life and death. They survived the interpretations of the unknown scribes who produced the texts which were gathered together as the Gospels. Christ's language witnessed reality in such a way that no organized power could control his meaning or profit from it. Even the subsequent compromises made by the Church in order to win support from the emperor and the bureaucratic officials in Rome did not limit the force of his actual words.

It was only thanks to the contested and late inclusion in the New Testament of the Book of Revelations that governments and the administrators of formal religion were able to gain control over Christ's language. Rome pushed hard for inclusion. Constantinople and the Church in the east were strongly opposed. This fourth-century argument was almost a rehearsal for the subsequent dispute over idolatry, which began in earnest with Damasus's election as Pope in 361 and dragged on until 841, when the iconoclastic struggle ended with virtual victory for Rome's position in favour of idol worship.

The premise of Revelations was that an old man called John, living on the island of Patmos, could deliver a prophesy revealed to him by the risen Jesus Christ. Five verses into the text, John establishes his privileged relationship by introducing Christ as "the faithful witness" who, with "a great voice as of a trumpet," instructs him to write. The "faithful witness" is the one who sees and speaks accurately and thus is to be trusted. John therefore goes on to convey Christ's message to the churches on earth. What follows are pages of raving. These include the entire pagan, superstitious, dark tradition which had dominated the Western barbarian imagination until the arrival of Christianity. Northrop Frye has shown that the Book of Revelations is nothing more than a compendium of mythological elements drawn from the Old Testament.[2] But this is precisely the sort of mythology which, when isolated from the main narrative, Judaism had in common with every other sect in the Mediterranean basin. The mesmerizing beauty of the words and images cannot be denied — majestic, filled with foreboding, threats and promises — offering a tantalizing physical view of heaven, which Christ had so carefully avoided; providing, in fact, a complete and complex model for the Christian imagination.

Once the Four Horsemen of the Apocalypse, the Seven Seals and the whores of Babylon, along with a false and facile division of the world into good and evil, had been given equal footing in the New Testament with the Sermon on the Mount, it was hardly surprising that the Christian language had been undermined to the point where it was as malleable as any old moon cult. In fact, more malleable. Pagan cults were often difficult for those in power to deform or manipulate because they combined strict public ritual with a narrow set of ironclad rules. Paul and his Epistles are often blamed for Christianity's strange tangents. But his contributions were merely politics and policy. John's Revelations altered the nature of the Christian ethic. It blew the Christian message so wide open that any extreme action, good or evil, could be justified — self-sacrifice, martyrdom, purity, devotion and concern for others had no greater purchase in Christ's official Testament than did racism, violence or absolutism of any sort. Whoever wrote John's text was consciously or unconsciously in the service of organized authority.

Official inclusion did not necessarily guarantee Revelations equal standing with those earlier Gospels which actually quoted the living Christ on the basis of firsthand evidence. Much of the credibility for a prophesy theoretically received from the risen Son of God came from a widespread belief that the author was the Disciple John who, years before, had also theoretically written one of the Gospels. Of course, anyone who wanted to know knew that they were two different people. For a start, the earliest manuscript of John's Gospel is in Greek, while that of Revelations is in Hebrew. The Church never actually said that the young fisherman/Disciple and the old man on the island of Patmos were one and the same. Instead the authorities remained vague on the subject. They permitted the misunderstanding to spread, which it did so successfully that most preachers, pastors and even priests still believe there was only one John.

For the quasi totality of believers who, from the fourth century on, simply accepted that one man wrote both texts, it was impossible not to give his later revelations equal value with his earlier work. If he lied on Patmos, then why would we believe his original Good News about Christ? And since his Gospel matches those of Matthew, Mark and Luke, if John lied, then why should anyone believe any of them?

Thousands of theologians would later contribute to the capture, binding and disarming of the original Christian language; Saint Augustine first among them. Perhaps the most effective method they found was the maintenance of the Bible in Latin, so that the original simple oral message could only be received in the form of an authorized interpretation by a priest. Even so, the real victory of official complexity over simple free language was already long over, having taken less than four hundred years from when Christ first preached.

The third and greatest breakout of language began tentatively inside the Christian church in the thirteenth century and eventually came to a culmination through the novel in the nineteenth and early twentieth centuries. It seems now to be almost over, our dominant language today being one of reassurance, confusion and control. That this revolution began in the Church was hardly surprising. Christianity was the universal truth of Western civilization. There was no serious dissenting position outside that idea. The obvious alternative, for anyone wishing to withdraw from the ideological and bureaucratic complexities of the Christian empire, was to return to the simplicity of the Church's founder.

Francis of Assisi, son of a rich merchant, set aside all the benefits of his civilization in 1206. His physical emulation of Christ's simple way of life was eloquent. More revolutionary, however, was his setting aside of a millennium of intricate theology and ideology to think and speak in the simple oral tongue of Christ.[3] This came in a world still dominated by the rich, mystical obscurity of another saint, Bernard of Clairvaux, who had died fifty years before. Francis's opting out was passive and suggested no challenge to authority. His message flashed through Europe like an electric current — oral and therefore intellectually invisible, escaping all ideological and theological structures, controls and traps. However, as with Socrates and Christ, oral dissent becomes the property of structures when the spokesman dies. The Church recuperated Francis's message by burying his memory in sainthoods, basilicas, writings and paintings — all the formal honours, in other words, that authority can dispense.

If there was to be an alternate model for the imagination it would have to come through the written word. This would have to begin unfolding through the forms which were already in existence — first poetry, then poetry on stage, then drama in prose, before evolving into the novel. The idea of narrative — of the story — was there from the beginning, inching its way through different media towards an autonomous existence. But perhaps the greatest works of genius came very early on, through the mechanisms of the older forms.

The fourteenth century was filled with these explosions of language, as Dante, then Boccaccio, Petrarch and Chaucer seized essentially secular local languages which they exploited in order to reflect human reality. But they also filled and formed them with their own genius and imagination. Poetry was therefore at the very centre of the public stage. Dante, a leader in Florentine city-state politics, was forced into exile in 1302 and consciously chose to write not in Vulgar Latin, but in a vulgar local dialect which was the fresh, straightforward and unchained language of the people. The same can be said of Petrarch, a papal courtier; Boccaccio, a Florentine public servant; and Chaucer, who was in the service of the king before becoming a civil servant. This humanist explosion was driven in part by a conviction that such poetry could have a profound effect on the reader. The writers were also fully conscious that they were sliding along a very thin line between social dissent, which could cost them their positions and perhaps their lives, and innocent verse, which wished merely to inform and to delight.

So long as the poem remained the weapon of men concerned by and involved in the real world, it maintained its popular force. The examples are endless. Alexander Pope, political meddler. John Milton, jailed for his political and religious beliefs. Walter Raleigh, adventurer and courtier. Aleksandr Pushkin, Decembrist sympathizer. Mikhail Lermontov, exiled for his poem attacking Pushkin's murderers — "You greedy crowd that round the sceptre crawl." Alphonse de Lamartine, leader of the 1848 Revolution. Victor Hugo, scourge of Louis-Napoléon.

That Hugo was among the most famous men of the second half of the nineteenth century and Byron nearly the most famous of the first does not really impress the world of contemporary literature. It merely seems to confirm that Romanticism didn't produce important verse. But the fame of Hugo and Byron had nothing to do with their style. It had to do with a willingness and an ability to reflect their own times. When Byron wrote, "All contemplative existence is bad. One should do something," he meant that words are what you do, not what you are. You must try to do something in the world — not in order to succeed, as if it were a matter of banal ambition, but in order to be there, in order to understand how to produce real words.

Throughout the long debate over the proper role of poetry, the Republic of Dubrovnik remained a peculiar and stable poetic example sitting on the edge of the West. Isolated and protected by the cliffs behind and the sea in front, Dubrovnik was the closest the Christian world ever came to recreating Athens. It was governed much of the time by its leading poets and lasted a thousand years, from the ninth to the nineteenth century, which also made it the longest lived of Western political organizations. The rectors of this city-state were changed monthly on a revolving basis. Their characteristics were a high level of education and, more often than not, an ability to denounce injustice and defend liberty through their verse.[4] In those thousand years, the city held off or maintained loose alliances with the Muslims, the Turks, the Venetians and the Austrians. Despite having one of the largest commercial fleets on the Mediterranean, they defended themselves without a navy or an army. Their strength was a remarkably astute foreign policy which neutralized their enemies. The poets also excelled in the particularly difficult negotiations which played the city's various rivals and enemies off against each other. Needless to say, it was Bonaparte, the destroyer of republics, who brought the by-then-aged system to an end.

Already in the early nineteenth century, the forces throughout the West that wished to drag poetry off into the wings of contemplation, specialization and elitism were growing. The centre stage was already being occupied by the novel. Later in the century, the shift was more or less complete. Even a genius like Baudelaire, who in some ways was one of the new inward-looking poets and yet who wrote with the full power of a popular wordsmith, was unable to find a window through to the public. "Any book," he wrote, "which does not address itself to the majority — in number and in intelligence — is a stupid book."[5] The burgeoning intellectual elites who "controlled" French poetry kept him out of the anthologies, school manuals and encyclopedias long after he was dead.

Similar battles took place in the theatre. Throughout the sixteenth and seventeenth centuries national languages were exploding on stages around Europe. Emotions, politics, national consciousness, love, ambition were all being expressed with an accuracy and originality never seen before. No one would have thought to differentiate between theatre for the elites and theatre for the people. The various parts of the audience took what suited them from plays like *King Lear* or *Hamlet*, whose staying power still seems to come in large part from this populist conception. Most of the audience, after all, was poor and uneducated. Molière came later in the evolution of French than Shakespeare did in English, so his role had less to do with explosive creativity than with a remarkable turning up of the lights of clarity and understanding. Although somewhat better educated than the Englishman, he, too, was an actor-producer-writer and by no means what his contemporaries would have considered a man of learning. He put on his plays both at court and in Paris and wrote for all parts of French society. The Church, the courtesans and the more serviceable pens were infuriated by his ability to expand apparently simple comedies, containing simple, accessible language, into social commentaries which directly attacked those who had money or who used the courts to advance their ambitions. They did everything they could to stop him and from time to time were able to close him down or turn the king against him.

But Molière's pen was faster and sharper and more popular than their backroom politics. Above all, he had the public with him because he reflected the world as it was. In the midst of the greatest controversy of his career, when he was under constant physical threat and the menace of being removed from court as well as shut down in Paris, he replied with a play which sent up his critics. In the middle of *La Critique de l'Ecole des Femmes* he paused to rub the noses of his literary rivals in their failure to carry the great public: "I'd just like to know," one of the characters mused, "whether the greatest rule of all the rules isn't to please."[6]

It was precisely this undefeatable power of the popular word — the word that pleases — which had driven Richelieu to create the French Academy. "The blows from a sword are easily healed," he wrote in his *Political Testament*. "But it is not the same with blows of the tongue."[7] The Academy was apparently devoted to developing language and literature. However, by its own internal logic, an official body devoted to language could only be driven by a desire for respectability and a conviction that if anyone was to be pleased, it was established authority. In more practical terms, a literary organization empowered to define could not help but be devoted to control.

Richelieu's understanding of systems and how they could be used to control ideas was, as always, astonishing. His use of the Academy to honour writers is still not generally understood to be a fine method for disarming dangerous language. If it had been understood, writers would not have run so eagerly to support other academies around the world. With the exception of a short period in the second half of the eighteenth century, when almost all French institutions were slipping out of control, the Academy has done precisely what the Cardinal expected. It has been a conservative force working against ungoverned explosions of language.

The essence of the faithful witness is that he seeks no honour for his words, except from the public. The ability to reflect accurately and to communicate directly requires an absolute freedom from any obligation as a writer to any organized structure. A writer can be involved in the world in a nonliterary capacity so long as his language is not directly bound to any interest. The worst of all possible combinations is to be out of the world as a man and yet bound to its structures as a writer.

The gradual marginalization of poetry and drama as the principle means of public communication can be attributed in part to such public ties. Never freed of their origins stretching back to Homer and increasingly imprisoned by the now stable national languages, poets found themselves writing more against their own past than to the reader. This poetry of reference, however brilliant and explosive, necessarily had to be turned inward, cutting off the public reflection. The growth of literary studies encouraged this, as did the growth of academies and prizes. What to intellectuals seemed revolutionary, to the outer world seemed elitism.

Poetry had at first been liberated by the exploitation of local languages that began in the fourteenth century. But the more poets plunged into local forms, the less sense their verse made in other tongues. To all intents and purposes it became untranslatable, although much of it was translated and published. The result is that the leading poets of the last hundred years are virtually unknown outside their own languages. Mallarmé influenced poets everywhere, but who else? Pound and Eliot wrote astonishing things about the modern world. How many French or Germans are aware of this? Rimbaud's myth as a tragic Hero has travelled, but not his poetry. Apollinaire, Éluard, Auden, Char, even Yeats, seem hopelessly limited by language.

Today there are poetry festivals almost every day in different universities throughout the West. There poets read to each other. This is not a forced imprisonment. Outside the Western democracies poets still communicate easily with the public through their verse. This is a prison constructed of the poets' own language in their own minds with materials such as dignity, formality, appropriate styles and appropriate structures — an imprisonment of the imagination by heightened self-consciousness. Theatre has been hampered by many of these same problems in addition to its dependence on a material infrastructure. The need to fill large halls with assembled crowds is not just an economic factor. It also creates a lack of flexibility — of light-footedness — which at the hint of political difficulties becomes a major disadvantage.

Those who first used the novel form were a minority voice in a civilization still dominated by religious parables, oral storytelling, traditional epic poetry and all the newer forms of poetry, theatre and essays. Yet even in its early picaresque appearances, the latent power of this new method came bursting out. *Amadis de Gaule*, perhaps the first real novel, was theoretically just an adventure story filled with the rules of well-bred worldliness. It appeared in Spain in 1508 and rapidly became one of the largest-selling books of all time, spreading throughout Europe and creating, as it went, a revolution in social perceptions. The curious, contradictory relationship between the rise of the novel and that of reason begins here. Machiavelli's *The Prince*, the first intellectual exposition of the new rational method, appeared in 1513. As for Amadis, he became the model for the wandering chivalrous individual of fiction. The twentieth-century existential heroes are reverberations of that knight, still fixated on the contradiction between the responsibility attached to honour, as opposed to their personal freedom, which requires staying outside all structures.

One way to understand the power in these books is to look at who wrote them. Cervantes: professional soldier, captured by the Turks, a slave for five years, one of the planners of the Armada. He was also jailed several times for fraud and murder. Rabelais: a physician devoted to theological law, politics, military strategy and botany. Daniel Defoe, author of the first modern English novel, *Robinson Crusoe*: merchant, rebel soldier under the Duke of Monmouth, secret agent for William III and journalist. Henry Fielding: lawyer and polemicist. In *The Welsh Opera*, he attacked the royal family and in *The Historical Annals*, turned on Walpole. He was eventually made a judge and set about writing *Tom Jones* as part of his dual campaign against poverty and dishonest judges. Jonathan Swift: political polemicist, Anglican priest and defender of Irish rights. He told Pope that his aim in writing *Gulliver* had been "to vex the world rather than to divert it." Voltaire: philosopher, polemicist, political agitator, courtier, imprisoned in the Bastille, exiled in England, adviser to both Empress Catherine the Great of Russia and Frederick the Great of Prussia, highly successful gentleman farmer and, as has already been noted, the most famous man of the eighteenth century. Lermontov: adventurer and professional soldier; died in a duel. Goethe: senior government official in Weimar. Tolstoy: professional soldier, political agitator and landowner devoted to experimental farming and revolutionary new farm management methods which, needless to say, included land reform and a new deal for the peasants.

All these people were searching about for new written forms which would break out of the established debates and have the sort of impact those in authority could not easily control. The novel rose in interwoven tandem with journalism and so novelists tended also to be pamphleteers and polemicists, writers of tracts and broadsides, political satirists and moralists. During his exile in England, Voltaire had seen the combination aggressively exploited by Swift. But that was not exceptional. Wherever there was a sufficient crack in the censorship laws to permit publication, novels and journalists rose like Siamese twins.

These driven men were not convinced, at least not in the early days, that a frivolous thing like the novel would help to change the world. Many of them had been taken in by the growing elitism which surrounded poetry and the stage. The superiority of those in decline seems always to undermine the self-confidence of those on the rise. Voltaire worked much harder at his poems and plays — nobler art forms, he believed — than at his novels. His epic poem *La Henriade* (1723) illustrated the life of Henri IV, who came closer than any other to the ideal of the good king. *Zaïre* (1732), an heroic tragedy written according to the established rules of the stage, played out the agonies of honour, power and betrayal. He was convinced that classic forms of literature, when combined with his influence on monarchs such as Catherine the Great and Frederick the Great, would create the maximum pressure for social and political change. He and others believed that these rational monarchs would respond with reforms. For decades he wasted time praising the Prussian King's endless and mediocre rhyming couplets. This shared devotion to the noblest of art forms seemed like a guarantee that change would come. Voltaire's poems and plays had great success but little secondary effect in the world outside books and theatres. They were eventually forgotten. But his frivolous little novels, thrown off more in frustration than out of any great belief in their artistic or moral value, immediately revealed a force of their own. Like his poems and plays, they had great popular success. But apart from the pleasure they brought the reader, novels like *Zadig* (1747) and *Candide* (1759) miraculously vaporized the dominant intellectual argument in favour of passivity before established systems. His fiction did not respond intellectually and win debates. It simply permitted readers to understand instinctively that such arguments were nonsense.

The secret of the novel seemed to be that, alone of the word forms, it created a complete world, and one which the public could easily penetrate. A novel belonged to the solitary reader in a way that no poem, play or essay could. It was free standing, three-dimensional and open to any man's view of it. The novelist seemed little more than a cipher for the public's reflection of itself. It was as if each reader had written the book himself. As if in some way each novel was read as an autobiography of the reader. Indeed, one of the novel's great strengths is that, at some unconscious level, each reader does believe he has written it. And he consciously believes that he could have written it. The greater the novel, the more easily the reader slips into this confusion. The novelist and his ego must obviously be invisible or such confusion would not be possible. The more the writer is visible in his fiction, the less the readers can participate. They must settle instead for a sort of intellectual voyeurism. While the role of the peeping tom may give pleasure, it is vastly inferior to that of the participant. The great novelists therefore disappeared from their books.

Perhaps most surprising was the ease with which this new form could be used by both writers and readers. There seemed to be neither inherent nor man-made limitations to the emotions it could provoke or to what it could evoke about public and private affairs. There were no arguments to be had over complex poetic forms. The only limitations were those the laws could impose. And unlike drama, there were no theatres for the authorities to close down. Books could be banned, but without great success since it was difficult to guess in advance what the public might read into a story. Governments could seize printing presses, but there were always more of these simple machines just across borders. And books slipped easily over borders and under counters. They were too small to be detected and too numerous to control. What's more, by writing in the language of the people, novelists ensured that the potential public included everyone who could read. In the 1530s Rabelais's *Gargantua* began its comic obscene romp across medieval good behaviour, attacking idle monks, pointless wars and dogmatism. Under the form of high comedy, he was offering a common sense view of man. Rabelais was constantly in trouble with the law, as was Fielding, until his *Tom Jones* began to undermine the credibility of courts throughout England.

There was in fact a solid wall between society and the reasonable use of words. That wall was established authority and structures, both civil and intellectual. The novelist, like a mortar, was able to lob the forces of language over the barrier of structure to society on the other side. The novel was the perfect missile, in that no effective antimissile could exist. There was nothing anyone could do to prevent its flight, apart from seize books, which was the equivalent of collecting mortar shells after they had hit their targets. Seizure was a tribute to the book and merely increased its success.

None of this quite explains the response of the public to an apparently frivolous means of entertainment. Narrative was at the core of the novel's success. It was the unassuming use of the story which made it possible for the reader to find his or her reflection in the novel. Beyond that was the sense that life came to life in fiction. Even facts took on a new kind of hardness within the novel. Truth seemed clearer and easier to state. Fiction could be far more real than real life. It could perceive the realities of man's inner and outer lives.

And although novels were theoretically limited by their devotion to popular and therefore local languages, it rapidly became clear that, compared to poetry and drama, they were easily translated. The narrative, characterizations, emotions and undogmatic style carried from one vernacular to another. *Gargantua* wasn't translated into English for a century (1653), but *The Princess of Clèves* appeared in 1679, a year after the French original. *Robinson Crusoe* was out in 1716 and soon being read throughout Europe; *Gil Blas* out in 1735 and into English by 1749. The conundrum of spreading literacy being limited to local languages could thus be bypassed by fiction.

Where in all this was the writer as artist? From the seventeenth to the early twentieth centuries, he was running to keep up with the growing popularity of the novel, while inventing new and better ways to communicate true reflections to the largest possible number of people. He was developing the technical skills to make his mortar shells fly higher and farther. If art entered the picture at all, it was only as a judgment made by society upon the writer's work long after it was written — more often than not as a sort of posthumous medal. And individuals do not go to war to win posthumous medals.

As the nineteenth century advanced, novelists discovered that they could have an enormous effect not just upon government and power structures, but upon all sorts of social expectations. Even an apparently passive force, like Jane Austen, had impact simply because her witnessing of the world was so exact and so lifelike that many readers saw themselves for the first time and thus were able to take a new critical distance from themselves and their society.

After the Reform Bill of 1832, British society remained uneasy for a good forty years. Political and social pressures were building on all sides for changes in such areas as the child labour laws, factory conditions and urban poverty. Into the midst of that unease Dickens dropped books like *Oliver Twist* and *Hard Times*. Most people knew that children were being exploited, the slums cruel and factory conditions intolerable. But that knowledge was abstract. Dickens took the middle-class husband and wife right into those slums and factories. He made them real places and therefore made the need for reform real. Alessandro Manzoni published his *The Betrothed* in 1825 with the same sort of effect. Theoretically it was an historical novel about the corrupt oppression of the Spanish rule in Lombardy. Everyone understood that it was really about the Austrians, the current masters of northern Italy. In two decades, from 1827 to 1847, Balzac wrote ninety-one interwoven volumes of his *Human Comedy*, perhaps the most astonishing accomplishment of modern fiction. He created a portrait of contemporary France, including all the tensions between Paris and the provinces, which had an enormous impact not only on the French but also on readers and writers throughout the West.

There was something in the novel's curious mixture of simple accessibility and complex content which made it the most accurate verbal reflection yet discovered. It permitted language to explode outwards again and again towards an ever-larger part of the population, as if humanity had finally invented a perpetual motion machine of the freed imagination. This could be seen in the books of Herman Melville, who — although a mystic as much as a novelist — nevertheless set his stories among the whale hunters (the oil industry) or in the navy or merchant marine.

Even Flaubert strengthened the novel's force as a public reflection by making the writer disappear absolutely from the reader's consciousness while at the same time creating reflections in which people of no particular worth became "heroes." Thus the fictional hero ceased being one with the rational, public Hero. Perhaps this was the first sign that novelists wanted to distance themselves from the rational society they had done so much to create. Emma Bovary, for example, was unintelligent, selfish and nastily ambitious. By making her the main character, the one with whom we are meant to identify, Flaubert jolted the reader into a more acute state of consciousness. In the process he was dragged through the law courts for offending public morals. Although Flaubert was acquitted, his trial was a warning of the new administrative controls which society was developing.

And yet fiction did not seem to have lost its steam by the century's end. In fact, Zola carried things a step further. He revived the old habits of the early "popular" novelists, like the elder Dumas, who had regularly gone out into society to research for three months and then returned to write for three. Year after year Dumas could be found in Russia studying the situation of the serfs, in Naples with Garibaldi, in Corsica with the bandits. Zola did not go so far afield, but he looked at his own society with an eye like a scalpel. He examined the stock exchanges and salons for *L'Argent* with the same detail as the slums and the mines for *Germinal*. It was as if the romantic eye of Dickens had been peeled of all its affectations. Zola found a way to bring to the page precisely what he saw. This concern carried him to the centre of the greatest crisis of the Third Republic — the Dreyfus Affair. With his open letter to the President of the Republic, *J'Accuse*, he intentionally libelled the military command to force them back into court, where Dreyfus's lawyers could cross-examine them. The immediate result was that the court condemned Zola and this inadvertently carried the *Affaire* to the highest degree of politicization. It was as if every citizen at last felt obliged to take a stand on one side or the other. During a second trial, Zola walked out in protest and fled to England. In his absence he was condemned to a year of prison. Eleven months later the *Affaire* had so evolved that he was able to come home.[8]

Although the literary community divided into pro- and anti-Dreyfus camps and writers seemed to be playing an ever-more-central role in public debates, in reality this was the high-water mark of the novelist's power. A new chorus of literary voices had been slowly growing during the last twenty years of the nineteenth century. They claimed that the novel had to be written as an art form and not as a reflection of reality. For them someone like Zola was dealing in crude reality and writing little more than journalism. Fiction, they believed, was the opposite of reality. Involvement with society would merely corrupt it. In order to demonstrate that Zola had abandoned the mainstream and slipped off into mere category or genre fiction, the growing establishment of literary experts called his books *naturalisme*, as if to say that they were only real and lacked style. Or they called them *roman-reportage*, as if they were not real fiction because they drew too much on the real world.

In truth Zola had simply strengthened the original link between the journalist-reporter-polemicist on the one hand, and the novelist on the other. Defoe, Swift, Voltaire, Diderot and hundreds of others had been products of that double approach. Zola had done no more than update the journalistic methods.

The transformation of the individual into a specialist was nevertheless well under way in the rest of society. It was increasingly difficult to stay both in the system and out. Any involvement in a profession carried with it either a contractual or a moral commitment to remain silent in public about what that profession involved. Any deviation from what was felt to be professional parameters indicated a lack of seriousness. What had once been relatively common — writers like Sheridan, Goethe and Lamartine holding public office — became a rarity. Disraeli was the last English novelist to hold an important political position and when, as leader of the Conservative party, he published a new novel, his reputation was damaged. What was true for politicians was doubly true for civil servants, officers and other employees. Even lawyers and doctors, if they worked in large groups, began to feel the pressures of professional solidarity and therefore public silence.

Those writers who wanted to remain part of the real world found that they were gradually being squeezed into an ever-narrower selection of professions. In fact, they were being squeezed out of the society they were meant to write about. They had always been marginal, but marginal had once described the privilege of free movement in and out. Now the rules proper to the boxes of expertise were keeping them on the outside. Only the rare individual could occupy more than one.

And if rational society were to have made an exception to this rule, the privilege certainly would not have been given to writers. After all, they were nonprofessional individuals who wished to communicate uncontrolled truths to masses of nonprofessional people.

What is more, through this process of exclusion, the writer was being denied the most sought-after reward of rational society — respectability. He had not sought it in the past because he had been greatly admired. Now the growing mass of the respectable — who were also the main readers of fiction — began to look down upon the novelists. They were irresponsible. They lived on the margins like dancers and actors, lost in a world of alcohol, drugs and prostitutes. As more novelists turned away from the real world in order to balance art with fantasy, they were accused of being what the early novelists had often pretended to be in order to avoid censorship — intellectual gypsies whose stories simply entertained innocent girls.

As late as 1918 the British army demobilization forms, which broke men down into eighteen social and professional categories, listed the novelist on the eighteenth level, which consisted of leftovers, marginals and nonprofessionals, including gypsies, vagrants and other nonproductive persons. Change, however, was well under way. Fiction was being converted into an art form. And, as with all self-declared interest groups, it began to spend as much time justifying itself as it did actually producing real fiction. The world of writers was becoming bloated with hangers-on: doctors of literary analysis, devotees of specific writers, advocates of particular literary styles, chroniclers of literary gossip, perpetual secretaries of literary organizations, linguists and literary historians, to name just a few. Once the main subjects had been analyzed, the next generation of literary doctors had to focus on smaller and smaller details. They spent decades giving meaning to the tiniest aspects of each writer's life and then snarled at each other over the corpse.

It was only a matter of time before the writer became a minority in his own world — in general, an underprivileged minority. The literary professionals had such things as long-term contracts, university tenure and pension plans. While most writers were renting space in marginal neighbourhoods, the experts had entered into the middle-class world of property ownership. The writers were gradually becoming more regional and travelled little, while the professors were constructing for themselves a prefinanced, international, self-perpetuating travel machine, which required them to move around the world in order to research literature and to discuss it with other experts. That many of their subjects were poorer and led less stable lives was extremely helpful. The more a novelist drank, divorced, went bankrupt and had mental breakdowns, the more interesting he was to study and the easier it was to equate internal anguish with creativity. An image of the writer as a suffering, tragic, foolish, obsessive soul began to emerge. Baudelaire: syphilitic and absinthe addict. Verlaine: alcoholic. Joyce: poor and blind. Proust: asthmatic, closet homosexual. Fitzgerald: poor, alcoholic and impotent. Hemingway: alcoholic suicide. Wilde: imprisoned homosexual martyr. Kerouac, Burroughs, and company: drink, drugs and family tragedy. Through all of this ran the almost unbroken theme of uncontrolled egos and of genius labouring unrecognized in poverty.

The career of the American writer Raymond Carver illustrated where all this would eventually lead. Specialists of literature fixed on him during the 1980s as a perfect, fresh example of the creator dogged by working-class roots plus family and alcohol problems. His work was rarely mentioned without reference to this personal colour. His premature death in 1989 came almost as a relief to his supporters. It freed them all to begin dividing the writer's body up into interesting morsels. That Carver died in his forties was a further benefit, confirming once again that writers are not made to live.

At first glance there is no reason why Carver or any other writer should take notice of this necrophagy, with its combination of the absurdly analytical and the ghoulish. But literary scientists are professionals in exactly the same way that political scientists are. And so, in whatever direction they drag literature, writers have difficulty not being dragged along. The idea that they could change the nature of fiction may at first have seemed ridiculous, but they are like royal courtesans or military baggage trains. A king who allowed his court to grow out of control was leeched by the courtesans until they destroyed him, just as a swollen baggage train, laden with whores, pillage, cooks and home comforts caused armies to lose battles.

Once the rational approach had provided literature with a multitude of specialized reasons for existing, its purpose could no longer be anything as base as communication with the reader. Instead, the relationship between the novel and its public came to be treated as an incidental or as an amusing subject worthy of gossip. That women had fainted when Byron read or that tens of thousands had welcomed Voltaire back to Paris in 1778 or that great crowds had come to hear Dickens, was the sort of information which belonged in light biographies. These were matters of little importance compared to the psychological interpretation of the writer and his words. Did Voltaire sleep with his niece? Was Byron bisexual? Did Dickens ever get over his childhood? The novel's relationship with the public came to be treated as indistinguishable from the writer's personal relationship with his public — simply illustrations of ego and of Hero worship. They were of tertiary importance behind the examination of the work's artistic worth and the revelation of personal meaning.

As Ford Madox Ford described the growing professionalism required by all this: "If you had told Flaubert or Conrad . . . that you were not convinced of the reality of Homais or Tuan Jim, as like as not they would have called you out and shot you." Whereas an English novelist of the new period "would have knocked you down if they could, supposing you had suggested that he was not a gentleman."[9] In other countries we can replace "gentleman" with "intellectual" or "artist" or "professional."

Although geniuses like Tolstoy and Mann were still writing and others like Orwell, Malraux, Hemingway, Greene and Camus were still to come, rules as to what constituted both a novel and a novelist were rapidly being written. Rebels like Julien Gracq would go on repeating, as he did in the 1960s, after refusing the principal accolade of the French literary establishment — the Prix Goncourt — for his novel *Les Rivages des Syrtes*, that "in art, there are no rules, there are only examples." But well before him Balzac had pointed out how self-serving the literary world had become — a world in which "one loves only one's inferiors." And Spengler, in his hodgepodge of curious ideas, was arguing between the two world wars that modern writers "do not possess [any] real standing in actual life. Not one of them has intervened effectively either in higher politics, in the development of modern technics, in matters of communications, in economics or in any other *big* actuality with a single act or a single compelling idea."

Aeronautics engineers know about airplanes and cardiologists know about hearts. But what does the average Western novelist now know? What is he to write about? What are his novels to contain? When Voltaire, Swift, Balzac and Zola wrote about government, industry, stock exchanges and science, they actually knew more than most of the people who were in those professions. The novelist was constantly pushing at the front edge of specific knowledge and understanding. Today's novelist, living as he usually does in the isolation of literature's own professional box, is unable to do this. What is it that he now knows profoundly enough to be able to write about? First, he knows about writing; second, about the world of writers; third, about the writer's inner life; and fourth, about his own practical situation, on the margins of the normal world, where he may exist in comfort or in poverty. At one extreme are those who write about writing — the university novelists and the experimentalists. At the other are those who, like Raymond Carver, refuse this self-indulgent cocoon in favour of charting their own experiences on the edge.

In neither case do we have the novelist running ahead of society, dragging everyone else behind. Walter Bagehot had already seen the problem looming late in the nineteenth century. "The reason why so few good books are written is that so few people who can write know anything."

As writers gradually lost their influence in society, so they fell back on the idea of art as its own justification. The seeds of this withdrawal were planted as early as Immanuel Kant and his "purposiveness without purpose" in art. It was not simply that a decadent school at the end of the nineteenth century had declared that art existed only for art's sake. Or that some genius like Wilde or Beaudelaire had added his weight to this argument. Language was gradually being brought under control by rational civilization and so the affected indifference of a few writers was not so much specific irresponsibility or egotism as one way of admitting defeat.

Rémy de Gourmont's aphorisms give a good sense of this petulant defeatism, which went as far as disgust for humanity. "Number LXXXIII — Better boredom than mediocre pleasure." Or, "we have no more principles and there are no more models; a writer creates his aesthetic by writing his books: we are reduced to relying on sensation, not judgment."[10]

The flamboyant withdrawal of the aesthetes obscured the real effect of much of the Modernist movement. Everywhere writers agreed on the need to reveal the individual's inner perceptions or psychology. But the practical expression of this need was the gradual withdrawal of fiction as a whole into style and form. These were the two measurable characteristics which could make the writer a professional like everyone else. The effect of this demotion of content, emotion and purpose can be seen as early as the Goncourt brothers. They thought their novels provided a realistic, detailed portrait of society. And yet what they really believed came out on page one of the *Journal* they began to keep on December 2, 1851, the day their first novel was published. It also turned out to be the day of Louis-Napoléon's successful coup d'état. The messenger who brought them the news of the coup was incensed when they enquired about the fate of the book — "Your novel . . . a novel . . . France couldn't give a damn for novels today, my boys!"[11] And he ran off to rejoin reality on the barricades, leaving them to mope in their study. The way the Goncourt brothers told the story, there was an assumption of art's fragility and irrelevance when faced by reality.

The self-hypnosis which the need to experiment with style and form was producing spread with astonishing rapidity. That this almost scientific approach was somehow related to unveiling the unconscious also made it seem to be relevant to the outside world. The excitement produced by radical changes in language and the genius, indeed madness, of many new practitioners, created a sense of progress. But the reality of this progress, when seen from the outside, was quite different. The writing profession was simply creating a dialect of its own — a dialect as inaccessible to nonprofessionals as that of doctors and economists. In other words, from the thirteenth century on, writers had sought and created ever-wider understanding. Now they themselves had opted to restrict the use of language.

The two most dramatic assertions of the death of literate, universal communications came early in the twentieth century with Marcel Proust and James Joyce. Once they had been adopted as the reigning geniuses of the modern revolution in literature, the novel was effectively dead as the leading linguistic tool for asking essential questions and changing society. What they did — inadvertently in the case of Proust — was to destroy both language and the story as bridges between the novel and the public. With a single stroke, they carried the novelist out of the domain of common sense and into that of reason maddened by logic.

What Proust wrote, and intended to write, was a strong social and political novel about the destruction of the aristocracy and the rough-handed rise of the middle classes. *A la Recherche du Temps Perdu* was filled with the traumas suffered by the Jews in France, the profound divisions caused by the Dreyfus Affair, the pitiful etiquette of a society in decline and the crude ambitions of those on the way up. The whole thing ended with the offstage massacre of World War I, and the grotesque postwar reconstitution of a society pretending to be unchanged. The language and the narrative were perhaps drawn out, but they were clear.

The literary community tended to focus its attention, however, on what it saw as a languid contemplation of the interior. From the charged story little more was retained than nostalgia. Proust was transformed from a terrorist into a custodian of memory — a dream master delivering the literary nostalgia of things past. This is not memory as an active agent, linking past and present. This is simply the past — passive and inoffensive. The overall effect of such an interpretation was to convert the "story" — which had always been the strength of the novel — into a coarse device that could be relegated to lesser categories of fiction.

The situation became even more confusing a few years later when another writer nullified Proust's revolution by doing the exact opposite. Louis-Ferdinand Céline was probably this century's most revolutionary writer in French. He exploded the language, exploded convention and broke through to the general reader with an extraordinarily modern directness which gave new meaning and power to the story. But the ideas he communicated came crawling out of the mud of the trenches, and his marginal mental stability caused him to turn this pessimism into the voice of man's dark side. In a sense he became a brilliant voice for the worst of our past. His ideas seemed to belong with Proust's style. If Proust had delivered his vision with Céline's power and revolutionary clarity, the French novel might still be the greatest force in the Western language.

The case of James Joyce was rather more straightforward. It is difficult to read his books as being written by other than an angry man filled with bitterness. He consciously felt himself to be the messiah of language and saw a cross on every corner. The anger he felt was in part the product of the divided society which had produced him — an anger undigested by his endless and unforgiving exile. He set out in his writing not, as is usually argued, to release the imprisoned word by destroying convention but to destroy communication itself. He closed *A Portrait of the Artist as a Young Man* with: "I go to encounter for the millionth time the reality of experience and to forge in the smithy of my soul the uncreated conscience of my race." What interests him is his own soul. There is no suggestion that he planned to pass on to others the forged results. And as first *Ulysses*, then *Finnegans Wake* demonstrated, indeed he did not.

Like Proust, he filled his books with social and political drama, but what dominated in the Joycean revolution was the obscure language, which was inaccessible to most of the public. This obscurity was not an accident. Joyce, in his messianic fervour, was fully aware that he was wrenching the novel away from the public — for whom it had been invented — and delivering it to the literary experts. The great novels of the nineteenth and early twentieth centuries had often been written by doctors, engineers, soldiers and landowners. Joyce knew that his major works would not even be accessible as reading material to the doctors, engineers, soldiers and landowners of the twentieth century. Among university students, only those specializing in literature would open his books. And only a small number would make their way to the end. Whatever his genius, Joyce provided the justification for an elitist revolution designed to steal fiction from the people. It was as if he knew that critics, not the public, were going to be the new priests of literature and the guarantors of immortality, and that he had therefore set about single-handedly creating modern literary criticism by writing fiction which was dependent on their expertise. There's a lot of fly food in *Ulysses* and it was put there for the flies. [12]

In the same period as *Ulysses*, another novel was written that broke down linguistic conventions with as much revolutionary fervour as Joyce's did. If anything, it did this better because it was driven by positive, not negative, impulses. Ford Madox Ford did not write with anger and hatred against humanity. And in *Parade's End* he broke up language narrative not as an intellectual trick or as a sort of revenge on the reader, but as a reflection of Western society breaking down during and after World War I.

If the literary community turned away from Ford and chose *Ulysses* over *Parade's End* as the turning point of twentieth-century fiction, it was largely because neither Ford nor *Parade's End* fitted the picture of modern literature. Ford was not a solitary, anguished, inward-looking novelist. He was a generous, gregarious man, filled with flaws but who gave much of his life to helping other writers. And *Parade's End* related directly to the real world. Ford did not devote his life with obsessive concentration to one or two works of genius, as the modern artist was meant to. He wrote endless books, some of them not very good, and some the best that could be written. Finally, Ford considered Joseph Conrad to be the greatest novelist of the twentieth century. This was an unforgivable flaw in a profession which required egocentric genius to believe, above all, in itself.

Conrad was and remains the source of the modern school of writers who have carried the inherent strengths of the novel into the twentieth century — a school which has stretched from Fitzgerald and Hemingway through Graham Greene and Gabriel García Márquez. It was not surprising that the literary professionals tended to fix Conrad in their intellectual class structure as a writer for boys.

In most introductions to Joyce's work, he is presented as the genius who encompassed the whole Modernist movement:

> To understand this form it was necessary to understand the limitations of fiction. It was necessary to comprehend that the novel had fully flowered and blossomed, that in Gustave Flaubert, and, after him, Henry James, the ultimate possibilities of characterization and mental and spiritual exploration and revelation had been exhausted. There was nothing to be done but to push the apparently set boundaries of the novel back still farther, to make possible the elaborations of that new factor in life — the subconscious.[13]

Of course, the only real set boundary of the novel was its ability to communicate with the reader. As for the elaboration of the subconscious, other novelists, Conrad and Hemingway for a start, were having no trouble finding new ways to express humanity's spiritual depths without turning the novel into a secret language. And why it is simply assumed, as an absolute truth, that the principal task of the novelist is to make technical progress is not made clear.

Yet Proust and Joyce became an intellectual wall behind which the literary experts could hide. It was not so much that generations of new writers would actually be influenced by them. They weren't. Rather, these two men were taken to be a signal that the literary profession had been officially constituted. Critics and writers could therefore begin acting as if style defined beauty and beauty was its own justification; as if politics had been proved irrelevant to fiction; as if the desire to communicate were old-fashioned, in fact retrograde, and a sign of intellectual inferiority; and as if success in building popular appeal were a sign of base commercialism.

This widespread evolution testified to three things at once: a defeat of the novelist by rational society, a coup d'état within the writing community by the camp followers, and a growing fatigue by an ever larger portion of the novelists as they gave in to the temptations and comforts of professional life. "Indifference to politics among artists has always been associated," Cyril Connolly wrote, "with a feeling of impotence. [This] crystallized into a theory that politics were harmful, that they were not artistic material of the first order."[14]

It looked almost as if many writers had changed enemies. Unjust authority and social conformity were being replaced by the "philistine" general public. How else could readers interpret the growing barriers between themselves and the written word? Or the conviction among intellectuals that what the public wanted was fiction of a lesser quality, which made it impossible to write for them?

Some novelists inexplicably assumed the exact opposite: that the public, desperate for literature, would make devoted suicidal attacks upon their impenetrable prose. It turned out, however, that the reader was not interested in a struggle with art. And so what came to be called serious fiction also remained largely unread, beginning with Joyce and Proust themselves. Most of the "important" writers of our time have fewer readers than a banal computer manual. This is a radical break with the past. Are these novelists actually important? Most of the great novelists of the last four centuries have been enormously popular in their own time or soon after. The talismans of modern literature are, if anything, even less read now than they were on publication. The strength of the novel from the beginning rested upon the fact that the greatest fiction was intellectually accessible to the full reading public. As the public grew, so the novel grew. Abruptly, in the twentieth century, this is no longer so. Many of the important novels are not even accessible to that part of the population that would have been literate in the eighteenth century. Gracq identified this phenomenon when he pointed out that literature had become something people talked about instead of reading — which was not particularly surprising given that it was no longer written to be read.

This does not mean that Proust and Joyce were not geniuses. A novel can be wonderful and surprising without being written on the main highway of communications, thought and argument. Life is filled with culs-de-sac, some of them extraordinarily interesting. Certainly the twentieth century has built two remarkable baroque villas off on a literary dead end which is worth a detour particularly for other writers, who may pick up ideas that can be adapted for use out on the main road. But what the literary profession has tried to do is to divert the main road into this cul-de-sac. And for the last sixty years it has spent most of its time trying to break through the privileged, walled gardens behind the Proustian and Joycean villas in the hope of discovering some nonexistent new highway.

The tools of this diversion have been almost entirely technical. Technique and more technique. For example, much of American fiction is dominated today by "important" writers who are either professors of creative writing or literature or products of those professors. The professor-novelist John Barth boasts that his students have been "involved in formally innovative writing of one sort or another."[15] How innovative writing can be formal is hard to tell, and yet *formal* is the correct word here. It describes a process which has nothing to do with the writer as faithful witness to the public and everything to do with an elite diligently elaborating its own self-protecting etiquette.

Producing novelists through these courses reinforces the isolation of a writing population that has little enough substantive training as it is to help it write about something. During the Middle Ages the aridity of the scholastic tradition came about in much the same way. Now as then, the scholastic approach can't help but define, categorize and create technical boundaries, when in reality the novel has none. It was not an accident that the historic strength of novelists came out of every domain except the scholastic, which — like those of the courtesans and eunuchs — thrived on structure and a worldview with itself at the centre. Now as then, the influence of scholastics turns on the assigning of jobs, titles, medals and prizes to the worthy. This obsession with control sidesteps the question of the reader's judgment and often causes the literary expert to forget one of the few truths about the novel, which Voltaire summarized as: "All styles are good except the boring."[16]

Of course, if Barth and others want to reduce themselves to the status of highly skilled castrati — the inevitable product of an overdeveloped court life — why shouldn't they? And every novelist has the right to be boring if he wishes. All the same, it is incomprehensible in a century overwhelmed by change and war and breakdown, by famine and the radical replacement of elites, that so many Western novelists have had so much trouble finding things to write about which do not centre on their personal state, the world of writers and technical skills. Consider, for example, the *nouveau roman*, manufactured more or less by Alain Robbe-Grillet and a handful of other intellectuals over a dinner table late at night as a clever way to cause a stir by launching verbal havoc. Consider the effort put into developing and analyzing this style by large parts of the literary world, and the eagerness with which universities in particular embraced this new generation of fly food. Or consider the method of analysis known as deconstructionism, which at first glance seems to offer a way to uncover new meaning hidden in the language of texts. Instead, the real intention of the method is to immobilize language and communication by making it impossible to agree upon meaning. How? "Authorial intentions are to be given no credence. The text subverts its own apparent meaning. The language of the text carries no reference to any mystical interior. Meaning is not contained in language."[17] This is not so much nihilism as it is advocacy of the return to a preliterate society.

The novelist who stays outside the specialist's box in which these kinds of debates take place is the closest thing to an enemy that the professionals have. The writer out in the real world is living proof that the novel was, and could still be, something else. Which is perhaps why

the professionals have made such an effort to divide Western fiction into
a maze of genres. Simplicity is no longer presented as a virtue. The
value of complex and difficult language has been preached with such
insistence that the public has begun to believe the lack of clarity must
be a sign of artistic talent. Even when simplicity appears in the form of
minimalism, the precedence given to style over any other aspects of
content is clear.

Most books dealing with the real world in an unaffected manner can
therefore automatically be cast into the lower reaches, where an array
of dismissive words has been developed to discount them. *Faction* had a
certain vogue. And *roman-reportage. Drawn from the author's experiences*.
These and other phrases are intended to imply that personal experiences
produce a less literary effect if they are gathered outside either the
author's psyche or the literary world. When André Malraux was asked
whether *Man's Fate* was a "lived" experience, he shot back:

> Listen, is there any such thing as "lived" anywhere? Isn't it just a kind
> of mirage? And who was considered to be the master of the "lived" [novel]
> in France? Balzac. But Baudelaire wrote that [Balzac] was the greatest
> visionary of our time.[18]

He was trying to explain the difference between the reflection produced
by the witness and the mere photo. Earlier in his life he had been
reduced to describing his own novels as "Greek tragedy invaded by
the police novel," as if some shocking formula were needed to destroy
the assumption that fiction was the opposite of fact, instead of being the
same thing through another eye.

Among those most successful at avoiding fiction's self-imposed limitations have been the writers who pretend to be writing nonfiction.
Long before he took the risk of publishing his first official novel, Tom
Wolfe was playing this trick. In reality he had always written fiction.
The Right Stuff was an almost Zola-like story. Truman Capote did the
same thing with *In Cold Blood*. And both men reached the full public in
a way that resembled the uncontrollable fictional appeals of the eighteenth century. Primo Levi with *Sequesto è un Uomo*, Ryszard Kapuściński with *The Emperor*, Shiva Naipaul with *North of South*, Bruce
Chatwin with *In Patagonia*, Jane Kramer in *The Last Cowboy* and even
Marguerite Yourcenar in *Hadrian's Memoirs* were all writing disguised
fiction. This allowed them to tell a story without being easily judged and
categorized by the literary community. The explosion in every sort of
nonfiction has been part of this same process.

Writers with something to say have been turning away from the novel
as if it were a mortally wounded means of communication. Many of
them, perhaps most, have dreamt of writing fiction. But their conviction

is that this would be an altruistic sacrifice — something to be risked someday when they are established as serious nonfiction writers. Their pessimism demonstrates how structure and professionalism can discourage those with talent.

Meanwhile the public has remained indifferent to the identification of reality as insufficiently literary. Readers have refused to abandon the story and so for decades have been embracing new means of communication that offer clear narrative. Fiction disguised as nonfiction has been one of the beneficiaries, so have various "categories" of the novel, such as the thriller. Throughout the West, people with the time and inclination to read can be overheard saying that they don't read novels anymore. Instead they read biographies. In describing a man's life, the biographer is obliged to tell a story. And with the breakdown of Victorian delicacy, these true stories have taken on the full flesh of fictional drama and character development. But no matter how extraordinary the subject's life, the writer is still limited by its direct attachment to reality. He is writing about his subject, while the novelist is writing about the reader. The faithful witness provides a reflection of the reader. The biographer can never offer more than voyeurism, examples and interpretation. All the same, he gives the public a story and some fictional vibrations. It's better than giving them nothing at all.

These struggles for control over fiction must be seen in the context of the novel's rise. Its force came from the fact that, unlike poetry and drama, it was not hemmed in by stultifying stylistic rules. The novel was therefore central to an uncontrolled explosion in language and understanding. Now Western fiction is restricted by stylistic boundaries, categories, high versus low art, appropriate subject matter and intellectual elites that both monitor all of the above and train their own successors. One of the novel's great strengths was the facility with which it could be translated from one vibrant regional language to another without any of that strength being lost. The scholasticism of the twentieth century has removed that facility, so that it is now common to find novels as difficult to translate as poetry. What all this indicates is that the novel is no longer a centre of linguistic freedom. It is now as much part of the problem of communication as it is of the solution.

The writers who have the greatest difficulty with what is now the literary status quo are those who make money from their books. This disapproval of novelists categorized as "commercial" comes without any direct mention of the public and the choice they exercise in reading one book rather than another. But the literary establishment cannot help noticing that most of what they consider to be good fiction is hidden deep in the wings, well off the public stage. This they blame on commercial fiction. Their view is that such commercial writers pander to the public's baser instincts. Had they not done this, the general reader would have been obliged to come to serious fiction on its own terms.

"Commercial" or "popular," fiction consists mainly of police novels, spy novels, thrillers, adventure novels, science fiction and romance fiction. These categories have been defined and separated by those in literary authority — professors, critics and publishers. Few of the writers placed inside these limiting walls would have put themselves there, apart perhaps from formula writers of supermarket romances and bus station mysteries.

The subject matter of "category" fiction usually occupies at least part of the territory once covered by the traditional mainstream novel. It is the category writers who now describe the real world and its crises. They may or may not do this honestly, with imagination or by rote, with great attention to detail or superficially. But even the hero of a third-rate adventure novel is closer to the real world than an obscure creation by Barth or Robbe-Grillet.

In 1976 the late Senator Frank Church, chairman of a U.S. congressional committee investigating the CIA, wrote in his report that the enormous power the new technologies of surveillance, indoctrination and mobilization had given to the state were capable of creating a Fascist regime overnight.[19] In some ways the spy novel is trying to deal with that situation. Equally, the growth in criminal violence, accompanied by a breakdown in our legal system, has fed the police novel. The steady growth in the arms trade has created a permanently escalating level of international violence, which has fed what is called the thriller.

The explanation for the extraordinary success of "category" fiction is not that the public is craven and uncultured. Times are confusing and citizens feel constrained by the narrow boxes of specialization into which rational structures have shut them. More than ever they need clear reflections of themselves and their world, which they feel they cannot see. The most successful works have always presented these reflections in the form of entertainment. Shakespeare and Molière, Goethe and Gogol all knew they had to entertain. There was never a suggestion that the pleasure this gave rendered their writing or their themes inconsequential.

Since this is no longer the case, why not simply leave literature in the comfortable refuge of the wings? New means of communication eager to take its place are not lacking. The images of film and television have already occupied the centre of the public stage once dominated by the novel. Even the most successful "category" fiction must struggle for a place at the feet of the electronic media which, without any effort on the part of the public, can instantly deliver perfect reflections. The new comic book has grabbed a place with a growing number of readers. In fact, the public stage is crowded today with a greater variety and quantity of communicators than the West has ever seen. And they all appear to be perfectly at ease in the limelight.

In this company the writer seems even more apart — often reluctant, dour, shy — and this in spite of centuries of public striving. Perhaps the explanation is simply that the sort of person who writes is no longer the same. Byron, for example, were he alive today, would probably be a rock star, driven to get through to the public by seizing hold of the microphone. Perhaps there has simply been a change of media on the public stage, but not of personnel.

However, these new media don't really give the public what it needs, either because they are too narrow or too easily manipulated. The popular song, for example, is more like an anthem or a slogan — more a raw, direct emotion than a witnessing. There was a return to the troubadour approach in the 1960s with poets like Leonard Cohen and Bob Dylan, but it was quickly overwhelmed by an explosion of electronic technique, in which words have played a very poor third to a complex packaging of sounds and, through video clips, of images. This ability to assemble electronically, note by note and instrument by instrument, is having an effect even on the reality of live classical music performance versus the superhuman arias and sonatas which are everywhere for sale. Just as the growth of the Hero feeds passivity and the worst kind of elitism, so these Heroic sounds, whether popular or classical, undermine the role of music as an active, binding phenomenon.

As for the comic book, whatever its strengths — and not to denigrate its popularity — it is primarily visual and its central force is illustration rather than verbal communication. Comics for children can easily sell hundreds of thousands of copies at a few dollars a piece. Adult comics or *BD* are more expensive but often sell a hundred thousand and average in the twenty thousand range. The average for novels in most countries is between two and five thousand. These comics play an essential role in the vibrancy of modern images. They can even take the place of the written word, but they do not replace it. They do not provide the practical mechanism of public language which permits the organization of daily life, general understanding and civilized change.

Finally, the electronic media suffer from weaknesses which are integral to their strengths — large physical infrastructures, high costs, corporate organization. Any means of communication which can be unplugged cannot be independent. Both film and television are easily controlled by political, military or administrative forces. Outside the handful of democracies, cinema and television screens are a barren land of official or harmless images. It used to be that during coups d'état the forces in revolt had to capture the presidential palace and the armories in order to succeed. Modern technology caused them to include the airports and radio stations. Now they must add the television studios as well.

The invention of the video cassette seemed to create a new element of freedom. A cassette is no more difficult to smuggle or hide than a book. Now, even in the most restrictive dictatorships, the elites who travel abroad return with cassettes. But only people rich enough to travel and to own a VCR are involved; people rich or powerful enough to ensure that they can watch the cassettes in absolute privacy.

The blatant controls enforced in some countries encourage us to think that the problem does not apply in the West. Yet in some ways our problem is worse. Nothing can appear on any of our screens without large inputs of cash from either advertisers or governments. Almost from the beginning the advertisers understood that, while they could not dictate content, it was easy to block whatever they didn't want on the air. All they had to do was not advertise it. Attempts by some networks to disarm this pressure by selling block advertising not assigned to specific programs has tended simply to obscure the problem by forcing advertisers to be more subtle when they apply pressure. The intelligent master never forbids. He shapes things in order to avoid undermining his own interests and to avoid open conflict. Television advertisers understand this and have therefore become the champions of inconsequential entertainment.

Meanwhile, throughout much of Europe, government funders understood from the beginning that they held controlling power. The result — in contrast to the early freedom on public television in a few countries such as the Netherlands, Britain, Germany, Canada and Australia — was organized propaganda, sometimes subtle, sometimes not. But even those few arm's-length governments gradually tired of being criticized by state corporations which exercised electronic free speech. Politicians began to respond with clumsy personal attacks on specific television programs and journalists, accusing them of antigovernment bias. This approach tended to backfire because it reminded the public of the 1930s, which had begun with governmental righteous indignation against free speech and ended with dictatorships across Europe. Governments therefore turned to bureaucratic manipulation. Budget restraints and political appointments proved so effective that producers soon understood there was little or no funding for real and sustained criticism. That was already the situation on private networks.

This atmosphere gradually created self-censorship, first among management and then among senior production staff. They found themselves becoming ever-more careful and ever-more "balanced," until they began to take extreme "care" each time a public issue arose.

But those who hold power already have an advantage over both the opposition and the press, which is why serious journalists have always tended towards a critical approach which seeks out faults. Governments and corporations have budgets and experts permanently assigned to the preparation of arguments designed to contradict all unfavourable judgments. These professional answers, when placed in opposition to most criticism, will at least create confusion and, at their most successful, cancel out the effect of the attack. Rigorous balance, when applied to television, gives a permanent advantage to those in power.

Nevertheless, budgetary and political manipulations are a complicated way to control freedom of speech. The solution has therefore increasingly been to commercialize television. After all, what attracts advertisers to television is precisely its ritualistic, reassuring smoothness.

Shocking and unsettling programs do not provide an effective background for marketing products. Distinctive programming detracts from the surrounding ads. What the sponsor seeks can be seen in the fact that ads are played at a higher sound level than the programs. On a scale of one to ten, programs vary from occasional silence to moments of maximum noise, but they run at average levels of four to six. Commercials are recorded at seven to eight, well above the program average. And while program sound fluctuates, ads hold a constant level for thirty seconds. This makes them seem even louder. The more commercial the overall television system, the more these ads tend towards eight or nine, as in the United States. But even at seven they are the dominant sound.

Ritual is a continuous and repetitive background phenomenon. Thus most programming is the background for commercial messages. The per-second production costs — what the industry calls "production values" — of advertisements are far higher than those of programming. In fact, most commercials are better television than the programs they finance, thanks to richer colour, more camera work and snappier scripting. If there is some benefit to be derived from dramatic surprise, it is saved for the advertiser.

The cinema has been just as easy to handle. American movies continue to dominate the screens of the world and Hollywood "standards" require budgets which make most truly independent production impossible. Cinema has come to resemble opera in that the apparatus for production is so heavy that those who have power and money inevitably control what will be produced. The financiers can hardly be blamed for financing only what they think is appropriate. As for social and political criticism, the heart of the film production system is financial, not moral. It is a high-risk business which produces ponderously via committees.

Films therefore rarely enter unresolved public debates. They tend rather to illustrate resolved opinion. And production is only the first step in this lengthy process. Distribution is equally dependent on financial risk and political complexities. Films may or may not cross borders because of a tangle of interests. They may be distributed widely or in a few theatres only. Films such as *La Bataille d'Alger* or Stanley Kubrick's *Paths of Glory* for a long time were simply not distributed in France. No one quite understood how it was done. Corporations own films in the absolute way that only an author, not a publisher, can own a book.

But the filmed image has other limitations. Even a brilliant, full-length motion picture made by a genius cannot be more than a narrow vision of limited events. It cannot, as a novel can, create an entire world and turn the reader's imagination loose within it. The genius of electronic communication turns on its ability to direct the viewer and to evoke responses. The genius of fiction turns on its ability to release the individual's emotions and thoughts. The electronic media require a more or less passive public. The novel needs an active one.

There is a simple technical illustration of this difference. The short story is a limited vehicle — not in artistic qualities, but in time, place, number of characters, complexity of story, emotional variety, and, of course, in the scope of the world reflected. At its best the short story is an object of single, intense, brilliant focus. It is a precise exercise in specific human emotions, while the novel, at its best, is a total release. After almost a century of converting the written word into film, the patterns of success and failure are fairly clear. Novels generally convert into bad films, good novels into particularly bad films. Short stories, on the other hand, have a relatively high success rate on the screen. They are sufficiently precise to avoid overwhelming the limited capabilities of the motion picture. In fact, the best movies are often drawn from mediocre or bad short stories, because even a good short story can be too complex for ninety or even one hundred and twenty minutes of screen time.

Television's greatest success has been in the area of sports broadcasting. Only there does the viewer feel he is getting the whole story. In no other area does the producer feel himself truly free to pursue the subject at hand. And nothing else can offer the advertiser guaranteed excitement free of socially relevant controversy. The sports formula has become increasingly important over the last forty years, with its most obvious by-product being a growing number of Heroic feature films on everything from boxing and baseball to Olympic running.

More important, however, has been the spread of this formula into cinema and television plots which have nothing to do with sports. On the surface they are war or crime stories or family sagas. Closer examination reveals that they have been reduced to the structure of a football drama. The key to this formula lies in its highly formal structures.

Clearly defined relationships are laid out. The real world is converted into a fixed pattern according to which predetermined actions will bring glory or tragedy. The excitement of this sports formula depends on a rigid system in which the unexpected can nevertheless happen. The established Hero, who may unexpectedly miss, lose, fall or in some way fail, is invariably pitted against the unproved player, who may unexpectedly save the day and become a Hero.

The reliance of all sports scenarios on this unexpected Hero to provide excitement is emotionally attractive, but it is also an insidious theme in a civilized society. It converts human relationships into little more than a lottery. Someone is going to win a million dollars. Someone is going to be the Hero in today's game. It raises the prospect of unfounded hope to the level of normalcy. That is why an increasing number of films — the vast majority, in fact — glorify the unexpected Hero. The day is endlessly being saved by the weak, the untrained, the fearful, the losers. This bears no relationship to what actually happens in the real world. The weak do not win battles anymore than the poor outsmart the rich or those who buy lottery tickets win the grand prize. From the very beginning, the moving picture has been addicted to happy endings. On television unhappy conclusions are almost unknown. In order to accomplish this, whole segments of Western fiction have had to be adapted; that is, twisted into suitably inspiring shapes. Thanks to Walt Disney and others, the tough realism of children's literature — from the Grimm Brothers and Hans Christian Andersen to Beatrix Potter and L. Frank Baum's Oz books — has been quite simply inverted. Some people would say that the little parables of the moving picture give hope to the underdog. In fact, they give a false reflection of reality and so weaken any hope for change.

The difficulty with the new devices for communication which crowd the public stage is that they minimize language or trivialize it or simply make no use of it. But you cannot have a postverbal civilization. Language is the one essential element in any society. It enables us to understand organizations and makes relationships possible. The word *civilization* itself rises out of the Roman civil law — the words which organized the relationship between individuals. What the electronic media have done is drown us in the sound of words but remove all sense of their meaning and overall shape.

The question which remains is whether the novel has the strength to do to the dictatorship of reason what it once did to the dictatorship of arbitrary power. One glance at much of the Western literary elites is enough to discourage that idea.

Outside the West the situation is quite different. In Central Europe and Latin America, the novel still reflects society. If writers played such an important role in the events of Central Europe in 1989, it was because they and their words had been the voice of opposition for forty years. In Africa and in much of Asia, where the nationalist era has only just begun and political instability is dangerous to anyone who speaks out, the novel is in full expansion. Put another way, the prisons of Eastern Europe and of the developing world have been populated with writers for the last forty years and the annual lists of political murders and executions are filled with novelists, essayists and journalists.

Any cursory glance back through the fiction which has made a profound impact in the West over the last half century turns up names like Arthur Koestler, Boris Pasternak, Gabriel García Márquez, Aleksandr Solzhenitsyn, Wole Soyinka, Jorge Amado, Ryszard Kapuściński, Mario Vargas Llosa and J. M. Coetzee. It is astonishing how many come from precisely those places on the edge of the West or completely outside where the novel is as important to local society as it was in Europe in the late eighteenth and nineteenth centuries. Or, indeed, there were Western writers like Albert Camus and Graham Greene, who found a certain strength by writing of the West in the context of the world outside. Today's reader takes from all these books the genuine reflection — the faithful witnessing — which the bulk of our own fiction no longer provides.

Only in the West, where the electronic media have taken over public communications, have the wordsmiths slipped off the public stage. There is a tendency to believe that the Rushdie affair in 1989 demonstrated just the opposite. But of course *The Satanic Verses* had nothing to do with a Western writer upsetting Western preconceptions. Instead, this novel was used as a lever by a factional political-religious leader to create a diplomatic incident between the West and the Islamic world. The incident resembled one of those nineteenth-century gunboat crises, only in reverse. We in the West used to seize regularly on some minor affront to our principles — such as free access for traders or missionaries to someone else's territory — and send off a military detachment to force major concessions. The Ayatollah Khomeini seized on an affront to his beliefs and sent off terrorists to destabilize the West and his Arab neighbours.

The threat to Salman Rushdie's life came on top of the ongoing threats by various governments for various reasons against hundreds of writers outside the West and the murder of dozens of novelists, journalists, playwrights and poets every year. Less than half a century ago we were doing the same sort of thing ourselves. And yet the West reacted to the Ayatollah Khomeini's threats with what can only be called embarrassment that words could have caused so much trouble. We insisted, and pressured Salman Rushdie to insist, that he hadn't intended to offend, that it was only a novel. But Rushdie was born a Muslim, was writing on one of his preferred subjects and knew what he was doing, just as Voltaire must have known when he attacked the Catholic Church or Tolstoy when he turned on the landowners or Fielding when he exposed legal corruption. As to Khomeini's reaction, it can hardly be considered surprising, coming as it did from the politically experienced leader of a radical wing of a religion six hundred years younger than our own and still caught up in the fervour of belief. After all, in the West religion lost most of its power two centuries ago and yet Christian sects are still murdering each other in Ireland.

Unacceptable though they may be, Khomeini's actions can be understood. The Western reaction was far more astonishing. An old man in a bankrupt developing country had only to utter a short sentence for our enormous infrastructure to go into spasms and begin turning in circles. Rational structures came up against belief and belief won with hardly a struggle. Most writers — no matter how withdrawn into their private world — supported Rushdie. A few, like the late Roald Dahl, did call on him to withdraw the book so that everyone could get on with their lives, thus suggesting that free speech was a valued part of society so long as it didn't cause delays or cost money. Even the vast majority of writers, who continue their support, seem to feel only that there has been a barbaric interference in the right of creativity, when what is at stake is creativity's right to interfere with barbarism and power, to say nothing of our own civilization's failure to identify with that right.

It is all the more surprising then that our wordsmiths have slipped off the public stage, turning away from society's need for reflection. Writers are at their best as terrorists — sometimes social terrorists, sometimes political, sometimes terrorists of the heart. If a writer is good, he will be all three at once. His weapons are words well used to disturb and to clarify thought, emotion and action. His genius, if he has it, will help him to explode self-satisfaction. He will create confusion in order to make clarity possible. Yet if the citizen wants to read about today's world — influenced as it is by rising crime, unmanageable drug use, directionless elites, contrasts of wealth and poverty, alienating cities and industrial structures dominated by arms production — he has a surprisingly limited number of writers among whom to choose. They must be supplemented by novelists from elsewhere, as well as large numbers who have been relegated to categories. Besides, much of the "category" fiction is very good. Long after Barth is buried and forgotten, Chandler's *The Big Sleep* and *The Long Goodbye* will be read as masterpieces.

What is it, then, which holds back the force of the written word in the West? Sclerosis? Gentility? The wrong people writing? Or is it something much more basic?

The novel, after all, rose with the struggle to advance reason. Fiction was the greatest enemy of the old system, but also the advance guard of the new. Even though the novel is a humanist and unmeasurable phenomenon, its most profound assumptions are indivisible from the dream of man's rational progress towards a better world. It is hardly surprising that when reason began to go off the tracks, novelists lost their way. They find it easy to criticize totalitarian regimes but are still congenitally blocked from getting at those elements in the foundations of reason which make the new totalitarian systems possible.

Those who do try to deal with today's problems have a tendency to draw the portrait of a civilization gone mad, as if betrayed by the survival of the pagan or dark side of man that predates reason. Kurt Vonnegut, Thomas Pynchon, Milan Kundera, Yann Queffélec, Ian McEwan, Martin Amis — most of them brilliant, a few simply hysterical — seem to find the inspiration for this shock treatment approach in the heavy parodies and satires of the eighteenth century. But the similarity is deceptive. *Gulliver*, *Zadig* and *Tom Jones* were also carefully aimed missiles. The reader immediately understood where the problem lay and in what direction society might move to improve itself. The modern equivalent expresses the confusion people feel, but the target is often less clear. In place of a reflection or witnessing the reader is offered participation of a cinematic sort. The problem these novels are trying to deal with has little to do with the anarchy of a modern madness and everything to do with a form of logical sanity which grinds on like a perpetual motion machine cut off from common sense.

To expect the novelist to deal with this dictatorship of reason is to hope that he will turn about and eat his own children. He must not only decide to do it, he must discover how it might be done. Most people now see the Western writer as uninvolved in that world which engages the bulk of the population. He appears to be off in a corner, comfortably shut up in his specialized box. But the writer himself also suffers from being just another expert in our civilization, exercising one of the thousands of professions available to an educated citizen. The complex demands of the publishing industry, the titles, prizes, tenures, grants and all the other honours he receives or, worse still, does not receive but needs to in order to survive — these are the chains which keep him in place.

In order to become the faithful witness again, he would have to regain the distrust, if not the hatred, of the established structures. He would need to cut away his literary chains and roam about as he once did, sometimes inside society, sometimes outside, seeking to release us from the prisons of rational language by finding new, alternate models for the imagination. Those writers who are solitary by nature, who walk alone and yet see everything around them, have an initial advantage. But even they have not cut themselves loose. "To write in plain, vigorous language . . . and to think fearlessly," Orwell said was his objective. Those skills both strengthen the writer and serve the public. "The spare word is the sword," wrote Robert Ford, "that guards better than silence."[20] With those weapons he can warn and win back the tribe to his reflections.

The standard analysis of a troubled society concentrates on its aging structures. Language, however, can be more important than those tangible forms. As time goes by, it is the established patterns of thought, the known arguments, the self-perpetuating truths which become the principal defenders of the structures in place. The older and more stable a society, the deeper down into our subconscious stretches the substructure of givens. These are the essential questions which are silently assumed to have been answered before a conversation begins or a word is written. The West has now built up layer upon layer of assumptions which cannot be addressed in any intelligent manner. The active vocabulary needed to question, even to simply discuss them, has withered away.

Worse still, these givens take on an enormous innate power. The last two centuries have fuelled a plethora of abstract givens which float in and out of fashion. Imperialism gives way to Socialism to Fascism to Capitalism to free peoples to free markets, efficiency, competition. Governments take great care to place themselves in chosen positions vis-à-vis these words, as do most organizations and individuals. They may wrap them as cloaks around themselves or heave them like boulders against other men.

There is no longer any need to corrupt the ideas born of reason. Anyone today may use a word such as *freedom* to mean everything under the sun. It is a concept which now has the intrinsic value of Weimar Republic paper money. There is no longer any emotional or sensible counterfeit detector which goes off when we hear the word incorrectly used.

Where earlier Western societies were built upon military or religious power, reason was constructed upon thought and language. The structures which at first released, then restrained, and now smother us are primarily the abstract manifestations of that thought and language.

There is no way out of the present confusion unless the writer leaves his specialist's box, abandons her professional privileges and begins stripping language down to its universal basics; what Mallarmé and Eliot called purifying.[21] Only they can demonstrate the folly of professional dialects which pretend to provide answers to everything, even though those answers reflect no reality. The reality of language is not to be right. The deformation such a hypocritical requirement brings to our essential means of communication can't help but create a prison for civilization.

The faithful witness, like Solon and Socrates, Voltaire and Swift, even Christ himself, is at his best when he concentrates on questioning and clarifying and avoids the specialist's obsession with solutions. He betrays society when he is silent or impenetrable or, worst of all, when he blithely reassures. He is true to himself and to the people when his clarity causes disquiet.

22

The Virtue of Doubt

The desert begins above the tree line in both North Africa and the Arctic. There is a certain obligatory clarity in these places where every individual has an unimpeded view. The severity of the heat or cold combines with the dryness to make these expanses of sand, rock and snow seem barren. To be exact, they are tightly strung. Life does prosper, but only by seizing its moment blade of grass by blade of grass at the specific time and place that each blade is available to be seized.

I was travelling a few years ago across the western end of the Sahara, the Rio d'Oro, in the protective hands of a guerrilla group known as the Polisario. They were then at the height of their war against the Moroccans and were given to sweeping out of the desert in their stripped-down, four-wheeled camels in the *razzia* style, fighting exactly the way the R'gibat tribe had for more than a millennium.

We were caught early one evening by a sudden, massive downpour. The seven of us were below ground in a covered dugout camouflaged in the middle of a dry riverbed. The ceiling was made of odd bits of lumber and mortar cases covered over by sand. It was the first rain in several years. The water ran across the desert like a wave across a paved surface towards the lowest ground and surrounded our little mound with a rising torrent which began to flood through the small exit. I suppose I would have been trapped down there, the only six-foot-two Celt ever to drown in the middle of the Rio d'Oro. However, the old R'gibat in charge got us up through the hole in time and out into a turbulent darkness. They managed to start the two Land Rovers before the motors were immersed and made a run for the dry bank with the rifles, mortars and the rest of us in a tangled mass behind.

At sunrise the next morning the barren sand was covered with sprouting plants. By midday the ground was laced with full-grown vines several metres long which flowered while we lunched under heavy wool blankets stretched between the Land Rovers to protect us from the sun. Fruit and gourds followed the flowers. By day's end they were ripe. The next morning the gourds were dry seedpods, dormant, waiting to be blown and buried until several years later another storm would come.

The same thing happens in the Arctic during the brief summer of unbroken sunlight. Not so fast, of course, because there the real extreme is the cold. But the plants complete in a few weeks the cycle which would have taken months elsewhere. They manage this in the few inches of tundra which the sun unfreezes and the result is an explosion of colour and fragrance.

The people who belong to these places are integrated with the extremes. Their civilization is taut. The slightest error is fatal, even with the addition of Western machinery. When a snowmobile or a Land Rover breaks down, the occupants' options are usually measured in hours. There are no rescues from boats overturned in the Arctic Sea. A moment's inattention can turn an innocent walk into a shapeless, lost eternity, in which death arrives rapidly.

These are not romantic civilizations or to be imitated, any more than any other. However, their dependence on the constant mastery of detail is hypnotizing to the Westerner. Or, rather, it is inconceivable. As is the attention they pay to everything that surrounds them. When the adaptability to circumstances of a desert dweller is compared to that of the typical urban Western adult, the latter seems very set in his ways.

I stayed recently with an Inuit hunter in a settlement on a small island north of the Arctic Circle. He lived in a basic Western-style house built by the government. The entrance was through an unheated porch stacked with frozen seal and whale meat. In the kitchen a thawed piece of raw caribou lay on a board on the floor in case anyone wished to slice off and nibble a bit. The first time I came in the hunter was repairing a hook. He spoke no English and had not been to school, but slipped across the room to show me the complex video he and his friends had just shot and acted in. That stretch between Stone Age culture and the nonchalant exploitation of the latest technology is startling.

But then the most striking things about these desert civilizations are their sophistication and their restraint. They are highly conscious cultures. Westerners float half awake through a padded world. The mechanisms and significance of most events escape us. There is no fault in that, except that we too easily accept such scandals as poverty among us. What's more, in general we occupy the world's temperate and rich zones so that the phenomenon of choice is neither a privilege nor a special event. It is a matter of course.

There is little choice of that sort among desert peoples. Instead there is the taut line of their civilization, which can be seen in something as simple as the care with which people move. Slowness is only in part a response to heat or cold. Above all, the movement is conscious. The Inuit are as clear on this as the R'gibat. I remember being slowed by a young woman in the Arctic who pointed out that my enthusiasm and surface energy would be misunderstood. If people in Igloolik, the village where we were, saw me moving so fast, they would think there was an emergency and, if no emergency, that I was deranged.

Careful action does not necessarily equate with reflection. However, the sort of outsiders who are attracted to the desert — not passersby like myself — tend to resemble each other. They seem to be seeking ways to strip off the padding of their own societies. Some are attracted by a false notion of romanticism, but they don't stay long. Those who remain tend to flex their consciousness and take an unromantic pleasure in doing so. You see this in the way they move, in their eyes, in a different cadence of speech. They seem to be attempting to reconstitute themselves as a whole being, including the rational, but also the emotive and what could be called the spirit or the soul. This would have made sense to Socrates — man as a trinity of intellect, spirit and appetite; the latter two essential but subordinated to coherent thinking.

The modern intellectual may find it difficult to equate the Socratic view with these minimalist efforts, which often have no verbal expression. Fulfilment without footnotes must belong to a lower order, fit only for sociological or anthropological study. Yet knowledge in these extreme places can quite easily take on its real meaning of understanding. The Socratic conviction that all virtues were forms of knowledge therefore holds firm, as does the result — "No man willingly does wrong."

This is the opposite of our elites. They often justify doing wrong because they do know. And this rational sophistication convinces them that structural inevitabilities must be accepted. In this curious inversion of the original Socratic intention, the sensible man is now one who understands that he must make do with the realities of the world, no matter how unfortunate. And so he is stuffed with knowledge, world weary and ready to accept the worst.

This seems far removed from Dante's launching of the humanist dream through virtue and knowledge. Even the most generous of observers would be hard put to discover any relationship between our modern elites and his model. There is, however, a link with the desert civilizations. And what Dante described was not an unrealizable ideal. The sixteenth-century architect Andrea Palladio believed that through his buildings man could reconstitute himself as a whole — history would be one with the future, nature with mathematical proportions, the soul with the public facade. "The city is nothing more than a great house and the house a small city." His buildings were to balance the beautiful with the useful, his interiors coordinated with the exteriors through a projection of the internal structure onto the facade.[1] In spite of his unifying, integrating themes, he saw himself as a rational architect. But that merely tells us how different the optimistic expectations of reason were from the divisive reality which even then was in preparation.

Apart from their self-assurance, the most common characteristics of our elites are cynicism, rhetoric and the worship of both ambition and power. These were also the characteristics of eighteenth-century courtesans. The assumption is that world-weary cynicism demonstrates intellectual superiority. In reality it indicates neither intelligence, experience nor accuracy. If anything, it demonstrates mediocrity and an inability to profit from experience. To be world weary is to be willing to go on repeating old mistakes.

We are now at one of those rare moments in history when the entire elite — military, governmental, business and university — will have an opportunity to prove that they are better than they seem. For the last three decades they have attempted to deal with baffling economic problems by spinning the wheels of military production, both for a nuclear arms race and for international weapon sales. The result is that our economic problems have not been solved. In the process, however, the Western industrial and financial infrastructure has become addicted to these artificial consumer goods. The worst thing about the addiction is that no one, not even the elites who provoked it, knows precisely how great the dependency is. The financing mechanisms, research priorities and production methods stretch far beyond apparent missile and tank contracts into every corner of the economy.

With the end of the Cold War, the justification for this economic option is gone. There is a popular assumption spread throughout the media that arms production will drop radically. But there is a difference between the reduction in stockpiled weapons and the shutting down of production. Nothing has been devised to replace the latter. A precipitous drop of even 10 percent would probably provoke massive industrial shudders. More than that would send the financial mechanisms of the West into shock. So far the reaction of the elites has been to ignore the problem. Their rhetoric for recovery concentrates on the ideology of market forces. Even a casual observation of reality indicates that they are confused and so far have devoted themselves to delaying tactics. The probable outcome will confirm them in their world-weary cynicism. The rise of uncountable new nationalist forces and at least two dozen unstable nations on the European continent will provide fresh arms markets as distrust and violence spread closer and closer to the Western enclave of stability. This will also justify new Western arms. They will have to be new because the threat will be of a nature different than that produced by superpower rivalries. Existing weaponry has no economic value. Our addicted structures require new production. And so, as the old nuclear-missile heavy-tank arsenal is reduced, a new conventional arsenal will be built.

To get through the confusion of the next few years our elites will need all of their rhetorical skills, providing streams of new answers before any serious questions are asked. They have begun by claiming the fall of Communism as a victory for Western methods, variously described as capitalism, the free market, individualism or democracy. This is not unlike the Jesuits' interpretation of the Lisbon earthquake as a judgment of God. After all, at least half the Soviet failure was the inheritance of centuries of Russian imperialism. The other half was the result of the uninhibited application of rational methods which came from the West.

Our civilization of sophists and pharisees will be fully tested by the next decade. And yet the rise of nationalism fits comfortably into rational methodology. After all, the nation-state received a first great boost thanks to its youthful and passionate marriage with reason — an embrace arranged in the early 1600s by a cardinal and an absolute monarch. Somehow, in preparation for this event, the rational method had already been severed from any humanist roots by Loyola, who demonstrated that reason was an unfettered weapon. The humanist dream is still with us, promising man as the measure of man, aesthetic values and moral virtue, but these have become marginal ideals, unattached to the realities of power. We began the seventeenth century in the grip of blind logic and we end the twentieth in the hands of blind reason, a sophisticated version of the former.

Spirit, appetite, faith, emotion, intuition, will, experience — none of these are relevant to the operations of our society. Instead we automatically assign blame for our failures and crimes to the irrational impulse. Our sense of man as a whole being — that is, our conscious memory — has been so fractured that we have neither any philosophical nor practical idea of how to hold our public and corporate authorities responsible for their actions. Deprived of our stabilizing humanist roots, we are horrified to discover that the perfectly natural emotive resources needed to deal with our civilization easily degenerate into base sentiment.

Our society was largely conceived by courtesans. They have therefore defined the idea of modernism in a way which reinforces their skills. And so we find ourselves almost automatically denigrating the forces of which they disapprove as being retrograde, inefficient, imprecise, simplistic — indeed, unprofessional. It isn't surprising that like most aging religions, reason is able to get away with presenting itself as the solution to the problems it creates. Nor that for the first time in Western history the courtesans don't need to change when they win power, that power having been designed in their image. After four and a half centuries of turning in circles around the same solutions, we have eliminated all practical memory of what came before. We are now as alone with our age as any civilization can be. There are no solid references to give us direction, no active contradictions. In effect we are now in our own past.

This rootless wandering is perhaps the explanation for the hypnotic effect which the idea of efficiency has upon us. Deprived of direction, we are determined to go there fast. And so we apply this minor sub-product of reason to our economies, administration, arts and even to our democratic process. We confuse intention with execution. Decision making with administration. Creation with accounting. On the dark plain where we wander, totems have been erected, not to indicate the way, but to provide hopeful relief. That of efficiency is one of the highest, a freestanding moral value.

It is difficult in this context to keep in mind that the essence of civilization should tend towards consideration, not speed. The easy answer is that decision making must be decoupled from administration; the former being organic and reflective, the latter linear and structured. But in a civilization which has mistaken management techniques for moral values, all answers are a trap.

Electronic communications further complicate the situation because they flourish on speed, formula truths and the appearance of change, which can be achieved simply by revolving the formulae. The new international news networks pride themselves on the immediacy with which they deliver enormous quantities of information. But as the Iraq campaign demonstrated, this seems to blur still further the line between reflection and action. The efficient delivery of undigestible quantities of information leaves the public little room to be more than a spectator.

The rational advocacy of efficiency more often than not produces inefficiency. It concentrates on how things are done and loses track of why. It measures specific costs without understanding real costs. This obsession with linear efficiency is one of the causes of our unending economic crisis. It produces the narrow logic which can demonstrate that arms production is the key to prosperity. Worst of all, it is capable of removing from democracy its greatest strength, the ability to act in a nonconventional manner, just as it removes from individuals their strength as nonlinear beings.

I am invariably struck when dealing with members of our elites by their profound pessimism. Above all, they are pessimistic about the human character. They consider it unlikely that the average individual will work hard enough or recognize beauty or vote for the best policies or even obey in a suitable manner. They take as a given that this individual cannot or will not understand the complexities of whatever responsibilities fate has thrust upon someone who has expertise and power.

This is particularly obvious today in what calls itself the Right. In fairness it should be said that the elites in general have been increasingly pessimistic about us for some time. The ideology-bound Left certainly felt that it knew what the people needed and would provide it for them. More moderate reformers have been somewhat the same and particularly devoted to the idea that the laws of the people could be administered in the most minute detail. At first glance the New Right seems quite different because it makes a point of praising individualism and attacking bureaucracy. However, this is a false debate. The question in their minds is not bureaucracy, but which bureaucracy. Wherever the Right holds power, the administrative elites of the large corporations and the financial sector grow. And those of government do not shrink. Programs aimed at social well-being are simply cut, while those which benefit the private administrations and certain categories of personal fortunes grow.

The arrival in force of the New Right is perhaps the inevitable result of the rational state gradually implementing the corporatist idea. How could a civilization devoted to structure, expertise and answers evolve into other than a coalition of professional groups? How, then, could the individual citizen not be seen as a serious impediment to getting on with business? This has been obscured by the proposition of painfully simplified abstract notions which are divorced from any social reality and presented as values. These are drawn in general from the Book of Revelations and other reserves of false mythology. For example, the ideal of the rugged individual opening up the American West is still applied as an essential truth to ten million citizens living in the small area of New York City, as if ten million bulls should and could be squeezed into a china shop.

In reality there is now a desperate need among technicians, manipulators of systems and profiteers to destroy any remaining evidence that Western society could function on the basis of humanist cooperation. Our elites need to be pessimistic about us in their own best interests. The establishment of self-interest as the prime driving force of the human character is the key to their approach. We are now crossing one of those difficult moments in history when any sensible approach seems unexciting and ineffective, while the forces of self-interest and structure appear tempting and unstoppable.

What hope can the singular considerations of an individual have when this rhetoric of false individualism is being shouted loud by those in power, leaving humanism with no mythology apart from that of the fringes? What hope there is lies precisely in the slow, close-to-reality enquiry and concern of the humanist. But first he, and perhaps more hopefully she, must stop believing that the accomplishments of the last few centuries are the result of rational methods, structure and self-interest, while the failures and violence are those of humanity and sensibility. In spite of the rhetoric which dominates our civilization, the opposite is true.

Jefferson put it that men by their constitution were naturally divided into two parts — those who fear and distrust the people versus those who identify with the people and have confidence in them. Our civilization has increasingly put those who fear and distrust in power over us. Those who have confidence have always argued that consciousness is the key to improvements in the human condition. But power structures have always treated consciousness in the citizenry as a danger which must first be lulled, then channelled towards the inoffensive through the mechanisms of language, mythology and structure.

Societies either roll on blindly to disaster or they find the inner strength to stop themselves long enough to find ways for reform from within. That was the meaning of the great Athenian pause, when Solon was brought forward and encouraged "to shake off the burdens." They believed, as he wrote, that "the public evil enters the house of every-man, the gates of his courtyard cannot keep it out."

The changes which might help us to deal with our own difficulties can be easily listed: reestablish the division between policy and admin-istration, for example, and end the cult of the Hero; widen the meaning of knowledge; end the alliance between barbarism (the generals, He-roes, stars, speculators) and technocracy; denigrate self-interest, mean-ingless power, cynicism, rhetoric; and, for that matter, simply change our elites.

But the void in our society has been produced by the absence of values. And values are not established by asserting issues. Victory over one issue or another is wonderfully orgasmic and quickly slips away. The constant base needed to supply values is the result of methodical participation. The individual gains his powers and responsibilities by being there. But we have no widespread belief in the value of partici-pation. The rational system has made us fear standing out in any serious way. Participation produces, but is also the product of, practical values and common sense, not expertise and reason.

The secret, then, is that we must alter our civilization from one of answers to one which feels satisfaction, not anxiety, when doubt is established. To be comfortable with panic when it is appropriate. If ours is the advanced civilization we pretend it is, there should be no need to act as if all decisions were designed to establish certainties. Grandiose issues should not need to be reduced to the simplistic state of for or against and then decided in a set period. This invariably means structuring public debate as a conflict between the rational and the irrational, in which common sense is reduced to a sort of Menshevik annoyance to be crushed between the two hard rocks of abstraction. "The historical process," Michael Howard has said, "through the very challenges it poses and the responses it evokes, itself creates the morality of mankind."[2] The true characteristics of civilization, after all, include taking one's time to work out what is to be done. Why, then, are we constantly bombarded with political, economic and social ultimatums?

A civilization of answers cannot help but be a civilization of swirling fads and facile emotions. What is to be done? What is to be done? For so long now so many people have been answering. Some with the power of life and death. Some with the desire to use that power. Some jocular salesmen of ideas. Some populist, elitist, sincere, income driven. So many answers. So many truths. What a disease this desire to answer has become, rushing through our veins like rats scurrying for truth in the endless corridors of expertise.

If the Socratic question can still be asked, it is certainly not rational. Voltaire pointed out that for the Romans, *sensus communis* meant common sense but also humanity and sensibility. It has been reduced to only good sense, "a state half-way between stupidity and intelligence." We have since reduced it still farther, as if appropriate only for manual labour and the education of small children. That is the narrowing effect of a civilization which seeks automatically to divide through answers when our desperate need is to unify the individual through questions.

Notes

CHAPTER ONE: IN WHICH THE NARRATOR POSITIONS HIMSELF

1. Voltaire quotes: "Tous les genres sont bons, hors le genre ennuyeux." *L'Enfant Prodigue*, préface, 1736. "Il faut avoir pour passion dominante l'amour du bien public." *Le Siècle de Louis XIV.* "Dieu n'est pas pour les gros bataillons, mais pour ceux qui tirent le mieux." *The Piccini Notebooks.*

2. Ludwig Wittgenstein, *Tractatus Logico-Philosophicus* (London: Routledge & Kegan Paul, 1961), 74. This is the last line of the book. The original publication was in the *Annalen der Naturphilosophie*, 1921: "Wovon man nicht sprechen kann, darüber muss man schweigen."

CHAPTER TWO: THE THEOLOGY OF POWER

1. Voltaire, *Dictionnaire Philosophique*, vol. 6 (Paris: Librairie de Fortic, 1826), 307. Under the entry "Juste (du) et de L'injuste," "Il est évident à toute la terre qu'un bienfait est plus honnête qu'un outrage, que la douceur est préférable à l'emportement. Il ne s'agit donc que de nous servir de notre raison pour discerner les nuances de l'honnête et du deshonnête."

2. Denis Diderot, *Encyclopédie*, ed. Alain Pons (Paris: Flammarion, 1987), vol. 1, 35. Originally published in 18 volumes between 1751 and 1766. The quotation is from Pons's introduction.

3. Oliver Germain-Thomas, *Retour à Bénarès* (Paris: Albin Michel, 1986), 56. "La cathédrale de mon pays n'est que le souvenir d'une culture alors qu'en ce temple tout parle, tout vibre, tout chante, tout vit."

4. *The Political Testament of Cardinal Richelieu* (Madison: University of Wisconsin Press, 1961), 45. A long controversy has surrounded the veracity of this document. It isn't unreasonable to believe that it is real. In any case, what the endless research has shown is that the material contained reflects accurately both other documents unquestionably written by Richelieu, as well as his general beliefs. If the document were, therefore, actually by his éminence grise, Father Joseph, or by a supporter drawing on documents after Richelieu's death to create a false testament that could be used against the then government, it would nevertheless be an accurate expression of Richelieu's beliefs. In that sense it may be more true than many autobiographies in which public figures take the time to rewrite history and their own opinions on it in light of later events. In fact, Richelieu's *Testament* is a perfect illustration of the current confusion between fact and truth. It may not be fact but it is true. Had he clearly written it for publication, it would have been a fact, but undoubtedly untrue.

5. Ordonnance No. 45-2283, du 9 octobre 1945, "Exposé des motifs." Michel Debré, *La Réforme de la Fonction Publique, 1945.*

6. Fernand Braudel, interviewed by Louis-Bernard Robitaille in *L'Actualité*, February 1986:

    Question. "Vous ne croyez pas que l'humanité, en se modernisant, soit devenue moins barbare?"

    Braudel. "Vous n'avez pas connu la Deuxième Guerre Mondiale! La différence c'est qu'on a moins d'excuse à être barbare. Je crois que les hommes sont profondément barbares."

CHAPTER THREE: THE RISE OF REASON

1. Cow example taken from Pierre Miguel, *Les Guerres de Religion* (Paris: Fayard, 1980), vol. 1, 53.

2. Isaiah Berlin, *The Age of Enlightenment* (Chicago: Mentor, 1956), 113.

3. Northrop Frye, Sheridan Baker, and George Perkins, eds. *The Harper Handbook to Literature* (New York: Harper & Row, 1988), 168, 169.

4. Diderot, *L'Encyclopédie*, vol. 2, 220. "Machiavélisme, espèce de politique détestable qu'on peut rendre en deux mots, par l'art de tyranniser."

5. See Ignatius Loyola, *Autobiographie*, trans. Alain Guillermou (Paris: Editions du Seuil, 1962), 45.

6. Ibid., 142. Notary public is an approximate translation for "*greffier publique*," a function which no longer exists in France.

7. The first summary of the institute, August 1539. The Papal Bull "Regimini Militantis," September 27, 1540, para. 1.

8. See Candido de Delmases, *Ignatius of Loyola, His Life and Work* (St. Louis: Institute of Jesuit Sources, 1985), 184–200. Quotation is from page 200.

9. Ibid.

10. Francis Bacon, *First Book of Aphorisms*, no. 12.

11. Michel Carmona, *Richelieu* (Paris: Fayard, 1983), 687.

12. Ibid., 393. "Six vices majeurs: l'incapacité, la lâcheté, l'ambition, l'avarice, l'ingratitude, et la fourberie."

13. *The Political Testament of Cardinal Richelieu*, 71.

14. Ibid., 84, 118.

15. Blaise Pascal, *Pensées*, chap. 23 (Paris: Editions du Seuil, 1962). Texte établi par Louis Lafuma, "TRANSITION," paragraph 200, 122. "Toute notre dignité consiste donc en la pensée. C'est de là qu'il nous faut relever. . . . Travaillons donc à bien penser: voilà le principe de la morale."

16. Carmona, *Richelieu*, 35.

17. Giambattista Vico, *La Méthode des Études de Notre Temps* (Paris: Grasset, 1981), 226–30.

18. Ibid.

19. Ibid., 203.

20. Corsica actually referred to itself as a kingdom, but Mary of the Immaculate Conception had the job of queen on a permanent basis and was not, of course, available for consultation. It was an elegant way to have a republic without shocking contemporary mores.

21. Joseph Foladare, *Boswell's Paoli* (Connecticut: Archon Books, 1979), 27. From a letter to Du Peyrou on 4 November 1764.
22. Ibid., 42.
23. Journal of the Rev. John Wesley, ed. Nehemiah Curnock (London: 1909–16), vol. 5, 342. Entry dated October 1767.
24. Jean-Jacques Rousseau, *The Social Contract* (London: Penguin Classics, 1968), 96. Originally published as *Du Contrat Social* (1762), book 2, chap. 10. "Il est encore en Europe un pays capable de législation, c'est l'Isle de Corse. La valeur et la constance avec laquelle ce brave peuple a su recouvrir et défendre sa liberté mériterait bien que quelque homme sage lui apprît à la conserver."
25. Foladare, *Boswell's Paoli*, 33.
26. Ibid., 160.
27. Voltaire, *Philosophical Dictionary* (London: Penguin Books, 1971), 327. Voltaire, *Dictionnaire Philosophique* (Paris: Librairie de Fortic, 1826), vol. 7, 252. "Celui qui brûle de l'ambition d'être édile, tribun, préteur, consul, dictateur, crie qu'il aime sa patrie, et il n'aime que lui-même." Originally published 1764.
28. Foladare, *Boswell's Paoli*, 154.
29. *International Herald Tribune*, 7 May 1987.
30. Edmund Burke, *Reflections on the Revolution in France*, 1790.
31. *The Life and Selected Writings of Thomas Jefferson* (New York: Modern Library, 1944), 51. Autobiography, 1821.
32. Ibid., 317. Paper, 28 April 1793.
33. Ibid., 373. Letter to Peter Carr, 19 August 1785.
34. Ibid., 576. Letter to Judge John Tyler, 28 June 1804.
35. Ibid., 448. Letter to E. Rutledge, 18 July 1788.
36. Ibid., 173. "The Character of George Washington."
37. Napoleon Bonaparte, *Voix de Napoléon* (Genève: Edition du Milieu du Monde), 27. May 1795 conversation with Madame de Chastenay. "En pareil cas il convient qu'une victoire complète soit à l'un des partis: dix mille par terre, d'un côté ou de l'autre. Autrement il faudra toujours recommencer." Second quote, June 1797: "Il leur faut de la gloire, les satisfactions de la vanité."
38. Ibid., 30. 10 December 1797. "Lorsque le bonheur du peuple français sera assis sur les meilleures lois organiques, l'Europe entière deviendra libre."
39. Ibid., 35. 9 November 1791. "Cet état de chose ne peut pas durer. Avant trois ans il nous menera au despotisme! Mais nous voulons la République assise sur les bases de l'égalité, de la morale, de la liberté civile et de la tolérance politique. Avec une bonne administration, tous les individus oublieront les factions dont on les a faits membres et il leur sera permis d'être Français!"
40. Ibid., 58, 21 February 1801. "Ceci est triste, général!" "Oui, comme la grandeur!"
41. Ibid., 193. To Narbonne in the Kremlin, 15 October 1812. "Moi, j'aime surtout la tragédie, haute, sublime, comme l'a faite Corneille. Les grands hommes y sont plus vrais que dans l'histoire. On ne les y voit que dans

les crises qu'ils développent, dans les moments de décision suprême; et on n'est pas surchargé de tout ce préparatoire de détails et de conjectures, que les historiens nous donne souvent à faux. C'est autant de gagné pour la gloire. Car, mon cher, il y a bien des misères dans l'homme, des fluctuations, des doutes. Tout cela doit disparaître dans le héros. C'est la statue monumentale, où ne s'aperçoivent plus les infirmités et les frissons de la chair. C'est *Le Persée* de Benvenuto Cellini, ce groupe correct et sublime, où on ne soupçonne guère, ma foi, la présence du plomb vil et des assiettes d'étain, que l'artiste en fureur avait jetés dans le moule bouillonnant, pour en faire sortir son demi-dieu."

42. Jefferson, *The Life*, 656, letter to Albert Gallatin, October 16, 1815; 683, letter to George Ticknor, November 25, 1817.

43. Ibid., letter to Count Dugnani, who had been Papal Nuncio in France in 1789, February 14, 1818, 684.

44. Léon Bloy, *L'Âme de Napoléon* (Paris: Mercure de France, 1912), 8. "Napoléon est inexplicable et, sans doute, le plus inexplicable des hommes, parce qu'il est, avant tout et surtout, le Préfigurant de CELUI qui doit venir et qui n'est peut-être plus bien loin."

45. Oswald Spengler, *The Decline of the West* (New York: Alfred A. Knopf, 1926), 81.

46. Spengler, *The Decline*, 28.

47. Elizabeth Becker, *When the War is Over* (New York: Simon & Schuster, 1986), 295.

CHAPTER FOUR: THE RATIONAL COURTESAN

1. Diderot, *L'Encyclopédie*, vol. 1, 320. See Cour: "des productions artificielles de la perfection la plus récherchée."

2. Duc de Saint-Simon, *Mémoires*, vol. 2, chap. 62. "C'était de ces insectes de cour qu'on est toujours surpris d'y voir et d'y trouver partout, et dont le peu de conséquence fait toute la consistance."

3. Baldesar Castiglione, *The Book of the Courtier* (New York: Doubleday, 1959), 299. First published in Italian in 1628.

4. Richard A. Gabriel, *Military Incompetence: Why the American Military Doesn't Win* (New York: Hill & Wang, 1985), 189.

5. Ibid.

6. Robert McNamara, *Blundering into Disaster* (New York: Pantheon, 1986), 24.

7. Charles de Gaulle, *Discours et Messages*, vol. 4, *1956–1965* (Paris: Plon, 1970), 85. Allocution prononcée à l'École Militaire, 15 février 1983, "Il est évident que, pour un pays, il n'y a plus d'indépendance imaginable s'il ne dispose pas d'un armement nucléaire, parce que, s'il n'en a pas, il est forcé de s'en remettre à un autre, qui en a, de sa sécurité et, par conséquent, de sa politique."

8. De Gaulle, *Discours et Messages*, vol. 5, *1966–1969*, 18, Conférence de presse tenue au Palais de l'Élysée, 21 février 1966, "Dans ce cas l'Europe serait automatiquement impliquée dans la lutte lors même qu'elle ne l'aurait pas voulu."

9. Gabriel, *Military Incompetence*, 3.
10. McNamara, *Blundering into Disaster*, 24, 26, 36. See also the interview given by McNamara to *Time* magazine, 11 February 1991, 62. Filled with touching modesty and real concerns for the well-being of man, at the same time its interpretation of past events is profoundly disturbing and reconfirms how McNamara came to do what he did when in power. For example, in agreeing that America had exaggerated the threat of the Cold War, he commented:

To begin with, the nuclear threat. And I'm not just talking about the missile gap. We could have maintained deterrence with a fraction of the number of warheads we built. The cost is tremendous — not just of warheads. It's research, and it's building all the goddamn bombers and missiles. Over the past 20 years the unnecessary costs are in the tens of billions. Insane. It was not necessary. And moreover, our actions stimulated the Russians ultimately.

The key five words in this otherwise accurate analysis are "over the past 20 years"; in other words, the problem began after his time in power.

His comments on the unsuccessful Vietnam bombing campaign are astonishing revelations of how his mind works — a talent for abstraction which makes practical humanism impossible, an automatic facility for blaming others.

Q. At the time you left government, the US was in the midst of one of the greatest bombing campaigns in the history of warfare. . . . You thought the bombing would work at the time?
A. No, I didn't think it would work at the time.
Q. Why undertake it then?
A. Because we had to try to prove it wouldn't work, number one, and other people thought it would work.
Q. What other people?
A. A majority of the senior military commanders, the Senate Armed Services Committee, the President.
Q. Were you opposed to it from the beginning?
A. It wasn't that I was opposed to it; I didn't think it would work from the beginning.

11. Nathaniel McKintterick, "The World Bank and McNamara's Legacy," *The National Interest* (Summer 1986).
12. Ibid.
13. Elio Gaspari, *New York Times*, November 2, 1983, Op. Ed. page.
14. Peter Jenkins, *Mrs. Thatcher's Revolution* (Harvard University Press, 1988), 197.
15. Mikhail Lermontov wrote "The Death of the Poet" on the day that Pushkin was provoked into a duel that he had no hope of winning and was killed. William Shawcross, *Sideshow* (New York: Simon & Schuster, 1979), 77.
16. Jean-Jacques Rousseau, *The Social Contract*, trans. Maurice Cranston (London: Penguin Books), chap. 10, "The People: Continued," 95. See

also the book Kissinger wrote in adulation of Clemens von Metternich, *A World Restored: Europe after Napoleon* (Gloucester, Mass.: Peter Smith, 1972).

17. Henry Kissinger, speech given at the Twenty-Eighth International Institute for Strategic Studies Conference, Kyoto, September 1986.

18. Seymour M. Hersh, *Atlantic Monthly*, May 1982.

19. Kissinger has denied this version of events. However, his taste for secrecy and his approach to the writing of the history in which he was involved leave a confused picture, as was demonstrated when William Shawcross's *Sideshow: Kissinger, Nixon and the Destruction of Cambodia* (New York: Simon & Schuster, 1979) was published while the first volume of Kissinger's memoirs, *The White House Years* (Boston: Little, Brown, 1979), was in proofs. Kissinger recalled the proofs in order to revise his portrait of events. He also repeatedly denied having done this. The *New York Times* (October 31, 1979) refuted his denial: "Kissinger revised his book more than he reported." For an in-depth description of these events and Kissinger's changes see William Shawcross, "The Literary Destruction of Henry Kissinger," *Far Eastern Economic Review*, January 2, 1981.

On the issue of Iran, arms, economic modernization, oil prices and inflation there is a surprising change of position between volume one and volume two of Kissinger's memoirs. In *The White House Years*, he wrote a strong defence of his Iran policy: "Nor can it be said that the Shah's arms purchases diverted resources from economic development, the conventional criticism of arms sales, to developing countries. The Shah did both. Iran's economic growth was not slowed nor was its political cohesion affected by its defense spending" (1260). What Kissinger doesn't mention is that by the early 1970s, the Shah's oil income was no longer sufficient to maintain the same level of arms purchases and economic development. There were only two ways out: reduce expenditures or increase the oil price. But Kissinger points out that the Shah had become an essential element in both American strategy and weapons sales policy; what is more, oil remained his source of income: "The vacuum left by British withdrawal, now menaced by Soviet intrusion and radical momentum, would be filled by a local power friendly to us. Iraq would be discouraged from adventures against the Emirates in the lower Gulf, and against Jordan and Saudi Arabia. A strong Iran could help dampen India's temptations to conclude its conquest of Pakistan. And all of this was achievable without any American resources, since the Shah was willing to pay for the equipment out of his oil revenues" (1264). Enormous military resources were needed to fill these roles. And Kissinger confirmed that the Shah had to raise oil prices to maintain his economic policies: "[the Shah's] motive for the original price rise was not political but economic; unlike some other countries, he wanted the maximum revenues for the development of his country" (1262). This sudden unwillingness to mention that "maximum revenues" were also needed to finance the military-arms strategy that the American government required in the eastern Mediterranean is, to put it politely, disingenuous. Kissinger then goes on to say, in support of the Shah's oil price policy: "In fact, the real price of oil declined by 15% from 1973 to 1978." What he doesn't say is that this decline was the result of a growing international inflation whose origins lay in the United States.

Kissinger's own description of the arms/oil price equation became part of a growing body of information that laid much of the responsibility at his door. In volume two of his memoirs — *Years of Upheaval* (Boston: Little, Brown, 1982) — he attempted to deny what he had already virtually admitted three years before: "Later on, it was sometimes claimed that the Nixon Administration's policy toward the Shah was influenced by our desire to increase his revenues so that he could buy additional military hardware. This is a reversal of the truth. . . . The most absurd example, perhaps, is the widely circulated claim that we were repeatedly warned of the danger of higher prices and turned it aside because Washington welcomed high oil revenues to finance Iranian rearmament. . . . [This argument was] demagogic ignorance" (857–858).

In the related footnote he continues: "This was the sophomoric thesis of a segment of CBS television's news program *60 Minutes*—'The Kissinger-Shah Connection?'—broadcast on May 4, 1980, as well as of numerous columns by Jack Anderson in *The Washington Post*, e.g., December 5, 10, and 26, 1979. See also the even more spurious account in Jean-Jacques Servan-Schreiber, *The World Challenge* (New York: Simon & Schuster, 1981), p. 51–56, 65–70)" (*Years of Upheaval*, 1252). If this denial is accurate, then it is unfortunate that Kissinger omits any mention of the most spurious of all sources: himself, in *The White House Years*, 1260–1264.

For a description of the astonishing growth in Iranian armaments and the resulting growth in U.S. arms industry dependence on Iran, see Anthony Sampson, *The Arms Bazaar* (London: Hodder & Stoughton, 1977), 241–259. This chapter, "The Arming of the Shah," also describes Kissinger's role in encouraging and helping the Shah to buy the most advanced weaponry.

20. Accounts of Simon Reisman's character abound in books and in the press. For an early description see Christina McCall-Newman, *Grits: An Intimate Portrait of the Liberal Party* (Toronto: Macmillan of Canada, 1982), 219–225, which mentions Reisman's role in defeating a guaranteed annual income (223) and describes the Reisman actions that led to new conflict-of-interest rules (page 444, footnote 197, of Part 4). For a more recent short description see John Sawatsky, *The Insiders: Government, Business and the Lobbyists* (Toronto: McClelland & Stewart, 1987), 184. For a description of Reisman in the FTA negotiations, see Linda McQuaig, *The Quick and the Dead: Brian Mulroney, Big Business and the Seduction of Canada* (Toronto: Viking, 1991), 1–7, 161–166.

Reisman's reputation for losing his temper or using outbursts as a negotiating technique has evolved over the years. At first, these tactics were seen by many as a tough and effective approach. Gradually, a body of opinion grew that what worked with subordinates and colleagues might actually backfire in international negotiations. Analysis of the FTA negotiations seems to be focusing gradually on Reisman's technique as one of the central factors in Canada's poor showing in the final treaty.

This evolution in public perception can be seen in the three books mentioned above. McCall-Newman talks almost admiringly of "a man given to cussing, yelling, laughing and smoking fat cigars" who would shout publicly at his Assistant Deputy Minister: "Listen, Tommy, knock it off! When I need your fucking advice, I'll ask for it" (219). Sawatsky calls him "a loud, arrogant and obnoxious, but effective, deputy minister of finance" (184). McQuaig describes FTA negotiating sessions in which the "enraged Simon Reisman" was "not likely to control himself for long. After all, he could only take so much." McQuaig believes that the Americans consciously provoked Reisman in the belief that his "fierce tirade[s] venting his rage" distracted the Canadians from arguing key points.

In checking the story surrounding the Canada-Europe bilateral negotiations in the Kennedy Round, I spoke with a number of people, including James Grandy (a brief telephone conversation) and Simon Reisman (a lengthy telephone conversation). Grandy, who took part in the Geneva session with Reisman, in general minimized the drama of what took place. He said, "We terminated the meeting." When asked whether that meant they had walked out, he eventually replied that they had "in effect walked out." He felt that the Europeans, rather than being shocked by Reisman's tactic, had "probably used it later as a stick to beat us with."

My conversation with Reisman could be seen as a demonstration of his negotiating methods. At first he minimized the incident, perhaps reflecting the growing criticism of his methods in the early 1990s. "There was a negotiation. It didn't go very well. . . . We had a good debate. . . . They thought we were being pretty hard on them [however] stories get enriched with the passage of time." When I asked whether they had walked out, he at first said no, then: "Walk out? Yeh! Well, we failed to reach an agreement." When asked whether he had lost his temper: "There was no such thing as temper tantrums. . . . It was a tough negotiation. . . . They left and we left. . . . The rest is gossip which gets enriched in telling!"

Our conversation began civilly. Gradually Reisman's voice rose and his tone became more vociferous. Eventually he was shouting about the Europeans who wanted Canada "to suck a hind teat"; about "some woman called Diebol or something" engaging in "irresponsible journalism . . . misleading the Canadian people!" (a reference to Linda Diebel of the *Toronto Star*); and eventually, about the person he was talking to, "You're looking for sensationalism! You describe yourself as an historian! More likely you're a muckraker! You've taken more than enough of my time!"

Whatever his reputation, it is nevertheless surprising to hear a leading public figure shout insults at someone he had never seen or met and said he did not know of; this despite the fact that he was simply being asked a series of information-oriented questions. If this was a sample of the methods he applied when negotiating with the Europeans during the Kennedy Round, it is difficult to imagine that Canada's position could not have been damaged.

21. See *Time*, 13 February 1989.
22. Ibid.

CHAPTER FIVE: VOLTAIRE'S CHILDREN

1. Descriptions of this process abound; some personal accounts, some devotional, some analytical. Four modern examples are Malachi Martin, *The Jesuits* (New York: Linden Press, 1987), 192, David Mitchell, *The Jesuits, A History* (New York: Watts, 1981), F. E. Peters, *Ours* (New York: Marek, 1981), *Les Jésuites: spiritualité et activité* (Paris: Éditions Beauchesne, 1974). Loyola's definition of obedience, quoted above, from Martin, *The Jesuits*, 196–199.
2. London Business School, "The Master's Programme," course presentation brochure. Quote from the foreword by the Programme Directors, Elroy Dimson and David Targett. Undated, probably 1986, 3.
3. "Course Development and Research Profile," Harvard Business School, 1986.
4. "The Business of the Harvard Business School," published by the school, probably in 1985.
5. Ibid.
6. Frank B. Copley, *Frederick W. Taylor, Father of Scientific Management*, 2 vols. (Harper's, 1923), vol. 1, 422.
7. Judith A. Merkle, *Management Ideology* (Berkeley: University of California Press, 1980), 15. Merkle's book provides a complete analysis of the whole Scientific Management phenomenon. See also, for basic documents, *Classics in Management*, ed. Harwood F. Merrill (New York: American Management Association, 1970).
8. V. I. Lenin, *Selected Works* (London: Lawrence and Wishard, 1937), vol. 3, 332. For a selection of Lenin's comments on Taylorism, see Merkle.
9. Merkle, *Management Ideology*, 291.
10. "The Business of the Harvard Business School."
11. For one personal description of the school, see Peter Cohen, *The Gospel According to the Harvard Business School* (Garden City, N.Y.: Doubleday, 1973).
12. Professor Abraham Zaleznik, "MBAs Learn Value of Home Life," *New York Times*, 16 October 1985, Living Section, 19.
13. British Business Schools, Report by The Rt. Hon. Lord Franks, British Institute of Management, London, 2 November 1963.
14. Graduate Management Admission Test (sometimes called the "Princeton Test"), see London Business School, "The Master's Programme," 5.
15. London Business School, *Annual Report, 1984/85*, and Harvard, "Course Development."
16. John F. Kennedy School of Government, Harvard University, Catalogue, 1982–1983.

17. Debré, *La Réforme*.
18. Quoted in Jean-Michel Gaillard, *Il Sera Président, Mon Fils* (Paris: Ramsay, 1987), 58.
19. Ibid., 23.
20. Ecole Nationale d'Administration, 1975, internal brochure number 36.
21. *Le Monde*, 16 Octobre 1986, 9. "Il faut donner à l'administration le sens de l'efficacité, du rendement et de la performance."
22. See materials published by ENA, for example, the annual *Remarques à l'usage des candidats et des preparateurs* prepared by the professors. Or for the sports exam, the document pamphlet, *Ecole Nationale d'Administration condition d'accès et régime de scolarité*, 1986.
23. Voltaire, *Philosophical Dictionary*, 149. Ibid., vol. 3, 246. "Un Parisien est tout surpris quand on lui dit que les Hottentots font couper à leurs enfants mâles un testicule. Les Hottentots sont peut-être surpris que les Parisiens en gardent deux."
24. Report by Forum of Educational Organization Leaders. Released in Washington and reported in *Herald Tribune*, 3 June 1967.
25. *Le Nouvel Observateur*, 29 August 1986. "To read you must invent" is part of the report.
26. Aspen Institute, "Can the Humanities Improve Management Effectiveness?" seminar given by Warren Edward Baunach (1986).
27. Harold Nicholson, *The Age of Reason* (London: Panther, 1930), 169.
28. Gaillard, *Il Sera Président*, 66.
29. Northrop Frye, "Acta Victoriana," installation address as president of Victoria College, Toronto (December 1959).
30. Jefferson, *The Life*. See, for example, his letters to Peter Carr, 19 August 1785 (373) and 10 August 1787 (428); to George Washington Lewis, 25 October 1825 (722); to James Madison, 17 February 1826 (726).
31. Ibid., letter to Henry Lee, 10 August 1824 (714).
32. Michael Beer, Bert Spector, Paul R. Lawrence, D. Quinn Mills, and Richard E. Walton, *Managing Human Assets: The Groundbreaking Harvard Business School Program* (New York: The Free Press, 1984).

CHAPTER SIX: THE FLOWERING OF ARMAMENTS

1. An ever-growing collection of institutes provides statistics, in many cases annually, on the arms phenomenon. Each comes to the subject with its own purpose and therefore weights the analysis of the same "facts" on its own side. Nothing as crude as distortion appears. It simply is not necessary. The numbers are fantastic enough to be beyond exaggeration. And there is not a single "hard" number in the arms business. It is dominated by hidden or overt government subsidies, as well as prices set in an artificial and political market. The same plane may be sold for ten times its cost or one-tenth of its cost. Institutes may make selective use of whatever figures they can get hold of. No one can accuse them of lack of professionalism if their figures are incomplete, because there are no complete figures. Public statistics on armaments make the old

nineteenth-century railway stock ventures seem honest in comparison. In fact, the institutes try their best in impossible circumstances.

The annual *Military Balance* of the International Institute of Strategic Studies in London gives an accounting of the results of this business — that is, of which armies have what arms. They are — more or less — sympathetic to what they see as the needs of Western defence. SIPRI (Stockholm International Peace Research Institute) publishes an annual accounting of arms sales. The Council of Economic Priorities in New York has attacked the subject in a number of reports which hold to the old liberal approach — that arms are a waste of money and that statistics prove it.

Dozens of books provide statistics. The earlier ones are particularly interesting because of their attempts to make sense of what was happening. A few useful titles are:

John Stanley and Maurice Pearton, *The International Trade in Arms* (London: International Institute for Strategic Studies [IISS], 1972).

Jean-François Dubos, *Ventes d'Armes: Une Politique* (Paris: Gallimard, 1974).

SIPRI, *The Arms Trade with the Third World* (New York: Council on Economic Priorities, 1977).

Steven Lydenberg, *Weapons for the World* (New York: Council on Economic Priorities, 1977).

The Brookings Institution, *Armed Forces as a Political Instrument* (Washington, D.C.: 1978).

Robert W. De Grasse, Jr., *Military Expansion — Economic Decline* (New York: Council on Economic Priorities, 1983).

William D. Hartung, *The Economic Consequences of a Nuclear Freeze* (New York: Council on Economic Priorities, 1984).

Carol Evans, "Reappraising Third World Arms Production" in *Survival* (March 1986).

James Adams, *Engines of War* (New York: Atlantic Monthly Press, 1990).

Martin Navias, *Ballistic Missile Proliferation in the Third World* (London: IISS/Brassey's 1990).

2. 1984 official figures of French capital goods exports:
    arms – 61.8 billion francs
    civil – 56.5 billion francs

3. On Dassault see John Ralston Saul, "The Evolution of Civil-Military Relations in France After the Algerian War," unpublished dissertation, Kings College, London, 1973, chap. 10, 439–456.

    For the statistics cited on this page and a more general analysis of the phenomenon, see:

Walter Goldstein, "The Opportunity Costs of Acting as a Superpower: U.S. Military Strategy in the 1980's," *Journal of Peace Research*, 18 (3) (1981), 248.

Stephen Strauss, "Defence Dominates Research," *Toronto Globe and Mail*, 14 January 1987.

Michael S. Serrill, "Boom into Bust," *Time*, 3 July 1989, 28–29.

4. For example, see *New York Times*, 12 February 1987, B13. Statement by Maurice N. Shuber, senior logistics officer in the Pentagon.

5. *International Herald Tribune*, 10 August 1988.

6. See Stanley and Pearton, *The International Trade in Arms*.

7. Charles de Gaulle, *Memoirs de Guerre*, vol. 1, *L'Appel* (Paris: Plon, 1954), 227. "Les Etats-Unis apportent aux grandes affaires des sentiments élémentaires et une politique compliquée." On McNamara, see a discussion of this approach in Stanley and Pearton, *International Trade in Arms*, 72–81.

8. Henry Kuss, speech to the American Ordnance Association, 20 October 1966. Quoted in *Arms Sales and Foreign Policy*, Staff study prepared for the use of the Committee on Foreign Relations, U.S. Senate (Washington: Government Printing Office, 1967), 4.

9. The other two were: (1) The U.S.–U.K. refusal to furnish Paris with nuclear information in the late fifties, even though the French had been central to wartime work on nuclear fission. (France's independent *force de frappe* was a direct result.) (2) De Gaulle's discovery that he couldn't give orders to his own Mediterranean fleet because it had been "integrated" into the NATO command, which was permanently led by Americans. He withdrew the fleet almost immediately.

10. Général Pierre Gallois, *Paradoxes de la Paix* (Paris: Presse du temps Présent, 1967), 126.

11. Robert Gilpin, *France in the Age of the Scientific State* (Princeton, N.J.: Princeton University Press, 1968), 252.

12. De Gaulle, *Discours*, vol. 3, 81, speech at the University of Toulouse, February 14, 1959. "C'est à l'Etat qu'il appartient de déterminer, dans le domaine de la Recherche, ce qui est le plus utile à l'intérêt publique et d'affecter à ces objectifs-là ce dont il dispose en fait de moyens et en fait d'hommes."

13. Bush quote: *Toronto Globe and Mail*, 14 January 1988.

14. Calculation agreed upon by most study groups. For example, *The Arms Trade with the Third World* (Stockholm: SIPRI, 1975), 12.

15. Quoted in Anthony Sampson, *The Arms Bazaar* (New York: Viking, 1977), 304.

16. Ibid., 114. The French title for the chief arms salesman is DMA or Délégué Ministériel pour l'Armement.

17. Pierre Briancon, "Editorial: Puissance de Feu," *Liberation*, 7–8 March 1987, 3. "Quelques envols un peu romantiques ont pu faire regretter que dans telle ou telle partie du globe, la fameuse 'politique de la France' se limite à celle d'un 'marchand de canons.' C'est oublier un peu vite qu'on ne peut avoir d'autre politique que celle de sa puissance, c'est-à-dire celle de ses canons: ceux que l'on possède, et ceux que l'on vend."

18. Quoted in *International Herald Tribune*, 24 February 1987, Business Section.

19. *New York Times*, 9 March 1991. See account of Secretary of State Baker's trip to the Middle East.

20. "Marchands de canons cherchent terre d'accueil," *Liberation*, 7–8 March 1987, 2. Henri Conze quote: "L'avenir est très incertain, mais les in-

dustriels ne doivent pas se laisser aller à la morosité. Les marches exis-
tent. Le problème est de savoir quand les clients disposeront à nouveau
de moyens financiers pour moderniser leur defense. Qui peut dire quel
sera le prix du pétrole dans un an?"

21. *Harper's Magazine* (January 1987), 50–51.
22. "Sweden's New Realities," *International Herald Tribune*, 3 June 1987,
     Special News Report, 7; on death of official see *Toronto Globe and Mail*,
     17 January 1987.
23. *The Arms Trade with the Third World*, 12; *Toronto Star*, 18 July 1988,
     A16; *Washington Post*, 27 January 1991, C1.
24. *Far Eastern Economic Review*, 9 July 1987, 28.
25. *The Arms Trade with the Third World*, 43.
26. *Toronto Globe and Mail*, July 1991, B11.
27. *Le Monde*, 10 August 1988, 3; *Washington Post*, 27 January 1991, C1.
28. *Far Eastern Economic Review*, 9 July 1987, 3.
29. *Annual Report to the Congress by the Secretary of Defense, Fiscal Year 1987*
     (Washington, D.C.: U.S. Government Printing Office, 1987), 293.
30. Michel Fourquet, *Revue de la Défense Nationale* (Paris: Ministère de la
     défense nationale, 1967), 756. General Fourquet was DMA from 1966 to
     1968 and Chef d'Etat-Major des Armées from 1968 to 1971. "*Admettre
     comme règle* que ces industries *doivent vivre de l'exportation.*"

CHAPTER SEVEN: THE QUESTION OF KILLING

1. On military and civilian deaths, see, for example, John Gellner, Editor
    of *Canadian Defense Quarterly*, in *Toronto Globe and Mail*, 31 December
    1980, 7. Figures such as these are always soft. A breakdown on war
    deaths from 1945 to 1989 has been done by William Eckhardt, research
    director of the Lentz Peace Research Institute. His figures are 13.3
    million civilian deaths and 6.8 million military deaths. These figures do
    not include conflicts with less than one thousand deaths per year. In
    their attempt to be "hard," they also leave out a large part of the guerrilla-
    and civilian-related casualties in more remote conflicts. The Burmese
    figures, for example, show 22,000 deaths. This is a conflict I have been
    following closely for a decade. A more accurate figure, given the disorder,
    violence and resulting poverty in the Shan States, might be 220,000.
    Another set of figures have been provided by Nicole Ball, National Se-
    curity Archives, Washington, D.C., as reported in the *Toronto Globe and
    Mail*, 30 September 1991: 40 million deaths altogether in 125 wars or
    conflicts since 1945.
2. Général F. Gambiez and Colonel M. Suire, *Histoire de la Première Guerre
    Mondiale* (Paris: Fayard, 1968), 216, provides the following figures on
    French soldiers killed in World War I:
    1914   300,000 in 4.5 months
    1915   31,000 per month
    1916   21,000 per month
    1917   13,500 per month
    1918   21,000 per month

3. Ibid., 124. "Notre âge sera celui des guerres plus ambitieuses et plus barbares que les autres."

4. Sun Tzu, *The Art of War*, trans. by Samuel B. Griffith; foreword by B. H. Liddell Hart (New York: Oxford University Press, 1963), vi.

5. Sun Tzu, *The Art of War*, 63.

6. C. Wright Mills, *The Power Elite* (New York: Oxford University Press, 1956), 171.

7. Pierre Lellouche, *L'Avenir de la Guerre* (Paris: Mazarine, 1985).

8. Ibid., 22.

CHAPTER EIGHT: LEARNING HOW TO ORGANIZE DEATH

1. Sun Tzu, *The Art of War*, 79.

2. Ibid., 73, 73, 76–78, 101, 102, 134.

3. Ibid., 91.

4. Quoted in Michael Elliott-Bateman, *Defeat in the East* (London: Oxford University Press, 1967), 171.

5. Sir Basil Liddell Hart, *A History of the First World War* (London, 1970 ed.), 80. First published in 1930.

6. Sir Basil Liddell Hart, *The Other Side of the Hill* (London: Pan, 1978), 31. First published in 1948.

7. Charles de Gaulle, *Le Fil de l'épée* (Paris: 10/18, 1964). First published in 1932.

8. Comte de Guibert, *Écrits Militaires 1772–1790*, préface et notes du Général Ménard (Paris: Editions Copernic, 1976), 192. "Si par hasard il s'élève dans une nation un bon général, la politique des ministres et les intrigues des courtisans ont soin de le tenir eloigné des troupes pendant la paix. On aime mieux confier ces troupes à des hommes médiocres, incapables de les former, mais passifs, dociles à toutes les volontés et à tous les systèmes. . . . La guerre arrive, les malheurs seuls peuvent ramener le choix sur le général habile."

9. Gambiez and Suire, *Histoire de la Première Guerre*, 105.

10. Liddell Hart, *The Other Side*, 32.

11. Brian Bond, *The Victorian Staff College* (London: Methuen, 1972), 169.

12. Ibid., 165. For a comparison in greater detail, with sources, see 162–69.

13. Quoted in Le Commandant Charles Bugnet, *En Ecoutant le Maréchal Foch* (Bernard Grasset, 1929), 39. Bugnet was one of Foch's aides. "La guerre a montré la nécessité pour la direction d'avoir un but, un plan et une méthode et d'en poursuivre l'application avec une active tenacité." He had begun by saying: "La guerre a montré la nécessité pour réussir d'avoir un but, un plan et une méthode."

14. Gambiez and Suire, *Histoire de la Première Guerre*, 330.

15. Bond, *The Victorian Staff College*, 279. Haig and Robertson quotes.

16. Ibid., 328.

CHAPTER NINE: PERSISTENT CONTINUITY AT THE HEART OF POWER

1. *Guardian Weekly*, 13 January 1991, 8, Jean Edward Smith's review of *Brute Force* by John Ellis (New York: Viking, 1991). "In the last 18

months of the war, the Allies deployed 80,000 tanks to the Germans' 20,000; 1.1 million trucks to 70,000; 235,000 combat aircraft to 45,000."

2. Quoted by Liddell Hart in *The Other Side of the Hill*, 26. It should be noted that in 1989, John J. Mearsheimer published an attack on Liddell Hart, minimizing his role in the overall development of tank strategy. Mearsheimer's book, *Liddell Hart and the Weight of History* (London: Brassey's Defence Publishers, 1989, 5) was put into a proper context by Sir Michael Howard in a review published by *The Spectator* (25 February 1989, 28) and in a letter from Alistair Horne (*The Spectator*, 18 March 1989, 22).

3. Ibid., 470.

4. Elliott-Bateman, *Defeat in the East*, 67. See also Major General Eric Dorman-Smith's description of both the Wavell and the Auchinleck campaigns in Liddell Hart's *Strategy*, 2nd rev. ed. (New York: Meridian, 1991), appendix 1. This is a letter written by Dorman-Smith to Liddell Hart in October 1942; in other words, not long after the second campaign. See also the review of this book in *The Spectator*, 30 March 1991.

5. Ibid., 67.

6. The words of Admiral Sir Rowland Jerram, quoted in Philip Warner, *Auchinleck, The Lonely Soldier* (London: Buchanard Enright, 1981), 253.

7. Gavin Stamp in *The Spectator*, 24 October 1987, 14.

8. Quoted in Charles J. Rolo, *Wingate Raiders* (London: Harrap, 1944).

9. See *The Chindit War*, Shelford Bidwell (London: Hodder & Stoughton, 1979), 38.

10. Sun Tzu, *The Art of War*, 101.

11. For example, Lellouche, *L'Avenir de la Guerre*, 13. He gives a figure of 160 for the Third World up to 1985.

12. William Manchester, *American Caesar: Douglas MacArthur: 1880–1964* (Boston: Little, Brown, 1978), 575.

13. Sun Tzu, *The Art of War*, 85.

14. Richard Gabriel and Paul Savage, *Crisis in Command* (New York: Hill & Wang, 1978), Table II. Gabriel, *Military Incompetence*, 21.

15. Gabriel, *Military Incompetence*, 184.

16. Guilbert, *Crises Militaires*, 107.

17. *Newsweek*, 31 August 1987, 14.

18. Gabriel, *Military Incompetence*, 27. See Gabriel for a full analysis of these problems of high technology versus the winning of wars.

19. *Guardian Weekly*, 24 March 1991, 18.

20. *International Herald Tribune*, 22 April 1991, 5.

21. *International Herald Tribune*, 15 April 1991, 3.

22. R. Jeffrey Smith, "The Patriot Less than a Hero," Washington Post Service, April 1991. See also:

William Safire, *International Herald Tribune*, 7 March 1991.
"Israeli scientists and officers say 0 to 20% of Scud missile warheads were destroyed by Patriots," *International Herald Tribune*, 2–3 November 1991.
New York Times, 9 January 1992, A8, *re* a 52-page report by Dr. The-

odore A. Postol, a physicist and former Pentagon science adviser, now professor of national security policy at MIT: "an almost total failure to intercept quite primitive attacking missiles."

23. Gabriel, *Military Incompetence*, 14.
24. As witnessed by the author, who happened to be in the Pentagon that morning for a meeting unrelated to Iran.
25. Gabriel, *Military Incompetence*, 185.
26. For a description of this phenomenon, see Robert Merle, *La Journée ne se lève pas pour nous* (Paris: Plon, 1986).
27. Sun Tzu, *The Art of War*, 143.

CHAPTER TEN: IN THE SERVICE OF THE GREATER SELF

1. The War of Jenkins' Ear began in 1739 after Robert Jenkins, master of a cargo ship, appeared before a committee of the British House of Commons with a box containing what he claimed was his own ear. This he said had been cut off by the Spanish coast guard in the West Indies, whom he said also pillaged his ship. The result was perhaps the first nation-state modern war in which artificially provoked national-racial outrage was used to advance raw commercial interests. Jingoism was an expression of blind patriotism invented in 1878 to encourage the sending of a British fleet into Turkish waters against the Russians. It came from a patriotic song called "By Jingo!"
2. See, for example, "Second Inaugural Address," Jefferson's *A Life*, 4 March 1805, 334.
3. Roger-Henri Guerrand, *Les Lieux* (Paris: Editions la Découverte, 1986), 43. In addition, the succeeding description of and statistics on one of the most extraordinary modern revolutions — the creation of sewage systems — are drawn from this remarkable book.
4. Jefferson, *The Life*, letter to the writer Thomas Law, 13 June 1814, 636.
5. Ibid., Letter to Peter Carr from Paris, 10 August 1787, 429.
6. There are many sources for Haussmann's rebuilding of Paris. For example, J. M. and Brian Chapman, *The Life and Times of Baron Haussmann* (London: Weidenfeld & Nicolson, 1957). Or William E. Echard, *Historical Dictionary of the French Second Empire 1852–1887* (Conn.: Greenwood Press, 1985). Or Stuart L. Campbell, *The Second Empire Revisited: a study in French Historiography* (New Brunswick, N.J.: Rutgers University Press, 1978).
7. Emile Zola, *L'Argent* (Paris: Bibliothèque-Charpentier 1893), 159.

Le coeur serré, madame Caroline examinait la cour, un terrain ravagé, que les ordures accumulées transformaient en un cloaque. On jetait tout là, il n'y avait ni fosse ni puisard, c'était un fumier sans cesse accru, empoisonnant l'air. . . . D'un pied inquiet, elle cherchait à éviter les débris de légumes et les os, en promenait ses regards aux deux bords, sur les habitations, des sortes de tanières sans nom, des rez-de-chaussées effondrés à demi, masures en ruines consolidées avec les matériaux les plus hétéroclites. Plusieurs étaient simplement couvertes de papier goud-ronné. Beaucoup n'avaient pas de porte, laissaient entrevoir des trous noir de cave, d'où sortait une halaine nauséabonde de misère. Des familles de huit et dix personnes s'entassaient dans ces charniers, sans même avoir un lit souvent, les hommes, les femmes, les enfants entas, se pourrissant les uns les autres, comme les fruits gâtés, livrés dès la petite enfance à l'instinctive luxure par la plus monstreuse des promis-cuités.

8. Albert Speer joined the National Socialist party in 1931; that is, before Hitler won power. His first position of authority was as Hitler's preferred architect, then as armaments minister. In Grand Admiral Karl Dönitz's short-lived 1945 government, he was reich minister of economy and production. His memoirs were called *Inside the Third Reich* (New York: Macmillan, 1970). An examination of Speer's attempt to defang the moral implications of his role can be found in Matthias Schmidt, *Albert Speer: The End of a Myth*, trans. Joachim Neugroschel (New York: St. Martin's Press, 1984). Originally published as *Albert Speer: Das Ende eines Mythos* (Munich: Bernard Scheiz Verlag).

9. Colin Campbell, *Government Under Stress* (Toronto: University of Toronto Press, 1983). Campbell looks at London, Ottawa and Washington. However, he pulls himself out of the reigning mythologies of the various systems only far enough to compare them; not to evaluate them.

10. Quoted in Theodore C. Sorensen, *Kennedy* (New York: Harper & Row, 1965), 283.

11. See Garry Wills, *The Kennedy Imprisonment* (Boston: Atlantic/Little, Brown, 1981), chap. 13, for a remarkable analysis of the Kennedy White House management style.

12. Jimmy Carter, *Why Not the Best?* (Nashville, Tenn.: Broadman Press, 1975).

13. The firings took place July 20–21, 1979.

14. *Independent* (London), 30 March 1990. Charles Powell, a civil servant and foreign affairs secretary to Mrs. Thatcher, lunched with Conrad Black, owner of the *Daily Telegraph*, to persuade him to give greater support to government.

15. François Mitterrand quoted in Catherine Nay, *Le Noir et le Rouge* (Paris: Grasset, 1984), 227. "Au niveau de l'homme politique, il n'y a qu'une ambition: gouverner."

16. *Le Monde*, 10 February 1989, 1.

17. Jefferson, *The Life*, letter to President George Washington, 23 May 1792, 513.

18. *New York Times*, 5 June 1989, 1. This article contains a breakdown of monies paid to senators and representatives by corporations and PACs.

19. See, for example, "Demand Grows for MPs in Business World," the *Independent* (London), 18 January 1989.

20. Anthony Sampson, *The Changing Anatomy of Britain* (London: Hodder & Stoughton, 1981), 181.

CHAPTER ELEVEN: THREE SHORT EXCURSIONS INTO THE UNREASONABLE

1. See, for example, Maurice F. Strong's address to the Harvard University Center for International Affairs, Cambridge, Mass., March 3, 1987.
2. For a full description, see Peter Ludlow, *The Making of the European Monetary System* (London: Butterworth Scientific, 1982).
3. Quotes on Robert Dole from *Life* magazine, September 1987, 63 and 64, in an article by George Gilder.
4. *International Herald Tribune*'s report of 21 January 1989, 4, taken from the Washington Post Service.
5. Quoted in the *New York Times*, 12 January 1989, 8.
6. Quoted in the *Independent* (London), 18 January 1989.
7. On Reagan's visit to Japan see *International Herald Tribune*, 12 May 1989, news story as well as column by William Safire. The Japanese company was the Fujisankei Group.
8. *London Times*, 13 February 1989.

CHAPTER TWELVE: THE ART OF THE SECRET

1. Sun Tzu, *The Art of War*, 144. Subsequent quotations, 147.
2. Desiderius Erasmus, *De Civilitate Morum Puerilium*, 1530. French version, 1544. Quoted in Guerrand, *Les Lieux*, 24.
3. Quoted in Harold Nicolson, *The Age of Reason* (London: Panther, 1930), 219.
4. Jefferson, *The Life*, three quotations: letter from Paris to James Madison, 20 December 1787, 436; Inauguration Address, 4 March 1801, 321; to the Secretary of the Treasury (Albert Gallatin), Washington, 1 April 1802, 566. On Alexander Hamilton and the Federalists, see the last chapter of James Thomas Flexner, *The Young Hamilton* (Boston: Little, Brown, 1978).
5. A standard text on Western approaches to toilet training and its results is Erik Erikson, *Childhood and Society* (London: Penguin, 1965).
6. Asa Briggs, *The Longman Encyclopedia* (London: Longmans, 1989).
7. Security figure: *International Herald Tribune*, 30 May 1986. Secrets figure: *International Herald Tribune*, 19 April 1990; editorial from *New York Times* entitled "6,796,501 Secrets." The actual number was 6,796,501.
8. *Times* (London), 11 February 1989.
9. The book in question is Alfred W. McCoy, *The Politics of Heroin in Southeast Asia* (New York: Harper & Row, 1972).
10. See, for example, *Le Monde*, 23 May 1986, article by Bernard Guetta.
11. *Daily Telegraph*, 12 May 1989.
12. *Toronto Star*, 21 June 1991. The Commissioner is John Grace.
13. First quote is from A. M. Rosenthal in *New York Times*, 11 June 1991, A15. Rosenthal was managing editor during the Pentagon Papers incident. His June 11 column summarized the events surrounding the whole incident.
14. See portrait of Robert Armstrong in chapter 4 of this book.
15. Re British SAS and Gibraltar, see the *Independent*, 27 January 1989, 1.

The Thames Television program was "Death on the Rock." The report was prepared by a former Conservative Home Office minister, Lord Windelesham, and Richard Rampton, QC.

16. Diderot: "On doit exiger de moi que je cherche la vérité, mais non que je la trouve."

17. Definitions, in order:

Johnson's Pocket Dictionary of the English Language (London: Chiswick, 1826)

E. Chambers, *Cyclopaedia: or an Universal Dictionary of Arts and Sciences* (London, 1738), 2 vols.

Dictionnaire Littré (Paris: Librairie Hachette, 1876): "Vérité — Qualité par laquelle les choses apparaissent telles qu'elles sont."

Noah Webster, *An American Dictionary of the English Language* (New York: S. Converse, 1828), 2 vols.

Le Petit Robert (Paris: Robert): "Vérité — Connaissance conforme au réel. Ce à quoi l'esprit peut et doit donner son assentiment."

18. Robert Calvi was involved as a high-profile banker in the obscure triangle linking the Vatican Bank, the Mafia and the world of finance during the 1980s. Igor Gouzenko was a cipher clerk at the Soviet Embassy in Ottawa. He defected in 1945. The information he provided on North American–based Soviet spy rings gave some early impetus to the red scare campaign of Senator Joseph McCarthy — which involved widespread, unsubstantiated attacks.

CHAPTER THIRTEEN: THE SECRETIVE KNIGHT

1. Jacob Bronowski, *Science and Human Values* (New York: Harper & Row, 1965), 59.

2. Michael Polanyi, "The Republic of Science," *Minerva* vol. 1 no. 1., (Autumn 1962), 53–73.

3. J. Robert Oppenheimer, *Science and the Common Understanding* (New York: Simon & Schuster, 1953), 85.

4. André Malraux, quoted in *Le Monde*, 5 July 1968, from an interview given late in his life.

5. John Ruskin, *Selections and Essays*, "Time and Tide: The White-Thorn Blossom," (New York: Charles Scribner's, 1918), 365. Originally written 1871.

6. Bronowski, *Science and Human Values*, 7 and 19.

7. John Ruskin, *Introduction to Modern Painters*, ed. David Barrie (London: André Deutsch, 1987), XXXII. Quote from Barrie's introduction.

8. Much of the discussion of nuclear responsibility here and in the next section is drawn from an unpublished paper written by John Polanyi, dated February 1986, including quotes from Polanyi and from the Franck Report. Supplied by the author.

9. Oppenheimer, *Science and the Common Understanding*, 4.

10. Quoted in *Le Canard Enchaîné*, 21 May 1987. "L'incident est d'une gravité . . . encore jamais recontrée jusqu'içi sur les réacteurs à eau pressurisée. . . . Une défaillance supplémentaire . . . aurait donc con-

duit à une perte complète des alimentations électroniques de puissance, saturation hors dimensionnement. . . . La nonfermeture des vannes aurait constitué une voie de dégénerescence supplémentaire de l'incident vers une situation difficilement contrôlable."

11. *Guardian*, 6 July 1987, 5.
12. Matthew L. Wald, "Can Nuclear Power Be Rehabilitated?" *New York Times*, 31 March 1991.
13. Reported in *International Herald Tribune*, 5 October 1988.
14. Martin Amis, *Einstein's Monsters* (London: Jonathan Cape, 1987), 8 and 9.
15. Quotes from *Guardian*, 10 November 1989, 1 and 7. See also *Financial Times*, 11 November 1989, 6.
16. See, for example, *Libération*, Paris, 24 avril 1991, 24: "Seule certitude: les centrales de demain seront sûres ou ne seront pas. C'est du moins ce qu'affirment les industriels. Leur nouveau credo: la 'sûreté passive.' " *New York Times*, 31 March 1991: "Can Nuclear Power Be Rehabilitated? The industry is trying to mend its image by curbing human errors."
17. A few references for these statements are:

On salmonella: *London Times*, 7 December 1988, Marian Burros; ibid., 10 February 1989, 1 and 12; ibid., 11 February 1989, 1 and 16; ibid., 13 February 1989, 10; ibid., 15 February 1989, 1

On hormones: *Le Monde*, October 1987, Philippe Lemaitre

On pesticides: *Toronto Star*, 3 January 1988, Andrew Chetley; *London Times*, 20 June 1989, Michael McCarthy

On fertilizers: *Toronto Star*, 28 August 1988, Lynda Hurst; *International Herald Tribune*, 9 August 1988, Steven Greenhouse; *New York Times*, 8 September 1989, 1, Keith Schneider

On nuclear plants: *International Herald Tribune*, 5 October 1988, Keith Schneider

CHAPTER FOURTEEN: OF PRINCES AND HEROES

1. There are many descriptions of the Calas case. Gustave Lanson's classic biography, *Voltaire*, published in 1906, provides a clear description of the context and I have drawn heavily on it. An excellent English translation was published in 1960 (*Voltaire* trans. Robert Wagoner [New York: published by John Wiley and Sons]).
2. *Oxford English Dictionary*, s.v. 3rd ed., "justice."
3. J. J. Rousseau, *The Social Contract*, 99.
4. Learned Hand, *The Spirit of Liberty: Papers and Addresses of Learned Hand* (Chicago: University of Chicago Press, 1952), 189.
5. Edmund Burke, 22 March 1775.
6. See Anthony Sampson's description of this debate in *The Changing Anatomy of Britain*, 159.
7. William Shawcross, "The Crips and the Bloods," *The Spectator*, 28 May 1988, 10.
8. Lord McCluskey, *Law, Justice and Democracy, The Reith Lectures* (London: Sweet and Maxwell, 1986), 2.

9. Quoted in Archibald Cox, "Storm Over the Supreme Court," Blumenthal Memorial Lecture, February 13, 1986, 21.

10. Montesquieu, *De L'Esprit des Lois*. Originally published in 1748. "Quand je vais dans un pays, je n'examine pas s'il y a des bonnes lois, mais si on exécute celles qui y sont, car il y a des bonnes lois partout."

11. McCluskey, *Law, Justice and Democracy*, 6.

12. "The Court's Pivot Man," *Time*, 6 July 1987, 8.

13. Supreme Court of the United States. *Payne* v. *Tennessee*. June 28, 1991. With Justice Marshall's resignation, seven out of nine justices will cast votes on the basis of ideology ranging from conservative to right-wing. See *New York Times*, 28 June 1991, A1, 10 and 11, for quotes from Justices Marshall, Stevens and Rehnquist.

14. Benjamin Hart, *The Task of the Third Generation; Young Conservatives Look to the Future*, forewords by Attorney General Edwin Meese and President Ronald Reagan (Washington, D.C.: Heritage Foundation/ Regenery Gateway, 1987).

15. Chief Justice Brian Dickson, address to the annual meeting of the Canadian Bar Association, August 24, 1987.

16. Quoted in *Time* magazine, 6 July 1987, 32.

17. *International Herald Tribune*, 20 May 1987.

18. *Financial Times*, 12 February 1992.

19. *Le Monde*, 26 January 1989, 14. Reported by Maurice Peyrot. La Fontaine: "Selon que vous serez puissant ou miserable . . ."

20. Jim Wolf, "CIA Says It Used BCCI Legally," *Toronto Globe and Mail*, August 1991, B11.

21. John Rawls, *A Theory of Justice* (Cambridge, Mass.: Harvard University Press, 1971).

22. Thomas Mann, *The Magic Mountain*, trans. H. Lowe Porter (Harmondsworth, England: Penguin, 1985), 513. First published in 1924.

23. *Voix de Napoleon*, 35. Speech given outside the Assembly on 18 Brumaire. "Qu'avez-vous fait de cette France que je vous avais laissée si brillante? Je vous ai laissé la paix et j'ai retrouvé la guerre! Je vous ai laissé des victoires et j'ai retrouvé des revers! Je vous ai laissé les millions d'Italie et j'ai retrouvé les lois spoliatrices et la misère! Qu'avez-vous fait de cent mille Français que je connaissais, mes compagnons de gloire? Ils sont mort! Cet état de choses ne peut pas durer."

24. Mann, *The Magic Mountain*, 464.

25. The subject of endless biographies, Garibaldi and the other players in the Risorgimento, such as Cavour and Mazzini, have been clearly and dispassionately described in a series of books published over the last few decades by Denis Mack Smith, from which much of this information is drawn.

CHAPTER FIFTEEN: THE HERO AND THE POLITICS OF IMMORTALITY

1. Erik Erikson, *Young Man Luther* (New York: Norton and Co., 1958), 75.

2. Schmidt, *Albert Speer: The End of a Myth*, 13–20.

3. Erikson, *Luther*, 109.
4. Jean Genet, *The Thief's Journal* (Harmondsworth: Penguin Modern Classics, 1967), 170. First published in French in 1949 as *Journal du Voleur*.
5. Jean Genet, *Le Balcon* (Lyon: Marc Barbezat, 1962), (37); le Juge: "Miroir qui me glorifie!" le Général: "Proche de la mort . . . où je ne serai rien, mais reflétée à l'infini dans ces miroirs que mon image" (55); le Chef de Police: "Non le cent millième reflet du'un miroir qui se répète; je serai l'Unique, en que cent mille verlent se confonde" (117); and le Chef de Police: "Mais dès que je me sentirai me multiplier infiniment, alors . . . alors, cessent d'être dur, j'irai pourrir dans les consciences" (219).

CHAPTER SIXTEEN: THE HIJACKING OF CAPITALISM

1. Ross Johnson rose to prominence as chief executive officer of R. J. R. Nabisco from 1984 to 1988. He was ejected from the company after an attempt to take over ownership of the company. Following the publication of *Barbarians at the Gate: The Fall of R. J. R. Nabisco* (New York: Harper & Row, 1990), he became a symbol, depending on your point of view, of extravagant or unacceptable or irresponsible financial management. See, for example, *Barbarians at the Gate*: "He would come to be the very symbol of the business world's 'Roaring Eighties' " (11). He had become a friend of Brian Mulroney in Montreal in the 1970s and played a key role in organizing American business to push the U.S.–Canada trade agreement through Congress. His fleet of ten corporate planes was used to fly around a wide range of business and sports figures as well as Mulroney and his wife. Mrs. Mulroney also became known as a shopping partner of Mrs. Johnson, who had access to a far larger income.
2. André Malraux, *La Condition Humaine* (Paris: Folio/Gallimard, 1977), 230. Original published 1933. "Le capitalisme moderne . . . est beaucoup plus volonté d'organisation que de puissance."
3. Rosabeth Moss Kanter, professor at the Harvard Business School, began her career with studies on the community and cooperative approach to economics. She has gradually moved through a justified critique of the large corporations to a view of the "postentrepreneurial economy." The quotation is from *Where Giants Learn to Dance: Mastering the Challenging Strategy, Management and Careers in the 1990s* (New York: Simon & Schuster, 1989), 52. This book ends with a section on "The Coming Demise of Bureaucracy and Hierarchy."

   In the context of this discussion, see a practical analysis in the humanist tradition: David Olive, *Just Rewards: The Case for Ethical Reform in Business* (Toronto: Penguin, 1987). See also Olive's program for reform of boards of directors — "Board Games" in *The Report on Business Magazine, Toronto Globe and Mail*, September 1991.
4. *Le Monde* 18 February 1989, 31.
5. *Far Eastern Economic Review*, 27 August 1987, 17; and *Newsweek*, 31 August 1987, 27.

6. Michael Porter, professor at the Harvard Business School and author of *Competition Strategy* (1980), *Competitive Advantage* (1985) and *The Competitive Advantage of Nations* (1990; all New York: Free Press). Interesting comments on his methods can be seen in "Competitiveness, Strategic Management, Democracy and Justice: The Bad News," a preliminary paper for a three-year study on the phenomenon of "competitiveness" as perceived by Porter. The study was led by Professor Jon Alexander of Carlton University, Ottawa. Preliminary conclusions are that Porter's approach would lead to governments abandoning social and economic leadership; instead limiting themselves to creating an environment "in which markets are free to adjudicate their own interests."

7. See a description of the Boeing situation in *International Herald Tribune*, 2 February 1989, Business Section, 1, by Laura Parker, Washington Post Service.

8. James G. Rogers of Butler, Rogers and Baskett, quoted in *New York Times*, 6 September 1987, R15.

9. Maurice F. Strong, "Opportunities for Real Growth in an Interdependent World, 17 May 1987, speech to Banff Conference.

10. Strong, speaking at the Harvard University Center for International Affairs, Cambridge, Mass., 3 March 1987.

11. Dominic Lawson in *Spectator*, 17 June 1989, 9.

12. All three examples are drawn from *Spectator*, lead article of 18 May 1991, 5.

13. Figures for this paragraph drawn from *International Herald Tribune*, 3 November 1988, 15; *Globe and Mail*, 2 January 1989, B7; *Bangkok Post*, 24 January 1990; *International Herald Tribune*, 26 January 1990.

14. Merger figures from IDD Information Services, reported in *Bangkok Post*, 24 January 1990. A more accurate calculation of the percentage of corporate cash flow absorbed by interest payments would be based on the $2.2 trillion plus the $1.1 trillion. The financial institution figures do not, of course, include the banks' proper role as intermediaries receiving deposits. Guidance in this area was received from economists at the Federal Reserve Bank (Robert Rewald and Sarah Holden).

    Guidance for British figures comes from the economists of The Bank of England.

    See also articles in: *Newsweek*, 7 November 1989; *Time*, 7 November, 1988; and *Globe and Mail*, 6 January 1989.

15. Quoted in *International Herald Tribune*, 1 November 1988, 13.

16. Akio Morita, with Edwin M. Reingold and Mitsuko Shimomura, *Made in Japan: Akio Morita and Sony* (New York: E. P. Dutton, 1987).

17. These and the immediately succeeding statistics are from Peter Drucker, writing in *Foreign Affairs*. They were quoted by Maurice F. Strong in a lecture to the University of Victoria, British Columbia, on October 30, 1986.

18. Strong, "Opportunities for Real Growth."

19. Friedrich Nietzsche, *Die Fröhliche Wissenschaft*, vol. 3, 16, "Moralität ist Herden-Instinkt, in Einzelnen."

20.　Sir Derek Alun-Jones, chairman of Ferranti International, quoted in the *Times* of London, 18 November 1989, 17. This article outlines the case.

21.　Socialist International Congress, Resolution, Vancouver, November 1978.

22.　Robert Engler, *The Brotherhood of Oil* (New York: New American Library, 1977), 9.

23.　Ibid., 51.

24.　See *The Brotherhood of Oil* and *Toronto Globe and Mail*, March 14, 1984.

25.　Diderot, *Encyclopédie*, vol. 2, 129: "*FORTUNE* (Morale): Les moyens de s'enrichir peuvent être *criminels* en morale, quoique permis par les lois."

CHAPTER SEVENTEEN: THE MIRACLE OF THE LOAVES

1.　Jim Slater's fall can be followed in *The Economist*, 1 June 1974, 95; 24 August 1974, 81; 1 November 1975, 72; 15 November 1975, 89; 18 September 1976, 115; 15 October 1977, 121. The whole phenomenon is analysed in Charles Raw, *Slater Walker* (London: André Deutsch, 1977).

2.　*The Economist*, 15 October 1977, 121.

3.　The Snake originally took shape in 1972, in the wake of the first major monetary crisis of the 1970s. The Snake is an exchange-rate regime in which countries must keep their currencies within agreed upper and lower margins determined by a grid which fixes the relative values of all participants. The EMS began in 1979 and is gradually evolving towards a single European currency or something not too distant from that ideal. For a good description of the origins of the EMS, see Ludlow, *The Making of the European Monetary System*.

4.　Quoted by Anthony Sampson in *International Herald Tribune*, 24 November 1982, 4.

5.　See Diane Cohen, "Signals of a Looming Depression," *Maclean's*, 25 August 1988, 7; Anthony Bianco, "The Casino Society," *Business Week*, 16 September 1985, 78; Rowan Bosworth-Davies, *Too Good to be True: How to Survive in the Casino Society* (London: Bodley Head, 1987); John Taylor, *Storming the Magic Kingdom* (New York: Alfred A. Knopf, 1987).

6.　Bianco, "The Casino Society," 79; and Cohen, "Signals."

7.　Jefferson, *The Life*, letter to James Madison, from Paris, 16 September 1789.

8.　Max Weber, *The Protestant Ethic and the Spirit of Capitalism*, trans. Talcott Parsons (New York: Charles Scribner's Sons, 1958), originally published in German 1904–5. See pages 177, 182 and the footnote to page 64.

9.　See Deuteronomy 23:20–21, Exodus 22:24, Leviticus 25:35–37, Ezekiel 18:13, the Psalmist 15:5.

10.　Émile Zola, *L'Argent* (Paris: Bibliothèque Charpentier, 1893), 107. "A quoi bon donner trente ans de sa vie, pour gagner un pauvre million, lorsque, en une heure, par une simple opération de Bourse, on peut le mettre dans sa poche? . . . Le pis est qu'on se dégoûte du gain légitime, qu'on finit même par perdre la notion de l'argent."

11.　See Harold Lever and Christopher Hulme, *Debt and Danger* (Boston: Atlantic Monthly Press, 1986).

12. As described in Anthony Storr, *Solitude — A Return to the Self* (New York: Free Press, 1988).

13. For descriptions of the Gulf-Pickens fight see *New York Times*, 1 November 1983, D9; *Financial Times*, 25 November 1983, 18; ibid., 28 November 1983, 7, full-page Gulf ad; ibid., 31 December 1983; *International Herald Tribune*, 31 December 1983, Business Section, 1.

14. *International Herald Tribune*, 27 May 1987, Business Section, 1.

15. For description of Beatrice takeover see *New York Times*, Sunday, 6 September 1987, Business Section, 1.

16. Warren Buffett, quoted by David Hilzenrath, *Sunday Star*, 1 September 1991. Rudolph Giuliani, quoted in Gail Sheehy, "Heaven's Hit Man," *Vanity Fair*, August 1987.

17. Quoted in Bosworth-Davies, *Too Good to Be True*.

18. Carol Ascher, "Can't Anyone Tell Right from Wrong?" in *Present Tense*, January–February 1987, 6–13.

19. Ibid.

20. *Times* (London), 24 April 1987.

21. Dome Petroleum had vast holdings in the Canadian High Arctic. Discoveries in the late 1970s were used to sell successive share offerings around the world and created a spectacular price rise. In the 1980s the company's debt situation, combined with the continuing difficulties of commercially exploiting such inaccessible reserves, led to a spectacular collapse.

22. Phil Roosevelt, "The Secretive Ways of George Soros," *International Herald Tribune*, 13 April 1987, 9.

23. See *Le Monde*, 14 February 1989, 21; ibid., 1 March 1989; *International Herald Tribune*, 15 April 1991.

24. For example, see *Le Monde*, 15 February 1989.

25. *Times* (London), 17 July 1989.

26. Sidney Homer, *A History of Interest Rates* (New Brunswick, N.J.: Rutgers University Press, 1972).

CHAPTER EIGHTEEN: IMAGES OF IMMORTALITY OR THE VICTORY OF IDOLATRY

1. There is a remarkable discussion and a detailed description of the rise of the Church in Rome and its relationship to Roman beliefs, architecture and images, as well as of the arrival of Greek magic and idolatry, in Richard Krautheimer, *Rome, Profile of a City 312–1308*, (Princeton, N.J.: Princeton University Press, 1980). I have drawn heavily from it in the references to Christianity and Rome.

2. Saint Augustine, *City of God* (Garden City, N.Y.: Doubleday, 1958), book 7, chap. 5, 136.

3. See H. Daniel-Rops, *The Church in the Dark Ages* (London: Dent, 1959), 556–62.

4. *The Koran*, trans. N. J. Dawood (Harmondsworth, England: Penguin, 1977), quoted from "The Merciful," 20. I have deleted the

chorus — "Which of your Lord's blessings do you deny?" — after each verse.

5. King James Version, 15:10; 18:4; 20:23.
6. The three most influential texts of the fifteenth-sixteenth-century transitional period were: Leon Battista Alberti, *On Painting* (1435), based on artistic changes in Florence; and Piero della Francesca; *De Prospectiva pingendi* (*On Perspective in Painting*) (1474–82) and *De quinque corporibus regularibus* (*On the Five Regular Bodies*) (after 1482).
7. Quoted in Claude Keisch, *Grand Empire — Virtue and Vice in the Napoleonic Empire* (New York: Hippocrene Books, 1990), 71.
8. R. G. Collingwood, *The Principles of Art* (London: Oxford University Press, 1974), 6. Originally published in 1938.
9. Both Francis Bacon quotes are from *The Spectator*, 25 May 1985, 36, in an interview with Alistair Hicks.
10. Aldous Huxley, *Brave New World* (Harmondsworth: Penguin, 1963), 134.
11. Marshall McLuhan, *Understanding Media: The Extensions of Man* (New York: New American Library, 1964), 269.
12. Ibid., 299.
13. See *Le Point*, Paris, 24–30 October 1988, 122.
14. Marshall McLuhan, *Letters of Marshall McLuhan* (Toronto: Oxford University Press, 1987), 220.
15. See, for example, by Liberatore and Tamburini, *RanXerox à New York*, (Paris: Albin Michel, 1982).
16. Bilal, *La Femme Piégé* (Paris: Dargand, 1986).
17. *Le Nouvel Observateur*, Paris, 29 August 1986.
18. Art Spiegelman, *Maus* (New York: Pantheon, 1986).
19. Quoted in Claude Marks, *World Artists, 1950–1980* (New York: H. W. Wilson Publishers, 1984), see Lichtenstein entry.
20. Chester Brown, "Returning to the Way Things Are," in *Yummy Fur*, no. 9 (Toronto: Vortex Publishing, 1988).
21. J. M. Le Clézio, *Le Procès-verbal* (Paris: Folio, 1963), 128. "Je suis pris dans la bande dessinée de mon choix."

CHAPTER NINETEEN: LIFE IN A BOX — SPECIALIZATION AND THE INDIVIDUAL

1. George Bernard Shaw, *You Never Can Tell*, The Bodley Head Bernard Shaw, vol. 1 (London: The Bodley Head, 1970), 671, 679, 685. Originally produced in 1899.
2. Mann, *The Magic Mountain*, 464.
3. John Stuart Mill, *Utilitarianism, Liberty, Representative Government* (London: Everyman Library [Dent], 1964), 131–158; from *On Liberty*, chaps. iv and v.
4. For first usage of the following words see the *Oxford English Dictionary*, 2nd ed., vol. xvi (Oxford: Clarendon Press, 1989), 152–153:

    Specialization: 1843, Mill, *Logic*, 270, "We have seen above in the words *pagan* and *villain*, remarkable examples of the specialization of the

meaning of words; 1865, Mill, *Comte*, 94, "The increasing specialisa-
tion of all employments . . . is not without inconveniences."

Specialise: 1865, M. Pattison, Oxford Ess., 292, "The very fact that the
new statue has restrained and specialised the subjects in the School of
Literal Humaniores . . ."

Specialist: 1862, Herbert Spencer, First Princ. II. 1. 36. 130, "Even the
most limited specialist would not describe as philosophical an essay
which . . ."

5. Charles Bonnet, *Palingènésie philosophique ou Idées sur l'état passé et l'état
    futur des êtres vivants*, 17ᵉ partie, chap. 4. "Je suis un être sentant et
    intelligent: il est dans la nature de tout être sentant et intelligent de
    vouloir sentir ou exister agréablement, et vouloir c'est cela s'aimer soi-
    même."

6. Learned Hand, *The Spirit of Liberty*, 7.

7. McLuhan, *Lettres*, 29 August 1973, to Commissioner Nicholas Johnson,
    U.S. Federal Communications Commission.

8. Both Strong and Polk quotes are from conversations with the author in
    1989.

9. Montesquieu, *Lettres Persanes* (Paris: Folio, 1981), 215, lettre LXXXIX,
    Usbeka à Ibben: "Tout homme est capable de faire du bien à un homme:
    mais c'est ressembler aux dieux que de contribuer au bonheur d'une
    société entière." Voltaire, "Poème sur le désastre de Lisbonne": "Et vous
    composerez dans ce chaos fatal/Des malheurs de chaque être un bonheur
    général!"

10. Jefferson, *The Life*, 711. Letter to Monsieur A. Coray, 31 October 1823.

11. "Happinees," TM Pending — "If you do it on your knees — HAP-
    PINEES — the ultimate knee protector." Happinees Inc., P.O. Box
    130, Station Z, Toronto, Canada M5N 2Z3.

12. Charles Murray quoted in *Sunday Telegraph*, 14 May 1989, 7.

13. *Vanity Fair*, August 1987, 134.

14. John F. Love, *McDonald's — Behind the Arches* (New York: Bantam
    Press, 1986), 15.

15. The description of the Hyatt Regency Waikoloa is drawn from *Time*, 27
    February 1989, 67.

16. Louis Harris, *Inside America* (New York: Random House, 1987). This
    includes the subsequent table.

17. See Walter Kenrick, *The Secret Museum: Pornography in Modern Culture*
    (New York: Viking, 1987). See also a review of this book by John Gross
    in the *New York Times*, 7 May 1987.

18. This pornography and its context are fully discussed in Steven Marcus,
    *The Other Victorians: a Study of Sexuality and Pornography in mid-
    Nineteenth Century England* (New York: Norton, 1985).

19. McLuhan, *Letters*. To Pierre Elliott Trudeau, 2 July 1975, 511.

20. American *Vogue*, June 1986, 236. Symposium, "American Men: What
    Do They Want?" quoted by Dr. Robert Goald, psychiatrist and professor
    at New York Medical College.

21. Conversation with the author in Belgrade, 22 October 1987.

22. André Malraux, quoted in *Le Monde*, 5 July 1986. This was a publication of a 1975 interview with Ion Mihaileanu. "Pour moi, le grand décalage, c'est que les terroristes que nous voyons à l'heure actuelle sont des personnages assez logiques alors que les terroristes que j'ai connus étaient assez près des nihilistes russes, c'est-à-dire au fond assez méta-physiciens."

23. List from "Rebirth of a Notion," by Marni Jackson, *Toronto* magazine, September 1988.

24. *International Herald Tribune*, October 1987. Italics added.

CHAPTER TWENTY: THE STARS

1. Thomas Jefferson, *The Life, Autobiography*, 104.

2. Quoted in Jesse Kornbluth, "Faye Fights Back," *Vanity Fair*, August 1987, 94.

3. C. Wright Mills, *The Power Elite*, 71.

4. Hand, *The Spirit of Liberty*, 38; from a speech called "The Preservation of Personality."

5. Mills, *The Power Elite*, 74.

6. The source of Goya's inspiration for this position has been endlessly debated. The art historian Jeanine Baticle attributes Goya's image to an engraving of the same scene by Miguel Bamborino. However, there is also *The Vision of the Apocalypse* by El Greco. It is in the Zuloaga Museum, Zumaya, and was painted in 1613. This was late in his life, when he had entered into his period of free-flowing, lyrical lunacy, which was not unlike the unchained self-absorbed vision of the modern painter. The main figure in this picture has his arms raised with the same ambiguous expression of joy and fear.

7. Eugène Delacroix, *Le 28 Juillet 1830 — La Liberté guidant le peuple*. Painted in 1831.

8. *Daily Mail*, 1 July 1987, 1.

9. *Times* (London), 20 June 1989, 42.

10. Quoted by William R. McMurtry, Q. C., in a speech to the Canadian Bar Association, Toronto, 16 January 1987.

11. Ibid.

12. Lannick Group ad in *Toronto Globe and Mail Report on Business Magazine*, August 1989.

13. See Albert Goldman's biography *The Lives of John Lennon* (New York: William Morrow, 1988). An example of the public reaction is the *New York Times* analysis on 12 September 1988, C15, by Allan Kozinn.

14. Christian de la Mazière quoted in *Paris-Match*, 15 May 1987, 75. Dalida quote from same article: "Je sers un art mineur mais c'est quand même une servitude qui implique d'aller jusqu'au bout de soi-même." "Loin dans la nuit, elle me confiait sa fascination pour le néant."

15. *New York Times*, September 8, 1987, A24.

16. Joseph Roth, *Confession of a Murderer, Told in One Night* (New York: Overlook Press, 1985), 107. Original edition published in 1937.

17. *New York Times Magazine*, 11 June 1989, 28.

18. For a description of the Presley house, see "Amazing Graceland," *Life* magazine, September 1987, 44.

19. David Bowie quoted in *Paris-Match*, 10 April 1987, 37.

Question: "Dans les années 70, vous clamiez votre bisexualité. Aujourd-'hui, vous vivez avec votre fils, Zowie, en Suisse près de Lausanne. Vous semblez avoir renoncé à vos extravagances."

Bowie:"J'ai beaucoup changé depuis mon départ des Etats-Unis, en 1976. Là-bas, je menais une vie stéréotypée, décadente. Je ne savais plus qui j'étais. Je suis retourné en Europe et j'ai décidé de consolider mon rôle de père. En vivant au côté de mon fils, j'ai grandi. J'ai mûri."

Question: "Vous avez dit un jour: 'Je veux traverser ma vie comme Superman. . . .'

Bowie: "Mon Dieu! Je devais être ivre mort. J'ai dû lire trop d'ouvrages de Nietzsche."

Question: "Quel est le plus grand risque que vous avez pris dans votre vie?"

Bowie: "Celui de me droguer. C'est un risque que je ne recommande à personne."

20. *Paris-Match*, 3 June 1988, 26.

Macciocchi sur le Pape: "J'avais rencontré Mao, de Gaulle, Hô Chi Minh, et un fois, tout au fond de Qom, la ville sainte de l'Iran, j'avais été reçue par le terrible Khomeini. Mais jamais je ne m'étais sentie aussi chiffonnée . . ."

Beatrice Dalle: "Moi scandaleuse? Jamais!" Et, "On me propose toujours des rôles de bête de sexe alors que je suis la réincarnation de la Sainte Vierge!"

Question: "C'est difficile d'être un sex-symbol?"

George Michael: "Il y a des hauts et des bas."

Le Pape: "Jean-Paul II Pasteur du Tiers Monde."

21. *Le Monde*, 20 May 1987, report on a poll carried out by IPSOS between May 6 and 13, 1987, among fifteen- to twenty-five-year-olds. The question was: "Quelles sont les personalités dont le nom vous vient à l'esprit lorsque vous pensez aux actions efficaces d'aide au développement?"
Forbes list of forty highest-paid entertainers, 21 September 1987. Some of the figures are for 1991. "Quelles sont les trois femmes célèbres sur lesquelles vous vous retourneriez en les croisant dans la rue?" *Le Monde*, 13 mai 1987, special insert, "Image de Femmes."

22. The description of the sale is largely drawn from Dominick Dunne, "The Windsor Epilogue," *Vanity Fair*, August 1987, 100.

23. See, for example, the profile by Sally Bedell Smith in *Vanity Fair*, July 1991.

24. *Paris-Match*:
"Si le sultan de Brunei achète le 'Nabila I' en mars, dans ce cas je ferai construire le 'Nabila II' qui est déjà dessiné. Il sera équipé d'un sous-

marin pouvant contenir six personnes et d'une caméra placée sous la coque, permettant de filmer les fonds marins. Chaque cabine aura son écran."

"Si les modérés prennent le pouvoir en Iran et si la paix avec l'Irak en découle, ce sont deux nations qu'il faudra reconstruire. Soit un marché de 170 milliards de dollars. Si nous obtenons le dixième de ce marché, cela fera 1,7 milliards de dollars!"

25. *International Herald Tribune*, 7 April 1987, 1.
26. Hebe Dorsey, "A Princely Birthday in Bavaria," *International Herald Tribune*, 10 June 1986, 10.
27. Details of the Grace Kelly–Rainier Grimaldi wedding taken from James Spada, *Grace: The Secret Lives of a Princess* (Garden City, N.Y.: Doubleday, 1987). The designer of the wedding dress was Helen Rose.
28. *Bangkok Post*, 28 January 1990.
29. Mills, *The Power Elite*, 75.
30. See cover of *Toronto* magazine, December 1989.
31. Re Sarah Bernhardt, see *Le Figaro, Journal des Débats, L'Intransigeant, Le Journal*, 26–30 March 1923. Re Edith Piaf (13–15 October 1963) and Gerard Philipe (26–29 November 1959), see *Le Monde, Le Figaro*, and *Combat*. Re Yves Montand: All of page 1: *Liberation, Quotidien de Paris, France-Soir*; half of page 1: *Figaro, Le Monde*; weekly covers: *Le Nouvel Observateur, L'Express, Événements de Jeudi, VSD*.
32. Ronald Reagan, *Where's the Rest of Me?* (1965), 51.
33. *Toronto Globe and Mail*, 6 May 1986, A13.
34. Trudeau's most controversial interview was on December 28, 1975, with Bruce Phillips and Carole Taylor on the CTV Network.

CHAPTER TWENTY-ONE: THE FAITHFUL WITNESS

1. There is a general consensus that Homer never existed as a single poet. He wrote the *Iliad* and the *Odyssey* in somewhat the same sense that Matthew wrote a Gospel.
2. On the question of Revelations' debt to the Old Testament, see Northrop Frye, *The Great Code: The Bible and Literature* (New York: Harcourt Brace Jovanovich, 1982), in general and specifically pp. 73 and 35. Regarding the confusion between the Apostle John and John of Patmos, it remains widespread. For example, the subject index of the Oxford University Press edition of the King James Version places the reference to John (of Revelations) under the entry for the Apostle John.
3. For a discussion of the linguistic phenomenon of Francis in the context of his time, see Erich Auerbach, *Mimesis, The Representation of Reality in Western Literature* (New York: Doubleday, 1953), chap. 7. Original German 1946.
4. Three of the best known rector poets were Dinko Ranjina (1536–1607), Dominko Zlataric (1558–1613) and Ivan Gundulic (1589–1638), who wrote Dubrovnik's greatest epic poem, *Osman*.

5. Charles Baudelaire, *Curiosités esthétiques*: "Tout livre qui ne s'adresse pas à la majorité — nombre et intelligence — est un sot livre."

6. Molière, *La Critique de l'Ecole des Femmes*, scene vi, Complete Works, vol. 2 (Paris: Flammarion, 1965), 132. "Je voudrais bien savoir si la grande règle de toutes les règles n'est pas de plaire . . ."

7. Richelieu, *Testament*, 41.

8. A whole literature exists on the Dreyfus affair. The finest single book is Jean-Denis Bredin, *L'Affaire* (Paris: Julliard, 1985). On Zola's involvement see part 3.

9. Ford Madox Ford, *The English Novel* (Manchester: Carcanet, 1983), 76. Original publication 1930.

    "En art il n'y a pas des règles, il n'y a que des exemples," Julien Gracq, quoted by Hubert Haddad in *Julien Gracq* (Paris: Le Castor Astral, 1986), 74.

    Balzac: "Ainsi va le monde littéraire. On n'y aime que ses inférieurs." *Une fille d'Eve.*

    Spengler, *The Decline of the West*, 32.

10. Rémy de Gourmont: "Nous n'avons plus de principes et il n'y a plus de modèles; un écrivain creé son esthétique en créant son oeuvre: nous en sommes réduits à faire appel à la sensation bien plus qu'au jugement," *Les Pas sur le Sable*, Le Livre des Masques, 2nd series.

11. Edmond and Jules de Goncourt: "Votre roman . . . un roman . . . la France se fiche pas mal des romans aujourd'hui, mes gaillards!" *Journal, Mémoires de la Vie Littéraire*, vol. 1, *1851–1861* (Paris: Pasquelles Editeurs), 9.

12. This phrase belongs to someone else. The American writer Stanley Crouch will know who.

13. Introduction by Herbert Gorman (1928) to James Joyce, *A Portrait of the Artist as a Young Man* (New York: Modern Library, 1944).

14. Cyril Connolly, *Enemies of Promise* (Harmondsworth: Penguin, 1938), 108.

15. Quoted in Bryan F. Griffin, "Panic Among the Philistines," *Harpers* (August 1981), 38.

16. Voltaire: "Tous les genres sont bons, hors le genre ennuyeux," *L'Enfant Prodigue*, preface.

17. See, for example, *The Fontana Dictionary of Modern Thought*, rev. ed., ed. Alan Bullock and Oliver Stallybrass (London: Fontana, 1988), 206.

18. Quoted in *Le Monde*, July 5, 1986, 19. "Écoutez, est-ce qu'il existe sérieusement du vécu quelque part? N'est-ce pas une espèce de chimère incroyable? Qu'a-t-on considéré comme le comble du vécu en France? Balzac. Mais Baudelaire écrivait qu'il est le plus grand visionnaire de notre temps."

19. Quoted in *New York Times* profile of I. F. Stone, 22 January 1978.

20. R. A. D. Ford, *Doors, Words and Silence* (Toronto: Mosaic Press, 1985).

21. T. S. Eliot, *Collected Poems 1909–1962* (London: Faber and Faber, 1974), 218. "Four Quartets, Little Gidding," originally published 1942.

CHAPTER TWENTY-TWO: THE VIRTUE OF DOUBT

1. For a discussion of Palladio, see Michelangelo Muraro, *Civilisation des Villas Vénitiennes* (Paris: Editions Mengès, 1987). Italian original 1986. See also various books and articles by James S. Ackerman, such as *Palladio* (Harmondsworth: Penguin, 1966).
2. Sir Michael Howard, "Process and Values in History" (Lecture given at Oxford University, 1989).

Acknowledgments

The writing of this book has gone on for over a decade and the list of people who have helped me is endless. What follows here is therefore incomplete. For that matter, some people may by now have forgotten giving advice or information. It goes without saying that in acknowledging help, I am not suggesting that anyone, from Maurice Strong on, agrees with what I have written. I'm simply thanking them.

First, there is Adrienne, for her advice, patience, encouragement and love.

Second, there is Adam Bellow, an extraordinary editor who has engaged in this long task with great imagination, care and consideration.

Third, there are the friends who have read drafts, made comments and suggestions and been supportive. Erwin Glikes, Laura Roebuck, Robin Straus, Mike Shaw, Michael Levine, Cynthia Good, Michelle Lapautre, Diana Mackay, Kirsten Hanson, Wendy Law-Yone, Linda Spalding, Vivienne Moody, Emile Martel, Ursula Bender, Roberto Santachiara and Olga Villalba.

Fourth, as someone virtually unable to write while sitting or lying at home, there are all the friends who have turned their houses into writing asylums. Bill and Cathy Graham in the Hockley Valley. Tim and Fran Lewis, as well as the late Roy Whitehead and Hillie in Bangkok. Bill Glassco at Tadoussac. Emile and Nicole Martel in Paris. Norm Lofts and Lisa Wood on Lake Joseph. Sandy and Jane Crews on Arma Island, Lake Joseph. John and Sue Polanyi on Sashile, Georgian Bay. Elizabeth Gordon at Seldom Seen. And, of course, my friends at Eygalières, who have put up with me wandering about distractedly.

Fifth is the astonishing number of people — some friends, some simply responding to requests — who helped in specific areas. In the swamp of philosophy, religion and history, I was periodically dragged back onto solid Buddhist ground by Sulak Sivaraksa and Father Joe Maier in Bangkok, Professor Andrew Watson in Toronto on Islamic and Arabic questions, Professor Alain Pons in Paris on Vico and the *Encyclopédistes*, Father Edgar Bull, John McMurtry, Len Pennachetti, Henri Robillot, Professor Marjory Rogers, Professor William Rogers and Olivier Todd. On the Jesuits, Michael Coren, André Fournier, S. J., and Professor Michael Higgens. On Arthurian mythology, David Staines. On torture, Professor Edward Peters.

On arms, the staff of the International Institute of Strategic Studies in London, Donald Agger in Washington and Anthony Sampson. On military questions, Professor Anthony Clayton at Sandhurst, Richard Gabriel, General Pierre Gallois, Sir Michael Howard, Jean Planchais and Professor John Polanyi, who was also a great help on the relationship between science and social responsibility. On cybernetics, Stephen Bingham.

On financial and economic questions, David Mitchell in New York; Robert Rewald and Sarah Holden at the Federal Reserve Bank in Washington; Samuel Brittan, Roger Garside, Simon Lovett, M. D. Craig of the Bank of England, all in Britain; Jack Belford, John Grant, Jim Laxer, Professor Abraham Rotstein, Mary E. Webb in Canada; and Alain Vernholes of *Le Monde* in Paris.

On government and administration, Romée de Bellescize, Georges Berthoin, Jean-Michel Gaillard, Charles Galtier, Richard Reeves and Glen Treverton. On legal questions, Michael Alexander, Maître Denis Debost, Professor William Graham, Q.C., Christopher Ives, and Martin Katz. On secrecy, Bernard Cadé and Johannes Gottwald, both of whom dragged out wonderful material.

On bullfighting, Luc Perrot and Aline Pélissier. On the image, Jean-Michel Beurdelay, Tim Clifford, Gérard Drouillet, Pierre Legué, Christopher Pratt, Mary Pratt and Bernard Paul. On writing, Julien Gracq, the late Terence Kilmartin and René de Obaldia. The late Sir Angus Wilson and Tony Garrett volunteered themselves as a two-man provençal *Encyclopédie* on a whole range of subjects.

And many other friends, including Diane de Bellescize, Bernard Bois, Guy Dupré, Mary Harrison, Odile Hellier, Phoebe Larmore, Bernard Kaplan, Bill McMurtry, Michael Ondaatje, Paulo and Marzia Perini, Jeremy Riley, Michael Robison, Sarah Thring, Martha Warnes and Julie Wadham, who, some time ago, before *The Birds of Prey*, helped me over the wall.

Index